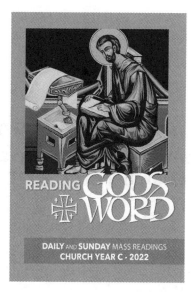

READING GOD'S WORD
Daily and Sunday Mass Readings
Church Year C 2022

Creative Communications for the Parish
1564 Fencorp Drive
Fenton, MO 63026
www.creativecommunications.com

READING GOD'S WORD
Daily and Sunday Mass Readings
Church Year C 2022

© *2021 Creative Communications for the Parish*

Published with the authority of the Committee on Divine Worship, United States Conference of Catholic Bishops.

ISBN Number: 978-1-68279-398-5

Cover Design: Jamie Wyatt
Cover Art: Shutterstock / Julia Raketic

INTRODUCTION

What began primarily as an aid to lectors preparing for Mass has now become a regular part of the daily prayer of Catholics who know the value of praying with Scripture. *Reading God's Word* helps us to follow the daily worship of the Church in a simple and convenient form.

Reading God's Word has the exact passages for daily Mass for an entire year, and they are available whenever you want them. More than simply convenient, *Reading God's Word* offers a way to respond to God's invitation to share his life. As the world Synod of Bishops on the "Word of God in the Life and Mission of the Church" noted in October 2008, Scripture represents God's desire to speak directly to us. When we take up the texts in *Reading God's Word*, we enter into a relationship with God in a profound way, and these living words begin to take root in our lives and bear fruit.

True, some of the words are so familiar as to be commonplace after years of hearing them proclaimed at Mass. At the same time, new circumstances in our lives as well as the action of grace can give new meaning to a text that we have heard since childhood. When we hear or read these words intently, we discover that as St. Paul has taught us (Romans 15:4), everything written in Scripture is written as instruction for our benefit.

May *Reading God's Word* richly benefit you all during the coming year.

Editorial Staff
Creative Communications for the Parish

Liturgical Celebrations

2021

First Sunday of Advent .... Nov. 28

Immaculate Conception *(holy day of obligation)* .... Wed., Dec. 8

Christmas *(holy day of obligation)* .... Sat., Dec. 25

The Holy Family of Jesus, Mary and Joseph .... Sun., Dec. 26

2022

The Octave Day of the Nativity of the Lord: Solemnity of Mary, the Holy
    Mother of God *(NOT a holy day of obligation)* .... Sat., Jan. 1

Epiphany .... Sun., Jan. 2

The Baptism of the Lord .... Sun., Jan. 9

The Presentation of the Lord .... Wed., Feb. 2

Ash Wednesday .... Mar. 2

St. Joseph, Spouse of the Blessed Virgin Mary .... Sat., Mar. 19

The Annunciation of the Lord .... Fri., Mar. 25

Palm Sunday of the Passion of the Lord .... Apr. 10

Holy Thursday .... Apr. 14

Good Friday .... Apr. 15

Holy Saturday .... Apr. 16

Easter Sunday of the Resurrection of the Lord .... Apr. 17

Ascension *(holy day of obligation)* .... Thu., May 26 or Sun., May 29

Pentecost Sunday .... June 5

The Most Holy Trinity .... Sun., June 12

The Most Holy Body and Blood of Christ .... Sun., June 19

The Nativity of St. John the Baptist .... Thu., June 23

The Most Sacred Heart of Jesus .... Fri., June 24

St. Peter and St. Paul .... Wed., June 29

The Transfiguration of the Lord .... Sat., Aug. 6

The Assumption of the Blessed Virgin Mary *(NOT a holy day of obligation)*
.... Mon., Aug. 15

The Exaltation of the Holy Cross .... Wed., Sept. 14

All Saints *(holy day of obligation)* .... Tues., Nov. 1

The Commemoration of All the Faithful Departed (All Souls' Day)
.... Wed., Nov. 2

The Dedication of the Lateran Basilica in Rome .... Wed., Nov. 9

Our Lord Jesus Christ, King of the Universe .... Sun., Nov. 20

First Sunday of Advent .... Nov. 27

NOTICE FOR LECTORS

If this book is used to prepare for reading at Mass, please note that the "announcement" formula is: *"A reading from the Book of ...,"* *"A reading from the Letter of ..."* or *"A reading from the holy Gospel according to ..."* We have placed *t* before the citation as a reminder of the announcement.

At the end of the readings, the lector or presider is to say, *"The word of the Lord."* We have placed ✛ at the end of texts as a reminder of that concluding declaration.

Also, herein the Responsorial Verse of each day's Psalm is printed only once in full, with an **R.** indicating where repetition is called for. The **R.** at the end of the Gospel Verse indicates that the response is one "Alleluia" or the acclamation used during Lent.

SUNDAY, NOVEMBER 28, 2021
FIRST SUNDAY OF ADVENT

† *Jeremiah 33:14-16*
I will raise up for David a just shoot.

The days are coming, says the LORD,
   when I will fulfill the promise
   I made to the house of Israel and Judah.
In those days, in that time,
   I will raise up for David a just shoot;
   he shall do what is right and just in the land.
In those days Judah shall be safe
   and Jerusalem shall dwell secure;
   this is what they shall call her:
"The LORD our justice." ✛

Psalm 25:4-5, 8-9, 10, 14
R. (1b) **To you, O Lord, I lift my soul.**
Your ways, O LORD, make known to me;
   teach me your paths,
guide me in your truth and teach me,
   for you are God my savior,
   and for you I wait all the day. **R.**
Good and upright is the LORD;
   thus he shows sinners the way.
He guides the humble to justice,
   and teaches the humble his way. **R.**
All the paths of the LORD are kindness and constancy
   toward those who keep his covenant and his decrees.
The friendship of the LORD is with those who fear him,
   and his covenant, for their instruction. **R.**

† *1 Thessalonians 3:12—4:2*
May the Lord strengthen your hearts at the coming of our Lord Jesus.

Brothers and sisters:
May the Lord make you increase and abound in love
   for one another and for all,
   just as we have for you,
   so as to strengthen your hearts,
   to be blameless in holiness before our God and Father
   at the coming of our Lord Jesus with all his holy ones. Amen.

Finally, brothers and sisters,
   we earnestly ask and exhort you in the Lord Jesus that,
   as you received from us

how you should conduct yourselves to please God
—and as you are conducting yourselves—
you do so even more.
For you know what instructions we gave you through the Lord
Jesus. ✛

Psalm 85:8
R. Alleluia, alleluia.
Show us, Lord, your love;
and grant us your salvation. **R.**

† Luke 21:25-28, 34-36
Your redemption is at hand.

Jesus said to his disciples:
"There will be signs in the sun, the moon, and the stars,
    and on earth nations will be in dismay,
    perplexed by the roaring of the sea and the waves.
People will die of fright
    in anticipation of what is coming upon the world,
    for the powers of the heavens will be shaken.
And then they will see the Son of Man
    coming in a cloud with power and great glory.
But when these signs begin to happen,
    stand erect and raise your heads
    because your redemption is at hand.

"Beware that your hearts do not become drowsy
    from carousing and drunkenness
    and the anxieties of daily life,
    and that day catch you by surprise like a trap.
For that day will assault everyone
    who lives on the face of the earth.
Be vigilant at all times
    and pray that you have the strength
    to escape the tribulations that are imminent
    and to stand before the Son of Man." ✛

MONDAY, NOVEMBER 29
ADVENT WEEKDAY

† Isaiah 2:1-5
*The LORD will gather all nations into
the eternal peace of the Kingdom of God.*

This is what Isaiah, son of Amoz,
    saw concerning Judah and Jerusalem.

In days to come,
The mountain of the LORD's house
   shall be established as the highest mountain
   and raised above the hills.
All nations shall stream toward it;
   many peoples shall come and say:
"Come, let us climb the LORD's mountain,
   to the house of the God of Jacob,
That he may instruct us in his ways,
   and we may walk in his paths."
For from Zion shall go forth instruction,
   and the word of the LORD from Jerusalem.
He shall judge between the nations,
   and impose terms on many peoples.
They shall beat their swords into plowshares
   and their spears into pruning hooks;
One nation shall not raise the sword against another,
   nor shall they train for war again.

O house of Jacob, come,
   let us walk in the light of the LORD! ✛

Psalm 122:1-2, 3-4b, 4cd-5, 6-7, 8-9
R. Let us go rejoicing to the house of the Lord.
I rejoiced because they said to me,
   "We will go up to the house of the LORD."
And now we have set foot
   within your gates, O Jerusalem. **R.**
Jerusalem, built as a city
   with compact unity.
To it the tribes go up,
   the tribes of the LORD. **R.**
According to the decree for Israel,
   to give thanks to the name of the LORD.
In it are set up judgment seats,
   seats for the house of David. **R.**
Pray for the peace of Jerusalem!
   May those who love you prosper!
May peace be within your walls,
   prosperity in your buildings. **R.**
Because of my relatives and friends
   I will say, "Peace be within you!"
Because of the house of the LORD, our God,
   I will pray for your good. **R.**

See Psalm 80:4

R. Alleluia, alleluia.

Come and save us, Lord our God;
let your face shine upon us, that we may be saved. **R.**

† *Matthew 8:5-11*

*Many will come from the east and
the west into the Kingdom of heaven.*

When Jesus entered Capernaum,
    a centurion approached him and appealed to him, saying,
    "Lord, my servant is lying at home paralyzed, suffering dreadfully."
He said to him, "I will come and cure him."
The centurion said in reply,
    "Lord, I am not worthy to have you enter under my roof;
    only say the word and my servant will be healed.
For I too am a man subject to authority,
    with soldiers subject to me.
And I say to one, 'Go,' and he goes;
    and to another, 'Come here,' and he comes;
    and to my slave, 'Do this,' and he does it."
When Jesus heard this, he was amazed and said to those following
    him,
    "Amen, I say to you, in no one in Israel have I found such faith.
I say to you, many will come from the east and the west,
    and will recline with Abraham, Isaac, and Jacob
    at the banquet in the Kingdom of heaven." ✛

TUESDAY, NOVEMBER 30
St. Andrew

† *Romans 10:9-18*

*Thus faith comes from what is heard,
and what is heard comes through the word of Christ.*

Brothers and sisters:
If you confess with your mouth that Jesus is Lord
    and believe in your heart that God raised him from the dead,
    you will be saved.
For one believes with the heart and so is justified,
    and one confesses with the mouth and so is saved.
The Scripture says,
    No one who believes in him will be put to shame.
There is no distinction between Jew and Greek;
    the same Lord is Lord of all,
    enriching all who call upon him.
For everyone who calls on the name of the Lord will be saved.

But how can they call on him in whom they have not believed?
And how can they believe in him of whom they have not heard?
And how can they hear without someone to preach?
And how can people preach unless they are sent?
As it is written,
How beautiful are the feet of those who bring the good news!
But not everyone has heeded the good news;
for Isaiah says, *Lord, who has believed what was heard from us?*
Thus faith comes from what is heard,
and what is heard comes through the word of Christ.
But I ask, did they not hear?
Certainly they did; for

*Their voice has gone forth to all the earth,
and their words to the ends of the world.* ✛

Psalm 19:8, 9, 10, 11
R. (10) **The judgments of the Lord are true, and all of them
are just.**
or
(John 6:63) **Your words, Lord, are Spirit and life.**
The law of the Lord is perfect,
refreshing the soul;
The decree of the Lord is trustworthy,
giving wisdom to the simple. **R.**
The precepts of the Lord are right,
rejoicing the heart;
The command of the Lord is clear,
enlightening the eye. **R.**
The fear of the Lord is pure,
enduring forever;
The ordinances of the Lord are true,
all of them just. **R.**
They are more precious than gold,
than a heap of purest gold;
Sweeter also than syrup
or honey from the comb. **R.**

Matthew 4:19
R. Alleluia, alleluia.
Come after me, says the Lord,
and I will make you fishers of men. **R.**

† *Matthew 4:18-22*
Immediately they left their nets and followed him.

As Jesus was walking by the Sea of Galilee, he saw two brothers,
Simon who is called Peter, and his brother Andrew,
casting a net into the sea; they were fishermen.
He said to them,
"Come after me, and I will make you fishers of men."
At once they left their nets and followed him.
He walked along from there and saw two other brothers,
James, the son of Zebedee, and his brother John.
They were in a boat, with their father Zebedee, mending their nets.
He called them, and immediately they left their boat and their father
and followed him. ✛

WEDNESDAY, DECEMBER 1
ADVENT WEEKDAY

† *Isaiah 25:6-10a*
*The LORD invites us to his feast and
will wipe away the tears from all faces.*

On this mountain the LORD of hosts
  will provide for all peoples
A feast of rich food and choice wines,
  juicy, rich food and pure, choice wines.
On this mountain he will destroy
  the veil that veils all peoples,
The web that is woven over all nations;
  he will destroy death forever.
The Lord GOD will wipe away
  the tears from all faces;
The reproach of his people he will remove
  from the whole earth; for the LORD has spoken.

  On that day it will be said:
"Behold our God, to whom we looked to save us!
  This is the LORD for whom we looked;
  let us rejoice and be glad that he has saved us!"
For the hand of the LORD will rest on this mountain. ✛

  Psalm 23:1b-3a, 3b-4, 5, 6
R. (6cd) **I shall live in the house of the Lord all the days of my
    life.**
The LORD is my shepherd; I shall not want.
  In verdant pastures he gives me repose;
Beside restful waters he leads me;
  he refreshes my soul. **R.**
He guides me in right paths
  for his name's sake.
Even though I walk in the dark valley
  I fear no evil; for you are at my side
With your rod and your staff
  that give me courage. **R.**
You spread the table before me
  in the sight of my foes;
You anoint my head with oil;
  my cup overflows. **R.**
Only goodness and kindness follow me
  all the days of my life;
And I shall dwell in the house of the LORD
  for years to come. **R.**

R. Alleluia, alleluia.
Behold, the Lord comes to save his people;
blessed are those prepared to meet him. **R.**

† Matthew 15:29-37
Jesus heals many and multiplies the bread.

At that time:
Jesus walked by the Sea of Galilee,
  went up on the mountain, and sat down there.
Great crowds came to him,
  having with them the lame, the blind, the deformed, the mute,
  and many others.
They placed them at his feet, and he cured them.
The crowds were amazed when they saw the mute speaking,
  the deformed made whole,
  the lame walking,
  and the blind able to see,
  and they glorified the God of Israel.

Jesus summoned his disciples and said,
  "My heart is moved with pity for the crowd,
  for they have been with me now for three days
  and have nothing to eat.
I do not want to send them away hungry,
  for fear they may collapse on the way."
The disciples said to him,
  "Where could we ever get enough bread in this deserted place
  to satisfy such a crowd?"
Jesus said to them, "How many loaves do you have?"
"Seven," they replied, "and a few fish."
He ordered the crowd to sit down on the ground.
Then he took the seven loaves and the fish,
  gave thanks, broke the loaves,
  and gave them to the disciples, who in turn gave them to the
    crowds.
They all ate and were satisfied.
They picked up the fragments left over—seven baskets full. ✝

THURSDAY, DECEMBER 2
ADVENT WEEKDAY

† *Isaiah 26:1-6*
Let in a nation that is just, one that keeps faith.

On that day they will sing this song in the land of Judah:

"A strong city have we;
  he sets up walls and ramparts to protect us.
Open up the gates
    to let in a nation that is just,
    one that keeps faith.
A nation of firm purpose you keep in peace;
    in peace, for its trust in you."

Trust in the LORD forever!
    For the LORD is an eternal Rock.
He humbles those in high places,
    and the lofty city he brings down;
He tumbles it to the ground,
    levels it with the dust.
It is trampled underfoot by the needy,
    by the footsteps of the poor. ✚

Psalm 118:1 and 8-9, 19-21, 25-27a

R. (26a) **Blessed is he who comes in the name of the Lord.**
  *(or **Alleluia.**)*

Give thanks to the LORD, for he is good,
    for his mercy endures forever.
It is better to take refuge in the LORD
    than to trust in man.
It is better to take refuge in the LORD
    than to trust in princes. **R.**

Open to me the gates of justice;
    I will enter them and give thanks to the LORD.
This gate is the LORD's;
    the just shall enter it.
I will give thanks to you, for you have answered me
    and have been my savior. **R.**

O LORD, grant salvation!
    O LORD, grant prosperity!
Blessed is he who comes in the name of the LORD;
    we bless you from the house of the LORD.
The LORD is God, and he has given us light. **R.**

Isaiah 55:6

R. Alleluia, alleluia.

Seek the LORD while he may be found;
call him while he is near. **R.**

† *Matthew 7:21, 24-27*
Whoever does the will of my Father will enter the Kingdom of heaven.

Jesus said to his disciples:
"Not everyone who says to me, 'Lord, Lord,'
   will enter the Kingdom of heaven,
   but only the one who does the will of my Father in heaven.

"Everyone who listens to these words of mine and acts on them
   will be like a wise man who built his house on rock.
The rain fell, the floods came,
   and the winds blew and buffeted the house.
But it did not collapse; it had been set solidly on rock.
And everyone who listens to these words of mine
   but does not act on them
   will be like a fool who built his house on sand.
The rain fell, the floods came,
   and the winds blew and buffeted the house.
And it collapsed and was completely ruined." ✝

FRIDAY, DECEMBER 3
ST. FRANCIS XAVIER

† *Isaiah 29:17-24*
On that day, the eyes of the blind shall see.

Thus says the Lord GOD:
But a very little while,
   and Lebanon shall be changed into an orchard,
   and the orchard be regarded as a forest!
On that day the deaf shall hear
   the words of a book;
And out of gloom and darkness,
   the eyes of the blind shall see.
The lowly will ever find joy in the LORD,
   and the poor rejoice in the Holy One of Israel.
For the tyrant will be no more
   and the arrogant will have gone;
All who are alert to do evil will be cut off,
   those whose mere word condemns a man,
Who ensnare his defender at the gate,
   and leave the just man with an empty claim.

Therefore thus says the LORD,
   the God of the house of Jacob,
   who redeemed Abraham:
Now Jacob shall have nothing to be ashamed of,
   nor shall his face grow pale.
When his children see
   the work of my hands in his midst,
They shall keep my name holy;
   they shall reverence the Holy One of Jacob,
   and be in awe of the God of Israel.
Those who err in spirit shall acquire understanding,
   and those who find fault shall receive instruction. ✦

Psalm 27:1, 4, 13-14
R. (1a) **The Lord is my light and my salvation.**
The LORD is my light and my salvation;
   whom should I fear?
The LORD is my life's refuge;
   of whom should I be afraid? **R.**
One thing I ask of the LORD;
   this I seek:
To dwell in the house of the LORD
   all the days of my life,
That I may gaze on the loveliness of the LORD
   and contemplate his temple. **R.**
I believe that I shall see the bounty of the LORD
   in the land of the living.
Wait for the LORD with courage;
   be stouthearted, and wait for the LORD. **R.**

R. Alleluia, alleluia.
Behold, our Lord shall come with power;
he will enlighten the eyes of his servants. **R.**

† *Matthew 9:27-31*
Believing in Jesus, two who were blind are cured.

As Jesus passed by, two blind men followed him, crying out,
   "Son of David, have pity on us!"
When he entered the house,
   the blind men approached him and Jesus said to them,
   "Do you believe that I can do this?"
"Yes, Lord," they said to him.
Then he touched their eyes and said,
   "Let it be done for you according to your faith."
And their eyes were opened.

Jesus warned them sternly,
"See that no one knows about this."
But they went out and spread word of him through all that land. ✢

SATURDAY, DECEMBER 4
ADVENT WEEKDAY, ST. JOHN DAMASCENE

† Isaiah 30:19-21, 23-26
The Merciful One will show you mercy when you cry out.

Thus says the Lord GOD,
  the Holy One of Israel:
O people of Zion, who dwell in Jerusalem,
  no more will you weep;
He will be gracious to you when you cry out,
  as soon as he hears he will answer you.
The Lord will give you the bread you need
  and the water for which you thirst.
No longer will your Teacher hide himself,
  but with your own eyes you shall see your Teacher,
While from behind, a voice shall sound in your ears:
  "This is the way; walk in it,"
  when you would turn to the right or to the left.

He will give rain for the seed
  that you sow in the ground,
And the wheat that the soil produces
  will be rich and abundant.
On that day your flock will be given pasture
  and the lamb will graze in spacious meadows;
The oxen and the asses that till the ground
  will eat silage tossed to them
  with shovel and pitchfork.
Upon every high mountain and lofty hill
  there will be streams of running water.
On the day of the great slaughter,
  when the towers fall,
The light of the moon will be like that of the sun
  and the light of the sun will be seven times greater
  like the light of seven days.
On the day the LORD binds up the wounds of his people,
  he will heal the bruises left by his blows. ✢

Psalm 147:1-2, 3-4, 5-6

R. (see Isaiah 30:18d) Blessed are all who wait for the Lord.

Praise the LORD, for he is good;
   sing praise to our God, for he is gracious;
   it is fitting to praise him.
The LORD rebuilds Jerusalem;
   the dispersed of Israel he gathers. **R.**
He heals the brokenhearted
   and binds up their wounds.
He tells the number of the stars;
   he calls each by name. **R.**
Great is our LORD and mighty in power:
   to his wisdom there is no limit.
The LORD sustains the lowly;
   the wicked he casts to the ground. **R.**

Isaiah 33:22

R. Alleluia, alleluia.

The LORD is our Judge, our Lawgiver, our King;
he it is who will save us. **R.**

† Matthew 9:35—10:1, 5a, 6-8

At the sight of the crowds, Jesus' heart was moved with pity for them.

Jesus went around to all the towns and villages,
   teaching in their synagogues,
   proclaiming the Gospel of the Kingdom,
   and curing every disease and illness.
At the sight of the crowds, his heart was moved with pity for them
   because they were troubled and abandoned,
   like sheep without a shepherd.
Then he said to his disciples,
   "The harvest is abundant but the laborers are few;
   so ask the master of the harvest
   to send out laborers for his harvest."

Then he summoned his Twelve disciples
   and gave them authority over unclean spirits to drive them out
   and to cure every disease and every illness.

Jesus sent out these twelve after instructing them thus,
   "Go to the lost sheep of the house of Israel.
As you go, make this proclamation: 'The Kingdom of heaven is at hand.'
Cure the sick, raise the dead,
   cleanse lepers, drive out demons.
Without cost you have received; without cost you are to give." ✚

SUNDAY, DECEMBER 5
SECOND SUNDAY OF ADVENT

† *Baruch 5:1-9*
Jerusalem, God will show your splendor.

Jerusalem, take off your robe of mourning and misery;
   put on the splendor of glory from God forever:
wrapped in the cloak of justice from God,
   bear on your head the mitre
   that displays the glory of the eternal name.
For God will show all the earth your splendor:
   you will be named by God forever
   the peace of justice, the glory of God's worship.

Up, Jerusalem! stand upon the heights;
   look to the east and see your children
gathered from the east and the west
   at the word of the Holy One,
   rejoicing that they are remembered by God.
Led away on foot by their enemies they left you:
   but God will bring them back to you
   borne aloft in glory as on royal thrones.
For God has commanded
   that every lofty mountain be made low,
and that the age-old depths and gorges
   be filled to level ground,
   that Israel may advance secure in the glory of God.
The forests and every fragrant kind of tree
   have overshadowed Israel at God's command;
for God is leading Israel in joy
   by the light of his glory,
   with his mercy and justice for company. ✝

   Psalm 126:1-2, 2-3, 4-5, 6
R. The Lord has done great things for us; we are filled with joy.
When the LORD brought back the captives of Zion,
   we were like men dreaming.
Then our mouth was filled with laughter,
   and our tongue with rejoicing. **R.**
Then they said among the nations,
   "The LORD has done great things for them."
The LORD has done great things for us;
   we are glad indeed. **R.**
Restore our fortunes, O LORD,
   like the torrents in the southern desert.

Those who sow in tears
  shall reap rejoicing. **R.**
Although they go forth weeping,
  carrying the seed to be sown,
They shall come back rejoicing,
  carrying their sheaves. **R.**

† *Philippians 1:4-6, 8-11*
Show yourselves pure and blameless for the day of Christ.

Brothers and sisters:
I pray always with joy in my every prayer for all of you,
  because of your partnership for the gospel
  from the first day until now.
I am confident of this,
  that the one who began a good work in you
  will continue to complete it
  until the day of Christ Jesus.
God is my witness,
  how I long for all of you with the affection of Christ Jesus.
And this is my prayer:
  that your love may increase ever more and more
  in knowledge and every kind of perception,
  to discern what is of value,
  so that you may be pure and blameless for the day of Christ,
  filled with the fruit of righteousness
  that comes through Jesus Christ
  for the glory and praise of God. ✤

Luke 3:4, 6
R. Alleluia, alleluia.
Prepare the way of the Lord, make straight his paths:
all flesh shall see the salvation of God. **R.**

† *Luke 3:1-6*
All flesh shall see the salvation of God.

In the fifteenth year of the reign of Tiberius Caesar,
  when Pontius Pilate was governor of Judea,
  and Herod was tetrarch of Galilee,
  and his brother Philip tetrarch of the region
    of Ituraea and Trachonitis,
  and Lysanias was tetrarch of Abilene,
  during the high priesthood of Annas and Caiaphas,
  the word of God came to John the son of Zechariah in the desert.
John went throughout the whole region of the Jordan,
  proclaiming a baptism of repentance for the forgiveness of sins,

as it is written in the book of the words of the prophet Isaiah:
A voice of one crying out in the desert:
"Prepare the way of the Lord,
  make straight his paths.
Every valley shall be filled
  and every mountain and hill shall be made low.
The winding roads shall be made straight,
  and the rough ways made smooth,
and all flesh shall see the salvation of God." ✝

MONDAY, DECEMBER 6
ADVENT WEEKDAY, ST. NICHOLAS

✝ *Isaiah 35:1-10*
God himself will come and save you.

The desert and the parched land will exult;
  the steppe will rejoice and bloom.
They will bloom with abundant flowers,
  and rejoice with joyful song.
The glory of Lebanon will be given to them,
  the splendor of Carmel and Sharon;
They will see the glory of the LORD,
  the splendor of our God.
Strengthen the hands that are feeble,
  make firm the knees that are weak,
Say to those whose hearts are frightened:
  Be strong, fear not!
Here is your God,
  he comes with vindication;
With divine recompense
  he comes to save you.
Then will the eyes of the blind be opened,
  the ears of the deaf be cleared;
Then will the lame leap like a stag,
  then the tongue of the mute will sing.

Streams will burst forth in the desert,
  and rivers in the steppe.
The burning sands will become pools,
  and the thirsty ground, springs of water;
The abode where jackals lurk
  will be a marsh for the reed and papyrus.
A highway will be there,
  called the holy way;

No one unclean may pass over it,
  nor fools go astray on it.
No lion will be there,
  nor beast of prey go up to be met upon it.
It is for those with a journey to make,
  and on it the redeemed will walk.
Those whom the LORD has ransomed will return
  and enter Zion singing,
  crowned with everlasting joy;
They will meet with joy and gladness,
  sorrow and mourning will flee. ✛

Psalm 85:9ab, 10, 11-12, 13-14
R. (Isaiah 35:4f) **Our God will come to save us!**
I will hear what God proclaims;
  the LORD—for he proclaims peace to his people.
Near indeed is his salvation to those who fear him,
  glory dwelling in our land. **R.**
Kindness and truth shall meet;
  justice and peace shall kiss.
Truth shall spring out of the earth,
  and justice shall look down from heaven. **R.**
The LORD himself will give his benefits;
  our land shall yield its increase.
Justice shall walk before him,
  and salvation, along the way of his steps. **R.**

R. Alleluia, alleluia.
Behold the king will come, the Lord of the earth,
and he himself will lift the yoke of our captivity. **R.**

† Luke 5:17-26
We have seen incredible things today.

One day as Jesus was teaching,
  Pharisees and teachers of the law,
  who had come from every village of Galilee and Judea and
    Jerusalem,
  were sitting there,
  and the power of the Lord was with him for healing.
And some men brought on a stretcher a man who was paralyzed;
  they were trying to bring him in and set him in his presence.
But not finding a way to bring him in because of the crowd,
  they went up on the roof
  and lowered him on the stretcher through the tiles
  into the middle in front of Jesus.

When Jesus saw their faith, he said,
"As for you, your sins are forgiven."

Then the scribes and Pharisees began to ask themselves,
"Who is this who speaks blasphemies?
Who but God alone can forgive sins?"
Jesus knew their thoughts and said to them in reply,
"What are you thinking in your hearts?
Which is easier, to say, 'Your sins are forgiven,'
or to say, 'Rise and walk'?
But that you may know
    that the Son of Man has authority on earth to forgive sins"—
he said to the one who was paralyzed,
"I say to you, rise, pick up your stretcher, and go home."

He stood up immediately before them,
    picked up what he had been lying on,
    and went home, glorifying God.
Then astonishment seized them all and they glorified God,
    and, struck with awe, they said,
"We have seen incredible things today." ✛

TUESDAY, DECEMBER 7
St. Ambrose

† Isaiah 40:1-11
God consoles his people.

Comfort, give comfort to my people,
    says your God.
Speak tenderly to Jerusalem, and proclaim to her
    that her service is at an end,
    her guilt is expiated;
Indeed, she has received from the hand of the LORD
    double for all her sins.

A voice cries out:
In the desert prepare the way of the LORD!
    Make straight in the wasteland a highway for our God!
Every valley shall be filled in,
    every mountain and hill shall be made low;
The rugged land shall be made a plain,
    the rough country, a broad valley.
Then the glory of the LORD shall be revealed,
    and all people shall see it together;
    for the mouth of the LORD has spoken.

A voice says, "Cry out!"
   I answer, "What shall I cry out?"
"All flesh is grass,
   and all their glory like the flower of the field.
The grass withers, the flower wilts,
   when the breath of the LORD blows upon it.
   So then, the people is the grass.
Though the grass withers and the flower wilts,
   the word of our God stands forever."

Go up onto a high mountain,
   Zion, herald of glad tidings;
Cry out at the top of your voice,
   Jerusalem, herald of good news!
Fear not to cry out
   and say to the cities of Judah:
   Here is your God!
Here comes with power
   the Lord GOD,
   who rules by his strong arm;
Here is his reward with him,
   his recompense before him.
Like a shepherd he feeds his flock;
   in his arms he gathers the lambs,
Carrying them in his bosom,
   and leading the ewes with care. ✛

Psalm 96:1-2, 3 and 10ac, 11-12, 13
R. (see Isaiah 40:10ab) **The Lord our God comes with power.**
Sing to the LORD a new song;
   sing to the LORD, all you lands.
Sing to the LORD; bless his name;
   announce his salvation, day after day. **R.**
Tell his glory among the nations;
   among all peoples, his wondrous deeds.
Say among the nations: The LORD is king;
   he governs the peoples with equity. **R.**
Let the heavens be glad and the earth rejoice;
   let the sea and what fills it resound;
   let the plains be joyful and all that is in them!
Then let all the trees of the forest rejoice. **R.**
They shall exult before the LORD, for he comes;
   for he comes to rule the earth.
He shall rule the world with justice
   and the peoples with his constancy. **R.**

R. Alleluia, alleluia.
The day of the Lord is near:
Behold, he comes to save us. **R.**

† *Matthew 18:12-14*
God does not will that the little ones be lost.

Jesus said to his disciples:
"What is your opinion?
If a man has a hundred sheep and one of them goes astray,
    will he not leave the ninety-nine in the hills
    and go in search of the stray?
And if he finds it, amen, I say to you, he rejoices more over it
    than over the ninety-nine that did not stray.
In just the same way, it is not the will of your heavenly Father
    that one of these little ones be lost." ✝

WEDNESDAY, DECEMBER 8
THE IMMACULATE CONCEPTION OF THE BLESSED VIRGIN MARY,
PATRONAL FEASTDAY OF THE UNITED STATES OF AMERICA

† *Genesis 3:9-15, 20*
I will put enmity between your offspring and hers.

After the man, Adam, had eaten of the tree,
    the LORD God called to the man and asked him, "Where are you?"
He answered, "I heard you in the garden;
    but I was afraid, because I was naked,
    so I hid myself."
Then he asked, "Who told you that you were naked?
You have eaten, then,
    from the tree of which I had forbidden you to eat!"
The man replied, "The woman whom you put here with me—
    she gave me fruit from the tree, and so I ate it."
The LORD God then asked the woman,
    "Why did you do such a thing?"
The woman answered, "The serpent tricked me into it, so I ate it."

Then the LORD God said to the serpent:
    "Because you have done this, you shall be banned
        from all the animals
        and from all the wild creatures;
    on your belly shall you crawl,
        and dirt shall you eat
        all the days of your life.
    I will put enmity between you and the woman,
        and between your offspring and hers;

he will strike at your head,
    while you strike at his heel."

The man called his wife Eve,
    because she became the mother of all the living. ✛

Psalm 98:1bcde, 2-3ab, 3cd-4
R. (1) **Sing to the Lord a new song, for he has done marvelous
    deeds.**
Sing to the Lord a new song,
    for he has done wondrous deeds;
his right hand has won victory for him,
    his holy arm. **R.**
The Lord has made his salvation known:
    in the sight of the nations he has revealed his justice.
He has remembered his kindness and his faithfulness
    toward the house of Israel. **R.**
All the ends of the earth have seen
    the salvation by our God.
Sing joyfully to the Lord, all you lands;
    break into song; sing praise. **R.**

† Ephesians 1:3-6, 11-12
He chose us in Christ before the foundation of the world.

Brothers and sisters:
Blessed be the God and Father of our Lord Jesus Christ,
    who has blessed us in Christ
    with every spiritual blessing in the heavens,
    as he chose us in him, before the foundation of the world,
    to be holy and without blemish before him.
In love he destined us for adoption to himself through Jesus Christ,
    in accord with the favor of his will,
    for the praise of the glory of his grace
    that he granted us in the beloved.

In him we were also chosen,
    destined in accord with the purpose of the One
    who accomplishes all things according to the intention of his will,
    so that we might exist for the praise of his glory,
    we who first hoped in Christ. ✛

See Luke 1:28
R. Alleluia, alleluia.
Hail, Mary, full of grace, the Lord is with you;
blessed are you among women. **R.**

† *Luke 1:26-38*
Hail, full of grace! The Lord is with you.

The angel Gabriel was sent from God
   to a town of Galilee called Nazareth,
   to a virgin betrothed to a man named Joseph,
   of the house of David,
   and the virgin's name was Mary.
And coming to her, he said,
   "Hail, full of grace! The Lord is with you."
But she was greatly troubled at what was said
   and pondered what sort of greeting this might be.
Then the angel said to her,
   "Do not be afraid, Mary,
   for you have found favor with God.
Behold, you will conceive in your womb and bear a son,
   and you shall name him Jesus.
He will be great and will be called Son of the Most High,
   and the Lord God will give him the throne of David his father,
   and he will rule over the house of Jacob forever,
   and of his Kingdom there will be no end."
But Mary said to the angel,
   "How can this be,
   since I have no relations with a man?"
And the angel said to her in reply,
   "The Holy Spirit will come upon you,
   and the power of the Most High will overshadow you.
Therefore the child to be born
   will be called holy, the Son of God.
And behold, Elizabeth, your relative,
   has also conceived a son in her old age,
   and this is the sixth month for her who was called barren;
   for nothing will be impossible for God."
Mary said, "Behold, I am the handmaid of the Lord.
May it be done to me according to your word."
Then the angel departed from her. ✙

THURSDAY, DECEMBER 9
ADVENT WEEKDAY, ST. JUAN DIEGO CUAUHTLATOATZIN

† *Isaiah 41:13-20*
I am your redeemer, the Holy One of Israel.

I am the LORD, your God,
   who grasp your right hand;

It is I who say to you, "Fear not,
  I will help you."
Fear not, O worm Jacob,
  O maggot Israel;
I will help you, says the LORD;
  your redeemer is the Holy One of Israel.
I will make of you a threshing sledge,
  sharp, new, and double-edged,
To thresh the mountains and crush them,
  to make the hills like chaff.
When you winnow them, the wind shall carry them off
  and the storm shall scatter them.
But you shall rejoice in the LORD,
  and glory in the Holy One of Israel.

The afflicted and the needy seek water in vain,
  their tongues are parched with thirst.
I, the LORD, will answer them;
  I, the God of Israel, will not forsake them.
I will open up rivers on the bare heights,
  and fountains in the broad valleys;
I will turn the desert into a marshland,
  and the dry ground into springs of water.
I will plant in the desert the cedar,
  acacia, myrtle, and olive;
I will set in the wasteland the cypress,
  together with the plane tree and the pine,
That all may see and know,
  observe and understand,
That the hand of the LORD has done this,
  the Holy One of Israel has created it. ✛

   Psalm 145:1, 9, 10-11, 12-13ab
R. (8) **The Lord is gracious and merciful; slow to anger, and
  of great kindness.**
I will extol you, O my God and King,
  and I will bless your name forever and ever.
The LORD is good to all
  and compassionate toward all his works. **R.**
Let all your works give you thanks, O LORD,
  and let your faithful ones bless you.
Let them discourse of the glory of your Kingdom
  and speak of your might. **R.**
Let them make known to men your might
  and the glorious splendor of your Kingdom.

Your Kingdom is a Kingdom for all ages,
and your dominion endures through all generations. **R.**

Isaiah 45:8
R. Alleluia, alleluia.
Let the clouds rain down the Just One,
and the earth bring forth a Savior. **R.**

✝ *Matthew 11:11-15*
None greater than John the Baptist has been born.

Jesus said to the crowds:
"Amen, I say to you,
among those born of women
there has been none greater than John the Baptist;
yet the least in the Kingdom of heaven is greater than he.
From the days of John the Baptist until now,
the Kingdom of heaven suffers violence,
and the violent are taking it by force.
All the prophets and the law prophesied up to the time of John.
And if you are willing to accept it,
he is Elijah, the one who is to come.
Whoever has ears ought to hear." ✝

FRIDAY, DECEMBER 10
ADVENT WEEKDAY, OUR LADY OF LORETO

✝ *Isaiah 48:17-19*
If only you would hearken to my commandments.

Thus says the LORD, your redeemer,
the Holy One of Israel:
I, the LORD, your God,
teach you what is for your good,
and lead you on the way you should go.
If you would hearken to my commandments,
your prosperity would be like a river,
and your vindication like the waves of the sea;
Your descendants would be like the sand,
and those born of your stock like its grains,
Their name never cut off
or blotted out from my presence. ✝

Psalm 1:1-2, 3, 4 and 6
R. (see John 8:12) **Those who follow you, Lord, will have the light of life.**
Blessed the man who follows not
the counsel of the wicked

Nor walks in the way of sinners,
  nor sits in the company of the insolent,
But delights in the law of the LORD
  and meditates on his law day and night. **R.**
He is like a tree
  planted near running water,
That yields its fruit in due season,
  and whose leaves never fade.
  Whatever he does, prospers. **R.**
Not so the wicked, not so;
  they are like chaff which the wind drives away.
For the LORD watches over the way of the just,
  but the way of the wicked vanishes. **R.**

R. Alleluia, alleluia.
The Lord will come; go out to meet him!
He is the prince of peace. **R.**

† *Matthew 11:16-19*
They listened to neither John nor to the Son of Man.

Jesus said to the crowds:
"To what shall I compare this generation?
It is like children who sit in marketplaces and call to one another,
  'We played the flute for you, but you did not dance,
  we sang a dirge but you did not mourn.'
For John came neither eating nor drinking, and they said,
  'He is possessed by a demon.'
The Son of Man came eating and drinking and they said,
  'Look, he is a glutton and a drunkard,
  a friend of tax collectors and sinners.'
But wisdom is vindicated by her works." ✛

SATURDAY, DECEMBER 11
ADVENT WEEKDAY, ST. POPE DAMASUS I

† *Sirach 48:1-4, 9-11*
Elijah was enveloped in a whirlwind.

In those days,
  like a fire there appeared the prophet Elijah
  whose words were as a flaming furnace.
Their staff of bread he shattered,
  in his zeal he reduced them to straits;
By the Lord's word he shut up the heavens
  and three times brought down fire.

How awesome are you, Elijah, in your wondrous deeds!
  Whose glory is equal to yours?
You were taken aloft in a whirlwind of fire,
  in a chariot with fiery horses.
You were destined, it is written, in time to come
  to put an end to wrath before the day of the LORD,
To turn back the hearts of fathers toward their sons,
  and to re-establish the tribes of Jacob.
Blessed is he who shall have seen you
  and who falls asleep in your friendship. ✙

Psalm 80:2ac and 3b, 15-16, 18-19
R. (4) **Lord, make us turn to you; let us see your face and we shall be saved.**
O shepherd of Israel, hearken,
From your throne upon the cherubim, shine forth.
Rouse your power. **R.**
Once again, O LORD of hosts,
  look down from heaven, and see;
Take care of this vine,
  and protect what your right hand has planted,
  the son of man whom you yourself made strong. **R.**
May your help be with the man of your right hand,
  with the son of man whom you yourself made strong.
Then we will no more withdraw from you;
  give us new life, and we will call upon your name. **R.**

Luke 3:4, 6
R. Alleluia, alleluia.
Prepare the way of the Lord, make straight his paths:
All flesh shall see the salvation of God. **R.**

✝ *Matthew 17:9a, 10-13*
Elijah has already come, and they did not recognize him.

As they were coming down from the mountain,
  the disciples asked Jesus,
  "Why do the scribes say that Elijah must come first?"
He said in reply, "Elijah will indeed come and restore all things;
  but I tell you that Elijah has already come,
  and they did not recognize him but did to him whatever they
    pleased.
So also will the Son of Man suffer at their hands."
Then the disciples understood
  that he was speaking to them of John the Baptist. ✙

SUNDAY, DECEMBER 12
THIRD SUNDAY OF ADVENT

† *Zephaniah 3:14-18a*
The Lord will rejoice over you with gladness.

Shout for joy, O daughter Zion!
  Sing joyfully, O Israel!
Be glad and exult with all your heart,
  O daughter Jerusalem!
The LORD has removed the judgment against you,
  he has turned away your enemies;
the King of Israel, the LORD, is in your midst,
  you have no further misfortune to fear.
On that day, it shall be said to Jerusalem:
  Fear not, O Zion, be not discouraged!
The LORD, your God, is in your midst,
  a mighty savior;
he will rejoice over you with gladness,
  and renew you in his love,
he will sing joyfully because of you,
  as one sings at festivals. ✛

Isaiah 12:2-3, 4, 5-6
**R. Cry out with joy and gladness: for among you is the great
    and Holy One of Israel.**
God indeed is my savior;
  I am confident and unafraid.
My strength and my courage is the LORD,
  and he has been my savior.
With joy you will draw water
  at the fountain of salvation. **R.**
Give thanks to the LORD, acclaim his name;
  among the nations make known his deeds,
  proclaim how exalted is his name. **R.**
Sing praise to the LORD for his glorious achievement;
  let this be known throughout all the earth.
Shout with exultation, O city of Zion,
  for great in your midst
  is the Holy One of Israel! **R.**

† *Philippians 4:4-7*
The Lord is near.

Brothers and sisters:
Rejoice in the Lord always.
I shall say it again: rejoice!

Your kindness should be known to all.
The Lord is near.
Have no anxiety at all, but in everything,
  by prayer and petition, with thanksgiving,
  make your requests known to God.
Then the peace of God that surpasses all understanding
  will guard your hearts and minds in Christ Jesus. ✛

Isaiah 61:1 (cited in Luke 4:18)
R. Alleluia, alleluia.
The Spirit of the Lord is upon me,
because he has anointed me
to bring glad tidings to the poor. **R.**

✝ *Luke 3:10-18*
What should we do?

The crowds asked John the Baptist,
  "What should we do?"
He said to them in reply,
  "Whoever has two cloaks
  should share with the person who has none.
And whoever has food should do likewise."
Even tax collectors came to be baptized and they said to him,
  "Teacher, what should we do?"
He answered them,
  "Stop collecting more than what is prescribed."
Soldiers also asked him,
  "And what is it that we should do?"
He told them,
  "Do not practice extortion,
  do not falsely accuse anyone,
  and be satisfied with your wages."

Now the people were filled with expectation,
  and all were asking in their hearts
  whether John might be the Christ.
John answered them all, saying,
  "I am baptizing you with water,
  but one mightier than I is coming.
I am not worthy to loosen the thongs of his sandals.
He will baptize you with the Holy Spirit and fire.
His winnowing fan is in his hand to clear his threshing floor
  and to gather the wheat into his barn,
  but the chaff he will burn with unquenchable fire."

Exhorting them in many other ways,
he preached good news to the people. ✛

MONDAY, DECEMBER 13
St. Lucy

† *Numbers 24:2-7, 15-17a*
A star shall advance from Jacob.

When Balaam raised his eyes and saw Israel encamped, tribe by
    tribe,
the spirit of God came upon him,
and he gave voice to his oracle:

The utterance of Balaam, son of Beor,
    the utterance of a man whose eye is true,
The utterance of one who hears what God says,
    and knows what the Most High knows,
Of one who sees what the Almighty sees,
    enraptured, and with eyes unveiled:
How goodly are your tents, O Jacob;
    your encampments, O Israel!
They are like gardens beside a stream,
    like the cedars planted by the Lord.
His wells shall yield free-flowing waters,
    he shall have the sea within reach;
His king shall rise higher,
    and his royalty shall be exalted.

Then Balaam gave voice to his oracle:

The utterance of Balaam, son of Beor,
    the utterance of the man whose eye is true,
The utterance of one who hears what God says,
    and knows what the Most High knows,
Of one who sees what the Almighty sees,
    enraptured, and with eyes unveiled.
I see him, though not now;
    I behold him, though not near:
A star shall advance from Jacob,
    and a staff shall rise from Israel. ✛

Psalm 25:4-5ab, 6 and 7bc, 8-9
R. (4) **Teach me your ways, O Lord.**
Your ways, O Lord, make known to me;
    teach me your paths,
Guide me in your truth and teach me,

for you are God my savior. **R.**
Remember that your compassion, O LORD,
 and your kindness are from of old.
In your kindness remember me,
 because of your goodness, O LORD. **R.**
Good and upright is the LORD;
 thus he shows sinners the way.
He guides the humble to justice,
 he teaches the humble his way. **R.**

Psalm 85:8
R. Alleluia, alleluia.
Show us, LORD, your love,
and grant us your salvation. **R.**

† Matthew 21:23-27
John's baptism: where did it come from?

When Jesus had come into the temple area,
 the chief priests and the elders of the people approached him
 as he was teaching and said,
 "By what authority are you doing these things?
And who gave you this authority?"
Jesus said to them in reply,
 "I shall ask you one question, and if you answer it for me,
 then I shall tell you by what authority I do these things.
Where was John's baptism from?
Was it of heavenly or of human origin?"
They discussed this among themselves and said,
 "If we say 'Of heavenly origin,' he will say to us,
 'Then why did you not believe him?'
But if we say, 'Of human origin,' we fear the crowd,
 for they all regard John as a prophet."
So they said to Jesus in reply, "We do not know."
He himself said to them,
 "Neither shall I tell you by what authority I do these things." ✛

TUESDAY, DECEMBER 14
ST. JOHN OF THE CROSS

† Zephaniah 3:1-2, 9-13
Messianic salvation is promised to all of the poor.

Thus says the LORD:
Woe to the city, rebellious and polluted,
 to the tyrannical city!
She hears no voice,
 accepts no correction;

In the LORD she has not trusted,
  to her God she has not drawn near.

For then I will change and purify
  the lips of the peoples,
That they all may call upon the name of the LORD,
  to serve him with one accord;
From beyond the rivers of Ethiopia
  and as far as the recesses of the North,
  they shall bring me offerings.

  On that day
You need not be ashamed
  of all your deeds,
  your rebellious actions against me;
For then will I remove from your midst
  the proud braggarts,
And you shall no longer exalt yourself
  on my holy mountain.
But I will leave as a remnant in your midst
  a people humble and lowly,
Who shall take refuge in the name of the LORD:
  the remnant of Israel.
They shall do no wrong
  and speak no lies;
Nor shall there be found in their mouths
  a deceitful tongue;
They shall pasture and couch their flocks
  with none to disturb them. ✤

Psalm 34:2-3, 6-7, 17-18, 19 and 23
R. (7a) **The Lord hears the cry of the poor.**
I will bless the LORD at all times;
  his praise shall be ever in my mouth.
Let my soul glory in the LORD;
  the lowly will hear me and be glad. **R.**
Look to him that you may be radiant with joy,
  and your faces may not blush with shame.
When the poor one called out, the LORD heard,
  and from all his distress he saved him. **R.**
The LORD confronts the evildoers,
  to destroy remembrance of them from the earth.
When the just cry out, the LORD hears them,
  and from all their distress he rescues them. **R.**

The LORD is close to the brokenhearted;
  and those who are crushed in spirit he saves.
The LORD redeems the lives of his servants;
  no one incurs guilt who takes refuge in him. **R.**
R. Alleluia, alleluia.
Come, O Lord, do not delay;
forgive the sins of your people. **R.**

† *Matthew 21:28-32*
John came and sinners believed in him.

Jesus said to the chief priests and the elders of the people:
"What is your opinion?
A man had two sons.
He came to the first and said,
  'Son, go out and work in the vineyard today.'
The son said in reply, 'I will not,'
  but afterwards he changed his mind and went.
The man came to the other son and gave the same order.
He said in reply, 'Yes, sir,' but did not go.
Which of the two did his father's will?"
They answered, "The first."
Jesus said to them, "Amen, I say to you,
  tax collectors and prostitutes
  are entering the Kingdom of God before you.
When John came to you in the way of righteousness,
  you did not believe him;
  but tax collectors and prostitutes did.
Yet even when you saw that,
  you did not later change your minds and believe him." ✝

WEDNESDAY, DECEMBER 15
ADVENT WEEKDAY

† *Isaiah 45:6c-8, 18, 21c-25*
Let the clouds rain down.

I am the LORD, there is no other;
  I form the light, and create the darkness,
I make well-being and create woe;
  I, the LORD, do all these things.
Let justice descend, O heavens, like dew from above,
  like gentle rain let the skies drop it down.
Let the earth open and salvation bud forth;
  let justice also spring up!
  I, the LORD, have created this.

For thus says the LORD,
The creator of the heavens,
  who is God,
The designer and maker of the earth
  who established it,
Not creating it to be a waste,
  but designing it be lived in:
I am the LORD, and there is no other.

Who announced this from the beginning
  and foretold it from of old?
Was it not I, the LORD,
  besides whom there is no other God?
There is no just and saving God but me.

Turn to me and be safe,
  all you ends of the earth,
  for I am God; there is no other!
By myself I swear,
  uttering my just decree
  and my unalterable word:
To me every knee shall bend;
  by me every tongue shall swear,
Saying, "Only in the LORD
  are just deeds and power.
Before him in shame shall come
  all who vent their anger against him.
In the LORD shall be the vindication and the glory
  of all the descendants of Israel." ✦

Psalm 85:9ab and 10, 11-12, 13-14
R. (Isaiah 45:8) **Let the clouds rain down the Just One, and
  the earth bring forth a Savior.**
I will hear what God proclaims;
  the LORD—for he proclaims peace to his people.
Near indeed is his salvation to those who fear him,
  glory dwelling in our land. **R.**
Kindness and truth shall meet;
  justice and peace shall kiss.
Truth shall spring out of the earth,
  and justice shall look down from heaven. **R.**
The LORD himself will give his benefits;
  our land shall yield its increase.
Justice shall walk before him,
  and salvation, along the way of his steps. **R.**

See Isaiah 40:9-10

R. Alleluia, alleluia.

Raise your voice and tell the Good News:

Behold, the Lord GOD comes with power. **R.**

† *Luke 7:18b-23*

Go back and tell John what you have seen and heard.

At that time,

John summoned two of his disciples and sent them to the Lord to ask,
  "Are you the one who is to come, or should we look for another?"
When the men came to the Lord, they said,
  "John the Baptist has sent us to you to ask,
  'Are you the one who is to come, or should we look for another?'"
At that time Jesus cured many of their diseases, sufferings, and evil
    spirits;
  he also granted sight to many who were blind.
And Jesus said to them in reply,
  "Go and tell John what you have seen and heard:
  the blind regain their sight,
  the lame walk,
  lepers are cleansed,
  the deaf hear, the dead are raised,
  the poor have the good news proclaimed to them.
And blessed is the one who takes no offense at me." ✢

THURSDAY, DECEMBER 16
ADVENT WEEKDAY

† *Isaiah 54:1-10*

Like a forsaken wife, the LORD has called you back.

Raise a glad cry, you barren one who did not bear,
  Break forth in jubilant song, you who were not in labor,
For more numerous are the children of the deserted wife
    than the children of her who has a husband,
    says the LORD.
Enlarge the space for your tent,
    spread out your tent cloths unsparingly;
    lengthen your ropes and make firm your stakes.
For you shall spread abroad to the right and to the left;
    your descendants shall dispossess the nations
    and shall people the desolate cities.

Fear not, you shall not be put to shame;
    you need not blush, for you shall not be disgraced.

The shame of your youth you shall forget,
 the reproach of your widowhood no longer remember.
For he who has become your husband is your Maker;
 his name is the LORD of hosts;
Your redeemer is the Holy One of Israel,
 called God of all the earth.
The LORD calls you back,
 like a wife forsaken and grieved in spirit,
A wife married in youth and then cast off,
 says your God.
For a brief moment I abandoned you,
 but with great tenderness I will take you back.
In an outburst of wrath, for a moment
 I hid my face from you;
but with enduring love I take pity on you,
 says the LORD, your redeemer.

This is for me like the days of Noah,
 when I swore that the waters of Noah
 should never again deluge the earth;
So I have sworn not to be angry with you,
 or to rebuke you.
Though the mountains leave their place
 and the hills be shaken,
My love shall never leave you
 nor my covenant of peace be shaken,
 says the LORD, who has mercy on you. ✛

Psalm 30:2 and 4, 5-6, 11-12a and 13b
R. (2a) **I will praise you, Lord, for you have rescued me.**
I will extol you, O LORD, for you drew me clear
 and did not let my enemies rejoice over me.
O LORD, you brought me up from the nether world;
 you preserved me from among those going down into the pit. **R.**

Sing praise to the LORD, you his faithful ones,
 and give thanks to his holy name.
For his anger lasts but a moment;
 a lifetime, his good will.
At nightfall, weeping enters in,
 but with the dawn, rejoicing. **R.**

"Hear, O LORD, and have pity on me;
 O LORD, be my helper."
You changed my mourning into dancing;
 O LORD, my God, forever will I give you thanks. **R.**

Luke 3:4, 6

R. Alleluia, alleluia.
Prepare the way of the Lord, make straight his paths;
All flesh shall see the salvation of God. **R.**

† *Luke 7:24-30*
John is the messenger who prepares the way of the Lord.

When the messengers of John the Baptist had left,
  Jesus began to speak to the crowds about John.
"What did you go out to the desert to see—a reed swayed by the
    wind?
Then what did you go out to see?
Someone dressed in fine garments?
Those who dress luxuriously and live sumptuously
    are found in royal palaces.
Then what did you go out to see?
A prophet? Yes, I tell you, and more than a prophet.
This is the one about whom Scripture says:

  Behold, I am sending my messenger ahead of you,
  he will prepare your way before you.

I tell you,
    among those born of women, no one is greater than John;
    yet the least in the Kingdom of God is greater than he."
(All the people who listened, including the tax collectors,
    who were baptized with the baptism of John,
    acknowledged the righteousness of God;
    but the Pharisees and scholars of the law,
    who were not baptized by him,
    rejected the plan of God for themselves.) ✢

FRIDAY, DECEMBER 17
ADVENT WEEKDAY

† *Genesis 49:2, 8-10*
The scepter shall not depart from Judah.

Jacob called his sons and said to them:
  "Assemble and listen, sons of Jacob,
    listen to Israel, your father.

  "You, Judah, shall your brothers praise
    —your hand on the neck of your enemies;
    the sons of your father shall bow down to you.
  Judah, like a lion's whelp,
    you have grown up on prey, my son.

He crouches like a lion recumbent,
the king of beasts—who would dare rouse him?
The scepter shall never depart from Judah,
or the mace from between his legs,
While tribute is brought to him,
and he receives the peoples' homage." ✛

Psalm 72:1-2, 3-4ab, 7-8, 17

R. (see 7) **Justice shall flourish in his time, and fullness of
peace for ever.**

O God, with your judgment endow the king,
and with your justice, the king's son;
He shall govern your people with justice
and your afflicted ones with judgment. **R.**
The mountains shall yield peace for the people,
and the hills justice.
He shall defend the afflicted among the people,
save the children of the poor. **R.**
Justice shall flower in his days,
and profound peace, till the moon be no more.
May he rule from sea to sea,
and from the River to the ends of the earth. **R.**
May his name be blessed forever;
as long as the sun his name shall remain.
In him shall all the tribes of the earth be blessed;
all the nations shall proclaim his happiness. **R.**

R. Alleluia, alleluia.
O Wisdom of our God Most High,
guiding creation with power and love:
come to teach us the path of knowledge! **R.**

† *Matthew 1:1-17*
The genealogy of Jesus Christ, son of David.

The book of the genealogy of Jesus Christ,
the son of David, the son of Abraham.

Abraham became the father of Isaac,
Isaac the father of Jacob,
Jacob the father of Judah and his brothers.
Judah became the father of Perez and Zerah,
whose mother was Tamar.
Perez became the father of Hezron,
Hezron the father of Ram,
Ram the father of Amminadab.

Amminadab became the father of Nahshon,
   Nahshon the father of Salmon,
   Salmon the father of Boaz,
   whose mother was Rahab.
Boaz became the father of Obed,
   whose mother was Ruth.
Obed became the father of Jesse,
   Jesse the father of David the king.

David became the father of Solomon,
   whose mother had been the wife of Uriah.
Solomon became the father of Rehoboam,
   Rehoboam the father of Abijah,
   Abijah the father of Asaph.
Asaph became the father of Jehoshaphat,
   Jehoshaphat the father of Joram,
   Joram the father of Uzziah.
Uzziah became the father of Jotham,
   Jotham the father of Ahaz,
   Ahaz the father of Hezekiah.
Hezekiah became the father of Manasseh,
   Manasseh the father of Amos,
   Amos the father of Josiah.
Josiah became the father of Jechoniah and his brothers
   at the time of the Babylonian exile.

After the Babylonian exile,
   Jechoniah became the father of Shealtiel,
   Shealtiel the father of Zerubbabel,
   Zerubbabel the father of Abiud.
Abiud became the father of Eliakim,
   Eliakim the father of Azor,
   Azor the father of Zadok.
Zadok became the father of Achim,
   Achim the father of Eliud,
   Eliud the father of Eleazar.
Eleazar became the father of Matthan,
   Matthan the father of Jacob,
   Jacob the father of Joseph, the husband of Mary.
Of her was born Jesus who is called the Christ.

Thus the total number of generations
   from Abraham to David
   is fourteen generations;
   from David to the Babylonian exile, fourteen generations;

from the Babylonian exile to the Christ,
fourteen generations. ✛

SATURDAY, DECEMBER 18
ADVENT WEEKDAY

† *Jeremiah 23:5-8*
I will raise up a righteous shoot to David.

Behold, the days are coming, says the LORD,
   when I will raise up a righteous shoot to David;
As king he shall reign and govern wisely,
   he shall do what is just and right in the land.
In his days Judah shall be saved,
   Israel shall dwell in security.
This is the name they give him:
   "The LORD our justice."

Therefore, the days will come, says the LORD,
   when they shall no longer say, "As the LORD lives,
   who brought the children of Israel out of the land of Egypt";
but rather, "As the LORD lives,
   who brought the descendants of the house of Israel
   up from the land of the north"—
and from all the lands to which I banished them;
   they shall again live on their own land. ✛

Psalm 72:1-2, 12-13, 18-19
R. (see 7) **Justice shall flourish in his time, and fullness of
   peace for ever.**
O God, with your judgment endow the king,
   and with your justice, the king's son;
He shall govern your people with justice
   and your afflicted ones with judgment. **R.**
For he shall rescue the poor when he cries out,
   and the afflicted when he has no one to help him.
He shall have pity for the lowly and the poor;
   the lives of the poor he shall save. **R.**
Blessed be the LORD, the God of Israel,
   who alone does wondrous deeds.
And blessed forever be his glorious name;
   may the whole earth be filled with his glory. **R.**

R. Alleluia, alleluia.
O Leader of the House of Israel,
giver of the Law to Moses on Sinai:
come to rescue us with your mighty power! **R.**

† *Matthew 1:18-25*

Jesus was born of Mary, the betrothed of Joseph, a son of David.

This is how the birth of Jesus Christ came about.
When his mother Mary was betrothed to Joseph,
    but before they lived together,
    she was found with child through the Holy Spirit.
Joseph her husband, since he was a righteous man,
    yet unwilling to expose her to shame,
    decided to divorce her quietly.
Such was his intention when, behold,
    the angel of the Lord appeared to him in a dream and said,
    "Joseph, son of David,
    do not be afraid to take Mary your wife into your home.
For it is through the Holy Spirit
    that this child has been conceived in her.
She will bear a son and you are to name him Jesus,
    because he will save his people from their sins."
All this took place to fulfill
    what the Lord had said through the prophet:

Behold, the virgin shall be with child and bear a son,
    and they shall name him Emmanuel,

    which means "God is with us."
When Joseph awoke,
    he did as the angel of the Lord had commanded him
    and took his wife into his home.
He had no relations with her until she bore a son,
    and he named him Jesus. ✛

SUNDAY, DECEMBER 19
FOURTH SUNDAY OF ADVENT

† *Micah 5:1-4a*

From you shall come forth the ruler of Israel.

Thus says the LORD:
You, Bethlehem-Ephrathah,
    too small to be among the clans of Judah,
from you shall come forth for me
    one who is to be ruler in Israel;
    whose origin is from of old,
    from ancient times.
    Therefore the Lord will give them up, until the time
        when she who is to give birth has borne,

and the rest of his kindred shall return
   to the children of Israel.
He shall stand firm and shepherd his flock
   by the strength of the LORD,
   in the majestic name of the LORD, his God;
and they shall remain, for now his greatness
   shall reach to the ends of the earth;
   he shall be peace. ✛

Psalm 80:2-3, 15-16, 18-19

**R. Lord, make us turn to you; let us see your face and we
   shall be saved.**

O shepherd of Israel, hearken,
   from your throne upon the cherubim, shine forth.
Rouse your power,
   and come to save us. **R.**
Once again, O LORD of hosts,
   look down from heaven, and see;
take care of this vine,
   and protect what your right hand has planted,
   the son of man whom you yourself made strong. **R.**
May your help be with the man of your right hand,
   the son of man whom you yourself made strong.
Then we will no more withdraw from you;
   give us new life, and we will call upon your name. **R.**

† Hebrews 10:5-10
Behold, I come to do your will.

Brothers and sisters:
When Christ came into the world, he said:
   "Sacrifice and offering you did not desire,
   but a body you prepared for me;
   in holocausts and sin offerings you took no delight.
   Then I said, 'As is written of me in the scroll,
   behold, I come to do your will, O God.'"

First he says, "Sacrifices and offerings,
   holocausts and sin offerings,
   you neither desired nor delighted in."
These are offered according to the law.
Then he says, "Behold, I come to do your will."
He takes away the first to establish the second.
By this "will," we have been consecrated
   through the offering of the body of Jesus Christ once for all. ✛

Luke 1:38
R. Alleluia, alleluia.
Behold, I am the handmaid of the Lord.
May it be done to me according to your word. **R.**

† *Luke 1:39-45*
And how does this happen to me, that the
mother of my Lord should come to me?

Mary set out
  and traveled to the hill country in haste
  to a town of Judah,
  where she entered the house of Zechariah
  and greeted Elizabeth.
When Elizabeth heard Mary's greeting,
  the infant leaped in her womb,
  and Elizabeth, filled with the Holy Spirit,
  cried out in a loud voice and said,
  "Blessed are you among women,
  and blessed is the fruit of your womb.
And how does this happen to me,
  that the mother of my Lord should come to me?
For at the moment the sound of your greeting reached my ears,
  the infant in my womb leaped for joy.
Blessed are you who believed
  that what was spoken to you by the Lord
  would be fulfilled." ✢

MONDAY, DECEMBER 20
ADVENT WEEKDAY

† *Isaiah 7:10-14*
Behold, the virgin shall be with child.

The LORD spoke to Ahaz:
Ask for a sign from the LORD, your God;
  let it be deep as the nether world, or high as the sky!
But Ahaz answered,
  "I will not ask! I will not tempt the LORD!"
Then Isaiah said:
  Listen, O house of David!
Is it not enough for you to weary men,
  must you also weary my God?
Therefore the Lord himself will give you this sign:
  the virgin shall conceive and bear a son,
  and shall name him Emmanuel. ✢

Psalm 24:1-2, 3-4ab, 5-6
R. (see 7c and 10b) **Let the Lord enter; he is the king of glory.**
The LORD's are the earth and its fullness;
   the world and those who dwell in it.
For he founded it upon the seas
   and established it upon the rivers. **R.**
Who can ascend the mountain of the LORD?
   or who may stand in his holy place?
He whose hands are sinless, whose heart is clean,
   who desires not what is vain. **R.**
He shall receive a blessing from the LORD,
   a reward from God his savior.
Such is the race that seeks for him,
   that seeks the face of the God of Jacob. **R.**

R. Alleluia, alleluia.
O Key of David,
opening the gates of God's eternal Kingdom:
come and free the prisoners of darkness! **R.**

† *Luke 1:26-38*
You will conceive in your womb and bear a son.

In the sixth month,
   the angel Gabriel was sent from God
   to a town of Galilee called Nazareth,
   to a virgin betrothed to a man named Joseph,
   of the house of David,
   and the virgin's name was Mary.
And coming to her, he said,
   "Hail, full of grace! The Lord is with you."
But she was greatly troubled at what was said
   and pondered what sort of greeting this might be.
Then the angel said to her,
   "Do not be afraid, Mary,
   for you have found favor with God.
Behold, you will conceive in your womb and bear a son,
   and you shall name him Jesus.
He will be great and will be called Son of the Most High,
   and the Lord God will give him the throne of David his father,
   and he will rule over the house of Jacob forever,
   and of his Kingdom there will be no end."

But Mary said to the angel,
   "How can this be,
   since I have no relations with a man?"

And the angel said to her in reply,
"The Holy Spirit will come upon you,
and the power of the Most High will overshadow you.
Therefore the child to be born
will be called holy, the Son of God.
And behold, Elizabeth, your relative,
has also conceived a son in her old age,
and this is the sixth month for her who was called barren;
for nothing will be impossible for God."

Mary said, "Behold, I am the handmaid of the Lord.
May it be done to me according to your word."
Then the angel departed from her. ✛

TUESDAY, DECEMBER 21
ADVENT WEEKDAY, ST. PETER CANISIUS

✝ *Song of Songs 2:8-14 (or Zephaniah 3:14-18a)*
Hark! my lover comes, springing across the mountains.

Hark! my lover—here he comes
springing across the mountains,
leaping across the hills.
My lover is like a gazelle
or a young stag.
Here he stands behind our wall,
gazing through the windows,
peering through the lattices.
My lover speaks; he says to me,
"Arise, my beloved, my dove, my beautiful one,
and come!
"For see, the winter is past,
the rains are over and gone.
The flowers appear on the earth,
the time of pruning the vines has come,
and the song of the dove is heard in our land.
The fig tree puts forth its figs,
and the vines, in bloom, give forth fragrance.
Arise, my beloved, my beautiful one,
and come!

"O my dove in the clefts of the rock,
in the secret recesses of the cliff,

Let me see you,
    let me hear your voice,
For your voice is sweet,
    and you are lovely." ✛

Psalm 33:2-3, 11-12, 20-21
R. (1a; 3a) **Exult, you just, in the Lord! Sing to him a new song.**
Give thanks to the Lord on the harp;
    with the ten-stringed lyre chant his praises.
Sing to him a new song;
    pluck the strings skillfully, with shouts of gladness. **R.**
But the plan of the Lord stands forever;
    the design of his heart, through all generations.
Blessed the nation whose God is the Lord,
    the people he has chosen for his own inheritance. **R.**
Our soul waits for the Lord,
    who is our help and our shield,
For in him our hearts rejoice;
    in his holy name we trust. **R.**

R. Alleluia, alleluia.
O Emmanuel, our King and Giver of Law:
come to save us, Lord our God! **R.**

† Luke 1:39-45
*And how does this happen to me, that the
mother of my Lord should come to me?*

Mary set out in those days
    and traveled to the hill country in haste
    to a town of Judah,
    where she entered the house of Zechariah
    and greeted Elizabeth.
When Elizabeth heard Mary's greeting,
    the infant leaped in her womb,
    and Elizabeth, filled with the Holy Spirit,
    cried out in a loud voice and said,
    "Most blessed are you among women,
    and blessed is the fruit of your womb.
And how does this happen to me,
    that the mother of my Lord should come to me?
For at the moment the sound of your greeting reached my ears,
    the infant in my womb leaped for joy.
Blessed are you who believed
    that what was spoken to you by the Lord
    would be fulfilled." ✛

WEDNESDAY, DECEMBER 22
ADVENT WEEKDAY

† 1 Samuel 1:24-28
Hannah gives thanks for the birth of Samuel.

In those days,
Hannah brought Samuel with her,
   along with a three-year-old bull,
   an ephah of flour, and a skin of wine,
   and presented him at the temple of the LORD in Shiloh.
After the boy's father had sacrificed the young bull,
   Hannah, his mother, approached Eli and said:
   "Pardon, my lord!
As you live, my lord,
   I am the woman who stood near you here, praying to the LORD.
I prayed for this child, and the LORD granted my request.
Now I, in turn, give him to the LORD;
   as long as he lives, he shall be dedicated to the LORD."
She left Samuel there. ✛

1 Samuel 2:1, 4-5, 6-7, 8abcd
R. (see 1a) **My heart exults in the Lord, my Savior.**
"My heart exults in the LORD,
   my horn is exalted in my God.
I have swallowed up my enemies;
   I rejoice in my victory." **R.**
"The bows of the mighty are broken,
   while the tottering gird on strength.
The well-fed hire themselves out for bread,
   while the hungry batten on spoil.
The barren wife bears seven sons,
   while the mother of many languishes." **R.**
"The LORD puts to death and gives life;
   he casts down to the nether world;
   he raises up again.
The LORD makes poor and makes rich,
   he humbles, he also exalts." **R.**
"He raises the needy from the dust;
   from the dung heap he lifts up the poor,
To seat them with nobles
   and make a glorious throne their heritage." **R.**

R. Alleluia, alleluia.
O King of all nations and keystone of the Church:
come and save man, whom you formed from the dust! **R.**

† *Luke 1:46-56*
The Mighty One has done great things for me.

Mary said:

"My soul proclaims the greatness of the Lord;
  my spirit rejoices in God my savior,
  for he has looked upon his lowly servant.
From this day all generations will call me blessed;
  the Almighty has done great things for me,
  and holy is his Name.
He has mercy on those who fear him
  in every generation.
He has shown the strength of his arm,
  and has scattered the proud in their conceit.
He has cast down the mighty from their thrones
  and has lifted up the lowly.
He has filled the hungry with good things,
  and the rich he has sent away empty.
He has come to the help of his servant Israel
  for he remembered his promise of mercy,
  the promise he made to our fathers,
  to Abraham and his children for ever."

Mary remained with Elizabeth about three months
  and then returned to her home. ✛

THURSDAY, DECEMBER 23
ADVENT WEEKDAY, ST. JOHN OF KANTY

† *Malachi 3:1-4, 23-24*
I will send you Elijah, the prophet, before the day of the LORD comes.

Thus says the Lord GOD:
Lo, I am sending my messenger
  to prepare the way before me;
And suddenly there will come to the temple
  the LORD whom you seek,
And the messenger of the covenant whom you desire.
  Yes, he is coming, says the LORD of hosts.
But who will endure the day of his coming?
  And who can stand when he appears?
For he is like the refiner's fire,
  or like the fuller's lye.
He will sit refining and purifying silver,
  and he will purify the sons of Levi,
Refining them like gold or like silver

that they may offer due sacrifice to the LORD.
Then the sacrifice of Judah and Jerusalem
will please the LORD,
as in the days of old, as in years gone by.

Lo, I will send you
Elijah, the prophet,
Before the day of the LORD comes,
the great and terrible day,
To turn the hearts of the fathers to their children,
and the hearts of the children to their fathers,
Lest I come and strike
the land with doom. ✝

Psalm 25:4-5ab, 8-9, 10 and 14
R. (see Luke 21:28) **Lift up your heads and see; your redemption is near at hand.**
Your ways, O LORD, make known to me;
teach me your paths,
Guide me in your truth and teach me,
for you are God my savior. **R.**
Good and upright is the LORD;
thus he shows sinners the way.
He guides the humble to justice,
he teaches the humble his way. **R.**
All the paths of the LORD are kindness and constancy
toward those who keep his covenant and his decrees.
The friendship of the LORD is with those who fear him,
and his covenant, for their instruction. **R.**

R. Alleluia, alleluia.
O King of all nations and keystone of the Church;
come and save man, whom you formed from the dust! **R.**

✝ Luke 1:57-66
The birth of John the Baptist.

When the time arrived for Elizabeth to have her child
she gave birth to a son.
Her neighbors and relatives heard
that the Lord had shown his great mercy toward her,
and they rejoiced with her.
When they came on the eighth day to circumcise the child,
they were going to call him Zechariah after his father,
but his mother said in reply,
"No. He will be called John."
But they answered her,

"There is no one among your relatives who has this name."
So they made signs, asking his father what he wished him to be
    called.
He asked for a tablet and wrote, "John is his name,"
    and all were amazed.
Immediately his mouth was opened, his tongue freed,
    and he spoke blessing God.
Then fear came upon all their neighbors,
    and all these matters were discussed
    throughout the hill country of Judea.
All who heard these things took them to heart, saying,
    "What, then, will this child be?"
For surely the hand of the Lord was with him. ✛

FRIDAY, DECEMBER 24
ADVENT WEEKDAY (MORNING)

† 2 Samuel 7:1-5, 8b-12, 14a, 16
The Kingdom of David shall endure forever in the sight of the LORD.

When King David was settled in his palace,
    and the LORD had given him rest from his enemies on every side,
    he said to Nathan the prophet,
    "Here I am living in a house of cedar,
    while the ark of God dwells in a tent!"
Nathan answered the king,
"Go, do whatever you have in mind,
    for the LORD is with you."
But that night the LORD spoke to Nathan and said:
    "Go, tell my servant David, 'Thus says the LORD:
    Should you build me a house to dwell in?

"'It was I who took you from the pasture
    and from the care of the flock
    to be commander of my people Israel.
I have been with you wherever you went,
    and I have destroyed all your enemies before you.
And I will make you famous like the great ones of the earth.
I will fix a place for my people Israel;
    I will plant them so that they may dwell in their place
    without further disturbance.
Neither shall the wicked continue to afflict them as they did of old,
    since the time I first appointed judges over my people Israel.
I will give you rest from all your enemies.
The LORD also reveals to you
    that he will establish a house for you.

And when your time comes and you rest with your ancestors,
  I will raise up your heir after you, sprung from your loins,
  and I will make his Kingdom firm.
I will be a father to him,
  and he shall be a son to me.
Your house and your Kingdom shall endure forever before me;
  your throne shall stand firm forever.'" ✝

Psalm 89:2-3, 4-5, 27 and 29
R. (2) **For ever I will sing the goodness of the Lord.**
The favors of the Lord I will sing forever;
  through all generations my mouth shall proclaim your faithfulness.
For you have said, "My kindness is established forever";
  in heaven you have confirmed your faithfulness. **R.**
"I have made a covenant with my chosen one,
  I have sworn to David my servant:
Forever will I confirm your posterity
  and establish your throne for all generations." **R.**
He shall say of me, "You are my father,
  my God, the rock, my savior."
Forever I will maintain my kindness toward him,
  and my covenant with him stands firm. **R.**

R. Alleluia, alleluia.
O Radiant Dawn,
splendor of eternal light, sun of justice:
come and shine on those who dwell in darkness and in the shadow
    of death. **R.**

✝ Luke 1:67-79
The daybreak from on high has visited us.

Zechariah his father, filled with the Holy Spirit, prophesied, saying:

"Blessed be the Lord, the God of Israel;
  for he has come to his people and set them free.
He has raised up for us a mighty Savior,
  born of the house of his servant David.
Through his prophets he promised of old
    that he would save us from our enemies,
    from the hands of all who hate us.
He promised to show mercy to our fathers
    and to remember his holy covenant.
This was the oath he swore to our father Abraham:
    to set us free from the hand of our enemies,
    free to worship him without fear,

holy and righteous in his sight
 all the days of our life.
You, my child, shall be called the prophet of the Most High,
 for you will go before the Lord to prepare his way,
 to give his people knowledge of salvation
 by the forgiveness of their sins.
In the tender compassion of our God
 the dawn from on high shall break upon us,
 to shine on those who dwell in darkness and the shadow of death,
 and to guide our feet into the way of peace."✙

SATURDAY, DECEMBER 25
THE NATIVITY OF THE LORD, CHRISTMAS

Below are readings for Mass at Midnight. For Vigil Mass: Isaiah 62:1-5 • Psalm 89:4-5,
16-17, 27, 29 • Acts 13:16-17, 22-25 • Matthew 1:1-25 or 1:18-25; At Dawn: Isaiah 62:11-12
 • Psalm 97:1, 6, 11-12 • Titus 3:4-7 • Luke 2:15-20; Mass during the Day (see below).

† Isaiah 9:1-6
A son is given us.

The people who walked in darkness
 have seen a great light;
upon those who dwelt in the land of gloom
 a light has shone.
You have brought them abundant joy
 and great rejoicing,
as they rejoice before you as at the harvest,
 as people make merry when dividing spoils.
For the yoke that burdened them,
 the pole on their shoulder,
and the rod of their taskmaster
 you have smashed, as on the day of Midian.
For every boot that tramped in battle,
 every cloak rolled in blood,
 will be burned as fuel for flames.
For a child is born to us, a son is given us;
 upon his shoulder dominion rests.
They name him Wonder-Counselor, God-Hero,
 Father-Forever, Prince of Peace.
His dominion is vast
 and forever peaceful,
from David's throne, and over his kingdom,
 which he confirms and sustains
by judgment and justice,
 both now and forever.
The zeal of the LORD of hosts will do this! ✙

Psalm 96:1-2, 2-3, 11-12, 13

R. (Luke 2:11) **Today is born our Savior, Christ the Lord.**

Sing to the LORD a new song;
  sing to the LORD, all you lands.
Sing to the LORD; bless his name. **R.**
Announce his salvation, day after day.
  Tell his glory among the nations;
  among all peoples, his wondrous deeds. **R.**
Let the heavens be glad and the earth rejoice;
  let the sea and what fills it resound;
  let the plains be joyful and all that is in them!
Then shall all the trees of the forest exult. **R.**
They shall exult before the LORD, for he comes;
  for he comes to rule the earth.
He shall rule the world with justice
  and the peoples with his constancy. **R.**

† *Titus 2:11-14*
The grace of God has appeared to all.

Beloved:
The grace of God has appeared, saving all
  and training us to reject godless ways and worldly desires
  and to live temperately, justly, and devoutly in this age,
  as we await the blessed hope,
  the appearance of the glory of our great God
  and savior Jesus Christ,
  who gave himself for us to deliver us from all lawlessness
  and to cleanse for himself a people as his own,
  eager to do what is good. ✛

Luke 2:10-11

R. Alleluia, alleluia.
I proclaim to you good news of great joy:
today a Savior is born for us,
Christ the Lord. **R.**

† *Luke 2:1-14*
Today a Savior has been born for you.

In those days a decree went out from Caesar Augustus
  that the whole world should be enrolled.
This was the first enrollment,
  when Quirinius was governor of Syria.
So all went to be enrolled, each to his own town.
And Joseph too went up from Galilee from the town of Nazareth
  to Judea, to the city of David that is called Bethlehem,

because he was of the house and family of David,
   to be enrolled with Mary, his betrothed, who was with child.
While they were there,
   the time came for her to have her child,
   and she gave birth to her firstborn son.
She wrapped him in swaddling clothes and laid him in a manger,
   because there was no room for them in the inn.

Now there were shepherds in that region living in the fields
   and keeping the night watch over their flock.
The angel of the Lord appeared to them
   and the glory of the Lord shone around them,
   and they were struck with great fear.
The angel said to them,
   "Do not be afraid;
   for behold, I proclaim to you good news of great joy
   that will be for all the people.
For today in the city of David
   a savior has been born for you who is Christ and Lord.
And this will be a sign for you:
   you will find an infant wrapped in swaddling clothes
   and lying in a manger."
And suddenly there was a multitude of the heavenly host with the
      angel,
   praising God and saying:
   "Glory to God in the highest
   and on earth peace to those on whom his favor rests." ✛

   Mass during the Day

† *Isaiah 52:7-10*
All the ends of the earth will behold the salvation of our God.

How beautiful upon the mountains
   are the feet of him who brings glad tidings,
announcing peace, bearing good news,
   announcing salvation, and saying to Zion,
   "Your God is King!"

Hark! Your sentinels raise a cry,
   together they shout for joy,
for they see directly, before their eyes,
   the Lord restoring Zion.
Break out together in song,
   O ruins of Jerusalem!
For the Lord comforts his people,
   he redeems Jerusalem.

The LORD has bared his holy arm
  in the sight of all the nations;
all the ends of the earth will behold
  the salvation of our God. ✛

Psalm 98:1, 2-3, 3-4, 5-6
R. All the ends of the earth have seen the saving power of God.
Sing to the LORD a new song,
  for he has done wondrous deeds;
His right hand has won victory for him,
  his holy arm. **R.**
The LORD has made his salvation known:
  in the sight of the nations he has revealed his justice.
He has remembered his kindness and his faithfulness
  toward the house of Israel. **R.**
All the ends of the earth have seen
  the salvation by our God.
Sing joyfully to the LORD, all you lands;
  break into song; sing praise. **R.**
Sing praise to the LORD with the harp,
  with the harp and melodious song.
With trumpets and the sound of the horn
  sing joyfully before the King, the LORD. **R.**

† *Hebrews 1:1-6*
God has spoken to us through the Son.

Brothers and sisters:
In times past, God spoke in partial and various ways
  to our ancestors through the prophets;
  in these last days, he has spoken to us through the Son,
  whom he made heir of all things
  and through whom he created the universe,
  who is the refulgence of his glory, the very imprint of his being,
  and who sustains all things by his mighty word.
  When he had accomplished purification from sins,
  he took his seat at the right hand of the Majesty on high,
  as far superior to the angels
  as the name he has inherited is more excellent than theirs.

For to which of the angels did God ever say:
  You are my son; this day I have begotten you?
Or again:
  I will be a father to him, and he shall be a son to me?
And again, when he leads the firstborn into the world, he says:
  Let all the angels of God worship him. ✛

R. Alleluia, alleluia.
A holy day has dawned upon us.
Come, you nations, and adore the Lord.
For today a great light has come upon the earth. **R.**

✝ *John 1:1-18 (or John 1:1-5, 9-14)*
The Word became flesh and made his dwelling among us.

In the beginning was the Word,
  and the Word was with God,
  and the Word was God.
He was in the beginning with God.
All things came to be through him,
  and without him nothing came to be.
What came to be through him was life,
  and this life was the light of the human race;
  the light shines in the darkness,
  and the darkness has not overcome it.
A man named John was sent from God.
He came for testimony, to testify to the light,
  so that all might believe through him.
He was not the light,
  but came to testify to the light.
The true light, which enlightens everyone, was coming into the
    world.
  He was in the world,
  and the world came to be through him,
  but the world did not know him.
He came to what was his own,
  but his own people did not accept him.

But to those who did accept him
  he gave power to become children of God,
  to those who believe in his name,
  who were born not by natural generation
  nor by human choice nor by a man's decision
  but of God.

And the Word became flesh
  and made his dwelling among us,
  and we saw his glory,
  the glory as of the Father's only Son,
  full of grace and truth.
John testified to him and cried out, saying,
  "This was he of whom I said,

'The one who is coming after me ranks ahead of me
because he existed before me.'"
From his fullness we have all received,
grace in place of grace,
because while the law was given through Moses,
grace and truth came through Jesus Christ.
No one has ever seen God.
The only Son, God, who is at the Father's side,
has revealed him. ✛

SUNDAY, DECEMBER 26
The Holy Family of Jesus, Mary and Joseph

✝ Sirach 3:2-6, 12-14 (or 1 Samuel 1:20-22, 24-28)
Those who fear the Lord honor their parents.

God sets a father in honor over his children;
a mother's authority he confirms over her sons.
Whoever honors his father atones for sins,
and preserves himself from them.
When he prays, he is heard;
he stores up riches who reveres his mother.
Whoever honors his father is gladdened by children,
and, when he prays, is heard.
Whoever reveres his father will live a long life;
he who obeys his father brings comfort to his mother.

My son, take care of your father when he is old;
grieve him not as long as he lives.
Even if his mind fail, be considerate of him;
revile him not all the days of his life;
kindness to a father will not be forgotten,
firmly planted against the debt of your sins
—a house raised in justice to you. ✛

Psalm 128:1-2, 3, 4-5 (or Psalm 84:2-3, 5-6, 9-10)
R. Blessed are those who fear the Lord and walk in his ways.
Blessed is everyone who fears the LORD,
who walks in his ways!
For you shall eat the fruit of your handiwork;
blessed shall you be, and favored. **R.**
Your wife shall be like a fruitful vine
in the recesses of your home;
your children like olive plants
around your table. **R.**
Behold, thus is the man blessed
who fears the LORD.

The LORD bless you from Zion:
may you see the prosperity of Jerusalem
all the days of your life. **R.**

✝ *Colossians 3:12-21 (or Colossians 3:12-17 or 1 John 3:1-2, 21-24)*
Family life in the Lord.

Brothers and sisters:
Put on, as God's chosen ones, holy and beloved,
heartfelt compassion, kindness, humility, gentleness, and patience,
bearing with one another and forgiving one another,
if one has a grievance against another;
as the Lord has forgiven you, so must you also do.
And over all these put on love,
that is, the bond of perfection.
And let the peace of Christ control your hearts,
the peace into which you were also called in one body.
And be thankful.
Let the word of Christ dwell in you richly,
as in all wisdom you teach and admonish one another,
singing psalms, hymns, and spiritual songs
with gratitude in your hearts to God.
And whatever you do, in word or in deed,
do everything in the name of the Lord Jesus,
giving thanks to God the Father through him.

Wives, be subordinate to your husbands,
as is proper in the Lord.
Husbands, love your wives,
and avoid any bitterness toward them.
Children, obey your parents in everything,
for this is pleasing to the Lord.
Fathers, do not provoke your children,
so they may not become discouraged. ✚

Colossians 3:15a, 16a (or see Acts 16:14b)
R. Alleluia, alleluia.
Let the peace of Christ control your hearts;
let the word of Christ dwell in you richly. **R.**

✝ *Luke 2:41-52*
His parents found Jesus sitting in the midst of the teachers.

Each year Jesus' parents went to Jerusalem for the feast of Passover,
and when he was twelve years old,
they went up according to festival custom.

After they had completed its days, as they were returning,
  the boy Jesus remained behind in Jerusalem,
  but his parents did not know it.
Thinking that he was in the caravan,
  they journeyed for a day
  and looked for him among their relatives and acquaintances,
  but not finding him,
  they returned to Jerusalem to look for him.
After three days they found him in the temple,
  sitting in the midst of the teachers,
  listening to them and asking them questions,
  and all who heard him were astounded
  at his understanding and his answers.
When his parents saw him,
  they were astonished,
  and his mother said to him,
  "Son, why have you done this to us?
Your father and I have been looking for you with great anxiety."
And he said to them,
  "Why were you looking for me?
Did you not know that I must be in my Father's house?"
But they did not understand what he said to them.
He went down with them and came to Nazareth,
  and was obedient to them;
  and his mother kept all these things in her heart.
And Jesus advanced in wisdom and age and favor
  before God and man. ✝

MONDAY, DECEMBER 27
St. John

✝ 1 John 1:1-4
What we have seen and heard we proclaim now to you.

Beloved:
  What was from the beginning,
  what we have heard,
  what we have seen with our eyes,
  what we looked upon
  and touched with our hands
  concerns the Word of life—
  for the life was made visible;
  we have seen it and testify to it
  and proclaim to you the eternal life
  that was with the Father and was made visible to us—
  what we have seen and heard

we proclaim now to you,
  so that you too may have fellowship with us;
  for our fellowship is with the Father
  and with his Son, Jesus Christ.
We are writing this so that our joy may be complete. ✛

Psalm 97:1-2, 5-6, 11-12
R. (12) **Rejoice in the Lord, you just!**
The Lord is king; let the earth rejoice;
  let the many isles be glad.
Clouds and darkness are around him,
  justice and judgment are the foundation of his throne. **R.**
The mountains melt like wax before the Lord,
  before the Lord of all the earth.
The heavens proclaim his justice,
  and all peoples see his glory. **R.**
Light dawns for the just;
  and gladness, for the upright of heart.
Be glad in the Lord, you just,
  and give thanks to his holy name. **R.**

See Te Deum
R. Alleluia, alleluia.
We praise you, O God,
we acclaim you as Lord;
the glorious company of Apostles praise you. **R.**

✝ *John 20:1a and 2-8*
The other disciple ran faster than Peter and arrived at the tomb first.

On the first day of the week,
  Mary Magdalene ran and went to Simon Peter
  and to the other disciple whom Jesus loved, and told them,
  "They have taken the Lord from the tomb,
  and we do not know where they put him."
So Peter and the other disciple went out and came to the tomb.
They both ran, but the other disciple ran faster than Peter
  and arrived at the tomb first;
  he bent down and saw the burial cloths there, but did not go in.
When Simon Peter arrived after him,
  he went into the tomb and saw the burial cloths there,
  and the cloth that had covered his head,
  not with the burial cloths but rolled up in a separate place.
Then the other disciple also went in,
  the one who had arrived at the tomb first,
  and he saw and believed. ✛

TUESDAY, DECEMBER 28
THE HOLY INNOCENTS

† 1 John 1:5—2:2
The Blood of his Son Jesus Christ cleanses us from all sin.

Beloved:
This is the message that we have heard from Jesus Christ
and proclaim to you:
God is light, and in him there is no darkness at all.
If we say, "We have fellowship with him,"
while we continue to walk in darkness,
we lie and do not act in truth.
But if we walk in the light as he is in the light,
then we have fellowship with one another,
and the Blood of his Son Jesus cleanses us from all sin.
If we say, "We are without sin,"
we deceive ourselves, and the truth is not in us.
If we acknowledge our sins, he is faithful and just
and will forgive our sins and cleanse us from every wrongdoing.
If we say, "We have not sinned," we make him a liar,
and his word is not in us.

My children, I am writing this to you
so that you may not commit sin.
But if anyone does sin, we have an Advocate with the Father,
Jesus Christ the righteous one.
He is expiation for our sins,
and not for our sins only but for those of the whole world. ✛

Psalm 124:2-3, 4-5, 7b-8
**R. (7) Our soul has been rescued like a bird from the fowler's
snare.**
Had not the LORD been with us—
When men rose up against us,
then would they have swallowed us alive,
When their fury was inflamed against us. **R.**
Then would the waters have overwhelmed us;
The torrent would have swept over us;
over us then would have swept the raging waters. **R.**
Broken was the snare,
and we were freed.
Our help is in the name of the LORD,
who made heaven and earth. **R.**

See Te Deum

R. Alleluia, alleluia.
We praise you, O God,
we acclaim you as Lord;
the white-robed army of martyrs praise you. **R.**

✝ *Matthew 2:13-18*
He ordered the massacre of all boys in Bethlehem.

When the magi had departed, behold,
the angel of the Lord appeared to Joseph in a dream and said,
"Rise, take the child and his mother, flee to Egypt,
and stay there until I tell you.
Herod is going to search for the child to destroy him."
Joseph rose and took the child and his mother by night
and departed for Egypt.
He stayed there until the death of Herod,
that what the Lord had said through the prophet might be fulfilled,
Out of Egypt I called my son.

When Herod realized that he had been deceived by the magi,
he became furious.
He ordered the massacre of all the boys in Bethlehem and its vicinity
two years old and under,
in accordance with the time he had ascertained from the magi.
Then was fulfilled what had been said through Jeremiah the prophet:

A voice was heard in Ramah,
sobbing and loud lamentation;
Rachel weeping for her children,
and she would not be consoled,
since they were no more. ✛

WEDNESDAY, DECEMBER 29
THE FIFTH DAY WITHIN THE OCTAVE OF THE NATIVITY OF THE LORD, ST. THOMAS BECKET

✝ *1 John 2:3-11*
Those who love their brother remain in the light.

Beloved:
The way we may be sure that we know Jesus
is to keep his commandments.
Whoever says, "I know him," but does not keep his commandments
is a liar, and the truth is not in him.
But whoever keeps his word,
the love of God is truly perfected in him.

This is the way we may know that we are in union with him:
   whoever claims to abide in him ought to walk just as he walked.

Beloved, I am writing no new commandment to you
   but an old commandment that you had from the beginning.
The old commandment is the word that you have heard.
And yet I do write a new commandment to you,
   which holds true in him and among you,
   for the darkness is passing away,
   and the true light is already shining.
Whoever says he is in the light,
   yet hates his brother, is still in the darkness.
Whoever loves his brother remains in the light,
   and there is nothing in him to cause a fall.
Whoever hates his brother is in darkness;
   he walks in darkness
   and does not know where he is going
   because the darkness has blinded his eyes. ✝

Psalm 96:1-2a, 2b-3, 5b-6
R. (11a) Let the heavens be glad and the earth rejoice!
Sing to the LORD a new song;
   sing to the LORD, all you lands.
Sing to the LORD; bless his name. **R.**
Announce his salvation, day after day.
Tell his glory among the nations;
   among all peoples, his wondrous deeds. **R.**
The LORD made the heavens.
Splendor and majesty go before him;
   praise and grandeur are in his sanctuary. **R.**

Luke 2:32
R. Alleluia, alleluia.
A light of revelation to the Gentiles
and glory for your people Israel. **R.**

✝ *Luke 2:22-35*
This is the light of revelation to the Gentiles.

When the days were completed for their purification
   according to the law of Moses,
   the parents of Jesus took him up to Jerusalem
   to present him to the Lord,
   just as it is written in the law of the Lord,
   Every male that opens the womb shall be consecrated to the Lord,
   and to offer the sacrifice of

a pair of turtledoves or two young pigeons,
in accordance with the dictate in the law of the Lord.

Now there was a man in Jerusalem whose name was Simeon.
This man was righteous and devout,
    awaiting the consolation of Israel,
    and the Holy Spirit was upon him.
It had been revealed to him by the Holy Spirit
    that he should not see death
    before he had seen the Christ of the Lord.
He came in the Spirit into the temple;
    and when the parents brought in the child Jesus
    to perform the custom of the law in regard to him,
    he took him into his arms and blessed God, saying:

"Lord, now let your servant go in peace;
    your word has been fulfilled:
my own eyes have seen the salvation
    which you prepared in the sight of every people,
a light to reveal you to the nations
    and the glory of your people Israel."

The child's father and mother were amazed at what was said about
        him;
    and Simeon blessed them and said to Mary his mother,
    "Behold, this child is destined
    for the fall and rise of many in Israel,
    and to be a sign that will be contradicted
    (and you yourself a sword will pierce)
    so that the thoughts of many hearts may be revealed." ✛

THURSDAY, DECEMBER 30
THE SIXTH DAY WITHIN THE OCTAVE OF THE NATIVITY OF THE LORD

✝ *1 John 2:12-17*
Those who do the will of God remain forever.

I am writing to you, children,
    because your sins have been forgiven for his name's sake.

I am writing to you, fathers,
    because you know him who is from the beginning.

I am writing to you, young men,
    because you have conquered the Evil One.

I write to you, children,
    because you know the Father.

I write to you, fathers,
   because you know him who is from the beginning.

I write to you, young men,
   because you are strong and the word of God remains in you,
   and you have conquered the Evil One.

Do not love the world or the things of the world.
If anyone loves the world, the love of the Father is not in him.
For all that is in the world,
   sensual lust, enticement for the eyes, and a pretentious life,
   is not from the Father but is from the world.
Yet the world and its enticement are passing away.
But whoever does the will of God remains forever. ✝

   Psalm 96:7-8a, 8b-9, 10
R. (11a) Let the heavens be glad and the earth rejoice!
Give to the LORD, you families of nations,
   give to the LORD glory and praise;
   give to the LORD the glory due his name! **R.**
Bring gifts, and enter his courts;
   worship the LORD in holy attire.
Tremble before him, all the earth. **R.**
Say among the nations: The LORD is king.
He has made the world firm, not to be moved;
   he governs the peoples with equity. **R.**

R. Alleluia, alleluia.
A holy day has dawned upon us.
Come, you nations, and adore the Lord.
Today a great light has come upon the earth. **R.**

   ✝ Luke 2:36-40
   She spoke about the child to all who were
   awaiting the redemption of Jerusalem.

There was a prophetess, Anna,
   the daughter of Phanuel, of the tribe of Asher.
She was advanced in years,
   having lived seven years with her husband after her marriage,
   and then as a widow until she was eighty-four.
She never left the temple,
   but worshiped night and day with fasting and prayer.
And coming forward at that very time,
   she gave thanks to God and spoke about the child
   to all who were awaiting the redemption of Jerusalem.

When they had fulfilled all the prescriptions
  of the law of the Lord,
  they returned to Galilee,
  to their own town of Nazareth.
The child grew and became strong, filled with wisdom;
  and the favor of God was upon him. ✛

FRIDAY, DECEMBER 31
THE SEVENTH DAY WITHIN THE OCTAVE OF THE NATIVITY OF THE LORD, ST. POPE SYLVESTER I

† *1 John 2:18-21*
You have the anointing that comes from the Holy One, and you have all knowledge.

Children, it is the last hour;
  and just as you heard that the antichrist was coming,
  so now many antichrists have appeared.
Thus we know this is the last hour.
They went out from us, but they were not really of our number;
  if they had been, they would have remained with us.
Their desertion shows that none of them was of our number.
But you have the anointing that comes from the Holy One,
  and you all have knowledge.
I write to you not because you do not know the truth
  but because you do, and because every lie is alien to the truth. ✛

Psalm 96:1-2, 11-12, 13
R. (11a) Let the heavens be glad and the earth rejoice!
Sing to the LORD a new song;
  sing to the LORD, all you lands.
Sing to the LORD; bless his name;
  announce his salvation, day after day. **R.**
Let the heavens be glad and the earth rejoice;
  let the sea and what fills it resound;
  let the plains be joyful and all that is in them!
Then shall all the trees of the forest exult before the LORD. **R.**
The LORD comes,
  he comes to rule the earth.
He shall rule the world with justice
  and the peoples with his constancy. **R.**

John 1:14a, 12a
R. Alleluia, alleluia.
The Word of God became flesh and dwelt among us.
To those who accepted him
he gave power to become the children of God. **R.**

† *John 1:1-18*

The Word became flesh.

In the beginning was the Word,
  and the Word was with God,
  and the Word was God.
He was in the beginning with God.
All things came to be through him,
  and without him nothing came to be.
What came to be through him was life,
  and this life was the light of the human race;
  the light shines in the darkness,
  and the darkness has not overcome it.

A man named John was sent from God.
He came for testimony, to testify to the light,
  so that all might believe through him.
He was not the light,
  but came to testify to the light.
The true light, which enlightens everyone, was coming into the
    world.

He was in the world,
  and the world came to be through him,
  but the world did not know him.
He came to what was his own,
  but his own people did not accept him.

But to those who did accept him
  he gave power to become children of God,
  to those who believe in his name,
  who were born not by natural generation
  nor by human choice nor by a man's decision
  but of God.

And the Word became flesh
  and made his dwelling among us,
  and we saw his glory,
  the glory as of the Father's only-begotten Son,
  full of grace and truth.

John testified to him and cried out, saying,
  "This was he of whom I said,
  'The one who is coming after me ranks ahead of me
  because he existed before me.'"

From his fullness we have all received,
  grace in place of grace,
  because while the law was given through Moses,
  grace and truth came through Jesus Christ.
No one has ever seen God.
The only-begotten Son, God, who is at the Father's side,
  has revealed him. ✛

SATURDAY, JANUARY 1, 2022
THE OCTAVE DAY OF THE NATIVITY OF THE LORD,
SOLEMNITY OF MARY, THE HOLY MOTHER OF GOD

† *Numbers 6:22-27*
They shall invoke my name upon the Israelites, and I will bless them.

The LORD said to Moses:
"Speak to Aaron and his sons and tell them:
   This is how you shall bless the Israelites.
Say to them:
   The LORD bless you and keep you!
   The LORD let his face shine upon you, and be gracious to you!
   The LORD look upon you kindly and give you peace!
So shall they invoke my name upon the Israelites,
   and I will bless them." †

Psalm 67:2-3, 5, 6, 8

R. May God bless us in his mercy.

May God have pity on us and bless us;
   may he let his face shine upon us.
So may your way be known upon earth;
   among all nations, your salvation. **R.**
May the nations be glad and exult
   because you rule the peoples in equity;
   the nations on the earth you guide. **R.**
May the peoples praise you, O God;
   may all the peoples praise you!
May God bless us,
   and may all the ends of the earth fear him! **R.**

† *Galatians 4:4-7*
God sent his Son, born of a woman.

Brothers and sisters:
When the fullness of time had come, God sent his Son,
   born of a woman, born under the law,
   to ransom those under the law,
   so that we might receive adoption as sons.
As proof that you are sons,
   God sent the Spirit of his Son into our hearts,
   crying out, "Abba, Father!"
So you are no longer a slave but a son,
   and if a son then also an heir, through God. †

Hebrews 1:1-2

R. Alleluia, alleluia.

In the past God spoke to our ancestors through the prophets;
in these last days, he has spoken to us through the Son. **R.**

† *Luke 2:16-21*
They found Mary and Joseph and the infant.
When the eight days were completed, he was named Jesus.

The shepherds went in haste to Bethlehem and found Mary and
　　Joseph,
　and the infant lying in the manger.
When they saw this,
　they made known the message
　that had been told them about this child.
All who heard it were amazed
　by what had been told them by the shepherds.
And Mary kept all these things,
　reflecting on them in her heart.
Then the shepherds returned,
　glorifying and praising God
　for all they had heard and seen,
　just as it had been told to them.

When eight days were completed for his circumcision,
　he was named Jesus, the name given him by the angel
　before he was conceived in the womb. ✛

SUNDAY, JANUARY 2
THE EPIPHANY OF THE LORD

† *Isaiah 60:1-6*
The glory of the LORD shines upon you.

Rise up in splendor, Jerusalem! Your light has come,
　the glory of the LORD shines upon you.
See, darkness covers the earth,
　and thick clouds cover the peoples;
but upon you the LORD shines,
　and over you appears his glory.
Nations shall walk by your light,
　and kings by your shining radiance.
Raise your eyes and look about;
　they all gather and come to you:
your sons come from afar,
　and your daughters in the arms of their nurses.

Then you shall be radiant at what you see,
  your heart shall throb and overflow,
for the riches of the sea shall be emptied out before you,
  the wealth of nations shall be brought to you.
Caravans of camels shall fill you,
  dromedaries from Midian and Ephah;
all from Sheba shall come
    bearing gold and frankincense,
    and proclaiming the praises of the LORD. ✢

Psalm 72:1-2, 7-8, 10-11, 12-13
R. Lord, every nation on earth will adore you.
O God, with your judgment endow the king,
  and with your justice, the king's son;
he shall govern your people with justice
  and your afflicted ones with judgment. **R.**
Justice shall flower in his days,
  and profound peace, till the moon be no more.
May he rule from sea to sea,
  and from the River to the ends of the earth. **R.**
The kings of Tarshish and the Isles shall offer gifts;
  the kings of Arabia and Seba shall bring tribute.
All kings shall pay him homage,
  all nations shall serve him. **R.**
For he shall rescue the poor when he cries out,
  and the afflicted when he has no one to help him.
He shall have pity for the lowly and the poor;
  the lives of the poor he shall save. **R.**

✝ *Ephesians 3:2-3a, 5-6*
Now it has been revealed that the Gentiles are coheirs of the promise.

Brothers and sisters:
You have heard of the stewardship of God's grace
  that was given to me for your benefit,
    namely, that the mystery was made known to me by revelation.
It was not made known to people in other generations
  as it has now been revealed
  to his holy apostles and prophets by the Spirit:
    that the Gentiles are coheirs, members of the same body,
    and copartners in the promise in Christ Jesus through the gospel. ✢

Matthew 2:2
R. Alleluia, alleluia.
We saw his star at its rising
and have come to do him homage. **R.**

† *Matthew 2:1-12*

We saw his star at its rising and have come to do him homage.

When Jesus was born in Bethlehem of Judea,
in the days of King Herod,
behold, magi from the east arrived in Jerusalem, saying,
"Where is the newborn king of the Jews?
We saw his star at its rising
and have come to do him homage."
When King Herod heard this,
he was greatly troubled,
and all Jerusalem with him.
Assembling all the chief priests and the scribes of the people,
he inquired of them where the Christ was to be born.
They said to him, "In Bethlehem of Judea,
for thus it has been written through the prophet:
And you, Bethlehem, land of Judah,
are by no means least among the rulers of Judah;
since from you shall come a ruler,
who is to shepherd my people Israel."
Then Herod called the magi secretly
and ascertained from them the time of the star's appearance.
He sent them to Bethlehem and said,
"Go and search diligently for the child.
When you have found him, bring me word,
that I too may go and do him homage."
After their audience with the king they set out.
And behold, the star that they had seen at its rising preceded them,
until it came and stopped over the place where the child was.
They were overjoyed at seeing the star,
and on entering the house
they saw the child with Mary his mother.
They prostrated themselves and did him homage.
Then they opened their treasures
and offered him gifts of gold, frankincense, and myrrh.
And having been warned in a dream not to return to Herod,
they departed for their country by another way. ✦

MONDAY, JANUARY 3
CHRISTMAS WEEKDAY, THE MOST HOLY NAME OF JESUS

† *1 John 3:22—4:6*

Test the spirits to see whether they belong to God.

Beloved:
We receive from him whatever we ask,

because we keep his commandments and do what pleases him.
And his commandment is this:
   we should believe in the name of his Son, Jesus Christ,
   and love one another just as he commanded us.
Those who keep his commandments remain in him, and he in them,
   and the way we know that he remains in us
   is from the Spirit whom he gave us.

Beloved, do not trust every spirit
   but test the spirits to see whether they belong to God,
   because many false prophets have gone out into the world.
This is how you can know the Spirit of God:
   every spirit that acknowledges Jesus Christ come in the flesh
   belongs to God,
   and every spirit that does not acknowledge Jesus
   does not belong to God.
This is the spirit of the antichrist
   who, as you heard, is to come,
   but in fact is already in the world.
You belong to God, children, and you have conquered them,
   for the one who is in you
   is greater than the one who is in the world.
They belong to the world;
   accordingly, their teaching belongs to the world,
   and the world listens to them.
We belong to God, and anyone who knows God listens to us,
   while anyone who does not belong to God refuses to hear us.
This is how we know the spirit of truth and the spirit of deceit. ✠

   Psalm 2:7bc-8, 10-12a
R. (8ab) **I will give you all the nations for an inheritance.**
The Lord said to me, "You are my Son;
   this day I have begotten you.
Ask of me and I will give you
   the nations for an inheritance
   and the ends of the earth for your possession." **R.**
And now, O kings, give heed;
   take warning, you rulers of the earth.
Serve the Lord with fear, and rejoice before him;
   with trembling, rejoice. **R.**

   Matthew 4:23
R. Alleluia, alleluia.
Jesus proclaimed the Gospel of the Kingdom
and cured every disease among the people. **R.**

† *Matthew 4:12-17, 23-25*
The Kingdom of heaven is at hand.

When Jesus heard that John had been arrested,
  he withdrew to Galilee.
He left Nazareth and went to live in Capernaum by the sea,
  in the region of Zebulun and Naphtali,
  that what had been said through Isaiah the prophet
  might be fulfilled:

> *Land of Zebulun and land of Naphtali,*
> * the way to the sea, beyond the Jordan,*
> * Galilee of the Gentiles,*
> *the people who sit in darkness*
> * have seen a great light,*
> *on those dwelling in a land overshadowed by death*
> * light has arisen.*

From that time on, Jesus began to preach and say,
  "Repent, for the Kingdom of heaven is at hand."

He went around all of Galilee,
  teaching in their synagogues, proclaiming the Gospel of the Kingdom,
  and curing every disease and illness among the people.
His fame spread to all of Syria,
  and they brought to him all who were sick with various diseases
  and racked with pain,
  those who were possessed, lunatics, and paralytics,
  and he cured them.
And great crowds from Galilee, the Decapolis, Jerusalem, and Judea,
  and from beyond the Jordan followed him. ✚

TUESDAY, JANUARY 4
St. Elizabeth Ann Seton

† *1 John 4:7-10*
God is love.

Beloved, let us love one another,
  because love is of God;
  everyone who loves is begotten by God and knows God.
Whoever is without love does not know God, for God is love.
In this way the love of God was revealed to us:
  God sent his only-begotten Son into the world
  so that we might have life through him.
In this is love:
  not that we have loved God, but that he loved us
  and sent his Son as expiation for our sins. ✚

Psalm 72:1-2, 3-4, 7-8

R. (see 11) **Lord, every nation on earth will adore you.**

O God, with your judgment endow the king,
  and with your justice, the king's son;
He shall govern your people with justice
  and your afflicted ones with judgment. **R.**

The mountains shall yield peace for the people,
  and the hills justice.
He shall defend the afflicted among the people,
  save the children of the poor. **R.**

Justice shall flower in his days,
  and profound peace, till the moon be no more.
May he rule from sea to sea,
  and from the River to the ends of the earth. **R.**

Luke 4:18

R. Alleluia, alleluia.

The Lord has sent me to bring glad tidings to the poor
and to proclaim liberty to captives. **R.**

† *Mark 6:34-44*

Multiplying the loaves, Jesus shows himself as a prophet.

When Jesus saw the vast crowd, his heart was moved with pity for
    them,
  for they were like sheep without a shepherd;
  and he began to teach them many things.
By now it was already late and his disciples approached him and said,
  "This is a deserted place and it is already very late.
Dismiss them so that they can go
  to the surrounding farms and villages
  and buy themselves something to eat."
He said to them in reply,
  "Give them some food yourselves."
But they said to him,
  "Are we to buy two hundred days' wages worth of food
  and give it to them to eat?"
He asked them, "How many loaves do you have? Go and see."
And when they had found out they said,
  "Five loaves and two fish."
So he gave orders to have them sit down in groups on the green
    grass.
The people took their places in rows by hundreds and by fifties.
Then, taking the five loaves and the two fish and looking up to
    heaven,
  he said the blessing, broke the loaves, and gave them to his disciples

to set before the people;
he also divided the two fish among them all.
They all ate and were satisfied.
And they picked up twelve wicker baskets full of fragments
and what was left of the fish.
Those who ate of the loaves were five thousand men. ✛

WEDNESDAY, JANUARY 5
St. John Neumann

† 1 John 4:11-18
If we love one another, God remains in us.

Beloved, if God so loved us,
we also must love one another.
No one has ever seen God.
Yet, if we love one another, God remains in us,
and his love is brought to perfection in us.

This is how we know that we remain in him and he in us,
that he has given us of his Spirit.
Moreover, we have seen and testify
that the Father sent his Son as savior of the world.
Whoever acknowledges that Jesus is the Son of God,
God remains in him and he in God.
We have come to know and to believe in the love God has for us.

God is love, and whoever remains in love remains in God and God in
him.
In this is love brought to perfection among us,
that we have confidence on the day of judgment
because as he is, so are we in this world.
There is no fear in love,
but perfect love drives out fear
because fear has to do with punishment,
and so one who fears is not yet perfect in love. ✛

Psalm 72:1-2,10, 12-13
R. (see 11) **Lord, every nation on earth will adore you.**
O God, with your judgment endow the king,
and with your justice, the king's son;
He shall govern your people with justice
and your afflicted ones with judgment. **R.**
The kings of Tarshish and the Isles shall offer gifts;
the kings of Arabia and Seba shall bring tribute. **R.**
For he shall rescue the poor when he cries out,
and the afflicted when he has no one to help him.

He shall have pity for the lowly and the poor;
  the lives of the poor he shall save. **R.**

See 1 Timothy 3:16
R. Alleluia, alleluia.
Glory to you, O Christ, proclaimed to the Gentiles.
Glory to you, O Christ, believed in throughout the world. **R.**

† *Mark 6:45-52*
They saw Jesus walking on the sea.

After the five thousand had eaten and were satisfied,
  Jesus made his disciples get into the boat
  and precede him to the other side toward Bethsaida,
  while he dismissed the crowd.
And when he had taken leave of them,
  he went off to the mountain to pray.
When it was evening,
  the boat was far out on the sea and he was alone on shore.
Then he saw that they were tossed about while rowing,
  for the wind was against them.
About the fourth watch of the night,
  he came toward them walking on the sea.
He meant to pass by them.
But when they saw him walking on the sea,
  they thought it was a ghost and cried out.
They had all seen him and were terrified.
But at once he spoke with them,
  "Take courage, it is I, do not be afraid!"
He got into the boat with them and the wind died down.
They were completely astounded.
They had not understood the incident of the loaves.
On the contrary, their hearts were hardened. ✛

THURSDAY, JANUARY 6
CHRISTMAS WEEKDAY, ST. ANDRÉ BESSETTE

† *1 John 4:19—5:4*
Those who love God must also love their brother and sister.

Beloved, we love God because
  he first loved us.
If anyone says, "I love God,"
  but hates his brother, he is a liar;
  for whoever does not love a brother whom he has seen
  cannot love God whom he has not seen.
This is the commandment we have from him:

Whoever loves God must also love his brother.

Everyone who believes that Jesus is the Christ is begotten by God,
    and everyone who loves the father
    loves also the one begotten by him.
In this way we know that we love the children of God
    when we love God and obey his commandments.
For the love of God is this,
    that we keep his commandments.
And his commandments are not burdensome,
    for whoever is begotten by God conquers the world.
And the victory that conquers the world is our faith. ✛

Psalm 72:1-2,14 and 15bc, 17
R. (see 11) **Lord, every nation on earth will adore you.**
O God, with your judgment endow the king,
    and with your justice, the king's son;
He shall govern your people with justice
    and your afflicted ones with judgment. **R.**
From fraud and violence he shall redeem them,
    and precious shall their blood be in his sight.
May they be prayed for continually;
    day by day shall they bless him. **R.**
May his name be blessed forever;
    as long as the sun his name shall remain.
In him shall all the tribes of the earth be blessed;
    all the nations shall proclaim his happiness. **R.**

Luke 4:18
R. Alleluia, alleluia.
The Lord has sent me to bring glad tidings to the poor
and to proclaim liberty to captives. **R.**

† *Luke 4:14-22a*
Today this Scripture passage is fulfilled.

Jesus returned to Galilee in the power of the Spirit,
    and news of him spread throughout the whole region.
He taught in their synagogues and was praised by all.

He came to Nazareth, where he had grown up,
    and went according to his custom
    into the synagogue on the sabbath day.
He stood up to read and was handed a scroll of the prophet Isaiah.
He unrolled the scroll and found the passage where it was written:
    The Spirit of the Lord is upon me,
        because he has anointed me

to bring glad tidings to the poor.
He has sent me to proclaim liberty to captives
and recovery of sight to the blind,
to let the oppressed go free,
and to proclaim a year acceptable to the Lord.

Rolling up the scroll, he handed it back to the attendant and sat
   down,
and the eyes of all in the synagogue looked intently at him.
He said to them,
"Today this Scripture passage is fulfilled in your hearing."
And all spoke highly of him
   and were amazed at the gracious words that came from his mouth. ✛

FRIDAY, JANUARY 7
CHRISTMAS WEEKDAY, ST. RAYMOND OF PENYAFORT

† *1 John 5:5-13*
The Spirit, the water, and the Blood.

Beloved:
Who indeed is the victor over the world
   but the one who believes that Jesus is the Son of God?

This is the one who came through water and Blood, Jesus Christ,
   not by water alone, but by water and Blood.
The Spirit is the one who testifies,
   and the Spirit is truth.
So there are three that testify,
   the Spirit, the water, and the Blood,
   and the three are of one accord.
If we accept human testimony,
   the testimony of God is surely greater.
Now the testimony of God is this,
   that he has testified on behalf of his Son.
Whoever believes in the Son of God
   has this testimony within himself.
Whoever does not believe God has made him a liar
   by not believing the testimony God has given about his Son.
And this is the testimony:
   God gave us eternal life,
   and this life is in his Son.
Whoever possesses the Son has life;
   whoever does not possess the Son of God does not have life.

I write these things to you so that you may know
  that you have eternal life,
  you who believe in the name of the Son of God. ✛

Psalm 147:12-13, 14-15, 19-20
R. (12a) **Praise the Lord, Jerusalem.** *(or* **Alleluia.***)*
Glorify the LORD, O Jerusalem;
  praise your God, O Zion.
For he has strengthened the bars of your gates;
  he has blessed your children within you. **R.**
He has granted peace in your borders;
  with the best of wheat he fills you.
He sends forth his command to the earth;
  swiftly runs his word! **R.**
He has proclaimed his word to Jacob,
  his statutes and his ordinances to Israel.
He has not done thus for any other nation;
  his ordinances he has not made known to them. Alleluia. **R.**

See Matthew 4:23
R. Alleluia, alleluia.
Jesus proclaimed the Gospel of the Kingdom
and cured every disease among the people. **R.**

† Luke 5:12-16
The leprosy left him immediately.

It happened that there was a man full of leprosy in one of the towns
  where Jesus was;
  and when he saw Jesus,
  he fell prostrate, pleaded with him, and said,
  "Lord, if you wish, you can make me clean."
Jesus stretched out his hand, touched him, and said,
  "I do will it. Be made clean."
And the leprosy left him immediately.
Then he ordered him not to tell anyone, but
  "Go, show yourself to the priest and offer for your cleansing
  what Moses prescribed; that will be proof for them."
The report about him spread all the more,
  and great crowds assembled to listen to him
  and to be cured of their ailments,
  but he would withdraw to deserted places to pray. ✛

SATURDAY, JANUARY 8
CHRISTMAS WEEKDAY

† 1 John 5:14-21
God hears us in regard to whatever we ask.

Beloved:
We have this confidence in him
  that if we ask anything according to his will, he hears us.
And if we know that he hears us in regard to whatever we ask,
  we know that what we have asked him for is ours.
If anyone sees his brother sinning, if the sin is not deadly,
  he should pray to God and he will give him life.
This is only for those whose sin is not deadly.
There is such a thing as deadly sin,
  about which I do not say that you should pray.
All wrongdoing is sin, but there is sin that is not deadly.

We know that anyone begotten by God does not sin;
  but the one begotten by God he protects,
  and the Evil One cannot touch him.
We know that we belong to God,
  and the whole world is under the power of the Evil One.
We also know that the Son of God has come
  and has given us discernment to know the one who is true.
And we are in the one who is true,
  in his Son Jesus Christ.
He is the true God and eternal life.
Children, be on your guard against idols. ✚

  Psalm 149:1-2, 3-4, 5-6a, 9b
R. The Lord takes delight in his people. *(or* **Alleluia.***)*
Sing to the LORD a new song
  of praise in the assembly of the faithful.
Let Israel be glad in their maker,
  let the children of Zion rejoice in their king. **R.**
Let them praise his name in the festive dance,
  let them sing praise to him with timbrel and harp.
For the LORD loves his people,
  and he adorns the lowly with victory. **R.**
Let the faithful exult in glory;
  let them sing for joy upon their couches;
Let the high praises of God be in their throats.
  This is the glory of all his faithful. Alleluia. **R.**

Matthew 4:16

R. Alleluia, alleluia.
The people who sit in darkness have seen a great light,
on those dwelling in a land overshadowed by death
light has arisen. **R.**

† John 3:22-30
The friend of the bridegroom rejoices at the bridegroom's voice.

Jesus and his disciples went into the region of Judea,
    where he spent some time with them baptizing.
John was also baptizing in Aenon near Salim,
    because there was an abundance of water there,
    and people came to be baptized,
    for John had not yet been imprisoned.
Now a dispute arose between the disciples of John and a Jew
    about ceremonial washings.
So they came to John and said to him,
    "Rabbi, the one who was with you across the Jordan,
    to whom you testified,
    here he is baptizing and everyone is coming to him."
John answered and said,
    "No one can receive anything except what has been given from
        heaven.
You yourselves can testify that I said that I am not the Christ,
    but that I was sent before him.
The one who has the bride is the bridegroom;
    the best man, who stands and listens for him,
    rejoices greatly at the bridegroom's voice.
So this joy of mine has been made complete.
He must increase; I must decrease." ✦

SUNDAY, JANUARY 9
THE BAPTISM OF THE LORD

† Isaiah 42:1-4, 6-7 *(or Isaiah 40:1-5, 9-11)*
Behold my servant with whom I am well pleased.

Thus says the LORD:
Here is my servant whom I uphold,
    my chosen one with whom I am pleased,
upon whom I have put my spirit;
    he shall bring forth justice to the nations,
not crying out, not shouting,
    not making his voice heard in the street.
A bruised reed he shall not break,
    and a smoldering wick he shall not quench,

until he establishes justice on the earth;
  the coastlands will wait for his teaching.

I, the LORD, have called you for the victory of justice,
  I have grasped you by the hand;
I formed you, and set you
    as a covenant of the people,
    a light for the nations,
to open the eyes of the blind,
    to bring out prisoners from confinement,
    and from the dungeon, those who live in darkness. ✛

Psalm 29:1bc-2, 3ac-4, 3b and 9c-10 (or Psalm 104:1b-2, 3-4, 24-25, 27-28, 29-30)
R. The Lord will bless his people with peace.
Give to the LORD, you sons of God,
  give to the LORD glory and praise,
give to the LORD the glory due his name;
  adore the LORD in holy attire. **R.**
The voice of the LORD is over the waters,
  the LORD, over vast waters.
The voice of the LORD is mighty;
  the voice of the LORD is majestic. **R.**
The God of glory thunders,
  and in his temple all say, "Glory!"
The LORD is enthroned above the flood;
  the LORD is enthroned as king forever. **R.**

✝ ***Acts 10:34-38*** *(or Titus 2:11-14; 3:4-7)*
God anointed him with the Holy Spirit.

Peter proceeded to speak to those gathered
  in the house of Cornelius, saying:
"In truth, I see that God shows no partiality.
Rather, in every nation whoever fears him and acts uprightly
  is acceptable to him.
You know the word that he sent to the Israelites
  as he proclaimed peace through Jesus Christ, who is Lord of all,
  what has happened all over Judea,
  beginning in Galilee after the baptism
  that John preached,
  how God anointed Jesus of Nazareth
  with the Holy Spirit and power.
He went about doing good
  and healing all those oppressed by the devil,
  for God was with him." ✛

See Mark 9:7 (or see Luke 3:16)
R. Alleluia, alleluia.
The heavens were opened and the voice of the Father thundered:
This is my beloved Son, listen to him. **R.**

† *Luke 3:15-16, 21-22*
When Jesus had been baptized and was praying, heaven was opened.

The people were filled with expectation,
    and all were asking in their hearts
    whether John might be the Christ.
John answered them all, saying,
    "I am baptizing you with water,
    but one mightier than I is coming.
I am not worthy to loosen the thongs of his sandals.
He will baptize you with the Holy Spirit and fire."

After all the people had been baptized
    and Jesus also had been baptized and was praying,
    heaven was opened and the Holy Spirit descended upon him
    in bodily form like a dove.
And a voice came from heaven,
    "You are my beloved Son;
    with you I am well pleased." ✛

MONDAY, JANUARY 10
WEEKDAY (FIRST WEEK IN ORDINARY TIME)

† *1 Samuel 1:1-8*
*Hannah's rival turned it into a constant reproach to her
that the LORD had left her barren.*

There was a certain man from Ramathaim, Elkanah by name,
    a Zuphite from the hill country of Ephraim.
He was the son of Jeroham, son of Elihu,
    son of Tohu, son of Zuph, an Ephraimite.
He had two wives, one named Hannah, the other Peninnah;
    Peninnah had children, but Hannah was childless.
This man regularly went on pilgrimage from his city
    to worship the LORD of hosts and to sacrifice to him at Shiloh,
    where the two sons of Eli, Hophni and Phinehas,
    were ministering as priests of the LORD.
When the day came for Elkanah to offer sacrifice,
    he used to give a portion each to his wife Peninnah
    and to all her sons and daughters,
    but a double portion to Hannah because he loved her,
    though the LORD had made her barren.

Her rival, to upset her, turned it into a constant reproach to her
　　that the Lord had left her barren.
This went on year after year;
　　each time they made their pilgrimage to the sanctuary of the Lord,
　　Peninnah would approach her,
　　and Hannah would weep and refuse to eat.
Her husband Elkanah used to ask her:
　　"Hannah, why do you weep, and why do you refuse to eat?
Why do you grieve?
Am I not more to you than ten sons?" ✛

　　Psalm 116:12-13, 14-17, 18-19
R. (17a) **To you, Lord, I will offer a sacrifice of praise.**
　　(or **Alleluia.***)*
How shall I make a return to the Lord
　　for all the good he has done for me?
The cup of salvation I will take up,
　　and I will call upon the name of the Lord. **R.**
My vows to the Lord I will pay
　　in the presence of all his people.
Precious in the eyes of the Lord
　　is the death of his faithful ones.
O Lord, I am your servant;
　　I am your servant, the son of your handmaid;
　　you have loosed my bonds. **R.**
My vows to the Lord I will pay
　　in the presence of all his people,
In the courts of the house of the Lord,
　　in your midst, O Jerusalem. **R.**

　　Mark 1:15
R. Alleluia, alleluia.
The Kingdom of God is at hand;
repent and believe in the Gospel. **R.**

† *Mark 1:14-20*
Repent, and believe in the Gospel.

After John had been arrested,
　　Jesus came to Galilee proclaiming the Gospel of God:
　　"This is the time of fulfillment.
The Kingdom of God is at hand.
Repent, and believe in the Gospel."

As he passed by the Sea of Galilee,
　　he saw Simon and his brother Andrew casting their nets into the sea;
　　they were fishermen.

Jesus said to them,
  "Come after me, and I will make you fishers of men."
Then they left their nets and followed him.
He walked along a little farther
  and saw James, the son of Zebedee, and his brother John.
They too were in a boat mending their nets.
Then he called them.
So they left their father Zebedee in the boat
  along with the hired men and followed him. ✛

TUESDAY, JANUARY 11
WEEKDAY

† 1 Samuel 1:9-20
The LORD God remembered Hannah, and she gave birth to Samuel.

Hannah rose after a meal at Shiloh,
  and presented herself before the LORD;
  at the time, Eli the priest was sitting on a chair
  near the doorpost of the LORD's temple.
In her bitterness she prayed to the LORD, weeping copiously,
  and she made a vow, promising: "O LORD of hosts,
  if you look with pity on the misery of your handmaid,
  if you remember me and do not forget me,
  if you give your handmaid a male child,
  I will give him to the LORD for as long as he lives;
  neither wine nor liquor shall he drink,
  and no razor shall ever touch his head."
As she remained long at prayer before the LORD,
  Eli watched her mouth, for Hannah was praying silently;
  though her lips were moving, her voice could not be heard.
Eli, thinking her drunk, said to her,
  "How long will you make a drunken show of yourself?
Sober up from your wine!"
"It isn't that, my lord," Hannah answered.
"I am an unhappy woman.
I have had neither wine nor liquor;
  I was only pouring out my troubles to the LORD.
Do not think your handmaid a ne'er-do-well;
  my prayer has been prompted by my deep sorrow and misery."
Eli said, "Go in peace,
  and may the God of Israel grant you what you have asked of him."
She replied, "Think kindly of your maidservant," and left.
She went to her quarters, ate and drank with her husband,
  and no longer appeared downcast.

Early the next morning they worshiped before the LORD,
   and then returned to their home in Ramah.

When Elkanah had relations with his wife Hannah,
   the LORD remembered her.
She conceived, and at the end of her term bore a son
   whom she called Samuel, since she had asked the LORD for him. ✛

1 Samuel 2:1, 4-5, 6-7, 8abcd
R. (see 1) **My heart exults in the Lord, my Savior.**
"My heart exults in the LORD,
   my horn is exalted in my God.
I have swallowed up my enemies;
   I rejoice in my victory." **R.**
"The bows of the mighty are broken,
   while the tottering gird on strength.
The well-fed hire themselves out for bread,
   while the hungry batten on spoil.
The barren wife bears seven sons,
   while the mother of many languishes." **R.**
"The LORD puts to death and gives life;
   he casts down to the nether world;
   he raises up again.
The LORD makes poor and makes rich;
   he humbles, he also exalts." **R.**
"He raises the needy from the dust;
   from the dung heap he lifts up the poor,
To seat them with nobles
   and make a glorious throne their heritage." **R.**

See 1 Thessalonians 2:13
R. Alleluia, alleluia.
Receive the word of God, not as the word of men,
but as it truly is, the word of God. **R.**

✝ *Mark 1:21-28*
Jesus taught them as one having authority.

Jesus came to Capernaum with his followers,
   and on the sabbath he entered the synagogue and taught.
The people were astonished at his teaching,
   for he taught them as one having authority and not as the scribes.
In their synagogue was a man with an unclean spirit;
   he cried out, "What have you to do with us, Jesus of Nazareth?
Have you come to destroy us?
I know who you are—the Holy One of God!"
Jesus rebuked him and said, "Quiet! Come out of him!"

The unclean spirit convulsed him and with a loud cry came out of him.
All were amazed and asked one another,
"What is this?
A new teaching with authority.
He commands even the unclean spirits and they obey him."
His fame spread everywhere throughout the whole region of Galilee. ✛

WEDNESDAY, JANUARY 12
WEEKDAY

† *1 Samuel 3:1-10, 19-20*
Speak, O LORD, for your servant is listening.

During the time young Samuel was minister to the LORD under Eli,
a revelation of the LORD was uncommon and vision infrequent.
One day Eli was asleep in his usual place.
His eyes had lately grown so weak that he could not see.
The lamp of God was not yet extinguished,
and Samuel was sleeping in the temple of the LORD
where the ark of God was.
The LORD called to Samuel, who answered, "Here I am."

Samuel ran to Eli and said, "Here I am. You called me."
"I did not call you," Eli said. "Go back to sleep."
So he went back to sleep.
Again the LORD called Samuel, who rose and went to Eli.
"Here I am," he said. "You called me."
But Eli answered, "I did not call you, my son. Go back to sleep."
At that time Samuel was not familiar with the LORD,
because the LORD had not revealed anything to him as yet.
The LORD called Samuel again, for the third time.
Getting up and going to Eli, he said, "Here I am.
You called me."
Then Eli understood that the LORD was calling the youth.
So Eli said to Samuel, "Go to sleep, and if you are called, reply,
'Speak, LORD, for your servant is listening.'"
When Samuel went to sleep in his place,
the LORD came and revealed his presence,
calling out as before, "Samuel, Samuel!"
Samuel answered, "Speak, for your servant is listening."

Samuel grew up, and the LORD was with him,
not permitting any word of his to be without effect.
Thus all Israel from Dan to Beersheba
came to know that Samuel was an accredited prophet of the LORD. ✛

Psalm 40:2 and 5, 7-8a, 8b-9, 10

R. (8a and 9a) **Here am I, Lord; I come to do your will.**

I have waited, waited for the LORD,
   and he stooped toward me and heard my cry.
Blessed the man who makes the LORD his trust;
   who turns not to idolatry
   or to those who stray after falsehood. **R.**
Sacrifice or oblation you wished not,
   but ears open to obedience you gave me.
Burnt offerings or sin-offerings you sought not;
   then said I, "Behold I come." **R.**
"In the written scroll it is prescribed for me.
To do your will, O my God, is my delight,
   and your law is within my heart!" **R.**
I announced your justice in the vast assembly;
   I did not restrain my lips, as you, O LORD, know. **R.**

John 10:27

R. Alleluia, alleluia.

My sheep hear my voice, says the Lord.
I know them, and they follow me. **R.**

† *Mark 1:29-39*

Jesus cured many who were sick with various diseases.

On leaving the synagogue
   Jesus entered the house of Simon and Andrew with James and John.
Simon's mother-in-law lay sick with a fever.
They immediately told him about her.
He approached, grasped her hand, and helped her up.
Then the fever left her and she waited on them.

When it was evening, after sunset,
   they brought to him all who were ill or possessed by demons.
The whole town was gathered at the door.
He cured many who were sick with various diseases,
   and he drove out many demons,
   not permitting them to speak because they knew him.

Rising very early before dawn,
   he left and went off to a deserted place, where he prayed.
Simon and those who were with him pursued him
   and on finding him said, "Everyone is looking for you."
He told them, "Let us go on to the nearby villages
   that I may preach there also.

For this purpose have I come."
So he went into their synagogues, preaching and driving out demons
   throughout the whole of Galilee. ✛

THURSDAY, JANUARY 13
WEEKDAY, ST. HILARY

† 1 Samuel 4:1-11
Israel was defeated and the ark of God was captured.

The Philistines gathered for an attack on Israel.
Israel went out to engage them in battle and camped at Ebenezer,
   while the Philistines camped at Aphek.
The Philistines then drew up in battle formation against Israel.
After a fierce struggle Israel was defeated by the Philistines,
   who slew about four thousand men on the battlefield.
When the troops retired to the camp, the elders of Israel said,
   "Why has the LORD permitted us to be defeated today by the
      Philistines?
Let us fetch the ark of the LORD from Shiloh
   that it may go into battle among us
   and save us from the grasp of our enemies."

So the people sent to Shiloh and brought from there
   the ark of the LORD of hosts, who is enthroned upon the cherubim.
The two sons of Eli, Hophni and Phinehas, were with the ark of God.
When the ark of the LORD arrived in the camp,
   all Israel shouted so loudly that the earth resounded.
The Philistines, hearing the noise of shouting, asked,
   "What can this loud shouting in the camp of the Hebrews mean?"
On learning that the ark of the LORD had come into the camp,
   the Philistines were frightened.
They said, "Gods have come to their camp."
They said also, "Woe to us! This has never happened before. Woe to us!
Who can deliver us from the power of these mighty gods?
These are the gods that struck the Egyptians
   with various plagues and with pestilence.
Take courage and be manly, Philistines;
   otherwise you will become slaves to the Hebrews,
   as they were your slaves.
So fight manfully!"
The Philistines fought and Israel was defeated;
   every man fled to his own tent.
It was a disastrous defeat,
   in which Israel lost thirty thousand foot soldiers.

The ark of God was captured,
and Eli's two sons, Hophni and Phinehas, were among the dead. ✙

Psalm 44:10-11, 14-15, 25-26

R. (27b) **Redeem us, Lord, because of your mercy.**
Yet now you have cast us off and put us in disgrace,
and you go not forth with our armies.
You have let us be driven back by our foes;
those who hated us plundered us at will. **R.**
You made us the reproach of our neighbors,
the mockery and the scorn of those around us.
You made us a byword among the nations,
a laughingstock among the peoples. **R.**
Why do you hide your face,
forgetting our woe and our oppression?
For our souls are bowed down to the dust,
our bodies are pressed to the earth. **R.**

See Matthew 4:23

R. Alleluia, alleluia.
Jesus preached the Gospel of the Kingdom
and cured every disease among the people. **R.**

† *Mark 1:40-45*
The leprosy left him, and he was made clean.

A leper came to him and kneeling down begged him and said,
"If you wish, you can make me clean."
Moved with pity, he stretched out his hand,
touched the leper, and said to him,
"I do will it. Be made clean."
The leprosy left him immediately, and he was made clean.
Then, warning him sternly, he dismissed him at once.
Then he said to him, "See that you tell no one anything,
but go, show yourself to the priest
and offer for your cleansing what Moses prescribed;
that will be proof for them."
The man went away and began to publicize the whole matter.
He spread the report abroad
so that it was impossible for Jesus to enter a town openly.
He remained outside in deserted places,
and people kept coming to him from everywhere. ✙

FRIDAY, JANUARY 14
WEEKDAY

† *1 Samuel 8:4-7, 10-22a*
You will complain against the king whom you have chosen,
but on that day the LORD will not answer you.

All the elders of Israel came in a body to Samuel at Ramah
and said to him, "Now that you are old,
and your sons do not follow your example,
appoint a king over us, as other nations have, to judge us."

Samuel was displeased when they asked for a king to judge them.
He prayed to the LORD, however, who said in answer:
"Grant the people's every request.
It is not you they reject, they are rejecting me as their king."

Samuel delivered the message of the LORD in full
to those who were asking him for a king.
He told them:
"The rights of the king who will rule you will be as follows:
He will take your sons and assign them to his chariots and horses,
and they will run before his chariot.
He will also appoint from among them his commanders of groups
of a thousand and of a hundred soldiers.
He will set them to do his plowing and his harvesting,
and to make his implements of war and the equipment of his
chariots.
He will use your daughters as ointment makers, as cooks, and as
bakers.
He will take the best of your fields, vineyards, and olive groves,
and give them to his officials.
He will tithe your crops and your vineyards,
and give the revenue to his eunuchs and his slaves.
He will take your male and female servants,
as well as your best oxen and your asses,
and use them to do his work.
He will tithe your flocks and you yourselves will become his slaves.
When this takes place,
you will complain against the king whom you have chosen,
but on that day the LORD will not answer you."

The people, however, refused to listen to Samuel's warning and said,
"Not so! There must be a king over us.
We too must be like other nations,
with a king to rule us and to lead us in warfare
and fight our battles."

When Samuel had listened to all the people had to say,
  he repeated it to the LORD, who then said to him,
  "Grant their request and appoint a king to rule them." ✛

Psalm 89:16-17, 18-19
R. (2) **For ever I will sing the goodness of the Lord.**
Blessed the people who know the joyful shout;
  in the light of your countenance, O LORD, they walk.
At your name they rejoice all the day,
  and through your justice they are exalted. **R.**
For you are the splendor of their strength,
  and by your favor our horn is exalted.
For to the LORD belongs our shield,
  and to the Holy One of Israel, our King. **R.**

Luke 7:16
R. Alleluia, alleluia.
A great prophet has arisen in our midst
and God has visited his people. **R.**

† *Mark 2:1-12*
The Son of Man has authority to forgive sins on earth.

When Jesus returned to Capernaum after some days,
  it became known that he was at home.
Many gathered together so that there was no longer room for them,
  not even around the door,
  and he preached the word to them.
They came bringing to him a paralytic carried by four men.
Unable to get near Jesus because of the crowd,
  they opened up the roof above him.
After they had broken through,
  they let down the mat on which the paralytic was lying.
When Jesus saw their faith, he said to him,
  "Child, your sins are forgiven."
Now some of the scribes were sitting there asking themselves,
  "Why does this man speak that way? He is blaspheming.
Who but God alone can forgive sins?'"
Jesus immediately knew in his mind what
  they were thinking to themselves,
  so he said, "Why are you thinking such things in your hearts?
Which is easier, to say to the paralytic,
  'Your sins are forgiven,'
  or to say, 'Rise, pick up your mat and walk'?
But that you may know
  that the Son of Man has authority to forgive sins on earth"
  —he said to the paralytic,

"I say to you, rise, pick up your mat, and go home."
He rose, picked up his mat at once,
    and went away in the sight of everyone.
They were all astounded
    and glorified God, saying, "We have never seen anything like
        this." ✛

SATURDAY, JANUARY 15
WEEKDAY, *[BVM]*

† *1 Samuel 9:1-4, 17-19; 10:1a*
This is the man of whom the LORD God spoke,
Saul who will rule his people.

There was a stalwart man from Benjamin named Kish,
    who was the son of Abiel, son of Zeror,
    son of Becorath, son of Aphiah, a Benjaminite.
He had a son named Saul, who was a handsome young man.
There was no other child of Israel more handsome than Saul;
    he stood head and shoulders above the people.

Now the asses of Saul's father, Kish, had wandered off.
Kish said to his son Saul, "Take one of the servants with you
    and go out and hunt for the asses."
Accordingly they went through the hill country of Ephraim,
    and through the land of Shalishah.
Not finding them there,
    they continued through the land of Shaalim without success.
They also went through the land of Benjamin,
    but they failed to find the animals.

When Samuel caught sight of Saul, the LORD assured him,
    "This is the man of whom I told you; he is to govern my people."

Saul met Samuel in the gateway and said,
    "Please tell me where the seer lives."
Samuel answered Saul: "I am the seer.
Go up ahead of me to the high place and eat with me today.
In the morning, before dismissing you,
    I will tell you whatever you wish."

Then, from a flask he had with him, Samuel poured oil on Saul's head;
    he also kissed him, saying:
    "The LORD anoints you commander over his heritage.
You are to govern the LORD's people Israel,
    and to save them from the grasp of their enemies roundabout.

"This will be the sign for you
that the LORD has anointed you commander over his heritage." ✛

Psalm 21:2-3, 4-5, 6-7

R. (2a) Lord, in your strength the king is glad.
O LORD, in your strength the king is glad;
  in your victory how greatly he rejoices!
You have granted him his heart's desire;
  you refused not the wish of his lips. **R.**
For you welcomed him with goodly blessings,
  you placed on his head a crown of pure gold.
He asked life of you: you gave him
  length of days forever and ever. **R.**
Great is his glory in your victory;
  majesty and splendor you conferred upon him.
For you made him a blessing forever;
  you gladdened him with the joy of your face. **R.**

Luke 4:18

R. Alleluia, alleluia.
The Lord sent me to bring glad tidings to the poor
and to proclaim liberty to captives. **R.**

✝Mark 2:13-17
I did not come to call the righteous but sinners.

Jesus went out along the sea.
All the crowd came to him and he taught them.
As he passed by, he saw Levi, son of Alphaeus,
  sitting at the customs post.
Jesus said to him, "Follow me."
And he got up and followed Jesus.
While he was at table in his house,
  many tax collectors and sinners sat with Jesus and his disciples;
  for there were many who followed him.
Some scribes who were Pharisees saw that Jesus was eating with
    sinners
  and tax collectors and said to his disciples,
  "Why does he eat with tax collectors and sinners?"
Jesus heard this and said to them,
  "Those who are well do not need a physician, but the sick do.
I did not come to call the righteous but sinners." ✛

SUNDAY, JANUARY 16
SECOND SUNDAY IN ORDINARY TIME

† *Isaiah 62:1-5*
The bridegroom rejoices in his bride.

For Zion's sake I will not be silent,
  for Jerusalem's sake I will not be quiet,
until her vindication shines forth like the dawn
  and her victory like a burning torch.

Nations shall behold your vindication,
  and all the kings your glory;
you shall be called by a new name
  pronounced by the mouth of the LORD.
You shall be a glorious crown in the hand of the LORD,
  a royal diadem held by your God.
No more shall people call you "Forsaken, "
  or your land "Desolate,"
but you shall be called "My Delight,"
  and your land "Espoused."
For the LORD delights in you
  and makes your land his spouse.
As a young man marries a virgin,
  your Builder shall marry you;
and as a bridegroom rejoices in his bride
  so shall your God rejoice in you. ✛

Psalm 96:1-2, 2-3, 7-8, 9-10
R. Proclaim his marvelous deeds to all the nations.
Sing to the LORD a new song;
  sing to the LORD, all you lands.
Sing to the LORD; bless his name. **R.**
Announce his salvation, day after day.
Tell his glory among the nations;
  among all peoples, his wondrous deeds. **R.**
Give to the LORD, you families of nations,
  give to the LORD glory and praise;
  give to the LORD the glory due his name! **R.**
Worship the LORD in holy attire.
  Tremble before him, all the earth;
say among the nations: The LORD is king.
  He governs the peoples with equity. **R.**

† 1 Corinthians 12:4-11
One and the same Spirit distributing them
individually to each person as he wishes.

Brothers and sisters:
There are different kinds of spiritual gifts but the same Spirit;
   there are different forms of service but the same Lord;
   there are different workings but the same God
   who produces all of them in everyone.
To each individual the manifestation of the Spirit
   is given for some benefit.
To one is given through the Spirit the expression of wisdom;
   to another, the expression of knowledge according to the same
      Spirit;
   to another, faith by the same Spirit;
   to another, gifts of healing by the one Spirit;
   to another, mighty deeds;
   to another, prophecy;
   to another, discernment of spirits;
   to another, varieties of tongues;
   to another, interpretation of tongues.
But one and the same Spirit produces all of these,
   distributing them individually to each person as he wishes. ✝

   See 2 Thessalonians 2:14
R. Alleluia, alleluia.
God has called us through the Gospel
to possess the glory of our Lord Jesus Christ. **R.**

† John 2:1-11
Jesus did this as the beginning of his signs at Cana in Galilee.

There was a wedding at Cana in Galilee,
   and the mother of Jesus was there.
Jesus and his disciples were also invited to the wedding.
When the wine ran short,
   the mother of Jesus said to him,
   "They have no wine."
And Jesus said to her,
   "Woman, how does your concern affect me?
My hour has not yet come."
His mother said to the servers,
   "Do whatever he tells you."
Now there were six stone water jars there for Jewish ceremonial
      washings,
   each holding twenty to thirty gallons.
Jesus told them,

"Fill the jars with water."
So they filled them to the brim.
Then he told them,
"Draw some out now and take it to the headwaiter."
So they took it.
And when the headwaiter tasted the water that had become wine,
   without knowing where it came from
   —although the servers who had drawn the water knew—,
   the headwaiter called the bridegroom and said to him,
   "Everyone serves good wine first,
   and then when people have drunk freely, an inferior one;
   but you have kept the good wine until now."
Jesus did this as the beginning of his signs at Cana in Galilee
   and so revealed his glory,
   and his disciples began to believe in him. ✛

MONDAY, JANUARY 17
St. Anthony

† 1 Samuel 15:16-23
*Obedience is better than sacrifice. Because you have rejected the command
of the Lord, he, too, has rejected you as ruler.*

Samuel said to Saul:
"Stop! Let me tell you what the Lord said to me last night."
Saul replied, "Speak!"
Samuel then said: "Though little in your own esteem,
   are you not leader of the tribes of Israel?
The Lord anointed you king of Israel and sent you on a mission, saying,
   'Go and put the sinful Amalekites under a ban of destruction.
Fight against them until you have exterminated them.'
Why then have you disobeyed the Lord?
You have pounced on the spoil, thus displeasing the Lord."
Saul answered Samuel: "I did indeed obey the Lord
   and fulfill the mission on which the Lord sent me.
I have brought back Agag, and I have destroyed Amalek under the ban.
But from the spoil the men took sheep and oxen,
   the best of what had been banned,
   to sacrifice to the Lord their God in Gilgal."
But Samuel said:
"Does the Lord so delight in burnt offerings and sacrifices
   as in obedience to the command of the Lord?
Obedience is better than sacrifice,
   and submission than the fat of rams.
For a sin like divination is rebellion,
   and presumption is the crime of idolatry.

Because you have rejected the command of the LORD,
    he, too, has rejected you as ruler." ✛

Psalm 50:8-9, 16bc-17, 21 and 23
R. (23b) **To the upright I will show the saving power of God.**
"Not for your sacrifices do I rebuke you,
    for your burnt offerings are before me always.
I take from your house no bullock,
    no goats out of your fold." **R.**
"Why do you recite my statutes,
    and profess my covenant with your mouth,
Though you hate discipline
    and cast my words behind you?" **R.**
"When you do these things, shall I be deaf to it?
    Or do you think that I am like yourself?
I will correct you by drawing them up before your eyes.
He that offers praise as a sacrifice glorifies me;
    and to him that goes the right way
        I will show the salvation of God." **R.**

Hebrews 4:12
R. Alleluia, alleluia.
The word of God is living and effective,
able to discern reflections and thoughts of the heart. **R.**

✝ *Mark 2:18-22*
The bridegroom is with them.

The disciples of John and of the Pharisees were accustomed to fast.
People came to Jesus and objected,
    "Why do the disciples of John and the disciples of the Pharisees
        fast,
    but your disciples do not fast?"
Jesus answered them,
    "Can the wedding guests fast while the bridegroom is with them?
As long as they have the bridegroom with them they cannot fast.
But the days will come when the bridegroom is taken away from
        them,
    and then they will fast on that day.
No one sews a piece of unshrunken cloth on an old cloak.
    If he does, its fullness pulls away,
    the new from the old, and the tear gets worse.
Likewise, no one pours new wine into old wineskins.
Otherwise, the wine will burst the skins,
    and both the wine and the skins are ruined.
Rather, new wine is poured into fresh wineskins." ✛

TUESDAY, JANUARY 18
WEEKDAY

† 1 Samuel 16:1-13
Samuel anointed David in the presence of his brothers,
and the Spirit of the LORD God rushed upon him.

The LORD said to Samuel:
"How long will you grieve for Saul,
    whom I have rejected as king of Israel?
Fill your horn with oil, and be on your way.
I am sending you to Jesse of Bethlehem,
    for I have chosen my king from among his sons."
But Samuel replied:
    "How can I go?
    Saul will hear of it and kill me."
To this the LORD answered:
    "Take a heifer along and say,
    'I have come to sacrifice to the LORD.'
Invite Jesse to the sacrifice, and I myself will tell you what to do;
    you are to anoint for me the one I point out to you."

Samuel did as the LORD had commanded him.
When he entered Bethlehem,
    the elders of the city came trembling to meet him and inquired,
    "Is your visit peaceful, O seer?"
He replied:
    "Yes! I have come to sacrifice to the LORD.
So cleanse yourselves and join me today for the banquet."
He also had Jesse and his sons cleanse themselves
    and invited them to the sacrifice.
As they came, he looked at Eliab and thought,
    "Surely the LORD's anointed is here before him."
But the LORD said to Samuel:
    "Do not judge from his appearance or from his lofty stature,
    because I have rejected him.
Not as man sees does God see,
    because he sees the appearance
    but the LORD looks into the heart."
Then Jesse called Abinadab and presented him before Samuel,
    who said, "The LORD has not chosen him."
Next Jesse presented Shammah, but Samuel said,
    "The LORD has not chosen this one either."
In the same way Jesse presented seven sons before Samuel,
    but Samuel said to Jesse,
    "The LORD has not chosen any one of these."

Then Samuel asked Jesse,
  "Are these all the sons you have?"
Jesse replied,
  "There is still the youngest, who is tending the sheep."
Samuel said to Jesse,
  "Send for him;
  we will not begin the sacrificial banquet until he arrives here."
Jesse sent and had the young man brought to them.
He was ruddy, a youth handsome to behold
  and making a splendid appearance.
The LORD said,
  "There—anoint him, for this is he!"
Then Samuel, with the horn of oil in hand,
  anointed him in the midst of his brothers;
  and from that day on, the Spirit of the LORD rushed upon David.
When Samuel took his leave, he went to Ramah. ✛

Psalm 89:20, 21-22, 27-28
R. (21a) **I have found David, my servant.**
Once you spoke in a vision,
  and to your faithful ones you said:
"On a champion I have placed a crown;
  over the people I have set a youth." **R.**
"I have found David, my servant;
  with my holy oil I have anointed him,
That my hand may be always with him,
  and that my arm may make him strong." **R.**
"He shall say of me, 'You are my father,
  my God, the Rock, my savior.'
And I will make him the first-born,
  highest of the kings of the earth." **R.**

See Ephesians 1:17-18
R. Alleluia, alleluia.
May the Father of our Lord Jesus Christ
enlighten the eyes of our hearts,
that we may know what is the hope
that belongs to our call. **R.**

† *Mark 2:23-28*
The sabbath was made for people, not people for the sabbath.

As Jesus was passing through a field of grain on the sabbath,
  his disciples began to make a path while picking the heads of grain.
At this the Pharisees said to him,
  "Look, why are they doing what is unlawful on the sabbath?"

He said to them,
"Have you never read what David did
when he was in need and he and his companions were hungry?
How he went into the house of God when Abiathar was high priest
and ate the bread of offering that only the priests could lawfully eat,
and shared it with his companions?"
Then he said to them,
"The sabbath was made for man, not man for the sabbath.
That is why the Son of Man is lord even of the sabbath." ✜

WEDNESDAY, JANUARY 19
WEEKDAY

† 1 Samuel 17:32-33, 37, 40-51
David overcame the Philistine with sling and stone.

David spoke to Saul:
"Let your majesty not lose courage.
I am at your service to go and fight this Philistine."
But Saul answered David,
"You cannot go up against this Philistine and fight with him,
for you are only a youth, while he has been a warrior from his
youth."

David continued:
"The LORD, who delivered me from the claws of the lion and the
bear,
will also keep me safe from the clutches of this Philistine."
Saul answered David, "Go! the LORD will be with you."

Then, staff in hand, David selected five smooth stones from the wadi
and put them in the pocket of his shepherd's bag.
With his sling also ready to hand, he approached the Philistine.

With his shield bearer marching before him,
the Philistine also advanced closer and closer to David.
When he had sized David up,
and seen that he was youthful, and ruddy, and handsome in
appearance,
the Philistine held David in contempt.
The Philistine said to David,
"Am I a dog that you come against me with a staff?"
Then the Philistine cursed David by his gods
and said to him, "Come here to me,
and I will leave your flesh for the birds of the air
and the beasts of the field."

David answered him:

"You come against me with sword and spear and scimitar,
but I come against you in the name of the LORD of hosts,
the God of the armies of Israel that you have insulted.
Today the LORD shall deliver you into my hand;
I will strike you down and cut off your head.
This very day I will leave your corpse
and the corpses of the Philistine army for the birds of the air
and the beasts of the field;
thus the whole land shall learn that Israel has a God.
All this multitude, too,
shall learn that it is not by sword or spear that the LORD saves.
For the battle is the LORD's and he shall deliver you into our hands."

The Philistine then moved to meet David at close quarters,
while David ran quickly toward the battle line
in the direction of the Philistine.
David put his hand into the bag and took out a stone,
hurled it with the sling,
and struck the Philistine on the forehead.
The stone embedded itself in his brow,
and he fell prostrate on the ground.
Thus David overcame the Philistine with sling and stone;
he struck the Philistine mortally, and did it without a sword.
Then David ran and stood over him;
with the Philistine's own sword which he drew from its sheath
he dispatched him and cut off his head. ✣

Psalm 144:1b, 2, 9-10

R. (1) Blessed be the Lord, my Rock!
Blessed be the LORD, my rock,
who trains my hands for battle, my fingers for war. **R.**
My refuge and my fortress,
my stronghold, my deliverer,
My shield, in whom I trust,
who subdues my people under me. **R.**
O God, I will sing a new song to you;
with a ten-stringed lyre I will chant your praise,
You who give victory to kings,
and deliver David, your servant, from the evil sword. **R.**

See Matthew 4:23

R. Alleluia, alleluia.
Jesus preached the Gospel of the Kingdom
and cured every disease among the people. **R.**

† *Mark 3:1-6*

Is it lawful on the sabbath to save life rather than to destroy it?

Jesus entered the synagogue.
There was a man there who had a withered hand.
They watched Jesus closely
   to see if he would cure him on the sabbath
   so that they might accuse him.
He said to the man with the withered hand,
   "Come up here before us."
Then he said to the Pharisees,
   "Is it lawful to do good on the sabbath rather than to do evil,
   to save life rather than to destroy it?"
But they remained silent.
Looking around at them with anger
   and grieved at their hardness of heart,
   Jesus said to the man, "Stretch out your hand."
He stretched it out and his hand was restored.
The Pharisees went out and immediately took counsel
   with the Herodians against him to put him to death. ✛

THURSDAY, JANUARY 20
WEEKDAY, ST. POPE FABIAN, ST. SEBASTIAN

† *1 Samuel 18:6-9; 19:1-7*
My father Saul is trying to kill you.

When David and Saul approached
   (on David's return after slaying the Philistine),
   women came out from each of the cities of Israel to meet King Saul,
   singing and dancing, with tambourines, joyful songs, and sistrums.
The women played and sang:

   "Saul has slain his thousands,
   and David his ten thousands."

Saul was very angry and resentful of the song, for he thought:
   "They give David ten thousands, but only thousands to me.
All that remains for him is the kingship."
And from that day on, Saul was jealous of David.

Saul discussed his intention of killing David
   with his son Jonathan and with all his servants.
But Saul's son Jonathan, who was very fond of David, told him:
   "My father Saul is trying to kill you.
Therefore, please be on your guard tomorrow morning;
   get out of sight and remain in hiding.

I, however, will go out and stand beside my father
in the countryside where you are, and will speak to him about you.
If I learn anything, I will let you know."

Jonathan then spoke well of David to his father Saul, saying to him:
"Let not your majesty sin against his servant David,
for he has committed no offense against you,
but has helped you very much by his deeds.
When he took his life in his hands and slew the Philistine,
and the LORD brought about a great victory
for all Israel through him,
you were glad to see it.
Why, then, should you become guilty of shedding innocent blood
by killing David without cause?"
Saul heeded Jonathan's plea and swore,
"As the LORD lives, he shall not be killed."
So Jonathan summoned David and repeated the whole conversation
to him.
Jonathan then brought David to Saul, and David served him as
before. ✛

Psalm 56:2-3, 9-10a, 10b-11, 12-13
R. (5b) **In God I trust; I shall not fear.**
Have mercy on me, O God, for men trample upon me;
all the day they press their attack against me.
My adversaries trample upon me all the day;
yes, many fight against me. **R.**
My wanderings you have counted;
my tears are stored in your flask;
are they not recorded in your book?
Then do my enemies turn back,
when I call upon you. **R.**
Now I know that God is with me.
In God, in whose promise I glory,
in God I trust without fear;
what can flesh do against me? **R.**
I am bound, O God, by vows to you;
your thank offerings I will fulfill.
For you have rescued me from death,
my feet, too, from stumbling;
that I may walk before God in the light of the living. **R.**

See 2 Timothy 1:10
R. Alleluia, alleluia.
Our Savior Jesus Christ has destroyed death
and brought life to light through the Gospel. **R.**

✝ Mark 3:7-12

The unclean spirits shouted, "You are the Son of God,"
but Jesus warned them sternly not to make him known.

Jesus withdrew toward the sea with his disciples.
A large number of people followed from Galilee and from Judea.
Hearing what he was doing,
  a large number of people came to him also from Jerusalem,
  from Idumea, from beyond the Jordan,
  and from the neighborhood of Tyre and Sidon.
He told his disciples to have a boat ready for him because of the
    crowd,
  so that they would not crush him.
He had cured many and, as a result, those who had diseases
  were pressing upon him to touch him.
And whenever unclean spirits saw him they would fall down before
    him
  and shout, "You are the Son of God."
He warned them sternly not to make him known. ✝

FRIDAY, JANUARY 21
ST. AGNES

✝ 1 Samuel 24:3-21

I will not raise a hand against my lord, for he is the LORD's anointed.

Saul took three thousand picked men from all Israel
  and went in search of David and his men
  in the direction of the wild goat crags.
When he came to the sheepfolds along the way, he found a cave,
  which he entered to relieve himself.
David and his men were occupying the inmost recesses of the cave.

David's servants said to him,
  "This is the day of which the LORD said to you,
  'I will deliver your enemy into your grasp;
  do with him as you see fit.'"
So David moved up and stealthily cut off an end of Saul's mantle.
Afterward, however, David regretted that he had cut off
  an end of Saul's mantle.
He said to his men,
  "The LORD forbid that I should do such a thing to my master,
  the LORD's anointed, as to lay a hand on him,
  for he is the LORD's anointed."
With these words David restrained his men
  and would not permit them to attack Saul.
Saul then left the cave and went on his way.

David also stepped out of the cave, calling to Saul,
  "My lord the king!"
When Saul looked back, David bowed to the ground in homage and
    asked Saul:
  "Why do you listen to those who say,
  'David is trying to harm you'?
You see for yourself today that the LORD just now delivered you
    into my grasp in the cave.
I had some thought of killing you, but I took pity on you instead.
I decided, 'I will not raise a hand against my lord,
    for he is the LORD's anointed and a father to me.'
Look here at this end of your mantle which I hold.
Since I cut off an end of your mantle and did not kill you,
    see and be convinced that I plan no harm and no rebellion.
I have done you no wrong,
    though you are hunting me down to take my life.
The LORD will judge between me and you,
    and the LORD will exact justice from you in my case.
I shall not touch you.
The old proverb says, 'From the wicked comes forth wickedness.'
So I will take no action against you.
Against whom are you on campaign, O king of Israel?
Whom are you pursuing? A dead dog, or a single flea!
The LORD will be the judge; he will decide between me and you.
May he see this, and take my part,
    and grant me justice beyond your reach!"

When David finished saying these things to Saul, Saul answered,
  "Is that your voice, my son David?"
And Saul wept aloud.
Saul then said to David: "You are in the right rather than I;
    you have treated me generously, while I have done you harm.
Great is the generosity you showed me today,
    when the LORD delivered me into your grasp
    and you did not kill me.
For if a man meets his enemy, does he send him away unharmed?
May the LORD reward you generously for what you have done this day.
And now, I know that you shall surely be king
    and that sovereignty over Israel shall come into your possession." ✛

  Psalm 57:2, 3-4, 6 and 11
R. (2a) Have mercy on me; God, have mercy.
Have mercy on me, O God; have mercy on me,
    for in you I take refuge.
In the shadow of your wings I take refuge,

till harm pass by. **R.**
I call to God the Most High,
to God, my benefactor.
May he send from heaven and save me;
may he make those a reproach who trample upon me;
may God send his mercy and his faithfulness. **R.**
Be exalted above the heavens, O God;
above all the earth be your glory!
For your mercy towers to the heavens,
and your faithfulness to the skies. **R.**

2 Corinthians 5:19
R. Alleluia, alleluia.
God was reconciling the world to himself in Christ,
and entrusting to us the message of reconciliation. **R.**

† *Mark 3:13-19*
Jesus summoned those whom he wanted and they came to him.

Jesus went up the mountain and summoned those whom he wanted
and they came to him.
He appointed Twelve, whom he also named Apostles,
that they might be with him
and he might send them forth to preach
and to have authority to drive out demons:
He appointed the Twelve:
Simon, whom he named Peter;
James, son of Zebedee,
and John the brother of James, whom he named Boanerges,
that is, sons of thunder;
Andrew, Philip, Bartholomew,
Matthew, Thomas, James the son of Alphaeus;
Thaddeus, Simon the Cananean,
and Judas Iscariot who betrayed him. ✛

SATURDAY, JANUARY 22
DAY OF PRAYER FOR THE LEGAL PROTECTION OF UNBORN CHILDREN

† *2 Samuel 1:1-4, 11-12, 19, 23-27*
How can the warriors have fallen in battle!

David returned from his defeat of the Amalekites
and spent two days in Ziklag.
On the third day a man came from Saul's camp,
with his clothes torn and dirt on his head.
Going to David, he fell to the ground in homage.
David asked him, "Where do you come from?"
He replied, "I have escaped from the camp of the children of Israel."

"Tell me what happened," David bade him.
He answered that many of the soldiers had fled the battle
    and that many of them had fallen and were dead,
    among them Saul and his son Jonathan.

David seized his garments and rent them,
    and all the men who were with him did likewise.
They mourned and wept and fasted until evening
    for Saul and his son Jonathan,
    and for the soldiers of the LORD of the clans of Israel,
    because they had fallen by the sword.

"Alas! the glory of Israel, Saul,
slain upon your heights;
how can the warriors have fallen!

"Saul and Jonathan, beloved and cherished,
    separated neither in life nor in death,
    swifter than eagles, stronger than lions!
Women of Israel, weep over Saul,
    who clothed you in scarlet and in finery,
    who decked your attire with ornaments of gold.

"How can the warriors have fallen—
    in the thick of the battle,
    slain upon your heights!

"I grieve for you, Jonathan my brother!
    most dear have you been to me;
    more precious have I held love for you than love for women.

"How can the warriors have fallen,
    the weapons of war have perished!" ✝

Psalm 80:2-3, 5-7
R. (4b) **Let us see your face, Lord, and we shall be saved.**
O shepherd of Israel, hearken,
    O guide of the flock of Joseph!
From your throne upon the cherubim, shine forth
    before Ephraim, Benjamin and Manasseh.
Rouse your power,
    and come to save us. **R.**
O LORD of hosts, how long will you burn with anger
    while your people pray?
You have fed them with the bread of tears
    and given them tears to drink in ample measure.

You have left us to be fought over by our neighbors,
and our enemies mock us. **R.**

See Acts 16:14b
R. Alleluia, alleluia.
Open our hearts, O Lord,
to listen to the words of your Son. **R.**

† *Mark 3:20-21*
They said, "He is out of his mind."

Jesus came with his disciples into the house.
Again the crowd gathered,
making it impossible for them even to eat.
When his relatives heard of this they set out to seize him,
for they said, "He is out of his mind." ✝

or, for the Day of Prayer
Any of the following readings from the Masses for "Various Needs and Occasions,"
(volume III, In Various Public Circumstances, 26A) or "For Giving Thanks to God for the
Gift of Human Life" (*Supplement*, numbers. 947A-947E): Genesis 1:1—2:2 (41) •
2 Maccabees 7:1, 20-31 (vol. II, 499) • Isaiah 49:1-6 (587) • Romans 11:33-36 (121) •
Ephesians 1:3-14 (104) • Ephesians 3:14-21 (vol. III, 476) • Colossians 1:12-20 (162) •
1 John 3:11-21 (208) • Matthew 18:1-5, 10, 12-14 (414) • Mark 9:30-37 (134) •
Luke 1:39-56 (622) • Luke 17:11-19 (144) • Luke 23:35-43 (162) • John 1:1-5, 9-14, 16-18
(755) • John 6:24-35 (113), or the *Lectionary for Mass* (volume IV),
the Mass "For Peace and Justice," numbers 887-891.

Readings from the Mass "For Peace and Justice"

† *James 3:13-18*
The fruit of righteousness is sown in peace for those who cultivate peace.

Beloved:
Who among you is wise and understanding?
Let him show his works by a good life
in the humility that comes from wisdom.
But if you have bitter jealousy and selfish ambition in your hearts,
do not boast and be false to the truth.
Wisdom of this kind does not come down from above
but is earthly, unspiritual, demonic.
For where jealousy and selfish ambition exist,
there is disorder and every foul practice.
But the wisdom from above is first of all pure,
the peaceable, gentle, compliant,
full of mercy and good fruits,
without inconstancy or insincerity.
And the fruit of righteousness is sown in peace
for those who cultivate peace. ✝

Psalm 85:9 and 10, 11-12, 13-14

R. (9b) **The Lord speaks of peace to his people.**

I will hear what God proclaims;
 the LORD—for he proclaims peace.
Near indeed is his salvation to those who fear him,
 glory dwelling in our land. **R.**
Kindness and truth shall meet;
 justice and peace shall kiss.
Truth shall spring out of the earth,
 and justice shall look down from heaven. **R.**
The LORD himself will give his benefits;
 our land shall yield its increase.
Justice shall walk before him,
 and salvation, along the way of his steps. **R.**

John 14:27

R. Alleluia, alleluia.

Peace I leave with you, says the Lord,
my peace I give to you. **R.**

✝ John 14:23-29

My peace I give to you.

Jesus said to his disciple, Jude:
"Whoever loves me will keep my word,
 and my Father will love him,
 and we will come to him and make our dwelling with him.
Whoever does not love me does not keep my words;
 yet the word you hear is not mine
 but that of the Father who sent me.

"I have told you this while I am with you.
The Advocate, the Holy Spirit—
 that the Father will send in my name—
 he will teach you everything
 and remind you of all that I told you.
Peace I leave with you; my peace I give to you.
Not as the world gives do I give it to you.
Do not let your hearts be troubled or afraid.
You heard me tell you,
 'I am going away and I will come back to you.'
If you loved me,
 you would rejoice that I am going to the Father;
 for the Father is greater than I.
And now I have told you this before it happens,
 so that when it happens you may believe." ✝

SUNDAY, JANUARY 23
THIRD SUNDAY IN ORDINARY TIME
† *Nehemiah 8:2-4a, 5-6, 8-10*
They read from the book of the Law and they understood what was read.

Ezra the priest brought the law before the assembly,
which consisted of men, women,
and those children old enough to understand.
Standing at one end of the open place that was before the Water Gate,
he read out of the book from daybreak till midday,
in the presence of the men, the women,
and those children old enough to understand;
and all the people listened attentively to the book of the law.
Ezra the scribe stood on a wooden platform
that had been made for the occasion.
He opened the scroll
so that all the people might see it
—for he was standing higher up than any of the people—;
and, as he opened it, all the people rose.
Ezra blessed the LORD, the great God,
and all the people, their hands raised high, answered,
"Amen, amen!"
Then they bowed down and prostrated themselves before the LORD,
their faces to the ground.
Ezra read plainly from the book of the law of God,
interpreting it so that all could understand what was read.
Then Nehemiah, that is, His Excellency, and Ezra the priest-scribe
and the Levites who were instructing the people
said to all the people:
"Today is holy to the LORD your God.
Do not be sad, and do not weep"—
for all the people were weeping as they heard the words of the law.
He said further: "Go, eat rich foods and drink sweet drinks,
and allot portions to those who had nothing prepared;
for today is holy to our LORD.
Do not be saddened this day,
for rejoicing in the LORD must be your strength!" ✛

Psalm 19:8, 9, 10, 15
R. Your words, Lord, are Spirit and life.
The law of the LORD is perfect,
refreshing the soul;
The decree of the LORD is trustworthy,
giving wisdom to the simple. **R.**

The precepts of the LORD are right,
  rejoicing the heart;
the command of the LORD is clear,
  enlightening the eye. **R.**
The fear of the LORD is pure,
  enduring forever;
the ordinances of the LORD are true,
  all of them just. **R.**
Let the words of my mouth and the thought of my heart
  find favor before you,
O LORD, my rock and my redeemer. **R.**

> **✝ 1 Corinthians 12:12-30** (or 1 Corinthians 12:12-14, 27)
> *You are Christ's body and individually parts of it.*

Brothers and sisters:
As a body is one though it has many parts,
  and all the parts of the body, though many, are one body,
  so also Christ.
For in one Spirit we were all baptized into one body,
whether Jews or Greeks, slaves or free persons,
  and we were all given to drink of one Spirit.

Now the body is not a single part, but many.
If a foot should say,
  "Because I am not a hand I do not belong to the body,"
  it does not for this reason belong any less to the body.
Or if an ear should say,
  "Because I am not an eye I do not belong to the body,"
  it does not for this reason belong any less to the body.
If the whole body were an eye, where would the hearing be?
If the whole body were hearing, where would the sense of smell be?
But as it is, God placed the parts,
  each one of them, in the body as he intended.
If they were all one part, where would the body be?
But as it is, there are many parts, yet one body.
The eye cannot say to the hand, "I do not need you,"
  nor again the head to the feet, "I do not need you."
Indeed, the parts of the body that seem to be weaker
  are all the more necessary,
  and those parts of the body that we consider less honorable
  we surround with greater honor,
  and our less presentable parts are treated with greater propriety,
  whereas our more presentable parts do not need this.
But God has so constructed the body
  as to give greater honor to a part that is without it,

so that there may be no division in the body,
but that the parts may have the same concern for one another.
If one part suffers, all the parts suffer with it;
if one part is honored, all the parts share its joy.

Now you are Christ's body, and individually parts of it.
Some people God has designated in the church
to be, first, apostles; second, prophets; third, teachers;
then, mighty deeds;
then gifts of healing, assistance, administration,
and varieties of tongues.
Are all apostles? Are all prophets? Are all teachers?
Do all work mighty deeds? Do all have gifts of healing?
Do all speak in tongues? Do all interpret? ✛

See Luke 4:18
R. Alleluia, alleluia.
The Lord sent me to bring glad tidings to the poor,
and to proclaim liberty to captives. **R.**

† *Luke 1:1-4; 4:14-21*
Today this Scripture passage is fulfilled.

Since many have undertaken to compile a narrative of the events
that have been fulfilled among us,
just as those who were eyewitnesses from the beginning
and ministers of the word have handed them down to us,
I too have decided,
after investigating everything accurately anew,
to write it down in an orderly sequence for you,
most excellent Theophilus,
so that you may realize the certainty of the teachings
you have received.

Jesus returned to Galilee in the power of the Spirit,
and news of him spread throughout the whole region.
He taught in their synagogues and was praised by all.

He came to Nazareth, where he had grown up,
and went according to his custom
into the synagogue on the sabbath day.
He stood up to read and was handed a scroll of the prophet Isaiah.
He unrolled the scroll and found the passage where it was written:
The Spirit of the LORD is upon me,
because he has anointed me
to bring glad tidings to the poor.

He has sent me to proclaim liberty to captives
   and recovery of sight to the blind,
   to let the oppressed go free,
   and to proclaim a year acceptable to the Lord.
Rolling up the scroll, he handed it back to the attendant and sat
   down,
and the eyes of all in the synagogue looked intently at him.
He said to them,
   "Today this Scripture passage is fulfilled in your hearing." ✝

MONDAY, JANUARY 24
ST. FRANCIS DE SALES

✝ *2 Samuel 5:1-7, 10*
You shall shepherd my people Israel.

All the tribes of Israel came to David in Hebron and said:
"Here we are, your bone and your flesh.
In days past, when Saul was our king,
   it was you who led the children of Israel out and brought them back.
And the LORD said to you, 'You shall shepherd my people Israel
   and shall be commander of Israel.'"
When all the elders of Israel came to David in Hebron,
   King David made an agreement with them there before the LORD,
   and they anointed him king of Israel.
David was thirty years old when he became king,
   and he reigned for forty years:
   seven years and six months in Hebron over Judah,
   and thirty-three years in Jerusalem
   over all Israel and Judah.

Then the king and his men set out for Jerusalem
   against the Jebusites who inhabited the region.
David was told, "You cannot enter here:
   the blind and the lame will drive you away!"
   which was their way of saying, "David cannot enter here."
But David did take the stronghold of Zion, which is the City of David.

David grew steadily more powerful,
   for the LORD of hosts was with him. ✝

Psalm 89:20, 21-22, 25-26
R. (25a) **My faithfulness and my mercy shall be with him.**
Once you spoke in a vision,
   and to your faithful ones you said:
"On a champion I have placed a crown;
   over the people I have set a youth." **R.**

"I have found David, my servant;
   with my holy oil I have anointed him,
That my hand may be always with him,
   and that my arm may make him strong." **R.**
"My faithfulness and my mercy shall be with him,
   and through my name shall his horn be exalted.
I will set his hand upon the sea,
   his right hand upon the rivers." **R.**

   See 2 Timothy 1:10
R. Alleluia, alleluia
Our Savior Jesus Christ has destroyed death
and brought life to light through the Gospel. **R.**

✛ Mark 3:22-30
It is the end of Satan.

The scribes who had come from Jerusalem said of Jesus,
   "He is possessed by Beelzebul," and
   "By the prince of demons he drives out demons."

Summoning them, he began to speak to them in parables,
   "How can Satan drive out Satan?
If a kingdom is divided against itself, that kingdom cannot stand.
And if a house is divided against itself,
   that house will not be able to stand.
And if Satan has risen up against himself and is divided,
   he cannot stand;
   that is the end of him.
But no one can enter a strong man's house to plunder his property
   unless he first ties up the strong man.
Then he can plunder his house.
Amen, I say to you, all sins and all blasphemies
   that people utter will be forgiven them.
But whoever blasphemes against the Holy Spirit
   will never have forgiveness,
   but is guilty of an everlasting sin."
For they had said, "He has an unclean spirit." ✛

TUESDAY, JANUARY 25
THE CONVERSION OF ST. PAUL

✛ Acts 22:3-16 *(or Acts 9:1-22)*
Get up and have yourself baptized and your sins washed away,
calling upon the name of Jesus.

Paul addressed the people in these words:
"I am a Jew, born in Tarsus in Cilicia,

but brought up in this city.
At the feet of Gamaliel I was educated strictly in our ancestral law
    and was zealous for God, just as all of you are today.
I persecuted this Way to death,
    binding both men and women and delivering them to prison.
Even the high priest and the whole council of elders
    can testify on my behalf.
For from them I even received letters to the brothers
    and set out for Damascus to bring back to Jerusalem
    in chains for punishment those there as well.

"On that journey as I drew near to Damascus,
    about noon a great light from the sky suddenly shone around me.
I fell to the ground and heard a voice saying to me,
    'Saul, Saul, why are you persecuting me?'
I replied, 'Who are you, sir?'
And he said to me,
    'I am Jesus the Nazorean whom you are persecuting.'
My companions saw the light
    but did not hear the voice of the one who spoke to me.
I asked, 'What shall I do, sir?'
The Lord answered me, 'Get up and go into Damascus,
    and there you will be told about everything
    appointed for you to do.'
Since I could see nothing because of the brightness of that light,
    I was led by hand by my companions and entered Damascus.

"A certain Ananias, a devout observer of the law,
    and highly spoken of by all the Jews who lived there,
    came to me and stood there and said,
    'Saul, my brother, regain your sight.'
And at that very moment I regained my sight and saw him.
Then he said,
    'The God of our ancestors designated you to know his will,
    to see the Righteous One, and to hear the sound of his voice;
    for you will be his witness before all
    to what you have seen and heard.
Now, why delay?
Get up and have yourself baptized and your sins washed away,
    calling upon his name.'" ✝

Psalm 117:1bc, 2
**R. (Mark 16:15) Go out to all the world and tell the Good
    News.** *(or Alleluia, alleluia.)*
Praise the LORD, all you nations;

glorify him, all you peoples! **R.**
For steadfast is his kindness toward us,
and the fidelity of the LORD endures forever. **R.**

See John 15:16
R. Alleluia, alleluia.
I chose you from the world,
to go and bear fruit that will last, says the Lord. **R.**

✝ *Mark 16:15-18*
Go out to all the world and tell the Good News.

Jesus appeared to the Eleven and said to them:
"Go into the whole world
and proclaim the Gospel to every creature.
Whoever believes and is baptized will be saved;
whoever does not believe will be condemned.
These signs will accompany those who believe:
in my name they will drive out demons,
they will speak new languages.
They will pick up serpents with their hands,
and if they drink any deadly thing, it will not harm them.
They will lay hands on the sick, and they will recover." ✛

WEDNESDAY, JANUARY 26
St. Timothy and St. Titus

✝ *2 Timothy 1:1-8 (or Titus 1:1-5)*
I recall your sincere faith.

Paul, an Apostle of Christ Jesus by the will of God
for the promise of life in Christ Jesus,
to Timothy, my dear child:
grace, mercy, and peace from God the Father
and Christ Jesus our Lord.

I am grateful to God,
whom I worship with a clear conscience as my ancestors did,
as I remember you constantly in my prayers, night and day.
I yearn to see you again, recalling your tears,
so that I may be filled with joy,
as I recall your sincere faith
that first lived in your grandmother Lois
and in your mother Eunice
and that I am confident lives also in you.

For this reason, I remind you to stir into flame
the gift of God that you have through the imposition of my hands.

For God did not give us a spirit of cowardice
  but rather of power and love and self-control.
So do not be ashamed of your testimony to our Lord,
  nor of me, a prisoner for his sake;
  but bear your share of hardship for the Gospel
  with the strength that comes from God. ✝

Psalm 96:1-2a, 2b-3, 7-8a, 10
R. (3) **Proclaim God's marvelous deeds to all the nations.**
Sing to the LORD a new song;
  sing to the LORD, all you lands.
Sing to the LORD; bless his name. **R.**
Announce his salvation, day after day.
Tell his glory among the nations;
  among all peoples, his wondrous deeds. **R.**
Give to the LORD, you families of nations,
  give to the LORD glory and praise;
  give to the LORD the glory due his name! **R.**
Say among the nations: The LORD is king.
He has made the world firm, not to be moved;
  he governs the peoples with equity. **R.**

R. Alleluia, alleluia.
The seed is the word of God, Christ is the sower;
all who come to him will live for ever. **R.**

✝ *Mark 4:1-20*
A sower went out to sow.

On another occasion, Jesus began to teach by the sea.
A very large crowd gathered around him
  so that he got into a boat on the sea and sat down.
And the whole crowd was beside the sea on land.
And he taught them at length in parables,
  and in the course of his instruction he said to them,
  "Hear this! A sower went out to sow.
And as he sowed, some seed fell on the path,
  and the birds came and ate it up.
Other seed fell on rocky ground where it had little soil.
It sprang up at once because the soil was not deep.
And when the sun rose, it was scorched and it withered for lack of
    roots.
Some seed fell among thorns, and the thorns grew up and choked it
  and it produced no grain.
And some seed fell on rich soil and produced fruit.
It came up and grew and yielded thirty, sixty, and a hundredfold."

He added, "Whoever has ears to hear ought to hear."

And when he was alone,
  those present along with the Twelve
  questioned him about the parables.
He answered them,
  "The mystery of the Kingdom of God has been granted to you.
But to those outside everything comes in parables, so that

they may look and see but not perceive,
  and hear and listen but not understand,
in order that they may not be converted and be forgiven."

Jesus said to them, "Do you not understand this parable?
Then how will you understand any of the parables?
The sower sows the word.
These are the ones on the path where the word is sown.
As soon as they hear, Satan comes at once
  and takes away the word sown in them.
And these are the ones sown on rocky ground who,
  when they hear the word, receive it at once with joy.
But they have no roots; they last only for a time.
Then when tribulation or persecution comes because of the word,
  they quickly fall away.
Those sown among thorns are another sort.
They are the people who hear the word,
  but worldly anxiety, the lure of riches,
  and the craving for other things intrude and choke the word,
  and it bears no fruit.
But those sown on rich soil are the ones who hear the word and
    accept it
  and bear fruit thirty and sixty and a hundredfold." ✛

THURSDAY, JANUARY 27
WEEKDAY, ST. ANGELA MERICI

† 2 Samuel 7:18-19, 24-29
Who am I, Lord GOD, and who are the members of my house?

After Nathan had spoken to King David,
  the king went in and sat before the LORD and said,
  "Who am I, Lord GOD, and who are the members of my house,
  that you have brought me to this point?
Yet even this you see as too little, Lord GOD;
  you have also spoken of the house of your servant
  for a long time to come:
  this too you have shown to man, Lord GOD!

"You have established for yourself your people Israel as yours forever,
and you, LORD, have become their God.
And now, LORD God, confirm for all time the prophecy you have made
concerning your servant and his house,
and do as you have promised.
Your name will be forever great, when men say,
'The LORD of hosts is God of Israel,'
and the house of your servant David stands firm before you.
It is you, LORD of hosts, God of Israel,
who said in a revelation to your servant,
'I will build a house for you.'
Therefore your servant now finds the courage to make this prayer to
you.
And now, Lord GOD, you are God and your words are truth;
you have made this generous promise to your servant.
Do, then, bless the house of your servant
that it may be before you forever;
for you, Lord GOD, have promised,
and by your blessing the house of your servant
shall be blessed forever." ✚

Psalm 132:1-2, 3-5, 11, 12, 13-14

R. (Luke 1:32b) **The Lord God will give him the throne of
David, his father.**

LORD, remember David
and all his anxious care;
How he swore an oath to the LORD,
vowed to the Mighty One of Jacob. **R.**
"I will not enter the house where I live,
nor lie on the couch where I sleep;
I will give my eyes no sleep,
my eyelids no rest,
Till I find a home for the LORD,
a dwelling for the Mighty One of Jacob." **R.**
The LORD swore an oath to David,
a firm promise from which he will not withdraw:
"Your own offspring
I will set upon your throne." **R.**
"If your sons keep my covenant,
and the decrees which I shall teach them,
Their sons, too, forever
shall sit upon your throne." **R.**
For the LORD has chosen Zion,
he prefers her for his dwelling:

"Zion is my resting place forever;
  in her I will dwell, for I prefer her." **R.**

Psalm 119:105
R. Alleluia, alleluia.
A lamp to my feet is your word,
a light to my path. **R.**

† *Mark 4:21-25*
A lamp is to be placed on a lampstand.
The measure with which you measure will be measured out to you.

Jesus said to his disciples,
  "Is a lamp brought in to be placed under a bushel basket
  or under a bed,
  and not to be placed on a lampstand?
For there is nothing hidden except to be made visible;
  nothing is secret except to come to light.
Anyone who has ears to hear ought to hear."
He also told them, "Take care what you hear.
The measure with which you measure will be measured out to you,
  and still more will be given to you.
To the one who has, more will be given;
  from the one who has not, even what he has will be taken away." ✛

FRIDAY, JANUARY 28
St. Thomas Aquinas

† *2 Samuel 11:1-4a, 5-10a, 13-17*
You have despised me and have taken the wife of Uriah to be your wife
(see 2 Samuel 12:10).

At the turn of the year, when kings go out on campaign,
  David sent out Joab along with his officers
  and the army of Israel,
  and they ravaged the Ammonites and besieged Rabbah.
David, however, remained in Jerusalem.
One evening David rose from his siesta
  and strolled about on the roof of the palace.
From the roof he saw a woman bathing, who was very beautiful.
David had inquiries made about the woman and was told,
  "She is Bathsheba, daughter of Eliam,
  and wife of Joab's armor bearer Uriah the Hittite."
Then David sent messengers and took her.
When she came to him, he had relations with her.
She then returned to her house.
But the woman had conceived,
  and sent the information to David, "I am with child."

Reading GOD'S WORD

David therefore sent a message to Joab,
  "Send me Uriah the Hittite."
So Joab sent Uriah to David.
When he came, David questioned him about Joab, the soldiers,
  and how the war was going, and Uriah answered that all was well.
David then said to Uriah, "Go down to your house and bathe your
    feet."
Uriah left the palace,
  and a portion was sent out after him from the king's table.
But Uriah slept at the entrance of the royal palace
  with the other officers of his lord, and did not go down
  to his own house.
David was told that Uriah had not gone home.
On the day following, David summoned him,
  and he ate and drank with David, who made him drunk.
But in the evening Uriah went out to sleep on his bed
  among his lord's servants, and did not go down to his home.
The next morning David wrote a letter to Joab
  which he sent by Uriah.
In it he directed:
  "Place Uriah up front, where the fighting is fierce.
Then pull back and leave him to be struck down dead."
So while Joab was besieging the city, he assigned Uriah
  to a place where he knew the defenders were strong.
When the men of the city made a sortie against Joab,
  some officers of David's army fell,
  and among them Uriah the Hittite died. ✢

  Psalm 51:3-4, 5-6a, 6bcd-7, 10-11
R. (see 3a) **Be merciful, O Lord, for we have sinned.**
Have mercy on me, O God, in your goodness;
  in the greatness of your compassion wipe out my offense.
Thoroughly wash me from my guilt
  and of my sin cleanse me. **R.**
For I acknowledge my offense,
  and my sin is before me always:
"Against you only have I sinned,
  and done what is evil in your sight." **R.**
I have done such evil in your sight
  that you are just in your sentence,
  blameless when you condemn.
True, I was born guilty,
  a sinner, even as my mother conceived me. **R.**
Let me hear the sounds of joy and gladness;
  the bones you have crushed shall rejoice.

Turn away your face from my sins,
  and blot out all my guilt. **R.**

  See Matthew 11:25
R. Alleluia, alleluia.
Blessed are you, Father, Lord of heaven and earth;
you have revealed to little ones the mysteries of the Kingdom. **R.**

✝ *Mark 4:26-34*
*A man scatters seed on the land and would sleep
and the seed would sprout and grow, he knows not how.*

Jesus said to the crowds:
"This is how it is with the Kingdom of God;
  it is as if a man were to scatter seed on the land
  and would sleep and rise night and day
  and the seed would sprout and grow,
  he knows not how.
Of its own accord the land yields fruit,
  first the blade, then the ear, then the full grain in the ear.
And when the grain is ripe, he wields the sickle at once,
  for the harvest has come."

He said,
  "To what shall we compare the Kingdom of God,
  or what parable can we use for it?
It is like a mustard seed that, when it is sown in the ground,
  is the smallest of all the seeds on the earth.
But once it is sown, it springs up and becomes the largest of plants
  and puts forth large branches,
  so that the birds of the sky can dwell in its shade."
With many such parables
  he spoke the word to them as they were able to understand it.
Without parables he did not speak to them,
  but to his own disciples he explained everything in private. ✛

SATURDAY, JANUARY 29
WEEKDAY, *[BVM]*

✝ *2 Samuel 12:1-7a, 10-17*
I have sinned against the LORD.

The LORD sent Nathan to David, and when he came to him,
  Nathan said: "Judge this case for me!
In a certain town there were two men, one rich, the other poor.
The rich man had flocks and herds in great numbers.
But the poor man had nothing at all
  except one little ewe lamb that he had bought.

He nourished her, and she grew up with him and his children.
She shared the little food he had
  and drank from his cup and slept in his bosom.
She was like a daughter to him.
Now, the rich man received a visitor,
  but he would not take from his own flocks and herds
  to prepare a meal for the wayfarer who had come to him.
Instead he took the poor man's ewe lamb
  and made a meal of it for his visitor."
David grew very angry with that man and said to him:
  "As the LORD lives, the man who has done this merits death!
He shall restore the ewe lamb fourfold
  because he has done this and has had no pity."

Then Nathan said to David: "You are the man!
Thus says the LORD God of Israel:
  'The sword shall never depart from your house,
  because you have despised me
  and have taken the wife of Uriah to be your wife.'
Thus says the LORD:
  'I will bring evil upon you out of your own house.
I will take your wives while you live to see it,
  and will give them to your neighbor.
He shall lie with your wives in broad daylight.
You have done this deed in secret,
  but I will bring it about in the presence of all Israel,
  and with the sun looking down.'"

Then David said to Nathan, "I have sinned against the LORD."
Nathan answered David: "The LORD on his part has forgiven your sin:
  you shall not die.
But since you have utterly spurned the LORD by this deed,
  the child born to you must surely die."
Then Nathan returned to his house.

The LORD struck the child that the wife of Uriah had borne to David,
  and it became desperately ill.
David besought God for the child.
He kept a fast, retiring for the night
  to lie on the ground clothed in sackcloth.
The elders of his house stood beside him
  urging him to rise from the ground; but he would not,
  nor would he take food with them. ✝

Psalm 51:12-13, 14-15, 16-17

R. (12a) **Create a clean heart in me, O God.**

A clean heart create for me, O God,
  and a steadfast spirit renew within me.
Cast me not out from your presence,
  and your Holy Spirit take not from me. **R.**
Give me back the joy of your salvation,
  and a willing spirit sustain in me.
I will teach transgressors your ways,
  and sinners shall return to you. **R.**
Free me from blood guilt, O God, my saving God;
  then my tongue shall revel in your justice.
O Lord, open my lips,
  and my mouth shall proclaim your praise. **R.**

John 3:16

R. Alleluia, alleluia.

God so loved the world that he gave his only-begotten Son,
so that everyone who believes in him might have eternal life. **R.**

✝ *Mark 4:35-41*
Who then is this whom even wind and sea obey?

On that day, as evening drew on, Jesus said to his disciples:
"Let us cross to the other side."
Leaving the crowd, they took Jesus with them in the boat just as he
  was.
And other boats were with him.
A violent squall came up and waves were breaking over the boat,
  so that it was already filling up.
Jesus was in the stern, asleep on a cushion.
They woke him and said to him,
  "Teacher, do you not care that we are perishing?"
He woke up,
  rebuked the wind, and said to the sea, "Quiet! Be still!"
The wind ceased and there was great calm.
Then he asked them, "Why are you terrified?
Do you not yet have faith?"
They were filled with great awe and said to one another,
  "Who then is this whom even wind and sea obey?" ✝

SUNDAY, JANUARY 30
FOURTH SUNDAY IN ORDINARY TIME

† *Jeremiah 1:4-5, 17-19*
A prophet to the nations I appointed you.

The word of the LORD came to me, saying:
Before I formed you in the womb I knew you,
before you were born I dedicated you,
a prophet to the nations I appointed you.

But do you gird your loins;
stand up and tell them
all that I command you.
Be not crushed on their account,
as though I would leave you crushed before them;
for it is I this day
who have made you a fortified city,
a pillar of iron, a wall of brass,
against the whole land:
against Judah's kings and princes,
against its priests and people.
They will fight against you but not prevail over you,
for I am with you to deliver you, says the LORD. ✛

Psalm 71:1-2, 3-4, 5-6, 15-17
R. (see 15ab) **I will sing of your salvation.**
In you, O LORD, I take refuge;
let me never be put to shame.
In your justice rescue me, and deliver me;
incline your ear to me, and save me. **R.**
Be my rock of refuge,
a stronghold to give me safety,
for you are my rock and my fortress.
O my God, rescue me from the hand of the wicked. **R.**
For you are my hope, O LORD;
my trust, O God, from my youth.
On you I depend from birth;
from my mother's womb you are my strength. **R.**
My mouth shall declare your justice,
day by day your salvation.
O God, you have taught me from my youth,
and till the present I proclaim your wondrous deeds. **R.**

✝ 1 Corinthians 12:31—13:13 (or *1 Corinthians 13:4-13*)
So faith, hope, love remain, these three; but the greatest of these is love.

Brothers and sisters:
Strive eagerly for the greatest spiritual gifts.
But I shall show you a still more excellent way.

If I speak in human and angelic tongues,
    but do not have love,
    I am a resounding gong or a clashing cymbal.
And if I have the gift of prophecy,
    and comprehend all mysteries and all knowledge;
    if I have all faith so as to move mountains,
    but do not have love, I am nothing.
If I give away everything I own,
    and if I hand my body over so that I may boast,
    but do not have love, I gain nothing.

Love is patient, love is kind.
It is not jealous, it is not pompous,
    It is not inflated, it is not rude,
    it does not seek its own interests,
    it is not quick-tempered, it does not brood over injury, it does not
        rejoice over wrongdoing
    but rejoices with the truth.
It bears all things, believes all things,
    hopes all things, endures all things.

Love never fails.
If there are prophecies, they will be brought to nothing;
    if tongues, they will cease;
    if knowledge, it will be brought to nothing.

For we know partially and we prophesy partially,
    but when the perfect comes, the partial will pass away.
When I was a child, I used to talk as a child,
    think as a child, reason as a child;
    when I became a man, I put aside childish things.
At present we see indistinctly, as in a mirror,
    but then face to face.
At present I know partially;
    then I shall know fully, as I am fully known.
So faith, hope, love remain, these three;
    but the greatest of these is love. ✛

Luke 4:18

R. Alleluia, alleluia.

The Lord sent me to bring glad tidings to the poor,
to proclaim liberty to captives. **R.**

† *Luke 4:21-30*

Like Elijah and Elisha, Jesus was not sent only to the Jews.

Jesus began speaking in the synagogue, saying:
   "Today this Scripture passage is fulfilled in your hearing."
And all spoke highly of him
   and were amazed at the gracious words that came from his mouth.
They also asked, "Isn't this the son of Joseph?"
He said to them, "Surely you will quote me this proverb,
   'Physician, cure yourself,' and say,
   'Do here in your native place
   the things that we heard were done in Capernaum.'"
And he said, "Amen, I say to you,
   no prophet is accepted in his own native place.
Indeed, I tell you,
   there were many widows in Israel in the days of Elijah
   when the sky was closed for three and a half years
   and a severe famine spread over the entire land.
It was to none of these that Elijah was sent,
   but only to a widow in Zarephath in the land of Sidon.
Again, there were many lepers in Israel
   during the time of Elisha the prophet;
   yet not one of them was cleansed, but only Naaman the Syrian."
When the people in the synagogue heard this,
   they were all filled with fury.
They rose up, drove him out of the town,
   and led him to the brow of the hill
   on which their town had been built,
   to hurl him down headlong.
But Jesus passed through the midst of them and went away. ✛

MONDAY, JANUARY 31
St. John Bosco

† *2 Samuel 15:13-14, 30; 16:5-13*

*Let us take flight, or none of us will escape from Absalom. Let Shimei alone
and let him curse, for the Lord has told him to.*

An informant came to David with the report,
   "The children of Israel have transferred their loyalty to Absalom."
At this, David said to all his servants
   who were with him in Jerusalem:

"Up! Let us take flight, or none of us will escape from Absalom.
Leave quickly, lest he hurry and overtake us,
   then visit disaster upon us and put the city to the sword."

As David went up the Mount of Olives, he wept without ceasing.
His head was covered, and he was walking barefoot.
All those who were with him also had their heads covered
   and were weeping as they went.

As David was approaching Bahurim,
   a man named Shimei, the son of Gera
   of the same clan as Saul's family,
   was coming out of the place, cursing as he came.
He threw stones at David and at all the king's officers,
   even though all the soldiers, including the royal guard,
   were on David's right and on his left.
Shimei was saying as he cursed:
   "Away, away, you murderous and wicked man!
The LORD has requited you for all the bloodshed in the family of Saul,
   in whose stead you became king,
   and the LORD has given over the kingdom to your son Absalom.
And now you suffer ruin because you are a murderer."
Abishai, son of Zeruiah, said to the king:
   "Why should this dead dog curse my lord the king?
Let me go over, please, and lop off his head."
But the king replied: "What business is it of mine or of yours,
   sons of Zeruiah, that he curses?
Suppose the LORD has told him to curse David;
   who then will dare to say, 'Why are you doing this?'"
Then the king said to Abishai and to all his servants:
   "If my own son, who came forth from my loins, is seeking my life,
   how much more might this Benjaminite do so?
Let him alone and let him curse, for the LORD has told him to.
Perhaps the LORD will look upon my affliction
   and make it up to me with benefits
   for the curses he is uttering this day."
David and his men continued on the road,
   while Shimei kept abreast of them on the hillside,
   all the while cursing and throwing stones and dirt as he went. ✛

Psalm 3:2-3, 4-5, 6-7

R. (8a) **Lord, rise up and save me.**

O LORD, how many are my adversaries!
   Many rise up against me!
Many are saying of me,

"There is no salvation for him in God." **R.**
But you, O Lord, are my shield;
  my glory, you lift up my head!
When I call out to the Lord,
  he answers me from his holy mountain. **R.**
When I lie down in sleep,
  I wake again, for the Lord sustains me.
I fear not the myriads of people
  arrayed against me on every side. **R.**

Luke 7:16
R. Alleluia, alleluia.
A great prophet has arisen in our midst
and God has visited his people. **R.**

† Mark 5:1-20
Unclean spirit, come out of the man!

Jesus and his disciples came to the other side of the sea,
  to the territory of the Gerasenes.
When he got out of the boat,
  at once a man from the tombs who had an unclean spirit met him.
The man had been dwelling among the tombs,
  and no one could restrain him any longer, even with a chain.
In fact, he had frequently been bound with shackles and chains,
    but the chains had been pulled apart by him and the shackles
      smashed,
    and no one was strong enough to subdue him.
Night and day among the tombs and on the hillsides
  he was always crying out and bruising himself with stones.
Catching sight of Jesus from a distance,
  he ran up and prostrated himself before him,
    crying out in a loud voice,
  "What have you to do with me, Jesus, Son of the Most High God?
I adjure you by God, do not torment me!"
(He had been saying to him, "Unclean spirit, come out of the man!")
He asked him, "What is your name?"
He replied, "Legion is my name. There are many of us."
And he pleaded earnestly with him
  not to drive them away from that territory.

Now a large herd of swine was feeding there on the hillside.
And they pleaded with him,
  "Send us into the swine. Let us enter them."
And he let them, and the unclean spirits came out and entered the
      swine.

The herd of about two thousand rushed down a steep bank into the
  sea,
  where they were drowned.
The swineherds ran away and reported the incident in the town
  and throughout the countryside.
And people came out to see what had happened.
As they approached Jesus,
  they caught sight of the man who had been possessed by Legion,
  sitting there clothed and in his right mind.
And they were seized with fear.
Those who witnessed the incident explained to them what had
  happened
  to the possessed man and to the swine.
Then they began to beg him to leave their district.
As he was getting into the boat,
  the man who had been possessed pleaded to remain with him.
But Jesus would not permit him but told him instead,
  "Go home to your family and announce to them
  all that the Lord in his pity has done for you."
Then the man went off and began to proclaim in the Decapolis
  what Jesus had done for him; and all were amazed. ✛

TUESDAY, FEBRUARY 1
WEEKDAY

† 2 Samuel 18:9-10, 14b, 24-25a, 30—19:3
My son Absalom, if only I had died instead of you.

Absalom unexpectedly came up against David's servants.
He was mounted on a mule,
   and, as the mule passed under the branches of a large terebinth,
   his hair caught fast in the tree.
He hung between heaven and earth
   while the mule he had been riding ran off.
Someone saw this and reported to Joab
   that he had seen Absalom hanging from a terebinth.
And taking three pikes in hand,
   he thrust for the heart of Absalom,
   still hanging from the tree alive.

Now David was sitting between the two gates,
   and a lookout went up to the roof of the gate above the city wall,
   where he looked about and saw a man running all alone.
The lookout shouted to inform the king, who said,
   "If he is alone, he has good news to report."
The king said, "Step aside and remain in attendance here."
So he stepped aside and remained there.
When the Cushite messenger came in, he said,
   "Let my lord the king receive the good news
   that this day the LORD has taken your part,
   freeing you from the grasp of all who rebelled against you."
But the king asked the Cushite, "Is young Absalom safe?"
The Cushite replied, "May the enemies of my lord the king
   and all who rebel against you with evil intent
   be as that young man!"

The king was shaken,
   and went up to the room over the city gate to weep.
He said as he wept,
   "My son Absalom! My son, my son Absalom!
If only I had died instead of you,
   Absalom, my son, my son!"

Joab was told that the king was weeping and mourning for Absalom;
   and that day's victory was turned into mourning for the whole army
   when they heard that the king was grieving for his son. ✚

Psalm 86:1-2, 3-4, 5-6

R. (1a) **Listen, Lord, and answer me.**

Incline your ear, O LORD; answer me,
   for I am afflicted and poor.
Keep my life, for I am devoted to you;
   save your servant who trusts in you.
You are my God. **R.**

Have mercy on me, O LORD,
   for to you I call all the day.
Gladden the soul of your servant,
   for to you, O LORD, I lift up my soul. **R.**

For you, O LORD, are good and forgiving,
   abounding in kindness to all who call upon you.
Hearken, O LORD, to my prayer
   and attend to the sound of my pleading. **R.**

Matthew 8:17

R. Alleluia, alleluia.

Christ took away our infirmities
and bore our diseases. **R.**

† *Mark 5:21-43*
Little girl, I say to you, arise!

When Jesus had crossed again in the boat to the other side,
   a large crowd gathered around him, and he stayed close to the sea.
One of the synagogue officials, named Jairus, came forward.
Seeing him he fell at his feet and pleaded earnestly with him, saying,
   "My daughter is at the point of death.
Please, come lay your hands on her
   that she may get well and live."
He went off with him
   and a large crowd followed him.

There was a woman afflicted with hemorrhages for twelve years.
She had suffered greatly at the hands of many doctors
   and had spent all that she had.
Yet she was not helped but only grew worse.
She had heard about Jesus and came up behind him in the crowd
   and touched his cloak.
She said, "If I but touch his clothes, I shall be cured."
Immediately her flow of blood dried up.
She felt in her body that she was healed of her affliction.
Jesus, aware at once that power had gone out from him,
   turned around in the crowd and asked, "Who has touched my
      clothes?"

But his disciples said to him,
"You see how the crowd is pressing upon you,
and yet you ask, Who touched me?"
And he looked around to see who had done it.
The woman, realizing what had happened to her,
approached in fear and trembling.
She fell down before Jesus and told him the whole truth.
He said to her, "Daughter, your faith has saved you.
Go in peace and be cured of your affliction."

While he was still speaking,
people from the synagogue official's house arrived and said,
"Your daughter has died; why trouble the teacher any longer?"
Disregarding the message that was reported,
Jesus said to the synagogue official,
"Do not be afraid; just have faith."
He did not allow anyone to accompany him inside
except Peter, James, and John, the brother of James.
When they arrived at the house of the synagogue official,
he caught sight of a commotion,
people weeping and wailing loudly.
So he went in and said to them,
"Why this commotion and weeping?
The child is not dead but asleep."
And they ridiculed him.
Then he put them all out.
He took along the child's father and mother
and those who were with him
and entered the room where the child was.
He took the child by the hand and said to her, *"Talitha koum,"*
which means, "Little girl, I say to you, arise!"
The girl, a child of twelve, arose immediately and walked around.
At that they were utterly astounded.
He gave strict orders that no one should know this
and said that she should be given something to eat. ✝

WEDNESDAY, FEBRUARY 2
THE PRESENTATION OF THE LORD

✝ *Malachi 3:1-4*
There will come to the temple the LORD whom you seek.

Thus says the Lord GOD:
Lo, I am sending my messenger
to prepare the way before me;
And suddenly there will come to the temple

the LORD whom you seek,
And the messenger of the covenant whom you desire.
　Yes, he is coming, says the LORD of hosts.
But who will endure the day of his coming?
　And who can stand when he appears?
For he is like the refiner's fire,
　or like the fuller's lye.
He will sit refining and purifying silver,
　and he will purify the sons of Levi,
Refining them like gold or like silver
　that they may offer due sacrifice to the LORD.
Then the sacrifice of Judah and Jerusalem
　will please the LORD,
　as in the days of old, as in years gone by. ✛

　Psalm 24:7, 8, 9, 10
R. (8) **Who is this king of glory? It is the Lord!**
Lift up, O gates, your lintels;
　reach up, you ancient portals,
　that the king of glory may come in! **R.**
Who is this king of glory?
　The LORD, strong and mighty,
　the LORD, mighty in battle. **R.**
Lift up, O gates, your lintels;
　reach up, you ancient portals,
　that the king of glory may come in! **R.**
Who is this king of glory?
　The LORD of hosts; he is the king of glory. **R.**

† *Hebrews 2:14-18*
He had to become like his brothers and sisters in every way.

Since the children share in blood and flesh,
　Jesus likewise shared in them,
　that through death he might destroy the one
　who has the power of death, that is, the Devil,
　and free those who through fear of death
　had been subject to slavery all their life.
Surely he did not help angels
　but rather the descendants of Abraham;
　therefore, he had to become like his brothers and sisters
　in every way,
　that he might be a merciful and faithful high priest before God
　to expiate the sins of the people.
Because he himself was tested through what he suffered,
　he is able to help those who are being tested. ✛

Luke 2:32

R. Alleluia, alleluia.

A light of revelation to the Gentiles,
and glory for your people Israel. **R.**

*† **Luke 2:22-40** (or Luke 2:22-32)*
My eyes have seen your salvation.

When the days were completed for their purification
according to the law of Moses,
Mary and Joseph took Jesus up to Jerusalem
to present him to the Lord,
just as it is written in the law of the Lord,
Every male that opens the womb shall be consecrated to the Lord,
and to offer the sacrifice of
a pair of turtledoves or two young pigeons,
in accordance with the dictate in the law of the Lord.

Now there was a man in Jerusalem whose name was Simeon.
This man was righteous and devout,
awaiting the consolation of Israel,
and the Holy Spirit was upon him.
It had been revealed to him by the Holy Spirit
that he should not see death
before he had seen the Christ of the Lord.
He came in the Spirit into the temple;
and when the parents brought in the child Jesus
to perform the custom of the law in regard to him,
he took him into his arms and blessed God, saying:

"Now, Master, you may let your servant go
in peace, according to your word,
for my eyes have seen your salvation,
which you prepared in sight of all the peoples:
a light for revelation to the Gentiles,
and glory for your people Israel."

The child's father and mother were amazed at what was said about
him;
and Simeon blessed them and said to Mary his mother,
"Behold, this child is destined
for the fall and rise of many in Israel,
and to be a sign that will be contradicted
—and you yourself a sword will pierce—
so that the thoughts of many hearts may be revealed."

There was also a prophetess, Anna,
  the daughter of Phanuel, of the tribe of Asher.
She was advanced in years,
  having lived seven years with her husband after her marriage,
  and then as a widow until she was eighty-four.
She never left the temple,
  but worshiped night and day with fasting and prayer.
And coming forward at that very time,
  she gave thanks to God and spoke about the child
  to all who were awaiting the redemption of Jerusalem.

When they had fulfilled all the prescriptions
  of the law of the Lord,
  they returned to Galilee, to their own town of Nazareth.
The child grew and became strong, filled with wisdom;
  and the favor of God was upon him. ✛

THURSDAY, FEBRUARY 3
WEEKDAY, ST. BLAISE, ST. ANSGAR

† 1 Kings 2:1-4, 10-12
I am going the way of all flesh. Take courage and be a man.

When the time of David's death drew near,
  he gave these instructions to his son Solomon:
  "I am going the way of all flesh.
Take courage and be a man.
Keep the mandate of the LORD, your God, following his ways
  and observing his statutes, commands, ordinances, and decrees
  as they are written in the law of Moses,
  that you may succeed in whatever you do,
  wherever you turn, and the LORD may fulfill
  the promise he made on my behalf when he said,
  'If your sons so conduct themselves
  that they remain faithful to me with their whole heart
  and with their whole soul,
  you shall always have someone of your line
  on the throne of Israel.'"

David rested with his ancestors and was buried in the City of David.
The length of David's reign over Israel was forty years:
  he reigned seven years in Hebron
  and thirty-three years in Jerusalem.

Solomon was seated on the throne of his father David,
  with his sovereignty firmly established. ✛

1 Chronicles 29:10, 11ab, 11d-12a, 12bcd

R. (12b) **Lord, you are exalted over all.**

"Blessed may you be, O LORD,
   God of Israel our father,
   from eternity to eternity." **R.**

"Yours, O LORD, are grandeur and power,
   majesty, splendor, and glory." **R.**

"LORD, you are exalted over all.
   Yours, O LORD, is the sovereignty;
   you are exalted as head over all.

Riches and honor are from you." **R.**

"In your hand are power and might;
   it is yours to give grandeur and strength to all." **R.**

Mark 1:15

R. Alleluia, alleluia.

The Kingdom of God is at hand;
repent and believe in the Gospel. **R.**

† Mark 6:7-13

Jesus summoned the Twelve and began to send them out.

Jesus summoned the Twelve and began to send them out two by two
   and gave them authority over unclean spirits.

He instructed them to take nothing for the journey but a walking
      stick
   —no food, no sack, no money in their belts.

They were, however, to wear sandals but not a second tunic.

He said to them,
   "Wherever you enter a house, stay there until you leave from there.

Whatever place does not welcome you or listen to you,
   leave there and shake the dust off your feet
   in testimony against them."

So they went off and preached repentance.

The Twelve drove out many demons,
   and they anointed with oil many who were sick and cured them. ✛

FRIDAY, FEBRUARY 4
WEEKDAY

† Sirach 47:2-11

With his every deed David offered thanks to God Most High;
in words of praise he loved his Maker.

Like the choice fat of the sacred offerings,
   so was David in Israel.

He made sport of lions as though they were kids,
   and of bears, like lambs of the flock.

As a youth he slew the giant
  and wiped out the people's disgrace,
When his hand let fly the slingstone
  that crushed the pride of Goliath.
Since he called upon the Most High God,
  who gave strength to his right arm
To defeat the skilled warrior
  and raise up the might of his people,
Therefore the women sang his praises,
    and ascribed to him tens of thousands
    and praised him when they blessed the LORD.
When he assumed the royal crown, he battled
  and subdued the enemy on every side.
He destroyed the hostile Philistines
  and shattered their power till our own day.
With his every deed he offered thanks
  to God Most High, in words of praise.
With his whole being he loved his Maker
  and daily had his praises sung;
He set singers before the altar and by their voices
  he made sweet melodies,
He added beauty to the feasts
  and solemnized the seasons of each year
So that when the Holy Name was praised,
  before daybreak the sanctuary would resound.
The LORD forgave him his sins
  and exalted his strength forever;
He conferred on him the rights of royalty
  and established his throne in Israel. ✛

Psalm 18:31, 47 and 50, 51
R. (see 47b) Blessed be God my salvation!
God's way is unerring,
  the promise of the LORD is fire-tried;
  he is a shield to all who take refuge in him. **R.**
The LORD live! And blessed be my Rock!
  Extolled be God my savior.
Therefore will I proclaim you, O LORD, among the nations,
  and I will sing praise to your name. **R.**
You who gave great victories to your king
  and showed kindness to your anointed,
  to David and his posterity forever. **R.**

See Luke 8:15
R. Alleluia, alleluia.
Blessed are they who have kept the word with a generous heart,
and yield a harvest through perseverance. **R.**

† *Mark 6:14-29*
It is John whom I beheaded. He has been raised up.

King Herod heard about Jesus, for his fame had become widespread,
and people were saying,
"John the Baptist has been raised from the dead;
that is why mighty powers are at work in him."
Others were saying, "He is Elijah";
still others, "He is a prophet like any of the prophets."
But when Herod learned of it, he said,
"It is John whom I beheaded. He has been raised up."

Herod was the one who had John arrested and bound in prison
on account of Herodias,
the wife of his brother Philip, whom he had married.
John had said to Herod,
"It is not lawful for you to have your brother's wife."
Herodias harbored a grudge against him
and wanted to kill him but was unable to do so.
Herod feared John, knowing him to be a righteous and holy man,
and kept him in custody.
When he heard him speak he was very much perplexed,
yet he liked to listen to him.
Herodias had an opportunity one day when Herod, on his birthday,
gave a banquet for his courtiers, his military officers,
and the leading men of Galilee.
His own daughter came in and performed a dance
that delighted Herod and his guests.
The king said to the girl,
"Ask of me whatever you wish and I will grant it to you."
He even swore many things to her,
"I will grant you whatever you ask of me,
even to half of my kingdom."
She went out and said to her mother,
"What shall I ask for?"
Her mother replied, "The head of John the Baptist."
The girl hurried back to the king's presence and made her request,
"I want you to give me at once on a platter
the head of John the Baptist."

The king was deeply distressed,
  but because of his oaths and the guests
  he did not wish to break his word to her.
So he promptly dispatched an executioner
  with orders to bring back his head.
He went off and beheaded him in the prison.
He brought in the head on a platter
  and gave it to the girl.
The girl in turn gave it to her mother.
When his disciples heard about it,
  they came and took his body and laid it in a tomb. ✚

SATURDAY, FEBRUARY 5
St. Agatha

✝ *1 Kings 3:4-13*
Give your servant an understanding heart to judge your people.

Solomon went to Gibeon to sacrifice there,
  because that was the most renowned high place.
Upon its altar Solomon offered a thousand burnt offerings.
In Gibeon the Lord appeared to Solomon in a dream at night.
God said, "Ask something of me and I will give it to you."
Solomon answered:
  "You have shown great favor to your servant, my father David,
  because he behaved faithfully toward you,
  with justice and an upright heart;
  and you have continued this great favor toward him, even today,
  seating a son of his on his throne.
O Lord, my God, you have made me, your servant,
  king to succeed my father David;
  but I am a mere youth, not knowing at all how to act.
I serve you in the midst of the people whom you have chosen,
  a people so vast that it cannot be numbered or counted.
Give your servant, therefore, an understanding heart
  to judge your people and to distinguish right from wrong.
For who is able to govern this vast people of yours?"

The Lord was pleased that Solomon made this request.
So God said to him: "Because you have asked for this—
  not for a long life for yourself,
  nor for riches, nor for the life of your enemies,
  but for understanding so that you may know what is right—
  I do as you requested.
I give you a heart so wise and understanding

that there has never been anyone like you up to now,
and after you there will come no one to equal you.
In addition, I give you what you have not asked for,
such riches and glory that among kings there is not your like." ✢

Psalm 119:9, 10, 11, 12, 13, 14
R. (12b) **Lord, teach me your statutes.**
How shall a young man be faultless in his way?
By keeping to your words. **R.**
With all my heart I seek you;
let me not stray from your commands. **R.**
Within my heart I treasure your promise,
that I may not sin against you. **R.**
Blessed are you, O LORD;
teach me your statutes. **R.**
With my lips I declare
all the ordinances of your mouth. **R.**
In the way of your decrees I rejoice,
as much as in all riches. **R.**

John 10:27
R. Alleluia, alleluia.
My sheep hear my voice, says the Lord;
I know them, and they follow me. **R.**

† *Mark 6:30-34*
They were like sheep without a shepherd.

The Apostles gathered together with Jesus
and reported all they had done and taught.
He said to them,
"Come away by yourselves to a deserted place and rest a while."
People were coming and going in great numbers,
and they had no opportunity even to eat.
So they went off in the boat by themselves to a deserted place.
People saw them leaving and many came to know about it.
They hastened there on foot from all the towns
and arrived at the place before them.

When Jesus disembarked and saw the vast crowd,
his heart was moved with pity for them,
for they were like sheep without a shepherd;
and he began to teach them many things. ✢

SUNDAY, FEBRUARY 6
FIFTH SUNDAY IN ORDINARY TIME

† *Isaiah 6:1-2a, 3-8*
Here I am! Send me.

In the year King Uzziah died,
   I saw the Lord seated on a high and lofty throne,
   with the train of his garment filling the temple.
Seraphim were stationed above.

They cried one to the other,
   "Holy, holy, holy is the LORD of hosts!
All the earth is filled with his glory!"
At the sound of that cry, the frame of the door shook
   and the house was filled with smoke.

Then I said, "Woe is me, I am doomed!
For I am a man of unclean lips,
   living among a people of unclean lips;
   yet my eyes have seen the King, the LORD of hosts!"
Then one of the seraphim flew to me,
   holding an ember that he had taken with tongs from the altar.

He touched my mouth with it, and said,
   "See, now that this has touched your lips,
   your wickedness is removed, your sin purged."

Then I heard the voice of the Lord saying,
   "Whom shall I send? Who will go for us?"
"Here I am," I said; "send me!" ✛

Psalm 138:1-2, 2-3, 4-5, 7-8
R. (1c) **In the sight of the angels I will sing your praises, Lord.**
I will give thanks to you, O LORD, with all my heart,
   for you have heard the words of my mouth;
   in the presence of the angels I will sing your praise;
I will worship at your holy temple
   and give thanks to your name. **R.**
Because of your kindness and your truth;
   for you have made great above all things
   your name and your promise.
When I called, you answered me;
   you built up strength within me. **R.**
All the kings of the earth shall give thanks to you, O LORD,
   when they hear the words of your mouth;

and they shall sing of the ways of the LORD:
"Great is the glory of the LORD." **R.**
Your right hand saves me.
The LORD will complete what he has done for me;
your kindness, O LORD, endures forever;
forsake not the work of your hands. **R.**

† *1 Corinthians 15:1-11 (or 1 Corinthians 15:3-8, 11)*
So we preached and so you believe.

I am reminding you, brothers and sisters,
of the gospel I preached to you,
which you indeed received and in which you also stand.
Through it you are also being saved,
if you hold fast to the word I preached to you,
unless you believed in vain.
For I handed on to you as of first importance what I also received:
that Christ died for our sins in accordance with the Scriptures;
that he was buried;
that he was raised on the third day in accordance with the
Scriptures;
that he appeared to Cephas, then to the Twelve.
After that, he appeared to more than five hundred brothers at once,
most of whom are still living,
though some have fallen asleep.
After that he appeared to James,
then to all the apostles.
Last of all, as to one born abnormally,
he appeared to me.
For I am the least of the apostles,
not fit to be called an apostle,
because I persecuted the church of God.
But by the grace of God I am what I am,
and his grace to me has not been ineffective.
Indeed, I have toiled harder than all of them;
not I, however, but the grace of God that is with me.
Therefore, whether it be I or they,
so we preach and so you believed. ✛

Matthew 4:19
R. Alleluia, alleluia.
Come after me
and I will make you fishers of men. **R.**

† *Luke 5:1-11*
They left everything and followed Jesus.

While the crowd was pressing in on Jesus and listening to the
    word of God,
  he was standing by the Lake of Gennesaret.
He saw two boats there alongside the lake;
  the fishermen had disembarked and were washing their nets.
Getting into one of the boats, the one belonging to Simon,
  he asked him to put out a short distance from the shore.
Then he sat down and taught the crowds from the boat.
After he had finished speaking, he said to Simon,
  "Put out into deep water and lower your nets for a catch."
Simon said in reply,
  "Master, we have worked hard all night and have caught nothing,
  but at your command I will lower the nets."
When they had done this, they caught a great number of fish
  and their nets were tearing.
They signaled to their partners in the other boat
  to come to help them.
They came and filled both boats
  so that the boats were in danger of sinking.
When Simon Peter saw this, he fell at the knees of Jesus and said,
  "Depart from me, Lord, for I am a sinful man."
For astonishment at the catch of fish they had made seized him
  and all those with him,
  and likewise James and John, the sons of Zebedee,
  who were partners of Simon.
Jesus said to Simon, "Do not be afraid;
  from now on you will be catching men."
When they brought their boats to the shore,
  they left everything and followed him. ✝

MONDAY, FEBRUARY 7
WEEKDAY

† *1 Kings 8:1-7, 9-13*
They brought the ark of the covenant into the holy of holies,
and a cloud filled the temple of the LORD.

The elders of Israel and all the leaders of the tribes,
  the princes in the ancestral houses of the children of Israel,
  came to King Solomon in Jerusalem,
  to bring up the ark of the LORD's covenant
  from the City of David, which is Zion.

All the people of Israel assembled before King Solomon
    during the festival in the month of Ethanim (the seventh month).
When all the elders of Israel had arrived,
    the priests took up the ark;
    they carried the ark of the LORD
    and the meeting tent with all the sacred vessels
    that were in the tent.
(The priests and Levites carried them.)

King Solomon and the entire community of Israel
    present for the occasion
    sacrificed before the ark sheep and oxen
    too many to number or count.
The priests brought the ark of the covenant of the LORD
    to its place beneath the wings of the cherubim in the sanctuary,
    the holy of holies of the temple.
The cherubim had their wings spread out over the place of the ark,
    sheltering the ark and its poles from above.
There was nothing in the ark but the two stone tablets
    which Moses had put there at Horeb,
    when the LORD made a covenant with the children of Israel
    at their departure from the land of Egypt.

When the priests left the holy place,
    the cloud filled the temple of the LORD
    so that the priests could no longer minister because of the cloud,
    since the LORD's glory had filled the temple of the LORD.
Then Solomon said, "The LORD intends to dwell in the dark cloud;
    I have truly built you a princely house,
    a dwelling where you may abide forever." ✛

Psalm 132:6-7, 8-10
R. (8a) Lord, go up to the place of your rest!
Behold, we heard of it in Ephrathah;
    we found it in the fields of Jaar.
Let us enter into his dwelling,
    let us worship at his footstool. **R.**
Advance, O LORD, to your resting place,
    you and the ark of your majesty.
May your priests be clothed with justice;
    let your faithful ones shout merrily for joy.
For the sake of David your servant,
    reject not the plea of your anointed. **R.**

See Matthew 4:23
R. Alleluia, alleluia.
Jesus preached the Gospel of the Kingdom
and cured every disease among the people. **R.**

✝ *Mark 6:53-56*
As many as touched it were healed.

After making the crossing to the other side of the sea,
Jesus and his disciples came to land at Gennesaret
and tied up there.
As they were leaving the boat, people immediately recognized him.
They scurried about the surrounding country
and began to bring in the sick on mats
to wherever they heard he was.
Whatever villages or towns or countryside he entered,
they laid the sick in the marketplaces
and begged him that they might touch only the tassel on his cloak;
and as many as touched it were healed. ✛

TUESDAY, FEBRUARY 8
WEEKDAY, ST. JEROME EMILIANI, ST. JOSEPHINE BAKHITA

✝ *1 Kings 8:22-23, 27-30*
You have said: My name shall be there, to hear the prayers of your people Israel.

Solomon stood before the altar of the LORD
in the presence of the whole community of Israel,
and stretching forth his hands toward heaven,
he said, "LORD, God of Israel,
there is no God like you in heaven above or on earth below;
you keep your covenant of mercy with your servants
who are faithful to you with their whole heart.

"Can it indeed be that God dwells on earth?
If the heavens and the highest heavens cannot contain you,
how much less this temple which I have built!
Look kindly on the prayer and petition of your servant, O LORD, my
God,
and listen to the cry of supplication which I, your servant,
utter before you this day.
May your eyes watch night and day over this temple,
the place where you have decreed you shall be honored;
may you heed the prayer which I, your servant, offer in this place.
Listen to the petitions of your servant and of your people Israel
which they offer in this place.
Listen from your heavenly dwelling and grant pardon." ✛

Psalm 84:3, 4, 5 and 10, 11
R. (2) **How lovely is your dwelling place, Lord, mighty God!**
My soul yearns and pines
  for the courts of the LORD.
My heart and my flesh
  cry out for the living God. **R.**
Even the sparrow finds a home,
  and the swallow a nest
  in which she puts her young—
Your altars, O LORD of hosts,
  my king and my God! **R.**
Blessed they who dwell in your house!
  continually they praise you.
O God, behold our shield,
  and look upon the face of your anointed. **R.**
I had rather one day in your courts
  than a thousand elsewhere;
I had rather lie at the threshold of the house of my God
  than dwell in the tents of the wicked. **R.**

Psalm 119:36, 29b
R. Alleluia, alleluia.
Incline my heart, O God, to your decrees;
and favor me with your law. **R.**

† *Mark 7:1-13*
You disregard God's commandment but cling to human tradition.

When the Pharisees with some scribes who had come from Jerusalem
  gathered around Jesus,
  they observed that some of his disciples ate their meals
  with unclean, that is, unwashed, hands.
(For the Pharisees and, in fact, all Jews,
  do not eat without carefully washing their hands,
  keeping the tradition of the elders.
And on coming from the marketplace
  they do not eat without purifying themselves.
And there are many other things that they have traditionally observed,
  the purification of cups and jugs and kettles and beds.)
So the Pharisees and scribes questioned him,
  "Why do your disciples not follow the tradition of the elders
  but instead eat a meal with unclean hands?"
He responded,
  "Well did Isaiah prophesy about you hypocrites,
  as it is written:

This people honors me with their lips,
  but their hearts are far from me;
in vain do they worship me,
  teaching as doctrines human precepts.

You disregard God's commandment but cling to human tradition."
He went on to say,
  "How well you have set aside the commandment of God
  in order to uphold your tradition!
For Moses said,
  Honor your father and your mother,
  and *Whoever curses father or mother shall die.*
Yet you say,
  'If someone says to father or mother,
  "Any support you might have had from me is *qorban*"'
  (meaning, dedicated to God),
  you allow him to do nothing more for his father or mother.
You nullify the word of God
  in favor of your tradition that you have handed on.
And you do many such things." ✛

WEDNESDAY, FEBRUARY 9
WEEKDAY

† 1 Kings 10:1-10
The Queen of Sheba saw all the wisdom of Solomon.

The queen of Sheba, having heard of Solomon's fame,
  came to test him with subtle questions.
She arrived in Jerusalem with a very numerous retinue,
  and with camels bearing spices,
  a large amount of gold, and precious stones.
She came to Solomon and questioned him on every subject
  in which she was interested.
King Solomon explained everything she asked about,
  and there remained nothing hidden from him
  that he could not explain to her.

When the queen of Sheba witnessed Solomon's great wisdom,
  the palace he had built, the food at his table,
  the seating of his ministers, the attendance and garb of his waiters,
  his banquet service,
  and the burnt offerings he offered in the temple of the LORD,
  she was breathless.
"The report I heard in my country
  about your deeds and your wisdom is true," she told the king.

"Though I did not believe the report until I came and saw with my
    own eyes,
I have discovered that they were not telling me the half.
Your wisdom and prosperity surpass the report I heard.
Blessed are your men, blessed these servants of yours,
    who stand before you always and listen to your wisdom.
Blessed be the Lord, your God,
    whom it has pleased to place you on the throne of Israel.
In his enduring love for Israel,
    the Lord has made you king to carry out judgment and justice."
Then she gave the king one hundred and twenty gold talents,
    a very large quantity of spices, and precious stones.
Never again did anyone bring such an abundance of spices
    as the queen of Sheba gave to King Solomon. ✝

Psalm 37:5-6, 30-31, 39-40
R. (30a) **The mouth of the just murmurs wisdom.**
Commit to the Lord your way;
    trust in him, and he will act.
He will make justice dawn for you like the light;
    bright as the noonday shall be your vindication. **R.**
The mouth of the just man tells of wisdom
    and his tongue utters what is right.
The law of his God is in his heart,
    and his steps do not falter. **R.**
The salvation of the just is from the Lord;
    he is their refuge in time of distress.
And the Lord helps them and delivers them;
    he delivers them from the wicked and saves them,
    because they take refuge in him. **R.**

See John 17:17b, 17a
R. Alleluia, alleluia.
Your word, O Lord, is truth:
consecrate us in the truth. **R.**

✝ Mark 7:14-23
What comes out of the man, that is what defiles him.

Jesus summoned the crowd again and said to them,
    "Hear me, all of you, and understand.
Nothing that enters one from outside can defile that person;
    but the things that come out from within are what defile."

When he got home away from the crowd
    his disciples questioned him about the parable.
He said to them,

"Are even you likewise without understanding?
Do you not realize that everything
    that goes into a person from outside cannot defile,
    since it enters not the heart but the stomach
    and passes out into the latrine?"
(Thus he declared all foods clean.)
"But what comes out of the man, that is what defiles him.
From within the man, from his heart,
    come evil thoughts, unchastity, theft, murder,
    adultery, greed, malice, deceit,
    licentiousness, envy, blasphemy, arrogance, folly.
All these evils come from within and they defile." ✛

THURSDAY, FEBRUARY 10
ST. SCHOLASTICA

† 1 Kings 11:4-13
*Since you have not kept my covenant, I will deprive you of the kingdom,
but I will leave your son one tribe for the sake of my servant David.*

When Solomon was old his wives had turned his heart to strange gods,
    and his heart was not entirely with the LORD, his God,
    as the heart of his father David had been.
By adoring Astarte, the goddess of the Sidonians,
    and Milcom, the idol of the Ammonites,
    Solomon did evil in the sight of the LORD;
    he did not follow him unreservedly as his father David had done.
Solomon then built a high place to Chemosh, the idol of Moab,
    and to Molech, the idol of the Ammonites,
    on the hill opposite Jerusalem.
He did the same for all his foreign wives
    who burned incense and sacrificed to their gods.
The LORD, therefore, became angry with Solomon,
    because his heart was turned away from the LORD, the God of Israel,
    who had appeared to him twice
    (for though the LORD had forbidden him
    this very act of following strange gods,
    Solomon had not obeyed him).

So the LORD said to Solomon: "Since this is what you want,
    and you have not kept my covenant and my statutes
    which I enjoined on you,
    I will deprive you of the kingdom and give it to your servant.
I will not do this during your lifetime, however,
    for the sake of your father David;
    it is your son whom I will deprive.

Nor will I take away the whole kingdom.
I will leave your son one tribe for the sake of my servant David
    and of Jerusalem, which I have chosen." ✝

Psalm 106:3-4, 35-36, 37 and 40

R. (4a) Remember us, O Lord, as you favor your people.
Blessed are they who observe what is right,
    who do always what is just.
Remember us, O LORD, as you favor your people;
    visit us with your saving help. **R.**
But they mingled with the nations
    and learned their works.
They served their idols,
    which became a snare for them. **R.**
They sacrificed their sons
    and their daughters to demons.
And the LORD grew angry with his people,
    and abhorred his inheritance. **R.**

James 1:21bc

R. Alleluia, alleluia.
Humbly welcome the word that has been planted in you
and is able to save your souls.

✝ Mark 7:24-30
The dogs under the table eat the children's scraps.

Jesus went to the district of Tyre.
He entered a house and wanted no one to know about it,
    but he could not escape notice.
Soon a woman whose daughter had an unclean spirit heard about him.
She came and fell at his feet.
The woman was a Greek, a Syrophoenician by birth,
    and she begged him to drive the demon out of her daughter.
He said to her, "Let the children be fed first.
For it is not right to take the food of the children
    and throw it to the dogs."
She replied and said to him,
    "Lord, even the dogs under the table eat the children's scraps."
Then he said to her, "For saying this, you may go.
The demon has gone out of your daughter."
When the woman went home, she found the child lying in bed
    and the demon gone. ✝

FRIDAY, FEBRUARY 11
WEEKDAY, OUR LADY OF LOURDES

† 1 Kings 11:29-32; 12:19
Israel went into rebellion against David's house to this day.

Jeroboam left Jerusalem,
  and the prophet Ahijah the Shilonite met him on the road.
The two were alone in the area,
  and the prophet was wearing a new cloak.
Ahijah took off his new cloak,
  tore it into twelve pieces, and said to Jeroboam:

"Take ten pieces for yourself;
  the LORD, the God of Israel, says:
  'I will tear away the kingdom from Solomon's grasp
  and will give you ten of the tribes.
One tribe shall remain to him for the sake of David my servant,
  and of Jerusalem,
  the city I have chosen out of all the tribes of Israel.'"

Israel went into rebellion against David's house to this day. ✛

Psalm 81:10-11ab, 12-13, 14-15
R. (11a and 9a) **I am the Lord, your God: hear my voice.**
"There shall be no strange god among you
  nor shall you worship any alien god.
I, the LORD, am your God
  who led you forth from the land of Egypt." **R.**
"My people heard not my voice,
  and Israel obeyed me not;
So I gave them up to the hardness of their hearts;
  they walked according to their own counsels." **R.**
"If only my people would hear me,
  and Israel walk in my ways,
Quickly would I humble their enemies;
  against their foes I would turn my hand." **R.**

See Acts 16:14b
R. Alleluia, alleluia.
Open our hearts, O Lord,
to listen to the words of your Son. **R.**

† Mark 7:31-37
He makes the deaf hear and the mute speak.

Jesus left the district of Tyre
  and went by way of Sidon to the Sea of Galilee,
  into the district of the Decapolis.

And people brought to him a deaf man who had a speech impediment
  and begged him to lay his hand on him.
He took him off by himself away from the crowd.
He put his finger into the man's ears
  and, spitting, touched his tongue;
  then he looked up to heaven and groaned, and said to him,
  "Ephphatha!" (that is, "Be opened!")
And immediately the man's ears were opened,
  his speech impediment was removed,
  and he spoke plainly.
He ordered them not to tell anyone.
But the more he ordered them not to,
  the more they proclaimed it.
They were exceedingly astonished and they said,
  "He has done all things well.
He makes the deaf hear and the mute speak." ✛

SATURDAY, FEBRUARY 12
WEEKDAY, *[BVM]*

† *1 Kings 12:26-32; 13:33-34*
Jeroboam made two golden calves.

Jeroboam thought to himself:
"The kingdom will return to David's house.
If now this people go up to offer sacrifices
  in the temple of the LORD in Jerusalem,
  the hearts of this people will return to their master,
  Rehoboam, king of Judah,
  and they will kill me."
After taking counsel, the king made two calves of gold
  and said to the people:
  "You have been going up to Jerusalem long enough.
Here is your God, O Israel, who brought you up from the land of
    Egypt."
And he put one in Bethel, the other in Dan.
This led to sin, because the people frequented those calves
  in Bethel and in Dan.
He also built temples on the high places
  and made priests from among the people who were not Levites.
Jeroboam established a feast in the eighth month
  on the fifteenth day of the month
  to duplicate in Bethel the pilgrimage feast of Judah,
  with sacrifices to the calves he had made;
  and he stationed in Bethel priests of the high places he had built.

Jeroboam did not give up his evil ways after this,
  but again made priests for the high places
  from among the common people.
Whoever desired it was consecrated
  and became a priest of the high places.
This was a sin on the part of the house of Jeroboam
  for which it was to be cut off and destroyed from the earth. ✛

Psalm 106:6-7ab, 19-20, 21-22
R. (4a) **Remember us, O Lord, as you favor your people.**
We have sinned, we and our fathers;
  we have committed crimes; we have done wrong.
Our fathers in Egypt
  considered not your wonders. **R.**
They made a calf in Horeb
  and adored a molten image;
They exchanged their glory
  for the image of a grass-eating bullock. **R.**
They forgot the God who had saved them,
  who had done great deeds in Egypt,
Wondrous deeds in the land of Ham,
  terrible things at the Red Sea. **R.**

Matthew 4:4b
R. Alleluia, alleluia.
One does not live on bread alone,
but on every word that comes forth from the mouth of God. **R.**

† *Mark 8:1-10*
They ate and were satisfied.

In those days when there again was a great crowd without anything
    to eat,
  Jesus summoned the disciples and said,
  "My heart is moved with pity for the crowd,
  because they have been with me now for three days
  and have nothing to eat.
If I send them away hungry to their homes,
  they will collapse on the way,
  and some of them have come a great distance."
His disciples answered him, "Where can anyone get enough bread
  to satisfy them here in this deserted place?"
Still he asked them, "How many loaves do you have?"
They replied, "Seven."
He ordered the crowd to sit down on the ground.
Then, taking the seven loaves he gave thanks, broke them,
  and gave them to his disciples to distribute,

and they distributed them to the crowd.
They also had a few fish.
He said the blessing over them
and ordered them distributed also.
They ate and were satisfied.
They picked up the fragments left over–seven baskets.
There were about four thousand people.

He dismissed the crowd and got into the boat with his disciples
and came to the region of Dalmanutha. ✛

SUNDAY, FEBRUARY 13
SIXTH SUNDAY IN ORDINARY TIME

† Jeremiah 17:5-8
Cursed is the one who trusts in human beings;
blessed is the one who trusts in the Lord.

Thus says the LORD:
Cursed is the one who trusts in human beings,
who seeks his strength in flesh,
whose heart turns away from the LORD.
He is like a barren bush in the desert
that enjoys no change of season,
but stands in a lava waste,
a salt and empty earth.
Blessed is the one who trusts in the LORD,
whose hope is the LORD.
He is like a tree planted beside the waters
that stretches out its roots to the stream:
it fears not the heat when it comes;
its leaves stay green;
in the year of drought it shows no distress,
but still bears fruit. ✛

Psalm 1:1-2, 3, 4 and 6
R. (40:5a) **Blessed are they who hope in the Lord.**
Blessed the man who follows not
the counsel of the wicked,
nor walks in the way of sinners,
nor sits in the company of the insolent,
but delights in the law of the LORD
and meditates on his law day and night. **R.**
He is like a tree
planted near running water,
that yields its fruit in due season,
and whose leaves never fade.

Whatever he does, prospers. **R.**
Not so the wicked, not so;
   they are like chaff which the wind drives away.
For the LORD watches over the way of the just,
   but the way of the wicked vanishes. **R.**

† 1 Corinthians 15:12, 16-20
If Christ has not been raised, your faith is in vain.

Brothers and sisters:
If Christ is preached as raised from the dead,
   how can some among you say there is no resurrection of the dead?
If the dead are not raised, neither has Christ been raised,
   and if Christ has not been raised, your faith is vain;
   you are still in your sins.
Then those who have fallen asleep in Christ have perished.
If for this life only we have hoped in Christ,
   we are the most pitiable people of all.

But now Christ has been raised from the dead,
   the firstfruits of those who have fallen asleep. ✛

Luke 6:23ab
R. Alleluia, alleluia.
Rejoice and be glad;
your reward will be great in heaven. **R.**

† Luke 6:17, 20-26
Blessed are the poor. Woe to you who are rich.

Jesus came down with the Twelve
   and stood on a stretch of level ground
   with a great crowd of his disciples
   and a large number of the people
   from all Judea and Jerusalem
   and the coastal region of Tyre and Sidon.
And raising his eyes toward his disciples he said:
   "Blessed are you who are poor,
     for the kingdom of God is yours.
   Blessed are you who are now hungry,
     for you will be satisfied.
   Blessed are you who are now weeping,
     for you will laugh.
   Blessed are you when people hate you,
     and when they exclude and insult you,
     and denounce your name as evil
     on account of the Son of Man.

Rejoice and leap for joy on that day!
Behold, your reward will be great in heaven.
For their ancestors treated the prophets in the same way.
　　But woe to you who are rich,
　　　　for you have received your consolation.
　　Woe to you who are filled now,
　　　　for you will be hungry.
　　Woe to you who laugh now,
　　　　for you will grieve and weep.
　　Woe to you when all speak well of you,
　　　　for their ancestors treated the false prophets in this way." ✛

MONDAY, FEBRUARY 14
St. Cyril, St. Monk and St. Methodius

† *James 1:1-11*
*The testing of your faith produces perseverance
so that you may be perfect and complete.*

James, a servant of God and of the Lord Jesus Christ,
　　to the twelve tribes in the dispersion, greetings.

Consider it all joy, my brothers and sisters,
　　when you encounter various trials,
　　for you know that the testing of your faith produces perseverance.
And let perseverance be perfect,
　　so that you may be perfect and complete, lacking in nothing.
But if any of you lacks wisdom,
　　he should ask God who gives to all generously and ungrudgingly,
　　and he will be given it.
But he should ask in faith, not doubting,
　　for the one who doubts is like a wave of the sea
　　that is driven and tossed about by the wind.
For that person must not suppose that he will receive anything from
　　　the Lord,
　　since he is a man of two minds, unstable in all his ways.

The brother in lowly circumstances
　　should take pride in high standing,
　　and the rich one in his lowliness,
　　for he will pass away "like the flower of the field."
For the sun comes up with its scorching heat and dries up the grass,
　　its flower droops, and the beauty of its appearance vanishes.
So will the rich person fade away in the midst of his pursuits. ✛

Psalm 119:67, 68, 71, 72, 75, 76
R. (77a) **Be kind to me, Lord, and I shall live.**
Before I was afflicted I went astray,
    but now I hold to your promise. **R.**
You are good and bountiful;
    teach me your statutes. **R.**
It is good for me that I have been afflicted,
    that I may learn your statutes. **R.**
The law of your mouth is to me more precious
    than thousands of gold and silver pieces. **R.**
I know, O LORD, that your ordinances are just,
    and in your faithfulness you have afflicted me. **R.**
Let your kindness comfort me
    according to your promise to your servants. **R.**

John 14:6
R. Alleluia, alleluia.
I am the way and the truth and the life, says the Lord;
no one comes to the Father except through me. **R.**

† *Mark 8:11-13*
Why does this generation seek a sign?

The Pharisees came forward and began to argue with Jesus,
    seeking from him a sign from heaven to test him.
He sighed from the depth of his spirit and said,
    "Why does this generation seek a sign?
Amen, I say to you, no sign will be given to this generation."
Then he left them, got into the boat again,
    and went off to the other shore. ✛

TUESDAY, FEBRUARY 15
WEEKDAY

† *James 1:12-18*
God himself tempts no one.

Blessed is he who perseveres in temptation,
    for when he has been proven he will receive the crown of life
    that he promised to those who love him.
No one experiencing temptation should say,
    "I am being tempted by God";
    for God is not subject to temptation to evil,
    and he himself tempts no one.
Rather, each person is tempted when lured and enticed by his desire.
Then desire conceives and brings forth sin,
    and when sin reaches maturity it gives birth to death.

Do not be deceived, my beloved brothers and sisters:
    all good giving and every perfect gift is from above,
    coming down from the Father of lights,
    with whom there is no alteration or shadow caused by change.
He willed to give us birth by the word of truth
    that we may be a kind of firstfruits of his creatures. ✛

Psalm 94:12-13a, 14-15, 18-19

R. (12a) **Blessed the man you instruct, O Lord.**

Blessed the man whom you instruct, O LORD,
    whom by your law you teach,
Giving him rest from evil days. **R.**
For the LORD will not cast off his people,
    nor abandon his inheritance;
But judgment shall again be with justice,
    and all the upright of heart shall follow it. **R.**
When I say, "My foot is slipping,"
    your mercy, O LORD, sustains me;
When cares abound within me,
    your comfort gladdens my soul. **R.**

John 14:23

R. Alleluia, alleluia.

Whoever loves me will keep my word, says the Lord;
and my Father will love him
and we will come to him. **R.**

† *Mark 8:14-21*

Watch out, guard against the leaven of the Pharisees and the leaven of Herod.

The disciples had forgotten to bring bread,
    and they had only one loaf with them in the boat.
Jesus enjoined them, "Watch out,
    guard against the leaven of the Pharisees
    and the leaven of Herod."
They concluded among themselves that
    it was because they had no bread.
When he became aware of this he said to them,
    "Why do you conclude that it is because you have no bread?
Do you not yet understand or comprehend?
Are your hearts hardened?
Do you have eyes and not see, ears and not hear?
And do you not remember,
    when I broke the five loaves for the five thousand,
    how many wicker baskets full of fragments you picked up?"
They answered him, "Twelve."

"When I broke the seven loaves for the four thousand,
  how many full baskets of fragments did you pick up?"
They answered him, "Seven."
He said to them, "Do you still not understand?" ✢

WEDNESDAY, FEBRUARY 16
WEEKDAY

† *James 1:19-27*
Be doers of the word and not hearers only.

Know this, my dear brothers and sisters:
  everyone should be quick to hear, slow to speak, slow to anger
  for anger does not accomplish
  the righteousness of God.
Therefore, put away all filth and evil excess
  and humbly welcome the word that has been planted in you
  and is able to save your souls.

Be doers of the word and not hearers only, deluding yourselves.
For if anyone is a hearer of the word and not a doer,
  he is like a man who looks at his own face in a mirror.
He sees himself, then goes off and promptly forgets
  what he looked like.
But the one who peers into the perfect law of freedom and perseveres,
  and is not a hearer who forgets but a doer who acts;
  such a one shall be blessed in what he does.

If anyone thinks he is religious and does not bridle his tongue
  but deceives his heart, his religion is vain.
Religion that is pure and undefiled before God and the Father is this:
  to care for orphans and widows in their affliction
  and to keep oneself unstained by the world. ✢

Psalm 15:2-3a, 3bc-4ab, 5
R. (1b) **Who shall live on your holy mountain, O Lord?**
He who walks blamelessly and does justice;
  who thinks the truth in his heart
  and slanders not with his tongue. **R.**
Who harms not his fellow man,
  nor takes up a reproach against his neighbor;
By whom the reprobate is despised,
  while he honors those who fear the LORD. **R.**
Who lends not his money at usury
  and accepts no bribe against the innocent.
He who does these things
  shall never be disturbed. **R.**

See Ephesians 1:17-18
R. Alleluia, alleluia.
May the Father of our Lord Jesus Christ
enlighten the eyes of our hearts,
that we may know what is the hope
that belongs to his call. **R.**

† *Mark 8:22-26*
His sight was restored and he could see everything distinctly.

When Jesus and his disciples arrived at Bethsaida,
  people brought to him a blind man and begged Jesus to touch him.
He took the blind man by the hand and led him outside the village.
Putting spittle on his eyes he laid his hands on the man and asked,
  "Do you see anything?"
Looking up the man replied, "I see people looking like trees and
  walking."
Then he laid hands on the man's eyes a second time and he saw
  clearly;
  his sight was restored and he could see everything distinctly.
Then he sent him home and said, "Do not even go into the village." ✢

THURSDAY, FEBRUARY 17
WEEKDAY, THE SEVEN HOLY FOUNDERS OF THE SERVITE ORDER

† *James 2:1-9*
Did not God choose those who are poor in the world?
You, however, dishonored the person who is poor.

My brothers and sisters, show no partiality
  as you adhere to the faith in our glorious Lord Jesus Christ.
For if a man with gold rings and fine clothes
  comes into your assembly,
  and a poor person with shabby clothes also comes in,
  and you pay attention to the one wearing the fine clothes
  and say, "Sit here, please,"
  while you say to the poor one, "Stand there," or "Sit at my feet,"
  have you not made distinctions among yourselves
  and become judges with evil designs?

Listen, my beloved brothers and sisters.
Did not God choose those who are poor in the world
  to be rich in faith and heirs of the Kingdom
  that he promised to those who love him?
But you dishonored the poor.
Are not the rich oppressing you?
And do they themselves not haul you off to court?

Is it not they who blaspheme the noble name that was invoked over
    you?
However, if you fulfill the royal law according to the Scripture,
    You shall love your neighbor as yourself, you are doing well.
But if you show partiality, you commit sin,
    and are convicted by the law as transgressors. ✤

    Psalm 34:2-3, 4-5, 6-7
R. (7a) **The Lord hears the cry of the poor.**
I will bless the LORD at all times;
    his praise shall be ever in my mouth.
Let my soul glory in the LORD;
    the lowly will hear me and be glad. **R.**
Glorify the LORD with me,
    let us together extol his name.
I sought the LORD, and he answered me
    and delivered me from all my fears. **R.**
Look to him that you may be radiant with joy,
    and your faces may not blush with shame.
When the poor one called out, the LORD heard,
    and from all his distress he saved him. **R.**

    See John 6:63c, 68c
R. Alleluia, alleluia.
Your words, Lord, are Spirit and life;
you have the words of everlasting life. **R.**

      † *Mark 8:27-33*
    You are the Christ. The Son of Man must suffer much.

Jesus and his disciples set out
    for the villages of Caesarea Philippi.
Along the way he asked his disciples,
    "Who do people say that I am?"
They said in reply,
    "John the Baptist, others Elijah,
    still others one of the prophets."
And he asked them,
    "But who do you say that I am?"
Peter said to him in reply,
    "You are the Christ."
Then he warned them not to tell anyone about him.

He began to teach them
    that the Son of Man must suffer greatly
    and be rejected by the elders, the chief priests, and the scribes,
    and be killed, and rise after three days.

He spoke this openly.
Then Peter took him aside and began to rebuke him.
At this he turned around and, looking at his disciples,
  rebuked Peter and said, "Get behind me, Satan.
You are thinking not as God does, but as human beings do." ✛

FRIDAY, FEBRUARY 18
WEEKDAY

† *James 2:14-24, 26*
For just as a body without a spirit is dead, so also faith without works is dead.

What good is it, my brothers and sisters,
  if someone says he has faith but does not have works?
Can that faith save him?
If a brother or sister has nothing to wear
  and has no food for the day,
  and one of you says to them,
  "Go in peace, keep warm, and eat well,"
  but you do not give them the necessities of the body,
  what good is it?
So also faith of itself,
  if it does not have works, is dead.

Indeed someone might say,
  "You have faith and I have works."
Demonstrate your faith to me without works,
  and I will demonstrate my faith to you from my works.
You believe that God is one.
You do well.
Even the demons believe that and tremble.
Do you want proof, you ignoramus,
  that faith without works is useless?
Was not Abraham our father justified by works
  when he offered his son Isaac upon the altar?
You see that faith was active along with his works,
  and faith was completed by the works.
Thus the Scripture was fulfilled that says,
  Abraham believed God,
  and it was credited to him as righteousness,
  and he was called *the friend of God.*
See how a person is justified by works and not by faith alone.
For just as a body without a spirit is dead,
  so also faith without works is dead. ✛

Psalm 112:1-2, 3-4, 5-6
R. (see 1b) **Blessed the man who greatly delights in the Lord's commands.**
Blessed the man who fears the LORD,
    who greatly delights in his commands.
His posterity shall be mighty upon the earth;
    the upright generation shall be blessed. **R.**
Wealth and riches shall be in his house;
    his generosity shall endure forever.
Light shines through the darkness for the upright;
    he is gracious and merciful and just. **R.**
Well for the man who is gracious and lends,
    who conducts his affairs with justice;
He shall never be moved;
    the just man shall be in everlasting remembrance. **R.**

John 15:15b
R. Alleluia, alleluia.
I call you my friends, says the Lord,
for I have made known to you all that the Father has told me. **R.**

† *Mark 8:34—9:1*
Those who lose their lives for my sake and that of the Gospel, will save them.

Jesus summoned the crowd with his disciples and said to them,
    "Whoever wishes to come after me must deny himself,
    take up his cross, and follow me.
For whoever wishes to save his life will lose it,
    but whoever loses his life for my sake
    and that of the Gospel will save it.
What profit is there for one to gain the whole world
    and forfeit his life?
What could one give in exchange for his life?
Whoever is ashamed of me and of my words
    in this faithless and sinful generation,
    the Son of Man will be ashamed of
    when he comes in his Father's glory with the holy angels."

He also said to them,
    "Amen, I say to you,
    there are some standing here who will not taste death
    until they see that the Kingdom of God has come in power." ✛

SATURDAY, FEBRUARY 19
WEEKDAY, *[BVM]*

† *James 3:1-10*
No human being can tame the tongue.

Not many of you should become teachers, my brothers and sisters,
   for you realize that we will be judged more strictly,
   for we all fall short in many respects.
If anyone does not fall short in speech, he is a perfect man,
   able to bridle the whole body also.
If we put bits into the mouths of horses to make them obey us,
   we also guide their whole bodies.
It is the same with ships:
   even though they are so large and driven by fierce winds,
   they are steered by a very small rudder
   wherever the pilot's inclination wishes.
In the same way the tounge is a samll member
   and yet has great pretensions.

Consider how small a fire can set a huge forest ablaze.
The tongue is also a fire.
It exists among our members as a worlds of malice,
   defiling the whole body
   and setting the entire course of our lives on fire,
   itself set on fire by Gehenna.
For every kind of beast and bird, of reptile and sea creature,
   can be tamed and has been tamed by the human species,
   but no man can tame the tongue.
It is a restless evil, full of deadly poison.
With it we bless the Lord and Father,
   and with it we curse men
   who are made in the likeness of God.
From the same mouth come blessing and cursing.
My brothers and sisters, this need not be so. ✛

Psalm 12:2-3, 4-5, 7-8
R. (8a) **You will protect us, Lord.**
Help, O LORD! for no one now is dutiful;
   faithfulness has vanished from among the children of men.
Everyone speaks falsehood to his neighbor;
   with smooth lips they speak, and double heart. **R.**

May the LORD destroy all smooth lips,
   every boastful tongue,
Those who say, "We are heroes with our tongues;
   our lips are our own; who is lord over us?" **R.**

The promises of the LORD are sure,
    like tried silver, freed from dross, sevenfold refined.
You, O LORD, will keep us
    and preserve us always from this generation. **R.**

See Mark 9:6
R. Alleluia, alleluia.
The heavens were opened and the voice of the Father thundered:
This is my beloved Son. Listen to him. **R.**

† *Mark 9:2-13*
Jesus was transfigured before them.

Jesus took Peter, James, and John
    and led them up a high mountain apart by themselves.
And he was transfigured before them,
    and his clothes became dazzling white,
    such as no fuller on earth could bleach them.
Then Elijah appeared to them along with Moses,
    and they were conversing with Jesus.
Then Peter said to Jesus in reply,
    "Rabbi, it is good that we are here!
Let us make three tents:
    one for you, one for Moses, and one for Elijah."
He hardly knew what to say, they were so terrified.
Then a cloud came, casting a shadow over them;
    then from the cloud came a voice,
    "This is my beloved Son. Listen to him."
Suddenly, looking around, the disciples no longer saw anyone
    but Jesus alone with them.

As they were coming down from the mountain,
    he charged them not to relate what they had seen to anyone,
    except when the Son of Man had risen from the dead.
So they kept the matter to themselves,
    questioning what rising from the dead meant.
Then they asked him,
    "Why do the scribes say that Elijah must come first?"
He told them, "Elijah will indeed come first and restore all things,
    yet how is it written regarding the Son of Man
    that he must suffer greatly and be treated with contempt?
But I tell you that Elijah has come
    and they did tohim whatever they pleased,
    as it is written of him." ✠

SUNDAY, FEBRUARY 20
SEVENTH SUNDAY IN ORDINARY TIME

† *1 Samuel 26:2, 7-9, 12-13, 22-23*
Though the Lord delivered you into my grasp, I would not harm you.

In those days, Saul went down to the desert of Ziph
  with three thousand picked men of Israel,
  to search for David in the desert of Ziph.
So David and Abishai went among Saul's soldiers by night
  and found Saul lying asleep within the barricade,
  with his spear thrust into the ground at his head
  and Abner and his men sleeping around him.

Abishai whispered to David:
  "God has delivered your enemy into your grasp this day.
Let me nail him to the ground with one thrust of the spear;
  I will not need a second thrust!"
But David said to Abishai, "Do not harm him,
  for who can lay hands on the LORD's anointed and remain
    unpunished?"
So David took the spear and the water jug from their place at Saul's
    head,
  and they got away without anyone's seeing or knowing or awakening.
All remained asleep,
  because the LORD had put them into a deep slumber.

Going across to an opposite slope,
  David stood on a remote hilltop
  at a great distance from Abner, son of Ner, and the troops.
He said: "Here is the king's spear.
Let an attendant come over to get it.
The LORD will reward each man for his justice and faithfulness.
Today, though the LORD delivered you into my grasp,
  I would not harm the LORD's anointed." ✝

Psalm 103:1-2, 3-4, 8, 10, 12-13
R. (8a) **The Lord is kind and merciful.**
Bless the LORD, O my soul;
  and all my being, bless his holy name.
Bless the LORD, O my soul,
  and forget not all his benefits. **R.**
He pardons all your iniquities,
  heals all your ills.
He redeems your life from destruction,
  crowns you with kindness and compassion. **R.**

Merciful and gracious is the LORD,
  slow to anger and abounding in kindness.
Not according to our sins does he deal with us,
  nor does he requite us according to our crimes. **R.**
As far as the east is from the west,
  so far has he put our transgressions from us.
As a father has compassion on his children,
  so the LORD has compassion on those who fear him. **R.**

✝ *1 Corinthians 15:45-49*
Just as we have borne the image of the earthly one,
we shall also bear the image of the heavenly one.

Brothers and sisters:
It is written, *The first man, Adam, became a living being,*
  the last Adam a life-giving spirit.
But the spiritual was not first;
  rather the natural and then the spiritual.
The first man was from the earth, earthly;
  the second man, from heaven.
As was the earthly one, so also are the earthly,
  and as is the heavenly one, so also are the heavenly.
Just as we have borne the image of the earthly one,
  we shall also bear the image of the heavenly one. ✛

  John 13:34
R. Alleluia, alleluia.
I give you a new commandment, says the Lord:
love one another as I have loved you. **R.**

✝ *Luke 6:27-38*
Be merciful, just as your Father is merciful.

Jesus said to his disciples:
"To you who hear I say,
  love your enemies, do good to those who hate you,
  bless those who curse you, pray for those who mistreat you.
To the person who strikes you on one cheek,
  offer the other one as well,
  and from the person who takes your cloak,
  do not withhold even your tunic
Give to everyone who asks of you,
  and from the one who takes what is yours do not demand it back.
Do to others as you would have them do to you.
For if you love those who love you,
  what credit is that to you?
Even sinners love those who love them.

And if you do good to those who do good to you,
   what credit is that to you?
Even sinners do the same.
If you lend money to those from whom you expect repayment,
   what credit is that to you?
Even sinners lend to sinners,
   and get back the same amount.
But rather, love your enemies and do good to them,
   and lend expecting nothing back;
   then your reward will be great
   and you will be children of the Most High,
   for he himself is kind to the ungrateful and the wicked.
Be merciful, just as your Father is merciful.

"Stop judging and you will not be judged.
Stop condemning and you will not be condemned.
Forgive and you will be forgiven.
Give, and gifts will be given to you;
   a good measure, packed together, shaken down, and overflowing,
   will be poured into your lap.
For the measure with which you measure
   will in return be measured out to you." ✛

MONDAY, FEBRUARY 21
WEEKDAY, ST. PETER DAMIAN

✝ *James 3:13-18*
*If you have bitter jealousy and selfish
ambition in your hearts, do not boast.*

Beloved:
Who among you is wise and understanding?
Let him show his works by a good life
   in the humility that comes from wisdom.
But if you have bitter jealousy and selfish ambition in your hearts,
   do not boast and be false to the truth.
Wisdom of this kind does not come down from above
   but is earthly, unspiritual, demonic.
For where jealousy and selfish ambition exist,
   there is disorder and every foul practice.
But the wisdom from above is first of all pure,
   then peaceable, gentle, compliant,
   full of mercy and good fruits,
   without inconstancy or insincerity.
And the fruit of righteousness is sown in peace
   for those who cultivate peace. ✛

Psalm 19:8, 9, 10, 15

R. (9a) **The precepts of the Lord give joy to the heart.**

The law of the Lord is perfect,
 refreshing the soul;
The decree of the Lord is trustworthy,
 giving wisdom to the simple. **R.**
The precepts of the Lord are right,
 rejoicing the heart;
The command of the Lord is clear,
 enlightening the eye. **R.**
The fear of the Lord is pure,
 enduring forever;
The ordinances of the Lord are true,
 all of them just. **R.**
Let the words of my mouth and the thought of my heart
 find favor before you,
 O Lord, my rock and my redeemer. **R.**

See 2 Timothy 1:10

R. Alleluia, alleluia.
Our Savior Jesus Christ has destroyed death
and brought life to light through the Gospel. **R.**

† *Mark 9:14-29*
I do believe, help my unbelief!

As Jesus came down from the mountain with Peter, James, and John
 and approached the other disciples,
 they saw a large crowd around them and scribes arguing with them.
Immediately on seeing him,
 the whole crowd was utterly amazed.
They ran up to him and greeted him.
He asked them, "What are you arguing about with them?"
Someone from the crowd answered him,
 "Teacher, I have brought to you my son possessed by a mute spirit.
Wherever it seizes him, it throws him down;
 he foams at the mouth, grinds his teeth, and becomes rigid.
I asked your disciples to drive it out, but they were unable to do so."
He said to them in reply,
 "O faithless generation, how long will I be with you?
How long will I endure you? Bring him to me."
They brought the boy to him.
And when he saw him,
 the spirit immediately threw the boy into convulsions.
As he fell to the ground, he began to roll around
 and foam at the mouth.

Then he questioned his father,
"How long has this been happening to him?"
He replied, "Since childhood.
It has often thrown him into fire and into water to kill him.
But if you can do anything, have compassion on us and help us."
Jesus said to him,
"'If you can!' Everything is possible to one who has faith."
Then the boy's father cried out, "I do believe, help my unbelief!"
Jesus, on seeing a crowd rapidly gathering,
    rebuked the unclean spirit and said to it,
    "Mute and deaf spirit, I command you:
    come out of him and never enter him again!"
Shouting and throwing the boy into convulsions, it came out.
He became like a corpse, which caused many to say, "He is dead!"
But Jesus took him by the hand, raised him, and he stood up.
When he entered the house, his disciples asked him in private,
    "Why could we not drive the spirit out?"
He said to them, "This kind can only come out through prayer." ✛

TUESDAY, FEBRUARY 22
THE CHAIR OF ST. PETER THE APOSTLE

† 1 Peter 5:1-4
As a fellow presbyter and witness to the sufferings of Christ.

Beloved:
I exhort the presbyters among you,
    as a fellow presbyter and witness to the sufferings of Christ
    and one who has a share in the glory to be revealed.
Tend the flock of God in your midst,
    overseeing not by constraint but willingly,
    as God would have it, not for shameful profit but eagerly.
Do not lord it over those assigned to you,
    but be examples to the flock.
And when the chief Shepherd is revealed,
    you will receive the unfading crown of glory. ✛

Psalm 23:1b-3a, 4, 5, 6
R. (1) **The Lord is my shepherd; there is nothing I shall want.**
The LORD is my shepherd; I shall not want.
    In verdant pastures he gives me repose;
Beside restful waters he leads me;
    he refreshes my soul. **R.**
Even though I walk in the dark valley
    I fear no evil; for you are at my side
With your rod and your staff

that give me courage. **R.**
You spread the table before me
  in the sight of my foes;
You anoint my head with oil;
  my cup overflows. **R.**
Only goodness and kindness follow me
  all the days of my life;
And I shall dwell in the house of the LORD
  for years to come. **R.**

Matthew 16:18
R. Alleluia, alleluia.
You are Peter, and upon this rock I will build my Church;
the gates of the netherworld shall not prevail against it. **R.**

† *Matthew 16:13-19*
You are Peter. I will give you the keys to the Kingdom of heaven.

When Jesus went into the region of Caesarea Philippi
  he asked his disciples,
  "Who do people say that the Son of Man is?"
They replied, "Some say John the Baptist, others Elijah,
  still others Jeremiah or one of the prophets."
He said to them, "But who do you say that I am?"
Simon Peter said in reply,
  "You are the Christ, the Son of the living God."
Jesus said to him in reply, "Blessed are you, Simon son of Jonah.
For flesh and blood has not revealed this to you, but my heavenly
    Father.
And so I say to you, you are Peter,
  and upon this rock I will build my Church,
  and the gates of the netherworld shall not prevail against it.
I will give you the keys to the Kingdom of heaven.
Whatever you bind on earth shall be bound in heaven;
  and whatever you loose on earth shall be loosed in heaven." ✛

WEDNESDAY, FEBRUARY 23
ST. POLYCARP

† *James 4:13-17*
*You have no idea what your life will be like
Instead you should say: If the Lord wills it.*

Beloved:
Come now, you who say,
  "Today or tomorrow we shall go into such and such a town,
  spend a year there doing business, and make a profit"—
  you have no idea what your life will be like tomorrow.

You are a puff of smoke that appears briefly and then disappears.
Instead you should say,
  "If the Lord wills it, we shall live to do this or that."
But now you are boasting in your arrogance.
All such boasting is evil.
So for one who knows the right thing to do
  and does not do it, it is a sin. ✙

Psalm 49:2-3, 6-7, 8-10, 11

R. (Matthew 5:3) **Blessed are the poor in spirit; the Kingdom
  of heaven is theirs!**
Hear this, all you peoples;
  hearken, all who dwell in the world,
Of lowly birth or high degree,
  rich and poor alike. **R.**
Why should I fear in evil days
  when my wicked ensnarers ring me round?
They trust in their wealth;
  the abundance of their riches is their boast. **R.**
Yet in no way can a man redeem himself,
  or pay his own ransom to God;
Too high is the price to redeem one's life; he would never have
    enough
  to remain alive always and not see destruction. **R.**
For he can see that wise men die,
  and likewise the senseless and the stupid pass away,
  leaving to others their wealth. **R.**

John 14:6

R. Alleluia, alleluia.
I am the way and the truth and the life, says the Lord;
no one comes to the Father except through me. **R.**

✝ *Mark 9:38-40*
Whoever is not against us is for us.

John said to Jesus,
  "Teacher, we saw someone driving out demons in your name,
  and we tried to prevent him because he does not follow us."
Jesus replied, "Do not prevent him.
There is no one who performs a mighty deed in my name
  who can at the same time speak ill of me.
For whoever is not against us is for us." ✙

THURSDAY, FEBRUARY 24
WEEKDAY

† *James 5:1-6*

The workers from whom you withheld the wages,
are crying aloud; their cries have reached the ears of the Lord of hosts.

Come now, you rich, weep and wail over your impending miseries.
Your wealth has rotted away, your clothes have become moth-eaten,
  your gold and silver have corroded,
  and that corrosion will be a testimony against you;
  it will devour your flesh like a fire.
You have stored up treasure for the last days.
Behold, the wages you withheld from the workers
  who harvested your fields are crying aloud;
  and the cries of the harvesters
  have reached the ears of the Lord of hosts.
You have lived on earth in luxury and pleasure;
  you have fattened your hearts for the day of slaughter.
You have condemned;
  you have murdered the righteous one;
  he offers you no resistance. ✚

Psalm 49:14-15ab, 15cd-16, 17-18, 19-20

R. (Matthew 5:3) **Blessed are the poor in spirit; the Kingdom of heaven is theirs!**

This is the way of those whose trust is folly,
  the end of those contented with their lot:
Like sheep they are herded into the nether world;
  death is their shepherd and the upright rule over them. **R.**

Quickly their form is consumed;
  the nether world is their palace.
But God will redeem me
  from the power of the nether world by receiving me. **R.**

Fear not when a man grows rich,
  when the wealth of his house becomes great,
For when he dies, he shall take none of it;
  his wealth shall not follow him down. **R.**

Though in his lifetime he counted himself blessed,
  "They will praise you for doing well for yourself,"
He shall join the circle of his forebears
  who shall never more see light. **R.**

See 1 Thessalonians 2:13

R. Alleluia, alleluia.
Receive the word of God, not as the word of men,
but as it truly is, the word of God. **R.**

† *Mark 9:41-50*

It is better for you to enter into life with one hand,
than with two hands to go into Gehenna.

Jesus said to his disciples:
"Anyone who gives you a cup of water to drink
    because you belong to Christ,
    amen, I say to you, will surely not lose his reward.

"Whoever causes one of these little ones who believe in me to sin,
    it would be better for him if a great millstone
    were put around his neck
    and he were thrown into the sea.
If your hand causes you to sin, cut it off.
It is better for you to enter into life maimed
    than with two hands to go into Gehenna,
    into the unquenchable fire.
And if your foot causes you to sin, cut if off.
It is better for you to enter into life crippled
    than with two feet to be thrown into Gehenna.
And if your eye causes you to sin, pluck it out.
Better for you to enter into the Kingdom of God with one eye
    than with two eyes to be thrown into Gehenna,
    where *their worm does not die, and the fire is not quenched.*

"Everyone will be salted with fire.
Salt is good, but if salt becomes insipid,
    with what will you restore its flavor?
Keep salt in yourselves and you will have peace with one another." ✝

FRIDAY, FEBRUARY 25
WEEKDAY

† *James 5:9-12*
The Judge is standing before the gates.

Do not complain, brothers and sisters, about one another,
    that you may not be judged.
Behold, the Judge is standing before the gates.
Take as an example of hardship and patience, brothers and sisters,
    the prophets who spoke in the name of the Lord.
Indeed we call blessed those who have persevered.
You have heard of the perseverance of Job,
    and you have seen the purpose of the Lord,
    because *the Lord is compassionate and merciful.*

But above all, my brothers and sisters, do not swear,
    either by heaven or by earth or with any other oath,

but let your "Yes" mean "Yes" and your "No" mean "No,"
that you may not incur condemnation. ✛

Psalm 103:1-2, 3-4, 8-9, 11-12

R. (8a) **The Lord is kind and merciful.**
Bless the LORD, O my soul;
  and all my being, bless his holy name.
Bless the LORD, O my soul,
  and forget not all his benefits. **R.**
He pardons all your iniquities,
  he heals all your ills.
He redeems your life from destruction,
  he crowns you with kindness and compassion. **R.**
Merciful and gracious is the LORD,
  slow to anger and abounding in kindness.
He will not always chide,
  nor does he keep his wrath forever. **R.**
For as the heavens are high above the earth,
  so surpassing is his kindness toward those who fear him.
As far as the east is from the west,
  so far has he put our transgressions from us. **R.**

See John 17:17b, 17a

R. Alleluia, alleluia.
Your word, O Lord, is truth;
consecrate us in the truth. **R.**

† *Mark 10:1-12*

What God has joined together, no human being must separate.

Jesus came into the district of Judea and across the Jordan.
Again crowds gathered around him and, as was his custom,
  he again taught them.
The Pharisees approached him and asked,
  "Is it lawful for a husband to divorce his wife?"
They were testing him.
He said to them in reply, "What did Moses command you?"
They replied,
  "Moses permitted a husband to write a bill of divorce
  and dismiss her."
But Jesus told them,
  "Because of the hardness of your hearts
  he wrote you this commandment.
But from the beginning of creation, *God made them male and female.*
For this reason a man shall leave his father and mother
  and be joined to his wife,
  and the two shall become one flesh.

So they are no longer two but one flesh.
Therefore what God has joined together,
   no human being must separate."
In the house the disciples again questioned Jesus about this.
He said to them,
   "Whoever divorces his wife and marries another
   commits adultery against her;
   and if she divorces her husband and marries another,
   she commits adultery." ✛

SATURDAY, FEBRUARY 26
WEEKDAY, [BVM]

✝ James 5:13-20
The fervent prayer of a righteous person is very powerful.

Beloved:
Is anyone among you suffering?
He should pray.
Is anyone in good spirits?
He should sing a song of praise.
Is anyone among you sick?
He should summon the presbyters of the Church,
   and they should pray over him
   and anoint him with oil in the name of the Lord.
The prayer of faith will save the sick person,
   and the Lord will raise him up.
If he has committed any sins, he will be forgiven.

Therefore, confess your sins to one another
   and pray for one another, that you may be healed.
The fervent prayer of a righteous person is very powerful.
Elijah was a man like us;
   yet he prayed earnestly that it might not rain,
   and for three years and six months it did not rain upon the land.
Then Elijah prayed again, and the sky gave rain
   and the earth produced its fruit.

My brothers and sisters,
   if anyone among you should stray from the truth
   and someone bring him back,
   he should know that whoever brings back a sinner
   from the error of his way will save his soul from death
   and will cover a multitude of sins. ✛

Psalm 141:1-2, 3 and 8

R. (2a) **Let my prayer come like incense before you.**
O LORD, to you I call; hasten to me;
    hearken to my voice when I call upon you.
Let my prayer come like incense before you;
    the lifting up of my hands, like the evening sacrifice. **R.**
O LORD, set a watch before my mouth,
    a guard at the door of my lips.
For toward you, O God, my LORD, my eyes are turned;
    in you I take refuge; strip me not of life. **R.**

See Matthew 11:25

R. Alleluia, alleluia.
Blessed are you, Father, Lord of heaven and earth;
you have revealed to little ones the mysteries of the Kingdom. **R.**

✝ *Mark 10:13-16*
*Whoever does not accept the Kingdom of God
like a child will not enter it.*

People were bringing children to Jesus that he might touch them,
    but the disciples rebuked them.
When Jesus saw this he became indignant and said to them,
    "Let the children come to me; do not prevent them,
    for the Kingdom of God belongs to such as these.
Amen, I say to you,
    whoever does not accept the Kingdom of God like a child
    will not enter it."
Then he embraced the children and blessed them,
    placing his hands on them. ✛

SUNDAY, FEBRUARY 27
EIGHTH SUNDAY IN ORDINARY TIME

✝ *Sirach 27:4-7*
Praise no on before he speaks.

When a sieve is shaken, the husks appear;
    so do one's faults when one speaks.
As the test of what the potter molds is in the furnace,
    so in tribulation is the test of the just.
The fruit of a tree shows the care it has had;
    so too does one's speech disclose the bent of one's mind.
Praise no one before he speaks,
    for it is then that people are tested. ✛

Psalm 92:2-3, 13-14, 15-16

R. Lord, it is good to give thanks to you.

It is good to give thanks to the LORD,
   to sing praise to your name, Most High,
To proclaim your kindness at dawn
   and your faithfulness throughout the night. **R.**
The just one shall flourish like the palm tree,
   like a cedar of Lebanon shall he grow.
They that are planted in the house of the LORD
   shall flourish in the courts of our God. **R.**
They shall bear fruit even in old age;
   vigorous and sturdy shall they be,
declaring how just is the LORD,
   my rock, in whom there is no wrong. **R.**

† *1 Corinthians 15:54-58*

God gives us victory through our Lord Jesus Christ.

Brothers and sisters:

When this which is corruptible clothes itself with incorruptibility
   and this which is mortal clothes itself with immortality,
   then the word that is written shall come about:
Death is swallowed up in victory.
Where, O death, is your victory?
Where, O death, is your sting?
The sting of death is sin,
   and the power of sin is the law.
But thanks be to God who gives us the victory
   through our Lord Jesus Christ.

Therefore, my beloved brothers and sisters,
   be firm, steadfast, always fully devoted to the work of the Lord,
   knowing that in the Lord your labor is not in vain. ✛

Philippians 2:15d, 16a

R. Alleluia, alleluia.

Shine like lights in the world
as you hold on to the word of life. **R.**

† *Luke 6:39-45*

From the fullness of the heart the mouth speaks.

Jesus told his disciples a parable,
"Can a blind person guide a blind person?
Will not both fall into a pit?
No disciple is superior to the teacher;
   but when fully trained,

every disciple will be like his teacher.
Why do you notice the splinter in your brother's eye,
 but do not perceive the wooden beam in your own?
How can you say to your brother,
 'Brother, let me remove that splinter in your eye,'
 when you do not even notice the wooden beam in your own eye?
You hypocrite! Remove the wooden beam from your eye first;
 then you will see clearly
 to remove the splinter in your brother's eye.

"A good tree does not bear rotten fruit,
 nor does a rotten tree bear good fruit.
For every tree is known by its own fruit.
For people do not pick figs from thornbushes,
 nor do they gather grapes from brambles.
A good person out of the store of goodness in his heart produces good,
 but an evil person out of a store of evil produces evil;
 for from the fullness of the heart the mouth speaks." ✛

MONDAY, FEBRUARY 28
WEEKDAY

† 1 Peter 1:3-9
Although you have not seen him, you love him;
you rejoice with an indescribable and glorious joy.

Blessed be the God and Father of our Lord Jesus Christ,
 who in his great mercy gave us a new birth to a living hope
 through the resurrection of Jesus Christ from the dead,
 to an inheritance that is imperishable, undefiled, and unfading,
 kept in heaven for you
 who by the power of God are safeguarded through faith,
 to a salvation that is ready to be revealed in the final time.
In this you rejoice, although now for a little while
 you may have to suffer through various trials,
 so that the genuineness of your faith,
 more precious than gold that is perishable even though tested by fire,
 may prove to be for praise, glory, and honor
 at the revelation of Jesus Christ.
Although you have not seen him you love him;
 even though you do not see him now yet you believe in him,
 you rejoice with an indescribable and glorious joy,
 as you attain the goal of faith, the salvation of your souls. ✛

Psalm 111:1-2, 5-6, 9 and 10c
R. (5) **The Lord will remember his covenant for ever.**
(or **Alleluia.***)*
I will give thanks to the LORD with all my heart
  in the company and assembly of the just.
Great are the works of the LORD,
  exquisite in all their delights. **R.**
He has given food to those who fear him;
  he will forever be mindful of his covenant.
He has made known to his people the power of his works,
  giving them the inheritance of the nations. **R.**
He has sent deliverance to his people;
  he has ratified his covenant forever;
  holy and awesome is his name.
His praise endures forever. **R.**

2 Corinthians 8:9
R. Alleluia, alleluia.
Jesus Christ became poor although he was rich,
so that by his poverty you might become rich. **R.**

† *Mark 10:17-27*
Go, sell what you have, and give to the poor.

As Jesus was setting out on a journey, a man ran up,
  knelt down before him, and asked him,
   "Good teacher, what must I do to inherit eternal life?"
Jesus answered him, "Why do you call me good?
No one is good but God alone.
You know the commandments: *You shall not kill;*
  you shall not commit adultery;
  you shall not steal;
  you shall not bear false witness;
  you shall not defraud;
  honor your father and your mother."
He replied and said to him,
  "Teacher, all of these I have observed from my youth."
Jesus, looking at him, loved him and said to him,
  "You are lacking in one thing.
Go, sell what you have, and give to the poor
  and you will have treasure in heaven; then come, follow me."
At that statement, his face fell,
  and he went away sad, for he had many possessions.

Jesus looked around and said to his disciples,
  "How hard it is for those who have wealth

to enter the Kingdom of God!"
The disciples were amazed at his words.
So Jesus again said to them in reply,
   "Children, how hard it is to enter the Kingdom of God!
It is easier for a camel to pass through the eye of a needle
   than for one who is rich to enter the Kingdom of God."
They were exceedingly astonished and said among themselves,
   "Then who can be saved?"
Jesus looked at them and said,
   "For men it is impossible, but not for God.
All things are possible for God." ✢

TUESDAY, MARCH 1
WEEKDAY

† 1 Peter 1:10-16

They prophesied about the grace that was to be yours; therefore, live soberly and set your hopes completely on the grace to be brought to you.

Beloved:
Concerning the salvation of your souls
  the prophets who prophesied about the grace that was to be yours
  searched and investigated it
  investigating the time and circumstances
  that the Spirit of Christ within them indicated
  when it testified in advance
  to the sufferings destined for Christ
  and the glories to follow them.
It was revealed to them that they were serving not themselves but you
  with regard to the things that have now been announced to you
  by those who preached the Good News to you
  through the Holy Spirit sent from heaven,
  things into which angels longed to look.

Therefore, gird up the loins of your mind, live soberly,
  and set your hopes completely on the grace to be brought to you
  at the revelation of Jesus Christ.
Like obedient children,
  do not act in compliance with the desires of your former ignorance
  but, as he who called you is holy,
  be holy yourselves in every aspect of your conduct,
  for it is written, *Be holy because I am holy.* ✛

Psalm 98:1, 2-3ab, 3cd-4

R. (2a) **The Lord has made known his salvation.**
Sing to the LORD a new song,
  for he has done wondrous deeds;
His right hand has won victory for him,
  his holy arm. **R.**
The LORD has made his salvation known:
  in the sight of the nations he has revealed his justice.
He has remembered his kindness and his faithfulness
  toward the house of Israel. **R.**
All the ends of the earth have seen
  the salvation by our God.
Sing joyfully to the LORD, all you lands;
  break into song; sing praise. **R.**

See Matthew 11:25
R. Alleluia, alleluia.
Blessed are you, Father, Lord of heaven and earth;
you have revealed to little ones the mysteries of the Kingdom. **R.**

† *Mark 10:28-31*
*You will receive a hundred times as much persecution in this
present age, and eternal life in the age to come.*

Peter began to say to Jesus,
    "We have given up everything and followed you."
Jesus said, "Amen, I say to you,
    there is no one who has given up house or brothers or sisters
    or mother or father or children or lands
    for my sake and for the sake of the Gospel
    who will not receive a hundred times more now in this present age:
    houses and brothers and sisters
    and mothers and children and lands,
    with persecutions, and eternal life in the age to come.
But many that are first will be last, and the last will be first." ✚

WEDNESDAY, MARCH 2
ASH WEDNESDAY

† *Joel 2:12-18*
Rend your hearts, not your garments.

Even now, says the LORD,
    return to me with your whole heart,
    with fasting, and weeping, and mourning;
Rend your hearts, not your garments,
    and return to the LORD, your God.
For gracious and merciful is he,
    slow to anger, rich in kindness,
    and relenting in punishment.
Perhaps he will again relent
    and leave behind him a blessing,
Offerings and libations
    for the LORD, your God.

Blow the trumpet in Zion!
    proclaim a fast,
    call an assembly;
Gather the people,
    notify the congregation;
Assemble the elders,
    gather the children

and the infants at the breast;
Let the bridegroom quit his room
  and the bride her chamber.
Between the porch and the altar
  let the priests, the ministers of the LORD, weep,
And say, "Spare, O LORD, your people,
  and make not your heritage a reproach,
  with the nations ruling over them!
Why should they say among the peoples,
  'Where is their God?'"

Then the LORD was stirred to concern for his land
  and took pity on his people. ✛

Psalm 51:3-4, 5-6ab, 12-13, 14 and 17
R. (see 3a) **Be merciful, O Lord, for we have sinned.**
Have mercy on me, O God, in your goodness;
  in the greatness of your compassion wipe out my offense.
Thoroughly wash me from my guilt
  and of my sin cleanse me. **R.**
For I acknowledge my offense,
  and my sin is before me always:
"Against you only have I sinned,
  and done what is evil in your sight." **R.**
A clean heart create for me, O God,
  and a steadfast spirit renew within me.
Cast me not out from your presence,
  and your Holy Spirit take not from me. **R.**
Give me back the joy of your salvation,
  and a willing spirit sustain in me.
O Lord, open my lips,
  and my mouth shall proclaim your praise. **R.**

✝ *2 Corinthians 5:20—6:2*
Be reconciled to God. Behold, now is the acceptable time.

Brothers and sisters:
We are ambassadors for Christ,
  as if God were appealing through us.
We implore you on behalf of Christ,
  be reconciled to God.
For our sake he made him to be sin who did not know sin,
  so that we might become the righteousness of God in him.

Working together, then,
  we appeal to you not to receive the grace of God in vain.

For he says:

In an acceptable time I heard you,
and on the day of salvation I helped you.

Behold, now is a very acceptable time;
behold, now is the day of salvation. ✛

See Psalm 95:8
R. Glory and praise to you, Lord Jesus Christ!
If today you hear his voice,
harden not your hearts. **R.**

† *Matthew 6:1-6, 16-18*
Your Father who sees in secret will repay you.

Jesus said to his disciples:
   "Take care not to perform righteous deeds
   in order that people may see them;
   otherwise, you will have no recompense from your heavenly Father.
When you give alms,
   do not blow a trumpet before you,
   as the hypocrites do in the synagogues and in the streets
   to win the praise of others.
Amen, I say to you,
   they have received their reward.
But when you give alms,
   do not let your left hand know what your right is doing,
   so that your almsgiving may be secret.
And your Father who sees in secret will repay you.

"When you pray,
   do not be like the hypocrites,
   who love to stand and pray in the synagogues and on street corners
   so that others may see them.
Amen, I say to you,
   they have received their reward.
But when you pray, go to your inner room,
   close the door, and pray to your Father in secret.
And your Father who sees in secret will repay you.

"When you fast,
   do not look gloomy like the hypocrites.
They neglect their appearance,
   so that they may appear to others to be fasting.
Amen, I say to you, they have received their reward.

But when you fast,
  anoint your head and wash your face,
  so that you may not appear to be fasting,
  except to your Father who is hidden.
And your Father who sees what is hidden will repay you." ✛

THURSDAY, MARCH 3
THURSDAY AFTER ASH WEDNESDAY, ST. KATHERINE DREXEL

† *Deuteronomy 30:15-20*
Behold, I set before you the blessing and the curse (Deuteronomy 11:26).

Moses said to the people:
"Today I have set before you
  life and prosperity, death and doom.
If you obey the commandments of the LORD, your God,
  which I enjoin on you today,
  loving him, and walking in his ways,
  and keeping his commandments, statutes and decrees,
  you will live and grow numerous,
  and the LORD, your God,
  will bless you in the land you are entering to occupy.
If, however, you turn away your hearts and will not listen,
  but are led astray and adore and serve other gods,
  I tell you now that you will certainly perish;
  you will not have a long life
  on the land that you are crossing the Jordan to enter and occupy.
I call heaven and earth today to witness against you:
  I have set before you life and death,
  the blessing and the curse.
Choose life, then,
  that you and your descendants may live, by loving the LORD, your
    God,
  heeding his voice, and holding fast to him.
For that will mean life for you,
  a long life for you to live on the land that the LORD swore
  he would give to your fathers Abraham, Isaac and Jacob." ✛

Psalm 1:1-2, 3, 4 and 6
R. (40:5a) **Blessed are they who hope in the Lord.**
Blessed the man who follows not
  the counsel of the wicked
Nor walks in the way of sinners,
  nor sits in the company of the insolent,
But delights in the law of the LORD
  and meditates on his law day and night. **R.**

He is like a tree
   planted near running water,
That yields its fruit in due season,
   and whose leaves never fade.
Whatever he does, prospers. **R.**
Not so the wicked, not so;
   they are like chaff which the wind drives away.
For the LORD watches over the way of the just,
   but the way of the wicked vanishes. **R.**

   Matthew 4:17
R. Glory and praise to you, Lord Jesus Christ!
Repent, says the Lord;
the Kingdom of heaven is at hand. **R.**

   ✝ Luke 9:22-25
   Whoever loses his life for my sake will save it.

Jesus said to his disciples:
   "The Son of Man must suffer greatly and be rejected
   by the elders, the chief priests, and the scribes,
   and be killed and on the third day be raised."

Then he said to all,
   "If anyone wishes to come after me, he must deny himself
   and take up his cross daily and follow me.
For whoever wishes to save his life will lose it,
   but whoever loses his life for my sake will save it.
What profit is there for one to gain the whole world
   yet lose or forfeit himself?" ✛

FRIDAY, MARCH 4
FRIDAY AFTER ASH WEDNESDAY, ST. CASIMIR

   ✝ Isaiah 58:1-9a
   Is this the manner of fasting I wish?

Thus says the Lord GOD:
Cry out full-throated and unsparingly,
   lift up your voice like a trumpet blast;
Tell my people their wickedness,
   and the house of Jacob their sins.
They seek me day after day,
   and desire to know my ways,
Like a nation that has done what is just
   and not abandoned the law of their God;
They ask me to declare what is due them,
   pleased to gain access to God.

"Why do we fast, and you do not see it?
afflict ourselves, and you take no note of it?"

Lo, on your fast day you carry out your own pursuits,
and drive all your laborers.
Yes, your fast ends in quarreling and fighting,
striking with wicked claw.
Would that today you might fast
so as to make your voice heard on high!
Is this the manner of fasting I wish,
of keeping a day of penance:
That a man bow his head like a reed
and lie in sackcloth and ashes?
Do you call this a fast,
a day acceptable to the LORD?
This, rather, is the fasting that I wish:
releasing those bound unjustly,
untying the thongs of the yoke;
Setting free the oppressed,
breaking every yoke;
Sharing your bread with the hungry,
sheltering the oppressed and the homeless;
Clothing the naked when you see them,
and not turning your back on your own.
Then your light shall break forth like the dawn,
and your wound shall quickly be healed;
Your vindication shall go before you,
and the glory of the LORD shall be your rear guard.
Then you shall call, and the LORD will answer,
you shall cry for help, and he will say: Here I am! ✙

Psalm 51:3-4, 5-6ab, 18-19

R. (19b) **A heart contrite and humbled, O God, you will not
spurn.**
Have mercy on me, O God, in your goodness;
in the greatness of your compassion wipe out my offense.
Thoroughly wash me from my guilt
and of my sin cleanse me. **R.**
For I acknowledge my offense,
and my sin is before me always:
"Against you only have I sinned,
and done what is evil in your sight." **R.**
For you are not pleased with sacrifices;
should I offer a burnt offering, you would not accept it.

My sacrifice, O God, is a contrite spirit;
    a heart contrite and humbled, O God, you will not spurn. **R.**

See Amos 5:14
R. Glory and praise to you, Lord Jesus Christ!
Seek good and not evil so that you may live,
and the Lord will be with you. **R.**

† *Matthew 9:14-15*
When the bridegroom is taken from them, then they will fast.

The disciples of John approached Jesus and said,
    "Why do we and the Pharisees fast much,
    but your disciples do not fast?"
Jesus answered them, "Can the wedding guests mourn
    as long as the bridegroom is with them?
The days will come when the bridegroom is taken away from them,
    and then they will fast." ✛

SATURDAY, MARCH 5
SATURDAY AFTER ASH WEDNESDAY

† *Isaiah 58:9b-14*
If you bestow your bread on the hungry,
then light shall rise for you in the darkness.

Thus says the LORD:
If you remove from your midst oppression,
    false accusation and malicious speech;
If you bestow your bread on the hungry
    and satisfy the afflicted;
Then light shall rise for you in the darkness,
    and the gloom shall become for you like midday;
Then the LORD will guide you always
    and give you plenty even on the parched land.
He will renew your strength,
    and you shall be like a watered garden,
    like a spring whose water never fails.
The ancient ruins shall be rebuilt for your sake,
    and the foundations from ages past you shall raise up;
"Repairer of the breach," they shall call you,
    "Restorer of ruined homesteads."

If you hold back your foot on the sabbath
    from following your own pursuits on my holy day;
If you call the sabbath a delight,
    and the LORD's holy day honorable;

If you honor it by not following your ways,
  seeking your own interests, or speaking with malice—
Then you shall delight in the LORD,
  and I will make you ride on the heights of the earth;
I will nourish you with the heritage of Jacob, your father,
  for the mouth of the LORD has spoken. ✝

Psalm 86:1-2, 3-4, 5-6
R. (11ab) **Teach me your way, O Lord, that I may walk in your
  truth.**
Incline your ear, O LORD; answer me,
  for I am afflicted and poor.
Keep my life, for I am devoted to you;
  save your servant who trusts in you.
  You are my God. **R.**
Have mercy on me, O Lord,
  for to you I call all the day.
Gladden the soul of your servant,
  for to you, O Lord, I lift up my soul. **R.**
For you, O Lord, are good and forgiving,
  abounding in kindness to all who call upon you.
Hearken, O LORD, to my prayer
  and attend to the sound of my pleading. **R.**

Ezekiel 33:11
R. Glory and praise to you, Lord Jesus Christ!
I take no pleasure in the death of the wicked man, says the Lord,
but rather in his conversion, that he may live. **R.**

† *Luke 5:27-32*
I have not come to call righteous to repentance but sinners.

Jesus saw a tax collector named Levi sitting at the customs post.
He said to him, "Follow me."
And leaving everything behind, he got up and followed him.
Then Levi gave a great banquet for him in his house,
  and a large crowd of tax collectors
  and others were at table with them.
The Pharisees and their scribes complained to his disciples, saying,
  "Why do you eat and drink with tax collectors and sinners?"
Jesus said to them in reply,
  "Those who are healthy do not need a physician, but the sick do.
I have not come to call the righteous to repentance but sinners." ✝

SUNDAY, MARCH 6
First Sunday of Lent

† *Deuteronomy 26:4-10*
The confession of faith of the chosen people.

Moses spoke to the people, saying:
"The priest shall receive the basket from you
and shall set it in front of the altar of the Lord, your God.

"Then you shall declare before the Lord, your God,
'My father was a wandering Aramean
who went down to Egypt with a small household
and lived there as an alien.
But there he became a nation
great, strong, and numerous.
When the Egyptians maltreated and oppressed us,
imposing hard labor upon us,
we cried to the Lord, the God of our fathers,
and he heard our cry
and saw our affliction, our toil, and our oppression.
He brought us out of Egypt
with his strong hand and outstretched arm,
with terrifying power, with signs and wonders;
and bringing us into this country,
he gave us this land flowing with milk and honey.
Therefore, I have now brought you the firstfruits
of the products of the soil
which you, O Lord, have given me.'
And having set them before the Lord, your God,
you shall bow down in his presence." ✤

Psalm 91:1-2, 10-11, 12-13, 14-15
R. (see 15b) **Be with me, Lord, when I am in trouble.**
You who dwell in the shelter of the Most High,
who abide in the shadow of the Almighty,
say to the Lord, "My refuge and fortress,
my God in whom I trust." R.
No evil shall befall you,
nor shall affliction come near your tent,
for to his angels he has given command about you,
that they guard you in all your ways. R.
Upon their hands they shall bear you up,
lest you dash your foot against a stone.
You shall tread upon the asp and the viper;
you shall trample down the lion and the dragon. R.

Because he clings to me, I will deliver him;
  I will set him on high because he acknowledges my name.
He shall call upon me, and I will answer him;
  I will be with him in distress;
I will deliver him and glorify him. **R.**

† *Romans 10:8-13*
The confession of faith of all believers in Christ.

Brothers and sisters:
What does Scripture say?
  The word is near you,
    in your mouth and in your heart
  —that is, the word of faith that we preach—,
  for, if you confess with your mouth that Jesus is Lord
  and believe in your heart that God raised him from the dead,
  you will be saved.
For one believes with the heart and so is justified,
  and one confesses with the mouth and so is saved.
For the Scripture says,
  No one who believes in him will be put to shame.
For there is no distinction between Jew and Greek;
  the same Lord is Lord of all,
  enriching all who call upon him.
For "everyone who calls on the name of the Lord will be saved." ✚

  Matthew 4:4b
R. Glory and praise to you, Lord Jesus Christ!
One does not live on bread alone,
but on every word that comes forth from the mouth of God. **R.**

† *Luke 4:1-13*
Jesus was led by the Spirit into the desert and was tempted.

Filled with the Holy Spirit, Jesus returned from the Jordan
  and was led by the Spirit into the desert for forty days,
  to be tempted by the devil.
He ate nothing during those days,
  and when they were over he was hungry.
The devil said to him,
  "If you are the Son of God,
  command this stone to become bread."
Jesus answered him,
  "It is written, *One does not live on bread alone.*"
Then he took him up and showed him
  all the kingdoms of the world in a single instant.

The devil said to him,
"I shall give to you all this power and glory;
for it has been handed over to me,
and I may give it to whomever I wish.
All this will be yours, if you worship me."
Jesus said to him in reply,
"It is written:
You shall worship the Lord, your God,
and him alone shall you serve."
Then he led him to Jerusalem,
made him stand on the parapet of the temple, and said to him,
"If you are the Son of God,
throw yourself down from here, for it is written:
He will command his angels concerning you, to guard you,
and:
With their hands they will support you,
lest you dash your foot against a stone."
Jesus said to him in reply,
"It also says,
You shall not put the Lord, your God, to the test."
When the devil had finished every temptation,
he departed from him for a time. ✛

MONDAY, MARCH 7
LENTEN WEEKDAY, ST. PERPETUA AND ST. FELICITY

† *Leviticus 19:1-2, 11-18*
Judge your fellow man justly.

The LORD said to Moses,
"Speak to the whole assembly of the children of Israel and tell them:
Be holy, for I, the LORD, your God, am holy.

"You shall not steal.
You shall not lie or speak falsely to one another.
You shall not swear falsely by my name,
thus profaning the name of your God.
I am the LORD.

"You shall not defraud or rob your neighbor.
You shall not withhold overnight the wages of your day laborer.
You shall not curse the deaf,
or put a stumbling block in front of the blind,
but you shall fear your God.
I am the LORD.

"You shall not act dishonestly in rendering judgment.

Show neither partiality to the weak nor deference to the mighty,
  but judge your fellow men justly.
You shall not go about spreading slander among your kin;
  nor shall you stand by idly when your neighbor's life is at stake.
I am the LORD.

"You shall not bear hatred for your brother in your heart.
Though you may have to reprove him,
  do not incur sin because of him.
Take no revenge and cherish no grudge against your fellow countrymen.
You shall love your neighbor as yourself.
I am the LORD." ✛

Psalm 19:8, 9, 10, 15
R. (John 6:63b) **Your words, Lord, are Spirit and life.**
The law of the LORD is perfect,
  refreshing the soul.
The decree of the LORD is trustworthy,
  giving wisdom to the simple. **R.**
The precepts of the LORD are right,
  rejoicing the heart.
The command of the LORD is clear,
  enlightening the eye. **R.**
The fear of the LORD is pure,
  enduring forever;
The ordinances of the LORD are true,
  all of them just. **R.**
Let the words of my mouth and the thought of my heart
  find favor before you,
  O LORD, my rock and my redeemer. **R.**

2 Corinthians 6:2b
R. Glory and praise to you, Lord Jesus Christ!
Behold, now is a very acceptable time;
behold, now is the day of salvation. **R.**

✝ Matthew 25:31-46
*Whatever you have done to the very least
of my brothers, you have done to me.*

Jesus said to his disciples:
  "When the Son of Man comes in his glory,
  and all the angels with him,
  he will sit upon his glorious throne,
  and all the nations will be assembled before him.
And he will separate them one from another,
  as a shepherd separates the sheep from the goats.

He will place the sheep on his right and the goats on his left.
Then the king will say to those on his right,
   'Come, you who are blessed by my Father.
Inherit the kingdom prepared for you from the foundation of the
     world.
For I was hungry and you gave me food,
   I was thirsty and you gave me drink,
   a stranger and you welcomed me,
   naked and you clothed me,
   ill and you cared for me,
   in prison and you visited me.'
Then the righteous will answer him and say,
   'Lord, when did we see you hungry and feed you,
   or thirsty and give you drink?
When did we see you a stranger and welcome you,
   or naked and clothe you?
When did we see you ill or in prison, and visit you?'
And the king will say to them in reply,
   'Amen, I say to you, whatever you did
   for one of these least brothers of mine, you did for me.'
Then he will say to those on his left,
   'Depart from me, you accursed,
   into the eternal fire prepared for the Devil and his angels.
For I was hungry and you gave me no food,
   I was thirsty and you gave me no drink,
   a stranger and you gave me no welcome,
   naked and you gave me no clothing,
   ill and in prison, and you did not care for me.'
Then they will answer and say,
   'Lord, when did we see you hungry or thirsty
   or a stranger or naked or ill or in prison,
   and not minister to your needs?'
He will answer them, 'Amen, I say to you,
   what you did not do for one of these least ones,
   you did not do for me.'
And these will go off to eternal punishment,
   but the righteous to eternal life." ✛

TUESDAY, MARCH 8
LENTEN WEEKDAY, ST. JOHN OF GOD

† Isaiah 55:10-11
My word will do whatever I will.

Thus says the LORD:
Just as from the heavens
 the rain and snow come down
And do not return there
 till they have watered the earth,
 making it fertile and fruitful,
Giving seed to the one who sows
 and bread to the one who eats,
So shall my word be
 that goes forth from my mouth;
It shall not return to me void,
 but shall do my will,
 achieving the end for which I sent it. ✛

Psalm 34:4-5, 6-7, 16-17, 18-19
R. (18b) **From all their distress God rescues the just.**
Glorify the LORD with me,
 let us together extol his name.
I sought the LORD, and he answered me
 and delivered me from all my fears. **R.**
Look to him that you may be radiant with joy,
 and your faces may not blush with shame.
When the poor one called out, the LORD heard,
 and from all his distress he saved him. **R.**
The LORD has eyes for the just,
 and ears for their cry.
The LORD confronts the evildoers,
 to destroy remembrance of them from the earth. **R.**
When the just cry out, the LORD hears them,
 and from all their distress he rescues them.
The LORD is close to the brokenhearted;
 and those who are crushed in spirit he saves. **R.**

Matthew 4:4b
R. Glory and praise to you, Lord Jesus Christ!
One does not live on bread alone,
but on every word that comes forth from the mouth of God. **R.**

† *Matthew 6:7-15*
This is how you are to pray.

Jesus said to his disciples:
"In praying, do not babble like the pagans,
who think that they will be heard because of their many words.
Do not be like them.
Your Father knows what you need before you ask him.

"This is how you are to pray:

Our Father who art in heaven,
hallowed be thy name,
thy Kingdom come,
thy will be done,
on earth as it is in heaven.
Give us this day our daily bread;
and forgive us our trespasses,
as we forgive those who trespass against us;
and lead us not into temptation,
but deliver us from evil.

"If you forgive men their transgressions,
your heavenly Father will forgive you.
But if you do not forgive men,
neither will your Father forgive your transgressions." ✛

WEDNESDAY, MARCH 9
LENTEN WEEKDAY, ST. FRANCES OF ROME

† *Jonah 3:1-10*
The Ninevites turned from their evil way.

The word of the LORD came to Jonah a second time:
"Set out for the great city of Nineveh,
and announce to it the message that I will tell you."
So Jonah made ready and went to Nineveh,
according to the LORD's bidding.
Now Nineveh was an enormously large city;
it took three days to go through it.
Jonah began his journey through the city,
and had gone but a single day's walk announcing,
"Forty days more and Nineveh shall be destroyed,"
when the people of Nineveh believed God;
they proclaimed a fast
and all of them, great and small, put on sackcloth.

When the news reached the king of Nineveh,
  he rose from his throne, laid aside his robe,
  covered himself with sackcloth, and sat in the ashes.
Then he had this proclaimed throughout Nineveh,
  by decree of the king and his nobles:
  "Neither man nor beast, neither cattle nor sheep,
  shall taste anything;
  they shall not eat, nor shall they drink water.
Man and beast shall be covered with sackcloth and call loudly to God;
  every man shall turn from his evil way
  and from the violence he has in hand.
Who knows, God may relent and forgive, and withhold his blazing
    wrath,
  so that we shall not perish."
When God saw by their actions how they turned from their evil way,
  he repented of the evil that he had threatened to do to them;
  he did not carry it out. ✛

  Psalm 51:3-4, 12-13, 18-19
**R. (19b) A heart contrite and humbled, O God, you will not
  spurn.**
Have mercy on me, O God, in your goodness;
  in the greatness of your compassion wipe out my offense.
Thoroughly wash me from my guilt
  and of my sin cleanse me. **R.**
A clean heart create for me, O God,
  and a steadfast spirit renew within me.
Cast me not out from your presence,
  and your Holy Spirit take not from me. **R.**
For you are not pleased with sacrifices;
  should I offer a burnt offering, you would not accept it.
My sacrifice, O God, is a contrite spirit;
  a heart contrite and humbled, O God, you will not spurn. **R.**

  Joel 2:12-13
R. Glory and praise to you, Lord Jesus Christ!
Even now, says the LORD,
return to me with your whole heart
for I am gracious and merciful. **R.**

† *Luke 11:29-32*
No sign will be given to this generation except the sign of Jonah.

While still more people gathered in the crowd, Jesus said to them,
  "This generation is an evil generation;
  it seeks a sign, but no sign will be given it,

except the sign of Jonah.
Just as Jonah became a sign to the Ninevites,
so will the Son of Man be to this generation.
At the judgment
the queen of the south will rise with the men of this generation
and she will condemn them,
because she came from the ends of the earth
to hear the wisdom of Solomon,
and there is something greater than Solomon here.
At the judgment the men of Nineveh will arise with this generation
and condemn it,
because at the preaching of Jonah they repented,
and there is something greater than Jonah here." ✛

THURSDAY, MARCH 10
LENTEN WEEKDAY

† *Esther C:12, 14-16, 23-25*
I have no protector other than you, LORD.

Queen Esther, seized with mortal anguish,
had recourse to the LORD.
She lay prostrate upon the ground, together with her handmaids,
from morning until evening, and said:
"God of Abraham, God of Isaac, and God of Jacob, blessed are you.
Help me, who am alone and have no help but you,
for I am taking my life in my hand.
As a child I used to hear from the books of my forefathers
that you, O LORD, always free those who are pleasing to you.
Now help me, who am alone and have no one but you,
O LORD, my God.

"And now, come to help me, an orphan.
Put in my mouth persuasive words in the presence of the lion
and turn his heart to hatred for our enemy,
so that he and those who are in league with him may perish.
Save us from the hand of our enemies;
turn our mourning into gladness
and our sorrows into wholeness." ✛

Psalm 138:1-2ab, 2cde-3, 7c-8
R. (3a) **Lord, on the day I called for help, you answered me.**
I will give thanks to you, O LORD, with all my heart,
for you have heard the words of my mouth;
in the presence of the angels I will sing your praise;
I will worship at your holy temple
and give thanks to your name. **R.**

Because of your kindness and your truth;
  for you have made great above all things
  your name and your promise.
When I called, you answered me;
  you built up strength within me. **R.**
Your right hand saves me.
The LORD will complete what he has done for me;
  your kindness, O LORD, endures forever;
  forsake not the work of your hands. **R.**

Psalm 51:12a, 14a
R. Glory and praise to you, Lord Jesus Christ!
A clean heart create for me, God;
give me back the joy of your salvation. **R.**

† *Matthew 7:7-12*
Everyone who asks, receives.

Jesus said to his disciples:
"Ask and it will be given to you;
  seek and you will find;
  knock and the door will be opened to you.
For everyone who asks, receives; and the one who seeks, finds;
  and to the one who knocks, the door will be opened.
Which one of you would hand his son a stone
  when he asked for a loaf of bread,
  or a snake when he asked for a fish?
If you then, who are wicked,
  know how to give good gifts to your children,
  how much more will your heavenly Father give good things
  to those who ask him.

"Do to others whatever you would have them do to you.
This is the law and the prophets." ✛

FRIDAY, MARCH 11
LENTEN WEEKDAY

† *Ezekiel 18:21-28*
*Do I derive any pleasure from the death of the wicked
and not rejoice when he turns from his evil way that he may live?*

Thus says the Lord GOD:
If the wicked man turns away from all the sins he committed,
  if he keeps all my statutes and does what is right and just,
  he shall surely live, he shall not die.
None of the crimes he committed shall be remembered against him;
  he shall live because of the virtue he has practiced.

Do I indeed derive any pleasure from the death of the wicked?
    says the Lord GOD.
Do I not rather rejoice when he turns from his evil way
    that he may live?

And if the virtuous man turns from the path of virtue to do evil,
    the same kind of abominable things that the wicked man does,
    can he do this and still live?
None of his virtuous deeds shall be remembered,
    because he has broken faith and committed sin;
    because of this, he shall die.
You say, "The LORD's way is not fair!"
Hear now, house of Israel:
    Is it my way that is unfair, or rather, are not your ways unfair?
When someone virtuous turns away from virtue to commit iniquity,
        and dies,
    it is because of the iniquity he committed that he must die.
But if the wicked, turning from the wickedness he has committed,
    does what is right and just,
    he shall preserve his life;
    since he has turned away from all the sins that he committed,
    he shall surely live, he shall not die. ✛

    Psalm 130:1-2, 3-4, 5-7a, 7bc-8
R. (3) **If you, O Lord, mark iniquities, who can stand?**
Out of the depths I cry to you, O LORD;
    LORD, hear my voice!
Let your ears be attentive
    to my voice in supplication. **R.**
If you, O LORD, mark iniquities,
    LORD, who can stand?
But with you is forgiveness,
    that you may be revered. **R.**
I trust in the LORD;
    my soul trusts in his word.
My soul waits for the LORD
    more than sentinels wait for the dawn.
    Let Israel wait for the LORD. **R.**
For with the LORD is kindness
    and with him is plenteous redemption;
And he will redeem Israel
    from all their iniquities. **R.**

Ezekiel 18:31

R. Glory and praise to you, Lord Jesus Christ!

Cast away from you all the crimes you have committed, says the LORD,
and make for yourselves a new heart and a new spirit. **R.**

† *Matthew 5:20-26*
Go first and be reconciled with your brother.

Jesus said to his disciples:
"I tell you,
   unless your righteousness surpasses that
   of the scribes and Pharisees,
   you will not enter into the Kingdom of heaven.

"You have heard that it was said to your ancestors,
   You shall not kill; and whoever kills will be liable to judgment.
But I say to you, whoever is angry with his brother
   will be liable to judgment,
   and whoever says to his brother, *Raqa,*
   will be answerable to the Sanhedrin,
   and whoever says, 'You fool,' will be liable to fiery Gehenna.
Therefore, if you bring your gift to the altar,
   and there recall that your brother
   has anything against you,
   leave your gift there at the altar,
   go first and be reconciled with your brother,
   and then come and offer your gift.
Settle with your opponent quickly while on the way to court.
Otherwise your opponent will hand you over to the judge,
   and the judge will hand you over to the guard,
   and you will be thrown into prison.
Amen, I say to you,
   you will not be released until you have paid the last penny." ✛

SATURDAY, MARCH 12
LENTEN WEEKDAY

† *Deuteronomy 26:16-19*
You will be a people sacred to the LORD God.

Moses spoke to the people, saying:
"This day the LORD, your God,
   commands you to observe these statutes and decrees.
Be careful, then,
   to observe them with all your heart and with all your soul.
Today you are making this agreement with the LORD:
   he is to be your God and you are to walk in his ways

and observe his statutes, commandments and decrees,
and to hearken to his voice.
And today the Lᴏʀᴅ is making this agreement with you:
you are to be a people peculiarly his own, as he promised you;
and provided you keep all his commandments,
he will then raise you high in praise and renown and glory
above all other nations he has made,
and you will be a people sacred to the Lᴏʀᴅ, your God,
as he promised." ✛

Psalm 119:1-2, 4-5, 7-8
R. (1b) Blessed are they who follow the law of the Lord!
Blessed are they whose way is blameless,
who walk in the law of the Lᴏʀᴅ.
Blessed are they who observe his decrees,
who seek him with all their heart. **R.**
You have commanded that your precepts
be diligently kept.
Oh, that I might be firm in the ways
of keeping your statutes! **R.**
I will give you thanks with an upright heart,
when I have learned your just ordinances.
I will keep your statutes;
do not utterly forsake me. **R.**

2 Corinthians 6:2b
R. Glory and praise to you, Lord Jesus Christ!
Behold, now is a very acceptable time;
behold, now is the day of salvation. **R.**

† *Matthew 5:43-48*
Be perfect, just as your heavenly Father is perfect.

Jesus said to his disciples:
"You have heard that it was said,
You shall love your neighbor and hate your enemy.
But I say to you, love your enemies,
and pray for those who persecute you,
that you may be children of your heavenly Father,
for he makes his sun rise on the bad and the good,
and causes rain to fall on the just and the unjust.
For if you love those who love you, what recompense will you have?
Do not the tax collectors do the same?
And if you greet your brothers and sisters only,
what is unusual about that?
Do not the pagans do the same?
So be perfect, just as your heavenly Father is perfect." ✛

SUNDAY, MARCH 13
SECOND SUNDAY OF LENT

† *Genesis 15:5-12, 17-18*
God made a covenant with Abraham, his faithful servant.

The Lord God took Abram outside and said,
  "Look up at the sky and count the stars, if you can.
Just so," he added, "shall your descendants be."
Abram put his faith in the LORD,
  who credited it to him as an act of righteousness.

He then said to him,
  "I am the LORD who brought you from Ur of the Chaldeans
  to give you this land as a possession."
"O Lord GOD, " he asked,
  "how am I to know that I shall possess it?"
He answered him,
  "Bring me a three-year-old heifer, a three-year-old she-goat,
  a three-year-old ram, a turtledove, and a young pigeon."
Abram brought him all these, split them in two,
  and placed each half opposite the other;
  but the birds he did not cut up.
Birds of prey swooped down on the carcasses,
  but Abram stayed with them.
As the sun was about to set, a trance fell upon Abram,
  and a deep, terrifying darkness enveloped him.

When the sun had set and it was dark,
  there appeared a smoking fire pot and a flaming torch,
  which passed between those pieces.
It was on that occasion that the LORD made a covenant with Abram,
  saying: "To your descendants I give this land,
  from the Wadi of Egypt to the Great River, the Euphrates." ✛

  Psalm 27:1, 7-8, 8-9, 13-14
R. (1a) **The Lord is my light and my salvation.**
The LORD is my light and my salvation;
  whom should I fear?
The LORD is my life's refuge;
  of whom should I be afraid? **R.**
Hear, O LORD, the sound of my call;
  have pity on me, and answer me.
Of you my heart speaks; you my glance seeks. **R.**
Your presence, O LORD, I seek.
  Hide not your face from me;

do not in anger repel your servant.
You are my helper: cast me not off. **R.**
I believe that I shall see the bounty of the LORD
in the land of the living.
Wait for the LORD with courage;
be stouthearted, and wait for the Lord. **R.**

† *Philippians 3:17—4:1 (or Philippians 3:20—4:1)*
Christ will change our lowly body to conform with his glorified body.

Join with others in being imitators of me, brothers and sisters,
and observe those who thus conduct themselves
according to the model you have in us.
For many, as I have often told you
and now tell you even in tears,
conduct themselves as enemies of the cross of Christ.
Their end is destruction.
Their God is their stomach;
their glory is in their "shame."
Their minds are occupied with earthly things.
But our citizenship is in heaven,
and from it we also await a savior, the Lord Jesus Christ.
He will change our lowly body
to conform with his glorified body
by the power that enables him also
to bring all things into subjection to himself.

Therefore, my brothers and sisters,
whom I love and long for, my joy and crown,
in this way stand firm in the Lord. ✛

See Matthew 17:5
R. Glory and praise to you, Lord Jesus Christ!
From the shining cloud the Father's voice is heard:
This is my beloved Son, hear him. **R.**

† *Luke 9:28b-36*
*While he was praying his face changed in appearance
and his clothing became dazzling white.*

Jesus took Peter, John, and James
and went up the mountain to pray.
While he was praying his face changed in appearance
and his clothing became dazzling white.
And behold, two men were conversing with him, Moses and Elijah,
who appeared in glory and spoke of his exodus
that he was going to accomplish in Jerusalem.

Peter and his companions had been overcome by sleep,
  but becoming fully awake,
  they saw his glory and the two men standing with him.

As they were about to part from him, Peter said to Jesus,
  "Master, it is good that we are here;
  let us make three tents,
  one for you, one for Moses, and one for Elijah."
But he did not know what he was saying.
While he was still speaking,
  a cloud came and cast a shadow over them,
  and they became frightened when they entered the cloud.
Then from the cloud came a voice that said,
  "This is my chosen Son; listen to him."
After the voice had spoken, Jesus was found alone.
They fell silent and did not at that time
  tell anyone what they had seen. ✛

MONDAY, MARCH 14
LENTEN WEEKDAY

✝ Daniel 9:4b-10
We have sinned, been wicked and done evil.

"LORD, great and awesome God,
  you who keep your merciful covenant toward those who love you
  and observe your commandments!
We have sinned, been wicked and done evil;
  we have rebelled and departed from your commandments and
    your laws.
We have not obeyed your servants the prophets,
  who spoke in your name to our kings, our princes,
  our fathers, and all the people of the land.
Justice, O Lord, is on your side;
  we are shamefaced even to this day:
  we, the men of Judah, the residents of Jerusalem,
  and all Israel, near and far,
  in all the countries to which you have scattered them
  because of their treachery toward you.
O LORD, we are shamefaced, like our kings, our princes, and our
    fathers,
  for having sinned against you.
But yours, O Lord, our God, are compassion and forgiveness!
Yet we rebelled against you
  and paid no heed to your command, O LORD, our God,
  to live by the law you gave us through your servants the prophets." ✛

Psalm 79:8, 9, 11 and 13

R. (see 103:10a) **Lord, do not deal with us according to our sins.**

Remember not against us the iniquities of the past;
   may your compassion quickly come to us,
   for we are brought very low. **R.**

Help us, O God our savior,
   because of the glory of your name;

Deliver us and pardon our sins
   for your name's sake. **R.**

Let the prisoners' sighing come before you;
   with your great power free those doomed to death.

Then we, your people and the sheep of your pasture,
   will give thanks to you forever;
   through all generations we will declare your praise. **R.**

See John 6:63c, 68c

R. Glory and praise to you, Lord Jesus Christ!

Your words, Lord, are Spirit and life;
you have the words of everlasting life. **R.**

† *Luke 6:36-38*
Forgive and you will be forgiven.

Jesus said to his disciples:
   "Be merciful, just as your Father is merciful.

"Stop judging and you will not be judged.
Stop condemning and you will not be condemned.
Forgive and you will be forgiven.
Give and gifts will be given to you;
   a good measure, packed together, shaken down, and overflowing,
   will be poured into your lap.
For the measure with which you measure
   will in return be measured out to you." ✛

TUESDAY, MARCH 15
LENTEN WEEKDAY

† *Isaiah 1:10, 16-20*
Learn to do good; make justice your aim.

Hear the word of the LORD,
   princes of Sodom!
Listen to the instruction of our God,
   people of Gomorrah!

   Wash yourselves clean!

Put away your misdeeds from before my eyes;
   cease doing evil; learn to do good.
Make justice your aim: redress the wronged,
   hear the orphan's plea, defend the widow.

Come now, let us set things right,
   says the LORD:
Though your sins be like scarlet,
   they may become white as snow;
Though they be crimson red,
   they may become white as wool.
If you are willing, and obey,
   you shall eat the good things of the land;
But if you refuse and resist,
   the sword shall consume you:
   for the mouth of the LORD has spoken! ✛

   Psalm 50:8-9, 16bc-17, 21 and 23

R. (23b) **To the upright I will show the saving power of God.**
"Not for your sacrifices do I rebuke you,
   for your burnt offerings are before me always.
I take from your house no bullock,
   no goats out of your fold." **R.**
"Why do you recite my statutes,
   and profess my covenant with your mouth,
Though you hate discipline
   and cast my words behind you?" **R.**
"When you do these things, shall I be deaf to it?
   Or do you think that I am like yourself?
   I will correct you by drawing them up before your eyes.
He that offers praise as a sacrifice glorifies me;
   and to him that goes the right way I will show the salvation of
      God." **R.**

   Ezekiel 18:31

R. Glory and praise to you, Lord Jesus Christ!
Cast away from you all the crimes you have committed, says the Lord,
and make for yourselves a new heart and a new spirit. **R.**

✝ *Matthew 23:1-12*
They preach but they do not practice.

Jesus spoke to the crowds and to his disciples, saying,
   "The scribes and the Pharisees
   have taken their seat on the chair of Moses.
Therefore, do and observe all things whatsoever they tell you,
   but do not follow their example.

For they preach but they do not practice.
They tie up heavy burdens hard to carry
    and lay them on people's shoulders,
    but they will not lift a finger to move them.
All their works are performed to be seen.
They widen their phylacteries and lengthen their tassels.
They love places of honor at banquets, seats of honor in synagogues,
    greetings in marketplaces, and the salutation 'Rabbi.'
As for you, do not be called 'Rabbi.'
You have but one teacher, and you are all brothers.
Call no one on earth your father;
    you have but one Father in heaven.
Do not be called 'Master';
    you have but one master, the Christ.
The greatest among you must be your servant.
Whoever exalts himself will be humbled;
    but whoever humbles himself will be exalted." ✛

WEDNESDAY, MARCH 16
LENTEN WEEKDAY

† *Jeremiah 18:18-20*
Come, let us persecute him.

The people of Judah and the citizens of Jerusalem said,
    "Come, let us contrive a plot against Jeremiah.
It will not mean the loss of instruction from the priests,
    nor of counsel from the wise, nor of messages from the prophets.
And so, let us destroy him by his own tongue;
    let us carefully note his every word."

Heed me, O LORD,
    and listen to what my adversaries say.
Must good be repaid with evil
    that they should dig a pit to take my life?
Remember that I stood before you
    to speak in their behalf,
    to turn away your wrath from them. ✛

Psalm 31:5-6, 14, 15-16
R. (17b) **Save me, O Lord, in your kindness.**
You will free me from the snare they set for me,
    for you are my refuge.
Into your hands I commend my spirit;
    you will redeem me, O LORD, O faithful God. **R.**
I hear the whispers of the crowd, that frighten me from every side,
    as they consult together against me, plotting to take my life. **R.**

But my trust is in you, O LORD;
  I say, "You are my God."
In your hands is my destiny; rescue me
  from the clutches of my enemies and my persecutors. **R.**

John 8:12
R. Glory and praise to you, Lord Jesus Christ!
I am the light of the world, says the Lord;
whoever follows me will have the light of life. **R.**

† *Matthew 20:17-28*
They will condemn the Son of Man to death.

As Jesus was going up to Jerusalem,
  he took the Twelve disciples aside by themselves,
  and said to them on the way,
  "Behold, we are going up to Jerusalem,
  and the Son of Man will be handed over to the chief priests
  and the scribes,
  and they will condemn him to death,
  and hand him over to the Gentiles
  to be mocked and scourged and crucified,
  and he will be raised on the third day."

Then the mother of the sons of Zebedee approached Jesus with her
    sons
  and did him homage, wishing to ask him for something.
He said to her, "What do you wish?"
She answered him,
  "Command that these two sons of mine sit,
  one at your right and the other at your left, in your kingdom."
Jesus said in reply,
  "You do not know what you are asking.
Can you drink the chalice that I am going to drink?"
They said to him, "We can."
He replied,
  "My chalice you will indeed drink,
  but to sit at my right and at my left,
  this is not mine to give
  but is for those for whom it has been prepared by my Father."
When the ten heard this,
  they became indignant at the two brothers.
But Jesus summoned them and said,
  "You know that the rulers of the Gentiles lord it over them,
  and the great ones make their authority over them felt.
But it shall not be so among you.

Rather, whoever wishes to be great among you shall be your servant;
   whoever wishes to be first among you shall be your slave.
Just so, the Son of Man did not come to be served but to serve
   and to give his life as a ransom for many." ✛

THURSDAY, MARCH 17
LENTEN WEEKDAY, ST. PATRICK

† *Jeremiah 17:5-10*
A curse on those who trust in mortals;
a blessing on those who trust in the Lord God.

Thus says the LORD:
Cursed is the man who trusts in human beings,
   who seeks his strength in flesh,
   whose heart turns away from the LORD.
He is like a barren bush in the desert
   that enjoys no change of season,
But stands in a lava waste,
   a salt and empty earth.
Blessed is the man who trusts in the LORD,
   whose hope is the LORD.
He is like a tree planted beside the waters
   that stretches out its roots to the stream:
It fears not the heat when it comes,
   its leaves stay green;
In the year of drought it shows no distress,
   but still bears fruit.
More tortuous than all else is the human heart,
   beyond remedy; who can understand it?
I, the LORD, alone probe the mind
   and test the heart,
To reward everyone according to his ways,
   according to the merit of his deeds. ✛

Psalm 1:1-2, 3, 4 and 6
R. (40:5a) **Blessed are they who hope in the Lord.**
Blessed the man who follows not
   the counsel of the wicked
Nor walks in the way of sinners,
   nor sits in the company of the insolent,
But delights in the law of the LORD
   and meditates on his law day and night. **R.**
He is like a tree
   planted near running water,
That yields its fruit in due season,

and whose leaves never fade.
  Whatever he does, prospers. **R.**
Not so, the wicked, not so;
  they are like chaff which the wind drives away.
For the LORD watches over the way of the just,
  but the way of the wicked vanishes. **R.**

See Luke 8:15
R. Glory and praise to you, Lord Jesus Christ!
Blessed are they who have kept the word with a generous heart
and yield a harvest through perseverance. **R.**

† *Luke 16:19-31*
Good things came to you and bad things to Lazarus;
now he is comforted while you are in agony.

Jesus said to the Pharisees:
"There was a rich man who dressed in purple garments and fine linen
  and dined sumptuously each day.
And lying at his door was a poor man named Lazarus, covered with
    sores,
  who would gladly have eaten his fill of the scraps
  that fell from the rich man's table.
Dogs even used to come and lick his sores.
When the poor man died,
  he was carried away by angels to the bosom of Abraham.
The rich man also died and was buried,
  and from the netherworld, where he was in torment,
  he raised his eyes and saw Abraham far off
  and Lazarus at his side.
And he cried out, 'Father Abraham, have pity on me.
Send Lazarus to dip the tip of his finger in water and cool my
    tongue,
  for I am suffering torment in these flames.'
Abraham replied, 'My child,
  remember that you received what was good during your lifetime
  while Lazarus likewise received what was bad;
  but now he is comforted here, whereas you are tormented.
Moreover, between us and you a great chasm is established
  to prevent anyone from crossing
  who might wish to go from our side to yours
  or from your side to ours.'
He said, 'Then I beg you, father, send him
  to my father's house,
  for I have five brothers, so that he may warn them,
  lest they too come to this place of torment.'

But Abraham replied, 'They have Moses and the prophets.
Let them listen to them.'
He said, 'Oh no, father Abraham,
  but if someone from the dead goes to them, they will repent.'
Then Abraham said,
  'If they will not listen to Moses and the prophets,
  neither will they be persuaded
  if someone should rise from the dead.'" ✛

FRIDAY, MARCH 18
LENTEN WEEKDAY, ST. CYRIL OF JERUSALEM

† *Genesis 37:3-4, 12-13a, 17b-28a*
Here comes the man of dreams; let us kill him.

Israel loved Joseph best of all his sons,
  for he was the child of his old age;
  and he had made him a long tunic.
When his brothers saw that their father loved him best of all his
    sons,
  they hated him so much that they would not even greet him.

One day, when his brothers had gone
  to pasture their father's flocks at Shechem,
  Israel said to Joseph,
  "Your brothers, you know, are tending our flocks at Shechem.
Get ready; I will send you to them."

So Joseph went after his brothers and caught up with them in Dothan.
They noticed him from a distance,
  and before he came up to them, they plotted to kill him.
They said to one another: "Here comes that master dreamer!
Come on, let us kill him and throw him into one of the cisterns here;
  we could say that a wild beast devoured him.
We shall then see what comes of his dreams."

When Reuben heard this,
  he tried to save him from their hands, saying,
  "We must not take his life.
Instead of shedding blood," he continued,
  "just throw him into that cistern there in the desert;
  but do not kill him outright."
His purpose was to rescue him from their hands
  and return him to his father.
So when Joseph came up to them,
  they stripped him of the long tunic he had on;

then they took him and threw him into the cistern,
which was empty and dry.

They then sat down to their meal.
Looking up, they saw a caravan of Ishmaelites coming from Gilead,
   their camels laden with gum, balm and resin
   to be taken down to Egypt.
Judah said to his brothers:
   "What is to be gained by killing our brother and concealing his
      blood?
Rather, let us sell him to these Ishmaelites,
   instead of doing away with him ourselves.
After all, he is our brother, our own flesh."
His brothers agreed.
They sold Joseph to the Ishmaelites for twenty pieces of silver. ✛

Psalm 105:16-17, 18-19, 20-21

R. (5a) Remember the marvels the Lord has done.
When the LORD called down a famine on the land
   and ruined the crop that sustained them,
He sent a man before them,
   Joseph, sold as a slave. **R.**
They had weighed him down with fetters,
   and he was bound with chains,
Till his prediction came to pass
   and the word of the LORD proved him true. **R.**
The king sent and released him,
   the ruler of the peoples set him free.
He made him lord of his house
   and ruler of all his possessions. **R.**

John 3:16

R. Glory and praise to you, Lord Jesus Christ!
God so loved the world that he gave his only-begotten Son;
so that everyone who believes in him might have eternal life. **R.**

✝ *Matthew 21:33-43, 45-46*
This is the heir; let us kill him.

Jesus said to the chief priests and the elders of the people:
"Hear another parable.
There was a landowner who planted a vineyard,
   put a hedge around it,
   dug a wine press in it, and built a tower.
Then he leased it to tenants and went on a journey.
When vintage time drew near,
   he sent his servants to the tenants to obtain his produce.

But the tenants seized the servants and one they beat,
   another they killed, and a third they stoned.
Again he sent other servants, more numerous than the first ones,
   but they treated them in the same way.
Finally, he sent his son to them,
   thinking, 'They will respect my son.'
But when the tenants saw the son, they said to one another,
   'This is the heir.
Come, let us kill him and acquire his inheritance.'
They seized him, threw him out of the vineyard, and killed him.
What will the owner of the vineyard do to those tenants when he
     comes?"
They answered him,
   "He will put those wretched men to a wretched death
   and lease his vineyard to other tenants
   who will give him the produce at the proper times."
Jesus said to them, "Did you never read in the Scriptures:

The stone that the builders rejected
   has become the cornerstone;
by the Lord has this been done,
   and it is wonderful in our eyes?

Therefore, I say to you,
   the Kingdom of God will be taken away from you
   and given to a people that will produce its fruit."
When the chief priests and the Pharisees heard his parables,
   they knew that he was speaking about them.
And although they were attempting to arrest him,
   they feared the crowds, for they regarded him as a prophet. ✛

SATURDAY, MARCH 19
St. Joseph, Spouse of the Blessed Virgin Mary
† 2 Samuel 7:4-5a, 12-14a, 16
The Lord God will give him the throne of David, his father (Luke 1:32).

The Lord spoke to Nathan and said:
"Go, tell my servant David,
   'When your time comes and you rest with your ancestors,
   I will raise up your heir after you, sprung from your loins,
   and I will make his kingdom firm.
It is he who shall build a house for my name.
And I will make his royal throne firm forever.
I will be a father to him,
   and he shall be a son to me.

Your house and your kingdom shall endure forever before me;
   your throne shall stand firm forever.'" ✝

   Psalm 89:2-3, 4-5, 27 and 29
R. (37) The son of David will live for ever.
The promises of the LORD I will sing forever;
   through all generations my mouth shall proclaim your faithfulness,
For you have said, "My kindness is established forever";
   in heaven you have confirmed your faithfulness. **R.**
"I have made a covenant with my chosen one,
   I have sworn to David my servant:
Forever will I confirm your posterity
   and establish your throne for all generations." **R.**
"He shall say of me, 'You are my father,
   my God, the Rock, my savior.'
Forever I will maintain my kindness toward him,
   and my covenant with him stands firm." **R.**

      ✝ Romans 4:13, 16-18, 22
      Abraham believed, hoping against hope.

Brothers and sisters:
It was not through the law
   that the promise was made to Abraham and his descendants
   that he would inherit the world,
   but through the righteousness that comes from faith.
For this reason, it depends on faith,
   so that it may be a gift,
   and the promise may be guaranteed to all his descendants,
   not to those who only adhere to the law
   but to those who follow the faith of Abraham,
   who is the father of all of us, as it is written,
   I have made you father of many nations.
He is our father in the sight of God,
   in whom he believed, who gives life to the dead
   and calls into being what does not exist.
He believed, hoping against hope,
   that he would become *the father of many nations,*
   according to what was said, *Thus shall your descendants be.*
That is why *it was credited to him as righteousness.* ✝

   Psalm 84:5
R. Glory and praise to you, Lord Jesus Christ!
Blessed are those who dwell in your house, O Lord;
they never cease to praise you. **R.**

✝Matthew 1:16, 18-21, 24a (or Luke 2:41-51a)
Joseph did as the angel of the Lord had commanded him.

Jacob was the father of Joseph, the husband of Mary.
Of her was born Jesus who is called the Christ.

Now this is how the birth of Jesus Christ came about.
When his mother Mary was betrothed to Joseph,
   but before they lived together,
   she was found with child through the Holy Spirit.
Joseph her husband, since he was a righteous man,
   yet unwilling to expose her to shame,
   decided to divorce her quietly.
Such was his intention when, behold,
   the angel of the Lord appeared to him in a dream and said,
   "Joseph, son of David,
   do not be afraid to take Mary your wife into your home.
For it is through the Holy Spirit
   that this child has been conceived in her.
She will bear a son and you are to name him Jesus,
   because he will save his people from their sins."
When Joseph awoke,
   he did as the angel of the Lord had commanded him
   and took his wife into his home. ✛

SUNDAY, MARCH 20
THIRD SUNDAY OF LENT

✝Exodus 3:1-8a, 13-15 (Scrutiny: Exodus 17:3-7)
"I AM" sent me to you.

Moses was tending the flock of his father-in-law Jethro,
   the priest of Midian.
Leading the flock across the desert, he came to Horeb,
   the mountain of God.
There an angel of the LORD appeared to Moses in fire
   flaming out of a bush.
As he looked on, he was surprised to see that the bush,
   though on fire, was not consumed.
So Moses decided,
   "I must go over to look at this remarkable sight,
   and see why the bush is not burned."

When the LORD saw him coming over to look at it more closely,
   God called out to him from the bush, "Moses! Moses!"
He answered, "Here I am."
God said, "Come no nearer!

Remove the sandals from your feet,
  for the place where you stand is holy ground.
I am the God of your fathers, " he continued,
  "the God of Abraham, the God of Isaac, the God of Jacob."
Moses hid his face, for he was afraid to look at God.
But the LORD said,
  "I have witnessed the affliction of my people in Egypt
  and have heard their cry of complaint against their slave drivers,
  so I know well what they are suffering.
Therefore I have come down to rescue them
  from the hands of the Egyptians
  and lead them out of that land into a good and spacious land,
  a land flowing with milk and honey."

Moses said to God, "But when I go to the Israelites
  and say to them, 'The God of your fathers has sent me to you,'
  if they ask me, 'What is his name?' what am I to tell them?"
God replied, "I am who am."
Then he added, "This is what you shall tell the Israelites:
  I AM sent me to you."

God spoke further to Moses, "Thus shall you say to the Israelites:
  The LORD, the God of your fathers,
  the God of Abraham, the God of Isaac, the God of Jacob,
  has sent me to you.

"This is my name forever;
  thus am I to be remembered through all generations." ✛

Psalm 103:1-2, 3-4, 6-7, 8, 11 (Scrutiny: Psalm 95:1-2, 6-7, 7-9)
R. (8a) **The Lord is kind and merciful.**
Bless the LORD, O my soul;
  and all my being, bless his holy name.
Bless the LORD, O my soul,
  and forget not all his benefits. **R.**
He pardons all your iniquities,
  heals all your ills,
He redeems your life from destruction,
  crowns you with kindness and compassion. **R.**
The LORD secures justice
  and the rights of all the oppressed.
He has made known his ways to Moses,
  and his deeds to the children of Israel. **R.**

Merciful and gracious is the LORD,
  slow to anger and abounding in kindness.
For as the heavens are high above the earth,
  so surpassing is his kindness toward those who fear him. **R.**

† *1 Corinthians 10:1-6, 10-12 (Scrutiny: Romans 5:1-2, 5-8)*
The life of the people with Moses in the desert
was written down as a warning to us.

I do not want you to be unaware, brothers and sisters,
  that our ancestors were all under the cloud
  and all passed through the sea,
  and all of them were baptized into Moses
  in the cloud and in the sea.
All ate the same spiritual food,
  and all drank the same spiritual drink,
  for they drank from a spiritual rock that followed them,
  and the rock was the Christ.
Yet God was not pleased with most of them,
  for they were struck down in the desert.

These things happened as examples for us,
  so that we might not desire evil things, as they did.
Do not grumble as some of them did,
  and suffered death by the destroyer.
These things happened to them as an example,
  and they have been written down as a warning to us,
  upon whom the end of the ages has come.
Therefore, whoever thinks he is standing secure
  should take care not to fall. ✛

  Matthew 4:17
R. Glory and praise to you, Lord Jesus Christ!
Repent, says the Lord;
the kingdom of heaven is at hand. **R.**

† *Luke 13:1-9*
(Scrutiny: John 4:5-42 or 4:5-15, 19b-26, 39a, 40-42)
If you do not repent, you will all perish as they did.

Some people told Jesus about the Galileans
  whose blood Pilate had mingled with the blood of their sacrifices.
Jesus said to them in reply,
  "Do you think that because these Galileans suffered in this way
  they were greater sinners than all other Galileans?
By no means!
But I tell you, if you do not repent,
  you will all perish as they did!

Or those eighteen people who were killed
  when the tower at Siloam fell on them—
  do you think they were more guilty
  than everyone else who lived in Jerusalem?
By no means!
But I tell you, if you do not repent,
  you will all perish as they did!"

And he told them this parable:
  "There once was a person who had a fig tree planted in his orchard,
  and when he came in search of fruit on it but found none,
  he said to the gardener,
  'For three years now I have come in search of fruit on this fig tree
  but have found none.
So cut it down.
Why should it exhaust the soil?'

He said to him in reply,
  'Sir, leave it for this year also,
  and I shall cultivate the ground around it and fertilize it;
  it may bear fruit in the future.
If not you can cut it down.'" ✝

MONDAY, MARCH 21
LENTEN WEEKDAY

✝ 2 Kings 5:1-15ab *(or any day this week, Exodus 17:1-7)*
There were many people with leprosy in Israel,
but none were made clean, except Naaman the Syrian (Luke 4:27).

Naaman, the army commander of the king of Aram,
  was highly esteemed and respected by his master,
  for through him the LORD had brought victory to Aram.
But valiant as he was, the man was a leper.
Now the Arameans had captured in a raid on the land of Israel
  a little girl, who became the servant of Naaman's wife.
"If only my master would present himself to the prophet in Samaria,"
  she said to her mistress, "he would cure him of his leprosy."
Naaman went and told his lord
  just what the slave girl from the land of Israel had said.
"Go," said the king of Aram.
"I will send along a letter to the king of Israel."
So Naaman set out, taking along ten silver talents,
  six thousand gold pieces, and ten festal garments.
To the king of Israel he brought the letter, which read:
  "With this letter I am sending my servant Naaman to you,
  that you may cure him of his leprosy."

When he read the letter,
   the king of Israel tore his garments and exclaimed:
   "Am I a god with power over life and death,
   that this man should send someone to me to be cured of leprosy?
Take note! You can see he is only looking for a quarrel with me!"
When Elisha, the man of God,
   heard that the king of Israel had torn his garments,
   he sent word to the king:
   "Why have you torn your garments?
Let him come to me and find out
   that there is a prophet in Israel."

Naaman came with his horses and chariots
   and stopped at the door of Elisha's house.
The prophet sent him the message:
   "Go and wash seven times in the Jordan,
   and your flesh will heal, and you will be clean."
But Naaman went away angry, saying,
   "I thought that he would surely come out and stand there
   to invoke the LORD his God,
   and would move his hand over the spot,
   and thus cure the leprosy.
Are not the rivers of Damascus, the Abana and the Pharpar,
   better than all the waters of Israel?
Could I not wash in them and be cleansed?"
With this, he turned about in anger and left.

But his servants came up and reasoned with him.
"My father," they said,
   "if the prophet had told you to do something extraordinary,
   would you not have done it?
All the more now, since he said to you,
   'Wash and be clean,' should you do as he said."
So Naaman went down and plunged into the Jordan seven times
   at the word of the man of God.
His flesh became again like the flesh of a little child, and he was
     clean.

He returned with his whole retinue to the man of God.
On his arrival he stood before him and said,
   "Now I know that there is no God in all the earth, except in
     Israel." ✤

Psalms 42:2, 3; 43:3, 4 (or Psalm 95:1-2, 6-7ab, 7c-9)

R. (see 42:3) **Athirst is my soul for the living God. When shall I go and behold the face of God?**

As the hind longs for the running waters,
  so my soul longs for you, O God. **R.**
Athirst is my soul for God, the living God.
  When shall I go and behold the face of God? **R.**
Send forth your light and your fidelity;
  they shall lead me on
And bring me to your holy mountain,
  to your dwelling-place. **R.**
Then will I go in to the altar of God,
  the God of my gladness and joy;
Then will I give you thanks upon the harp,
  O God, my God! **R.**

See Psalm 130:5, 7

R. Glory and praise to you, Lord Jesus Christ!
I hope in the Lord, I trust in his word;
with him there is kindness and plenteous redemption. **R.**

> **† Luke 4:24-30** *(or any day this week, John 4:5-42)*
> *Like Elijah and Elisha, Jesus was sent not only to the Jews.*

Jesus said to the people in the synagogue at Nazareth:
"Amen, I say to you,
  no prophet is accepted in his own native place.
Indeed, I tell you, there were many widows in Israel
  in the days of Elijah
    when the sky was closed for three and a half years
    and a severe famine spread over the entire land.
It was to none of these that Elijah was sent,
  but only to a widow in Zarephath in the land of Sidon.
Again, there were many lepers in Israel
  during the time of Elisha the prophet;
  yet not one of them was cleansed, but only Naaman the Syrian."
When the people in the synagogue heard this,
  they were all filled with fury.
They rose up, drove him out of the town,
  and led him to the brow of the hill
  on which their town had been built,
  to hurl him down headlong.
But he passed through the midst of them and went away. **✝**

TUESDAY, MARCH 22
LENTEN WEEKDAY

† *Daniel 3:25, 34-43*
We ask you to receive us with humble and contrite hearts.

Azariah stood up in the fire and prayed aloud:

"For your name's sake, O Lord, do not deliver us up forever,
    or make void your covenant.
Do not take away your mercy from us,
    for the sake of Abraham, your beloved,
    Isaac your servant, and Israel your holy one,
To whom you promised to multiply their offspring
    like the stars of heaven,
    or the sand on the shore of the sea.
For we are reduced, O Lord, beyond any other nation,
    brought low everywhere in the world this day
    because of our sins.
We have in our day no prince, prophet, or leader,
    no burnt offering, sacrifice, oblation, or incense,
    no place to offer first fruits, to find favor with you.
But with contrite heart and humble spirit
    let us be received;
As though it were burnt offerings of rams and bullocks,
    or thousands of fat lambs,
So let our sacrifice be in your presence today
    as we follow you unreservedly;
    for those who trust in you cannot be put to shame.
And now we follow you with our whole heart,
    we fear you and we pray to you.
Do not let us be put to shame,
    but deal with us in your kindness and great mercy.
Deliver us by your wonders,
    and bring glory to your name, O Lord." ✝

Psalm 25:4-5ab, 6 and 7bc, 8-9
R. (6a) **Remember your mercies, O Lord.**
Your ways, O LORD, make known to me;
    teach me your paths,
Guide me in your truth and teach me,
    for you are God my savior. **R.**
Remember that your compassion, O LORD,
    and your kindness are from of old.
In your kindness remember me,
    because of your goodness, O LORD. **R.**

Good and upright is the LORD;
　　thus he shows sinners the way.
He guides the humble to justice,
　　he teaches the humble his way. **R.**

　　Joel 2:12-13
R. Glory and praise to you, Lord Jesus Christ!
Even now, says the LORD,
return to me with your whole heart;
for I am gracious and merciful.

† *Matthew 18:21-35*
Unless each of you forgives your brother and sister, the Father will not forgive you.

Peter approached Jesus and asked him,
　　"Lord, if my brother sins against me,
　　how often must I forgive him?
As many as seven times?"
Jesus answered, "I say to you, not seven times but seventy-seven
　　　times.
That is why the Kingdom of heaven may be likened to a king
　　who decided to settle accounts with his servants.
When he began the accounting,
　　a debtor was brought before him who owed him a huge amount.
Since he had no way of paying it back,
　　his master ordered him to be sold,
　　along with his wife, his children, and all his property,
　　in payment of the debt.
At that, the servant fell down, did him homage, and said,
　　'Be patient with me, and I will pay you back in full.'
Moved with compassion the master of that servant
　　let him go and forgave him the loan.
When that servant had left, he found one of his fellow servants
　　who owed him a much smaller amount.
He seized him and started to choke him, demanding,
　　'Pay back what you owe.'
Falling to his knees, his fellow servant begged him,
　　'Be patient with me, and I will pay you back.'
But he refused.
Instead, he had him put in prison
　　until he paid back the debt.
Now when his fellow servants saw what had happened,
　　they were deeply disturbed, and went to their master
　　and reported the whole affair.
His master summoned him and said to him, 'You wicked servant!
I forgave you your entire debt because you begged me to.

Should you not have had pity on your fellow servant,
 as I had pity on you?'
Then in anger his master handed him over to the torturers
 until he should pay back the whole debt.
So will my heavenly Father do to you,
 unless each of you forgives your brother from your heart." ✝

WEDNESDAY, MARCH 23
Lenten Weekday, St. Turibius of Mogrovejo

† *Deuteronomy 4:1, 5-9*
Keep the commandments and your work will be complete.

Moses spoke to the people and said:
"Now, Israel, hear the statutes and decrees
 which I am teaching you to observe,
 that you may live, and may enter in and take possession of the
 land
 which the Lord, the God of your fathers, is giving you.
Therefore, I teach you the statutes and decrees
 as the Lord, my God, has commanded me,
 that you may observe them in the land you are entering to occupy.
Observe them carefully,
 for thus will you give evidence
 of your wisdom and intelligence to the nations,
 who will hear of all these statutes and say,
 'This great nation is truly a wise and intelligent people.'
For what great nation is there
 that has gods so close to it as the Lord, our God, is to us
 whenever we call upon him?
Or what great nation has statutes and decrees
 that are as just as this whole law
 which I am setting before you today?

"However, take care and be earnestly on your guard
 not to forget the things which your own eyes have seen,
 nor let them slip from your memory as long as you live,
 but teach them to your children and to your children's children." ✝

Psalm 147:12-13, 15-16, 19-20
R. (12a) **Praise the Lord, Jerusalem.**
Glorify the Lord, O Jerusalem;
 praise your God, O Zion.
For he has strengthened the bars of your gates;
 he has blessed your children within you. **R.**
He sends forth his command to the earth;
 swiftly runs his word!

He spreads snow like wool;
   frost he strews like ashes. **R.**
He has proclaimed his word to Jacob,
   his statutes and his ordinances to Israel.
He has not done thus for any other nation;
   his ordinances he has not made known to them. **R.**

   See John 6:63c, 68c
R. Glory and praise to you, Lord Jesus Christ!
Your words, Lord, are Spirit and life;
you have the words of everlasting life. **R.**

† *Matthew 5:17-19*
Whoever keeps and teaches the law will be called great.

Jesus said to his disciples:
"Do not think that I have come to abolish the law or the prophets.
I have come not to abolish but to fulfill.
Amen, I say to you, until heaven and earth pass away,
   not the smallest letter or the smallest part of a letter
   will pass from the law,
   until all things have taken place.
Therefore, whoever breaks one of the least of these commandments
   and teaches others to do so
   will be called least in the Kingdom of heaven.
But whoever obeys and teaches these commandments
   will be called greatest in the Kingdom of heaven." ✦

THURSDAY, MARCH 24
LENTEN WEEKDAY

† *Jeremiah 7:23-28*
This is the nation that will not listen to the voice of the LORD God.

Thus says the LORD:
   This is what I commanded my people:
      Listen to my voice;
      then I will be your God and you shall be my people.
   Walk in all the ways that I command you,
      so that you may prosper.

But they obeyed not, nor did they pay heed.
They walked in the hardness of their evil hearts
   and turned their backs, not their faces, to me.
From the day that your fathers left the land of Egypt even to this day,
   I have sent you untiringly all my servants the prophets.
Yet they have not obeyed me nor paid heed;
   they have stiffened their necks and done worse than their fathers.

When you speak all these words to them,
    they will not listen to you either;
    when you call to them, they will not answer you.
Say to them:
    This is the nation that does not listen
    to the voice of the LORD, its God,
    or take correction.
Faithfulness has disappeared;
    the word itself is banished from their speech. ✛

Psalm 95:1b-2, 6-7ab, 7c-9
R. (8) **If today you hear his voice, harden not your hearts.**
Come, let us sing joyfully to the LORD;
    let us acclaim the Rock of our salvation.
Let us come into his presence with thanksgiving;
    let us joyfully sing psalms to him. **R.**
Come, let us bow down in worship;
    let us kneel before the LORD who made us.
For he is our God,
    and we are the people he shepherds, the flock he guides. **R.**
Oh, that today you would hear his voice:
    "Harden not your hearts as at Meribah,
    as in the day of Massah in the desert,
Where your fathers tempted me;
    they tested me though they had seen my works." **R.**

Joel 2:12-13
R. Glory and praise to you, Lord Jesus Christ!
Even now, says the LORD,
return to me with your whole heart,
for I am gracious and merciful. **R.**

† *Luke 11:14-23*
Whoever is not with me is against me.

Jesus was driving out a demon that was mute,
    and when the demon had gone out,
    the mute man spoke and the crowds were amazed.
Some of them said, "By the power of Beelzebul, the prince of demons,
    he drives out demons."
Others, to test him, asked him for a sign from heaven.
But he knew their thoughts and said to them,
    "Every kingdom divided against itself will be laid waste
    and house will fall against house.
And if Satan is divided against himself,
    how will his kingdom stand?
For you say that it is by Beelzebul that I drive out demons.

If I, then, drive out demons by Beelzebul,
  by whom do your own people drive them out?
Therefore they will be your judges.
But if it is by the finger of God that I drive out demons,
  then the Kingdom of God has come upon you.
When a strong man fully armed guards his palace,
  his possessions are safe.
But when one stronger than he attacks and overcomes him,
    he takes away the armor on which he relied
    and distributes the spoils.
Whoever is not with me is against me,
  and whoever does not gather with me scatters." ✛

FRIDAY, MARCH 25
THE ANNUNCIATION OF THE LORD

† *Isaiah 7:10-14; 8:10*
Behold, the virgin shall conceive.

The LORD spoke to Ahaz, saying:
  Ask for a sign from the LORD, your God;
  let it be deep as the nether world, or high as the sky!
But Ahaz answered,
  "I will not ask! I will not tempt the LORD!"

Then Isaiah said:
  Listen, O house of David!
Is it not enough for you to weary people,
  must you also weary my God?
Therefore the Lord himself will give you this sign:
  the virgin shall be with child, and bear a son,
  and shall name him Emmanuel,
  which means "God is with us!" ✛

Psalm 40:7-8a, 8b-9, 10, 11

R. (8a and 9a) **Here I am, Lord; I come to do your will.**
Sacrifice or oblation you wished not,
  but ears open to obedience you gave me.
Holocausts or sin-offerings you sought not;
  then said I, "Behold I come." **R.**
"In the written scroll it is prescribed for me,
To do your will, O my God, is my delight,
  and your law is within my heart!" **R.**
I announced your justice in the vast assembly;
  I did not restrain my lips, as you, O LORD, know. **R.**
Your justice I kept not hid within my heart;

your faithfulness and your salvation I have spoken of;
I have made no secret of your kindness and your truth
in the vast assembly. **R.**

† *Hebrews 10:4-10*
As is written of me in the scroll, behold, I come to do your will, O God.

Brothers and sisters:
It is impossible that the blood of bulls and goats
  take away sins.
For this reason, when Christ came into the world, he said:
  "Sacrifice and offering you did not desire,
  but a body you prepared for me;
  in holocausts and sin offerings you took no delight.
Then I said, 'As is written of me in the scroll,
  behold, I come to do your will, O God.'"

First he says, "Sacrifices and offerings,
  holocausts and sin offerings,
  you neither desired nor delighted in."
These are offered according to the law.
Then he says, "Behold, I come to do your will."
He takes away the first to establish the second.
By this "will," we have been consecrated
  through the offering of the Body of Jesus Christ once for all. ✛

John 1:14ab
R. Alleluia, alleluia.
The Word of God became flesh and made his dwelling among us;
and we saw his glory. **R.**

† *Luke 1:26-38*
Behold, you will conceive in your womb and bear a son.

The angel Gabriel was sent from God
  to a town of Galilee called Nazareth,
  to a virgin betrothed to a man named Joseph,
  of the house of David,
  and the virgin's name was Mary.
And coming to her, he said,
  "Hail, full of grace! The Lord is with you."
But she was greatly troubled at what was said
  and pondered what sort of greeting this might be.
Then the angel said to her,
  "Do not be afraid, Mary,
  for you have found favor with God.
Behold, you will conceive in your womb and bear a son,

and you shall name him Jesus.
He will be great and will be called Son of the Most High,
   and the Lord God will give him the throne of David his father,
   and he will rule over the house of Jacob forever,
   and of his Kingdom there will be no end."
But Mary said to the angel,
   "How can this be,
   since I have no relations with a man?"
And the angel said to her in reply,
   "The Holy Spirit will come upon you,
   and the power of the Most High will overshadow you.
Therefore the child to be born
   will be called holy, the Son of God.
And behold, Elizabeth, your relative,
   has also conceived a son in her old age,
   and this is the sixth month for her who was called barren;
   for nothing will be impossible for God."
Mary said, "Behold, I am the handmaid of the Lord.
May it be done to me according to your word."
Then the angel departed from her. ✢

SATURDAY, MARCH 26
LENTEN WEEKDAY

† Hosea 6:1-6
What I want is love, not sacrifice.

"Come, let us return to the LORD,
   it is he who has rent, but he will heal us;
   he has struck us, but he will bind our wounds.
He will revive us after two days;
   on the third day he will raise us up,
   to live in his presence.
Let us know, let us strive to know the LORD;
   as certain as the dawn is his coming,
   and his judgment shines forth like the light of day!
He will come to us like the rain,
   like spring rain that waters the earth."

What can I do with you, Ephraim?
What can I do with you, Judah?
Your piety is like a morning cloud,
   like the dew that early passes away.
For this reason I smote them through the prophets,
   I slew them by the words of my mouth;

For it is love that I desire, not sacrifice,
and knowledge of God rather than burnt offerings. ✛

Psalm 51:3-4, 18-19, 20-21ab
R. (see Hosea 6:6) **It is mercy I desire, and not sacrifice.**
Have mercy on me, O God, in your goodness;
in the greatness of your compassion wipe out my offense.
Thoroughly wash me from my guilt
and of my sin cleanse me. **R.**
For you are not pleased with sacrifices;
should I offer a burnt offering, you would not accept it.
My sacrifice, O God, is a contrite spirit;
a heart contrite and humbled, O God, you will not spurn. **R.**
Be bountiful, O LORD, to Zion in your kindness
by rebuilding the walls of Jerusalem;
Then shall you be pleased with due sacrifices,
burnt offerings and holocausts. **R.**

Psalm 95:8
R. Glory and praise to you, Lord Jesus Christ!
If today you hear his voice,
harden not your hearts. **R.**

† *Luke 18:9-14*
The tax collector went home justified, not the Pharisee.

Jesus addressed this parable
to those who were convinced of their own righteousness
and despised everyone else.
"Two people went up to the temple area to pray;
one was a Pharisee and the other was a tax collector.
The Pharisee took up his position and spoke this prayer to himself,
'O God, I thank you that I am not like the rest of humanity—
greedy, dishonest, adulterous—or even like this tax collector.
I fast twice a week,
and I pay tithes on my whole income.'
But the tax collector stood off at a distance
and would not even raise his eyes to heaven
but beat his breast and prayed,
'O God, be merciful to me a sinner.'
I tell you, the latter went home justified, not the former;
for everyone who exalts himself will be humbled,
and the one who humbles himself will be exalted." ✛

SUNDAY, MARCH 27
FOURTH SUNDAY OF LENT

✝ *Joshua 5:9a, 10-12 (Scrutiny: 1 Samuel 16:1b, 6-7, 10-13a)*
The people of God entered the promised land and there kept the Passover.

The LORD said to Joshua,
"Today I have removed the reproach of Egypt from you."

While the Israelites were encamped at Gilgal on the plains of Jericho,
   they celebrated the Passover
   on the evening of the fourteenth of the month.
On the day after the Passover,
   they ate of the produce of the land
   in the form of unleavened cakes and parched grain.
On that same day after the Passover,
   on which they ate of the produce of the land, the manna ceased.
No longer was there manna for the Israelites,
   who that year ate of the yield of the land of Canaan. ✝

Psalm 34:2-3, 4-5, 6-7 (Scrutiny: Psalm 23:1-3a, 3b-4, 5, 6, (1))
R. (9a) Taste and see the goodness of the Lord.
I will bless the LORD at all times;
   his praise shall be ever in my mouth.
Let my soul glory in the LORD;
   the lowly will hear me and be glad. **R.**
Glorify the LORD with me,
   let us together extol his name.
I sought the LORD, and he answered me
   and delivered me from all my fears. **R.**
Look to him that you may be radiant with joy,
   and your faces may not blush with shame.
When the poor one called out, the LORD heard,
   and from all his distress he saved him. **R.**

✝ *2 Corinthians 5:17-21 (Scrutiny: Ephesians 5:8-14)*
God reconciled us to himself through Christ.

Brothers and sisters:
Whoever is in Christ is a new creation:
   the old things have passed away;
   behold, new things have come.
And all this is from God,
   who has reconciled us to himself through Christ
   and given us the ministry of reconciliation,
   namely, God was reconciling the world to himself in Christ,

not counting their trespasses against them
and entrusting to us the message of reconciliation.
So we are ambassadors for Christ,
as if God were appealing through us.
We implore you on behalf of Christ,
be reconciled to God.
For our sake he made him to be sin who did not know sin,
so that we might become the righteousness of God in him. ✛

Luke 15:18

R. Glory and praise to you, Lord Jesus Christ!
I will get up and go to my Father and shall say to him:
Father, I have sinned against heaven and against you. **R.**

†*Luke 15:1-3, 11-32*
(Scrutiny: John 9:1-41 or 9:1, 6-9, 13-17, 34-38)
Your brother was dead and has come to life again.

Tax collectors and sinners were all drawing near to listen to Jesus,
but the Pharisees and scribes began to complain, saying,
"This man welcomes sinners and eats with them."
So to them Jesus addressed this parable:
"A man had two sons, and the younger son said to his father,
'Father give me the share of your estate that should come to me.'
So the father divided the property between them.
After a few days, the younger son collected all his belongings
and set off to a distant country
where he squandered his inheritance on a life of dissipation.
When he had freely spent everything,
a severe famine struck that country,
and he found himself in dire need.
So he hired himself out to one of the local citizens
who sent him to his farm to tend the swine.
And he longed to eat his fill of the pods on which the swine fed,
but nobody gave him any.
Coming to his senses he thought,
'How many of my father's hired workers
have more than enough food to eat,
but here am I, dying from hunger.
I shall get up and go to my father and I shall say to him,
"Father, I have sinned against heaven and against you.
I no longer deserve to be called your son;
treat me as you would treat one of your hired workers."'
So he got up and went back to his father.
While he was still a long way off,
his father caught sight of him, and was filled with compassion.

He ran to his son, embraced him and kissed him.
His son said to him,
   'Father, I have sinned against heaven and against you;
   I no longer deserve to be called your son.'
But his father ordered his servants,
   'Quickly bring the finest robe and put it on him;
   put a ring on his finger and sandals on his feet.
Take the fattened calf and slaughter it.
Then let us celebrate with a feast,
   because this son of mine was dead, and has come to life again;
   he was lost, and has been found.'
Then the celebration began.
Now the older son had been out in the field
   and, on his way back, as he neared the house,
   he heard the sound of music and dancing.
He called one of the servants and asked what this might mean.
The servant said to him,
   'Your brother has returned
   and your father has slaughtered the fattened calf
   because he has him back safe and sound.'
He became angry,
   and when he refused to enter the house,
   his father came out and pleaded with him.
He said to his father in reply,
   'Look, all these years I served you
   and not once did I disobey your orders;
   yet you never gave me even a young goat to feast on with my
      friends.
But when your son returns
   who swallowed up your property with prostitutes,
   for him you slaughter the fattened calf.'
He said to him,
   'My son, you are here with me always;
   everything I have is yours.
But now we must celebrate and rejoice,
   because your brother was dead and has come to life again;
   he was lost and has been found.'" ✝

MONDAY, MARCH 28
LENTEN WEEKDAY

†Isaiah 65:17-21 *(or any day this week, Micah 7:7-9)*
No longer shall the sound of weeping or the sound of crying be heard.

Thus says the LORD:
Lo, I am about to create new heavens
    and a new earth;
The things of the past shall not be remembered
    or come to mind.
Instead, there shall always be rejoicing and happiness
    in what I create;
For I create Jerusalem to be a joy
    and its people to be a delight;
I will rejoice in Jerusalem
    and exult in my people.
No longer shall the sound of weeping be heard there,
    or the sound of crying;
No longer shall there be in it
    an infant who lives but a few days,
    or an old man who does not round out his full lifetime;
He dies a mere youth who reaches but a hundred years,
    and he who fails of a hundred shall be thought accursed.
They shall live in the houses they build,
    and eat the fruit of the vineyards they plant. ✛

Psalm 30:2 and 4, 5-6, 11-12a and 13b
(or Psalm 27:1, 7-8a, 8b-9abc, 13-14)
R. (2a) I will praise you, Lord, for you have rescued me.
I will extol you, O LORD, for you drew me clear
    and did not let my enemies rejoice over me.
O LORD, you brought me up from the nether world;
    you preserved me from among those going down into the pit. **R.**
Sing praise to the LORD, you his faithful ones,
    and give thanks to his holy name.
For his anger lasts but a moment;
    a lifetime, his good will.
At nightfall, weeping enters in,
    but with the dawn, rejoicing. **R.**
"Hear, O LORD, and have pity on me;
    O LORD, be my helper."
You changed my mourning into dancing;
    O LORD, my God, forever will I give you thanks. **R.**

Amos 5:14

R. Glory and praise to you, Lord Jesus Christ!
Seek good and not evil so that you may live,
and the LORD will be with you. **R.**

> **† *John 4:43-54*** *(or any day this week, John 9:1-41)*
> *Go, your son will live.*

At that time Jesus left [Samaria] for Galilee.
For Jesus himself testified
   that a prophet has no honor in his native place.
When he came into Galilee, the Galileans welcomed him,
   since they had seen all he had done in Jerusalem at the feast;
   for they themselves had gone to the feast.

Then he returned to Cana in Galilee,
   where he had made the water wine.
Now there was a royal official whose son was ill in Capernaum.
When he heard that Jesus had arrived in Galilee from Judea,
   he went to him and asked him to come down
   and heal his son, who was near death.
Jesus said to him,
   "Unless you people see signs and wonders, you will not believe."
The royal official said to him,
   "Sir, come down before my child dies."
Jesus said to him, "You may go; your son will live."
The man believed what Jesus said to him and left.
While the man was on his way back,
   his slaves met him and told him that his boy would live.
He asked them when he began to recover.
They told him,
   "The fever left him yesterday, about one in the afternoon."
The father realized that just at that time Jesus had said to him,
   "Your son will live,"
   and he and his whole household came to believe.
Now this was the second sign Jesus did
   when he came to Galilee from Judea. ✢

TUESDAY, MARCH 29
LENTEN WEEKDAY

† *Ezekiel 47:1-9, 12*

I saw water flowing from the temple, and all who
were touched by it were saved (see Roman Missal).

The angel brought me, Ezekiel,
   back to the entrance of the temple of the LORD,
   and I saw water flowing out
   from beneath the threshold of the temple toward the east,
   for the façade of the temple was toward the east;
   the water flowed down from the right side of the temple,
   south of the altar.
He led me outside by the north gate,
   and around to the outer gate facing the east,
   where I saw water trickling from the right side.
Then when he had walked off to the east
   with a measuring cord in his hand,
   he measured off a thousand cubits
   and had me wade through the water,
   which was ankle-deep.
He measured off another thousand
   and once more had me wade through the water,
   which was now knee-deep.
Again he measured off a thousand and had me wade;
   the water was up to my waist.
Once more he measured off a thousand,
   but there was now a river through which I could not wade;
   for the water had risen so high it had become a river
   that could not be crossed except by swimming.
He asked me, "Have you seen this, son of man?"
Then he brought me to the bank of the river, where he had me sit.
Along the bank of the river I saw very many trees on both sides.
He said to me,
   "This water flows into the eastern district down upon the Arabah,
   and empties into the sea, the salt waters, which it makes fresh.
Wherever the river flows,
   every sort of living creature that can multiply shall live,
   and there shall be abundant fish,
   for wherever this water comes the sea shall be made fresh.
Along both banks of the river, fruit trees of every kind shall grow;
   their leaves shall not fade, nor their fruit fail.
Every month they shall bear fresh fruit,
   for they shall be watered by the flow from the sanctuary.
Their fruit shall serve for food, and their leaves for medicine." ✦

Psalm 46:2-3, 5-6, 8-9

R. (8) **The Lord of hosts is with us; our stronghold is the God of Jacob.**

God is our refuge and our strength,
    an ever-present help in distress.
Therefore we fear not, though the earth be shaken
    and mountains plunge into the depths of the sea. **R.**
There is a stream whose runlets gladden the city of God,
    the holy dwelling of the Most High.
God is in its midst; it shall not be disturbed;
    God will help it at the break of dawn. **R.**
The LORD of hosts is with us;
    our stronghold is the God of Jacob.
Come! behold the deeds of the LORD,
    the astounding things he has wrought on earth. **R.**

Psalm 51:12a, 14a

R. Glory and praise to you, Lord Jesus Christ!

A clean heart create for me, O God;
give me back the joy of your salvation. **R.**

† *John 5:1-16*
Immediately the man became well.

There was a feast of the Jews, and Jesus went up to Jerusalem.
Now there is in Jerusalem at the Sheep Gate
    a pool called in Hebrew Bethesda, with five porticoes.
In these lay a large number of ill, blind, lame, and crippled.
One man was there who had been ill for thirty-eight years.
When Jesus saw him lying there
    and knew that he had been ill for a long time, he said to him,
    "Do you want to be well?"
The sick man answered him,
    "Sir, I have no one to put me into the pool
    when the water is stirred up;
    while I am on my way, someone else gets down there before me."
Jesus said to him, "Rise, take up your mat, and walk."
Immediately the man became well, took up his mat, and walked.

Now that day was a sabbath.
So the Jews said to the man who was cured,
    "It is the sabbath, and it is not lawful for you to carry your mat."
He answered them, "The man who made me well told me,
    'Take up your mat and walk.'"
They asked him,
    "Who is the man who told you, 'Take it up and walk'?"

The man who was healed did not know who it was,
for Jesus had slipped away, since there was a crowd there.
After this Jesus found him in the temple area and said to him,
"Look, you are well; do not sin any more,
so that nothing worse may happen to you."
The man went and told the Jews
that Jesus was the one who had made him well.
Therefore, the Jews began to persecute Jesus
because he did this on a sabbath. ✛

WEDNESDAY, MARCH 30
Lenten Weekday

† Isaiah 49:8-15
I have given you as a covenant to the people, to restore the land.

Thus says the Lord:
In a time of favor I answer you,
on the day of salvation I help you;
and I have kept you and given you as a covenant to the people,
To restore the land
and allot the desolate heritages,
Saying to the prisoners: Come out!
To those in darkness: Show yourselves!
Along the ways they shall find pasture,
on every bare height shall their pastures be.
They shall not hunger or thirst,
nor shall the scorching wind or the sun strike them;
For he who pities them leads them
and guides them beside springs of water.
I will cut a road through all my mountains,
and make my highways level.
See, some shall come from afar,
others from the north and the west,
and some from the land of Syene.
Sing out, O heavens, and rejoice, O earth,
break forth into song, you mountains.
For the Lord comforts his people
and shows mercy to his afflicted.

But Zion said, "The Lord has forsaken me;
my Lord has forgotten me."
Can a mother forget her infant,
be without tenderness for the child of her womb?
Even should she forget,
I will never forget you. ✛

Psalm 145:8-9, 13cd-14, 17-18

R. (8a) **The Lord is gracious and merciful.**

The LORD is gracious and merciful,
 slow to anger and of great kindness.
The LORD is good to all
 and compassionate toward all his works. **R.**
The LORD is faithful in all his words
 and holy in all his works.
The LORD lifts up all who are falling
 and raises up all who are bowed down. **R.**
The LORD is just in all his ways
 and holy in all his works.
The LORD is near to all who call upon him,
 to all who call upon him in truth. **R.**

John 11:25a, 26

R. Glory and praise to you, Lord Jesus Christ!

I am the resurrection and the life, says the Lord;
whoever believes in me will never die. **R.**

† *John 5:17-30*

As the Father raises the dead and gives them life,
so also does the Son give life to those whom he chooses.

Jesus answered the Jews:
"My Father is at work until now, so I am at work."
For this reason they tried all the more to kill him,
 because he not only broke the sabbath
 but he also called God his own father, making himself equal to God.

Jesus answered and said to them,
 "Amen, amen, I say to you, the Son cannot do anything on his own,
 but only what he sees the Father doing;
 for what he does, the Son will do also.
For the Father loves the Son
 and shows him everything that he himself does,
 and he will show him greater works than these,
 so that you may be amazed.
For just as the Father raises the dead and gives life,
 so also does the Son give life to whomever he wishes.
Nor does the Father judge anyone,
 but he has given all judgment to the Son,
 so that all may honor the Son just as they honor the Father.
Whoever does not honor the Son
 does not honor the Father who sent him.

Amen, amen, I say to you, whoever hears my word
  and believes in the one who sent me
  has eternal life and will not come to condemnation,
  but has passed from death to life.
Amen, amen, I say to you, the hour is coming and is now here
  when the dead will hear the voice of the Son of God,
  and those who hear will live.
For just as the Father has life in himself,
  so also he gave to the Son the possession of life in himself.
And he gave him power to exercise judgment,
  because he is the Son of Man.
Do not be amazed at this,
  because the hour is coming in which all who are in the tombs
  will hear his voice and will come out,
  those who have done good deeds
  to the resurrection of life,
  but those who have done wicked deeds
  to the resurrection of condemnation.

"I cannot do anything on my own;
  I judge as I hear, and my judgment is just,
  because I do not seek my own will
  but the will of the one who sent me." ✛

THURSDAY, MARCH 31
LENTEN WEEKDAY

† *Exodus 32:7-14*
Relent in punishing your people.

The LORD said to Moses,
  "Go down at once to your people
  whom you brought out of the land of Egypt,
  for they have become depraved.
They have soon turned aside from the way I pointed out to them,
  making for themselves a molten calf and worshiping it,
  sacrificing to it and crying out,
  'This is your God, O Israel,
  who brought you out of the land of Egypt!'"
The LORD said to Moses,
  "I see how stiff-necked this people is.
Let me alone, then,
  that my wrath may blaze up against them to consume them.
Then I will make of you a great nation."

But Moses implored the LORD, his God, saying,
"Why, O LORD, should your wrath blaze up against your own
people,
whom you brought out of the land of Egypt
with such great power and with so strong a hand?
Why should the Egyptians say,
'With evil intent he brought them out,
that he might kill them in the mountains
and exterminate them from the face of the earth'?
Let your blazing wrath die down;
relent in punishing your people.
Remember your servants Abraham, Isaac and Israel,
and how you swore to them by your own self, saying,
'I will make your descendants as numerous as the stars in the sky;
and all this land that I promised,
I will give your descendants as their perpetual heritage.'"
So the LORD relented in the punishment
he had threatened to inflict on his people. ✢

Psalm 106:19-20, 21-22, 23
R. (4a) Remember us, O Lord, as you favor your people.
Our fathers made a calf in Horeb
and adored a molten image;
They exchanged their glory
for the image of a grass-eating bullock. **R.**
They forgot the God who had saved them,
who had done great deeds in Egypt,
Wondrous deeds in the land of Ham,
terrible things at the Red Sea. **R.**
Then he spoke of exterminating them,
but Moses, his chosen one,
Withstood him in the breach
to turn back his destructive wrath. **R.**

John 3:16
R. Glory and praise to you, Lord Jesus Christ!
God so loved the world that he gave his only-begotten Son,
so that everyone who believes in him might have eternal life. **R.**

✝ John 5:31-47
The one who will accuse you is Moses, in whom you have placed your hope.

Jesus said to the Jews:
"If I testify on my own behalf, my testimony is not true.
But there is another who testifies on my behalf,
and I know that the testimony he gives on my behalf is true.

You sent emissaries to John, and he testified to the truth.
I do not accept human testimony,
   but I say this so that you may be saved.
He was a burning and shining lamp,
   and for a while you were content to rejoice in his light.
But I have testimony greater than John's.
The works that the Father gave me to accomplish,
   these works that I perform testify on my behalf
   that the Father has sent me.
Moreover, the Father who sent me has testified on my behalf.
But you have never heard his voice nor seen his form,
   and you do not have his word remaining in you,
   because you do not believe in the one whom he has sent.
You search the Scriptures,
   because you think you have eternal life through them;
   even they testify on my behalf.
But you do not want to come to me to have life.

"I do not accept human praise;
   moreover, I know that you do not have the love of God in you.
I came in the name of my Father,
   but you do not accept me;
   yet if another comes in his own name,
   you will accept him.
How can you believe, when you accept praise from one another
   and do not seek the praise that comes from the only God?
Do not think that I will accuse you before the Father:
   the one who will accuse you is Moses,
   in whom you have placed your hope.
For if you had believed Moses,
   you would have believed me,
   because he wrote about me.
But if you do not believe his writings,
   how will you believe my words?" ✛

FRIDAY, APRIL 1
LENTEN WEEKDAY

† *Wisdom 2:1a, 12-22*
Let us condemn him to a shameful death.

The wicked said among themselves,
 thinking not aright:
"Let us beset the just one, because he is obnoxious to us;
 he sets himself against our doings,
Reproaches us for transgressions of the law
 and charges us with violations of our training.
He professes to have knowledge of God
 and styles himself a child of the LORD.
To us he is the censure of our thoughts;
 merely to see him is a hardship for us,
Because his life is not like that of others,
 and different are his ways.
He judges us debased;
 he holds aloof from our paths as from things impure.
He calls blest the destiny of the just
 and boasts that God is his Father.
Let us see whether his words be true;
 let us find out what will happen to him.
For if the just one be the son of God, he will defend him
 and deliver him from the hand of his foes.
With revilement and torture let us put him to the test
 that we may have proof of his gentleness
 and try his patience.
Let us condemn him to a shameful death;
 for according to his own words, God will take care of him."
These were their thoughts, but they erred;
 for their wickedness blinded them,
and they knew not the hidden counsels of God;
 neither did they count on a recompense of holiness
 nor discern the innocent souls' reward. ✜

Psalm 34:17-18, 19-20, 21 and 23
R. (19a) **The Lord is close to the brokenhearted.**
The LORD confronts the evildoers,
 to destroy remembrance of them from the earth.
When the just cry out, the LORD hears them,
 and from all their distress he rescues them. **R.**
The LORD is close to the brokenhearted;
 and those who are crushed in spirit he saves.

Many are the troubles of the just man,
  but out of them all the LORD delivers him. **R.**
He watches over all his bones;
  not one of them shall be broken.
The LORD redeems the lives of his servants;
  no one incurs guilt who takes refuge in him. **R.**

  Matthew 4:4b
R. Glory and praise to you, Lord Jesus Christ!
One does not live on bread alone,
but on every word that comes forth from the mouth of God. **R.**

† *John 7:1-2, 10, 25-30*
They tried to arrest him, but his hour had not yet come.

Jesus moved about within Galilee;
  he did not wish to travel in Judea,
  because the Jews were trying to kill him.
But the Jewish feast of Tabernacles was near.

But when his brothers had gone up to the feast,
  he himself also went up, not openly but as it were in secret.

Some of the inhabitants of Jerusalem said,
  "Is he not the one they are trying to kill?
And look, he is speaking openly and they say nothing to him.
Could the authorities have realized that he is the Christ?
But we know where he is from.
When the Christ comes, no one will know where he is from."
So Jesus cried out in the temple area as he was teaching and said,
  "You know me and also know where I am from.
Yet I did not come on my own,
  but the one who sent me, whom you do not know, is true.
I know him, because I am from him, and he sent me."
So they tried to arrest him,
  but no one laid a hand upon him,
  because his hour had not yet come. ✛

SATURDAY, APRIL 2
LENTEN WEEKDAY, ST. FRANCIS OF PAOLA

† *Jeremiah 11:18-20*
I am like a trusting lamb led to slaughter.

I knew their plot because the LORD informed me;
  at that time you, O LORD, showed me their doings.

Yet I, like a trusting lamb led to slaughter,
  had not realized that they were hatching plots against me:

"Let us destroy the tree in its vigor;
let us cut him off from the land of the living,
so that his name will be spoken no more."

But, you, O LORD of hosts, O just Judge,
    searcher of mind and heart,
Let me witness the vengeance you take on them,
    for to you I have entrusted my cause! ✚

Psalm 7:2-3, 9bc-10, 11-12

R. (2a) O Lord, my God, in you I take refuge.
O LORD, my God, in you I take refuge;
    save me from all my pursuers and rescue me,
Lest I become like the lion's prey,
    to be torn to pieces, with no one to rescue me. **R.**
Do me justice, O LORD, because I am just,
    and because of the innocence that is mine.
Let the malice of the wicked come to an end,
    but sustain the just,
    O searcher of heart and soul, O just God. **R.**
A shield before me is God,
    who saves the upright of heart;
A just judge is God,
    a God who punishes day by day. **R.**

See Luke 8:15

R. Glory and praise to you, Lord Jesus Christ!
Blessed are they who have kept the word with a generous heart
and yield a harvest through perseverance. **R.**

✝ *John 7:40-53*
The Christ will not come from Galilee, will he?

Some in the crowd who heard these words of Jesus said,
    "This is truly the Prophet."
Others said, "This is the Christ."
But others said, "The Christ will not come from Galilee, will he?
Does not Scripture say that the Christ will be of David's family
    and come from Bethlehem, the village where David lived?"
So a division occurred in the crowd because of him.
Some of them even wanted to arrest him,
    but no one laid hands on him.

So the guards went to the chief priests and Pharisees,
    who asked them, "Why did you not bring him?"
The guards answered, "Never before has anyone spoken like this man."
So the Pharisees answered them, "Have you also been deceived?

Have any of the authorities or the Pharisees believed in him?
But this crowd, which does not know the law, is accursed."
Nicodemus, one of their members who had come to him earlier, said
　　to them,
　"Does our law condemn a man before it first hears him
　and finds out what he is doing?"
They answered and said to him,
　"You are not from Galilee also, are you?
Look and see that no prophet arises from Galilee."

Then each went to his own house. ✛

SUNDAY, APRIL 3
FIFTH SUNDAY OF LENT

✝Isaiah 43:16-21 (Scrutiny: Ezekiel 37:12-14)
See, I am doing something new and I give my people drink.

Thus says the LORD,
　who opens a way in the sea
　and a path in the mighty waters,
who leads out chariots and horsemen,
　a powerful army,
till they lie prostrate together, never to rise,
　snuffed out and quenched like a wick.
Remember not the events of the past,
　the things of long ago consider not;
see, I am doing something new!
　Now it springs forth, do you not perceive it?
In the desert I make a way,
　in the wasteland, rivers.
Wild beasts honor me,
　jackals and ostriches,
for I put water in the desert
　and rivers in the wasteland
　for my chosen people to drink,
the people whom I formed for myself,
　that they might announce my praise. ✛

Psalm 126:1-2, 2-3, 4-5, 6 (Scrutiny: Psalm 130:1-2, 3-4, 5-6,
7-8, (7))

R. (3) **The Lord has done great things for us; we are filled
　with joy.**
When the LORD brought back the captives of Zion,
　we were like men dreaming.
Then our mouth was filled with laughter,
　and our tongue with rejoicing. **R.**

Then they said among the nations,
  "The LORD has done great things for them."
The LORD has done great things for us;
  we are glad indeed. **R.**
Restore our fortunes, O LORD,
  like the torrents in the southern desert.
Those that sow in tears
  shall reap rejoicing. **R.**
Although they go forth weeping,
  carrying the seed to be sown,
they shall come back rejoicing,
  carrying their sheaves. **R.**

† *Philippians 3:8-14* (Scrutiny: Romans 8:8-11)
Because of Christ, I consider everything as a loss, being conformed to his death.

Brothers and sisters:
I consider everything as a loss
  because of the supreme good of knowing Christ Jesus my Lord.
For his sake I have accepted the loss of all things
  and I consider them so much rubbish,
  that I may gain Christ and be found in him,
  not having any righteousness of my own based on the law
  but that which comes through faith in Christ,
  the righteousness from God,
  depending on faith to know him and the power of his resurrection
  and the sharing of his sufferings by being conformed to his death,
  if somehow I may attain the resurrection from the dead.

It is not that I have already taken hold of it
  or have already attained perfect maturity,
  but I continue my pursuit in hope that I may possess it,
  since I have indeed been taken possession of by Christ Jesus.
Brothers and sisters, I for my part
  do not consider myself to have taken possession.
Just one thing: forgetting what lies behind
  but straining forward to what lies ahead,
  I continue my pursuit toward the goal,
  the prize of God's upward calling, in Christ Jesus. ✠

Joel 2:12-13
R. Glory and praise to you, Lord Jesus Christ!
Even now, says the Lord,
return to me with your whole heart;
for I am gracious and merciful. **R.**

† *John 8:1-11* *(Scrutiny: John 11:1-45*
or 11:3-7, 17, 20-27, 33b-45)
Let the one among you who is without sin be the first to throw a stone at her.

Jesus went to the Mount of Olives.
But early in the morning he arrived again in the temple area,
   and all the people started coming to him,
   and he sat down and taught them.
Then the scribes and the Pharisees brought a woman
   who had been caught in adultery
   and made her stand in the middle.
They said to him,
   "Teacher, this woman was caught
   in the very act of committing adultery.
Now in the law, Moses commanded us to stone such women.
So what do you say?"
They said this to test him,
   so that they could have some charge to bring against him.
Jesus bent down and began to write on the ground with his finger.
But when they continued asking him,
   he straightened up and said to them,
   "Let the one among you who is without sin
   be the first to throw a stone at her."
Again he bent down and wrote on the ground.
And in response, they went away one by one,
   beginning with the elders.
So he was left alone with the woman before him.
Then Jesus straightened up and said to her,
   "Woman, where are they?
Has no one condemned you?"
She replied, "No one, sir."
Then Jesus said, "Neither do I condemn you.
Go, and from now on do not sin any more." ✠

MONDAY, APRIL 4
LENTEN WEEKDAY, ST. ISIDORE

† *Daniel 13:1-9, 15-17, 19-30, 33-62* *(or Daniel 13:41c-62)*
(or any day this week, 2 Kings 4:18b-21, 32-37)
Here I am about to die, though I have done none of the things charged against me.

In Babylon there lived a man named Joakim,
   who married a very beautiful and God-fearing woman, Susanna,
   the daughter of Hilkiah;
   her pious parents had trained their daughter
   according to the law of Moses.

Joakim was very rich;
  he had a garden near his house,
  and the Jews had recourse to him often
  because he was the most respected of them all.

That year, two elders of the people were appointed judges,
  of whom the Lord said, "Wickedness has come out of Babylon:
  from the elders who were to govern the people as judges."
These men, to whom all brought their cases,
  frequented the house of Joakim.
When the people left at noon,
  Susanna used to enter her husband's garden for a walk.
When the old men saw her enter every day for her walk,
  they began to lust for her.
They suppressed their consciences;
  they would not allow their eyes to look to heaven,
  and did not keep in mind just judgments.

One day, while they were waiting for the right moment,
  she entered the garden as usual, with two maids only.
She decided to bathe, for the weather was warm.
Nobody else was there except the two elders,
  who had hidden themselves and were watching her.
"Bring me oil and soap," she said to the maids,
  "and shut the garden doors while I bathe."

As soon as the maids had left,
  the two old men got up and hurried to her.
"Look," they said, "the garden doors are shut, and no one can see us;
  give in to our desire, and lie with us.
If you refuse, we will testify against you
  that you dismissed your maids because a young man was here
    with you."

"I am completely trapped," Susanna groaned.
"If I yield, it will be my death;
  if I refuse, I cannot escape your power.
Yet it is better for me to fall into your power without guilt
  than to sin before the Lord."
Then Susanna shrieked, and the old men also shouted at her,
  as one of them ran to open the garden doors.
When the people in the house heard the cries from the garden,
  they rushed in by the side gate to see what had happened to her.
At the accusations by the old men,
  the servants felt very much ashamed,
  for never had any such thing been said about Susanna.

When the people came to her husband Joakim the next day,
 the two wicked elders also came,
 fully determined to put Susanna to death.
Before all the people they ordered:
 "Send for Susanna, the daughter of Hilkiah,
 the wife of Joakim."
When she was sent for,
 she came with her parents, children and all her relatives.
All her relatives and the onlookers were weeping.

In the midst of the people the two elders rose up
 and laid their hands on her head.
Through tears she looked up to heaven,
 for she trusted in the Lord wholeheartedly.
The elders made this accusation:
 "As we were walking in the garden alone,
 this woman entered with two girls
 and shut the doors of the garden, dismissing the girls.
A young man, who was hidden there, came and lay with her.
When we, in a corner of the garden, saw this crime,
 we ran toward them.
We saw them lying together,
 but the man we could not hold, because he was stronger than we;
 he opened the doors and ran off.
Then we seized her and asked who the young man was,
 but she refused to tell us.
We testify to this."
The assembly believed them,
 since they were elders and judges of the people,
 and they condemned her to death.

But Susanna cried aloud:
 "O eternal God, you know what is hidden
 and are aware of all things before they come to be:
 you know that they have testified falsely against me.
Here I am about to die,
 though I have done none of the things
 with which these wicked men have charged me."

The Lord heard her prayer.
As she was being led to execution,
 God stirred up the holy spirit of a young boy named Daniel,
 and he cried aloud:
 "I will have no part in the death of this woman."
All the people turned and asked him, "What is this you are saying?"

He stood in their midst and continued,
  "Are you such fools, O children of Israel!
To condemn a woman of Israel without examination
  and without clear evidence?
Return to court, for they have testified falsely against her."

Then all the people returned in haste.
To Daniel the elders said,
  "Come, sit with us and inform us,
  since God has given you the prestige of old age."
But he replied,
  "Separate these two far from each other that I may examine them."

After they were separated one from the other,
  he called one of them and said:
  "How you have grown evil with age!
Now have your past sins come to term:
  passing unjust sentences, condemning the innocent,
  and freeing the guilty, although the Lord says,
  'The innocent and the just you shall not put to death.'
Now, then, if you were a witness,
  tell me under what tree you saw them together."
"Under a mastic tree," he answered.
Daniel replied, "Your fine lie has cost you your head,
  for the angel of God shall receive the sentence from him
  and split you in two."
Putting him to one side, he ordered the other one to be brought.
Daniel said to him,
  "Offspring of Canaan, not of Judah, beauty has seduced you,
  lust has subverted your conscience.
This is how you acted with the daughters of Israel,
  and in their fear they yielded to you;
  but a daughter of Judah did not tolerate your wickedness.
Now, then, tell me under what tree you surprised them together."
"Under an oak," he said.
Daniel replied, "Your fine lie has cost you also your head,
  for the angel of God waits with a sword to cut you in two
  so as to make an end of you both."

The whole assembly cried aloud,
  blessing God who saves those who hope in him.
They rose up against the two elders,
  for by their own words Daniel had convicted them of perjury.
According to the law of Moses,
  they inflicted on them

the penalty they had plotted to impose on their neighbor:
they put them to death.
Thus was innocent blood spared that day. ✛

Psalm 23:1b-3a, 3b-4, 5, 6 (or Psalm 17:1bcd, 6-7, 8b and 15)
R. (4ab) **Even though I walk in the dark valley I fear no evil;
for you are at my side.**
The LORD is my shepherd; I shall not want.
    In verdant pastures he gives me repose;
Beside restful waters he leads me;
    he refreshes my soul. **R.**
He guides me in right paths
    for his name's sake.
Even though I walk in the dark valley
    I fear no evil; for you are at my side
With your rod and your staff
    that give me courage. **R.**
You spread the table before me
    in the sight of my foes;
You anoint my head with oil;
    my cup overflows. **R.**
Only goodness and kindness follow me
    all the days of my life;
And I shall dwell in the house of the LORD
    for years to come. **R.**

Ezekiel 33:11
R. Glory and praise to you, Lord Jesus Christ!
I take no pleasure in the death of the wicked man, says the Lord,
but rather in his conversion, that he may live. **R.**

✝John 8:12-20 (or John 8:1-11)
I am the light of the world.

Jesus spoke to them again, saying,
    "I am the light of the world.
Whoever follows me will not walk in darkness,
    but will have the light of life."
So the Pharisees said to him,
    "You testify on your own behalf,
    so your testimony cannot be verified."
Jesus answered and said to them,
    "Even if I do testify on my own behalf, my testimony can be verified,
    because I know where I came from and where I am going.
But you do not know where I come from or where I am going.
You judge by appearances, but I do not judge anyone.

And even if I should judge, my judgment is valid,
  because I am not alone,
  but it is I and the Father who sent me.
Even in your law it is written
  that the testimony of two men can be verified.
I testify on my behalf and so does the Father who sent me."
So they said to him, "Where is your father?"
Jesus answered, "You know neither me nor my Father.
If you knew me, you would know my Father also."
He spoke these words
  while teaching in the treasury in the temple area.
But no one arrested him, because his hour had not yet come. ✢

The Gospel from the Fifth Sunday of Lent (John 11:1-45) may be used any day this week (with the other alternate Readings).

TUESDAY, APRIL 5
LENTEN WEEKDAY, ST. VINCENT FERRER

† *Numbers 21:4-9*
Whoever looks at the bronze serpent, shall live.

From Mount Hor the children of Israel set out on the Red Sea road,
  to bypass the land of Edom.
But with their patience worn out by the journey,
  the people complained against God and Moses,
  "Why have you brought us up from Egypt to die in this desert,
  where there is no food or water?
We are disgusted with this wretched food!"

In punishment the LORD sent among the people saraph serpents,
  which bit the people so that many of them died.
Then the people came to Moses and said,
  "We have sinned in complaining against the LORD and you.
Pray the LORD to take the serpents away from us."
So Moses prayed for the people, and the LORD said to Moses,
  "Make a saraph and mount it on a pole,
  and whoever looks at it after being bitten will live."
Moses accordingly made a bronze serpent and mounted it on a pole,
  and whenever anyone who had been bitten by a serpent
  looked at the bronze serpent, he lived. ✢

Psalm 102:2-3, 16-18, 19-21
R. (2) O Lord, hear my prayer, and let my cry come to you.
O LORD, hear my prayer,
  and let my cry come to you.

Hide not your face from me
　in the day of my distress.
Incline your ear to me;
　in the day when I call, answer me speedily. **R.**
The nations shall revere your name, O LORD,
　and all the kings of the earth your glory,
When the LORD has rebuilt Zion
　and appeared in his glory;
When he has regarded the prayer of the destitute,
　and not despised their prayer. **R.**
Let this be written for the generation to come,
　and let his future creatures praise the LORD:
"The LORD looked down from his holy height,
　from heaven he beheld the earth,
To hear the groaning of the prisoners,
　to release those doomed to die." **R.**

R. Glory and praise to you, Lord Jesus Christ!

The seed is the word of God, Christ is the sower;
all who come to him will live for ever. **R.**

† *John 8:21-30*

*When you have lifted up the Son of Man,
then you will know that I am he.*

Jesus said to the Pharisees:
"I am going away and you will look for me,
　but you will die in your sin.
Where I am going you cannot come."
So the Jews said,
　"He is not going to kill himself, is he,
　because he said, 'Where I am going you cannot come'?"
He said to them, "You belong to what is below,
　I belong to what is above.
You belong to this world,
　but I do not belong to this world.
That is why I told you that you will die in your sins.
For if you do not believe that I AM,
　you will die in your sins."
So they said to him, "Who are you?"
Jesus said to them, "What I told you from the beginning.
I have much to say about you in condemnation.
But the one who sent me is true,
　and what I heard from him I tell the world."
They did not realize that he was speaking to them of the Father.

So Jesus said to them,
    "When you lift up the Son of Man,
    then you will realize that I AM,
    and that I do nothing on my own,
    but I say only what the Father taught me.
The one who sent me is with me.
He has not left me alone,
    because I always do what is pleasing to him."
Because he spoke this way, many came to believe in him. ✛

WEDNESDAY, APRIL 6
Lenten Weekday

✝ Daniel 3:14-20, 91-92, 95
The Lord has sent his angel to deliver his servants.

King Nebuchadnezzar said:
"Is it true, Shadrach, Meshach, and Abednego,
    that you will not serve my god,
    or worship the golden statue that I set up?
Be ready now to fall down and worship the statue I had made,
    whenever you hear the sound of the trumpet,
    flute, lyre, harp, psaltery, bagpipe,
    and all the other musical instruments;
    otherwise, you shall be instantly cast into the white-hot furnace;
    and who is the God who can deliver you out of my hands?"
Shadrach, Meshach, and Abednego answered King Nebuchadnezzar,
    "There is no need for us to defend ourselves before you
    in this matter.
If our God, whom we serve,
    can save us from the white-hot furnace
    and from your hands, O king, may he save us!
But even if he will not, know, O king,
    that we will not serve your god
    or worship the golden statue that you set up."

King Nebuchadnezzar's face became livid with utter rage
    against Shadrach, Meshach, and Abednego.
He ordered the furnace to be heated seven times more than usual
    and had some of the strongest men in his army
    bind Shadrach, Meshach, and Abednego
    and cast them into the white-hot furnace.

Nebuchadnezzar rose in haste and asked his nobles,
    "Did we not cast three men bound into the fire?"
"Assuredly, O king," they answered.

"But," he replied, "I see four men unfettered and unhurt,
   walking in the fire, and the fourth looks like a son of God."
Nebuchadnezzar exclaimed,
   "Blessed be the God of Shadrach, Meshach, and Abednego,
   who sent his angel to deliver the servants who trusted in him;
   they disobeyed the royal command and yielded their bodies
   rather than serve or worship any god
   except their own God." ✛

   Daniel 3:52, 53, 54, 55, 56
R. (52b) **Glory and praise for ever!**
"Blessed are you, O Lord, the God of our fathers,
   praiseworthy and exalted above all forever;
And blessed is your holy and glorious name,
   praiseworthy and exalted above all for all ages." **R.**
"Blessed are you in the temple of your holy glory,
   praiseworthy and exalted above all forever." **R.**
"Blessed are you on the throne of your Kingdom,
   praiseworthy and exalted above all forever." **R.**
"Blessed are you who look into the depths
   from your throne upon the cherubim;
   praiseworthy and exalted above all forever." **R.**
"Blessed are you in the firmament of heaven,
   praiseworthy and glorious forever." **R.**

   See Luke 8:15
R. Glory and praise to you, Lord Jesus Christ!
Blessed are they who have kept the word with a generous heart
and yield a harvest through perseverance. **R.**

† *John 8:31-42*
If the Son makes you free, you will be free indeed.

Jesus said to those Jews who believed in him,
   "If you remain in my word, you will truly be my disciples,
   and you will know the truth, and the truth will set you free."
They answered him, "We are descendants of Abraham
   and have never been enslaved to anyone.
How can you say, 'You will become free'?"
Jesus answered them, "Amen, amen, I say to you,
   everyone who commits sin is a slave of sin.
A slave does not remain in a household forever,
   but a son always remains.
So if the Son frees you, then you will truly be free.
I know that you are descendants of Abraham.
But you are trying to kill me,
   because my word has no room among you.

I tell you what I have seen in the Father's presence;
   then do what you have heard from the Father."

They answered and said to him, "Our father is Abraham."
Jesus said to them, "If you were Abraham's children,
   you would be doing the works of Abraham.
But now you are trying to kill me,
   a man who has told you the truth that I heard from God;
   Abraham did not do this.
You are doing the works of your father!"
So they said to him, "We were not born of fornication.
We have one Father, God."
Jesus said to them, "If God were your Father, you would love me,
   for I came from God and am here;
   I did not come on my own, but he sent me." ✛

THURSDAY, APRIL 7
LENTEN WEEKDAY, ST. JOHN BAPTIST DE LA SALLE

† *Genesis 17:3-9*
You will be the father of a multitude of nations.

When Abram prostrated himself, God spoke to him:
"My covenant with you is this:
   you are to become the father of a host of nations.
No longer shall you be called Abram;
   your name shall be Abraham,
   for I am making you the father of a host of nations.
I will render you exceedingly fertile;
   I will make nations of you;
   kings shall stem from you.
I will maintain my covenant with you
   and your descendants after you
   throughout the ages as an everlasting pact,
   to be your God and the God of your descendants after you.
I will give to you
   and to your descendants after you
   the land in which you are now staying,
   the whole land of Canaan, as a permanent possession;
   and I will be their God."

God also said to Abraham:
   "On your part, you and your descendants after you
   must keep my covenant throughout the ages." ✛

Psalm 105:4-5, 6-7, 8-9
R. (8a) **The Lord remembers his covenant for ever.**
Look to the Lord in his strength;
  seek to serve him constantly.
Recall the wondrous deeds that he has wrought,
  his portents, and the judgments he has uttered. **R.**
You descendants of Abraham, his servants,
  sons of Jacob, his chosen ones!
He, the Lord, is our God;
  throughout the earth his judgments prevail. **R.**
He remembers forever his covenant
  which he made binding for a thousand generations—
Which he entered into with Abraham
  and by his oath to Isaac. **R.**

Psalm 95:8
R. Glory and praise to you, Lord Jesus Christ!
If today you hear his voice,
harden not your hearts. **R.**

✝ *John 8:51-59*
Your father, Abraham, rejoiced because he saw my day.

Jesus said to the Jews:
"Amen, amen, I say to you,
  whoever keeps my word will never see death."
So the Jews said to him,
  "Now we are sure that you are possessed.
Abraham died, as did the prophets, yet you say,
  'Whoever keeps my word will never taste death.'
Are you greater than our father Abraham, who died?
Or the prophets, who died?
Who do you make yourself out to be?"
Jesus answered, "If I glorify myself, my glory is worth nothing;
  but it is my Father who glorifies me,
  of whom you say, 'He is our God.'
You do not know him, but I know him.
And if I should say that I do not know him,
  I would be like you a liar.
But I do know him and I keep his word.
Abraham your father rejoiced to see my day;
  he saw it and was glad."
So the Jews said to him,
  "You are not yet fifty years old and you have seen Abraham?"
Jesus said to them, "Amen, amen, I say to you,
  before Abraham came to be, I AM."

So they picked up stones to throw at him;
but Jesus hid and went out of the temple area. ✛

FRIDAY, APRIL 8
LENTEN WEEKDAY

† *Jeremiah 20:10-13*
The LORD God is with me, a mighty hero.

I hear the whisperings of many:
"Terror on every side!
Denounce! let us denounce him!"
All those who were my friends
are on the watch for any misstep of mine.
"Perhaps he will be trapped; then we can prevail,
and take our vengeance on him."
But the LORD is with me, like a mighty champion:
my persecutors will stumble, they will not triumph.
In their failure they will be put to utter shame,
to lasting, unforgettable confusion.
O LORD of hosts, you who test the just,
who probe mind and heart,
Let me witness the vengeance you take on them,
for to you I have entrusted my cause.
Sing to the LORD,
praise the LORD,
For he has rescued the life of the poor
from the power of the wicked! ✛

Psalm 18:2-3a, 3bc-4, 5-6, 7
R. (see 7) **In my distress I called upon the Lord, and he heard
my voice.**
I love you, O LORD, my strength,
O LORD, my rock, my fortress, my deliverer. **R.**
My God, my rock of refuge,
my shield, the horn of my salvation, my stronghold!
Praised be the LORD, I exclaim,
and I am safe from my enemies. **R.**
The breakers of death surged round about me,
the destroying floods overwhelmed me;
The cords of the nether world enmeshed me,
the snares of death overtook me. **R.**
In my distress I called upon the LORD
and cried out to my God;
From his temple he heard my voice,
and my cry to him reached his ears. **R.**

See John 6:63c, 68c
R. Glory and praise to you, Lord Jesus Christ!
Your words, Lord, are Spirit and life;
you have the words of everlasting life. **R.**

† John 10:31-42
They wanted to arrest Jesus, but he eluded them.

The Jews picked up rocks to stone Jesus.
Jesus answered them, "I have shown you many good works from my
  Father.
For which of these are you trying to stone me?"
The Jews answered him,
  "We are not stoning you for a good work but for blasphemy.
You, a man, are making yourself God."
Jesus answered them,
  "Is it not written in your law, 'I said, "You are gods"'?
If it calls them gods to whom the word of God came,
  and Scripture cannot be set aside,
  can you say that the one
  whom the Father has consecrated and sent into the world
  blasphemes because I said, 'I am the Son of God'?
If I do not perform my Father's works, do not believe me;
  but if I perform them, even if you do not believe me,
  believe the works, so that you may realize and understand
  that the Father is in me and I am in the Father."
Then they tried again to arrest him;
  but he escaped from their power.

He went back across the Jordan
  to the place where John first baptized, and there he remained.
Many came to him and said,
  "John performed no sign,
  but everything John said about this man was true."
And many there began to believe in him. ✛

SATURDAY, APRIL 9
LENTENT WEEKDAY

† Ezekiel 37:21-28
I will make them into one nation.

Thus says the Lord GOD:
I will take the children of Israel from among the nations
  to which they have come,
  and gather them from all sides to bring them back to their land.

I will make them one nation upon the land,
in the mountains of Israel,
and there shall be one prince for them all.
Never again shall they be two nations,
and never again shall they be divided into two kingdoms.

No longer shall they defile themselves with their idols,
their abominations, and all their transgressions.
I will deliver them from all their sins of apostasy,
and cleanse them so that they may be my people
and I may be their God.
My servant David shall be prince over them,
and there shall be one shepherd for them all;
they shall live by my statutes and carefully observe my decrees.
They shall live on the land that I gave to my servant Jacob,
the land where their fathers lived;
they shall live on it forever,
they, and their children, and their children's children,
with my servant David their prince forever.
I will make with them a covenant of peace;
it shall be an everlasting covenant with them,
and I will multiply them, and put my sanctuary among them forever.
My dwelling shall be with them;
I will be their God, and they shall be my people.
Thus the nations shall know that it is I, the LORD,
who make Israel holy,
when my sanctuary shall be set up among them forever. ✚

Jeremiah 31:10, 11-12abcd, 13
R. (see 10d) **The Lord will guard us, as a shepherd guards his flock.**
Hear the word of the LORD, O nations,
proclaim it on distant isles, and say:
He who scattered Israel, now gathers them together,
he guards them as a shepherd his flock. **R.**
The LORD shall ransom Jacob,
he shall redeem him from the hand of his conqueror.
Shouting, they shall mount the heights of Zion,
they shall come streaming to the LORD's blessings:
The grain, the wine, and the oil,
the sheep and the oxen. **R.**
Then the virgins shall make merry and dance,
and young men and old as well.
I will turn their mourning into joy,
I will console and gladden them after their sorrows. **R.**

Ezekiel 18:31

R. Glory and praise to you, Lord Jesus Christ!
Cast away from you all the crimes you have committed, says the LORD,
and make for yourselves a new heart and a new spirit. **R.**

✝ *John 11:45-56*
To gather together in unity the scattered children of God.

Many of the Jews who had come to Mary
    and seen what Jesus had done began to believe in him.
But some of them went to the Pharisees
    and told them what Jesus had done.
So the chief priests and the Pharisees
    convened the Sanhedrin and said,
    "What are we going to do?
This man is performing many signs.
If we leave him alone, all will believe in him,
    and the Romans will come
    and take away both our land and our nation."
But one of them, Caiaphas,
    who was high priest that year, said to them,
    "You know nothing,
    nor do you consider that it is better for you
    that one man should die instead of the people,
    so that the whole nation may not perish."
He did not say this on his own,
    but since he was high priest for that year,
    he prophesied that Jesus was going to die for the nation,
    and not only for the nation,
    but also to gather into one the dispersed children of God.
So from that day on they planned to kill him.

So Jesus no longer walked about in public among the Jews,
    but he left for the region near the desert,
    to a town called Ephraim,
    and there he remained with his disciples.

Now the Passover of the Jews was near,
    and many went up from the country to Jerusalem
    before Passover to purify themselves.
They looked for Jesus and said to one another
    as they were in the temple area, "What do you think?
That he will not come to the feast?" ✛

SUNDAY, APRIL 10
PALM SUNDAY OF THE PASSION OF THE LORD
(At the Procession with Palms)

† *Luke 19:28-40*
Blessed is he who comes in the name of the Lord.

Jesus proceeded on his journey up to Jerusalem.
As he drew near to Bethphage and Bethany
    at the place called the Mount of Olives,
    he sent two of his disciples.
He said, "Go into the village opposite you,
    and as you enter it you will find a colt tethered
    on which no one has ever sat.
Untie it and bring it here.
And if anyone should ask you,
    'Why are you untying it?'
    you will answer,
    'The Master has need of it.'"
So those who had been sent went off
    and found everything just as he had told them.
And as they were untying the colt, its owners said to them,
    "Why are you untying this colt?"
They answered,
    "The Master has need of it."
So they brought it to Jesus,
    threw their cloaks over the colt,
    and helped Jesus to mount.
As he rode along,
    the people were spreading their cloaks on the road;
    and now as he was approaching the slope of the Mount of Olives,
    the whole multitude of his disciples
    began to praise God aloud with joy
    for all the mighty deeds they had seen.
They proclaimed:
    "Blessed is the king who comes
        in the name of the Lord.
    Peace in heaven
        and glory in the highest."
Some of the Pharisees in the crowd said to him,
    "Teacher, rebuke your disciples."
He said in reply,
    "I tell you, if they keep silent,
    the stones will cry out!" ✛

(At Mass)

† *Isaiah 50:4-7*
*My face I did not shield from buffets and spitting
knowing that I shall not be put to shame.*

The Lord GOD has given me
   a well-trained tongue,
that I might know how to speak to the weary
   a word that will rouse them.
Morning after morning
   he opens my ear that I may hear;
and I have not rebelled,
   have not turned back.
I gave my back to those who beat me,
   my cheeks to those who plucked my beard;
my face I did not shield
   from buffets and spitting.

The Lord GOD is my help,
   therefore I am not disgraced;
I have set my face like flint,
   knowing that I shall not be put to shame. ✢

Psalm 22:8-9, 17-18, 19-20, 23-24
R. (2a) **My God, my God, why have you abandoned me?**
All who see me scoff at me;
   they mock me with parted lips, they wag their heads:
"He relied on the LORD; let him deliver him,
   let him rescue him, if he loves him." **R.**
Indeed, many dogs surround me,
   a pack of evildoers closes in upon me;
they have pierced my hands and my feet;
   I can count all my bones. **R.**
They divide my garments among them,
   and for my vesture they cast lots.
But you, O LORD, be not far from me;
   O my help, hasten to aid me. **R.**
I will proclaim your name to my brethren;
   in the midst of the assembly I will praise you:
"You who fear the LORD, praise him;
   all you descendants of Jacob, give glory to him;
   revere him, all you descendants of Israel!" **R.**

† *Philippians 2:6-11*
Christ humbled himself. Because of this God greatly exalted him.

Christ Jesus, though he was in the form of God,
  did not regard equality with God
  something to be grasped.
Rather, he emptied himself,
  taking the form of a slave,
  coming in human likeness;
  and found human in appearance,
  he humbled himself,
  becoming obedient to the point of death,
  even death on a cross.
Because of this, God greatly exalted him
  and bestowed on him the name
  which is above every name,
  that at the name of Jesus
  every knee should bend,
  of those in heaven and on earth and under the earth,
  and every tongue confess that
  Jesus Christ is Lord,
  to the glory of God the Father. ✛

Philippians 2:8-9
R. Glory and praise to you, Lord Jesus Christ!
Christ became obedient to the point of death,
even death on a cross.
Because of this, God greatly exalted him
and bestowed on him the name which is above every name. **R.**

† *Luke 22:14—23:56 (or Luke 23:1-49)*
The Passion of our Lord Jesus Christ.

When the hour came,
  Jesus took his place at table with the apostles.
He said to them,
  "I have eagerly desired to eat this Passover with you before I suffer,
  for, I tell you, I shall not eat it again
  until there is fulfillment in the kingdom of God."
Then he took a cup, gave thanks, and said,
  "Take this and share it among yourselves;
  for I tell you that from this time on
  I shall not drink of the fruit of the vine
  until the kingdom of God comes."
Then he took the bread, said the blessing,
  broke it, and gave it to them, saying,

"This is my body, which will be given for you;
do this in memory of me."
And likewise the cup after they had eaten, saying,
"This cup is the new covenant in my blood,
which will be shed for you.

"And yet behold, the hand of the one who is to betray me
is with me on the table;
for the Son of Man indeed goes as it has been determined;
but woe to that man by whom he is betrayed."
And they began to debate among themselves
who among them would do such a deed.

Then an argument broke out among them
about which of them should be regarded as the greatest.
He said to them,
"The kings of the Gentiles lord it over them
and those in authority over them are addressed as 'Benefactors';
but among you it shall not be so.
Rather, let the greatest among you be as the youngest,
and the leader as the servant.
For who is greater:
the one seated at table or the one who serves?
Is it not the one seated at table?
I am among you as the one who serves.
It is you who have stood by me in my trials;
and I confer a kingdom on you,
just as my Father has conferred one on me,
that you may eat and drink at my table in my kingdom;
and you will sit on thrones
judging the twelve tribes of Israel.

"Simon, Simon, behold Satan has demanded
to sift all of you like wheat,
but I have prayed that your own faith may not fail;
and once you have turned back,
you must strengthen your brothers."
He said to him,
"Lord, I am prepared to go to prison and to die with you."
But he replied,
"I tell you, Peter, before the cock crows this day,
you will deny three times that you know me."

He said to them,
"When I sent you forth without a money bag or a sack or sandals,
were you in need of anything?"

"No, nothing," they replied.
He said to them,
  "But now one who has a money bag should take it,
  and likewise a sack,
  and one who does not have a sword
  should sell his cloak and buy one.
For I tell you that this Scripture must be fulfilled in me,
  namely, *He was counted among the wicked;*
  and indeed what is written about me is coming to fulfillment."
Then they said,
  "Lord, look, there are two swords here."
But he replied, "It is enough!"

Then going out, he went, as was his custom, to the Mount of Olives,
  and the disciples followed him.
When he arrived at the place he said to them,
  "Pray that you may not undergo the test."
After withdrawing about a stone's throw from them and kneeling,
  he prayed, saying, "Father, if you are willing,
  take this cup away from me;
  still, not my will but yours be done."
And to strengthen him an angel from heaven appeared to him.
He was in such agony and he prayed so fervently
  that his sweat became like drops of blood
  falling on the ground.
When he rose from prayer and returned to his disciples,
  he found them sleeping from grief.
He said to them, "Why are you sleeping?
Get up and pray that you may not undergo the test."

While he was still speaking, a crowd approached
  and in front was one of the Twelve, a man named Judas.
He went up to Jesus to kiss him.
Jesus said to him,
  "Judas, are you betraying the Son of Man with a kiss?"
His disciples realized what was about to happen, and they asked,
  "Lord, shall we strike with a sword?"
And one of them struck the high priest's servant
  and cut off his right ear.
But Jesus said in reply,
  "Stop, no more of this!"
Then he touched the servant's ear and healed him.
And Jesus said to the chief priests and temple guards
  and elders who had come for him,
  "Have you come out as against a robber, with swords and clubs?

Day after day I was with you in the temple area,
  and you did not seize me;
  but this is your hour, the time for the power of darkness."

After arresting him they led him away
  and took him into the house of the high priest;
  Peter was following at a distance.
They lit a fire in the middle of the courtyard and sat around it,
  and Peter sat down with them.
When a maid saw him seated in the light,
  she looked intently at him and said,
  "This man too was with him."
But he denied it saying,
  "Woman, I do not know him."
A short while later someone else saw him and said,
  "You too are one of them";
  but Peter answered, "My friend, I am not."
About an hour later, still another insisted,
  "Assuredly, this man too was with him,
  for he also is a Galilean."
But Peter said,
  "My friend, I do not know what you are talking about."
Just as he was saying this, the cock crowed,
  and the Lord turned and looked at Peter;
  and Peter remembered the word of the Lord,
  how he had said to him,
  "Before the cock crows today, you will deny me three times."
He went out and began to weep bitterly.
The men who held Jesus in custody were ridiculing and beating him.
They blindfolded him and questioned him, saying,
  "Prophesy! Who is it that struck you?"
And they reviled him in saying many other things against him.

When day came the council of elders of the people met,
  both chief priests and scribes,
  and they brought him before their Sanhedrin.
They said, "If you are the Christ, tell us, "
  but he replied to them, "If I tell you, you will not believe,
  and if I question, you will not respond.
But from this time on the Son of Man will be seated
  at the right hand of the power of God."
They all asked, "Are you then the Son of God?"
He replied to them, "You say that I am."
Then they said, "What further need have we for testimony?
We have heard it from his own mouth."

Then the whole assembly of them arose and brought him before Pilate.
They brought charges against him, saying,
  "We found this man misleading our people;
  he opposes the payment of taxes to Caesar
  and maintains that he is the Christ, a king."
Pilate asked him, "Are you the king of the Jews?"
He said to him in reply, "You say so."
Pilate then addressed the chief priests and the crowds,
  "I find this man not guilty."
But they were adamant and said,
  "He is inciting the people with his teaching throughout all Judea,
  from Galilee where he began even to here."

On hearing this Pilate asked if the man was a Galilean;
  and upon learning that he was under Herod's jurisdiction,
  he sent him to Herod who was in Jerusalem at that time.
Herod was very glad to see Jesus;
  he had been wanting to see him for a long time,
  for he had heard about him
  and had been hoping to see him perform some sign.
He questioned him at length,
  but he gave him no answer.
The chief priests and scribes, meanwhile,
  stood by accusing him harshly.
Herod and his soldiers treated him contemptuously and mocked him,
  and after clothing him in resplendent garb,
  he sent him back to Pilate.
Herod and Pilate became friends that very day,
  even though they had been enemies formerly.
Pilate then summoned the chief priests, the rulers, and the people
  and said to them, "You brought this man to me
  and accused him of inciting the people to revolt.
I have conducted my investigation in your presence
  and have not found this man guilty
  of the charges you have brought against him,
  nor did Herod, for he sent him back to us.
So no capital crime has been committed by him.
Therefore I shall have him flogged and then release him."

But all together they shouted out,
  "Away with this man!
  Release Barabbas to us."
—Now Barabbas had been imprisoned for a rebellion
  that had taken place in the city and for murder.—

Again Pilate addressed them, still wishing to release Jesus,
    but they continued their shouting,
    "Crucify him! Crucify him!"
Pilate addressed them a third time,
    "What evil has this man done?
    I found him guilty of no capital crime.
Therefore I shall have him flogged and then release him."
With loud shouts, however,
    they persisted in calling for his crucifixion,
    and their voices prevailed.
The verdict of Pilate was that their demand should be granted.
So he released the man who had been imprisoned
    for rebellion and murder, for whom they asked,
    and he handed Jesus over to them to deal with as they wished.

As they led him away
    they took hold of a certain Simon, a Cyrenian,
    who was coming in from the country;
    and after laying the cross on him,
    they made him carry it behind Jesus.
A large crowd of people followed Jesus,
    including many women who mourned and lamented him.
Jesus turned to them and said,
    "Daughters of Jerusalem, do not weep for me;
    weep instead for yourselves and for your children
    for indeed, the days are coming when people will say,
    'Blessed are the barren,
    the wombs that never bore
    and the breasts that never nursed.'
At that time people will say to the mountains,
    'Fall upon us!'
    and to the hills, 'Cover us!'
    for if these things are done when the wood is green
    what will happen when it is dry?"
Now two others, both criminals,
    were led away with him to be executed.

When they came to the place called the Skull,
    they crucified him and the criminals there,
    one on his right, the other on his left.
Then Jesus said,
    "Father, forgive them, they know not what they do."
They divided his garments by casting lots.
The people stood by and watched;
    the rulers, meanwhile, sneered at him and said,

"He saved others, let him save himself
if he is the chosen one, the Christ of God."
Even the soldiers jeered at him.
As they approached to offer him wine they called out,
"If you are King of the Jews, save yourself."
Above him there was an inscription that read,
"This is the King of the Jews."

Now one of the criminals hanging there reviled Jesus, saying,
"Are you not the Christ?
Save yourself and us."
The other, however, rebuking him, said in reply,
"Have you no fear of God,
for you are subject to the same condemnation?
And indeed, we have been condemned justly,
for the sentence we received corresponds to our crimes,
but this man has done nothing criminal."
Then he said,
"Jesus, remember me when you come into your kingdom."
He replied to him,
"Amen, I say to you,
today you will be with me in Paradise."

It was now about noon and darkness came over the whole land
until three in the afternoon
because of an eclipse of the sun.
Then the veil of the temple was torn down the middle.
Jesus cried out in a loud voice,
"Father, into your hands I commend my spirit";
and when he had said this he breathed his last.

(Here all kneel and pause for a short time.)

The centurion who witnessed what had happened glorified God and
said,
"This man was innocent beyond doubt."
When all the people who had gathered for this spectacle saw what
had happened,
they returned home beating their breasts;
but all his acquaintances stood at a distance,
including the women who had followed him from Galilee
and saw these events.

Now there was a virtuous and righteous man named Joseph who,
though he was a member of the council,
had not consented to their plan of action.

He came from the Jewish town of Arimathea
   and was awaiting the kingdom of God.
He went to Pilate and asked for the body of Jesus.
After he had taken the body down,
   he wrapped it in a linen cloth
   and laid him in a rock-hewn tomb
   in which no one had yet been buried.
It was the day of preparation,
   and the sabbath was about to begin.
The women who had come from Galilee with him followed behind,
   and when they had seen the tomb
   and the way in which his body was laid in it,
   they returned and prepared spices and perfumed oils.
Then they rested on the sabbath according to the commandment. ✤

MONDAY, APRIL 11
MONDAY OF HOLY WEEK

† Isaiah 42:1-7
He will not cry out, nor make his voice heard in the street.
(First oracle of the Servant of the Lord)

Here is my servant whom I uphold,
   my chosen one with whom I am pleased,
Upon whom I have put my Spirit;
   he shall bring forth justice to the nations,
Not crying out, not shouting,
   not making his voice heard in the street.
A bruised reed he shall not break,
   and a smoldering wick he shall not quench,
Until he establishes justice on the earth;
   the coastlands will wait for his teaching.

Thus says God, the LORD,
   who created the heavens and stretched them out,
   who spreads out the earth with its crops,
Who gives breath to its people
   and spirit to those who walk on it:
I, the LORD, have called you for the victory of justice,
   I have grasped you by the hand;
I formed you, and set you
   as a covenant of the people,
   a light for the nations,
To open the eyes of the blind,
   to bring out prisoners from confinement,
   and from the dungeon, those who live in darkness. ✤

Psalm 27:1, 2, 3, 13-14

R. (1a) **The Lord is my light and my salvation.**

The LORD is my light and my salvation;
  whom should I fear?
The LORD is my life's refuge;
  of whom should I be afraid? **R.**
When evildoers come at me
  to devour my flesh,
My foes and my enemies
  themselves stumble and fall. **R.**
Though an army encamp against me,
  my heart will not fear;
Though war be waged upon me,
  even then will I trust. **R.**
I believe that I shall see the bounty of the LORD
  in the land of the living.
Wait for the LORD with courage;
  be stouthearted, and wait for the LORD. **R.**

R. Glory and praise to you, Lord Jesus Christ!

Hail to you, our King;
you alone are compassionate with our faults. **R.**

† *John 12:1-11*
Let her keep this for the day of my burial.

Six days before Passover Jesus came to Bethany,
  where Lazarus was, whom Jesus had raised from the dead.
They gave a dinner for him there, and Martha served,
  while Lazarus was one of those reclining at table with him.
Mary took a liter of costly perfumed oil
  made from genuine aromatic nard
  and anointed the feet of Jesus and dried them with her hair;
  the house was filled with the fragrance of the oil.
Then Judas the Iscariot, one of his disciples,
  and the one who would betray him, said,
  "Why was this oil not sold for three hundred days' wages
  and given to the poor?"
He said this not because he cared about the poor
  but because he was a thief and held the money bag
  and used to steal the contributions.
So Jesus said, "Leave her alone.
Let her keep this for the day of my burial.
You always have the poor with you, but you do not always have me."

The large crowd of the Jews found out that he was there and came,
  not only because of him, but also to see Lazarus,
  whom he had raised from the dead.
And the chief priests plotted to kill Lazarus too,
  because many of the Jews were turning away
  and believing in Jesus because of him. ✛

TUESDAY, APRIL 12
TUESDAY OF HOLY WEEK

† *Isaiah 49:1-6*

*I will make you a light to the nations, that my salvation may reach
to the ends of the earth. (Second oracle of the Servant of the Lord)*

Hear me, O islands,
  listen, O distant peoples.
The LORD called me from birth,
  from my mother's womb he gave me my name.
He made of me a sharp-edged sword
  and concealed me in the shadow of his arm.
He made me a polished arrow,
  in his quiver he hid me.
You are my servant, he said to me,
  Israel, through whom I show my glory.

Though I thought I had toiled in vain,
  and for nothing, uselessly, spent my strength,
Yet my reward is with the LORD,
  my recompense is with my God.
For now the LORD has spoken
  who formed me as his servant from the womb,
That Jacob may be brought back to him
  and Israel gathered to him;
And I am made glorious in the sight of the LORD,
  and my God is now my strength!
It is too little, he says, for you to be my servant,
  to raise up the tribes of Jacob,
  and restore the survivors of Israel;
I will make you a light to the nations,
  that my salvation may reach to the ends of the earth. ✛

Psalm 71:1-2, 3-4a, 5ab-6ab, 15 and 17
R. (see 15ab) **I will sing of your salvation.**
In you, O LORD, I take refuge;
  let me never be put to shame.
In your justice rescue me, and deliver me;
  incline your ear to me, and save me. **R.**

Be my rock of refuge,
  a stronghold to give me safety,
  for you are my rock and my fortress.
O my God, rescue me from the hand of the wicked. **R.**
For you are my hope, O Lord;
  my trust, O God, from my youth.
On you I depend from birth;
  from my mother's womb you are my strength. **R.**
My mouth shall declare your justice,
  day by day your salvation.
O God, you have taught me from my youth,
  and till the present I proclaim your wondrous deeds. **R.**

R. Glory and praise to you, Lord Jesus Christ!
Hail to you, our King, obedient to the Father;
you were led to your crucifixion like a gentle lamb to the slaughter. **R.**

† *John 13:21-33, 36-38*
One of you will betray me; the cock will not crow before you deny me three times.

Reclining at table with his disciples, Jesus was deeply troubled
    and testified,
  "Amen, amen, I say to you, one of you will betray me."
The disciples looked at one another, at a loss as to whom he meant.
One of his disciples, the one whom Jesus loved,
  was reclining at Jesus' side.
So Simon Peter nodded to him to find out whom he meant.
He leaned back against Jesus' chest and said to him,
  "Master, who is it?"
Jesus answered,
  "It is the one to whom I hand the morsel after I have dipped it."
So he dipped the morsel and took it and handed it to Judas,
  son of Simon the Iscariot.
After Judas took the morsel, Satan entered him.
So Jesus said to him, "What you are going to do, do quickly."
Now none of those reclining at table realized why he said this to him.
Some thought that since Judas kept the money bag, Jesus had told
    him,
  "Buy what we need for the feast,"
  or to give something to the poor.
So Judas took the morsel and left at once. And it was night.

When he had left, Jesus said,
  "Now is the Son of Man glorified, and God is glorified in him.
If God is glorified in him, God will also glorify him in himself,
  and he will glorify him at once.

My children, I will be with you only a little while longer.
You will look for me, and as I told the Jews,
  'Where I go you cannot come,' so now I say it to you."

Simon Peter said to him, "Master, where are you going?"
Jesus answered him,
  "Where I am going, you cannot follow me now,
  though you will follow later."
Peter said to him,
  "Master, why can I not follow you now?
  I will lay down my life for you."
Jesus answered, "Will you lay down your life for me?
Amen, amen, I say to you, the cock will not crow
  before you deny me three times." ✛

WEDNESDAY, APRIL 13
WEDNESDAY OF HOLY WEEK

† Isaiah 50:4-9a
My face I did not shield from buffets and spitting.
(Third oracle of the Servant of the Lord)

The Lord GOD has given me
  a well-trained tongue,
That I might know how to speak to the weary
  a word that will rouse them.
Morning after morning
  he opens my ear that I may hear;
And I have not rebelled,
  have not turned back.
I gave my back to those who beat me,
  my cheeks to those who plucked my beard;
My face I did not shield
  from buffets and spitting.

The Lord GOD is my help,
  therefore I am not disgraced;
I have set my face like flint,
  knowing that I shall not be put to shame.
He is near who upholds my right;
  if anyone wishes to oppose me,
  let us appear together.
Who disputes my right?
  Let him confront me.
See, the Lord GOD is my help;
  who will prove me wrong? ✛

Psalm 69:8-10, 21-22, 31 and 33-34

R. (14c) Lord, in your great love, answer me.

For your sake I bear insult,
  and shame covers my face.
I have become an outcast to my brothers,
  a stranger to my mother's sons,
because zeal for your house consumes me,
  and the insults of those who blaspheme you fall upon me. **R.**
Insult has broken my heart, and I am weak,
  I looked for sympathy, but there was none;
  for consolers, not one could I find.
Rather they put gall in my food,
  and in my thirst they gave me vinegar to drink. **R.**
I will praise the name of God in song,
  and I will glorify him with thanksgiving:
"See, you lowly ones, and be glad;
  you who seek God, may your hearts revive!
For the LORD hears the poor,
  and his own who are in bonds he spurns not." **R.**

R. Glory and praise to you, Lord Jesus Christ!

Hail to you, our King;
you alone are compassionate with our errors. **R.**
or
Hail to you, our King, obedient to the Father;
you were led to your crucifixion like a gentle lamb to the slaughter. **R.**

† *Matthew 26:14-25*

The Son of Man indeed goes, as it is written of him,
but woe to that man by whom the Son of Man is betrayed.

One of the Twelve, who was called Judas Iscariot,
  went to the chief priests and said,
  "What are you willing to give me
  if I hand him over to you?"
They paid him thirty pieces of silver,
  and from that time on he looked for an opportunity to hand him over.

On the first day of the Feast of Unleavened Bread,
  the disciples approached Jesus and said,
  "Where do you want us to prepare
  for you to eat the Passover?"
He said,
  "Go into the city to a certain man and tell him,
  'The teacher says, "My appointed time draws near;
  in your house I shall celebrate the Passover with my disciples."'"

The disciples then did as Jesus had ordered,
    and prepared the Passover.

When it was evening,
    he reclined at table with the Twelve.
And while they were eating, he said,
    "Amen, I say to you, one of you will betray me."
Deeply distressed at this,
    they began to say to him one after another,
    "Surely it is not I, Lord?"
He said in reply,
    "He who has dipped his hand into the dish with me
    is the one who will betray me.
The Son of Man indeed goes, as it is written of him,
    but woe to that man by whom the Son of Man is betrayed.
It would be better for that man if he had never been born."
Then Judas, his betrayer, said in reply,
    "Surely it is not I, Rabbi?"
He answered, "You have said so." ✚

THURSDAY, APRIL 14
THURSDAY OF HOLY WEEK (HOLY THURSDAY)
EVENING MASS OF THE LORD'S SUPPER

† *Exodus 12:1-8, 11-14*
The law regarding the Passover meal.

The LORD said to Moses and Aaron in the land of Egypt,
    "This month shall stand at the head of your calendar;
    you shall reckon it the first month of the year.
Tell the whole community of Israel:
    On the tenth of this month every one of your families
    must procure for itself a lamb, one apiece for each household.
If a family is too small for a whole lamb,
    it shall join the nearest household in procuring one
    and shall share in the lamb
    in proportion to the number of persons who partake of it.
The lamb must be a year-old male and without blemish.
You may take it from either the sheep or the goats.
You shall keep it until the fourteenth day of this month,
    and then, with the whole assembly of Israel present,
    it shall be slaughtered during the evening twilight.
They shall take some of its blood
    and apply it to the two doorposts and the lintel
    of every house in which they partake of the lamb.

That same night they shall eat its roasted flesh
   with unleavened bread and bitter herbs.

"This is how you are to eat it:
   with your loins girt, sandals on your feet and your staff in hand,
   you shall eat like those who are in flight.
It is the Passover of the LORD.
For on this same night I will go through Egypt,
   striking down every firstborn of the land, both man and beast,
   and executing judgment on all the gods of Egypt—I, the LORD!
But the blood will mark the houses where you are.
Seeing the blood, I will pass over you;
   thus, when I strike the land of Egypt,
   no destructive blow will come upon you.

"This day shall be a memorial feast for you,
   which all your generations shall celebrate
   with pilgrimage to the LORD, as a perpetual institution." ✛

   Psalm 116:12-13, 15-16bc, 17-18
R. (see 1 Corinthians 10:16) **Our blessing-cup is a communion
   with the Blood of Christ.**
How shall I make a return to the LORD
   for all the good he has done for me?
The cup of salvation I will take up,
   and I will call upon the name of the LORD. **R.**
Precious in the eyes of the LORD
   is the death of his faithful ones.
I am your servant, the son of your handmaid;
   you have loosed my bonds. **R.**
To you will I offer sacrifice of thanksgiving,
   and I will call upon the name of the LORD.
My vows to the LORD I will pay
   in the presence of all his people. **R.**

✝ *1 Corinthians 11:23-26*
*For as often as you eat this bread and drink the cup,
you proclaim the death of the Lord.*

Brothers and sisters:
I received from the Lord what I also handed on to you,
   that the Lord Jesus, on the night he was handed over,
   took bread, and, after he had given thanks,
   broke it and said, "This is my body that is for you.
Do this in remembrance of me."
In the same way also the cup, after supper, saying,
   "This cup is the new covenant in my blood.

Do this, as often as you drink it, in remembrance of me."
For as often as you eat this bread and drink the cup,
 you proclaim the death of the Lord until he comes. ✛

John 13:34

R. Glory and praise to you, Lord Jesus Christ!
I give you a new commandment, says the Lord:
love one another as I have loved you. **R.**

✝ John 13:1-15
Jesus loved them to the end.

Before the feast of Passover,
 Jesus knew that his hour had come
 to pass from this world to the Father.
He loved his own in the world and he loved them to the end.
The devil had already induced Judas, son of Simon the Iscariot, to
 hand him over.
So, during supper,
 fully aware that the Father had put everything into his power
 and that he had come from God and was returning to God,
 he rose from supper and took off his outer garments.
He took a towel and tied it around his waist.
Then he poured water into a basin
 and began to wash the disciples' feet
 and dry them with the towel around his waist.
He came to Simon Peter, who said to him,
 "Master, are you going to wash my feet?"
Jesus answered and said to him,
 "What I am doing, you do not understand now,
 but you will understand later."
Peter said to him, "You will never wash my feet."
Jesus answered him,
 "Unless I wash you, you will have no inheritance with me."
Simon Peter said to him,
 "Master, then not only my feet, but my hands and head as well."
Jesus said to him,
 "Whoever has bathed has no need except to have his feet washed,
 for he is clean all over;
 so you are clean, but not all."
For he knew who would betray him;
 for this reason, he said, "Not all of you are clean."

So when he had washed their feet
 and put his garments back on and reclined at table again,
 he said to them, "Do you realize what I have done for you?

You call me 'teacher' and 'master,' and rightly so, for indeed I am.
If I, therefore, the master and teacher, have washed your feet,
  you ought to wash one another's feet.
I have given you a model to follow,
  so that as I have done for you, you should also do." ✛

FRIDAY, APRIL 15
FRIDAY OF THE PASSION OF THE LORD (GOOD FRIDAY)

† *Isaiah 52:13—53:12*
He himself was wounded for our sins.
(Fourth oracle of the Servant of the Lord)

See, my servant shall prosper,
  he shall be raised high and greatly exalted.
Even as many were amazed at him—
  so marred was his look beyond human semblance
  and his appearance beyond that of the sons of man—
so shall he startle many nations,
  because of him kings shall stand speechless;
for those who have not been told shall see,
  those who have not heard shall ponder it.

Who would believe what we have heard?
  To whom has the arm of the LORD been revealed?
He grew up like a sapling before him,
  like a shoot from the parched earth;
there was in him no stately bearing to make us look at him,
  nor appearance that would attract us to him.
He was spurned and avoided by people,
  a man of suffering, accustomed to infirmity,
one of those from whom people hide their faces,
  spurned, and we held him in no esteem.

Yet it was our infirmities that he bore,
  our sufferings that he endured,
while we thought of him as stricken,
  as one smitten by God and afflicted.
But he was pierced for our offenses,
  crushed for our sins;
upon him was the chastisement that makes us whole,
  by his stripes we were healed.
We had all gone astray like sheep,
  each following his own way;
but the LORD laid upon him
  the guilt of us all.

Though he was harshly treated, he submitted
and opened not his mouth;
like a lamb led to the slaughter
or a sheep before the shearers,
he was silent and opened not his mouth.
Oppressed and condemned, he was taken away,
and who would have thought any more of his destiny?
When he was cut off from the land of the living,
and smitten for the sin of his people,
a grave was assigned him among the wicked
and a burial place with evildoers,
though he had done no wrong
nor spoken any falsehood.
But the LORD was pleased
to crush him in infirmity.

If he gives his life as an offering for sin,
he shall see his descendants in a long life,
and the will of the LORD shall be accomplished through him.

Because of his affliction
he shall see the light in fullness of days;
through his suffering, my servant shall justify many,
and their guilt he shall bear.
Therefore I will give him his portion among the great,
and he shall divide the spoils with the mighty,
because he surrendered himself to death
and was counted among the wicked;
and he shall take away the sins of many,
and win pardon for their offenses. ✛

Psalm 31:2 and 6, 12-13, 15-16, 17 and 25
R. (Luke 23:46) **Father, into your hands I commend my spirit.**
In you, O LORD, I take refuge;
let me never be put to shame.
In your justice rescue me.
Into your hands I commend my spirit;
you will redeem me, O LORD, O faithful God. **R.**
For all my foes I am an object of reproach,
a laughingstock to my neighbors, and a dread to my friends;
they who see me abroad flee from me.
I am forgotten like the unremembered dead;
I am like a dish that is broken. **R.**
But my trust is in you, O LORD;
I say, "You are my God.

In your hands is my destiny; rescue me
  from the clutches of my enemies and my persecutors." **R.**
Let your face shine upon your servant;
  save me in your kindness.
Take courage and be stouthearted,
  all you who hope in the LORD. **R.**

† Hebrews 4:14-16; 5:7-9

*Jesus learned obedience and became
the source of salvation for all who obey him.*

Brothers and sisters:
Since we have a great high priest who has passed through the heavens,
  Jesus, the Son of God,
  let us hold fast to our confession.
For we do not have a high priest
  who is unable to sympathize with our weaknesses,
  but one who has similarly been tested in every way,
  yet without sin.
So let us confidently approach the throne of grace
  to receive mercy and to find grace for timely help.

In the days when Christ was in the flesh,
  he offered prayers and supplications with loud cries and tears
  to the one who was able to save him from death,
  and he was heard because of his reverence.
Son though he was, he learned obedience from what he suffered;
  and when he was made perfect,
  he became the source of eternal salvation for all who obey him. ✝

Philippians 2:8-9

R. Glory and praise to you, Lord Jesus Christ!
Christ became obedient to the point of death,
even death on a cross.
Because of this, God greatly exalted him
and bestowed on him the name which is above every other name. **R.**

† John 18:1—19:42

The Passion of our Lord Jesus Christ.

Jesus went out with his disciples across the Kidron valley
  to where there was a garden,
  into which he and his disciples entered.
Judas his betrayer also knew the place,
  because Jesus had often met there with his disciples.
So Judas got a band of soldiers and guards
  from the chief priests and the Pharisees
  and went there with lanterns, torches, and weapons.

Jesus, knowing everything that was going to happen to him,
  went out and said to them, "Whom are you looking for?"
They answered him, "Jesus the Nazorean."
He said to them, "I AM."
Judas his betrayer was also with them.
When he said to them, "I AM,"
  they turned away and fell to the ground.
So he again asked them,
  "Whom are you looking for?"
They said, "Jesus the Nazorean."
Jesus answered,
  "I told you that I AM.
So if you are looking for me, let these men go."
This was to fulfill what he had said,
  "I have not lost any of those you gave me."
Then Simon Peter, who had a sword, drew it,
  struck the high priest's slave, and cut off his right ear.
The slave's name was Malchus.
Jesus said to Peter,
  "Put your sword into its scabbard.
Shall I not drink the cup that the Father gave me?"

So the band of soldiers, the tribune, and the Jewish guards seized
    Jesus,
  bound him, and brought him to Annas first.
He was the father-in-law of Caiaphas,
  who was high priest that year.
It was Caiaphas who had counseled the Jews
  that it was better that one man should die rather than the people.

Simon Peter and another disciple followed Jesus.
Now the other disciple was known to the high priest,
  and he entered the courtyard of the high priest with Jesus.
But Peter stood at the gate outside.
So the other disciple, the acquaintance of the high priest,
  went out and spoke to the gatekeeper and brought Peter in.
Then the maid who was the gatekeeper said to Peter,
  "You are not one of this man's disciples, are you?"
He said, "I am not."
Now the slaves and the guards were standing around a charcoal fire
  that they had made, because it was cold,
    and were warming themselves.
Peter was also standing there keeping warm.

The high priest questioned Jesus
  about his disciples and about his doctrine.
Jesus answered him,
  "I have spoken publicly to the world.
I have always taught in a synagogue
  or in the temple area where all the Jews gather,
  and in secret I have said nothing. Why ask me?
Ask those who heard me what I said to them.
They know what I said."
When he had said this,
  one of the temple guards standing there struck Jesus and said,
  "Is this the way you answer the high priest?"
Jesus answered him,
  "If I have spoken wrongly, testify to the wrong;
  but if I have spoken rightly, why do you strike me?"
Then Annas sent him bound to Caiaphas the high priest.

Now Simon Peter was standing there keeping warm.
And they said to him,
  "You are not one of his disciples, are you?"
He denied it and said,
  "I am not."
One of the slaves of the high priest,
  a relative of the one whose ear Peter had cut off, said,
  "Didn't I see you in the garden with him?"
Again Peter denied it.
And immediately the cock crowed.

Then they brought Jesus from Caiaphas to the praetorium.
It was morning.
And they themselves did not enter the praetorium,
  in order not to be defiled so that they could eat the Passover.
So Pilate came out to them and said,
  "What charge do you bring against this man?"
They answered and said to him,
  "If he were not a criminal,
  we would not have handed him over to you."
At this, Pilate said to them,
  "Take him yourselves, and judge him according to your law."
The Jews answered him,
  "We do not have the right to execute anyone, "
  in order that the word of Jesus might be fulfilled
  that he said indicating the kind of death he would die.
So Pilate went back into the praetorium
  and summoned Jesus and said to him,

"Are you the King of the Jews?"
Jesus answered,
"Do you say this on your own
or have others told you about me?"
Pilate answered,
"I am not a Jew, am I?
Your own nation and the chief priests handed you over to me.
What have you done?"
Jesus answered,
"My kingdom does not belong to this world.
If my kingdom did belong to this world,
my attendants would be fighting
to keep me from being handed over to the Jews.
But as it is, my kingdom is not here."
So Pilate said to him,
"Then you are a king?"
Jesus answered,
"You say I am a king.
For this I was born and for this I came into the world,
to testify to the truth.
Everyone who belongs to the truth listens to my voice."
Pilate said to him, "What is truth?"

When he had said this,
he again went out to the Jews and said to them,
"I find no guilt in him.
But you have a custom that I release one prisoner to you at Passover.
Do you want me to release to you the King of the Jews?"
They cried out again,
"Not this one but Barabbas!"
Now Barabbas was a revolutionary.

Then Pilate took Jesus and had him scourged.
And the soldiers wove a crown out of thorns and placed it on his head,
and clothed him in a purple cloak,
and they came to him and said,
"Hail, King of the Jews!"
And they struck him repeatedly.
Once more Pilate went out and said to them,
"Look, I am bringing him out to you,
so that you may know that I find no guilt in him."
So Jesus came out,
wearing the crown of thorns and the purple cloak.
And he said to them, "Behold, the man!"

When the chief priests and the guards saw him they cried out,
  "Crucify him, crucify him!"
Pilate said to them,
  "Take him yourselves and crucify him.
I find no guilt in him."
The Jews answered,
  "We have a law, and according to that law he ought to die,
  because he made himself the Son of God."
Now when Pilate heard this statement,
  he became even more afraid,
  and went back into the praetorium and said to Jesus,
  "Where are you from?"
Jesus did not answer him.
So Pilate said to him,
  "Do you not speak to me?
Do you not know that I have power to release you
  and I have power to crucify you?"
Jesus answered him,
  "You would have no power over me
  if it had not been given to you from above.
For this reason the one who handed me over to you
  has the greater sin."
Consequently, Pilate tried to release him; but the Jews cried out,
  "If you release him, you are not a Friend of Caesar.
Everyone who makes himself a king opposes Caesar."

When Pilate heard these words he brought Jesus out
  and seated him on the judge's bench
  in the place called Stone Pavement, in Hebrew, Gabbatha.
It was preparation day for Passover, and it was about noon.
And he said to the Jews,
  "Behold, your king!"
They cried out,
  "Take him away, take him away! Crucify him!"
Pilate said to them,
  "Shall I crucify your king?"
The chief priests answered,
  "We have no king but Caesar."
Then he handed him over to them to be crucified.

So they took Jesus, and, carrying the cross himself,
  he went out to what is called the Place of the Skull,
  in Hebrew, Golgotha.
There they crucified him, and with him two others,
  one on either side, with Jesus in the middle.

Pilate also had an inscription written and put on the cross.
It read,
   "Jesus the Nazorean, the King of the Jews."
Now many of the Jews read this inscription,
   because the place where Jesus was crucified was near the city;
   and it was written in Hebrew, Latin, and Greek.
So the chief priests of the Jews said to Pilate,
   "Do not write 'The King of the Jews,'
   but that he said, 'I am the King of the Jews.'"
Pilate answered,
   "What I have written, I have written."

When the soldiers had crucified Jesus,
   they took his clothes and divided them into four shares,
   a share for each soldier.
They also took his tunic, but the tunic was seamless,
   woven in one piece from the top down.
So they said to one another,
   "Let's not tear it, but cast lots for it to see whose it will be,"
   in order that the passage of Scripture might be fulfilled that says:
      They divided my garments among them,
         and for my vesture they cast lots.
This is what the soldiers did.

Standing by the cross of Jesus were his mother
   and his mother's sister, Mary the wife of Clopas,
   and Mary of Magdala.
When Jesus saw his mother and the disciple there whom he loved
   he said to his mother, "Woman, behold, your son."
Then he said to the disciple,
   "Behold, your mother."
And from that hour the disciple took her into his home.

After this, aware that everything was now finished,
   in order that the Scripture might be fulfilled,
   Jesus said, "I thirst."
There was a vessel filled with common wine.
So they put a sponge soaked in wine on a sprig of hyssop
   and put it up to his mouth.
When Jesus had taken the wine, he said,
   "It is finished."
And bowing his head, he handed over the spirit.

   (Here all kneel and pause for a short time.)

Now since it was preparation day,
    in order that the bodies might not remain on the cross on the
        sabbath,
    for the sabbath day of that week was a solemn one,
    the Jews asked Pilate that their legs be broken
    and that they be taken down.
So the soldiers came and broke the legs of the first
    and then of the other one who was crucified with Jesus.
But when they came to Jesus and saw that he was already dead,
    they did not break his legs,
    but one soldier thrust his lance into his side,
    and immediately blood and water flowed out.
An eyewitness has testified, and his testimony is true;
    he knows that he is speaking the truth,
    so that you also may come to believe.
For this happened so that the Scripture passage might be fulfilled:
    Not a bone of it will be broken.
And again another passage says:
    They will look upon him whom they have pierced.

After this, Joseph of Arimathea,
    secretly a disciple of Jesus for fear of the Jews,
    asked Pilate if he could remove the body of Jesus.
And Pilate permitted it.
So he came and took his body.
Nicodemus, the one who had first come to him at night,
    also came bringing a mixture of myrrh and aloes
    weighing about one hundred pounds.
They took the body of Jesus
    and bound it with burial cloths along with the spices,
    according to the Jewish burial custom.
Now in the place where he had been crucified there was a garden,
    and in the garden a new tomb, in which no one had yet been buried.
So they laid Jesus there because of the Jewish preparation day;
    for the tomb was close by. ✚

SATURDAY, APRIL 16
HOLY SATURDAY: EASTER VIGIL MASS

Nine readings are assigned to the Easter Vigil: seven from the Old Testament and two from the New. If circumstances demand in individual cases, the number of prescribed readings may be reduced. Three selections from the Old Testament, however, should be read before the epistle and Gospel, although when necessary, two may be read. In any case, the reading from Exodus about the escape through the Red Sea (reading 3) should never be omitted.

(Other readings for the Easter Vigil liturgy are: Genesis 1:1—2:2 or Genesis 1:1, 26-31a • Psalm 104:1-2, 5-6, 10 and 12, 13-14, 24 and 35c or Psalm 33:4-5, 6-7, 12-13, 20 and 22 • Genesis 22:1-18 or 22:1-2, 9a, 10-13, 15-18 • Psalm 16:5 and 8, 9-10, 11 • Isaiah 54:5-14 • Psalm 30:2 and 4, 5-6, 11-12a and 13b • Isaiah 55:1-11 • Isaiah 12:2-3, 4bcd, 5-6 • Baruch 3:9-15, 32—4:4 • Psalm 19:8, 9, 10, 11 • Ezekiel 36:16-17a, 18-28 • Psalm 42:3, 5; 43:3, 4 or Isaiah 12:2-3, 4bcd, 5-6 or Psalm 51:12-13, 14-15, 18-19.)

† *Exodus 14:15—15:1*
The Israelites marched on dry land through the midst of the sea.

The LORD said to Moses, "Why are you crying out to me?
Tell the Israelites to go forward.
And you, lift up your staff and, with hand outstretched over the sea,
    split the sea in two,
    that the Israelites may pass through it on dry land.
But I will make the Egyptians so obstinate
    that they will go in after them.
Then I will receive glory through Pharaoh and all his army,
    his chariots and charioteers.
The Egyptians shall know that I am the LORD,
    when I receive glory through Pharaoh
    and his chariots and charioteers."

The angel of God, who had been leading Israel's camp,
    now moved and went around behind them.
The column of cloud also, leaving the front,
    took up its place behind them,
    so that it came between the camp of the Egyptians
    and that of Israel.
But the cloud now became dark, and thus the night passed
    without the rival camps coming any closer together all night long.
Then Moses stretched out his hand over the sea,
    and the LORD swept the sea
    with a strong east wind throughout the night
    and so turned it into dry land.
When the water was thus divided,
    the Israelites marched into the midst of the sea on dry land,
    with the water like a wall to their right and to their left.

The Egyptians followed in pursuit;
   all Pharaoh's horses and chariots and charioteers went after them
   right into the midst of the sea.
In the night watch just before dawn
   the LORD cast through the column of the fiery cloud
   upon the Egyptian force a glance that threw it into a panic;
   and he so clogged their chariot wheels
   that they could hardly drive.
With that the Egyptians sounded the retreat before Israel,
   because the LORD was fighting for them against the Egyptians.

Then the LORD told Moses, "Stretch out your hand over the sea,
   that the water may flow back upon the Egyptians,
   upon their chariots and their charioteers."
So Moses stretched out his hand over the sea,
   and at dawn the sea flowed back to its normal depth.
The Egyptians were fleeing head on toward the sea,
   when the LORD hurled them into its midst.
As the water flowed back,
   it covered the chariots and the charioteers of Pharaoh's whole army
   which had followed the Israelites into the sea.
Not a single one of them escaped.
But the Israelites had marched on dry land
   through the midst of the sea,
   with the water like a wall to their right and to their left.
Thus the LORD saved Israel on that day
   from the power of the Egyptians.
When Israel saw the Egyptians lying dead on the seashore
   and beheld the great power that the LORD
   had shown against the Egyptians,
   they feared the LORD and believed in him and in his servant Moses.

Then Moses and the Israelites sang this song to the LORD:
   I will sing to the LORD, for he is gloriously triumphant;
   horse and chariot he has cast into the sea. ✝

Exodus 15:1-2, 3-4, 5-6, 17-18
R. (1b) **Let us sing to the Lord; he has covered himself in glory.**
I will sing to the LORD, for he is gloriously triumphant;
   horse and chariot he has cast into the sea.
My strength and my courage is the LORD,
   and he has been my savior.
He is my God, I praise him;
   the God of my father, I extol him. **R.**

The LORD is a warrior,
    LORD is his name!
Pharaoh's chariots and army he hurled into the sea;
    the elite of his officers were submerged in the Red Sea. **R.**
The flood waters covered them,
    they sank into the depths like a stone.
Your right hand, O LORD, magnificent in power,
    your right hand, O LORD, has shattered the enemy. **R.**
You brought in the people you redeemed
    and planted them on the mountain of your inheritance—
the place where you made your seat, O LORD,
    the sanctuary, LORD, which your hands established.
The LORD shall reign forever and ever. **R.**

† *Romans 6:3-11*
Christ, raised from the dead, dies no more.

Brothers and sisters:
Are you unaware that we who were baptized into Christ Jesus
    were baptized into his death?
We were indeed buried with him through baptism into death,
    so that, just as Christ was raised from the dead
    by the glory of the Father,
    we too might live in newness of life.

For if we have grown into union with him through a death like his,
    we shall also be united with him in the resurrection.
We know that our old self was crucified with him,
    so that our sinful body might be done away with,
    that we might no longer be in slavery to sin.
For a dead person has been absolved from sin.
If, then, we have died with Christ,
    we believe that we shall also live with him.
We know that Christ, raised from the dead, dies no more;
    death no longer has power over him.
As to his death, he died to sin once and for all;
    as to his life, he lives for God.
Consequently, you too must think of yourselves as being dead to sin
    and living for God in Christ Jesus. ✛

Psalm 118:1-2, 16-17, 22-23
R. Alleluia, alleluia, alleluia.
Give thanks to the LORD, for he is good,
    for his mercy endures forever.
Let the house of Israel say,
    "His mercy endures forever." **R.**

The right hand of the Lᴏʀᴅ has struck with power;
 the right hand of the Lᴏʀᴅ is exalted.
I shall not die, but live,
 and declare the works of the Lᴏʀᴅ. **R.**
The stone which the builders rejected
 has become the cornerstone.
By the Lᴏʀᴅ has this been done;
 it is wonderful in our eyes. **R.**

† *Luke 24:1-12*

Why do you seek the Living One among the dead?

At daybreak on the first day of the week
 the women who had come from Galilee with Jesus
 took the spices they had prepared
 and went to the tomb.
They found the stone rolled away from the tomb;
 but when they entered,
 they did not find the body of the Lord Jesus.
While they were puzzling over this, behold,
 two men in dazzling garments appeared to them.
They were terrified and bowed their faces to the ground.
They said to them,
 "Why do you seek the living one among the dead?
He is not here, but he has been raised.
Remember what he said to you while he was still in Galilee,
 that the Son of Man must be handed over to sinners
 and be crucified, and rise on the third day."
And they remembered his words.
Then they returned from the tomb
 and announced all these things to the eleven
 and to all the others.
The women were Mary Magdalene, Joanna, and Mary the mother of
  James;
 the others who accompanied them also told this to the apostles,
 but their story seemed like nonsense
 and they did not believe them.
But Peter got up and ran to the tomb,
 bent down, and saw the burial cloths alone;
 then he went home amazed at what had happened. ✛

SUNDAY, APRIL 17
EASTER SUNDAY OF THE RESURRECTION OF THE LORD

✝ Acts of the Apostles 10:34a, 37-43
We ate and drank with him after he rose from the dead.

Peter proceeded to speak and said:
"You know what has happened all over Judea,
beginning in Galilee after the baptism
that John preached,
how God anointed Jesus of Nazareth
with the Holy Spirit and power.
He went about doing good
and healing all those oppressed by the devil,
for God was with him.
We are witnesses of all that he did
both in the country of the Jews and in Jerusalem.
They put him to death by hanging him on a tree.
This man God raised on the third day and granted that he be visible,
not to all the people, but to us,
the witnesses chosen by God in advance,
who ate and drank with him after he rose from the dead.
He commissioned us to preach to the people
and testify that he is the one appointed by God
as judge of the living and the dead.
To him all the prophets bear witness,
that everyone who believes in him
will receive forgiveness of sins through his name." ✙

Psalm 118:1-2, 16-17, 22-23
R. (24) **This is the day the Lord has made; let us rejoice and
be glad.** *(or **Alleluia**.)*
Give thanks to the LORD, for he is good,
for his mercy endures forever.
Let the house of Israel say,
"His mercy endures forever." **R.**
"The right hand of the LORD has struck with power;
the right hand of the LORD is exalted.
I shall not die, but live,
and declare the works of the LORD." **R.**
The stone which the builders rejected
has become the cornerstone.
By the LORD has this been done;
it is wonderful in our eyes. **R.**

† *Colossians 3:1-4* *(or 1 Corinthians 5:6b-8)*
Seek what is above, where Christ is.

Brothers and sisters:
If then you were raised with Christ, seek what is above,
    where Christ is seated at the right hand of God.
Think of what is above, not of what is on earth.
For you have died, and your life is hidden with Christ in God.
When Christ your life appears,
    then you too will appear with him in glory. ✤

SEQUENCE: Victimae paschali laudes
Christians, to the Paschal Victim
    Offer your thankful praises!
A Lamb the sheep redeems;
    Christ, who only is sinless,
    Reconciles sinners to the Father.
Death and life have contended in that combat stupendous:
    The Prince of life, who died, reigns immortal.
Speak, Mary, declaring
    What you saw, wayfaring.
"The tomb of Christ, who is living,
    The glory of Jesus' resurrection;
Bright angels attesting,
    The shroud and napkin resting.
Yes, Christ my hope is arisen;
    to Galilee he goes before you."
Christ indeed from death is risen, our new life obtaining.
    Have mercy, victor King, ever reigning!
    Amen. Alleluia.

See 1 Corinthians 5:7b-8a
R. Alleluia, alleluia.
Christ, our paschal lamb, has been sacrificed;
let us then feast with joy in the Lord. **R.**

† *John 20:1-9* *(or Luke 24:1-12 or,*
at an afternoon or evening Mass, Luke 24:13-35)
He had to rise from the dead.

On the first day of the week,
    Mary of Magdala came to the tomb early in the morning,
    while it was still dark,
    and saw the stone removed from the tomb.
So she ran and went to Simon Peter
    and to the other disciple whom Jesus loved, and told them,
    "They have taken the Lord from the tomb,
    and we don't know where they put him."
So Peter and the other disciple went out and came to the tomb.

They both ran, but the other disciple ran faster than Peter
    and arrived at the tomb first;
    he bent down and saw the burial cloths there, but did not go in.
When Simon Peter arrived after him,
    he went into the tomb and saw the burial cloths there,
    and the cloth that had covered his head,
    not with the burial cloths but rolled up in a separate place.
Then the other disciple also went in,
    the one who had arrived at the tomb first,
    and he saw and believed.
For they did not yet understand the Scripture
    that he had to rise from the dead. ✛

MONDAY, APRIL 18
MONDAY WITHIN THE OCTAVE OF EASTER

† *Acts of the Apostles 2:14, 22-33*
God raised this Jesus; of this we are all witnesses.

On the day of Pentecost, Peter stood up with the Eleven,
    raised his voice, and proclaimed:
    "You who are Jews, indeed all of you staying in Jerusalem.
Let this be known to you, and listen to my words.

"You who are children of Israel, hear these words.
Jesus the Nazorean was a man commended to you by God
    with mighty deeds, wonders, and signs,
    which God worked through him in your midst, as you yourselves
        know.
This man, delivered up by the set plan and foreknowledge of God,
    you killed, using lawless men to crucify him.
But God raised him up, releasing him from the throes of death,
    because it was impossible for him to be held by it.
For David says of him:

I saw the Lord ever before me,
    with him at my right hand I shall not be disturbed.
Therefore my heart has been glad and my tongue has exulted;
    my flesh, too, will dwell in hope,
because you will not abandon my soul to the nether world,
    nor will you suffer your holy one to see corruption.
You have made known to me the paths of life;
    you will fill me with joy in your presence.

My brothers, one can confidently say to you
    about the patriarch David that he died and was buried,
    and his tomb is in our midst to this day.

But since he was a prophet and knew that God had sworn an oath to
    him
  that he would set one of his descendants upon his throne,
  he foresaw and spoke of the resurrection of the Christ,
  that neither was he abandoned to the netherworld
  nor did his flesh see corruption.
God raised this Jesus;
  of this we are all witnesses.
Exalted at the right hand of God,
  he poured forth the promise of the Holy Spirit
  that he received from the Father, as you both see and hear." ✛

Psalm 16:1b-2a and 5, 7-8, 9-10, 11
R. (1) Keep me safe, O God; you are my hope. *(or* **Alleluia.***)*
Keep me, O God, for in you I take refuge;
  I say to the LORD, "My Lord are you."
O LORD, my allotted portion and my cup,
  you it is who hold fast my lot. **R.**
I bless the LORD who counsels me;
  even in the night my heart exhorts me.
I set the LORD ever before me;
  with him at my right hand I shall not be disturbed. **R.**
Therefore my heart is glad and my soul rejoices,
  my body, too, abides in confidence;
Because you will not abandon my soul to the nether world,
  nor will you suffer your faithful one to undergo corruption. **R.**
You will show me the path to life,
  fullness of joys in your presence,
  the delights at your right hand forever. **R.**

Psalm 118:24
R. Alleluia, alleluia.
This is the day the LORD has made;
let us be glad and rejoice in it. **R.**

† *Matthew 28:8-15*
Go tell my brothers to go to Galilee, and there they will see me.

Mary Magdalene and the other Mary went away quickly from the
    tomb,
  fearful yet overjoyed,
  and ran to announce the news to his disciples.
And behold, Jesus met them on their way and greeted them.
They approached, embraced his feet, and did him homage.
Then Jesus said to them, "Do not be afraid.
Go tell my brothers to go to Galilee,
  and there they will see me."

While they were going, some of the guard went into the city
  and told the chief priests all that had happened.
The chief priests assembled with the elders and took counsel;
  then they gave a large sum of money to the soldiers,
  telling them, "You are to say,
  'His disciples came by night and stole him while we were asleep.'
And if this gets to the ears of the governor,
  we will satisfy him and keep you out of trouble."
The soldiers took the money and did as they were instructed.
And this story has circulated among the Jews to the present day. ✦

TUESDAY, APRIL 19
TUESDAY WITHIN THE OCTAVE OF EASTER

† Acts of the Apostles 2:36-41
Repent and be baptized, every one of you, in the name of Jesus Christ.

On the day of Pentecost, Peter said to the Jewish people,
  "Let the whole house of Israel know for certain
  that God has made him both Lord and Christ,
  this Jesus whom you crucified."

Now when they heard this, they were cut to the heart,
  and they asked Peter and the other Apostles,
  "What are we to do, my brothers?"
Peter said to them,
  "Repent and be baptized, every one of you,
  in the name of Jesus Christ, for the forgiveness of your sins;
  and you will receive the gift of the Holy Spirit.
For the promise is made to you and to your children
  and to all those far off,
  whomever the Lord our God will call."
He testified with many other arguments, and was exhorting them,
  "Save yourselves from this corrupt generation."
Those who accepted his message were baptized,
  and about three thousand persons were added that day. ✦

Psalm 33:4-5, 18-19, 20 and 22
R. (5b) **The earth is full of the goodness of the Lord.**
  (*or* **Alleluia.***)*
Upright is the word of the LORD,
  and all his works are trustworthy.
He loves justice and right;
  of the kindness of the LORD the earth is full. **R.**
See, the eyes of the LORD are upon those who fear him,
  upon those who hope for his kindness,

To deliver them from death
  and preserve them in spite of famine. **R.**
Our soul waits for the LORD,
  who is our help and our shield.
May your kindness, O LORD, be upon us
  who have put our hope in you. **R.**

  Psalm 118:24
R. Alleluia, alleluia.
This is the day the LORD has made;
let us be glad and rejoice in it. **R.**

† *John 20:11-18*
I have seen the Lord, and he said these things to me.

Mary Magdalene stayed outside the tomb weeping.
And as she wept, she bent over into the tomb
  and saw two angels in white sitting there,
  one at the head and one at the feet
  where the Body of Jesus had been.
And they said to her, "Woman, why are you weeping?"
She said to them, "They have taken my Lord,
  and I don't know where they laid him."
When she had said this, she turned around and saw Jesus there,
  but did not know it was Jesus.
Jesus said to her, "Woman, why are you weeping?
Whom are you looking for?"
She thought it was the gardener and said to him,
  "Sir, if you carried him away,
  tell me where you laid him,
  and I will take him."
Jesus said to her, "Mary!"
She turned and said to him in Hebrew, "Rabbouni,"
  which means Teacher.
Jesus said to her, "Stop holding on to me,
  for I have not yet ascended to the Father.
But go to my brothers and tell them,
  'I am going to my Father and your Father,
  to my God and your God.'"
Mary went and announced to the disciples,
  "I have seen the Lord,"
  and then reported what he had told her. ✛

WEDNESDAY, APRIL 20
WEDNESDAY WITHIN THE OCTAVE OF EASTER

† *Acts of the Apostles 3:1-10*
What I do have I give you: in the name of the Lord Jesus, rise and walk.

Peter and John were going up to the temple area
for the three o'clock hour of prayer.
And a man crippled from birth was carried
and placed at the gate of the temple called "the Beautiful Gate"
every day
to beg for alms from the people who entered the temple.
When he saw Peter and John about to go into the temple,
he asked for alms.
But Peter looked intently at him, as did John,
and said, "Look at us."
He paid attention to them, expecting to receive something from them.
Peter said, "I have neither silver nor gold,
but what I do have I give you:
in the name of Jesus Christ the Nazorean, rise and walk."
Then Peter took him by the right hand and raised him up,
and immediately his feet and ankles grew strong.
He leaped up, stood, and walked around,
and went into the temple with them,
walking and jumping and praising God.
When all the people saw him walking and praising God,
they recognized him as the one
who used to sit begging at the Beautiful Gate of the temple,
and they were filled with amazement and astonishment
at what had happened to him. ✛

Psalm 105:1-2, 3-4, 6-7, 8-9
R. (3b) **Rejoice, O hearts that seek the Lord.** *(or* **Alleluia.***)*
Give thanks to the LORD, invoke his name;
make known among the nations his deeds.
Sing to him, sing his praise,
proclaim all his wondrous deeds. **R.**
Glory in his holy name;
rejoice, O hearts that seek the LORD!
Look to the LORD in his strength;
seek to serve him constantly. **R.**
You descendants of Abraham, his servants,
sons of Jacob, his chosen ones!
He, the LORD, is our God;
throughout the earth his judgments prevail. **R.**

He remembers forever his covenant
  which he made binding for a thousand generations—
Which he entered into with Abraham
  and by his oath to Isaac. **R.**

  Psalm 118:24
R. Alleluia, alleluia.
This is the day the LORD has made;
let us be glad and rejoice in it. **R.**

† Luke 24:13-35
They recognized Jesus in the breaking of the bread.

That very day, the first day of the week,
  two of Jesus' disciples were going
  to a village seven miles from Jerusalem called Emmaus,
  and they were conversing about all the things that had occurred.
And it happened that while they were conversing and debating,
  Jesus himself drew near and walked with them,
  but their eyes were prevented from recognizing him.
He asked them,
  "What are you discussing as you walk along?"
They stopped, looking downcast.
One of them, named Cleopas, said to him in reply,
  "Are you the only visitor to Jerusalem
  who does not know of the things
  that have taken place there in these days?"
And he replied to them, "What sort of things?"
They said to him,
  "The things that happened to Jesus the Nazarene,
  who was a prophet mighty in deed and word
  before God and all the people,
  how our chief priests and rulers both handed him over
  to a sentence of death and crucified him.
But we were hoping that he would be the one to redeem Israel;
  and besides all this,
  it is now the third day since this took place.
Some women from our group, however, have astounded us:
  they were at the tomb early in the morning
  and did not find his Body;
  they came back and reported
  that they had indeed seen a vision of angels
  who announced that he was alive.
Then some of those with us went to the tomb
  and found things just as the women had described,
  but him they did not see."

And he said to them, "Oh, how foolish you are!
How slow of heart to believe all that the prophets spoke!
Was it not necessary that the Christ should suffer these things
   and enter into his glory?"
Then beginning with Moses and all the prophets,
   he interpreted to them what referred to him
   in all the Scriptures.
As they approached the village to which they were going,
   he gave the impression that he was going on farther.
But they urged him, "Stay with us,
   for it is nearly evening and the day is almost over."
So he went in to stay with them.
And it happened that, while he was with them at table,
   he took bread, said the blessing,
   broke it, and gave it to them.
With that their eyes were opened and they recognized him,
   but he vanished from their sight.
Then they said to each other,
   "Were not our hearts burning within us
   while he spoke to us on the way and opened the Scriptures to us?"
So they set out at once and returned to Jerusalem
   where they found gathered together
   the Eleven and those with them who were saying,
   "The Lord has truly been raised and has appeared to Simon!"
Then the two recounted what had taken place on the way
   and how he was made known to them in the breaking of the
     bread. ✛

THURSDAY, APRIL 21
THURSDAY WITHIN THE OCTAVE OF EASTER

† *Acts of the Apostles 3:11-26*
The author of life you put to death, but God raised him from the dead.

As the crippled man who had been cured clung to Peter and John,
   all the people hurried in amazement toward them
   in the portico called "Solomon's Portico."
When Peter saw this, he addressed the people,
   "You children of Israel, why are you amazed at this,
   and why do you look so intently at us
   as if we had made him walk by our own power or piety?
The God of Abraham, the God of Isaac, and the God of Jacob,
   the God of our fathers, has glorified his servant Jesus
   whom you handed over and denied in Pilate's presence,
   when he had decided to release him.

You denied the Holy and Righteous One
and asked that a murderer be released to you.
The author of life you put to death,
but God raised him from the dead; of this we are witnesses.
And by faith in his name,
this man, whom you see and know, his name has made strong,
and the faith that comes through it
has given him this perfect health,
in the presence of all of you.
Now I know, brothers and sisters,
that you acted out of ignorance, just as your leaders did;
but God has thus brought to fulfillment
what he had announced beforehand
through the mouth of all the prophets,
that his Christ would suffer.
Repent, therefore, and be converted, that your sins may be wiped away,
and that the Lord may grant you times of refreshment
and send you the Christ already appointed for you, Jesus,
whom heaven must receive until the times of universal restoration
of which God spoke through the mouth
of his holy prophets from of old.
For Moses said:

A prophet like me will the Lord, your God, raise up for you
from among your own kin;
to him you shall listen in all that he may say to you.
Everyone who does not listen to that prophet
will be cut off from the people.

"Moreover, all the prophets who spoke,
from Samuel and those afterwards, also announced these days.
You are the children of the prophets
and of the covenant that God made with your ancestors
when he said to Abraham,
In your offspring all the families of the earth shall be blessed.
For you first, God raised up his servant and sent him to bless you
by turning each of you from your evil ways." ✛

Psalm 8:2ab and 5, 6-7, 8-9
**R. (2ab) O Lord, our God, how wonderful your name in all the
earth!** *(or* **Alleluia.***)*
O LORD, our Lord,
how glorious is your name over all the earth!
What is man that you should be mindful of him,
or the son of man that you should care for him? **R.**

You have made him little less than the angels,
  and crowned him with glory and honor.
You have given him rule over the works of your hands,
  putting all things under his feet. **R.**
All sheep and oxen,
  yes, and the beasts of the field,
The birds of the air, the fishes of the sea,
  and whatever swims the paths of the seas. **R.**

Psalm 118:24
R. Alleluia, alleluia.
This is the day the LORD has made;
let us be glad and rejoice in it. **R.**

† *Luke 24:35-48*
*Thus it was written that the Christ would suffer
and rise from the dead on the third day.*

The disciples of Jesus recounted what had taken place along the way,
  and how they had come to recognize him in the breaking of bread.

While they were still speaking about this,
  he stood in their midst and said to them,
  "Peace be with you."
But they were startled and terrified
  and thought that they were seeing a ghost.
Then he said to them, "Why are you troubled?
And why do questions arise in your hearts?
Look at my hands and my feet, that it is I myself.
Touch me and see, because a ghost does not have flesh and bones
  as you can see I have."
And as he said this,
  he showed them his hands and his feet.
While they were still incredulous for joy and were amazed,
  he asked them, "Have you anything here to eat?"
They gave him a piece of baked fish;
  he took it and ate it in front of them.

He said to them,
  "These are my words that I spoke to you while I was still with you,
  that everything written about me in the law of Moses
  and in the prophets and psalms must be fulfilled."
Then he opened their minds to understand the Scriptures.
And he said to them,
  "Thus it is written that the Christ would suffer
  and rise from the dead on the third day

and that repentance, for the forgiveness of sins,
would be preached in his name
to all the nations, beginning from Jerusalem.
You are witnesses of these things." ✝

FRIDAY, APRIL 22
FRIDAY WITHIN THE OCTAVE OF EASTER

✝ Acts of the Apostles 4:1-12
There is no salvation through anyone else.

After the crippled man had been cured,
while Peter and John were still speaking to the people,
the priests, the captain of the temple guard,
and the Sadducees confronted them,
disturbed that they were teaching the people
and proclaiming in Jesus the resurrection of the dead.
They laid hands on Peter and John
and put them in custody until the next day,
since it was already evening.
But many of those who heard the word came to believe
and the number of men grew to about five thousand.

On the next day, their leaders, elders, and scribes
were assembled in Jerusalem, with Annas the high priest,
Caiaphas, John, Alexander,
and all who were of the high-priestly class.
They brought them into their presence and questioned them,
"By what power or by what name have you done this?"
Then Peter, filled with the Holy Spirit, answered them,
"Leaders of the people and elders:
If we are being examined today
about a good deed done to a cripple,
namely, by what means he was saved,
then all of you and all the people of Israel should know
that it was in the name of Jesus Christ the Nazorean
whom you crucified, whom God raised from the dead;
in his name this man stands before you healed.
He is *the stone rejected by you, the builders,*
which has become the cornerstone.
There is no salvation through anyone else,
nor is there any other name under heaven
given to the human race by which we are to be saved." ✝

Psalm 118:1-2 and 4, 22-24, 25-27a

R. (22) **The stone rejected by the builders has become the cornerstone.** *(or* **Alleluia.***)*

Give thanks to the Lord, for he is good,
   for his mercy endures forever.
Let the house of Israel say,
   "His mercy endures forever."
Let those who fear the Lord say,
   "His mercy endures forever." **R.**
The stone which the builders rejected
   has become the cornerstone.
By the Lord has this been done;
   it is wonderful in our eyes.
This is the day the Lord has made;
   let us be glad and rejoice in it. **R.**
O Lord, grant salvation!
   O Lord, grant prosperity!
Blessed is he who comes in the name of the Lord;
   we bless you from the house of the Lord.
The Lord is God, and he has given us light. **R.**

Psalm 118:24

R. Alleluia, alleluia.

This is the day the Lord has made;
let us be glad and rejoice in it. **R.**

† *John 21:1-14*

*Jesus came over and took the bread and gave it to them,
and in like manner the fish.*

Jesus revealed himself again to his disciples at the Sea of Tiberias.
He revealed himself in this way.
Together were Simon Peter, Thomas called Didymus,
   Nathanael from Cana in Galilee,
   Zebedee's sons, and two others of his disciples.
Simon Peter said to them, "I am going fishing."
They said to him, "We also will come with you."
So they went out and got into the boat,
   but that night they caught nothing.
When it was already dawn, Jesus was standing on the shore;
   but the disciples did not realize that it was Jesus.
Jesus said to them, "Children, have you caught anything to eat?"
They answered him, "No."
So he said to them, "Cast the net over the right side of the boat
   and you will find something."

So they cast it, and were not able to pull it in
  because of the number of fish.
So the disciple whom Jesus loved said to Peter, "It is the Lord."
When Simon Peter heard that it was the Lord,
  he tucked in his garment, for he was lightly clad,
  and jumped into the sea.
The other disciples came in the boat,
  for they were not far from shore, only about a hundred yards,
  dragging the net with the fish.
When they climbed out on shore,
  they saw a charcoal fire with fish on it and bread.
Jesus said to them, "Bring some of the fish you just caught."
So Simon Peter went over and dragged the net ashore
  full of one hundred fifty-three large fish.
Even though there were so many, the net was not torn.
Jesus said to them, "Come, have breakfast."
And none of the disciples dared to ask him, "Who are you?"
  because they realized it was the Lord.
Jesus came over and took the bread and gave it to them,
  and in like manner the fish.
This was now the third time Jesus was revealed to his disciples
  after being raised from the dead. ✝

SATURDAY, APRIL 23
SATURDAY WITHIN THE OCTAVE OF EASTER

✝ Acts of the Apostles 4:13-21
It is impossible for us not to speak about what we have seen and heard.

Observing the boldness of Peter and John
  and perceiving them to be uneducated, ordinary men,
  the leaders, elders, and scribes were amazed,
  and they recognized them as the companions of Jesus.
Then when they saw the man who had been cured standing there
    with them,
  they could say nothing in reply.
So they ordered them to leave the Sanhedrin,
  and conferred with one another, saying,
  "What are we to do with these men?
Everyone living in Jerusalem knows that a remarkable sign
  was done through them, and we cannot deny it.
But so that it may not be spread any further among the people,
  let us give them a stern warning
  never again to speak to anyone in this name."

So they called them back
  and ordered them not to speak or teach at all in the name of Jesus.
Peter and John, however, said to them in reply,
  "Whether it is right in the sight of God
  for us to obey you rather than God, you be the judges.
It is impossible for us not to speak about what we have seen and
    heard."
After threatening them further,
  they released them,
  finding no way to punish them,
  on account of the people who were all praising God
  for what had happened. ✛

Psalm 118:1 and 14-15ab, 16-18, 19-21
R. (21a) **I will give thanks to you, for you have answered me.**
  (or **Alleluia.***)*
Give thanks to the LORD, for he is good,
  for his mercy endures forever.
My strength and my courage is the LORD,
  and he has been my savior.
The joyful shout of victory
  in the tents of the just. **R.**
"The right hand of the LORD is exalted;
  the right hand of the LORD has struck with power."
I shall not die, but live,
  and declare the works of the LORD.
Though the LORD has indeed chastised me,
  yet he has not delivered me to death. **R.**
Open to me the gates of justice;
  I will enter them and give thanks to the LORD.
This is the gate of the LORD;
  the just shall enter it.
I will give thanks to you, for you have answered me
  and have been my savior. **R.**

Psalm 118:24
R. Alleluia, alleluia.
This is the day the LORD has made;
  let us be glad and rejoice in it. **R.**

† *Mark 16:9-15*
Go into the whole world and proclaim the Gospel to every creature.

When Jesus had risen, early on the first day of the week,
  he appeared first to Mary Magdalene,
  out of whom he had driven seven demons.

She went and told his companions who were mourning and weeping.
When they heard that he was alive
  and had been seen by her, they did not believe.

After this he appeared in another form
  to two of them walking along on their way to the country.
They returned and told the others;
  but they did not believe them either.

But later, as the Eleven were at table, he appeared to them
  and rebuked them for their unbelief and hardness of heart
  because they had not believed those
  who saw him after he had been raised.
He said to them, "Go into the whole world
  and proclaim the Gospel to every creature." ✛

SUNDAY, APRIL 24
SECOND SUNDAY OF EASTER OR SUNDAY OF DIVINE MERCY

† Acts of the Apostles 5:12-16
More than ever, believers in the Lord,
great numbers of men and women, were added to them.

Many signs and wonders were done among the people
  at the hands of the apostles.
They were all together in Solomon's portico.
None of the others dared to join them, but the people esteemed them.
Yet more than ever, believers in the Lord,
  great numbers of men and women, were added to them.
Thus they even carried the sick out into the streets
  and laid them on cots and mats
  so that when Peter came by,
  at least his shadow might fall on one or another of them.
A large number of people from the towns
  in the vicinity of Jerusalem also gathered,
  bringing the sick and those disturbed by unclean spirits,
  and they were all cured. ✛

Psalm 118:2-4, 13-15, 22-24
**R. Give thanks to the Lord, for he is good, his love is ever-
  lasting.** *(or* **Alleluia.***)*
Let the house of Israel say,
  "His mercy endures forever."
Let the house of Aaron say,
  "His mercy endures forever."
Let those who fear the LORD say,
  "His mercy endures forever." **R.**

I was hard pressed and was falling,
  but the Lord helped me.
My strength and my courage is the Lord,
  and he has been my savior.
The joyful shout of victory
  in the tents of the just: **R.**
The stone which the builders rejected
  has become the cornerstone.
By the Lord has this been done;
  it is wonderful in our eyes.
This is the day the Lord has made;
  let us be glad and rejoice in it. **R.**

† *Revelation 1:9-11a, 12-13, 17-19*
I was dead, but now I am alive forever and ever.

I, John, your brother, who share with you
  the distress, the kingdom, and the endurance we have in Jesus,
  found myself on the island called Patmos
  because I proclaimed God's word and gave testimony to Jesus.
I was caught up in spirit on the Lord's day
  and heard behind me a voice as loud as a trumpet, which said,
  "Write on a scroll what you see."
Then I turned to see whose voice it was that spoke to me,
  and when I turned, I saw seven gold lampstands
  and in the midst of the lampstands one like a son of man,
  wearing an ankle-length robe, with a gold sash around his chest.

When I caught sight of him, I fell down at his feet as though dead.
He touched me with his right hand and said, "Do not be afraid.
I am the first and the last, the one who lives.
Once I was dead, but now I am alive forever and ever.
I hold the keys to death and the netherworld.
Write down, therefore, what you have seen,
  and what is happening, and what will happen afterwards." ✛

John 20:29
R. Alleluia, alleluia.
You believe in me, Thomas, because you have seen me, says the Lord;
blessed are they who have not seen me, but still believe! **R.**

† *John 20:19-31*

Eight days later Jesus came and stood in their midst.

On the evening of that first day of the week,
  when the doors were locked, where the disciples were,
  for fear of the Jews,
  Jesus came and stood in their midst
  and said to them, "Peace be with you."
When he had said this, he showed them his hands and his side.
The disciples rejoiced when they saw the Lord.
Jesus said to them again, "Peace be with you.
As the Father has sent me, so I send you."
And when he had said this, he breathed on them and said to them,
  "Receive the Holy Spirit.
Whose sins you forgive are forgiven them,
  and whose sins you retain are retained."

Thomas, called Didymus, one of the Twelve,
  was not with them when Jesus came.
So the other disciples said to him, "We have seen the Lord."
But he said to them,
  "Unless I see the mark of the nails in his hands
  and put my finger into the nailmarks
  and put my hand into his side, I will not believe."

Now a week later his disciples were again inside
  and Thomas was with them.
Jesus came, although the doors were locked,
  and stood in their midst and said, "Peace be with you."
Then he said to Thomas, "Put your finger here and see my hands,
  and bring your hand and put it into my side,
  and do not be unbelieving, but believe."
Thomas answered and said to him, "My Lord and my God!"
Jesus said to him, "Have you come to believe because you have seen
      me?
Blessed are those who have not seen and have believed."

Now Jesus did many other signs in the presence of his disciples
  that are not written in this book.
But these are written that you may come to believe
  that Jesus is the Christ, the Son of God,
  and that through this belief you may have life in his name. ✝

MONDAY, APRIL 25
St. Mark

† *1 Peter 5:5b-14*
Mark, my son, sends you greetings.

Beloved:
Clothe yourselves with humility
in your dealings with one another, for

*God opposes the proud
but bestows favor on the humble.*

So humble yourselves under the mighty hand of God,
that he may exalt you in due time.
Cast all your worries upon him because he cares for you.

Be sober and vigilant.
Your opponent the Devil is prowling around like a roaring lion
looking for someone to devour.
Resist him, steadfast in faith,
knowing that your brothers and sisters throughout the world
undergo the same sufferings.
The God of all grace
who called you to his eternal glory through Christ Jesus
will himself restore, confirm, strengthen, and establish you
after you have suffered a little.
To him be dominion forever. Amen.

I write you this briefly through Silvanus,
whom I consider a faithful brother,
exhorting you and testifying that this is the true grace of God.
Remain firm in it.
The chosen one at Babylon sends you greeting, as does Mark, my son.
Greet one another with a loving kiss.
Peace to all of you who are in Christ. ✛

Psalm 89:2-3, 6-7, 16-17
R. (2) For ever I will sing the goodness of the Lord.
(or **Alleluia.***)*
The favors of the Lord I will sing forever;
through all generations my mouth shall proclaim your faithfulness.
For you have said, "My kindness is established forever";
in heaven you have confirmed your faithfulness. **R.**
The heavens proclaim your wonders, O Lord,
and your faithfulness, in the assembly of the holy ones.
For who in the skies can rank with the Lord?
Who is like the Lord among the sons of God? **R.**

Blessed the people who know the joyful shout;
  in the light of your countenance, O Lᴏʀᴅ, they walk.
At your name they rejoice all the day,
  and through your justice they are exalted. **R.**

1 Corinthians 1:23a-24b
R. Alleluia, alleluia.
We proclaim Christ crucified;
he is the power of God and the wisdom of God. **R.**

† Mark 16:15-20
Proclaim the Gospel to every creature.

Jesus appeared to the Eleven and said to them:
"Go into the whole world
  and proclaim the Gospel to every creature.
Whoever believes and is baptized will be saved;
  whoever does not believe will be condemned.
These signs will accompany those who believe:
  in my name they will drive out demons,
  they will speak new languages.
They will pick up serpents with their hands,
  and if they drink any deadly thing, it will not harm them.
They will lay hands on the sick, and they will recover."

Then the Lord Jesus, after he spoke to them,
  was taken up into heaven
  and took his seat at the right hand of God.
But they went forth and preached everywhere,
  while the Lord worked with them
  and confirmed the word through accompanying signs. **✝**

TUESDAY, APRIL 26
Eᴀsᴛᴇʀ Wᴇᴇᴋᴅᴀʏ

† Acts of the Apostles 4:32-37
The community of believers was of one heart and mind.

The community of believers was of one heart and mind,
  and no one claimed that any of his possessions was his own,
  but they had everything in common.
With great power the Apostles bore witness
  to the resurrection of the Lord Jesus,
  and great favor was accorded them all.
There was no needy person among them,
  for those who owned property or houses would sell them,
  bring the proceeds of the sale,

and put them at the feet of the Apostles,
and they were distributed to each according to need.

Thus Joseph, also named by the Apostles Barnabas
(which is translated "son of encouragement"),
a Levite, a Cypriot by birth,
sold a piece of property that he owned,
then brought the money and put it at the feet of the Apostles. ✛

Psalm 93:1ab, 1cd-2, 5

R. (1a) **The Lord is king; he is robed in majesty.** *(or **Alleluia**.)*
The LORD is king, in splendor robed;
  robed is the LORD and girt about with strength. **R.**
And he has made the world firm,
  not to be moved.
Your throne stands firm from of old;
  from everlasting you are, O LORD. **R.**
Your decrees are worthy of trust indeed:
  holiness befits your house,
  O LORD, for length of days. **R.**

John 3:14-15

R. Alleluia, alleluia.
The Son of Man must be lifted up,
so that everyone who believes in him
may have eternal life. **R.**

† *John 3:7b-15*

*No one has gone up to heaven except the one
who has come down from heaven, the Son of Man.*

Jesus said to Nicodemus:
  "'You must be born from above.'
The wind blows where it wills, and you can hear the sound it makes,
  but you do not know where it comes from or where it goes;
  so it is with everyone who is born of the Spirit."
Nicodemus answered and said to him,
  "How can this happen?"
Jesus answered and said to him,
  "You are the teacher of Israel and you do not understand this?
Amen, amen, I say to you,
  we speak of what we know and we testify to what we have seen,
  but you people do not accept our testimony.
If I tell you about earthly things and you do not believe,
  how will you believe if I tell you about heavenly things?
No one has gone up to heaven
  except the one who has come down from heaven, the Son of Man.

And just as Moses lifted up the serpent in the desert,
  so must the Son of Man be lifted up,
  so that everyone who believes in him may have eternal life." ✛

WEDNESDAY, APRIL 27
Easter Weekday

✝ Acts of the Apostles 5:17-26
The men whom you put in prison are in the temple area
and are teaching the people.

The high priest rose up and all his companions,
  that is, the party of the Sadducees,
  and, filled with jealousy,
  laid hands upon the Apostles and put them in the public jail.
But during the night, the angel of the Lord opened the doors of the
      prison,
  led them out, and said,
  "Go and take your place in the temple area,
  and tell the people everything about this life."
When they heard this,
  they went to the temple early in the morning and taught.
When the high priest and his companions arrived,
  they convened the Sanhedrin,
  the full senate of the children of Israel,
  and sent to the jail to have them brought in.
But the court officers who went did not find them in the prison,
  so they came back and reported,
  "We found the jail securely locked
  and the guards stationed outside the doors,
  but when we opened them, we found no one inside."
When the captain of the temple guard and the chief priests heard
      this report,
  they were at a loss about them,
  as to what this would come to.
Then someone came in and reported to them,
  "The men whom you put in prison are in the temple area
  and are teaching the people."
Then the captain and the court officers went and brought them,
  but without force,
  because they were afraid of being stoned by the people. ✛

Psalm 34:2-3, 4-5, 6-7, 8-9

R. (7a) **The Lord hears the cry of the poor.** *(or* **Alleluia.***)*

I will bless the LORD at all times;
  his praise shall be ever in my mouth.
Let my soul glory in the LORD;
  the lowly will hear me and be glad. **R.**
Glorify the LORD with me,
  let us together extol his name.
I sought the LORD, and he answered me
  and delivered me from all my fears. **R.**
Look to him that you may be radiant with joy,
  and your faces may not blush with shame.
When the poor one called out, the LORD heard,
  and from all his distress he saved him. **R.**
The angel of the LORD encamps
  around those who fear him, and delivers them.
Taste and see how good the LORD is;
  blessed the man who takes refuge in him. **R.**

John 3:16

R. Alleluia, alleluia.

God so loved the world that he gave his only-begotten Son,
so that everyone who believes in him might have eternal life. **R.**

† *John 3:16-21*

God sent his Son that the world might be saved through him.

God so loved the world that he gave his only-begotten Son,
  so that everyone who believes in him might not perish
  but might have eternal life.
For God did not send his Son into the world to condemn the world,
  but that the world might be saved through him.
Whoever believes in him will not be condemned,
  but whoever does not believe has already been condemned,
  because he has not believed in the name of the only-begotten Son
    of God.
And this is the verdict,
  that the light came into the world,
  but people preferred darkness to light,
  because their works were evil.
For everyone who does wicked things hates the light
  and does not come toward the light,
  so that his works might not be exposed.
But whoever lives the truth comes to the light,
  so that his works may be clearly seen as done in God. ✛

THURSDAY, APRIL 28
EASTER WEEKDAY, ST. PETER CHANEL, ST. LOUIS GRIGNION DE MONTFORT

† *Acts of the Apostles 5:27-33*
We are witnesses of these words, as is the Holy Spirit.

When the court officers had brought the Apostles in
and made them stand before the Sanhedrin,
the high priest questioned them,
"We gave you strict orders did we not,
to stop teaching in that name.
Yet you have filled Jerusalem with your teaching
and want to bring this man's blood upon us."
But Peter and the Apostles said in reply,
"We must obey God rather than men.
The God of our ancestors raised Jesus,
though you had him killed by hanging him on a tree.
God exalted him at his right hand as leader and savior
to grant Israel repentance and forgiveness of sins.
We are witnesses of these things,
as is the Holy Spirit whom God has given to those who obey him."

When they heard this,
they became infuriated and wanted to put them to death. ✛

Psalm 34:2 and 9, 17-18, 19-20
R. (7a) **The Lord hears the cry of the poor.** *(or* **Alleluia.***)*
I will bless the LORD at all times;
his praise shall be ever in my mouth.
Taste and see how good the LORD is;
blessed the man who takes refuge in him. **R.**
The LORD confronts the evildoers,
to destroy remembrance of them from the earth.
When the just cry out, the LORD hears them,
and from all their distress he rescues them. **R.**
The LORD is close to the brokenhearted;
and those who are crushed in spirit he saves.
Many are the troubles of the just man,
but out of them all the LORD delivers him. **R.**

John 20:29
R. Alleluia, alleluia.
You believe in me, Thomas, because you have seen me, says the Lord;
blessed are those who have not seen, but still believe! **R.**

✝ *John 3:31-36*

The Father loves the Son and has given everything over to him.

The one who comes from above is above all.
The one who is of the earth is earthly and speaks of earthly things.
But the one who comes from heaven is above all.
He testifies to what he has seen and heard,
   but no one accepts his testimony.
Whoever does accept his testimony certifies that God is trustworthy.
For the one whom God sent speaks the words of God.
He does not ration his gift of the Spirit.
The Father loves the Son and has given everything over to him.
Whoever believes in the Son has eternal life,
   but whoever disobeys the Son will not see life,
   but the wrath of God remains upon him. ✝

FRIDAY, APRIL 29
ST. CATHERINE OF SIENA

✝ *Acts of the Apostles 5:34-42*

The Apostles went out rejoicing that they had been found worthy
to suffer dishonor for the sake of the name.

A Pharisee in the Sanhedrin named Gamaliel,
   a teacher of the law, respected by all the people,
   stood up, ordered the Apostles to be put outside for a short time,
   and said to the Sanhedrin, "Fellow children of Israel,
   be careful what you are about to do to these men.
Some time ago, Theudas appeared, claiming to be someone important,
   and about four hundred men joined him, but he was killed,
   and all those who were loyal to him
   were disbanded and came to nothing.
After him came Judas the Galilean at the time of the census.
He also drew people after him,
   but he too perished and all who were loyal to him were scattered.
So now I tell you,
   have nothing to do with these men, and let them go.
For if this endeavor or this activity is of human origin,
   it will destroy itself.
But if it comes from God, you will not be able to destroy them;
   you may even find yourselves fighting against God."
They were persuaded by him.
After recalling the Apostles, they had them flogged,
   ordered them to stop speaking in the name of Jesus,
   and dismissed them.

So they left the presence of the Sanhedrin,
  rejoicing that they had been found worthy
  to suffer dishonor for the sake of the name.
And all day long, both at the temple and in their homes,
  they did not stop teaching and proclaiming the Christ, Jesus. ✛

Psalm 27:1, 4, 13-14

R. (see 4abc) **One thing I seek: to dwell in the house of the
  Lord.** *(or* **Alleluia.***)*

The LORD is my light and my salvation;
  whom should I fear?
The LORD is my life's refuge;
  of whom should I be afraid? **R.**

One thing I ask of the LORD;
  this I seek:
To dwell in the house of the LORD;
  all the days of my life,
That I may gaze on the loveliness of the LORD
  and contemplate his temple. **R.**

I believe that I shall see the bounty of the LORD
  in the land of the living.
Wait for the LORD with courage;
  be stouthearted, and wait for the LORD. **R.**

Matthew 4:4b

R. Alleluia, alleluia.
One does not live on bread alone,
but on every word that comes forth from the mouth of God. **R.**

† *John 6:1-15*
Jesus distributed to those who were reclining as much as they wanted.

Jesus went across the Sea of Galilee.
A large crowd followed him,
  because they saw the signs he was performing on the sick.
Jesus went up on the mountain,
  and there he sat down with his disciples.
The Jewish feast of Passover was near.
When Jesus raised his eyes and saw that a large crowd was coming
    to him,
  he said to Philip, "Where can we buy enough food for them to eat?"
He said this to test him,
  because he himself knew what he was going to do.
Philip answered him,
  "Two hundred days' wages worth of food would not be enough
  for each of them to have a little."

One of his disciples,
   Andrew, the brother of Simon Peter, said to him,
   "There is a boy here who has five barley loaves and two fish;
   but what good are these for so many?"
Jesus said, "Have the people recline."
Now there was a great deal of grass in that place.
So the men reclined, about five thousand in number.
Then Jesus took the loaves, gave thanks,
   and distributed them to those who were reclining,
   and also as much of the fish as they wanted.
When they had had their fill, he said to his disciples,
   "Gather the fragments left over,
   so that nothing will be wasted."
So they collected them,
   and filled twelve wicker baskets with fragments
   from the five barley loaves that had been more than they could eat.
When the people saw the sign he had done, they said,
   "This is truly the Prophet, the one who is to come into the world."
Since Jesus knew that they were going to come and carry him off
   to make him king,
   he withdrew again to the mountain alone. ✛

SATURDAY, APRIL 30
EASTER WEEKDAY, ST. POPE PIUS V

† *Acts of the Apostles 6:1-7*
They chose seven men filled with the Holy Spirit.

As the number of disciples continued to grow,
   the Hellenists complained against the Hebrews
   because their widows
   were being neglected in the daily distribution.
So the Twelve called together the community of the disciples and said,
   "It is not right for us to neglect the word of God to serve at table.
Brothers, select from among you seven reputable men,
   filled with the Spirit and wisdom,
   whom we shall appoint to this task,
   whereas we shall devote ourselves to prayer
   and to the ministry of the word."
The proposal was acceptable to the whole community,
   so they chose Stephen, a man filled with faith and the Holy Spirit,
   also Philip, Prochorus, Nicanor, Timon, Parmenas,
   and Nicholas of Antioch, a convert to Judaism.
They presented these men to the Apostles
   who prayed and laid hands on them.

The word of God continued to spread,
   and the number of the disciples in Jerusalem increased greatly;
   even a large group of priests were becoming obedient to the faith. ✛

Psalm 33:1-2, 4-5, 18-19

R. (22) Lord, let your mercy be on us, as we place our trust in you. *(or* **Alleluia.***)*

Exult, you just, in the LORD;
   praise from the upright is fitting.
Give thanks to the LORD on the harp;
   with the ten-stringed lyre chant his praises. **R.**
Upright is the word of the LORD,
   and all his works are trustworthy.
He loves justice and right;
   of the kindness of the LORD the earth is full. **R.**
See, the eyes of the LORD are upon those who fear him,
   upon those who hope for his kindness,
To deliver them from death
   and preserve them in spite of famine. **R.**

R. Alleluia, alleluia.
Christ is risen, who made all things;
he has shown mercy on all people. **R.**

✝ *John 6:16-21*
They saw Jesus, walking on the sea.

When it was evening, the disciples of Jesus went down to the sea,
   embarked in a boat, and went across the sea to Capernaum.
It had already grown dark, and Jesus had not yet come to them.
The sea was stirred up because a strong wind was blowing.
When they had rowed about three or four miles,
   they saw Jesus walking on the sea and coming near the boat,
   and they began to be afraid.
But he said to them, "It is I. Do not be afraid."
They wanted to take him into the boat,
   but the boat immediately arrived at the shore
   to which they were heading. ✛

SUNDAY, MAY 1
THIRD SUNDAY OF EASTER

† *Acts of the Apostles 5:27-32, 40b-41*
We are witnesses of these words as is the Holy Spirit.

When the captain and the court officers had brought the apostles in
and made them stand before the Sanhedrin,
the high priest questioned them,
"We gave you strict orders, did we not,
to stop teaching in that name?
Yet you have filled Jerusalem with your teaching
and want to bring this man's blood upon us."
But Peter and the apostles said in reply,
"We must obey God rather than men.
The God of our ancestors raised Jesus,
though you had him killed by hanging him on a tree.
God exalted him at his right hand as leader and savior
to grant Israel repentance and forgiveness of sins.
We are witnesses of these things,
as is the Holy Spirit whom God has given to those who obey him."

The Sanhedrin ordered the apostles
to stop speaking in the name of Jesus, and dismissed them.
So they left the presence of the Sanhedrin,
rejoicing that they had been found worthy
to suffer dishonor for the sake of the name. ✚

Psalm 30:2, 4, 5-6, 11-12, 13
R. (2a) **I will praise you, Lord, for you have rescued me.**
(or **Alleluia.***)*
I will extol you, O LORD, for you drew me clear
and did not let my enemies rejoice over me.
O LORD, you brought me up from the netherworld;
you preserved me from among those going down into the pit. **R.**
Sing praise to the LORD, you his faithful ones,
and give thanks to his holy name.
For his anger lasts but a moment;
a lifetime, his good will.
At nightfall, weeping enters in,
but with the dawn, rejoicing. **R.**
Hear, O LORD, and have pity on me;
O LORD, be my helper.
You changed my mourning into dancing;
O LORD, my God, forever will I give you thanks. **R.**

† *Revelation 5:11-14*
Worthy is the Lamb that was slain to receive power and riches.

I, John, looked and heard the voices of many angels
who surrounded the throne
and the living creatures and the elders.
They were countless in number, and they cried out in a loud voice:
"Worthy is the Lamb that was slain
to receive power and riches, wisdom and strength,
honor and glory and blessing."
Then I heard every creature in heaven and on earth
and under the earth and in the sea,
everything in the universe, cry out:
"To the one who sits on the throne and to the Lamb
be blessing and honor, glory and might,
forever and ever."
The four living creatures answered, "Amen,"
and the elders fell down and worshiped. ✛

R. Alleluia, alleluia.
Christ is risen, creator of all;
he has shown pity on all people. **R.**

† *John 21:1-19* (or *John 21:1-14*)
Jesus came and took the bread and gave it to them and in like manner the fish.

At that time, Jesus revealed himself again to his disciples at the
Sea of Tiberias.
He revealed himself in this way.
Together were Simon Peter, Thomas called Didymus,
Nathanael from Cana in Galilee,
Zebedee's sons, and two others of his disciples.
Simon Peter said to them, "I am going fishing."
They said to him, "We also will come with you."
So they went out and got into the boat,
but that night they caught nothing.
When it was already dawn, Jesus was standing on the shore;
but the disciples did not realize that it was Jesus.
Jesus said to them, "Children, have you caught anything to eat?"
They answered him, "No."
So he said to them, "Cast the net over the right side of the boat
and you will find something."
So they cast it, and were not able to pull it in
because of the number of fish.
So the disciple whom Jesus loved said to Peter, "It is the Lord."
When Simon Peter heard that it was the Lord,

he tucked in his garment, for he was lightly clad,
and jumped into the sea.
The other disciples came in the boat,
for they were not far from shore, only about a hundred yards,
dragging the net with the fish.
When they climbed out on shore,
they saw a charcoal fire with fish on it and bread.
Jesus said to them, "Bring some of the fish you just caught."
So Simon Peter went over and dragged the net ashore
full of one hundred fifty-three large fish.
Even though there were so many, the net was not torn.
Jesus said to them, "Come, have breakfast."
And none of the disciples dared to ask him, "Who are you?"
because they realized it was the Lord.
Jesus came over and took the bread and gave it to them,
and in like manner the fish.
This was now the third time Jesus was revealed to his disciples
after being raised from the dead.

When they had finished breakfast, Jesus said to Simon Peter,
"Simon, son of John, do you love me more than these?"
Simon Peter answered him, "Yes, Lord, you know that I love you."
Jesus said to him, "Feed my lambs."
He then said to Simon Peter a second time,
"Simon, son of John, do you love me?"
Simon Peter answered him, "Yes, Lord, you know that I love you."
Jesus said to him, "Tend my sheep."
Jesus said to him the third time,
"Simon, son of John, do you love me?"
Peter was distressed that Jesus had said to him a third time,
"Do you love me?" and he said to him,
"Lord, you know everything; you know that I love you."
Jesus said to him, "Feed my sheep.   ·
Amen, amen, I say to you, when you were younger,
you used to dress yourself and go where you wanted;
but when you grow old, you will stretch out your hands,
and someone else will dress you
and lead you where you do not want to go."
He said this signifying by what kind of death he would glorify God.
And when he had said this, he said to him, "Follow me." ✛

MONDAY, MAY 2
St. Athanasius

† *Acts of the Apostles 6:8-15*
They could not withstand the wisdom and the Spirit with which he spoke.

Stephen, filled with grace and power,
  was working great wonders and signs among the people.
Certain members of the so-called Synagogue of Freedmen,
  Cyreneans, and Alexandrians,
  and people from Cilicia and Asia,
  came forward and debated with Stephen,
  but they could not withstand the wisdom and the Spirit with
    which he spoke.
Then they instigated some men to say,
  "We have heard him speaking blasphemous words
  against Moses and God."
They stirred up the people, the elders, and the scribes,
  accosted him, seized him,
  and brought him before the Sanhedrin.
They presented false witnesses who testified,
  "This man never stops saying things against this holy place and
    the law.
For we have heard him claim
  that this Jesus the Nazorean will destroy this place
  and change the customs that Moses handed down to us."
All those who sat in the Sanhedrin looked intently at him
  and saw that his face was like the face of an angel. ✛

Psalm 119:23-24, 26-27, 29-30
R. (1ab) **Blessed are they who follow the law of the Lord!**
  (or Alleluia.)
Though princes meet and talk against me,
  your servant meditates on your statutes.
Yes, your decrees are my delight;
  they are my counselors. **R.**
I declared my ways, and you answered me;
  teach me your statutes.
Make me understand the way of your precepts,
  and I will meditate on your wondrous deeds. **R.**
Remove from me the way of falsehood,
  and favor me with your law.
The way of truth I have chosen;
  I have set your ordinances before me. **R.**

Matthew 4:4b
R. Alleluia, alleluia.
One does not live on bread alone
but on every word that comes forth from the mouth of God. **R.**

† *John 6:22-29*
Do not work for food that perishes
but for food that endures for eternal life.

[**A**fter Jesus had fed the five thousand men, his disciples saw him
    walking on the sea.]
The next day, the crowd that remained across the sea
    saw that there had been only one boat there,
    and that Jesus had not gone along with his disciples in the boat,
    but only his disciples had left.
Other boats came from Tiberias
    near the place where they had eaten the bread
    when the Lord gave thanks.
When the crowd saw that neither Jesus nor his disciples were there,
    they themselves got into boats
    and came to Capernaum looking for Jesus.
And when they found him across the sea they said to him,
    "Rabbi, when did you get here?"
Jesus answered them and said,
    "Amen, amen, I say to you, you are looking for me
    not because you saw signs
    but because you ate the loaves and were filled.
Do not work for food that perishes
    but for the food that endures for eternal life,
    which the Son of Man will give you.
For on him the Father, God, has set his seal."
So they said to him,
    "What can we do to accomplish the works of God?"
Jesus answered and said to them,
    "This is the work of God, that you believe in the one he sent." ✛

TUESDAY, MAY 3
St. Philip and St. James

† *1 Corinthians 15:1-8*
After that he appeared to James, then to all the Apostles.

I am reminding you, brothers and sisters,
    of the Gospel I preached to you,
    which you indeed received and in which you also stand.
Through it you are also being saved,
    if you hold fast to the word I preached to you,

unless you believed in vain.
For I handed on to you as of first importance what I also received:
    that Christ died for our sins
        in accordance with the Scriptures;
    that he was buried;
    that he was raised on the third day
        in accordance with the Scriptures;
    that he appeared to Cephas, then to the Twelve.
After that, he appeared to more
    than five hundred brothers and sisters at once,
    most of whom are still living,
    though some have fallen asleep.
After that he appeared to James,
    then to all the Apostles.
Last of all, as to one born abnormally,
    he appeared to me. ✝

    Psalm 19:2-3, 4-5

R. (5) **Their message goes out through all the earth.**
    (or **Alleluia.***)*
The heavens declare the glory of God;
    and the firmament proclaims his handiwork.
Day pours out the word to day;
    and night to night imparts knowledge. **R.**
Not a word nor a discourse
    whose voice is not heard;
Through all the earth their voice resounds,
    and to the ends of the world, their message. **R.**

    John 14:6b, 9c

R. Alleluia, alleluia.
I am the way, the truth, and the life, says the Lord;
Philip, whoever has seen me has seen the Father. **R.**

✝ *John 14:6-14*

Have I been with you so long and you still do not know me?

Jesus said to Thomas, "I am the way and the truth and the life.
No one comes to the Father except through me.
If you know me, then you will also know my Father.
From now on you do know him and have seen him."
Philip said to him,
    "Master, show us the Father, and that will be enough for us."
Jesus said to him, "Have I been with you for so long a time
    and you still do not know me, Philip?
Whoever has seen me has seen the Father.

How can you say, 'Show us the Father'?
Do you not believe that I am in the Father and the Father is in me?
The words that I speak to you I do not speak on my own.
The Father who dwells in me is doing his works.
Believe me that I am in the Father and the Father is in me,
   or else, believe because of the works themselves.
Amen, amen, I say to you,
   whoever believes in me will do the works that I do,
   and will do greater ones than these,
   because I am going to the Father.
And whatever you ask in my name, I will do,
   so that the Father may be glorified in the Son.
If you ask anything of me in my name, I will do it." ✚

WEDNESDAY, MAY 4
EASTER WEEKDAY

† *Acts of the Apostles 8:1b-8*
They went about preaching the word.

There broke out a severe persecution of the Church in Jerusalem,
   and all were scattered
   throughout the countryside of Judea and Samaria,
   except the Apostles.
Devout men buried Stephen and made a loud lament over him.
Saul, meanwhile, was trying to destroy the Church;
   entering house after house and dragging out men and women,
   he handed them over for imprisonment.

Now those who had been scattered went about preaching the word.
Thus Philip went down to the city of Samaria
   and proclaimed the Christ to them.
With one accord, the crowds paid attention to what was said by Philip
   when they heard it and saw the signs he was doing.
For unclean spirits, crying out in a loud voice,
   came out of many possessed people,
   and many paralyzed and crippled people were cured.
There was great joy in that city. ✚

Psalm 66:1b-3a, 4-5, 6-7a
R. (1) **Let all the earth cry out to God with joy.** (or **Alleluia.**)
Shout joyfully to God, all the earth,
   sing praise to the glory of his name;
   proclaim his glorious praise.
Say to God, "How tremendous are your deeds!" **R.**
"Let all on earth worship and sing praise to you,
   sing praise to your name!"

Come and see the works of God,
his tremendous deeds among the children of Adam. **R.**
He has changed the sea into dry land;
through the river they passed on foot;
therefore let us rejoice in him.
He rules by his might forever. **R.**

See John 6:40
R. Alleluia, alleluia.
Everyone who believes in the Son has eternal life,
and I shall raise him on the last day, says the Lord. **R.**

† *John 6:35-40*
*This is the will of my Father, that all
who see the Son may have eternal life.*

Jesus said to the crowds,
"I am the bread of life;
whoever comes to me will never hunger,
and whoever believes in me will never thirst.
But I told you that although you have seen me,
you do not believe.
Everything that the Father gives me will come to me,
and I will not reject anyone who comes to me,
because I came down from heaven not to do my own will
but the will of the one who sent me.
And this is the will of the one who sent me,
that I should not lose anything of what he gave me,
but that I should raise it on the last day.
For this is the will of my Father,
that everyone who sees the Son and believes in him
may have eternal life,
and I shall raise him on the last day." ✝

THURSDAY, MAY 5
EASTER WEEKDAY

† *Acts of the Apostles 8:26-40*
Look, there is water. What is to prevent my being baptized?

The angel of the Lord spoke to Philip,
"Get up and head south on the road
that goes down from Jerusalem to Gaza, the desert route."
So he got up and set out.
Now there was an Ethiopian eunuch,
a court official of the Candace,
that is, the queen of the Ethiopians,

in charge of her entire treasury,
who had come to Jerusalem to worship, and was returning home.
Seated in his chariot, he was reading the prophet Isaiah.
The Spirit said to Philip,
"Go and join up with that chariot."
Philip ran up and heard him reading Isaiah the prophet and said,
"Do you understand what you are reading?"
He replied,
"How can I, unless someone instructs me?"
So he invited Philip to get in and sit with him.
This was the Scripture passage he was reading:

Like a sheep he was led to the slaughter,
and as a lamb before its shearer is silent,
so he opened not his mouth.
In his humiliation justice was denied him.
Who will tell of his posterity?
For his life is taken from the earth.

Then the eunuch said to Philip in reply,
"I beg you, about whom is the prophet saying this?
About himself, or about someone else?"
Then Philip opened his mouth and, beginning with this Scripture
   passage,
he proclaimed Jesus to him.
As they traveled along the road
   they came to some water,
and the eunuch said, "Look, there is water.
What is to prevent my being baptized?"
Then he ordered the chariot to stop,
   and Philip and the eunuch both went down into the water,
   and he baptized him.
When they came out of the water,
   the Spirit of the Lord snatched Philip away,
   and the eunuch saw him no more,
   but continued on his way rejoicing.
Philip came to Azotus, and went about proclaiming the good news
   to all the towns until he reached Caesarea. ✝

   Psalm 66:8-9, 16-17, 20
R. (1) **Let all the earth cry out to God with joy.** *(or* **Alleluia.***)*
Bless our God, you peoples,
   loudly sound his praise;
He has given life to our souls,
   and has not let our feet slip. **R.**

Hear now, all you who fear God, while I declare
  what he has done for me.
When I appealed to him in words,
  praise was on the tip of my tongue. **R.**
Blessed be God who refused me not
  my prayer or his kindness! **R.**

John 6:51

R. Alleluia, alleluia.

I am the living bread that came down from heaven, says the Lord;
whoever eats this bread will live forever. **R.**

† *John 6:44-51*
I am the living bread that came down from heaven.

Jesus said to the crowds:
"No one can come to me unless the Father who sent me draw him,
  and I will raise him on the last day.
It is written in the prophets:

  They shall all be taught by God.

Everyone who listens to my Father and learns from him comes to me.
Not that anyone has seen the Father
  except the one who is from God;
  he has seen the Father.
Amen, amen, I say to you,
  whoever believes has eternal life.
I am the bread of life.
Your ancestors ate the manna in the desert, but they died;
  this is the bread that comes down from heaven
  so that one may eat it and not die.
I am the living bread that came down from heaven;
  whoever eats this bread will live forever;
  and the bread that I will give
  is my Flesh for the life of the world." ✛

FRIDAY, MAY 6
EASTER WEEKDAY

† *Acts of the Apostles 9:1-20*
This man is a chosen instrument of mine
to carry my name before the Gentiles.

Saul, still breathing murderous threats against the disciples of the
  Lord,
  went to the high priest and asked him
  for letters to the synagogues in Damascus, that,

if he should find any men or women who belonged to the Way,
he might bring them back to Jerusalem in chains.
On his journey, as he was nearing Damascus,
a light from the sky suddenly flashed around him.
He fell to the ground and heard a voice saying to him,
"Saul, Saul, why are you persecuting me?"
He said, "Who are you, sir?"
The reply came, "I am Jesus, whom you are persecuting.
Now get up and go into the city and you will be told what you must do."
The men who were traveling with him stood speechless,
for they heard the voice but could see no one.
Saul got up from the ground,
but when he opened his eyes he could see nothing;
so they led him by the hand and brought him to Damascus.
For three days he was unable to see, and he neither ate nor drank.

There was a disciple in Damascus named Ananias,
and the Lord said to him in a vision, "Ananias."
He answered, "Here I am, Lord."
The Lord said to him, "Get up and go to the street called Straight
and ask at the house of Judas for a man from Tarsus named Saul.
He is there praying,
and in a vision he has seen a man named Ananias
come in and lay his hands on him,
that he may regain his sight."
But Ananias replied,
"Lord, I have heard from many sources about this man,
what evil things he has done to your holy ones in Jerusalem.
And here he has authority from the chief priests
to imprison all who call upon your name."
But the Lord said to him,
"Go, for this man is a chosen instrument of mine
to carry my name before Gentiles, kings, and children of Israel,
and I will show him what he will have to suffer for my name."
So Ananias went and entered the house;
laying his hands on him, he said,
"Saul, my brother, the Lord has sent me,
Jesus who appeared to you on the way by which you came,
that you may regain your sight and be filled with the Holy Spirit."
Immediately things like scales fell from his eyes
and he regained his sight.
He got up and was baptized,
and when he had eaten, he recovered his strength.

He stayed some days with the disciples in Damascus,
   and he began at once to proclaim Jesus in the synagogues,
   that he is the Son of God. ✚

   Psalm 117:1bc, 2

**R. (Mark 16:15) Go out to all the world and tell the Good
News.** *(or **Alleluia**.)*
Praise the LORD, all you nations;
   glorify him, all you peoples! **R.**
For steadfast is his kindness toward us,
   and the fidelity of the LORD endures forever. **R.**

   John 6:56

R. Alleluia, alleluia.
Whoever eats my Flesh and drinks my Blood,
remains in me and I in him, says the Lord. **R.**

† *John 6:52-59*
My Flesh is true food, and my Blood is true drink.

The Jews quarreled among themselves, saying,
   "How can this man give us his Flesh to eat?"
Jesus said to them,
   "Amen, amen, I say to you,
   unless you eat the Flesh of the Son of Man and drink his Blood,
   you do not have life within you.
Whoever eats my Flesh and drinks my Blood
   has eternal life,
   and I will raise him on the last day.
For my Flesh is true food,
   and my Blood is true drink.
Whoever eats my Flesh and drinks my Blood
   remains in me and I in him.
Just as the living Father sent me
   and I have life because of the Father,
   so also the one who feeds on me will have life because of me.
This is the bread that came down from heaven.
Unlike your ancestors who ate and still died,
   whoever eats this bread will live forever."
These things he said while teaching in the synagogue in Capernaum. ✚

SATURDAY, MAY 7
EASTER WEEKDAY

✝ Acts of the Apostles 9:31-42
*The Church was being built up, and with the consolation
of the Holy Spirit she grew in numbers.*

The Church throughout all Judea, Galilee, and Samaria
was at peace.
She was being built up and walked in the fear of the Lord,
and with the consolation of the Holy Spirit she grew in numbers.

As Peter was passing through every region,
he went down to the holy ones living in Lydda.
There he found a man named Aeneas,
who had been confined to bed for eight years, for he was paralyzed.
Peter said to him,
"Aeneas, Jesus Christ heals you. Get up and make your bed."
He got up at once.
And all the inhabitants of Lydda and Sharon saw him,
and they turned to the Lord.

Now in Joppa there was a disciple named Tabitha
(which translated is Dorcas).
She was completely occupied with good deeds and almsgiving.
Now during those days she fell sick and died,
so after washing her, they laid her out in a room upstairs.
Since Lydda was near Joppa,
the disciples, hearing that Peter was there,
sent two men to him with the request,
"Please come to us without delay."
So Peter got up and went with them.
When he arrived, they took him to the room upstairs
where all the widows came to him weeping
and showing him the tunics and cloaks
that Dorcas had made while she was with them.
Peter sent them all out and knelt down and prayed.
Then he turned to her body and said, "Tabitha, rise up."
She opened her eyes, saw Peter, and sat up.
He gave her his hand and raised her up,
and when he had called the holy ones and the widows,
he presented her alive.
This became known all over Joppa,
and many came to believe in the Lord. ✛

Psalm 116:12-13, 14-15, 16-17

R. (12) How shall I make a return to the Lord for all the good he has done for me? *(or* **Alleluia.***)*

How shall I make a return to the L‏ORD
  for all the good he has done for me?
The cup of salvation I will take up,
  and I will call upon the name of the L‏ORD. **R.**
My vows to the L‏ORD I will pay
  in the presence of all his people.
Precious in the eyes of the L‏ORD
  is the death of his faithful ones. **R.**
O L‏ORD, I am your servant;
  I am your servant, the son of your handmaid;
  you have loosed my bonds.
To you will I offer sacrifice of thanksgiving,
  and I will call upon the name of the L‏ORD. **R.**

See John 6:63c, 68c

R. Alleluia, alleluia.

Your words, Lord, are Spirit and life;
you have the words of everlasting life. **R.**

† *John 6:60-69*

To whom shall we go? You have the words of eternal life.

Many of the disciples of Jesus who were listening said,
  "This saying is hard; who can accept it?"
Since Jesus knew that his disciples were murmuring about this,
  he said to them, "Does this shock you?
What if you were to see the Son of Man ascending to where he was
    before?
It is the Spirit that gives life, while the flesh is of no avail.
The words I have spoken to you are Spirit and life.
But there are some of you who do not believe."
Jesus knew from the beginning the ones who would not believe
  and the one who would betray him.
And he said, "For this reason I have told you that no one can come
    to me
  unless it is granted him by my Father."

As a result of this,
  many of his disciples returned to their former way of life
  and no longer walked with him.
Jesus then said to the Twelve, "Do you also want to leave?"

Simon Peter answered him, "Master, to whom shall we go?
You have the words of eternal life.
We have come to believe
    and are convinced that you are the Holy One of God." ✛

SUNDAY, MAY 8
FOURTH SUNDAY OF EASTER

✝ Acts of the Apostles 13:14, 43-52
We now turn to the Gentiles.

Paul and Barnabas continued on from Perga
    and reached Antioch in Pisidia.
On the sabbath they entered the synagogue and took their seats.
Many Jews and worshipers who were converts to Judaism
    followed Paul and Barnabas, who spoke to them
    and urged them to remain faithful to the grace of God.

On the following sabbath almost the whole city gathered
    to hear the word of the Lord.
When the Jews saw the crowds, they were filled with jealousy
    and with violent abuse contradicted what Paul said.
Both Paul and Barnabas spoke out boldly and said,
    "It was necessary that the word of God be spoken to you first,
    but since you reject it
    and condemn yourselves as unworthy of eternal life,
    we now turn to the Gentiles.
For so the Lord has commanded us,
    I have made you a light to the Gentiles,
    that you may be an instrument of salvation
    to the ends of the earth."

The Gentiles were delighted when they heard this
    and glorified the word of the Lord.
All who were destined for eternal life came to believe,
    and the word of the Lord continued to spread
    through the whole region.
The Jews, however, incited the women of prominence who were
        worshipers
    and the leading men of the city,
    stirred up a persecution against Paul and Barnabas,
    and expelled them from their territory.
So they shook the dust from their feet in protest against them,
    and went to Iconium.
The disciples were filled with joy and the Holy Spirit. ✛

Psalm 100:1-2, 3, 5

R. (3c) **We are his people, the sheep of his flock.** *(or* **Alleluia.***)*

Sing joyfully to the LORD, all you lands;
  serve the LORD with gladness;
  come before him with joyful song. **R.**
Know that the LORD is God;
  he made us, his we are;
  his people, the flock he tends. **R.**
The LORD is good:
  his kindness endures forever,
  and his faithfulness, to all generations. **R.**

† *Revelation 7:9, 14b-17*
The Lamb will shepherd them and lead them to springs of life-giving water.

I, John, had a vision of a great multitude,
  which no one could count,
  from every nation, race, people, and tongue.
They stood before the throne and before the Lamb,
  wearing white robes and holding palm branches in their hands.

Then one of the elders said to me,
  "These are the ones who have survived the time of great distress;
  they have washed their robes
  and made them white in the blood of the Lamb.

  "For this reason they stand before God's throne
    and worship him day and night in his temple.
  The one who sits on the throne will shelter them.
  They will not hunger or thirst anymore,
    nor will the sun or any heat strike them.
  For the Lamb who is in the center of the throne
    will shepherd them
    and lead them to springs of life-giving water,
    and God will wipe away every tear from their eyes." ✝

John 10:14

R. Alleluia, alleluia.
I am the good shepherd, says the Lord;
I know my sheep, and mine know me. **R.**

† *John 10:27-30*
I give my sheep eternal life.

Jesus said:
"My sheep hear my voice;
  I know them, and they follow me.
I give them eternal life, and they shall never perish.

No one can take them out of my hand.
My Father, who has given them to me, is greater than all,
　　and no one can take them out of the Father's hand.
The Father and I are one." ✛

MONDAY, MAY 9
EASTER WEEKDAY

†Acts of the Apostles 11:1-18
God has then granted life-giving repentance to the Gentiles too.

The Apostles and the brothers who were in Judea
　　heard that the Gentiles too had accepted the word of God.
So when Peter went up to Jerusalem
　　the circumcised believers confronted him, saying,
　　"You entered the house of uncircumcised people and ate with them."
Peter began and explained it to them step by step, saying,
　　"I was at prayer in the city of Joppa
　　when in a trance I had a vision,
　　something resembling a large sheet coming down,
　　lowered from the sky by its four corners, and it came to me.
Looking intently into it,
　　I observed and saw the four-legged animals of the earth,
　　the wild beasts, the reptiles, and the birds of the sky.
I also heard a voice say to me, 'Get up, Peter. Slaughter and eat.'
But I said, 'Certainly not, sir,
　　because nothing profane or unclean has ever entered my mouth.'
But a second time a voice from heaven answered,
　　'What God has made clean, you are not to call profane.'
This happened three times,
　　and then everything was drawn up again into the sky.
Just then three men appeared at the house where we were,
　　who had been sent to me from Caesarea.
The Spirit told me to accompany them without discriminating.
These six brothers also went with me,
　　and we entered the man's house.
He related to us how he had seen the angel standing in his house,
　　　　saying,
　　'Send someone to Joppa and summon Simon, who is called Peter,
　　who will speak words to you
　　by which you and all your household will be saved.'
As I began to speak, the Holy Spirit fell upon them
　　as it had upon us at the beginning,
　　and I remembered the word of the Lord, how he had said,
　　'John baptized with water
　　but you will be baptized with the Holy Spirit.'

If then God gave them the same gift he gave to us
  when we came to believe in the Lord Jesus Christ,
  who was I to be able to hinder God?"
When they heard this,
  they stopped objecting and glorified God, saying,
  "God has then granted life-giving repentance to the Gentiles too." ✛

Psalms 42:2-3; 43:3, 4

R. (see 3a) **Athirst is my soul for the living God.** *(or* **Alleluia.***)*
As the hind longs for the running waters,
  so my soul longs for you, O God.
Athirst is my soul for God, the living God.
  When shall I go and behold the face of God? **R.**
Send forth your light and your fidelity;
  they shall lead me on
And bring me to your holy mountain,
  to your dwelling-place. **R.**
Then will I go in to the altar of God,
  the God of my gladness and joy;
Then will I give you thanks upon the harp,
  O God, my God! **R.**

John 10:14

R. Alleluia, alleluia.
I am the good shepherd, says the Lord;
I know my sheep, and mine know me. **R.**

✝ *John 10:1-10*
I am the gate for the sheep.

Jesus said:
"Amen, amen, I say to you,
  whoever does not enter a sheepfold through the gate
  but climbs over elsewhere is a thief and a robber.
But whoever enters through the gate is the shepherd of the sheep.
The gatekeeper opens it for him, and the sheep hear his voice,
  as he calls his own sheep by name and leads them out.
When he has driven out all his own,
  he walks ahead of them, and the sheep follow him,
  because they recognize his voice.
But they will not follow a stranger;
  they will run away from him,
  because they do not recognize the voice of strangers."
Although Jesus used this figure of speech,
  they did not realize what he was trying to tell them.

So Jesus said again, "Amen, amen, I say to you,
   I am the gate for the sheep.
All who came before me are thieves and robbers,
   but the sheep did not listen to them.
I am the gate.
Whoever enters through me will be saved,
   and will come in and go out and find pasture.
A thief comes only to steal and slaughter and destroy;
   I came so that they might have life and have it more abundantly." ✛

TUESDAY, MAY 10
Easter Weekday, St. Damien de Veuster

† Acts of the Apostles 11:19-26
*They began speaking to the Greeks as well,
proclaiming the Good News of Jesus Christ.*

Those who had been scattered by the persecution
   that arose because of Stephen
   went as far as Phoenicia, Cyprus, and Antioch,
   preaching the word to no one but Jews.
There were some Cypriots and Cyrenians among them, however,
   who came to Antioch and began to speak to the Greeks as well,
   proclaiming the Lord Jesus.
The hand of the Lord was with them
   and a great number who believed turned to the Lord.
The news about them reached the ears of the Church in Jerusalem,
   and they sent Barnabas to go to Antioch.
When he arrived and saw the grace of God,
   he rejoiced and encouraged them all
   to remain faithful to the Lord in firmness of heart,
   for he was a good man, filled with the Holy Spirit and faith.
And a large number of people was added to the Lord.
Then he went to Tarsus to look for Saul,
   and when he had found him he brought him to Antioch.
For a whole year they met with the Church
   and taught a large number of people,
   and it was in Antioch that the disciples
   were first called Christians. ✛

Psalm 87:1b-3, 4-5, 6-7
R. (117:1a) **All you nations, praise the Lord.** *(or Alleluia.)*
His foundation upon the holy mountains
   the Lord loves:
The gates of Zion,
   more than any dwelling of Jacob.

Glorious things are said of you,
  O city of God! **R.**
I tell of Egypt and Babylon
  among those who know the LORD;
Of Philistia, Tyre, Ethiopia:
  "This man was born there."
And of Zion they shall say:
  "One and all were born in her;
And he who has established her
  is the Most High LORD." **R.**
They shall note, when the peoples are enrolled:
  "This man was born there."
And all shall sing, in their festive dance:
  "My home is within you." **R.**

John 10:27

R. Alleluia, alleluia.
My sheep hear my voice, says the Lord;
I know them, and they follow me. **R.**

† *John 10:22-30*
The Father and I are one.

The feast of the Dedication was taking place in Jerusalem.
It was winter.
And Jesus walked about in the temple area on the Portico of Solomon.
So the Jews gathered around him and said to him,
  "How long are you going to keep us in suspense?
If you are the Christ, tell us plainly."
Jesus answered them, "I told you and you do not believe.
The works I do in my Father's name testify to me.
But you do not believe, because you are not among my sheep.
My sheep hear my voice;
  I know them, and they follow me.
I give them eternal life, and they shall never perish.
No one can take them out of my hand.
My Father, who has given them to me, is greater than all,
  and no one can take them out of the Father's hand.
The Father and I are one." ✛

WEDNESDAY, MAY 11
EASTER WEEKDAY

✝ *Acts of the Apostles 12:24—13:5a*
Set apart for me Barnabas and Saul.

The word of God continued to spread and grow.

After Barnabas and Saul completed their relief mission,
   they returned to Jerusalem,
   taking with them John, who is called Mark.

Now there were in the Church at Antioch prophets and teachers:
   Barnabas, Symeon who was called Niger, Lucius of Cyrene,
   Manaen who was a close friend of Herod the tetrarch, and Saul.
While they were worshiping the Lord and fasting, the Holy Spirit
   said,
   "Set apart for me Barnabas and Saul
   for the work to which I have called them."
Then, completing their fasting and prayer,
   they laid hands on them and sent them off.

So they, sent forth by the Holy Spirit,
   went down to Seleucia
   and from there sailed to Cyprus.
When they arrived in Salamis,
   they proclaimed the word of God in the Jewish synagogues. ✝

Psalm 67:2-3, 5, 6 and 8
R. (4) **O God, let all the nations praise you!** (*or* **Alleluia.**)
May God have pity on us and bless us;
   may he let his face shine upon us.
So may your way be known upon earth;
   among all nations, your salvation. **R.**
May the nations be glad and exult
   because you rule the peoples in equity;
   the nations on the earth you guide. **R.**
May the peoples praise you, O God;
   may all the peoples praise you!
May God bless us,
   and may all the ends of the earth fear him! **R.**

John 8:12
R. Alleluia, alleluia.
I am the light of the world, says the Lord;
whoever follows me will have the light of life. **R.**

† *John 12:44-50*
I came into the world as light.

Jesus cried out and said,
"Whoever believes in me believes not only in me
 but also in the one who sent me,
 and whoever sees me sees the one who sent me.
I came into the world as light,
 so that everyone who believes in me might not remain in darkness.
And if anyone hears my words and does not observe them,
 I do not condemn him,
 for I did not come to condemn the world but to save the world.
Whoever rejects me and does not accept my words
 has something to judge him: the word that I spoke,
 it will condemn him on the last day,
 because I did not speak on my own,
 but the Father who sent me commanded me what to say and speak.
And I know that his commandment is eternal life.
So what I say, I say as the Father told me." †

THURSDAY, MAY 12
EASTER WEEKDAY; ST. NEREUS AND ST. ACHILLEUS; ST. PANCRAS

† *Acts of the Apostles 13:13-25*
*From this man's descendants God, according to his promise,
has brought to Israel a savior, Jesus.*

From Paphos, Paul and his companions
 set sail and arrived at Perga in Pamphylia.
But John left them and returned to Jerusalem.
They continued on from Perga and reached Antioch in Pisidia.
On the sabbath they entered into the synagogue and took their seats.
After the reading of the law and the prophets,
 the synagogue officials sent word to them,
 "My brothers, if one of you has a word of exhortation
 for the people, please speak."

So Paul got up, motioned with his hand, and said,
 "Fellow children of Israel and you others who are God-fearing,
   listen.
The God of this people Israel chose our ancestors
 and exalted the people during their sojourn in the land of Egypt.
With uplifted arms he led them out,
 and for about forty years he put up with them in the desert.
When he had destroyed seven nations in the land of Canaan,
 he gave them their land as an inheritance
 at the end of about four hundred and fifty years.

After these things he provided judges up to Samuel the prophet.
Then they asked for a king.
God gave them Saul, son of Kish,
  a man from the tribe of Benjamin, for forty years.
Then he removed him and raised up David as their king;
  of him he testified,
  I have found David, son of Jesse, a man after my own heart;
  he will carry out my every wish.
From this man's descendants God, according to his promise,
  has brought to Israel a savior, Jesus.
John heralded his coming by proclaiming a baptism of repentance
  to all the people of Israel;
  and as John was completing his course, he would say,
  'What do you suppose that I am? I am not he.
Behold, one is coming after me;
  I am not worthy to unfasten the sandals of his feet.'" ✛

Psalm 89:2-3, 21-22, 25 and 27

R. (2) **For ever I will sing the goodness of the Lord.**
  (or **Alleluia.***)*
The favors of the LORD I will sing forever;
  through all generations my mouth shall proclaim your faithfulness.
For you have said, "My kindness is established forever";
  in heaven you have confirmed your faithfulness. **R.**
"I have found David, my servant;
  with my holy oil I have anointed him,
That my hand may be always with him,
  and that my arm may make him strong." **R.**
"My faithfulness and my mercy shall be with him,
  and through my name shall his horn be exalted.
He shall say of me, 'You are my father,
  my God, the Rock, my savior.'" **R.**

See Revelation 1:5ab

R. Alleluia, alleluia.
Jesus Christ, you are the faithful witness,
the firstborn of the dead,
you have loved us and freed us from our sins by your Blood. **R.**

† *John 13:16-20*
Whoever receives the one I send receives me.

When Jesus had washed the disciples' feet, he said to them:
"Amen, amen, I say to you, no slave is greater than his master
  nor any messenger greater than the one who sent him.
If you understand this, blessed are you if you do it.

I am not speaking of all of you.
I know those whom I have chosen.
But so that the Scripture might be fulfilled,
The one who ate my food has raised his heel against me.
From now on I am telling you before it happens,
so that when it happens you may believe that I AM.
Amen, amen, I say to you, whoever receives the one I send
receives me, and whoever receives me receives the one who sent
me." ✛

FRIDAY, MAY 13
EASTER WEEKDAY, OUR LADY OF FATIMA

† *Acts of the Apostles 13:26-33*
God has fulfilled his promise by raising Jesus from the dead.

When Paul came to Antioch in Pisidia, he said in the synagogue:
"My brothers, children of the family of Abraham,
and those others among you who are God-fearing,
to us this word of salvation has been sent.
The inhabitants of Jerusalem and their leaders failed to recognize him,
and by condemning him they fulfilled the oracles of the prophets
that are read sabbath after sabbath.
For even though they found no grounds for a death sentence,
they asked Pilate to have him put to death,
and when they had accomplished all that was written about him,
they took him down from the tree and placed him in a tomb.
But God raised him from the dead,
and for many days he appeared to those
who had come up with him from Galilee to Jerusalem.
These are now his witnesses before the people.
We ourselves are proclaiming this good news to you
that what God promised our fathers
he has brought to fulfillment for us, their children, by raising up
Jesus,
as it is written in the second psalm,
You are my Son; this day I have begotten you." ✛

Psalm 2:6-7, 8-9, 10-11ab
R. (7bc) **You are my Son; this day I have begotten you.**
(*or* **Alleluia.**)
"I myself have set up my king
on Zion, my holy mountain."
I will proclaim the decree of the LORD:
The LORD said to me, "You are my Son;
this day I have begotten you." **R.**

"Ask of me and I will give you
the nations for an inheritance
and the ends of the earth for your possession.
You shall rule them with an iron rod;
you shall shatter them like an earthen dish." **R.**
And now, O kings, give heed;
take warning, you rulers of the earth.
Serve the LORD with fear, and rejoice before him;
with trembling rejoice. **R.**

John 14:6
R. Alleluia, alleluia.
I am the way and the truth and the life, says the Lord;
no one comes to the Father except through me. **R.**

✝ *John 14:1-6*
I am the way and the truth and the life.

Jesus said to his disciples:
"Do not let your hearts be troubled.
You have faith in God; have faith also in me.
In my Father's house there are many dwelling places.
If there were not,
would I have told you that I am going to prepare a place for you?
And if I go and prepare a place for you,
I will come back again and take you to myself,
so that where I am you also may be.
Where I am going you know the way."
Thomas said to him,
"Master, we do not know where you are going;
how can we know the way?"
Jesus said to him, "I am the way and the truth and the life.
No one comes to the Father except through me." ✛

SATURDAY, MAY 14
ST. MATTHIAS

✝ *Acts of the Apostles 1:15-17, 20-26*
The lot fell upon Matthias, and he was counted with the Eleven Apostles.

Peter stood up in the midst of the brothers and sisters
(there was a group of about one hundred and twenty persons in
the one place).
He said, "My brothers and sisters,
the Scripture had to be fulfilled
which the Holy Spirit spoke beforehand
through the mouth of David, concerning Judas,
who was the guide for those who arrested Jesus.

Judas was numbered among us
  and was allotted a share in this ministry.
For it is written in the Book of Psalms:

  Let his encampment become desolate,
    and may no one dwell in it.
and:

  May another take his office.

Therefore, it is necessary that one of the men
  who accompanied us the whole time
  the Lord Jesus came and went among us,
  beginning from the baptism of John
  until the day on which he was taken up from us,
  become with us a witness to his resurrection."
So they proposed two, Joseph called Barsabbas,
  who was also known as Justus, and Matthias.
Then they prayed,
  "You, Lord, who know the hearts of all,
  show which one of these two you have chosen
  to take the place in this apostolic ministry
  from which Judas turned away to go to his own place."
Then they gave lots to them, and the lot fell upon Matthias,
  and he was counted with the Eleven Apostles. ✠

  Psalm 113:1b-2, 3-4, 5-6, 7-8
R. (8) **The Lord will give him a seat with the leaders of his
  people.** *(or* **Alleluia.***)*
Praise, you servants of the LORD,
  praise the name of the LORD.
Blessed be the name of the LORD
  both now and forever. **R.**
From the rising to the setting of the sun
  is the name of the LORD to be praised.
High above all nations is the LORD;
  above the heavens is his glory. **R.**
Who is like the LORD, our God, who is enthroned on high
  and looks upon the heavens and the earth below? **R.**
He raises up the lowly from the dust;
  from the dunghill he lifts up the poor
To seat them with princes,
  with the princes of his own people. **R.**

See *John 15:16*
R. Alleluia, alleluia.
I chose you from the world,
to go and bear fruit that will last, says the Lord. **R.**

† *John 15:9-17*
It was not you who chose me, but I who chose you.

Jesus said to his disciples:
"As the Father loves me, so I also love you.
Remain in my love.
If you keep my commandments, you will remain in my love,
    just as I have kept my Father's commandments
    and remain in his love.

"I have told you this so that my joy might be in you
    and your joy might be complete.
This is my commandment: love one another as I love you.
No one has greater love than this,
    to lay down one's life for one's friends.
You are my friends if you do what I command you.
I no longer call you slaves,
    because a slave does not know what his master is doing.
I have called you friends,
    because I have told you everything I have heard from my Father.
It was not you who chose me, but I who chose you
    and appointed you to go and bear fruit that will remain,
    so that whatever you ask the Father in my name he may give you.
This I command you: love one another." ✛

SUNDAY, MAY 15
FIFTH SUNDAY OF EASTER

† *Acts of the Apostles 14:21-27*
*They called the Church together and
reported what God had done with them.*

After Paul and Barnabas had proclaimed the good news to that city
    and made a considerable number of disciples,
    they returned to Lystra and to Iconium and to Antioch.
They strengthened the spirits of the disciples
    and exhorted them to persevere in the faith, saying,
    "It is necessary for us to undergo many hardships
    to enter the kingdom of God."
They appointed elders for them in each church and,
    with prayer and fasting, commended them to the Lord
    in whom they had put their faith.

Then they traveled through Pisidia and reached Pamphylia.
After proclaiming the word at Perga they went down to Attalia.
From there they sailed to Antioch,
> where they had been commended to the grace of God
> for the work they had now accomplished.
And when they arrived, they called the church together
> and reported what God had done with them
> and how he had opened the door of faith to the Gentiles. ✝

Psalm 145:8-9, 10-11, 12-13

R. (see 1) **I will praise your name for ever, my king and my God.** *(or* **Alleluia.***)*

The LORD is gracious and merciful,
> slow to anger and of great kindness.
The LORD is good to all
> and compassionate toward all his works. **R.**

Let all your works give you thanks, O LORD,
> and let your faithful ones bless you.
Let them discourse of the glory of your kingdom
> and speak of your might. **R.**

Let them make known your might to the children of Adam,
> and the glorious splendor of your kingdom.
Your kingdom is a kingdom for all ages,
> and your dominion endures through all generations. **R.**

✝ *Revelation 21:1-5a*
God will wipe every tear from their eyes.

Then I, John, saw a new heaven and a new earth.
The former heaven and the former earth had passed away,
> and the sea was no more.
I also saw the holy city, a new Jerusalem,
> coming down out of heaven from God,
> prepared as a bride adorned for her husband.
I heard a loud voice from the throne saying,
> "Behold, God's dwelling is with the human race.
He will dwell with them and they will be his people
> and God himself will always be with them as their God.
He will wipe every tear from their eyes,
> and there shall be no more death or mourning, wailing or pain,
> for the old order has passed away."

The One who sat on the throne said,
> "Behold, I make all things new." ✝

John 13:34
R. Alleluia, alleluia.
I give you a new commandment, says the Lord:
love one another as I have loved you. **R.**

† *John 13:31-33a, 34-35*
I give you a new commandment: love one another.

When Judas had left them, Jesus said,
"Now is the Son of Man glorified, and God is glorified in him.
If God is glorified in him,
    God will also glorify him in himself,
    and God will glorify him at once.
My children, I will be with you only a little while longer.
I give you a new commandment: love one another.
As I have loved you, so you also should love one another.
This is how all will know that you are my disciples,
    if you have love for one another." ✛

MONDAY, MAY 16
EASTER WEEKDAY

† *Acts of the Apostles 14:5-18*
*We proclaim to you Good News that you should
turn from these idols to the living God.*

There was an attempt in Iconium
    by both the Gentiles and the Jews,
    together with their leaders,
    to attack and stone Paul and Barnabas.
They realized it,
    and fled to the Lycaonian cities of Lystra and Derbe
    and to the surrounding countryside,
    where they continued to proclaim the Good News.

At Lystra there was a crippled man, lame from birth,
    who had never walked.
He listened to Paul speaking, who looked intently at him,
    saw that he had the faith to be healed,
    and called out in a loud voice, "Stand up straight on your feet."
He jumped up and began to walk about.
When the crowds saw what Paul had done,
    they cried out in Lycaonian,
    "The gods have come down to us in human form."
They called Barnabas "Zeus" and Paul "Hermes,"
    because he was the chief speaker.

And the priest of Zeus, whose temple was at the entrance to the city,
   brought oxen and garlands to the gates,
   for he together with the people intended to offer sacrifice.

The Apostles Barnabas and Paul tore their garments
   when they heard this and rushed out into the crowd, shouting,
   "Men, why are you doing this?
We are of the same nature as you, human beings.
We proclaim to you good news
   that you should turn from these idols to the living God,
   who made heaven and earth and sea and all that is in them.
In past generations he allowed all Gentiles to go their own ways;
   yet, in bestowing his goodness,
   he did not leave himself without witness,
   for he gave you rains from heaven and fruitful seasons,
   and filled you with nourishment and gladness for your hearts."
Even with these words, they scarcely restrained the crowds
   from offering sacrifice to them. ✛

   Psalm 115:1-2, 3-4, 15-16
R. (1ab) Not to us, O Lord, but to your name give the glory.
   (or Alleluia.)
Not to us, O LORD, not to us
   but to your name give glory
   because of your mercy, because of your truth.
Why should the pagans say,
   "Where is their God?" **R.**
Our God is in heaven;
   whatever he wills, he does.
Their idols are silver and gold,
   the handiwork of men. **R.**
May you be blessed by the LORD,
   who made heaven and earth.
Heaven is the heaven of the LORD,
   but the earth he has given to the children of men. **R.**

   John 14:26
R. Alleluia, alleluia.
The Holy Spirit will teach you everything
and remind you of all I told you. **R.**

† John 14:21-26
The Advocate whom the Father will send will teach you everything.

Jesus said to his disciples:
"Whoever has my commandments and observes them
  is the one who loves me.
Whoever loves me will be loved by my Father,
  and I will love him and reveal myself to him."
Judas, not the Iscariot, said to him,
  "Master, then what happened that you will reveal yourself to us
  and not to the world?"
Jesus answered and said to him,
  "Whoever loves me will keep my word,
  and my Father will love him,
  and we will come to him and make our dwelling with him.
Whoever does not love me does not keep my words;
  yet the word you hear is not mine
  but that of the Father who sent me.

"I have told you this while I am with you.
The Advocate, the Holy Spirit
  whom the Father will send in my name—
  he will teach you everything
  and remind you of all that I told you." ✛

TUESDAY, MAY 17
EASTER WEEKDAY

† Acts of the Apostles 14:19-28
*They called the Church together and
reported what God had done with them.*

In those days, some Jews from Antioch and Iconium
  arrived and won over the crowds.
They stoned Paul and dragged him out of the city,
  supposing that he was dead.
But when the disciples gathered around him,
  he got up and entered the city.
On the following day he left with Barnabas for Derbe.

After they had proclaimed the good news to that city
  and made a considerable number of disciples,
  they returned to Lystra and to Iconium and to Antioch.
They strengthened the spirits of the disciples
  and exhorted them to persevere in the faith, saying,
  "It is necessary for us to undergo many hardships
  to enter the Kingdom of God."

They appointed presbyters for them in each Church and,
   with prayer and fasting, commended them to the Lord
   in whom they had put their faith.
Then they traveled through Pisidia and reached Pamphylia.
After proclaiming the word at Perga they went down to Attalia.
From there they sailed to Antioch,
   where they had been commended to the grace of God
   for the work they had now accomplished.
And when they arrived, they called the Church together
   and reported what God had done with them
   and how he had opened the door of faith to the Gentiles.
Then they spent no little time with the disciples. ✛

Psalm 145:10-11, 12-13ab, 21
R. (see 12) **Your friends make known, O Lord, the glorious
   splendor of your kingdom.** *(or* **Alleluia.***)*
Let all your works give you thanks, O LORD,
   and let your faithful ones bless you.
Let them discourse of the glory of your kingdom
   and speak of your might. **R.**
Making known to men your might
   and the glorious splendor of your kingdom.
Your kingdom is a kingdom for all ages,
   and your dominion endures through all generations. **R.**
May my mouth speak the praise of the LORD,
   and may all flesh bless his holy name forever and ever. **R.**

See Luke 24:46, 26
R. Alleluia, alleluia.
Christ had to suffer and to rise from the dead,
and so enter into his glory. **R.**

† *John 14:27-31a*
My peace I give to you.

Jesus said to his disciples:
"Peace I leave with you; my peace I give to you.
Not as the world gives do I give it to you.
Do not let your hearts be troubled or afraid.
You heard me tell you,
   'I am going away and I will come back to you.'
If you loved me,
   you would rejoice that I am going to the Father;
   for the Father is greater than I.
And now I have told you this before it happens,
   so that when it happens you may believe.

I will no longer speak much with you,
  for the ruler of the world is coming.
He has no power over me,
  but the world must know that I love the Father
  and that I do just as the Father has commanded me." ✛

WEDNESDAY, MAY 18
EASTER WEEKDAY, ST. POPE JOHN I

† Acts of the Apostles 15:1-6
*They decided to go up to Jerusalem to the Apostles
and presbyters about this question.*

Some who had come down from Judea were instructing the brothers,
  "Unless you are circumcised according to the Mosaic practice,
  you cannot be saved."
Because there arose no little dissension and debate
  by Paul and Barnabas with them,
  it was decided that Paul, Barnabas, and some of the others
  should go up to Jerusalem to the Apostles and presbyters
  about this question.
They were sent on their journey by the Church,
  and passed through Phoenicia and Samaria
  telling of the conversion of the Gentiles,
  and brought great joy to all the brethren.
When they arrived in Jerusalem,
  they were welcomed by the Church,
  as well as by the Apostles and the presbyters,
  and they reported what God had done with them.
But some from the party of the Pharisees who had become believers
  stood up and said, "It is necessary to circumcise them
  and direct them to observe the Mosaic law."

The Apostles and the presbyters met together to see about this
    matter. ✛

Psalm 122:1-2, 3-4ab, 4cd-5
R. (see 1) **Let us go rejoicing to the house of the Lord.**
  (or **Alleluia.***)*
I rejoiced because they said to me,
  "We will go up to the house of the LORD."
And now we have set foot
  within your gates, O Jerusalem. **R.**
Jerusalem, built as a city
  with compact unity.
To it the tribes go up,
  the tribes of the LORD. **R.**

According to the decree for Israel,
  to give thanks to the name of the LORD.
In it are set up judgment seats,
  seats for the house of David. **R.**

John 15:4a, 5b
R. Alleluia, alleluia.
Remain in me, as I remain in you, says the Lord;
whoever remains in me will bear much fruit. **R.**

† *John 15:1-8*
Whoever remains in me and I in him will bear much fruit.

Jesus said to his disciples:
"I am the true vine, and my Father is the vine grower.
He takes away every branch in me that does not bear fruit,
  and everyone that does he prunes so that it bears more fruit.
You are already pruned because of the word that I spoke to you.
Remain in me, as I remain in you.
Just as a branch cannot bear fruit on its own
  unless it remains on the vine,
  so neither can you unless you remain in me.
I am the vine, you are the branches.
Whoever remains in me and I in him will bear much fruit,
  because without me you can do nothing.
Anyone who does not remain in me
  will be thrown out like a branch and wither;
  people will gather them and throw them into a fire
  and they will be burned.
If you remain in me and my words remain in you,
  ask for whatever you want and it will be done for you.
By this is my Father glorified,
  that you bear much fruit and become my disciples." ✛

THURSDAY, MAY 19
EASTER WEEKDAY

† *Acts of the Apostles 15:7-21*
*It is my judgment, therefore, that we ought to stop
troubling the Gentiles who turn to God.*

After much debate had taken place,
  Peter got up and said to the Apostles and the presbyters,
  "My brothers, you are well aware that from early days
  God made his choice among you that through my mouth
  the Gentiles would hear the word of the Gospel and believe.
And God, who knows the heart,
  bore witness by granting them the Holy Spirit

just as he did us.
He made no distinction between us and them,
  for by faith he purified their hearts.
Why, then, are you now putting God to the test
  by placing on the shoulders of the disciples
  a yoke that neither our ancestors nor we have been able to bear?
On the contrary, we believe that we are saved
  through the grace of the Lord Jesus, in the same way as they."
The whole assembly fell silent,
  and they listened
  while Paul and Barnabas described the signs and wonders
  God had worked among the Gentiles through them.

After they had fallen silent, James responded,
  "My brothers, listen to me.
Symeon has described how God first concerned himself
  with acquiring from among the Gentiles a people for his name.
The words of the prophets agree with this, as is written:

After this I shall return
  and rebuild the fallen hut of David;
from its ruins I shall rebuild it
  and raise it up again,
so that the rest of humanity may seek out the Lord,
  even all the Gentiles on whom my name is invoked.
Thus says the Lord who accomplishes these things,
  known from of old.

It is my judgment, therefore,
  that we ought to stop troubling the Gentiles who turn to God,
  but tell them by letter to avoid pollution from idols,
  unlawful marriage, the meat of strangled animals, and blood.
For Moses, for generations now,
  has had those who proclaim him in every town,
  as he has been read in the synagogues every sabbath." ✛

  Psalm 96:1-2a, 2b-3, 10
R. (3) **Proclaim God's marvelous deeds to all the nations.**
  *(or **Alleluia**.)*
Sing to the LORD a new song;
  sing to the LORD, all you lands.
Sing to the LORD; bless his name. **R.**
Announce his salvation, day after day.
Tell his glory among the nations;
  among all peoples, his wondrous deeds. **R.**

Say among the nations: The LORD is king.
He has made the world firm, not to be moved;
 he governs the peoples with equity. **R.**

John 10:27
R. Alleluia, alleluia.
My sheep hear my voice, says the Lord;
I know them, and they follow me. **R.**

† *John 15:9-11*
Remain in my love, that your joy might be complete.

Jesus said to his disciples:
"As the Father loves me, so I also love you.
Remain in my love.
If you keep my commandments, you will remain in my love,
 just as I have kept my Father's commandments
 and remain in his love.

"I have told you this so that
 my joy might be in you and
 your joy might be complete." ✛

FRIDAY, MAY 20
EASTER WEEKDAY, ST. BERNARDINE OF SIENA

† *Acts of the Apostles 15:22-31*
*It is the decision of the Holy Spirit and of us not to place on you
any burden beyond these necessities.*

The Apostles and presbyters, in agreement with the whole Church,
 decided to choose representatives
 and to send them to Antioch with Paul and Barnabas.
The ones chosen were Judas, who was called Barsabbas,
 and Silas, leaders among the brothers.
This is the letter delivered by them:
"The Apostles and the presbyters, your brothers,
 to the brothers in Antioch, Syria, and Cilicia
 of Gentile origin: greetings.
Since we have heard that some of our number
 who went out without any mandate from us
 have upset you with their teachings
 and disturbed your peace of mind,
 we have with one accord decided to choose representatives
 and to send them to you along with our beloved Barnabas and Paul,
 who have dedicated their lives to the name of our Lord Jesus Christ.
So we are sending Judas and Silas
 who will also convey this same message by word of mouth:

'It is the decision of the Holy Spirit and of us
not to place on you any burden beyond these necessities,
namely, to abstain from meat sacrificed to idols,
from blood, from meats of strangled animals,
and from unlawful marriage.
If you keep free of these,
you will be doing what is right. Farewell.'"

And so they were sent on their journey.
Upon their arrival in Antioch
they called the assembly together and delivered the letter.
When the people read it, they were delighted with the exhortation. ✛

Psalm 57:8-9, 10 and 12
R. (10a) **I will give you thanks among the peoples, O Lord.**
(or **Alleluia.***)*
My heart is steadfast, O God; my heart is steadfast;
I will sing and chant praise.
Awake, O my soul; awake, lyre and harp!
I will wake the dawn. **R.**
I will give thanks to you among the peoples, O LORD,
I will chant your praise among the nations.
For your mercy towers to the heavens,
and your faithfulness to the skies.
Be exalted above the heavens, O God;
above all the earth be your glory! **R.**

John 15:15b
R. Alleluia, alleluia.
I call you my friends, says the Lord,
for I have made known to you all that the Father has told me. **R.**

✝John 15:12-17
This is my commandment: love one another.

Jesus said to his disciples:
"This is my commandment: love one another as I love you.
No one has greater love than this,
to lay down one's life for one's friends.
You are my friends if you do what I command you.
I no longer call you slaves,
because a slave does not know what his master is doing.
I have called you friends,
because I have told you everything I have heard from my Father.

It was not you who chose me, but I who chose you
  and appointed you to go and bear fruit that will remain,
  so that whatever you ask the Father in my name he may give you.
This I command you: love one another." ✛

SATURDAY, MAY 21
Easter Weekday, St. Christopher Magallanes and Companions

✝ *Acts of the Apostles 16:1-10*
Come over to Macedonia and help us.

Paul reached also Derbe and Lystra
  where there was a disciple named Timothy,
  the son of a Jewish woman who was a believer,
  but his father was a Greek.
The brothers in Lystra and Iconium spoke highly of him,
  and Paul wanted him to come along with him.
On account of the Jews of that region, Paul had him circumcised,
  for they all knew that his father was a Greek.
As they traveled from city to city,
  they handed on to the people for observance the decisions
  reached by the Apostles and presbyters in Jerusalem.
Day after day the churches grew stronger in faith
  and increased in number.

They traveled through the Phrygian and Galatian territory
  because they had been prevented by the Holy Spirit
  from preaching the message in the province of Asia.
When they came to Mysia, they tried to go on into Bithynia,
  but the Spirit of Jesus did not allow them,
  so they crossed through Mysia and came down to Troas.
During the night Paul had a vision.
A Macedonian stood before him and implored him with these words,
  "Come over to Macedonia and help us."
When he had seen the vision,
  we sought passage to Macedonia at once,
  concluding that God had called us to proclaim the Good News to
    them. ✛

Psalm 100:1b-2, 3, 5
R. (2a) Let all the earth cry out to God with joy. *(or* **Alleluia.***)*
Sing joyfully to the LORD, all you lands;
  serve the LORD with gladness;
  come before him with joyful song. **R.**
Know that the LORD is God;
  he made us, his we are;
  his people, the flock he tends. **R.**

The LORD is good:
  his kindness endures forever,
  and his faithfulness, to all generations. **R.**

  Colossians 3:1
R. Alleluia, alleluia.
If then you were raised with Christ,
seek what is above,
where Christ is seated at the right hand of God. **R.**

✝ *John 15:18-21*
You do not belong to the world,
and I have chosen you out of the world.

Jesus said to his disciples:
"If the world hates you, realize that it hated me first.
If you belonged to the world, the world would love its own;
  but because you do not belong to the world,
  and I have chosen you out of the world,
  the world hates you.
Remember the word I spoke to you,
  'No slave is greater than his master.'
If they persecuted me, they will also persecute you.
If they kept my word, they will also keep yours.
And they will do all these things to you on account of my name,
  because they do not know the one who sent me." ✛

SUNDAY, MAY 22
SIXTH SUNDAY OF EASTER
(When the Ascension of the Lord is celebrated on the following Sunday, the Second Reading
and Gospel from the Seventh Sunday of Easter may be read on the Sixth Sunday of Easter.)

✝ *Acts of the Apostles 15:1-2, 22-29*
It is the decision of the Holy Spirit and of us not to place on you
any burden beyond these necessities.

Some who had come down from Judea were instructing the brothers,
  "Unless you are circumcised according to the Mosaic practice,
  you cannot be saved."
Because there arose no little dissension and debate
  by Paul and Barnabas with them,
  it was decided that Paul, Barnabas, and some of the others
  should go up to Jerusalem to the apostles and elders
  about this question.

The apostles and elders, in agreement with the whole church,
  decided to choose representatives
  and to send them to Antioch with Paul and Barnabas.

The ones chosen were Judas, who was called Barsabbas,
   and Silas, leaders among the brothers.
This is the letter delivered by them:

"The apostles and the elders, your brothers,
   to the brothers in Antioch, Syria, and Cilicia
   of Gentile origin: greetings.
Since we have heard that some of our number
   who went out without any mandate from us
   have upset you with their teachings
   and disturbed your peace of mind,
   we have with one accord decided to choose representatives
   and to send them to you along with our beloved Barnabas and Paul,
   who have dedicated their lives to the name of our Lord Jesus Christ.
So we are sending Judas and Silas
   who will also convey this same message by word of mouth:
   'It is the decision of the Holy Spirit and of us
   not to place on you any burden beyond these necessities,
   namely, to abstain from meat sacrificed to idols,
   from blood, from meats of strangled animals,
   and from unlawful marriage.
If you keep free of these,
   you will be doing what is right. Farewell.'" ✠

   Psalm 67:2-3, 5, 6, 8
R. O God, let all the nations praise you! *(or* **Alleluia.***)*
May God have pity on us and bless us;
   may he let his face shine upon us.
So may your way be known upon earth;
   among all nations, your salvation. **R.**
May the nations be glad and exult
   because you rule the peoples in equity;
   the nations on the earth you guide. **R.**
May the peoples praise you, O God;
   may all the peoples praise you!
May God bless us,
   and may all the ends of the earth fear him! **R.**

   ✝ Revelation 21:10-14, 22-23 (or Revelation 22:12-14, 16-17, 20)
   The angel showed me the holy city coming down out of heaven.

The angel took me in spirit to a great, high mountain
   and showed me the holy city Jerusalem
   coming down out of heaven from God.
It gleamed with the splendor of God.

Its radiance was like that of a precious stone,
    like jasper, clear as crystal.
It had a massive, high wall,
    with twelve gates where twelve angels were stationed
    and on which names were inscribed,
    the names of the twelve tribes of the Israelites.
There were three gates facing east,
    three north, three south, and three west.
The wall of the city had twelve courses of stones as its foundation,
    on which were inscribed the twelve names
    of the twelve apostles of the Lamb.

I saw no temple in the city
    for its temple is the Lord God almighty and the Lamb.
The city had no need of sun or moon to shine on it,
    for the glory of God gave it light,
    and its lamp was the Lamb. ✛

John 14:23
R. Alleluia, alleluia.
Whoever loves me will keep my word, says the Lord,
and my Father will love him and we will come to him. **R.**

✝ ***John 14:23-29*** *(or John 17:20-26)*
*The Holy Spirit will teach you everything
and remind you of all that I told you.*

Jesus said to his disciples:
    "Whoever loves me will keep my word,
    and my Father will love him,
    and we will come to him and make our dwelling with him.
Whoever does not love me does not keep my words;
    yet the word you hear is not mine
    but that of the Father who sent me.

"I have told you this while I am with you.
The Advocate, the Holy Spirit,
    whom the Father will send in my name,
    will teach you everything
    and remind you of all that I told you.
Peace I leave with you; my peace I give to you.
Not as the world gives do I give it to you.
Do not let your hearts be troubled or afraid.
You heard me tell you,
    'I am going away and I will come back to you.'

If you loved me,
　　you would rejoice that I am going to the Father;
　　for the Father is greater than I.
And now I have told you this before it happens,
　　so that when it happens you may believe." ✢

MONDAY, MAY 23
EASTER WEEKDAY

† *Acts of the Apostles 16:11-15*
The Lord opened her heart to pay attention to what Paul taught.

We set sail from Troas, making a straight run for Samothrace,
　　and on the next day to Neapolis, and from there to Philippi,
　　a leading city in that district of Macedonia and a Roman colony.
We spent some time in that city.
On the sabbath we went outside the city gate along the river
　　where we thought there would be a place of prayer.
We sat and spoke with the women who had gathered there.
One of them, a woman named Lydia, a dealer in purple cloth,
　　from the city of Thyatira, a worshiper of God, listened,
　　and the Lord opened her heart to pay attention
　　to what Paul was saying.
After she and her household had been baptized,
　　she offered us an invitation,
　　"If you consider me a believer in the Lord,
　　come and stay at my home," and she prevailed on us. ✢

Psalm 149:1b-2, 3-4, 5-6a and 9b
R. (see 4a) **The Lord takes delight in his people.** *(or* **Alleluia.***)*
Sing to the LORD a new song
　　of praise in the assembly of the faithful.
Let Israel be glad in their maker,
　　let the children of Zion rejoice in their king. **R.**
Let them praise his name in the festive dance,
　　let them sing praise to him with timbrel and harp.
For the LORD loves his people,
　　and he adorns the lowly with victory. **R.**
Let the faithful exult in glory;
　　let them sing for joy upon their couches.
Let the high praises of God be in their throats.
　　This is the glory of all his faithful. Alleluia. **R.**

John 15:26b, 27a
R. Alleluia, alleluia.
The Spirit of truth will testify to me, says the Lord,
and you also will testify. **R.**

† John 15:26—16:4a
The Spirit of truth will testify to me.

J esus said to his disciples:
"When the Advocate comes whom I will send you from the Father,
   the Spirit of truth who proceeds from the Father,
   he will testify to me.
And you also testify,
   because you have been with me from the beginning.

"I have told you this so that you may not fall away.
They will expel you from the synagogues;
   in fact, the hour is coming when everyone who kills you
   will think he is offering worship to God.
They will do this because they have not known either the Father or
      me.
I have told you this so that when their hour comes
   you may remember that I told you." ✛

TUESDAY, MAY 24
EASTER WEEKDAY

† Acts of the Apostles 16:22-34
Believe in the Lord Jesus and you and your household will be saved.

T he crowd in Philippi joined in the attack on Paul and Silas,
   and the magistrates had them stripped
   and ordered them to be beaten with rods.
After inflicting many blows on them,
   they threw them into prison
   and instructed the jailer to guard them securely.
When he received these instructions, he put them in the innermost cell
   and secured their feet to a stake.

About midnight, while Paul and Silas were praying
   and singing hymns to God as the prisoners listened,
   there was suddenly such a severe earthquake
   that the foundations of the jail shook;
   all the doors flew open, and the chains of all were pulled loose.
When the jailer woke up and saw the prison doors wide open,
   he drew his sword and was about to kill himself,
   thinking that the prisoners had escaped.
But Paul shouted out in a loud voice,
   "Do no harm to yourself; we are all here."
He asked for a light and rushed in and,
   trembling with fear, he fell down before Paul and Silas.

Then he brought them out and said,
 "Sirs, what must I do to be saved?"
And they said, "Believe in the Lord Jesus
 and you and your household will be saved."
So they spoke the word of the Lord to him and to everyone in his
 house.
He took them in at that hour of the night and bathed their wounds;
 then he and all his family were baptized at once.
He brought them up into his house and provided a meal
 and with his household rejoiced at having come to faith in God. ✝

Psalm 138:1-2ab, 2cde-3, 7c-8
R. (7c) **Your right hand saves me, O Lord.** *(or* **Alleluia.***)*
I will give thanks to you, O Lord, with all my heart,
 for you have heard the words of my mouth;
 in the presence of the angels I will sing your praise;
I will worship at your holy temple,
 and give thanks to your name. **R.**
Because of your kindness and your truth,
 you have made great above all things
 your name and your promise.
When I called, you answered me;
 you built up strength within me. **R.**
Your right hand saves me.
The Lord will complete what he has done for me;
 your kindness, O Lord, endures forever;
 forsake not the work of your hands. **R.**

See John 16:7, 13
R. Alleluia, alleluia.
I will send to you the Spirit of truth, says the Lord;
he will guide you to all truth. **R.**

✝ *John 16:5-11*
For if I do not go, the Advocate will not come to you.

Jesus said to his disciples:
"Now I am going to the one who sent me,
 and not one of you asks me, 'Where are you going?'
But because I told you this, grief has filled your hearts.
But I tell you the truth, it is better for you that I go.
For if I do not go, the Advocate will not come to you.
But if I go, I will send him to you.
And when he comes he will convict the world
 in regard to sin and righteousness and condemnation:
 sin, because they do not believe in me;

righteousness, because I am going to the Father
and you will no longer see me;
condemnation, because the ruler of this world has been
   condemned." ✛

WEDNESDAY, MAY 25
EASTER WEEKDAY, ST. BEDE THE VENERABLE,
ST. POPE GREGORY VII, ST. MARY MAGDALENE DE' PAZZI

† *Acts of the Apostles 17:15, 22—18:1*
What therefore you unknowingly worship, I proclaim to you.

After Paul's escorts had taken him to Athens,
   they came away with instructions for Silas and Timothy
   to join him as soon as possible.

Then Paul stood up at the Areopagus and said:
   "You Athenians, I see that in every respect
   you are very religious.
For as I walked around looking carefully at your shrines,
   I even discovered an altar inscribed, 'To an Unknown God.'
What therefore you unknowingly worship, I proclaim to you.
The God who made the world and all that is in it,
   the Lord of heaven and earth,
   does not dwell in sanctuaries made by human hands,
   nor is he served by human hands because he needs anything.
Rather it is he who gives to everyone life and breath and everything.
He made from one the whole human race
   to dwell on the entire surface of the earth,
   and he fixed the ordered seasons and the boundaries of their regions,
   so that people might seek God,
   even perhaps grope for him and find him,
   though indeed he is not far from any one of us.
For 'In him we live and move and have our being,'
   as even some of your poets have said,
   'For we too are his offspring.'
Since therefore we are the offspring of God,
   we ought not to think that the divinity is like an image
   fashioned from gold, silver, or stone by human art and imagination.
God has overlooked the times of ignorance,
   but now he demands that all people everywhere repent
   because he has established a day on which he will 'judge the world
   with justice' through a man he has appointed,
   and he has provided confirmation for all
   by raising him from the dead."

When they heard about resurrection of the dead,
  some began to scoff, but others said,
  "We should like to hear you on this some other time."
And so Paul left them.
But some did join him, and became believers.
Among them were Dionysius,
  a member of the Court of the Areopagus,
  a woman named Damaris, and others with them.

After this he left Athens and went to Corinth. ✝

  Psalm 148:1-2, 11-12, 13, 14
R. Heaven and earth are full of your glory. *(or* **Alleluia.***)*
Praise the LORD from the heavens;
  praise him in the heights.
Praise him, all you his angels;
  praise him, all you his hosts. **R.**
Let the kings of the earth and all peoples,
  the princes and all the judges of the earth,
Young men too, and maidens,
  old men and boys. **R.**
Praise the name of the LORD,
  for his name alone is exalted;
His majesty is above earth and heaven. **R.**
He has lifted up the horn of his people;
Be this his praise from all his faithful ones,
  from the children of Israel, the people close to him.
  Alleluia. **R.**

  John 14:16
R. Alleluia, alleluia.
I will ask the Father
and he will give you another Advocate
to be with you always. **R.**

✝ *John 16:12-15*
When the Spirit of truth comes, he will guide you to all truth.

Jesus said to his disciples:
"I have much more to tell you, but you cannot bear it now.
But when he comes, the Spirit of truth,
  he will guide you to all truth.
He will not speak on his own,
  but he will speak what he hears,
  and will declare to you the things that are coming.
He will glorify me,
  because he will take from what is mine and declare it to you.

Everything that the Father has is mine;
    for this reason I told you that he will take from what is mine
    and declare it to you." ✝

THURSDAY, MAY 26
THE ASCENSION OF THE LORD
(If the Ascension is celebrated on the Seventh Sunday of Easter, May 29,
the readings today are for an Easter Weekday:
Acts of the Apostles 18:1-8 • Psalm 98:1, 2-3ab, 3cd-4 • John 16:16-20 [294].)

† *Acts of the Apostles 1:1-11*
As the Apostles were looking on, Jesus was taken up.

In the first book, Theophilus,
    I dealt with all that Jesus did and taught
    until the day he was taken up,
    after giving instructions through the Holy Spirit
    to the apostles whom he had chosen.
He presented himself alive to them
    by many proofs after he had suffered,
    appearing to them during forty days
    and speaking about the kingdom of God.
While meeting with them,
    he enjoined them not to depart from Jerusalem,
    but to wait for "the promise of the Father
    about which you have heard me speak;
    for John baptized with water,
    but in a few days you will be baptized with the Holy Spirit."

When they had gathered together they asked him,
    "Lord, are you at this time going to restore the kingdom to Israel?"
He answered them,
    "It is not for you to know the times or seasons
    that the Father has established by his own authority.
But you will receive power when the Holy Spirit comes upon you,
    and you will be my witnesses in Jerusalem,
    throughout Judea and Samaria,
    and to the ends of the earth."
When he had said this, as they were looking on,
    he was lifted up, and a cloud took him from their sight.
While they were looking intently at the sky as he was going,
    suddenly two men dressed in white garments stood beside them.
They said, "Men of Galilee,
    why are you standing there looking at the sky?

This Jesus who has been taken up from you into heaven
   will return in the same way as you have seen him going into
      heaven." ✝

Psalm 47:2-3, 6-7, 8-9

R. (6) God mounts his throne to shouts of joy: a blare of
   trumpets for the Lord. *(or* **Alleluia.***)*

All you peoples, clap your hands,
   shout to God with cries of gladness,
for the LORD, the Most High, the awesome,
   is the great king over all the earth. **R.**
God mounts his throne amid shouts of joy;
   the LORD, amid trumpet blasts.
Sing praise to God, sing praise;
   sing praise to our king, sing praise. **R.**
For king of all the earth is God;
   sing hymns of praise.
God reigns over the nations,
   God sits upon his holy throne. **R.**

*✝ **Ephesians 1:17-23** (or Hebrews 9:24-28; 10:19-23)*
God seated Jesus at his right hand in the heavens.

Brothers and sisters:
May the God of our Lord Jesus Christ, the Father of glory,
   give you a Spirit of wisdom and revelation
   resulting in knowledge of him.
May the eyes of your hearts be enlightened,
   that you may know what is the hope that belongs to his call,
   what are the riches of glory
   in his inheritance among the holy ones,
   and what is the surpassing greatness of his power
   for us who believe,
   in accord with the exercise of his great might:
   which he worked in Christ,
   raising him from the dead
   and seating him at his right hand in the heavens,
   far above every principality, authority, power, and dominion,
   and every name that is named
   not only in this age but also in the one to come.
And he put all things beneath his feet
   and gave him as head over all things to the church,
   which is his body,
   the fullness of the one who fills all things in every way. ✝

Matthew 28:19a, 20b
R. Alleluia, alleluia.
Go and teach all nations, says the Lord;
I am with you always, until the end of the world. **R.**

✝ *Luke 24:46-53*
As he blessed them, he was taken up to heaven.

Jesus said to his disciples:
"Thus it is written that the Christ would suffer
and rise from the dead on the third day
and that repentance, for the forgiveness of sins,
would be preached in his name
to all the nations, beginning from Jerusalem.
You are witnesses of these things.
And behold I am sending the promise of my Father upon you;
but stay in the city
until you are clothed with power from on high."

Then he led them out as far as Bethany,
raised his hands, and blessed them.
As he blessed them he parted from them
and was taken up to heaven.
They did him homage
and then returned to Jerusalem with great joy,
and they were continually in the temple praising God. ✛

FRIDAY, MAY 27
EASTER WEEKDAY, ST. AUGUSTINE OF CANTERBURY

✝ *Acts of the Apostles 18:9-18*
I have many people in this city.

One night while Paul was in Corinth, the Lord said to him in a vision,
"Do not be afraid.
Go on speaking, and do not be silent, for I am with you.
No one will attack and harm you,
for I have many people in this city."
He settled there for a year and a half
and taught the word of God among them.

But when Gallio was proconsul of Achaia,
the Jews rose up together against Paul
and brought him to the tribunal, saying,
"This man is inducing people to worship God contrary to the law."
When Paul was about to reply, Gallio spoke to the Jews,
"If it were a matter of some crime or malicious fraud,
I should with reason hear the complaint of you Jews;

but since it is a question of arguments over doctrine and titles
and your own law, see to it yourselves.
I do not wish to be a judge of such matters."
And he drove them away from the tribunal.
They all seized Sosthenes, the synagogue official,
and beat him in full view of the tribunal.
But none of this was of concern to Gallio.

Paul remained for quite some time,
and after saying farewell to the brothers he sailed for Syria,
together with Priscilla and Aquila.
At Cenchreae he had shaved his head because he had taken a vow. ✛

Psalm 47:2-3, 4-5, 6-7
R. (8a) **God is king of all the earth.** *(or* **Alleluia.***)*
All you peoples, clap your hands,
shout to God with cries of gladness,
For the LORD, the Most High, the awesome,
is the great king over all the earth. **R.**
He brings people under us;
nations under our feet.
He chooses for us our inheritance,
the glory of Jacob, whom he loves. **R.**
God mounts his throne amid shouts of joy;
the LORD, amid trumpet blasts.
Sing praise to God, sing praise;
sing praise to our king, sing praise. **R.**

See Luke 24:46, 26
R. Alleluia, alleluia.
Christ had to suffer and to rise from the dead,
and so enter into his glory. **R.**

† *John 16:20-23*
No one will take your joy away from you.

Jesus said to his disciples:
"Amen, amen, I say to you, you will weep and mourn,
while the world rejoices;
you will grieve, but your grief will become joy.
When a woman is in labor, she is in anguish because her hour has
arrived;
but when she has given birth to a child,
she no longer remembers the pain because of her joy
that a child has been born into the world.
So you also are now in anguish.   .

But I will see you again, and your hearts will rejoice,
  and no one will take your joy away from you.
On that day you will not question me about anything.
Amen, amen, I say to you,
  whatever you ask the Father in my name he will give you." ✛

SATURDAY, MAY 28
Easter Weekday

† Acts of the Apostles 18:23-28
Apollos established from the Scriptures that the Christ is Jesus.

After staying in Antioch some time,
  Paul left and traveled in orderly sequence
  through the Galatian country and Phrygia,
  bringing strength to all the disciples.

A Jew named Apollos, a native of Alexandria,
  an eloquent speaker, arrived in Ephesus.
He was an authority on the Scriptures.
He had been instructed in the Way of the Lord and,
  with ardent spirit, spoke and taught accurately about Jesus,
  although he knew only the baptism of John.
He began to speak boldly in the synagogue;
  but when Priscilla and Aquila heard him,
  they took him aside
  and explained to him the Way of God more accurately.
And when he wanted to cross to Achaia,
  the brothers encouraged him
  and wrote to the disciples there to welcome him.
After his arrival he gave great assistance
  to those who had come to believe through grace.
He vigorously refuted the Jews in public,
  establishing from the Scriptures that the Christ is Jesus. ✛

Psalm 47:2-3, 8-9, 10
R. (8a) **God is king of all the earth.** *(or* **Alleluia.***)*
All you peoples, clap your hands;
  shout to God with cries of gladness.
For the Lord, the Most High, the awesome,
  is the great king over all the earth. **R.**
For king of all the earth is God;
  sing hymns of praise.
God reigns over the nations,
  God sits upon his holy throne. **R.**

The princes of the peoples are gathered together
  with the people of the God of Abraham.
For God's are the guardians of the earth;
  he is supreme. **R.**

John 16:28
R. Alleluia, alleluia.
I came from the Father and have come into the world;
now I am leaving the world and going back to the Father. **R.**

✝ *John 16:23b-28*
My Father loves you because you have loved me and believed in me.

Jesus said to his disciples:
"Amen, amen, I say to you,
  whatever you ask the Father in my name he will give you.
Until now you have not asked anything in my name;
  ask and you will receive, so that your joy may be complete.

"I have told you this in figures of speech.
The hour is coming when I will no longer speak to you in figures
  but I will tell you clearly about the Father.
On that day you will ask in my name,
  and I do not tell you that I will ask the Father for you.
For the Father himself loves you, because you have loved me
  and have come to believe that I came from God.
I came from the Father and have come into the world.
Now I am leaving the world and going back to the Father." ✝

SUNDAY, MAY 29
SEVENTH SUNDAY OF EASTER
(If the Ascension is celebrated today, use the readings given for Thursday, May 26.)

✝ *Acts 7:55-60*
I see the Son of Man standing at the right hand of God.

Stephen, filled with the Holy Spirit,
  looked up intently to heaven and saw the glory of God
  and Jesus standing at the right hand of God,
  and Stephen said, "Behold, I see the heavens opened
  and the Son of Man standing at the right hand of God."
But they cried out in a loud voice,
  covered their ears, and rushed upon him together.
They threw him out of the city, and began to stone him.
The witnesses laid down their cloaks
  at the feet of a young man named Saul.

As they were stoning Stephen, he called out,
"Lord Jesus, receive my spirit."
Then he fell to his knees and cried out in a loud voice,
"Lord, do not hold this sin against them";
and when he said this, he fell asleep. ✛

Psalm 97:1-2, 6-7, 9

R. (1a and 9a) **The Lord is king, the most high over all the
earth.** (*or* **Alleluia.**)
The LORD is king; let the earth rejoice;
let the many islands be glad.
Justice and judgment are the foundation of his throne. **R.**
The heavens proclaim his justice,
and all peoples see his glory.
All gods are prostrate before him. **R.**
You, O LORD, are the Most High over all the earth,
exalted far above all gods. **R.**

† *Revelation 22:12-14, 16-17, 20*
Come, Lord Jesus!

I, John, heard a voice saying to me:
"Behold, I am coming soon.
I bring with me the recompense I will give to each
according to his deeds.
I am the Alpha and the Omega, the first and the last,
the beginning and the end."

Blessed are they who wash their robes
so as to have the right to the tree of life
and enter the city through its gates.

"I, Jesus, sent my angel to give you this testimony for the churches.
I am the root and offspring of David,
the bright morning star."

The Spirit and the bride say, "Come."
Let the hearer say, "Come."
Let the one who thirsts come forward,
and the one who wants it receive the gift of life-giving water.

The one who gives this testimony says, "Yes, I am coming soon."
Amen! Come, Lord Jesus! ✛

See John 14:18

R. Alleluia, alleluia.
I will not leave you orphans, says the Lord.
I will come back to you, and your hearts will rejoice. **R.**

† *John 17:20-26*
That they may be brought to perfection as one!

Lifting up his eyes to heaven, Jesus prayed, saying:
  "Holy Father, I pray not only for them,
  but also for those who will believe in me through their word,
  so that they may all be one,
  as you, Father, are in me and I in you,
  that they also may be in us,
  that the world may believe that you sent me.
And I have given them the glory you gave me,
  so that they may be one, as we are one,
  I in them and you in me,
  that they may be brought to perfection as one,
  that the world may know that you sent me,
  and that you loved them even as you loved me.
Father, they are your gift to me.
I wish that where I am they also may be with me,
  that they may see my glory that you gave me,
  because you loved me before the foundation of the world.
Righteous Father, the world also does not know you,
  but I know you, and they know that you sent me.
I made known to them your name and I will make it known,
  that the love with which you loved me
  may be in them and I in them." ✛

MONDAY, MAY 30
EASTER WEEKDAY

† *Acts of the Apostles 19:1-8*
Did you receive the Holy Spirit when you became believers?

While Apollos was in Corinth,
  Paul traveled through the interior of the country
  and down to Ephesus where he found some disciples.
He said to them,
  "Did you receive the Holy Spirit when you became believers?"
They answered him,
  "We have never even heard that there is a Holy Spirit."
He said, "How were you baptized?"
They replied, "With the baptism of John."
Paul then said, "John baptized with a baptism of repentance,
  telling the people to believe in the one who was to come after him,
  that is, in Jesus."
When they heard this,
  they were baptized in the name of the Lord Jesus.

And when Paul laid his hands on them,
the Holy Spirit came upon them,
and they spoke in tongues and prophesied.
Altogether there were about twelve men.

He entered the synagogue, and for three months debated boldly
with persuasive arguments about the Kingdom of God. ✛

Psalm 68:2-3ab, 4-5acd, 6-7ab
R. (33a) **Sing to God, O kingdoms of the earth.** *(or* **Alleluia.***)*
God arises; his enemies are scattered,
and those who hate him flee before him.
As smoke is driven away, so are they driven;
as wax melts before the fire. **R.**
But the just rejoice and exult before God;
they are glad and rejoice.
Sing to God, chant praise to his name;
whose name is the LORD. **R.**
The father of orphans and the defender of widows
is God in his holy dwelling.
God gives a home to the forsaken;
he leads forth prisoners to prosperity. **R.**

Colossians 3:1
R. Alleluia, alleluia.
If then you were raised with Christ,
seek what is above,
where Christ is seated at the right hand of God. **R.**

† *John 16:29-33*
Take courage, I have conquered the world.

The disciples said to Jesus,
"Now you are talking plainly, and not in any figure of speech.
Now we realize that you know everything
and that you do not need to have anyone question you.
Because of this we believe that you came from God."
Jesus answered them, "Do you believe now?
Behold, the hour is coming and has arrived
when each of you will be scattered to his own home
and you will leave me alone.
But I am not alone, because the Father is with me.
I have told you this so that you might have peace in me.
In the world you will have trouble,
but take courage, I have conquered the world." ✛

TUESDAY, MAY 31
THE VISITATION OF THE BLESSED VIRGIN MARY

† Zephaniah 3:14-18a (or Romans 12:9-16)
The King of Israel, the Lord, is in your midst.

Shout for joy, O daughter Zion!
  Sing joyfully, O Israel!
Be glad and exult with all your heart,
  O daughter Jerusalem!
The LORD has removed the judgment against you,
  he has turned away your enemies;
The King of Israel, the LORD, is in your midst,
  you have no further misfortune to fear.
On that day, it shall be said to Jerusalem:
  Fear not, O Zion, be not discouraged!
The LORD, your God, is in your midst,
  a mighty savior;
He will rejoice over you with gladness,
  and renew you in his love,
He will sing joyfully because of you,
  as one sings at festivals. ✛

Isaiah 12:2-3, 4bcd, 5-6
R. (6) **Among you is the great and Holy One of Israel.**
  (or **Alleluia.**)
God indeed is my savior;
  I am confident and unafraid.
My strength and my courage is the LORD,
  and he has been my savior.
With joy you will draw water
  at the fountain of salvation. **R.**
Give thanks to the LORD, acclaim his name;
  among the nations make known his deeds,
  proclaim how exalted is his name. **R.**
Sing praise to the LORD for his glorious achievement;
  let this be known throughout all the earth.
Shout with exultation, O city of Zion,
  for great in your midst
  is the Holy One of Israel! **R.**

See Luke 1:45
R. Alleluia, alleluia.
Blessed are you, O Virgin Mary, who believed
that what was spoken to you by the Lord would be fulfilled. **R.**

† *Luke 1:39-56*

And how does this happen to me, that the mother of my Lord should come to me?

Mary set out
 and traveled to the hill country in haste
 to a town of Judah,
 where she entered the house of Zechariah
 and greeted Elizabeth.
When Elizabeth heard Mary's greeting,
 the infant leaped in her womb,
 and Elizabeth, filled with the Holy Spirit,
 cried out in a loud voice and said,
 "Most blessed are you among women,
 and blessed is the fruit of your womb.
And how does this happen to me,
 that the mother of my Lord should come to me?
For at the moment the sound of your greeting reached my ears,
 the infant in my womb leaped for joy.
Blessed are you who believed
 that what was spoken to you by the Lord
 would be fulfilled."

And Mary said:
"My soul proclaims the greatness of the Lord;
 my spirit rejoices in God my Savior,
 for he has looked with favor on his lowly servant.
From this day all generations will call me blessed:
 the Almighty has done great things for me,
 and holy is his Name.

He has mercy on those who fear him
 in every generation.
He has shown the strength of his arm,
 he has scattered the proud in their conceit.
He has cast down the mighty from their thrones,
 and has lifted up the lowly.
He has filled the hungry with good things,
 and the rich he has sent away empty.
He has come to the help of his servant Israel
 for he has remembered his promise of mercy,
 the promise he made to our fathers,
 to Abraham and his children for ever."

Mary remained with her about three months
 and then returned to her home. ✛

WEDNESDAY, JUNE 1
St. Justin

† *Acts 20:28-38*
*I commend you to God who has the power to build you up
and to give you an inheritance.*

At Miletus, Paul spoke to the presbyters of the Church of Ephesus:
"Keep watch over yourselves and over the whole flock
  of which the Holy Spirit has appointed you overseers,
  in which you tend the Church of God
  that he acquired with his own Blood.
I know that after my departure savage wolves will come among you,
  and they will not spare the flock.
And from your own group, men will come forward perverting the truth
  to draw the disciples away after them.
So be vigilant and remember that for three years, night and day,
  I unceasingly admonished each of you with tears.
And now I commend you to God
  and to that gracious word of his that can build you up
  and give you the inheritance among all who are consecrated.
I have never wanted anyone's silver or gold or clothing.
You know well that these very hands
  have served my needs and my companions.
In every way I have shown you that by hard work of that sort
  we must help the weak,
  and keep in mind the words of the Lord Jesus who himself said,
  'It is more blessed to give than to receive.'"

When he had finished speaking
  he knelt down and prayed with them all.
They were all weeping loudly
  as they threw their arms around Paul and kissed him,
  for they were deeply distressed that he had said
  that they would never see his face again.
Then they escorted him to the ship. ✝

Psalm 68:29-30, 33-35a, 35bc-36ab
R. (33a) **Sing to God, O kingdoms of the earth.** *(or* **Alleluia.***)*
Show forth, O God, your power,
  the power, O God, with which you took our part;
For your temple in Jerusalem
  let the kings bring you gifts. **R.**
You kingdoms of the earth, sing to God,
  chant praise to the LORD
  who rides on the heights of the ancient heavens.

Behold, his voice resounds, the voice of power:
  "Confess the power of God!" **R.**
Over Israel is his majesty;
  his power is in the skies.
Awesome in his sanctuary is God, the God of Israel;
  he gives power and strength to his people. **R.**

See John 17:17b, 17a
R. Alleluia, alleluia.
Your word, O Lord, is truth;
consecrate us in the truth. **R.**

† *John 17:11b-19*

May they be one just as we are one.

Lifting up his eyes to heaven, Jesus prayed, saying:
"Holy Father, keep them in your name
  that you have given me,
  so that they may be one just as we are one.
When I was with them I protected them in your name that you gave
    me,
  and I guarded them, and none of them was lost
  except the son of destruction,
  in order that the Scripture might be fulfilled.
But now I am coming to you.
I speak this in the world
  so that they may share my joy completely.
I gave them your word, and the world hated them,
  because they do not belong to the world
  any more than I belong to the world.
I do not ask that you take them out of the world
  but that you keep them from the Evil One.
They do not belong to the world
  any more than I belong to the world.
Consecrate them in the truth.
Your word is truth.
As you sent me into the world,
  so I sent them into the world.
And I consecrate myself for them,
  so that they also may be consecrated in truth." ✛

THURSDAY, JUNE 2
EASTER WEEKDAY, ST. MARCELLINUS AND ST. PETER

† *Acts of the Apostles 22:30; 23:6-11*
You must bear witness in Rome.

Wishing to determine the truth
about why Paul was being accused by the Jews,
the commander freed him
and ordered the chief priests and the whole Sanhedrin to convene.
Then he brought Paul down and made him stand before them.

Paul was aware that some were Sadducees and some Pharisees,
so he called out before the Sanhedrin,
"My brothers, I am a Pharisee, the son of Pharisees;
I am on trial for hope in the resurrection of the dead."
When he said this,
a dispute broke out between the Pharisees and Sadducees,
and the group became divided.
For the Sadducees say that there is no resurrection
or angels or spirits,
while the Pharisees acknowledge all three.
A great uproar occurred,
and some scribes belonging to the Pharisee party
stood up and sharply argued,
"We find nothing wrong with this man.
Suppose a spirit or an angel has spoken to him?"
The dispute was so serious that the commander,
afraid that Paul would be torn to pieces by them,
ordered his troops to go down and rescue Paul from their midst
and take him into the compound.
The following night the Lord stood by him and said, "Take courage.
For just as you have borne witness to my cause in Jerusalem,
so you must also bear witness in Rome." ✜

Psalm 16:1b-2a and 5, 7-8, 9-10, 11
R. (1) Keep me safe, O God; you are my hope. *(or* **Alleluia.***)*
Keep me, O God, for in you I take refuge;
I say to the LORD, "My Lord are you."
O LORD, my allotted portion and my cup,
you it is who hold fast my lot. **R.**
I bless the LORD who counsels me;
even in the night my heart exhorts me.
I set the LORD ever before me;
with him at my right hand I shall not be disturbed. **R.**

Therefore my heart is glad and my soul rejoices,
   my body, too, abides in confidence;
Because you will not abandon my soul to the nether world,
   nor will you suffer your faithful one to undergo corruption. **R.**
You will show me the path to life,
   fullness of joys in your presence,
   the delights at your right hand forever. **R.**

   John 17:21
R. Alleluia, alleluia.
May they all be one as you, Father, are in me and I in you,
that the world may believe that you sent me, says the Lord. **R.**

✝ John 17:20-26
May they all be one.

Lifting up his eyes to heaven, Jesus prayed saying:
"I pray not only for these,
   but also for those who will believe in me through their word,
   so that they may all be one,
   as you, Father, are in me and I in you,
   that they also may be in us,
   that the world may believe that you sent me.
And I have given them the glory you gave me,
   so that they may be one, as we are one,
   I in them and you in me,
   that they may be brought to perfection as one,
   that the world may know that you sent me,
   and that you loved them even as you loved me.
Father, they are your gift to me.
I wish that where I am they also may be with me,
   that they may see my glory that you gave me,
   because you loved me before the foundation of the world.
Righteous Father, the world also does not know you,
   but I know you, and they know that you sent me.
I made known to them your name and I will make it known,
   that the love with which you loved me
   may be in them and I in them." ✛

FRIDAY, JUNE 3
St. Charles Lwanga and Companions

† Acts of the Apostles 25:13b-21
Jesus was dead, whom Paul claimed to be alive.

King Agrippa and Bernice arrived in Caesarea
on a visit to Festus.
Since they spent several days there,
Festus referred Paul's case to the king, saying,
"There is a man here left in custody by Felix.
When I was in Jerusalem the chief priests and the elders of the Jews
brought charges against him and demanded his condemnation.
I answered them that it was not Roman practice
to hand over an accused person before he has faced his accusers
and had the opportunity to defend himself against their charge.
So when they came together here, I made no delay;
the next day I took my seat on the tribunal
and ordered the man to be brought in.
His accusers stood around him,
but did not charge him with any of the crimes I suspected.
Instead they had some issues with him about their own religion
and about a certain Jesus who had died
but who Paul claimed was alive.
Since I was at a loss how to investigate this controversy,
I asked if he were willing to go to Jerusalem
and there stand trial on these charges.
And when Paul appealed that he be held in custody
for the Emperor's decision,
I ordered him held until I could send him to Caesar." **+**

Psalm 103:1-2, 11-12, 19-20ab
R. (19a) **The Lord has established his throne in heaven.**
(or **Alleluia.***)*
Bless the LORD, O my soul;
and all my being, bless his holy name.
Bless the LORD, O my soul,
and forget not all his benefits. **R.**
For as the heavens are high above the earth,
so surpassing is his kindness toward those who fear him.
As far as the east is from the west,
so far has he put our transgressions from us. **R.**
The LORD has established his throne in heaven,
and his kingdom rules over all.
Bless the LORD, all you his angels,
you mighty in strength, who do his bidding. **R.**

John 14:26

R. Alleluia, alleluia.

The Holy Spirit will teach you everything
and remind you of all I told you. **R.**

† John 21:15-19
Feed my lambs, feed my sheep.

After Jesus had revealed himself to his disciples and eaten breakfast
　　with them,
　　he said to Simon Peter,
　　"Simon, son of John, do you love me more than these?"
Simon Peter answered him, "Yes, Lord, you know that I love you."
Jesus said to him, "Feed my lambs."
He then said to Simon Peter a second time,
　　"Simon, son of John, do you love me?"
Simon Peter answered him, "Yes, Lord, you know that I love you."
He said to him, "Tend my sheep."
He said to him the third time,
　　"Simon, son of John, do you love me?"
Peter was distressed that he had said to him a third time,
　　"Do you love me?" and he said to him,
　　"Lord, you know everything; you know that I love you."
Jesus said to him, "Feed my sheep.
Amen, amen, I say to you, when you were younger,
　　you used to dress yourself and go where you wanted;
　　but when you grow old, you will stretch out your hands,
　　and someone else will dress you
　　and lead you where you do not want to go."
He said this signifying by what kind of death he would glorify God.
And when he had said this, he said to him, "Follow me." ✛

SATURDAY, JUNE 4
EASTER WEEKDAY

(Morning) † Acts of the Apostles 28:16-20, 30-31
Paul remained at Rome, proclaiming the Kingdom of God.

When he entered Rome, Paul was allowed to live by himself,
　　with the soldier who was guarding him.

Three days later he called together the leaders of the Jews.
When they had gathered he said to them, "My brothers,
　　although I had done nothing against our people
　　or our ancestral customs,
　　I was handed over to the Romans as a prisoner from Jerusalem.

After trying my case the Romans wanted to release me,
    because they found nothing against me deserving the death penalty.
But when the Jews objected, I was obliged to appeal to Caesar,
    even though I had no accusation to make against my own nation.
This is the reason, then, I have requested to see you
    and to speak with you, for it is on account of the hope of Israel
    that I wear these chains."

He remained for two full years in his lodgings.
He received all who came to him, and with complete assurance
    and without hindrance he proclaimed the Kingdom of God
    and taught about the Lord Jesus Christ. ✝

  Psalm 11:4, 5 and 7
R. (see 7b) **The just will gaze on your face, O Lord.** (*or* **Alleluia.***)
The LORD is in his holy temple;
    the LORD's throne is in heaven.
His eyes behold,
    his searching glance is on mankind. **R.**
The LORD searches the just and the wicked;
    the lover of violence he hates.
For the LORD is just, he loves just deeds;
    the upright shall see his face. **R.**

  John 16:7, 13
R. Alleluia, alleluia.
I will send to you the Spirit of truth, says the Lord;
he will guide you to all truth. **R.**

  ✝ *John 21:20-25*
  This is the disciple who has written these things and his testimony is true.

Peter turned and saw the disciple following whom Jesus loved,
    the one who had also reclined upon his chest during the supper
    and had said, "Master, who is the one who will betray you?"
When Peter saw him, he said to Jesus, "Lord, what about him?"
Jesus said to him, "What if I want him to remain until I come?
What concern is it of yours?
You follow me."
So the word spread among the brothers that that disciple would not
    die.
But Jesus had not told him that he would not die,
    just "What if I want him to remain until I come?
What concern is it of yours?"

It is this disciple who testifies to these things
    and has written them, and we know that his testimony is true.

There are also many other things that Jesus did,
  but if these were to be described individually,
  I do not think the whole world would contain the books
  that would be written. ✛

SUNDAY, JUNE 5
PENTECOST SUNDAY
(The Pentecost Vigil Readings are: Genesis 11:1-9 or Exodus 19:3-8a, 16-20b or
Ezekiel 37:1-14 or Joel 3:1-5 • Psalm 104:1-2, 24, 35, 27-28, 29-30 • Romans 8:22-27 •
John 7:37-39. The Extended Vigil: Genesis 11:1-9 • Psalm 33:10-15 • Exodus 19:3-8a,
16-20b • Daniel 3:52-56 or Psalm 19:8-11• Ezekiel 37:1-14 • Psalm 107:2-9 • Joel 3:1-5 •
Psalm 104:1-2, 24, 35, 27-28, 29, 30 • Romans 8:22-27 • John 7:37-39 [62].)

† *Acts of the Apostles 2:1-11*
They were filled with the Holy Spirit and began to speak.

When the time for Pentecost was fulfilled,
  they were all in one place together.
And suddenly there came from the sky
  a noise like a strong driving wind,
  and it filled the entire house in which they were.
Then there appeared to them tongues as of fire,
  which parted and came to rest on each one of them.
And they were all filled with the Holy Spirit
  and began to speak in different tongues,
  as the Spirit enabled them to proclaim.

Now there were devout Jews from every nation under heaven
  staying in Jerusalem.
At this sound, they gathered in a large crowd,
  but they were confused
  because each one heard them speaking in his own language.
They were astounded, and in amazement they asked,
  "Are not all these people who are speaking Galileans?
Then how does each of us hear them in his native language?
We are Parthians, Medes, and Elamites,
  inhabitants of Mesopotamia, Judea and Cappadocia,
  Pontus and Asia, Phrygia and Pamphylia,
  Egypt and the districts of Libya near Cyrene,
  as well as travelers from Rome,
  both Jews and converts to Judaism, Cretans and Arabs,
  yet we hear them speaking in our own tongues
  of the mighty acts of God." ✛

Psalm 104:1, 24, 29-30, 31, 34

R. (see 30) **Lord, send out your Spirit, and renew the face of the earth.** *(or* **Alleluia.***)*

Bless the LORD, O my soul!

O LORD, my God, you are great indeed!

How manifold are your works, O LORD!
  The earth is full of your creatures. **R.**

If you take away their breath, they perish
  and return to their dust.

When you send forth your spirit, they are created,
  and you renew the face of the earth. **R.**

May the glory of the LORD endure forever;
  may the LORD be glad in his works!

Pleasing to him be my theme;
  I will be glad in the LORD. **R.**

✝ 1 Corinthians 12:3b-7, 12-13 *(or Romans 8:8-17)*
In one Spirit we were all baptized into one body.

Brothers and sisters:

No one can say, "Jesus is Lord," except by the Holy Spirit.

There are different kinds of spiritual gifts but the same Spirit;
  there are different forms of service but the same Lord;
  there are different workings but the same God
  who produces all of them in everyone.

To each individual the manifestation of the Spirit
  is given for some benefit.

As a body is one though it has many parts,
  and all the parts of the body, though many, are one body,
  so also Christ.

For in one Spirit we were all baptized into one body,
  whether Jews or Greeks, slaves or free persons,
  and we were all given to drink of one Spirit. ✝

PENTECOST SEQUENCE: Veni, Sancte Spiritus

Come, Holy Spirit, come!

And from your celestial home
  Shed a ray of light divine!

Come, Father of the poor!

Come, source of all our store!
  Come, within our bosoms shine.

You, of comforters the best;

You, the soul's most welcome guest;
  Sweet refreshment here below;

In our labor, rest most sweet;

Grateful coolness in the heat;
   Solace in the midst of woe.
O most blessed Light divine,
Shine within these hearts of yours,
   And our inmost being fill!
Where you are not, we have naught,
Nothing good in deed or thought,
   Nothing free from taint of ill.
Heal our wounds, our strength renew;
On our dryness pour your dew;
   Wash the stains of guilt away:
Bend the stubborn heart and will;
Melt the frozen, warm the chill;
   Guide the steps that go astray.
On the faithful, who adore
And confess you, evermore
   In your sevenfold gift descend;
Give them virtue's sure reward;
Give them your salvation, Lord;
   Give them joys that never end. Amen.
   Alleluia.

R. Alleluia, alleluia.

Come, Holy Spirit, fill the hearts of your faithful
and kindle in them the fire of your love. **R.**

✝ *John 20:19-23* (or *John 14:15-16, 23b-26*)
As the Father sent me, so I send you. Receive the Holy Spirit.

On the evening of that first day of the week,
   when the doors were locked, where the disciples were,
   for fear of the Jews,
   Jesus came and stood in their midst
   and said to them, "Peace be with you."
When he had said this, he showed them his hands and his side.
The disciples rejoiced when they saw the Lord.
Jesus said to them again, "Peace be with you.
As the Father has sent me, so I send you."
And when he had said this, he breathed on them and said to them,
   "Receive the Holy Spirit.
Whose sins you forgive are forgiven them,
   and whose sins you retain are retained." ✛

MONDAY, JUNE 6
The Blessed Virgin Mary, Mother of the Church
(Tenth Week in Ordinary Time)

† Genesis 3:9-15, 20 (or Acts 1:12-14)
The mother of all the living.

After Adam had eaten of the tree,
  the Lord God called to him and asked him, "Where are you?"
He answered, "I heard you in the garden;
  but I was afraid, because I was naked,
  so I hid myself."
Then he asked, "Who told you that you were naked?
You have eaten, then,
  from the tree of which I had forbidden you to eat!"
The man replied, "The woman whom you put here with me—
  she gave me fruit from the tree, and so I ate it."
The Lord God then asked the woman,
  "Why did you do such a thing?"
The woman answered, "The serpent tricked me into it, so I ate it."

Then the Lord God said to the serpent:
  "Because you have done this, you shall be banned
    from all the animals
    and from all the wild creatures;
  On your belly shall you crawl,
    and dirt shall you eat
    all the days of your life.
  I will put enmity between you and the woman,
    and between your offspring and hers;
  He will strike at your head,
    while you strike at his heel."
The man called his wife Eve,
  because she became the mother of all the living. ✙

Psalm 87:1-2, 3 and 5, 6-7
R. (3) **Glorious things are told of you, O city of God.**
His foundation upon the holy mountains
  the Lord loves:
The gates of Zion,
  more than any dwelling of Jacob. **R.**
Glorious things are said of you,
  O city of God!
And of Zion they shall say:
  "One and all were born in her;
And he who has established her
  is the Most High Lord." **R.**

They shall note, when the peoples are enrolled:
"This man was born there."
And all shall sing, in their festive dance:
"My home is within you." **R.**

R. Alleluia, alleluia.
O happy Virgin, you gave birth to the Lord;
O blessed mother of the Church,
you warm our hearts with the Spirit of your Son Jesus Christ. **R.**

✝ John 19:25-34
Woman, behold your son. Behold your mother.

Standing by the cross of Jesus were his mother
and his mother's sister, Mary the wife of Clopas,
and Mary of Magdala.
When Jesus saw his mother and the disciple there whom he loved,
he said to his mother, "Woman, behold, your son."
Then he said to the disciple,
"Behold, your mother."
And from that hour the disciple took her into his home.
After this, aware that everything was now finished,
in order that the Scripture might be fulfilled,
Jesus said, "I thirst."
There was a vessel filled with common wine.
So they put a sponge soaked in wine on a sprig of hyssop
and put it up to his mouth.
When Jesus had taken the wine, he said,
"It is finished."
And bowing his head, he handed over the spirit.

Now since it was preparation day,
in order that the bodies might not remain on the cross on the
sabbath,
for the sabbath day of that week was a solemn one,
the Jews asked Pilate that their legs be broken
and they be taken down.
So the soldiers came and broke the legs of the first
and then of the other one who was crucified with Jesus.
But when they came to Jesus and saw that he was already dead,
they did not break his legs,
but one soldier thrust his lance into his side,
and immediately Blood and water flowed out. ✛

TUESDAY, JUNE 7
WEEKDAY

† *1 Kings 17:7-16*
The jar of flour shall not go empty,
as the LORD had foretold through Elijah.

The brook near where Elijah was hiding ran dry,
 because no rain had fallen in the land.
So the LORD said to Elijah:
 "Move on to Zarephath of Sidon and stay there.
I have designated a widow there to provide for you."
He left and went to Zarephath.
As he arrived at the entrance of the city,
 a widow was gathering sticks there; he called out to her,
 "Please bring me a small cupful of water to drink."
She left to get it, and he called out after her,
 "Please bring along a bit of bread."
She answered, "As the LORD, your God, lives,
 I have nothing baked;
 there is only a handful of flour in my jar
 and a little oil in my jug.
Just now I was collecting a couple of sticks,
 to go in and prepare something for myself and my son;
 when we have eaten it, we shall die."
Elijah said to her, "Do not be afraid.
Go and do as you propose.
But first make me a little cake and bring it to me.
Then you can prepare something for yourself and your son.
For the LORD, the God of Israel, says,
 'The jar of flour shall not go empty,
 nor the jug of oil run dry,
 until the day when the LORD sends rain upon the earth.'"
She left and did as Elijah had said.
She was able to eat for a year, and Elijah and her son as well;
 the jar of flour did not go empty,
 nor the jug of oil run dry,
 as the LORD had foretold through Elijah. ✚

Psalm 4:2-3, 4-5, 7b-8
R. (7a) **Lord, let your face shine on us.**
When I call, answer me, O my just God,
 you who relieve me when I am in distress;
 Have pity on me, and hear my prayer!
Men of rank, how long will you be dull of heart?
 Why do you love what is vain and seek after falsehood? **R.**

Know that the LORD does wonders for his faithful one;
   the LORD will hear me when I call upon him.
Tremble, and sin not;
   reflect, upon your beds, in silence. **R.**
O LORD, let the light of your countenance shine upon us!
You put gladness into my heart,
   more than when grain and wine abound. **R.**

   Matthew 5:16
R. Alleluia, alleluia.
Let your light shine before others
that they may see your good deeds and glorify your heavenly Father. **R.**

† *Matthew 5:13-16*
You are the light of the world.

Jesus said to his disciples:
"You are the salt of the earth.
But if salt loses its taste, with what can it be seasoned?
It is no longer good for anything
   but to be thrown out and trampled underfoot.
You are the light of the world.
A city set on a mountain cannot be hidden.
Nor do they light a lamp and then put it under a bushel basket;
   it is set on a lampstand,
   where it gives light to all in the house.
Just so, your light must shine before others,
   that they may see your good deeds
   and glorify your heavenly Father." ✛

WEDNESDAY, JUNE 8
WEEKDAY

† *1 Kings 18:20-39*
Let it be known this day that you, LORD, are God.

Ahab sent to all the children of Israel
   and had the prophets assemble on Mount Carmel.

Elijah appealed to all the people and said,
   "How long will you straddle the issue?
If the LORD is God, follow him; if Baal, follow him."
The people, however, did not answer him.
So Elijah said to the people,
   "I am the only surviving prophet of the LORD,
   and there are four hundred and fifty prophets of Baal.
Give us two young bulls.

Let them choose one, cut it into pieces, and place it on the wood,
  but start no fire.
I shall prepare the other and place it on the wood,
  but shall start no fire.
You shall call on your gods, and I will call on the LORD.
The God who answers with fire is God."
All the people answered, "Agreed!"

Elijah then said to the prophets of Baal,
  "Choose one young bull and prepare it first,
  for there are more of you.
Call upon your gods, but do not start the fire."
Taking the young bull that was turned over to them, they prepared it
  and called on Baal from morning to noon, saying,
  "Answer us, Baal!"
But there was no sound, and no one answering.
And they hopped around the altar they had prepared.
When it was noon, Elijah taunted them:
  "Call louder, for he is a god and may be meditating,
  or may have retired, or may be on a journey.
Perhaps he is asleep and must be awakened."
They called out louder and slashed themselves with swords and
      spears,
  as was their custom, until blood gushed over them.
Noon passed and they remained in a prophetic state
  until the time for offering sacrifice.
But there was not a sound;
  no one answered, and no one was listening.

Then Elijah said to all the people, "Come here to me."
When the people had done so, he repaired the altar of the LORD
  that had been destroyed.
He took twelve stones, for the number of tribes of the sons of Jacob,
  to whom the LORD had said, "Your name shall be Israel."
He built an altar in honor of the LORD with the stones,
  and made a trench around the altar
  large enough for two measures of grain.
When he had arranged the wood,
  he cut up the young bull and laid it on the wood.
"Fill four jars with water," he said,
  "and pour it over the burnt offering and over the wood."
"Do it again," he said, and they did it again.
"Do it a third time," he said,
  and they did it a third time.

The water flowed around the altar,
  and the trench was filled with the water.

At the time for offering sacrifice,
  the prophet Elijah came forward and said,
"LORD, God of Abraham, Isaac, and Israel,
  let it be known this day that you are God in Israel
  and that I am your servant
  and have done all these things by your command.
Answer me, LORD!
Answer me, that this people may know that you, LORD, are God
  and that you have brought them back to their senses."
The LORD's fire came down
  and consumed the burnt offering, wood, stones, and dust,
  and it lapped up the water in the trench.
Seeing this, all the people fell prostrate and said,
  "The LORD is God! The LORD is God!" ✛

   Psalm 16:1b-2ab, 4, 5ab and 8, 11
R. (1b) **Keep me safe, O God; you are my hope.**
Keep me, O God, for in you I take refuge;
  I say to the LORD, "My Lord are you." **R.**
They multiply their sorrows
  who court other gods.
Blood libations to them I will not pour out,
  nor will I take their names upon my lips. **R.**
O LORD, my allotted portion and cup,
  you it is who hold fast my lot.
I set the LORD ever before me;
  with him at my right hand I shall not be disturbed. **R.**
You will show me the path to life,
  fullness of joys in your presence,
  the delights at your right hand forever. **R.**

   Psalm 25:4b, 5a
R. Alleluia, alleluia.
Teach me your paths, my God,
and guide me in your truth. **R.**

   †Matthew 5:17-19
   I have come not to abolish the law, but to fulfill it.

Jesus said to his disciples:
"Do not think that I have come to abolish the law or the prophets.
I have come not to abolish but to fulfill.
Amen, I say to you, until heaven and earth pass away,
  not the smallest letter or the smallest part of a letter

will pass from the law,
until all things have taken place.
Therefore, whoever breaks one of the least of these commandments
and teaches others to do so
will be called least in the Kingdom of heaven.
But whoever obeys and teaches these commandments
will be called greatest in the Kingdom of heaven." ✟

THURSDAY, JUNE 9
WEEKDAY, ST. EPHREM

✝ *1 Kings 18:41-46*
Elijah prayed and the sky gave rain (James 5:18).

Elijah said to Ahab, "Go up, eat and drink,
for there is the sound of a heavy rain."
So Ahab went up to eat and drink,
while Elijah climbed to the top of Carmel,
crouched down to the earth,
and put his head between his knees.
"Climb up and look out to sea," he directed his servant,
who went up and looked, but reported, "There is nothing."
Seven times he said, "Go, look again!"
And the seventh time the youth reported,
"There is a cloud as small as a man's hand rising from the sea."
Elijah said, "Go and say to Ahab,
'Harness up and leave the mountain before the rain stops you.'"
In a trice the sky grew dark with clouds and wind,
and a heavy rain fell.
Ahab mounted his chariot and made for Jezreel.
But the hand of the LORD was on Elijah,
who girded up his clothing and ran before Ahab
as far as the approaches to Jezreel. ✟

Psalm 65:10, 11, 12-13
R. (2a) **It is right to praise you in Zion, O God.**
You have visited the land and watered it;
greatly have you enriched it.
God's watercourses are filled;
you have prepared the grain. **R.**
Thus have you prepared the land:
drenching its furrows, breaking up its clods,
Softening it with showers,
blessing its yield. **R.**
You have crowned the year with your bounty,
and your paths overflow with a rich harvest;

The untilled meadows overflow with it,
and rejoicing clothes the hills. **R.**

John 13:34
R. Alleluia, alleluia.
I give you a new commandment:
love one another as I have loved you. **R.**

† *Matthew 5:20-26*
Whoever is angry with his brother will be liable to judgment.

Jesus said to his disciples:
"I tell you, unless your righteousness surpasses that
of the scribes and Pharisees,
you will not enter into the Kingdom of heaven.

"You have heard that it was said to your ancestors,
You shall not kill; and whoever kills will be liable to judgment.
But I say to you, whoever is angry with his brother
will be liable to judgment,
and whoever says to his brother, *Raqa,*
will be answerable to the Sanhedrin,
and whoever says, 'You fool,' will be liable to fiery Gehenna.
Therefore, if you bring your gift to the altar,
and there recall that your brother
has anything against you,
leave your gift there at the altar,
go first and be reconciled with your brother,
and then come and offer your gift.
Settle with your opponent quickly while on the way to court with him.
Otherwise your opponent will hand you over to the judge,
and the judge will hand you over to the guard,
and you will be thrown into prison.
Amen, I say to you,
you will not be released until you have paid the last penny." ✛

FRIDAY, JUNE 10
WEEKDAY

† *1 Kings 19:9a, 11-16*
Stand on the mountain before the LORD.

At the mountain of God, Horeb,
Elijah came to a cave, where he took shelter.
But the word of the LORD came to him,
"Go outside and stand on the mountain before the LORD;
the LORD will be passing by."

A strong and heavy wind was rending the mountains
  and crushing rocks before the LORD—
  but the LORD was not in the wind.
After the wind there was an earthquake—
  but the LORD was not in the earthquake.
After the earthquake there was fire—
  but the LORD was not in the fire.
After the fire there was a tiny whispering sound.
When he heard this,
  Elijah hid his face in his cloak
  and went and stood at the entrance of the cave.
A voice said to him, "Elijah, why are you here?"
He replied, "I have been most zealous for the LORD,
  the God of hosts.
But the children of Israel have forsaken your covenant,
  torn down your altars,
  and put your prophets to the sword.
I alone am left, and they seek to take my life."
The LORD said to him,
  "Go, take the road back to the desert near Damascus.
When you arrive, you shall anoint Hazael as king of Aram.
Then you shall anoint Jehu, son of Nimshi, as king of Israel,
  and Elisha, son of Shaphat of Abel-meholah,
  as prophet to succeed you." ✛

Psalm 27:7-8a, 8b-9abc, 13-14
R. (8b) **I long to see your face, O Lord.**
Hear, O LORD, the sound of my call;
  have pity on me, and answer me.
Of you my heart speaks; you my glance seeks. **R.**
Your presence, O LORD, I seek.
Hide not your face from me;
  do not in anger repel your servant.
You are my helper: cast me not off. **R.**
I believe that I shall see the bounty of the LORD
  in the land of the living.
Wait for the LORD with courage;
  be stouthearted, and wait for the LORD. **R.**

Philippians 2:15d, 16a
R. Alleluia, alleluia.
Shine like lights on the world,
  as you hold on to the word of life. **R.**

† *Matthew 5:27-32*
*Everyone who looks at a woman with lust has already
committed adultery with her in his heart.*

Jesus said to his disciples:
"You have heard that it was said, *You shall not commit adultery.*
But I say to you,
  everyone who looks at a woman with lust
  has already committed adultery with her in his heart.
If your right eye causes you to sin,
  tear it out and throw it away.
It is better for you to lose one of your members
  than to have your whole body thrown into Gehenna.
And if your right hand causes you to sin,
  cut it off and throw it away.
It is better for you to lose one of your members
  than to have your whole body go into Gehenna.

"It was also said,
Whoever divorces his wife must give her a bill of divorce.
But I say to you,
  whoever divorces his wife (unless the marriage is unlawful)
  causes her to commit adultery,
  and whoever marries a divorced woman commits adultery." ✛

SATURDAY, JUNE 11
St. Barnabas

† *Acts 11:21b-26; 13:1-3*
Barnabas was a good man, filled with the Holy Spirit and with faith.

In those days a great number who believed turned to the Lord.
The news about them reached the ears of the Church in Jerusalem,
  and they sent Barnabas to go to Antioch.
When he arrived and saw the grace of God,
  he rejoiced and encouraged them all
  to remain faithful to the Lord in firmness of heart,
  for he was a good man, filled with the Holy Spirit and faith.
And a large number of people was added to the Lord.
Then he went to Tarsus to look for Saul,
  and when he had found him he brought him to Antioch.
For a whole year they met with the Church
  and taught a large number of people,
  and it was in Antioch that the disciples
  were first called Christians.

Now there were in the Church at Antioch prophets and teachers:
  Barnabas, Symeon who was called Niger,
  Lucius of Cyrene,
  Manaen who was a close friend of Herod the tetrarch, and Saul.
While they were worshiping the Lord and fasting, the Holy Spirit said,
  "Set apart for me Barnabas and Saul
  for the work to which I have called them."
Then, completing their fasting and prayer,
  they laid hands on them and sent them off. ✛

Psalm 98:1bcde, 2-3ab, 3cd-4, 5-6
R. (see 2b) **The Lord has revealed to the nations his saving
  power.**
Sing to the LORD a new song,
  for he has done wondrous deeds;
His right hand has won victory for him,
  his holy arm. **R.**
The LORD has made his salvation known:
  in the sight of the nations he has revealed his justice.
He has remembered his kindness and his faithfulness
  toward the house of Israel. **R.**
All the ends of the earth have seen
  the salvation by our God.
Sing joyfully to the LORD, all you lands;
  break into song; sing praise. **R.**
Sing praise to the LORD with the harp,
  with the harp and melodious song.
With trumpets and the sound of the horn
  sing joyfully before the King, the LORD. **R.**

Psalm 119:36a, 29b
R. Alleluia, alleluia.
Incline my heart, O God, to your decrees;
and favor me with your law. **R.**

✝ *Matthew 5:33-37*
I say to you, do not swear at all.

Jesus said to his disciples:
"You have heard that it was said to your ancestors,
  Do not take a false oath,
  but make good to the Lord all that you vow.
But I say to you, do not swear at all;
  not by heaven, for it is God's throne;
  nor by the earth, for it is his footstool;
  nor by Jerusalem, for it is the city of the great King.

Do not swear by your head,
   for you cannot make a single hair white or black.
Let your 'Yes' mean 'Yes,' and your 'No' mean 'No.'
Anything more is from the Evil One." ✛

SUNDAY, JUNE 12
THE MOST HOLY TRINITY

✝ Proverbs 8:22-31
Before the earth was made, Wisdom was conceived.

Thus says the wisdom of God:
"The LORD possessed me, the beginning of his ways,
   the forerunner of his prodigies of long ago;
from of old I was poured forth,
   at the first, before the earth.
When there were no depths I was brought forth,
   when there were no fountains or springs of water;
before the mountains were settled into place,
   before the hills, I was brought forth;
while as yet the earth and fields were not made,
   nor the first clods of the world.

"When the Lord established the heavens I was there,
   when he marked out the vault over the face of the deep;
when he made firm the skies above,
   when he fixed fast the foundations of the earth;
when he set for the sea its limit,
   so that the waters should not transgress his command;
then was I beside him as his craftsman,
   and I was his delight day by day,
playing before him all the while,
   playing on the surface of his earth;
and I found delight in the human race." ✛

Psalm 8:4-5, 6-7, 8-9
R. (2a) **O Lord, our God, how wonderful your name in all the
   earth!**
When I behold your heavens, the work of your fingers,
   the moon and the stars which you set in place—
what is man that you should be mindful of him,
   or the son of man that you should care for him? **R.**
You have made him little less than the angels,
   and crowned him with glory and honor.
You have given him rule over the works of your hands,
   putting all things under his feet. **R.**

All sheep and oxen,
  yes, and the beasts of the field,
the birds of the air, the fishes of the sea,
  and whatever swims the paths of the seas. **R.**

† *Romans 5:1-5*

To God, through Christ, in love poured out through the Holy Spirit.

Brothers and sisters:
Therefore, since we have been justified by faith,
  we have peace with God through our Lord Jesus Christ,
  through whom we have gained access by faith
  to this grace in which we stand,
  and we boast in hope of the glory of God.
Not only that, but we even boast of our afflictions,
  knowing that affliction produces endurance,
  and endurance, proven character,
  and proven character, hope,
  and hope does not disappoint,
  because the love of God has been poured out into our hearts
  through the Holy Spirit that has been given to us. ✛

See Revelation 1:8

R. Alleluia, alleluia.
Glory to the Father, the Son, and the Holy Spirit;
to God who is, who was, and who is to come. **R.**

† *John 16:12-15*

Everything that the Father has is mine;
the Spirit will take from what is mine and declare it to you.

Jesus said to his disciples:
  "I have much more to tell you, but you cannot bear it now.
But when he comes, the Spirit of truth,
  he will guide you to all truth.
He will not speak on his own,
  but he will speak what he hears,
  and will declare to you the things that are coming.
He will glorify me,
  because he will take from what is mine and declare it to you.
Everything that the Father has is mine;
  for this reason I told you that he will take from what is mine
  and declare it to you." ✛

MONDAY, JUNE 13
St. Anthony of Padua (Eleventh Week in Ordinary Time)

† *1 Kings 21:1-16*
Naboth has been stoned to death.

Naboth the Jezreelite had a vineyard in Jezreel
   next to the palace of Ahab, king of Samaria.
Ahab said to Naboth, "Give me your vineyard to be my vegetable
      garden,
   since it is close by, next to my house.
I will give you a better vineyard in exchange, or,
   if you prefer, I will give you its value in money."
Naboth answered him, "The LORD forbid
   that I should give you my ancestral heritage."
Ahab went home disturbed and angry at the answer
   Naboth the Jezreelite had made to him:
   "I will not give you my ancestral heritage."
Lying down on his bed, he turned away from food and would not eat.

His wife Jezebel came to him and said to him,
   "Why are you so angry that you will not eat?"
He answered her, "Because I spoke to Naboth the Jezreelite
   and said to him, 'Sell me your vineyard, or,
   if you prefer, I will give you a vineyard in exchange.'
But he refused to let me have his vineyard."
His wife Jezebel said to him,
   "A fine ruler over Israel you are indeed!
Get up.
Eat and be cheerful.
I will obtain the vineyard of Naboth the Jezreelite for you."

So she wrote letters in Ahab's name and,
   having sealed them with his seal,
   sent them to the elders and to the nobles
   who lived in the same city with Naboth.
This is what she wrote in the letters:
   "Proclaim a fast and set Naboth at the head of the people.
Next, get two scoundrels to face him
   and accuse him of having cursed God and king.
Then take him out and stone him to death."
His fellow citizens—the elders and nobles who dwelt in his city—
   did as Jezebel had ordered them in writing,
   through the letters she had sent them.
They proclaimed a fast and placed Naboth at the head of the people.

Two scoundrels came in and confronted him with the accusation,
"Naboth has cursed God and king."
And they led him out of the city and stoned him to death.
Then they sent the information to Jezebel
that Naboth had been stoned to death.

When Jezebel learned that Naboth had been stoned to death,
she said to Ahab,
"Go on, take possession of the vineyard
of Naboth the Jezreelite that he refused to sell you,
because Naboth is not alive, but dead."
On hearing that Naboth was dead, Ahab started off on his way
down to the vineyard of Naboth the Jezreelite,
to take possession of it. ✝

Psalm 5:2-3ab, 4b-6a, 6b-7
R. (2b) **Lord, listen to my groaning.**
Hearken to my words, O LORD,
    attend to my sighing.
Heed my call for help,
    my king and my God! **R.**
At dawn I bring my plea expectantly before you.
For you, O God, delight not in wickedness;
    no evil man remains with you;
    the arrogant may not stand in your sight. **R.**
You hate all evildoers.
    You destroy all who speak falsehood;
The bloodthirsty and the deceitful
    the LORD abhors. **R.**

Psalm 119:105
R. Alleluia, alleluia.
A lamp to my feet is your word,
a light to my path. **R.**

✝ *Matthew 5:38-42*
But I say to you, offer no resistance to one who is evil.

Jesus said to his disciples:
"You have heard that it was said,
    An eye for an eye and a tooth for a tooth.
But I say to you, offer no resistance to one who is evil.
When someone strikes you on your right cheek,
    turn the other one to him as well.
If anyone wants to go to law with you over your tunic,
    hand him your cloak as well.

Should anyone press you into service for one mile,
  go with him for two miles.
Give to the one who asks of you,
  and do not turn your back on one who wants to borrow." ✛

TUESDAY, JUNE 14
WEEKDAY

† *1 Kings 21:17-29*
You have provoked me by leading Israel into sin.

After the death of Naboth the Lord said to Elijah the Tishbite:
  "Start down to meet Ahab, king of Israel,
  who rules in Samaria.
He will be in the vineyard of Naboth,
  of which he has come to take possession.
This is what you shall tell him,
  'The Lord says: After murdering, do you also take possession?
For this, the Lord says:
  In the place where the dogs licked up the blood of Naboth,
  the dogs shall lick up your blood, too.'"
Ahab said to Elijah, "Have you found me out, my enemy?"
"Yes," he answered.
"Because you have given yourself up to doing evil in the Lord's sight,
  I am bringing evil upon you: I will destroy you
  and will cut off every male in Ahab's line,
  whether slave or freeman, in Israel.
I will make your house like that of Jeroboam, son of Nebat,
  and like that of Baasha, son of Ahijah,
  because of how you have provoked me by leading Israel into sin."
(Against Jezebel, too, the Lord declared,
  "The dogs shall devour Jezebel in the district of Jezreel.")
"When one of Ahab's line dies in the city,
  dogs will devour him;
  when one of them dies in the field,
  the birds of the sky will devour him."
Indeed, no one gave himself up to the doing of evil
  in the sight of the Lord as did Ahab,
  urged on by his wife Jezebel.
He became completely abominable by following idols,
  just as the Amorites had done,
  whom the Lord drove out before the children of Israel.

When Ahab heard these words, he tore his garments
  and put on sackcloth over his bare flesh.
He fasted, slept in the sackcloth, and went about subdued.

Then the LORD said to Elijah the Tishbite,
"Have you seen that Ahab has humbled himself before me?
Since he has humbled himself before me,
I will not bring the evil in his time.
I will bring the evil upon his house during the reign of his son." ✛

Psalm 51:3-4, 5-6ab, 11 and 16
R. (see 3a) **Be merciful, O Lord, for we have sinned.**
Have mercy on me, O God, in your goodness;
in the greatness of your compassion wipe out my offense.
Thoroughly wash me from my guilt
and of my sin cleanse me. **R.**
For I acknowledge my offense,
and my sin is before me always:
"Against you only have I sinned,
and done what is evil in your sight." **R.**
Turn away your face from my sins,
and blot out all my guilt.
Free me from blood guilt, O God, my saving God;
then my tongue shall revel in your justice. **R.**

John 13:34
R. Alleluia, alleluia.
I give you a new commandment:
love one another as I have loved you. **R.**

✝ Matthew 5:43-48
Love your enemies.

Jesus said to his disciples:
"You have heard that it was said,
You shall love your neighbor and hate your enemy.
But I say to you, love your enemies
and pray for those who persecute you,
that you may be children of your heavenly Father,
for he makes his sun rise on the bad and the good,
and causes rain to fall on the just and the unjust.
For if you love those who love you, what recompense will you have?
Do not the tax collectors do the same?
And if you greet your brothers only,
what is unusual about that?
Do not the pagans do the same?
So be perfect, just as your heavenly Father is perfect." ✛

WEDNESDAY, JUNE 15
WEEKDAY

† *2 Kings 2:1, 6-14*
A flaming chariot came between them, and Elijah went up to heaven.

When the LORD was about to take Elijah up to heaven in a whirlwind,
  he and Elisha were on their way from Gilgal.
Elijah said to Elisha, "Please stay here;
  the LORD has sent me on to the Jordan."
"As the LORD lives, and as you yourself live,
  I will not leave you," Elisha replied.
And so the two went on together.
Fifty of the guild prophets followed and
  when the two stopped at the Jordan,
  they stood facing them at a distance.
Elijah took his mantle, rolled it up
  and struck the water, which divided,
  and both crossed over on dry ground.

When they had crossed over, Elijah said to Elisha,
  "Ask for whatever I may do for you, before I am taken from you."
Elisha answered, "May I receive a double portion of your spirit."
"You have asked something that is not easy," Elijah replied.
"Still, if you see me taken up from you,
  your wish will be granted; otherwise not."
As they walked on conversing,
  a flaming chariot and flaming horses came between them,
  and Elijah went up to heaven in a whirlwind.
When Elisha saw it happen he cried out,
  "My father! my father! Israel's chariots and drivers!"
But when he could no longer see him,
  Elisha gripped his own garment and tore it in two.

Then he picked up Elijah's mantle that had fallen from him,
  and went back and stood at the bank of the Jordan.
Wielding the mantle that had fallen from Elijah,
  Elisha struck the water in his turn and said,
  "Where is the LORD, the God of Elijah?"
When Elisha struck the water it divided and he crossed over. ✛

Psalm 31:20, 21, 24

R. (25) **Let your hearts take comfort, all who hope in the
  Lord.**
How great is the goodness, O LORD,
  which you have in store for those who fear you,
And which, toward those who take refuge in you,

you show in the sight of the children of men. **R.**
You hide them in the shelter of your presence
  from the plottings of men;
You screen them within your abode
  from the strife of tongues. **R.**
Love the LORD, all you his faithful ones!
  The LORD keeps those who are constant,
  but more than requites those who act proudly. **R.**

John 14:23
R. Alleluia, alleluia.
Whoever loves me will keep my word,
and my Father will love him
and we will come to him. **R.**

† *Matthew 6:1-6, 16-18*
And your Father who sees what is hidden will repay you.

Jesus said to his disciples:
"Take care not to perform righteous deeds
  in order that people may see them;
  otherwise, you will have no recompense from your heavenly Father.
When you give alms, do not blow a trumpet before you,
  as the hypocrites do in the synagogues and in the streets
  to win the praise of others.
Amen, I say to you, they have received their reward.
But when you give alms,
  do not let your left hand know what your right is doing,
  so that your almsgiving may be secret.
And your Father who sees in secret will repay you.

"When you pray, do not be like the hypocrites,
  who love to stand and pray in the synagogues and on street corners
  so that others may see them.
Amen, I say to you, they have received their reward.
But when you pray, go to your inner room, close the door,
  and pray to your Father in secret.
And your Father who sees in secret will repay you.

"When you fast, do not look gloomy like the hypocrites.
They neglect their appearance,
  so that they may appear to others to be fasting.
Amen, I say to you, they have received their reward.
But when you fast, anoint your head and wash your face,
  so that you may not appear to others to be fasting,
  except to your Father who is hidden.
And your Father who sees what is hidden will repay you." †

THURSDAY, JUNE 16
WEEKDAY

† *Sirach 48:1-14*
*Elijah was enveloped in a whirlwind, and Elisha was filled
with the twofold portion of his spirit.*

Like a fire there appeared the prophet Elijah
  whose words were as a flaming furnace.
Their staff of bread he shattered,
  in his zeal he reduced them to straits;
By the Lord's word he shut up the heavens
  and three times brought down fire.
How awesome are you, Elijah, in your wondrous deeds!
  Whose glory is equal to yours?
You brought a dead man back to life
  from the nether world, by the will of the LORD.
You sent kings down to destruction,
  and easily broke their power into pieces.
You brought down nobles, from their beds of sickness.
You heard threats at Sinai,
  at Horeb avenging judgments.
You anointed kings who should inflict vengeance,
  and a prophet as your successor.
You were taken aloft in a whirlwind of fire,
  in a chariot with fiery horses.
You were destined, it is written, in time to come
  to put an end to wrath before the day of the LORD,
To turn back the hearts of fathers toward their sons,
  and to re-establish the tribes of Jacob.
Blessed is he who shall have seen you
And who falls asleep in your friendship.
For we live only in our life,
  but after death our name will not be such.
  O Elijah, enveloped in the whirlwind!

Then Elisha, filled with the twofold portion of his spirit,
  wrought many marvels by his mere word.
During his lifetime he feared no one,
  nor was any man able to intimidate his will.
Nothing was beyond his power;
  beneath him flesh was brought back into life.
In life he performed wonders,
  and after death, marvelous deeds. ✛

Psalm 97:1-2, 3-4, 5-6, 7
R. (12a) Rejoice in the Lord, you just!
The LORD is king; let the earth rejoice;
   let the many isles be glad.
Clouds and darkness are round about him,
   justice and judgment are the foundation of his throne. **R.**
Fire goes before him
   and consumes his foes round about.
His lightnings illumine the world;
   the earth sees and trembles. **R.**
The mountains melt like wax before the LORD,
   before the Lord of all the earth.
The heavens proclaim his justice,
   and all peoples see his glory. **R.**
All who worship graven things are put to shame,
   who glory in the things of nought;
   all gods are prostrate before him. **R.**

Romans 8:15bc
R. Alleluia, alleluia.
You have received a spirit of adoption as sons
through which we cry: Abba! Father! **R.**

† *Matthew 6:7-15*
This is how you are to pray.

Jesus said to his disciples:
   "In praying, do not babble like the pagans,
   who think that they will be heard because of their many words.
Do not be like them.
Your Father knows what you need before you ask him.

"This is how you are to pray:

   'Our Father who art in heaven,
      hallowed be thy name,
      thy Kingdom come,
   thy will be done,
      on earth as it is in heaven.
   Give us this day our daily bread;
   and forgive us our trespasses,
      as we forgive those who trespass against us;
   and lead us not into temptation,
      but deliver us from evil.'

"If you forgive others their transgressions,
   your heavenly Father will forgive you.

But if you do not forgive others,
neither will your Father forgive your transgressions." ✛

FRIDAY, JUNE 17
WEEKDAY

† *2 Kings 11:1-4, 9-18, 20*
They anointed him and shouted: "Long live the king!"

When Athaliah, the mother of Ahaziah,
saw that her son was dead,
she began to kill off the whole royal family.
But Jehosheba, daughter of King Jehoram and sister of Ahaziah,
took Joash, his son, and spirited him away, along with his nurse,
from the bedroom where the princes were about to be slain.
She concealed him from Athaliah, and so he did not die.
For six years he remained hidden in the temple of the LORD,
while Athaliah ruled the land.

But in the seventh year,
Jehoiada summoned the captains of the Carians
and of the guards.
He had them come to him in the temple of the LORD,
exacted from them a sworn commitment,
and then showed them the king's son.

The captains did just as Jehoiada the priest commanded.
Each one with his men, both those going on duty for the sabbath
and those going off duty that week,
came to Jehoiada the priest.
He gave the captains King David's spears and shields,
which were in the temple of the LORD.
And the guards, with drawn weapons,
lined up from the southern to the northern limit of the enclosure,
surrounding the altar and the temple on the king's behalf.
Then Jehoiada led out the king's son
and put the crown and the insignia upon him.
They proclaimed him king and anointed him,
clapping their hands and shouting, "Long live the king!"

Athaliah heard the noise made by the people,
and appeared before them in the temple of the LORD.
When she saw the king standing by the pillar, as was the custom,
and the captains and trumpeters near him,
with all the people of the land rejoicing and blowing trumpets,
she tore her garments and cried out, "Treason, treason!"

Then Jehoiada the priest instructed the captains
in command of the force:
"Bring her outside through the ranks.
If anyone follows her," he added, "let him die by the sword."
He had given orders that she
should not be slain in the temple of the LORD.
She was led out forcibly to the horse gate of the royal palace,
where she was put to death.

Then Jehoiada made a covenant between the LORD as one party
and the king and the people as the other,
by which they would be the LORD's people;
and another covenant, between the king and the people.
Thereupon all the people of the land went to the temple of Baal
and demolished it.
They shattered its altars and images completely,
and slew Mattan, the priest of Baal, before the altars.
Jehoiada appointed a detachment for the temple of the LORD.
All the people of the land rejoiced and the city was quiet,
now that Athaliah had been slain with the sword
at the royal palace. ✝

Psalm 132:11, 12, 13-14, 17-18
R. (13) **The Lord has chosen Zion for his dwelling.**
The LORD swore to David
a firm promise from which he will not withdraw:
"Your own offspring
I will set upon your throne." **R.**
"If your sons keep my covenant
and the decrees which I shall teach them,
Their sons, too, forever
shall sit upon your throne." **R.**
For the LORD has chosen Zion;
he prefers her for his dwelling.
"Zion is my resting place forever;
in her will I dwell, for I prefer her." **R.**
"In her will I make a horn to sprout forth for David;
I will place a lamp for my anointed.
His enemies I will clothe with shame,
but upon him my crown shall shine." **R.**

Matthew 5:3
R. Alleluia, alleluia.
Blessed are the poor in spirit;
for theirs is the Kingdom of heaven. **R.**

† *Matthew 6:19-23*

For where your treasure is, there also will your heart be.

Jesus said to his disciples:
"Do not store up for yourselves treasures on earth,
  where moth and decay destroy, and thieves break in and steal.
But store up treasures in heaven,
  where neither moth nor decay destroys, nor thieves break in and
    steal.
For where your treasure is, there also will your heart be.

"The lamp of the body is the eye.
If your eye is sound, your whole body will be filled with light;
  but if your eye is bad, your whole body will be in darkness.
And if the light in you is darkness, how great will the darkness be." ✛

SATURDAY, JUNE 18
WEEKDAY, *[BVM]*

† *2 Chronicles 24:17-25*

They murdered Zechariah between the
sanctuary and the altar (Matthew 23:35).

After the death of Jehoiada,
  the princes of Judah came and paid homage to King Joash,
  and the king then listened to them.
They forsook the temple of the LORD, the God of their fathers,
  and began to serve the sacred poles and the idols;
  and because of this crime of theirs,
  wrath came upon Judah and Jerusalem.
Although prophets were sent to them to convert them to the LORD,
  the people would not listen to their warnings.
Then the Spirit of God possessed Zechariah,
  son of Jehoiada the priest.
He took his stand above the people and said to them:
  "God says, 'Why are you transgressing the LORD's commands,
  so that you cannot prosper?
Because you have abandoned the LORD, he has abandoned you.'"
But they conspired against him,
  and at the king's order they stoned him to death
  in the court of the LORD's temple.
Thus King Joash was unmindful of the devotion shown him
  by Jehoiada, Zechariah's father, and slew his son.
And as Zechariah was dying, he said, "May the LORD see and
    avenge."

At the turn of the year a force of Arameans came up against Joash.
They invaded Judah and Jerusalem,
   did away with all the princes of the people,
   and sent all their spoil to the king of Damascus.
Though the Aramean force came with few men,
   the LORD surrendered a very large force into their power,
   because Judah had abandoned the LORD, the God of their fathers.
So punishment was meted out to Joash.
After the Arameans had departed from him,
   leaving him in grievous suffering,
   his servants conspired against him
   because of the murder of the son of Jehoiada the priest.
He was buried in the City of David,
   but not in the tombs of the kings. ✝

Psalm 89:4-5, 29-30, 31-32, 33-34

R. (29a) **For ever I will maintain my love for my servant.**
"I have made a covenant with my chosen one,
   I have sworn to David my servant:
Forever will I confirm your posterity
   and establish your throne for all generations." **R.**
"Forever I will maintain my kindness toward him,
   and my covenant with him stands firm.
I will make his posterity endure forever
   and his throne as the days of heaven." **R.**
"If his sons forsake my law
   and walk not according to my ordinances,
If they violate my statutes
   and keep not my commands." **R.**
"I will punish their crime with a rod
   and their guilt with stripes.
Yet my mercy I will not take from him,
   nor will I belie my faithfulness." **R.**

2 Corinthians 8:9

R. Alleluia, alleluia.
Jesus Christ became poor although he was rich,
so that by his poverty you might become rich. **R.**

✝ Matthew 6:24-34
Do not worry about tomorrow.

Jesus said to his disciples:
"No one can serve two masters.
He will either hate one and love the other,
   or be devoted to one and despise the other.
You cannot serve God and mammon.

"Therefore I tell you, do not worry about your life,
   what you will eat or drink,
   or about your body, what you will wear.
Is not life more than food and the body more than clothing?
Look at the birds in the sky;
   they do not sow or reap, they gather nothing into barns,
   yet your heavenly Father feeds them.
Are not you more important than they?
Can any of you by worrying add a single moment to your life-span?
Why are you anxious about clothes?
Learn from the way the wild flowers grow.
They do not work or spin.
But I tell you that not even Solomon in all his splendor
   was clothed like one of them.
If God so clothes the grass of the field,
   which grows today and is thrown into the oven tomorrow,
   will he not much more provide for you, O you of little faith?
So do not worry and say, 'What are we to eat?'
   or 'What are we to drink?' or 'What are we to wear?'
All these things the pagans seek.
Your heavenly Father knows that you need them all.
But seek first the Kingdom of God and his righteousness,
   and all these things will be given you besides.
Do not worry about tomorrow; tomorrow will take care of itself.
Sufficient for a day is its own evil." ✛

SUNDAY, JUNE 19
The Most Holy Body and Blood of Christ (Corpus Christi)

† Genesis 14:18-20
Melchizedek brought out bread and wine.

In those days, Melchizedek, king of Salem, brought out bread and
   wine,
   and being a priest of God Most High,
   he blessed Abram with these words:
   "Blessed be Abram by God Most High,
      the creator of heaven and earth;
   and blessed be God Most High,
      who delivered your foes into your hand."
Then Abram gave him a tenth of everything. ✛

Psalm 110:1, 2, 3, 4
R. (4b) **You are a priest for ever, in the line of Melchizedek.**
The Lord said to my Lord: "Sit at my right hand
   till I make your enemies your footstool." **R.**

The scepter of your power the LORD will stretch forth from Zion:
"Rule in the midst of your enemies." **R.**
"Yours is princely power in the day of your birth, in holy splendor;
before the daystar, like the dew, I have begotten you." **R.**
The LORD has sworn, and he will not repent:
"You are a priest forever, according to the order of Melchizedek." **R.**

† *1 Corinthians 11:23-26*
For as often as you eat and drink,
you proclaim the death of the Lord.

Brothers and sisters:
I received from the Lord what I also handed on to you,
that the Lord Jesus, on the night he was handed over,
took bread, and, after he had given thanks,
broke it and said, "This is my body that is for you.
Do this in remembrance of me."
In the same way also the cup, after supper, saying,
"This cup is the new covenant in my blood.
Do this, as often as you drink it, in remembrance of me."
For as often as you eat this bread and drink the cup,
you proclaim the death of the Lord until he comes. ✝

The sequence Laud, O Zion (Lauda Sion)*, or the shorter form beginning with the verse* Lo! the angel's food is given*, may be sung optionally before the Alleluia.*

John 6:51
R. Alleluia, alleluia.
I am the living bread that came down from heaven, says the Lord;
whoever eats this bread will live forever. **R.**

† *Luke 9:11b-17*
They all ate and were satisfied.

Jesus spoke to the crowds about the kingdom of God,
and he healed those who needed to be cured.
As the day was drawing to a close,
the Twelve approached him and said,
"Dismiss the crowd
so that they can go to the surrounding villages and farms
and find lodging and provisions;
for we are in a deserted place here."
He said to them, "Give them some food yourselves."
They replied, "Five loaves and two fish are all we have,
unless we ourselves go and buy food for all these people."
Now the men there numbered about five thousand.

Then he said to his disciples,
   "Have them sit down in groups of about fifty."
They did so and made them all sit down.
Then taking the five loaves and the two fish,
   and looking up to heaven,
   he said the blessing over them, broke them,
   and gave them to the disciples to set before the crowd.
They all ate and were satisfied.
And when the leftover fragments were picked up,
   they filled twelve wicker baskets. ✛

MONDAY, JUNE 20
WEEKDAY (TWELFTH WEEK IN ORDINARY TIME)

✝ 2 Kings 17:5-8, 13-15a, 18
In his great anger against Israel, the LORD put them away out of his sight.
Only the tribe of Judah was left.

Shalmaneser, king of Assyria, occupied the whole land
   and attacked Samaria, which he besieged for three years.
In the ninth year of Hoshea, king of Israel,
   the king of Assyria took Samaria,
   and deported the children of Israel to Assyria,
   settling them in Halah, at the Habor, a river of Gozan,
   and the cities of the Medes.

This came about because the children of Israel sinned against the LORD,
   their God, who had brought them up from the land of Egypt,
   from under the domination of Pharaoh, king of Egypt,
   and because they venerated other gods.
They followed the rites of the nations
   whom the LORD had cleared out of the way of the children of Israel
   and the kings of Israel whom they set up.

And though the LORD warned Israel and Judah
   by every prophet and seer,
   "Give up your evil ways and keep my commandments and statutes,
   in accordance with the entire law which I enjoined on your fathers
   and which I sent you by my servants the prophets,"
   they did not listen, but were as stiff-necked as their fathers,
   who had not believed in the LORD, their God.
They rejected his statutes,
   the covenant which he had made with their fathers,
   and the warnings which he had given them, till,
   in his great anger against Israel,
   the LORD put them away out of his sight.
Only the tribe of Judah was left. ✛

Psalm 60:3, 4-5, 12-13

R. (7b) **Help us with your right hand, O Lord, and answer us.**

O God, you have rejected us and broken our defenses;
  you have been angry; rally us! **R.**
You have rocked the country and split it open;
  repair the cracks in it, for it is tottering.
You have made your people feel hardships;
  you have given us stupefying wine. **R.**
Have not you, O God, rejected us,
  so that you go not forth, O God, with our armies?
Give us aid against the foe,
  for worthless is the help of men. **R.**

Hebrews 4:12

R. Alleluia, alleluia.

The word of God is living and effective,
able to discern reflections and thoughts of the heart. **R.**

† *Matthew 7:1-5*
Remove the wooden beam from your eye first.

Jesus said to his disciples:
"Stop judging, that you may not be judged.
For as you judge, so will you be judged,
  and the measure with which you measure will be measured out to
    you.
Why do you notice the splinter in your brother's eye,
  but do not perceive the wooden beam in your own eye?
How can you say to your brother,
  'Let me remove that splinter from your eye,'
  while the wooden beam is in your eye?
You hypocrite, remove the wooden beam from your eye first;
  then you will see clearly
  to remove the splinter from your brother's eye." ✛

TUESDAY, JUNE 21
St. Aloysius Gonzaga

† *2 Kings 19:9b-11, 14-21, 31-35a, 36*
*I will shield and save this city for my own sake
and for the sake of my servant David.*

Sennacherib, king of Assyria, sent envoys to Hezekiah
  with this message:
"Thus shall you say to Hezekiah, king of Judah:
  'Do not let your God on whom you rely deceive you
  by saying that Jerusalem will not be handed over
  to the king of Assyria.

You have heard what the kings of Assyria have done
   to all other countries: they doomed them!
Will you, then, be saved?'"

Hezekiah took the letter from the hand of the messengers and read it;
   then he went up to the temple of the LORD,
   and spreading it out before him,
   he prayed in the LORD's presence:
   "O LORD, God of Israel, enthroned upon the cherubim!
You alone are God over all the kingdoms of the earth.
You have made the heavens and the earth.
Incline your ear, O LORD, and listen!
Open your eyes, O LORD, and see!
Hear the words of Sennacherib which he sent to taunt the living God.
Truly, O LORD, the kings of Assyria have laid waste the nations
   and their lands, and cast their gods into the fire;
   they destroyed them because they were not gods,
   but the work of human hands, wood and stone.
Therefore, O LORD, our God, save us from the power of this man,
   that all the kingdoms of the earth may know
   that you alone, O LORD, are God."

Then Isaiah, son of Amoz, sent this message to Hezekiah:
   "Thus says the LORD, the God of Israel,
   in answer to your prayer for help against Sennacherib, king of
      Assyria:
   I have listened!
This is the word the LORD has spoken concerning him:

   "'She despises you, laughs you to scorn,
      the virgin daughter Zion!
   Behind you she wags her head,
      daughter Jerusalem.

   "'For out of Jerusalem shall come a remnant,
      and from Mount Zion, survivors.
   The zeal of the LORD of hosts shall do this.'

"Therefore, thus says the LORD concerning the king of Assyria:
   'He shall not reach this city, nor shoot an arrow at it,
   nor come before it with a shield,
   nor cast up siege-works against it.
He shall return by the same way he came,
   without entering the city, says the LORD.
I will shield and save this city for my own sake,
   and for the sake of my servant David.'"

That night the angel of the Lord went forth and struck down
　one hundred and eighty-five thousand men in the Assyrian camp.
So Sennacherib, the king of Assyria, broke camp,
　and went back home to Nineveh. ✛

　Psalm 48:2-3ab, 3cd-4, 10-11
R. (see 9d) **God upholds his city for ever.**
Great is the Lord and wholly to be praised
　in the city of our God.
His holy mountain, fairest of heights,
　is the joy of all the earth. **R.**
Mount Zion, "the recesses of the North,"
　is the city of the great King.
God is with her castles;
　renowned is he as a stronghold. **R.**
O God, we ponder your mercy
　within your temple.
As your name, O God, so also your praise
　reaches to the ends of the earth.
Of justice your right hand is full. **R.**

　John 8:12
R. Alleluia, alleluia.
I am the light of the world, says the Lord;
whoever follows me will have the light of life. **R.**

†*Matthew 7:6, 12-14*
Do to others whatever you would have them do to you.

Jesus said to his disciples:
"Do not give what is holy to dogs, or throw your pearls before swine,
　lest they trample them underfoot, and turn and tear you to pieces.

"Do to others whatever you would have them do to you.
This is the Law and the Prophets.

"Enter through the narrow gate;
　for the gate is wide and the road broad that leads to destruction,
　and those who enter through it are many.
How narrow the gate and constricted the road that leads to life.
And those who find it are few." ✛

WEDNESDAY, JUNE 22
WEEKDAY, ST. PAULINUS OF NOLA, ST. JOHN FISHER AND ST. THOMAS MORE

† *2 Kings 22:8-13; 23:1-3*
The king had the book that had been found in the temple read out to them,
and he made a covenant before the LORD.

The high priest Hilkiah informed the scribe Shaphan,
"I have found the book of the law in the temple of the LORD."
Hilkiah gave the book to Shaphan, who read it.
Then the scribe Shaphan went to the king and reported,
  "Your servants have smelted down the metals available in the temple
  and have consigned them to the master workmen
  in the temple of the LORD."
The scribe Shaphan also informed the king
  that the priest Hilkiah had given him a book,
  and then read it aloud to the king.
When the king heard the contents of the book of the law,
  he tore his garments and issued this command to Hilkiah the priest,
  Ahikam, son of Shaphan,
  Achbor, son of Micaiah, the scribe Shaphan,
  and the king's servant Asaiah:
"Go, consult the LORD for me, for the people, for all Judah,
  about the stipulations of this book that has been found,
  for the anger of the LORD has been set furiously ablaze against us,
  because our fathers did not obey the stipulations of this book,
  nor fulfill our written obligations."

The king then had all the elders of Judah
  and of Jerusalem summoned together before him.
The king went up to the temple of the LORD with all the men of Judah
  and all the inhabitants of Jerusalem:
  priests, prophets, and all the people, small and great.
He had the entire contents of the book of the covenant
  that had been found in the temple of the LORD, read out to them.
Standing by the column, the king made a covenant before the LORD
  that they would follow him
  and observe his ordinances, statutes and decrees
  with their whole hearts and souls,
  thus reviving the terms of the covenant
  which were written in this book.
And all the people stood as participants in the covenant. ✛

Psalm 119:33, 34, 35, 36, 37, 40
R. (33a) **Teach me the way of your decrees, O Lord.**
Instruct me, O LORD, in the way of your statutes,
  that I may exactly observe them. **R.**

Give me discernment, that I may observe your law
   and keep it with all my heart. **R.**
Lead me in the path of your commands,
   for in it I delight. **R.**
Incline my heart to your decrees
   and not to gain. **R.**
Turn away my eyes from seeing what is vain:
   by your way give me life. **R.**
Behold, I long for your precepts;
   in your justice give me life. **R.**

John 15:4a, 5b
R. Alleluia, alleluia.
Remain in me, as I remain in you, says the Lord;
whoever remains in me will bear much fruit. **R.**

† *Matthew 7:15-20*
By their fruits you will know them.

Jesus said to his disciples:
"Beware of false prophets, who come to you in sheep's clothing,
   but underneath are ravenous wolves.
By their fruits you will know them.
Do people pick grapes from thornbushes, or figs from thistles?
Just so, every good tree bears good fruit,
   and a rotten tree bears bad fruit.
A good tree cannot bear bad fruit,
   nor can a rotten tree bear good fruit.
Every tree that does not bear good fruit will be cut down
   and thrown into the fire.
So by their fruits you will know them." ✛

THURSDAY, JUNE 23
THE NATIVITY OF ST. JOHN THE BAPTIST
(The Vigil Readings for the Nativity of St. John the Baptist are: Jeremiah 1:4-10 •
Psalm 71:1-2, 3-4a, 5-6ab, 15ab and 17 • 1 Peter 1:8-12 • Luke 1:5-17 [586].)

† *Isaiah 49:1-6*
I will make you a light to the nations.

Hear me, O coastlands,
   listen, O distant peoples.
The LORD called me from birth,
   from my mother's womb he gave me my name.
He made of me a sharp-edged sword
   and concealed me in the shadow of his arm.

He made me a polished arrow,
  in his quiver he hid me.
You are my servant, he said to me,
  Israel, through whom I show my glory.

Though I thought I had toiled in vain,
  and for nothing, uselessly, spent my strength,
yet my reward is with the LORD,
  my recompense is with my God.
For now the LORD has spoken
  who formed me as his servant from the womb,
that Jacob may be brought back to him
  and Israel gathered to him;
and I am made glorious in the sight of the LORD,
  and my God is now my strength!
It is too little, he says, for you to be my servant,
  to raise up the tribes of Jacob,
  and restore the survivors of Israel;
I will make you a light to the nations,
  that my salvation may reach to the ends of the earth. ✢

Psalm 139:1b-3, 13-14ab, 14c-15
R. (14) **I praise you, for I am wonderfully made.**
O LORD, you have probed me, you know me:
  you know when I sit and when I stand;
  you understand my thoughts from afar.
My journeys and my rest you scrutinize,
  with all my ways you are familiar. **R.**
Truly you have formed my inmost being;
  you knit me in my mother's womb.
I give you thanks that I am fearfully, wonderfully made;
  wonderful are your works. **R.**
My soul also you knew full well;
  nor was my frame unknown to you
When I was made in secret,
  when I was fashioned in the depths of the earth. **R.**

† Acts 13:22-26
John heralded his coming by proclaiming a baptism of repentance.

In those days, Paul said:
"God raised up David as king;
  of him God testified,
  I have found David, son of Jesse, a man after my own heart;
  he will carry out my every wish.

From this man's descendants God, according to his promise,
    has brought to Israel a savior, Jesus.
John heralded his coming by proclaiming a baptism of repentance
    to all the people of Israel;
    and as John was completing his course, he would say,
    'What do you suppose that I am? I am not he.
Behold, one is coming after me;
    I am not worthy to unfasten the sandals of his feet.'

"My brothers, sons of the family of Abraham,
    and those others among you who are God-fearing,
    to us this word of salvation has been sent." ✛

See Luke 1:76
R. Alleluia, alleluia.
You, child, will be called prophet of the Most High,
for you will go before the Lord to prepare his way. **R.**

✝ *Luke 1:57-66, 80*
John is his name.

When the time arrived for Elizabeth to have her child
    she gave birth to a son.
Her neighbors and relatives heard
    that the Lord had shown his great mercy toward her,
    and they rejoiced with her.
When they came on the eighth day to circumcise the child,
    they were going to call him Zechariah after his father,
    but his mother said in reply,
    "No. He will be called John."
But they answered her,
    "There is no one among your relatives who has this name."
So they made signs, asking his father what he wished him to be called.
He asked for a tablet and wrote, "John is his name,"
    and all were amazed.
Immediately his mouth was opened, his tongue freed,
    and he spoke blessing God.
Then fear came upon all their neighbors,
    and all these matters were discussed
    throughout the hill country of Judea.
All who heard these things took them to heart, saying,
    "What, then, will this child be?"
For surely the hand of the Lord was with him.

The child grew and became strong in spirit,
    and he was in the desert until the day
    of his manifestation to Israel. ✛

FRIDAY, JUNE 24
THE MOST SACRED HEART OF JESUS

† *Ezekiel 34:11-16*
I myself will pasture my sheep and I myself will give them rest.

Thus says the Lord GOD:
  I myself will look after and tend my sheep.
As a shepherd tends his flock
  when he finds himself among his scattered sheep,
  so will I tend my sheep.
I will rescue them from every place where they were scattered
  when it was cloudy and dark.
I will lead them out from among the peoples
  and gather them from the foreign lands;
  I will bring them back to their own country
  and pasture them upon the mountains of Israel
  in the land's ravines and all its inhabited places.
In good pastures will I pasture them,
  and on the mountain heights of Israel
  shall be their grazing ground.
There they shall lie down on good grazing ground,
  and in rich pastures shall they be pastured
  on the mountains of Israel.
I myself will pasture my sheep;
  I myself will give them rest, says the Lord GOD.
The lost I will seek out,
  the strayed I will bring back,
  the injured I will bind up,
  the sick I will heal,
  but the sleek and the strong I will destroy,
  shepherding them rightly. ✚

Psalm 23:1-3a, 3b-4, 5, 6
R. (1) **The Lord is my shepherd; there is nothing I shall want.**
The LORD is my shepherd; I shall not want.
  In verdant pastures he gives me repose;
beside restful waters he leads me;
  he refreshes my soul. **R.**
He guides me in right paths
  for his name's sake.
Even though I walk in the dark valley
  I fear no evil; for you are at my side
with your rod and your staff
  that give me courage. **R.**

You spread the table before me
   in the sight of my foes;
you anoint my head with oil;
   my cup overflows. **R.**
Only goodness and kindness follow me
   all the days of my life;
and I shall dwell in the house of the LORD
   for years to come. **R.**

† *Romans 5:5b-11*

God proves his love for us.

Brothers and sisters:
The love of God has been poured out into our hearts
   through the Holy Spirit that has been given to us.
For Christ, while we were still helpless,
   died at the appointed time for the ungodly.
Indeed, only with difficulty does one die for a just person,
   though perhaps for a good person
   one might even find courage to die.
But God proves his love for us
   in that while we were still sinners Christ died for us.
How much more then, since we are now justified by his blood,
   will we be saved through him from the wrath.
Indeed, if, while we were enemies,
   we were reconciled to God through the death of his Son,
   how much more, once reconciled,
   will we be saved by his life.
Not only that,
   but we also boast of God through our Lord Jesus Christ,
   through whom we have now received reconciliation. ✛

   Matthew 11:29ab
R. Alleluia, alleluia.
Take my yoke upon you, says the Lord,
and learn from me, for I am meek and humble of heart. **R.**
or

   John 10:14
R. Alleluia, alleluia.
I am the good shepherd, says the Lord,
I know my sheep, and mine know me. **R.**

†Luke 15:3-7
Rejoice with me because I have found my lost sheep.

Jesus addressed this parable to the Pharisees and scribes:
"What man among you having a hundred sheep and losing one of them
    would not leave the ninety-nine in the desert
    and go after the lost one until he finds it?
And when he does find it,
    he sets it on his shoulders with great joy
    and, upon his arrival home,
    he calls together his friends and neighbors and says to them,
    'Rejoice with me because I have found my lost sheep.'
I tell you, in just the same way
    there will be more joy in heaven over one sinner who repents
    than over ninety-nine righteous people
    who have no need of repentance." ✛

SATURDAY, JUNE 25
THE IMMACULATE HEART OF THE BLESSED VIRGIN MARY

†Lamentations 2:2, 10-14, 18-19
Cry out to the Lord over the fortresses of daughter Zion.

The Lord has consumed without pity
    all the dwellings of Jacob;
He has torn down in his anger
    the fortresses of daughter Judah;
He has brought to the ground in dishonor
    her king and her princes.

On the ground in silence sit
    the old men of daughter Zion;
They strew dust on their heads
    and gird themselves with sackcloth;
The maidens of Jerusalem
    bow their heads to the ground.

Worn out from weeping are my eyes,
    within me all is in ferment;
My gall is poured out on the ground
    because of the downfall of the daughter of my people,
As child and infant faint away
    in the open spaces of the town.

In vain they ask their mothers,
    "Where is the grain?"

As they faint away like the wounded
  in the streets of the city,
And breathe their last
  in their mothers' arms.

To what can I liken or compare you,
  O daughter Jerusalem?
What example can I show you for your comfort,
  virgin daughter Zion?
For great as the sea is your downfall;
  who can heal you?

Your prophets had for you
  false and specious visions;
They did not lay bare your guilt,
  to avert your fate;
They beheld for you in vision
  false and misleading portents.

Cry out to the Lord;
  moan, O daughter Zion!
Let your tears flow like a torrent
  day and night;
Let there be no respite for you,
  no repose for your eyes.

Rise up, shrill in the night,
  at the beginning of every watch;
Pour out your heart like water
  in the presence of the Lord;
Lift up your hands to him
  for the lives of your little ones
Who faint from hunger
  at the corner of every street. ✦

Psalm 74:1b-2, 3-5, 6-7, 20-21
R. (19b) **Lord, forget not the souls of your poor ones.**
Why, O God, have you cast us off forever?
  Why does your anger smolder against the sheep of your pasture?
Remember your flock which you built up of old,
  the tribe you redeemed as your inheritance,
  Mount Zion, where you took up your abode. **R.**
Turn your steps toward the utter ruins;
  toward all the damage the enemy has done in the sanctuary.
Your foes roar triumphantly in your shrine;
  they have set up their tokens of victory.

They are like men coming up with axes to a clump of trees. **R.**
With chisel and hammer they hack at all the paneling of the sanctuary.
They set your sanctuary on fire;
    the place where your name abides they have razed and profaned. **R.**
Look to your covenant,
    for the hiding places in the land and the plains are full of violence.
May the humble not retire in confusion;
    may the afflicted and the poor praise your name. **R.**

See Luke 2:19
R. Alleluia, alleluia.
Blessed is the Virgin Mary who kept the word of God
and pondered it in her heart. **R.**

† *Luke 2:41-51*
His mother kept all these things in her heart.

Each year Jesus' parents went to Jerusalem for the feast of Passover,
    and when he was twelve years old,
    they went up according to festival custom.
After they had completed its days, as they were returning,
    the boy Jesus remained behind in Jerusalem,
    but his parents did not know it.
Thinking that he was in the caravan,
    they journeyed for a day
    and looked for him among their relatives and acquaintances,
    but not finding him,
    they returned to Jerusalem to look for him.
After three days they found him in the temple,
    sitting in the midst of the teachers,
    listening to them and asking them questions,
    and all who heard him were astounded
    at his understanding and his answers.
When his parents saw him,
    they were astonished,
    and his mother said to him,
    "Son, why have you done this to us?
Your father and I have been looking for you with great anxiety."
And he said to them,
    "Why were you looking for me?
Did you not know that I must be in my Father's house?"
But they did not understand what he said to them.
He went down with them and came to Nazareth,
    and was obedient to them;
    and his mother kept all these things in her heart. ✛

SUNDAY, JUNE 26
THIRTEENTH SUNDAY IN ORDINARY TIME

† 1 Kings 19:16b, 19-21
Then Elisha left and followed Elijah as his attendant.

The LORD said to Elijah:
"You shall anoint Elisha, son of Shaphat of Abel-meholah,
   as prophet to succeed you."

Elijah set out and came upon Elisha, son of Shaphat,
   as he was plowing with twelve yoke of oxen;
   he was following the twelfth.

Elijah went over to him and threw his cloak over him.
Elisha left the oxen, ran after Elijah, and said,
   "Please, let me kiss my father and mother goodbye,
   and I will follow you."
Elijah answered, "Go back!
Have I done anything to you?"
Elisha left him, and taking the yoke of oxen, slaughtered them;
   he used the plowing equipment for fuel to boil their flesh,
   and gave it to his people to eat.
Then Elisha left and followed Elijah as his attendant. ✛

Psalm 16:1-2, 5, 7-8, 9-10, 11

R. (see 5a) **You are my inheritance, O Lord.**
Keep me, O God, for in you I take refuge;
   I say to the LORD, "My Lord are you.
O LORD, my allotted portion and my cup,
   you it is who hold fast my lot." **R.**
I bless the LORD who counsels me;
   even in the night my heart exhorts me.
I set the LORD ever before me;
   with him at my right hand I shall not be disturbed. **R.**
Therefore my heart is glad and my soul rejoices,
   my body, too, abides in confidence
because you will not abandon my soul to the netherworld,
   nor will you suffer your faithful one to undergo corruption. **R.**
You will show me the path to life,
   fullness of joys in your presence,
   the delights at your right hand forever. **R.**

✝ *Galatians 5:1, 13-18*
You were called for freedom.

Brothers and sisters:
For freedom Christ set us free;
    so stand firm and do not submit again to the yoke of slavery.

For you were called for freedom, brothers and sisters.
But do not use this freedom
    as an opportunity for the flesh;
    rather, serve one another through love.
For the whole law is fulfilled in one statement,
    namely, *You shall love your neighbor as yourself.*
But if you go on biting and devouring one another,
    beware that you are not consumed by one another.

I say, then: live by the Spirit
    and you will certainly not gratify the desire of the flesh.
For the flesh has desires against the Spirit,
    and the Spirit against the flesh;
    these are opposed to each other,
    so that you may not do what you want.
But if you are guided by the Spirit, you are not under the law. ✛

1 Samuel 3:9; John 6:68c
R. Alleluia, alleluia.
Speak, Lord, your servant is listening;
you have the words of everlasting life. **R.**

✝ *Luke 9:51-62*
He resolutely determined to journey to Jerusalem.
I will follow you wherever you go.

When the days for Jesus' being taken up were fulfilled,
    he resolutely determined to journey to Jerusalem,
    and he sent messengers ahead of him.
On the way they entered a Samaritan village
    to prepare for his reception there,
    but they would not welcome him
    because the destination of his journey was Jerusalem.
When the disciples James and John saw this they asked,
    "Lord, do you want us to call down fire from heaven
    to consume them?"
Jesus turned and rebuked them, and they journeyed to another village.

As they were proceeding on their journey someone said to him,
  "I will follow you wherever you go."
Jesus answered him,
  "Foxes have dens and birds of the sky have nests,
  but the Son of Man has nowhere to rest his head."

And to another he said, "Follow me."
But he replied, "Lord, let me go first and bury my father."
But he answered him, "Let the dead bury their dead.
But you, go and proclaim the kingdom of God."
And another said, "I will follow you, Lord,
  but first let me say farewell to my family at home."
To him Jesus said, "No one who sets a hand to the plow
  and looks to what was left behind is fit for the kingdom of God." ✢

MONDAY, JUNE 27
WEEKDAY, ST. CYRIL OF ALEXANDRIA

†Amos 2:6-10, 13-16
They trample the heads of the weak into the dust of the earth.

Thus says the LORD:
For three crimes of Israel, and for four,
  I will not revoke my word;
Because they sell the just man for silver,
  and the poor man for a pair of sandals.
They trample the heads of the weak
  into the dust of the earth,
  and force the lowly out of the way.
Son and father go to the same prostitute,
  profaning my holy name.
Upon garments taken in pledge
  they recline beside any altar;
And the wine of those who have been fined
  they drink in the house of their god.

Yet it was I who destroyed the Amorites before them,
  who were as tall as the cedars,
  and as strong as the oak trees.
I destroyed their fruit above,
  and their roots beneath.
It was I who brought you up from the land of Egypt,
  and who led you through the desert for forty years,
  to occupy the land of the Amorites.

Beware, I will crush you into the ground
  as a wagon crushes when laden with sheaves.

Flight shall perish from the swift,
    and the strong man shall not retain his strength;
The warrior shall not save his life,
    nor the bowman stand his ground;
The swift of foot shall not escape,
    nor the horseman save his life.
And the most stouthearted of warriors
    shall flee naked on that day, says the LORD. ✛

Psalm 50:16bc-17, 18-19, 20-21, 22-23
R. (22a) **Remember this, you who never think of God.**
"Why do you recite my statutes,
    and profess my covenant with your mouth,
Though you hate discipline
    and cast my words behind you?" **R.**
"When you see a thief, you keep pace with him,
    and with adulterers you throw in your lot.
To your mouth you give free rein for evil,
    you harness your tongue to deceit." **R.**
"You sit speaking against your brother;
    against your mother's son you spread rumors.
When you do these things, shall I be deaf to it?
    Or do you think that I am like yourself?
    I will correct you by drawing them up before your eyes." **R.**
"Consider this, you who forget God,
    lest I rend you and there be no one to rescue you.
He that offers praise as a sacrifice glorifies me;
    and to him that goes the right way I will show the salvation of
        God." **R.**

Psalm 95:8
R. **Alleluia, alleluia.**
If today you hear his voice,
harden not your hearts. **R.**

† *Matthew 8:18-22*
Follow me.

When Jesus saw a crowd around him,
    he gave orders to cross to the other shore.
A scribe approached and said to him,
    "Teacher, I will follow you wherever you go."
Jesus answered him, "Foxes have dens and birds of the sky have
        nests,
    but the Son of Man has nowhere to rest his head."

Another of his disciples said to him,
  "Lord, let me go first and bury my father."
But Jesus answered him, "Follow me,
  and let the dead bury their dead." ✢

TUESDAY, JUNE 28
St. Irenaeus

†*Amos 3:1-8; 4:11-12*
The Lord God speaks—who will not prophesy!

Hear this word, O children of Israel, that the Lord pronounces
    over you,
  over the whole family that I brought up from the land of Egypt:

You alone have I favored,
    more than all the families of the earth;
  Therefore I will punish you
    for all your crimes.

Do two walk together
    unless they have agreed?
  Does a lion roar in the forest
    when it has no prey?
  Does a young lion cry out from its den
    unless it has seized something?
  Is a bird brought to earth by a snare
    when there is no lure for it?
  Does a snare spring up from the ground
    without catching anything?
  If the trumpet sounds in a city,
    will the people not be frightened?
  If evil befalls a city,
    has not the Lord caused it?
  Indeed, the Lord God does nothing
    without revealing his plan
    to his servants, the prophets.

The lion roars—
    who will not be afraid!
  The Lord God speaks—
    who will not prophesy!

I brought upon you such upheaval
    as when God overthrew Sodom and Gomorrah:
    you were like a brand plucked from the fire;

Yet you returned not to me,
     says the LORD.

So now I will deal with you in my own way, O Israel!
     and since I will deal thus with you,
     prepare to meet your God, O Israel. ✛

Psalm 5:4b-6a, 6b-7, 8
R. (9a) **Lead me in your justice, Lord.**
At dawn I bring my plea expectantly before you.
For you, O God, delight not in wickedness;
     no evil man remains with you;
     the arrogant may not stand in your sight. **R.**
You hate all evildoers;
     you destroy all who speak falsehood;
The bloodthirsty and the deceitful
     the LORD abhors. **R.**
But I, because of your abundant mercy,
     will enter your house;
I will worship at your holy temple
     in fear of you, O LORD. **R.**

Psalm 130:5
R. Alleluia, alleluia.
I trust in the LORD;
my soul trusts in his word. **R.**

† *Matthew 8:23-27*
Jesus rebuked the winds and the sea, and there was great calm.

As Jesus got into a boat, his disciples followed him.
Suddenly a violent storm came up on the sea,
     so that the boat was being swamped by waves;
     but he was asleep.
They came and woke him, saying,
     "Lord, save us! We are perishing!"
He said to them, "Why are you terrified, O you of little faith?"
Then he got up, rebuked the winds and the sea,
     and there was great calm.
The men were amazed and said, "What sort of man is this,
     whom even the winds and the sea obey?" ✛

WEDNESDAY, JUNE 29
St. Peter and St. Paul

(Readings for the Vigil Mass are: Acts 3:1-10 • Psalm 19:2-3, 4-5 •
Galatians 1:11-20 • John 21:15-19 [590].)

† Acts 12:1-11
*Now I know for certain that the Lord
rescued me from the hand of Herod.*

In those days, King Herod laid hands upon some members of the
    Church to harm them.
He had James, the brother of John, killed by the sword,
    and when he saw that this was pleasing to the Jews
    he proceeded to arrest Peter also.
—It was the feast of Unleavened Bread.—
He had him taken into custody and put in prison
    under the guard of four squads of four soldiers each.
He intended to bring him before the people after Passover.
Peter thus was being kept in prison,
    but prayer by the Church was fervently being made
    to God on his behalf.

On the very night before Herod was to bring him to trial,
    Peter, secured by double chains,
    was sleeping between two soldiers,
    while outside the door guards kept watch on the prison.
Suddenly the angel of the Lord stood by him,
    and a light shone in the cell.
He tapped Peter on the side and awakened him, saying,
    "Get up quickly."
The chains fell from his wrists.
The angel said to him, "Put on your belt and your sandals."
He did so.
Then he said to him, "Put on your cloak and follow me."
So he followed him out,
    not realizing that what was happening through the angel was real;
    he thought he was seeing a vision.
They passed the first guard, then the second,
    and came to the iron gate leading out to the city,
    which opened for them by itself.
They emerged and made their way down an alley,
    and suddenly the angel left him.
Then Peter recovered his senses and said,
    "Now I know for certain

that the Lord sent his angel
and rescued me from the hand of Herod
and from all that the Jewish people had been expecting." ✛

Psalm 34:2-3, 4-5, 6-7, 8-9

R. (5) **The angel of the Lord will rescue those who fear him.**
I will bless the LORD at all times;
   his praise shall be ever in my mouth.
Let my soul glory in the LORD;
   the lowly will hear me and be glad. **R.**
Glorify the LORD with me,
   let us together extol his name.
I sought the LORD, and he answered me
   and delivered me from all my fears. **R.**
Look to him that you may be radiant with joy,
   and your faces may not blush with shame.
When the poor one called out, the LORD heard,
   and from all his distress he saved him. **R.**
The angel of the LORD encamps
   around those who fear him, and delivers them.
Taste and see how good the LORD is;
   blessed the man who takes refuge in him. **R.**

† *2 Timothy 4:6-8, 17-18*
From now on the crown of righteousness awaits me.

I, Paul, am already being poured out like a libation,
   and the time of my departure is at hand.
I have competed well; I have finished the race;
   I have kept the faith.
From now on the crown of righteousness awaits me,
   which the Lord, the just judge,
   will award to me on that day, and not only to me,
   but to all who have longed for his appearance.

The Lord stood by me and gave me strength,
   so that through me the proclamation might be completed
   and all the Gentiles might hear it.
And I was rescued from the lion's mouth.
The Lord will rescue me from every evil threat
   and will bring me safe to his heavenly Kingdom.
To him be glory forever and ever. Amen. ✛

Matthew 16:18

R. Alleluia, alleluia.
You are Peter and upon this rock I will build my Church,
and the gates of the netherworld shall not prevail against it. **R.**

† *Matthew 16:13-19*

You are Peter, and I will give you the keys to the Kingdom of heaven.

When Jesus went into the region of Caesarea Philippi
   he asked his disciples,
"Who do people say that the Son of Man is?"
They replied, "Some say John the Baptist, others Elijah,
   still others Jeremiah or one of the prophets."
He said to them, "But who do you say that I am?"
Simon Peter said in reply,
   "You are the Christ, the Son of the living God."
Jesus said to him in reply, "Blessed are you, Simon son of Jonah.
For flesh and blood has not revealed this to you, but my heavenly
    Father.
And so I say to you, you are Peter,
   and upon this rock I will build my Church,
   and the gates of the netherworld shall not prevail against it.
I will give you the keys to the Kingdom of heaven.
Whatever you bind on earth shall be bound in heaven;
   and whatever you loose on earth shall be loosed in heaven." ✢

THURSDAY, JUNE 30
WEEKDAY, THE FIRST MARTYRS OF THE HOLY ROMAN CHURCH

† *Amos 7:10-17*

Go, prophesy to my people Israel.

Amaziah, the priest of Bethel, sent word to Jeroboam, king of Israel:
   "Amos has conspired against you here within Israel;
   the country cannot endure all his words.
For this is what Amos says:
   Jeroboam shall die by the sword, and Israel shall surely be exiled
    from its land."

To Amos, Amaziah said:
   "Off with you, visionary, flee to the land of Judah!
There earn your bread by prophesying,
   but never again prophesy in Bethel;
   for it is the king's sanctuary and a royal temple."
Amos answered Amaziah, "I was no prophet,
   nor have I belonged to a company of prophets;
   I was a shepherd and a dresser of sycamores.
The LORD took me from following the flock, and said to me,
   'Go, prophesy to my people Israel.'
Now hear the word of the LORD!"

You say: prophesy not against Israel,
   preach not against the house of Isaac.
      Now thus says the LORD:
Your wife shall be made a harlot in the city,
   and your sons and daughters shall fall by the sword;
Your land shall be divided by measuring line,
   and you yourself shall die in an unclean land;
      Israel shall be exiled far from its land. ✛

Psalm 19:8, 9, 10, 11
**R. (10cd) The judgments of the Lord are true, and all of them
are just.**
The law of the LORD is perfect,
   refreshing the soul;
The decree of the LORD is trustworthy,
   giving wisdom to the simple. **R.**
The precepts of the LORD are right,
   rejoicing the heart;
The command of the LORD is clear,
   enlightening the eye. **R.**
The fear of the LORD is pure,
   enduring forever;
The ordinances of the LORD are true,
   all of them just. **R.**
They are more precious than gold,
   than a heap of purest gold;
Sweeter also than syrup
   or honey from the comb. **R.**

2 Corinthians 5:19
R. Alleluia, alleluia.
God was reconciling the world to himself in Christ
and entrusting to us the message of reconciliation. **R.**

† *Matthew 9:1-8*
They glorified God who had given such authority to men.

After entering a boat, Jesus made the crossing, and came into his
   own town.
And there people brought to him a paralytic lying on a stretcher.
When Jesus saw their faith, he said to the paralytic,
   "Courage, child, your sins are forgiven."
At that, some of the scribes said to themselves,
   "This man is blaspheming."
Jesus knew what they were thinking, and said,
   "Why do you harbor evil thoughts?

Which is easier, to say, 'Your sins are forgiven,'
    or to say, 'Rise and walk'?
But that you may know that the Son of Man
    has authority on earth to forgive sins"—
    he then said to the paralytic,
    "Rise, pick up your stretcher, and go home."
He rose and went home.
When the crowds saw this they were struck with awe
    and glorified God who had given such authority to men. ✝

FRIDAY, JULY 1
WEKDAY, ST. JUNÍPERO SERRA

† *Amos 8:4-6, 9-12*

I will send famine upon the land: not a famine of bread or thirst for water,
but for hearing the word of the LORD.

Hear this, you who trample upon the needy
and destroy the poor of the land!
"When will the new moon be over," you ask,
"that we may sell our grain,
and the sabbath, that we may display the wheat?
We will diminish the containers for measuring,
add to the weights,
and fix our scales for cheating!
We will buy the lowly man for silver,
and the poor man for a pair of sandals;
even the refuse of the wheat we will sell!"

On that day, says the Lord GOD,
I will make the sun set at midday
and cover the earth with darkness in broad daylight.
I will turn your feasts into mourning
and all your songs into lamentations.
I will cover the loins of all with sackcloth
and make every head bald.
I will make them mourn as for an only son,
and bring their day to a bitter end.

Yes, days are coming, says the Lord GOD,
when I will send famine upon the land:
Not a famine of bread, or thirst for water,
but for hearing the word of the LORD.
Then shall they wander from sea to sea
and rove from the north to the east
In search of the word of the LORD,
but they shall not find it. ✛

Psalm 119:2, 10, 20, 30, 40, 131

R. (Matthew 4:4) **One does not live by bread alone, but by**
every word that comes from the mouth of God.
Blessed are they who observe his decrees,
who seek him with all their heart. **R.**
With all my heart I seek you;
let me not stray from your commands. **R.**
My soul is consumed with longing
for your ordinances at all times. **R.**

The way of truth I have chosen;
  I have set your ordinances before me. **R.**
Behold, I long for your precepts;
  in your justice give me life. **R.**
I gasp with open mouth
  in my yearning for your commands. **R.**

Matthew 11:28
R. Alleluia, alleluia.
Come to me, all you who labor and are burdened,
and I will give you rest, says the Lord. **R.**

† *Matthew 9:9-13*
Those who are well do not need a physician; I desire mercy, not sacrifice.

As Jesus passed by,
  he saw a man named Matthew sitting at the customs post.
He said to him, "Follow me."
And he got up and followed him.
While he was at table in his house,
  many tax collectors and sinners came
  and sat with Jesus and his disciples.
The Pharisees saw this and said to his disciples,
  "Why does your teacher eat with tax collectors and sinners?"
He heard this and said,
  "Those who are well do not need a physician, but the sick do.
Go and learn the meaning of the words,
  I desire mercy, not sacrifice.
I did not come to call the righteous but sinners." ✛

SATURDAY, JULY 2
WEEKDAY, *[BVM]*

† *Amos 9:11-15*
I will bring about the restoration of my people Israel;
I will plant them upon their own ground.

Thus says the LORD:
On that day I will raise up
  the fallen hut of David;
I will wall up its breaches,
  raise up its ruins,
  and rebuild it as in the days of old,
That they may conquer what is left of Edom
  and all the nations that shall bear my name,
  say I, the LORD, who will do this.
Yes, days are coming,
  says the LORD,

When the plowman shall overtake the reaper,
  and the vintager, him who sows the seed;
The juice of grapes shall drip down the mountains,
  and all the hills shall run with it.
I will bring about the restoration of my people Israel;
  they shall rebuild and inhabit their ruined cities,
Plant vineyards and drink the wine,
  set out gardens and eat the fruits.
I will plant them upon their own ground;
  never again shall they be plucked
From the land I have given them,
  say I, the LORD, your God. ✢

  Psalm 85:9ab and 10, 11-12, 13-14
R. (see 9b) **The Lord speaks of peace to his people.**
I will hear what God proclaims;
  the LORD—for he proclaims peace to his people.
Near indeed is his salvation to those who fear him,
  glory dwelling in our land. **R.**
Kindness and truth shall meet;
  justice and peace shall kiss.
Truth shall spring out of the earth,
  and justice shall look down from heaven. **R.**
The LORD himself will give his benefits;
  our land shall yield its increase.
Justice shall walk before him,
  and salvation, along the way of his steps. **R.**

  John 10:27
R. Alleluia, alleluia.
My sheep hear my voice, says the Lord;
I know them, and they follow me. **R.**

  ✝ Matthew 9:14-17
Can the wedding guests mourn as long as the bridegroom is with them?

The disciples of John approached Jesus and said,
  "Why do we and the Pharisees fast much,
  but your disciples do not fast?"
Jesus answered them, "Can the wedding guests mourn
  as long as the bridegroom is with them?
The days will come when the bridegroom is taken away from them,
  and then they will fast.
No one patches an old cloak with a piece of unshrunken cloth,
  for its fullness pulls away from the cloak and the tear gets worse.
People do not put new wine into old wineskins.

Otherwise the skins burst, the wine spills out, and the skins are
   ruined.
Rather, they pour new wine into fresh wineskins, and both are
   preserved." ✝

SUNDAY, JULY 3
FOURTEENTH SUNDAY IN ORDINARY TIME

✝ Isaiah 66:10-14c
Behold, I will spread prosperity over her like a river.

Thus says the LORD:
Rejoice with Jerusalem and be glad because of her,
   all you who love her;
exult, exult with her,
   all you who were mourning over her!
Oh, that you may suck fully
   of the milk of her comfort,
that you may nurse with delight
   at her abundant breasts!
For thus says the LORD:
Lo, I will spread prosperity over Jerusalem like a river,
   and the wealth of the nations like an overflowing torrent.
As nurslings, you shall be carried in her arms,
   and fondled in her lap;
as a mother comforts her child,
   so will I comfort you;
   in Jerusalem you shall find your comfort.

When you see this, your heart shall rejoice
   and your bodies flourish like the grass;
the LORD's power shall be known to his servants. ✝

Psalm 66:1-3, 4-5, 6-7, 16, 20
R. (1) Let all the earth cry out to God with joy.
Shout joyfully to God, all the earth,
   sing praise to the glory of his name;
   proclaim his glorious praise.
Say to God, "How tremendous are your deeds!" **R.**
"Let all on earth worship and sing praise to you,
   sing praise to your name!"
Come and see the works of God,
   his tremendous deeds among the children of Adam. **R.**
He has changed the sea into dry land;
   through the river they passed on foot;
   therefore let us rejoice in him.

He rules by his might forever. **R.**
Hear now, all you who fear God,
 while I declare what he has done for me.
Blessed be God who refused me not
 my prayer or his kindness! **R.**

† *Galatians 6:14-18*
I bear the marks of Jesus on my body.

Brothers and sisters:
May I never boast except in the cross of our Lord Jesus Christ,
 through which the world has been crucified to me,
 and I to the world.
For neither does circumcision mean anything, nor does uncircumcision,
 but only a new creation.
Peace and mercy be to all who follow this rule
 and to the Israel of God.

From now on, let no one make troubles for me;
 for I bear the marks of Jesus on my body.

The grace of our Lord Jesus Christ be with your spirit,
 brothers and sisters. Amen. ✤

Colossians 3:15a, 16a
R. Alleluia, alleluia.
Let the peace of Christ control your hearts;
let the word of Christ dwell in you richly. **R.**

† *Luke 10:1-12, 17-20* (or *Luke 10:1-9*)
Your peace will rest on that person.

At that time the Lord appointed seventy-two others
 whom he sent ahead of him in pairs
 to every town and place he intended to visit.
He said to them,
 "The harvest is abundant but the laborers are few;
 so ask the master of the harvest
 to send out laborers for his harvest.
Go on your way;
 behold, I am sending you like lambs among wolves.
Carry no money bag, no sack, no sandals;
 and greet no one along the way.
Into whatever house you enter, first say,
 'Peace to this household.'
If a peaceful person lives there,
 your peace will rest on him;
 but if not, it will return to you.

Stay in the same house and eat and drink what is offered to you,
  for the laborer deserves his payment.
Do not move about from one house to another.
Whatever town you enter and they welcome you,
  eat what is set before you,
  cure the sick in it and say to them,
  'The kingdom of God is at hand for you.'
Whatever town you enter and they do not receive you,
  go out into the streets and say,
  'The dust of your town that clings to our feet,
  even that we shake off against you.'
Yet know this: the kingdom of God is at hand.
I tell you,
  it will be more tolerable for Sodom on that day than for that town."

The seventy-two returned rejoicing, and said,
  "Lord, even the demons are subject to us because of your name."
Jesus said, "I have observed Satan fall like lightning from the sky.
Behold, I have given you the power to 'tread upon serpents' and
    scorpions
and upon the full force of the enemy and nothing will harm you.
Nevertheless, do not rejoice because the spirits are subject to you,
  but rejoice because your names are written in heaven." ✛

MONDAY, JULY 4
Weekday, Independence Day, U.S.A.
(For Independence Day, any readings from the *Lectionary for Mass* (volume IV),
the Mass "For the Country or a City," numbers 882–886,
or "For Peace and Justice," numbers 887–891.)

† Hosea 2:16, 17c-18, 21-22
I will espouse you to me forever.

Thus says the LORD:
I will allure her;
  I will lead her into the desert
  and speak to her heart.
She shall respond there as in the days of her youth,
  when she came up from the land of Egypt.

  On that day, says the LORD,
She shall call me "My husband,"
  and never again "My baal."

I will espouse you to me forever:
  I will espouse you in right and in justice,
  in love and in mercy;

I will espouse you in fidelity,
   and you shall know the LORD. ✛

   Psalm 145:2-3, 4-5, 6-7, 8-9
R. (8a) **The Lord is gracious and merciful.**
Every day will I bless you,
   and I will praise your name forever and ever.
Great is the LORD and highly to be praised;
   his greatness is unsearchable. **R.**
Generation after generation praises your works
   and proclaims your might.
They speak of the splendor of your glorious majesty
   and tell of your wondrous works. **R.**
They discourse of the power of your terrible deeds
   and declare your greatness.
They publish the fame of your abundant goodness
   and joyfully sing of your justice. **R.**
The LORD is gracious and merciful,
   slow to anger and of great kindness.
The LORD is good to all
   and compassionate toward all his works. **R.**

   See 2 Timothy 1:10
R. Alleluia, alleluia.
Our Savior Jesus Christ has destroyed death
and brought life to light through the Gospel. **R.**

† Matthew 9:18-26
My daughter has just died, but come and she will live.

While Jesus was speaking, an official came forward,
   knelt down before him, and said,
   "My daughter has just died.
But come, lay your hand on her, and she will live."
Jesus rose and followed him, and so did his disciples.
A woman suffering hemorrhages for twelve years came up behind him
   and touched the tassel on his cloak.
She said to herself, "If only I can touch his cloak, I shall be cured."
Jesus turned around and saw her, and said,
   "Courage, daughter! Your faith has saved you."
And from that hour the woman was cured.

When Jesus arrived at the official's house
   and saw the flute players and the crowd who were making a
      commotion,
   he said, "Go away! The girl is not dead but sleeping."

And they ridiculed him.
When the crowd was put out, he came and took her by the hand,
and the little girl arose.
And news of this spread throughout all that land. ✝

TUESDAY, JULY 5
Weekday, St. Anthony Zaccaria, St. Elizabeth of Portugal

† *Hosea 8:4-7, 11-13*
When they sow the wind, they shall reap the whirlwind.

Thus says the LORD:
They made kings in Israel, but not by my authority;
    they established princes, but without my approval.
With their silver and gold they made
    idols for themselves, to their own destruction.
Cast away your calf, O Samaria!
    my wrath is kindled against them;
How long will they be unable to attain
    innocence in Israel?
The work of an artisan,
    no god at all,
Destined for the flames—
    such is the calf of Samaria!

When they sow the wind,
    they shall reap the whirlwind;
The stalk of grain that forms no ear
    can yield no flour;
Even if it could,
    strangers would swallow it.

When Ephraim made many altars to expiate sin,
    his altars became occasions of sin.
Though I write for him my many ordinances,
    they are considered as a stranger's.
Though they offer sacrifice,
    immolate flesh and eat it,
    the LORD is not pleased with them.
He shall still remember their guilt
    and punish their sins;
    they shall return to Egypt. ✝

Psalm 115:3-4, 5-6, 7ab-8, 9-10
R. (9a) **The house of Israel trusts in the Lord.** *(or* **Alleluia.***)*
Our God is in heaven;
 whatever he wills, he does.
Their idols are silver and gold,
 the handiwork of men. **R.**
They have mouths but speak not;
 they have eyes but see not;
They have ears but hear not;
 they have noses but smell not. **R.**
They have hands but feel not;
 they have feet but walk not.
Their makers shall be like them,
 everyone that trusts in them. **R.**

John 10:14
R. Alleluia, alleluia.
I am the good shepherd, says the Lord;
I know my sheep, and mine know me. **R.**

† *Matthew 9:32-38*
The harvest is abundant but the laborers are few.

A demoniac who could not speak was brought to Jesus,
 and when the demon was driven out the mute man spoke.
The crowds were amazed and said,
 "Nothing like this has ever been seen in Israel."
But the Pharisees said,
 "He drives out demons by the prince of demons."

Jesus went around to all the towns and villages,
 teaching in their synagogues,
 proclaiming the Gospel of the Kingdom,
 and curing every disease and illness.
At the sight of the crowds, his heart was moved with pity for them
 because they were troubled and abandoned,
 like sheep without a shepherd.
Then he said to his disciples,
 "The harvest is abundant but the laborers are few;
 so ask the master of the harvest
 to send out laborers for his harvest." ✛

WEDNESDAY, JULY 6
WEEKDAY, ST. MARIA GORETTI

† *Hosea 10:1-3, 7-8, 12*
It is time to seek the LORD.

Israel is a luxuriant vine
  whose fruit matches its growth.
The more abundant his fruit,
  the more altars he built;
The more productive his land,
  the more sacred pillars he set up.
Their heart is false,
  now they pay for their guilt;
God shall break down their altars
  and destroy their sacred pillars.
If they would say,
  "We have no king"—
Since they do not fear the LORD,
  what can the king do for them?

The king of Samaria shall disappear,
  like foam upon the waters.
The high places of Aven shall be destroyed,
  the sin of Israel;
  thorns and thistles shall overgrow their altars.
Then they shall cry out to the mountains, "Cover us!"
  and to the hills, "Fall upon us!"

"Sow for yourselves justice,
  reap the fruit of piety;
break up for yourselves a new field,
  for it is time to seek the LORD,
  till he come and rain down justice upon you." ✛

Psalm 105:2-3, 4-5, 6-7
R. (4b) **Seek always the face of the Lord.** *(or* **Alleluia.***)*
Sing to him, sing his praise,
  proclaim all his wondrous deeds.
Glory in his holy name;
  rejoice, O hearts that seek the LORD! **R.**
Look to the LORD in his strength;
  seek to serve him constantly.
Recall the wondrous deeds that he has wrought,
  his portents, and the judgments he has uttered. **R.**
You descendants of Abraham, his servants,
  sons of Jacob, his chosen ones!

He, the LORD, is our God;
   throughout the earth his judgments prevail. **R.**

   Mark 1:15
R. Alleluia, alleluia.
The Kingdom of God is at hand:
repent and believe in the Gospel. **R.**

† *Matthew 10:1-7*
Go rather to the lost sheep of the house of Israel.

Jesus summoned his Twelve disciples
   and gave them authority over unclean spirits to drive them out
   and to cure every disease and every illness.
The names of the Twelve Apostles are these:
   first, Simon called Peter, and his brother Andrew;
   James, the son of Zebedee, and his brother John;
   Philip and Bartholomew,
   Thomas and Matthew the tax collector;
   James, the son of Alphaeus, and Thaddeus;
   Simon the Cananean, and Judas Iscariot
   who betrayed Jesus.

Jesus sent out these Twelve after instructing them thus,
   "Do not go into pagan territory or enter a Samaritan town.
Go rather to the lost sheep of the house of Israel.
As you go, make this proclamation: 'The Kingdom of heaven is at
      hand.'" ✤

THURSDAY, JULY 7
WEEKDAY

† *Hosea 11:1-4, 8e-9*
My heart is overwhelmed.

Thus says the LORD:
When Israel was a child I loved him,
   out of Egypt I called my son.
The more I called them,
   the farther they went from me,
Sacrificing to the Baals
   and burning incense to idols.
Yet it was I who taught Ephraim to walk,
   who took them in my arms;
I drew them with human cords,
   with bands of love;
I fostered them like one
   who raises an infant to his cheeks;

Yet, though I stooped to feed my child,
  they did not know that I was their healer.

My heart is overwhelmed,
  my pity is stirred.
I will not give vent to my blazing anger,
  I will not destroy Ephraim again;
For I am God and not man,
  the Holy One present among you;
I will not let the flames consume you. ✛

Psalm 80:2ac and 3b, 15-16
R. (4b) Let us see your face, Lord, and we shall be saved.
O shepherd of Israel, hearken.
From your throne upon the cherubim, shine forth.
Rouse your power. **R.**
Once again, O LORD of hosts,
  look down from heaven, and see:
Take care of this vine,
  and protect what your right hand has planted,
  the son of man whom you yourself made strong. **R.**

Mark 1:15
R. Alleluia, alleluia.
The Kingdom of God is at hand:
repent and believe in the Gospel. **R.**

✝ *Matthew 10:7-15*
Without cost you have received; without cost you are to give.

Jesus said to his Apostles:
"As you go, make this proclamation:
  'The Kingdom of heaven is at hand.'
Cure the sick, raise the dead,
  cleanse the lepers, drive out demons.
Without cost you have received; without cost you are to give.
Do not take gold or silver or copper for your belts;
  no sack for the journey, or a second tunic,
  or sandals, or walking stick.
The laborer deserves his keep.
Whatever town or village you enter, look for a worthy person in it,
  and stay there until you leave.
As you enter a house, wish it peace.
If the house is worthy,
  let your peace come upon it;
  if not, let your peace return to you.

Whoever will not receive you or listen to your words—
   go outside that house or town and shake the dust from your feet.
Amen, I say to you, it will be more tolerable
   for the land of Sodom and Gomorrah on the day of judgment
   than for that town." ✝

FRIDAY, JULY 8
WEEKDAY

† *Hosea 14:2-10*
We shall say no more "Our god" to the work of our hands.

Thus says the LORD:
Return, O Israel, to the LORD, your God;
   you have collapsed through your guilt.
Take with you words,
   and return to the LORD;
Say to him, "Forgive all iniquity,
   and receive what is good, that we may render
   as offerings the bullocks from our stalls.
Assyria will not save us,
   nor shall we have horses to mount;
We shall say no more, 'Our god,'
   to the work of our hands;
   for in you the orphan finds compassion."
I will heal their defection, says the LORD,
   I will love them freely;
   for my wrath is turned away from them.
I will be like the dew for Israel:
   he shall blossom like the lily;
He shall strike root like the Lebanon cedar,
   and put forth his shoots.
His splendor shall be like the olive tree
   and his fragrance like the Lebanon cedar.
Again they shall dwell in his shade
   and raise grain;
They shall blossom like the vine,
   and his fame shall be like the wine of Lebanon.

Ephraim! What more has he to do with idols?
   I have humbled him, but I will prosper him.
"I am like a verdant cypress tree"—
   because of me you bear fruit!

Let him who is wise understand these things;
   let him who is prudent know them.

Straight are the paths of the LORD,
  in them the just walk,
  but sinners stumble in them. ✛

Psalm 51:3-4, 8-9, 12-13, 14 and 17
R. (17b) **My mouth will declare your praise.**
Have mercy on me, O God, in your goodness;
  in the greatness of your compassion wipe out my offense.
Thoroughly wash me from my guilt
  and of my sin cleanse me. **R.**
Behold, you are pleased with sincerity of heart,
  and in my inmost being you teach me wisdom.
Cleanse me of sin with hyssop, that I may be purified;
  wash me, and I shall be whiter than snow. **R.**
A clean heart create for me, O God,
  and a steadfast spirit renew within me.
Cast me not out from your presence,
  and your Holy Spirit take not from me. **R.**
Give me back the joy of your salvation,
  and a willing spirit sustain in me.
O Lord, open my lips,
  and my mouth shall proclaim your praise. **R.**

John 16:13a; 14:26d
R. Alleluia, alleluia.
When the Spirit of truth comes,
he will guide you to all truth
and remind you of all I told you. **R.**

✝ Matthew 10:16-23
For it will not be you who speak,
but the Spirit of your Father speaking through you.

Jesus said to his Apostles:
"Behold, I am sending you like sheep in the midst of wolves;
  so be shrewd as serpents and simple as doves.
But beware of men,
  for they will hand you over to courts
  and scourge you in their synagogues,
  and you will be led before governors and kings for my sake
  as a witness before them and the pagans.
When they hand you over,
  do not worry about how you are to speak
  or what you are to say.
You will be given at that moment what you are to say.
For it will not be you who speak
  but the Spirit of your Father speaking through you.

Brother will hand over brother to death,
  and the father his child;
  children will rise up against parents and have them put to death.
You will be hated by all because of my name,
  but whoever endures to the end will be saved.
When they persecute you in one town, flee to another.
Amen, I say to you, you will not finish the towns of Israel
  before the Son of Man comes." ✛

SATURDAY, JULY 9
WEEKDAY, ST. AUGUSTINE ZHAO RONG AND COMPANIONS, [BVM]

† Isaiah 6:1-8
I am a man of unclean lips; yet my eyes have seen the King, the LORD of hosts!

In the year King Uzziah died,
  I saw the Lord seated on a high and lofty throne,
  with the train of his garment filling the temple.
Seraphim were stationed above; each of them had six wings:
  with two they veiled their faces,
  with two they veiled their feet,
  and with two they hovered aloft.

They cried one to the other,
  "Holy, holy, holy is the LORD of hosts!
All the earth is filled with his glory!"
At the sound of that cry, the frame of the door shook
  and the house was filled with smoke.

Then I said, "Woe is me, I am doomed!
For I am a man of unclean lips,
  living among a people of unclean lips;
  yet my eyes have seen the King, the LORD of hosts!"
Then one of the seraphim flew to me,
  holding an ember that he had taken with tongs from the altar.

He touched my mouth with it and said,
  "See, now that this has touched your lips,
  your wickedness is removed, your sin purged."

Then I heard the voice of the LORD saying,
  "Whom shall I send? Who will go for us?"
"Here I am," I said; "send me!" ✛

Psalm 93:1ab, 1cd-2, 5
R. (1a) **The Lord is king; he is robed in majesty.**
The LORD is king, in splendor robed;
  robed is the LORD and girt about with strength. **R.**

And he has made the world firm,
   not to be moved.
Your throne stands firm from of old;
   from everlasting you are, O LORD. **R.**
Your decrees are worthy of trust indeed:
   holiness befits your house,
   O LORD, for length of days. **R.**

   1 Peter 4:14

R. Alleluia, alleluia.

If you are insulted for the name of Christ, blessed are you,
for the Spirit of God rests upon you. **R.**

† *Matthew 10:24-33*

Do not be afraid of those who kill the body.

Jesus said to his Apostles:
"No disciple is above his teacher,
   no slave above his master.
It is enough for the disciple that he become like his teacher,
   for the slave that he become like his master.
If they have called the master of the house Beelzebul,
   how much more those of his household!

"Therefore do not be afraid of them.
Nothing is concealed that will not be revealed,
   nor secret that will not be known.
What I say to you in the darkness, speak in the light;
   what you hear whispered, proclaim on the housetops.
And do not be afraid of those who kill the body but cannot kill the soul;
   rather, be afraid of the one who can destroy
   both soul and body in Gehenna.
Are not two sparrows sold for a small coin?
Yet not one of them falls to the ground without your Father's
      knowledge.
Even all the hairs of your head are counted.
So do not be afraid; you are worth more than many sparrows.
Everyone who acknowledges me before others
   I will acknowledge before my heavenly Father.
But whoever denies me before others,
   I will deny before my heavenly Father." ✛

SUNDAY, JULY 10
FIFTEENTH SUNDAY IN ORDINARY TIME

† *Deuteronomy 30:10-14*
The word is very near to you: you have only to carry it out.

Moses said to the people:
"If only you would heed the voice of the LORD, your God,
and keep his commandments and statutes
that are written in this book of the law,
when you return to the LORD, your God,
with all your heart and all your soul.

"For this command that I enjoin on you today
is not too mysterious and remote for you.
It is not up in the sky, that you should say,
'Who will go up in the sky to get it for us
and tell us of it, that we may carry it out?'
Nor is it across the sea, that you should say,
'Who will cross the sea to get it for us
and tell us of it, that we may carry it out?'
No, it is something very near to you,
already in your mouths and in your hearts;
you have only to carry it out." ✛

Psalm 69:14, 17, 30-31, 33-34, 36, 37 (or Psalm 19:8, 9, 10, 11)
R. (see 33) **Turn to the Lord in your need, and you will live.**
I pray to you, O LORD,
for the time of your favor, O God!
In your great kindness answer me
with your constant help.
Answer me, O LORD, for bounteous is your kindness:
in your great mercy turn toward me. **R.**
I am afflicted and in pain;
let your saving help, O God, protect me.
I will praise the name of God in song,
and I will glorify him with thanksgiving. **R.**
"See, you lowly ones, and be glad;
you who seek God, may your hearts revive!
For the LORD hears the poor,
and his own who are in bonds he spurns not." **R.**
For God will save Zion
and rebuild the cities of Judah.
The descendants of his servants shall inherit it,
and those who love his name shall inhabit it. **R.**

† *Colossians 1:15-20*
All things were created through him and for him.

Christ Jesus is the image of the invisible God,
   the firstborn of all creation.
For in him were created all things in heaven and on earth,
   the visible and the invisible,
   whether thrones or dominions or principalities or powers;
   all things were created through him and for him.
He is before all things,
   and in him all things hold together.
He is the head of the body, the church.
He is the beginning, the firstborn from the dead,
   that in all things he himself might be preeminent.
For in him all the fullness was pleased to dwell,
   and through him to reconcile all things for him,
   making peace by the blood of his cross
   through him, whether those on earth or those in heaven. ✛

   See John 6:63c, 68c
R. Alleluia, alleluia.
Your words, Lord, are Spirit and life;
you have the words of everlasting life. **R.**

† *Luke 10:25-37*
Who is my neighbor?

There was a scholar of the law who stood up to test Jesus and said,
   "Teacher, what must I do to inherit eternal life?"
Jesus said to him, "What is written in the law?
How do you read it?"
He said in reply,
   "You shall love the Lord, your God,
   with all your heart,
   with all your being,
   with all your strength,
   and with all your mind,
   and your neighbor as yourself."
He replied to him, "You have answered correctly;
   do this and you will live."

But because he wished to justify himself, he said to Jesus,
   "And who is my neighbor?"
Jesus replied,
   "A man fell victim to robbers
   as he went down from Jerusalem to Jericho.
They stripped and beat him and went off leaving him half-dead.

A priest happened to be going down that road,
  but when he saw him, he passed by on the opposite side.
Likewise a Levite came to the place,
  and when he saw him, he passed by on the opposite side.
But a Samaritan traveler who came upon him
  was moved with compassion at the sight.
He approached the victim,
  poured oil and wine over his wounds and bandaged them.
Then he lifted him up on his own animal,
  took him to an inn, and cared for him.
The next day he took out two silver coins
  and gave them to the innkeeper with the instruction,
  'Take care of him.
If you spend more than what I have given you,
  I shall repay you on my way back.'
Which of these three, in your opinion,
  was neighbor to the robbers' victim?"
He answered, "The one who treated him with mercy."
Jesus said to him, "Go and do likewise." ✚

MONDAY, JULY 11
St. Benedict

†Isaiah 1:10-17
Wash yourselves clean! Put away your misdeeds from before my eyes.

Hear the word of the Lord,
  princes of Sodom!
Listen to the instruction of our God,
  people of Gomorrah!
What care I for the number of your sacrifices?
  says the Lord.
I have had enough of whole-burnt rams
  and fat of fatlings;
In the blood of calves, lambs and goats
  I find no pleasure.

When you come in to visit me,
  who asks these things of you?
Trample my courts no more!
  Bring no more worthless offerings;
  your incense is loathsome to me.
New moon and sabbath, calling of assemblies,
  octaves with wickedness: these I cannot bear.
Your new moons and festivals I detest;
  they weigh me down, I tire of the load.

When you spread out your hands,
  I close my eyes to you;
Though you pray the more,
  I will not listen.
Your hands are full of blood!
  Wash yourselves clean!
Put away your misdeeds from before my eyes;
  cease doing evil; learn to do good.
Make justice your aim: redress the wronged,
  hear the orphan's plea, defend the widow. ✛

Psalm 50:8-9, 16bc-17, 21 and 23
R. (23b) **To the upright I will show the saving power of God.**
"Not for your sacrifices do I rebuke you,
  for your burnt offerings are before me always.
I take from your house no bullock,
  no goats out of your fold." **R.**
"Why do you recite my statutes,
  and profess my covenant with your mouth,
Though you hate discipline
  and cast my words behind you?" **R.**
"When you do these things, shall I be deaf to it?
  Or do you think that I am like yourself?
  I will correct you by drawing them up before your eyes.
He that offers praise as a sacrifice glorifies me;
  and to him that goes the right way I will show the salvation of
    God." **R.**

Matthew 5:10
R. Alleluia, alleluia.
Blessed are they who are persecuted for the sake of righteousness,
for theirs is the Kingdom of heaven. **R.**

† Matthew 10:34—11:1
I have come to bring not peace, but the sword.

Jesus said to his Apostles:
"Do not think that I have come to bring peace upon the earth.
I have come to bring not peace but the sword.
For I have come to set
  a man against his father,
    a daughter against her mother,
  and a daughter-in-law against her mother-in-law;
    and one's enemies will be those of his household.

"Whoever loves father or mother more than me is not worthy of me,
   and whoever loves son or daughter more than me is not worthy of
      me;
   and whoever does not take up his cross
   and follow after me is not worthy of me.
Whoever finds his life will lose it,
   and whoever loses his life for my sake will find it.

"Whoever receives you receives me,
   and whoever receives me receives the one who sent me.
Whoever receives a prophet because he is a prophet
   will receive a prophet's reward,
   and whoever receives a righteous man
   because he is righteous
   will receive a righteous man's reward.
And whoever gives only a cup of cold water
   to one of these little ones to drink
   because he is a disciple—
   amen, I say to you, he will surely not lose his reward."

When Jesus finished giving these commands to his Twelve disciples,
   he went away from that place to teach and to preach in their
      towns. ✛

TUESDAY, JULY 12
WEEKDAY

✝ Isaiah 7:1-9
Unless your faith is firm, you shall not be firm!

In the days of Ahaz, king of Judah, son of Jotham, son of Uzziah,
   Rezin, king of Aram,
   and Pekah, king of Israel, son of Remaliah,
   went up to attack Jerusalem,
   but they were not able to conquer it.
When word came to the house of David that Aram
   was encamped in Ephraim,
   the heart of the king and the heart of the people trembled,
   as the trees of the forest tremble in the wind.

Then the LORD said to Isaiah: Go out to meet Ahaz,
   you and your son Shear-jashub,
   at the end of the conduit of the upper pool,
   on the highway of the fuller's field, and say to him:
   Take care you remain tranquil and do not fear;
   let not your courage fail
   before these two stumps of smoldering brands

the blazing anger of Rezin and the Arameans,
and of the son Remaliah,
because of the mischief that
Aram, Ephraim and the son of Remaliah,
plots against you, saying,
"Let us go up and tear Judah asunder, make it our own by force,
and appoint the son of Tabeel king there."

Thus says the LORD:
    This shall not stand, it shall not be!
Damascus is the capital of Aram,
    and Rezin is the head of Damascus;
Samaria is the capital of Ephraim,
    and Remaliah's son the head of Samaria.

But within sixty years and five,
    Ephraim shall be crushed, no longer a nation.
Unless your faith is firm
    you shall not be firm! ✢

Psalm 48:2-3a, 3b-4, 5-6, 7-8
R. (see 9d) **God upholds his city for ever.**
Great is the LORD and wholly to be praised
    in the city of our God.
His holy mountain, fairest of heights,
    is the joy of all the earth. **R.**
Mount Zion, "the recesses of the North,"
    is the city of the great King.
God is with her castles;
    renowned is he as a stronghold. **R.**
For lo! the kings assemble,
    they come on together;
They also see, and at once are stunned,
    terrified, routed. **R.**
Quaking seizes them there;
    anguish, like a woman's in labor,
As though a wind from the east
    were shattering ships of Tarshish. **R.**

Psalm 95:8
R. Alleluia, alleluia.
If today you hear his voice,
harden not your hearts. **R.**

† Matthew 11:20-24
*It will be more tolerable for Tyre and Sidon and
for the land of Sodom on the day of judgment than for you.*

Jesus began to reproach the towns
  where most of his mighty deeds had been done,
  since they had not repented.
"Woe to you, Chorazin! Woe to you, Bethsaida!
For if the mighty deeds done in your midst
  had been done in Tyre and Sidon,
  they would long ago have repented in sackcloth and ashes.
But I tell you, it will be more tolerable
  for Tyre and Sidon on the day of judgment than for you.
And as for you, Capernaum:

*Will you be exalted to heaven?
  You will go down to the nether world.*

For if the mighty deeds done in your midst had been done in Sodom,
  it would have remained until this day.
But I tell you, it will be more tolerable
  for the land of Sodom on the day of judgment than for you." ✛

WEDNESDAY, JULY 13
WEEKDAY, ST. HENRY

† Isaiah 10:5-7, 13b-16
Will the axe boast against the one who hews with it?

Thus says the LORD:
Woe to Assyria! My rod in anger,
  my staff in wrath.
Against an impious nation I send him,
  and against a people under my wrath I order him
To seize plunder, carry off loot,
  and tread them down like the mud of the streets.
But this is not what he intends,
  nor does he have this in mind;
Rather, it is in his heart to destroy,
  to make an end of nations not a few.

  For he says:
"By my own power I have done it,
  and by my wisdom, for I am shrewd.
I have moved the boundaries of peoples,
  their treasures I have pillaged,
  and, like a giant, I have put down the enthroned.

My hand has seized like a nest
  the riches of nations;
As one takes eggs left alone,
  so I took in all the earth;
No one fluttered a wing,
  or opened a mouth, or chirped!"

Will the axe boast against him who hews with it?
  Will the saw exalt itself above him who wields it?
As if a rod could sway him who lifts it,
  or a staff him who is not wood!
Therefore the Lord, the LORD of hosts,
  will send among his fat ones leanness,
And instead of his glory there will be kindling
  like the kindling of fire. ✛

Psalm 94:5-6, 7-8, 9-10, 14-15
R. (14a) The Lord will not abandon his people.
Your people, O LORD, they trample down,
  your inheritance they afflict.
Widow and stranger they slay,
  the fatherless they murder. **R.**
And they say, "The LORD sees not;
  the God of Jacob perceives not."
Understand, you senseless ones among the people;
  and, you fools, when will you be wise? **R.**
Shall he who shaped the ear not hear?
  or he who formed the eye not see?
Shall he who instructs nations not chastise,
  he who teaches men knowledge? **R.**
For the LORD will not cast off his people,
  nor abandon his inheritance;
But judgment shall again be with justice,
  and all the upright of heart shall follow it. **R.**

Matthew 11:25
R. Alleluia, alleluia.
Blessed are you, Father, Lord of heaven and earth,
you have revealed to little ones the mysteries of the Kingdom. **R.**

† *Matthew 11:25-27*

Although you have hidden these things from the wise and the learned
you have revealed them to the childlike.

At that time Jesus exclaimed:
"I give praise to you, Father, Lord of heaven and earth,
for although you have hidden these things
from the wise and the learned
you have revealed them to the childlike.
Yes, Father, such has been your gracious will.
All things have been handed over to me by my Father.
No one knows the Son except the Father,
and no one knows the Father except the Son
and anyone to whom the Son wishes to reveal him." ✛

THURSDAY, JULY 14
St. Kateri Tekakwitha

† *Isaiah 26:7-9, 12, 16-19*

Awake and sing, you who lie in the dust.

The way of the just is smooth;
the path of the just you make level.
Yes, for your way and your judgments, O Lord,
we look to you;
Your name and your title
are the desire of our souls.
My soul yearns for you in the night,
yes, my spirit within me keeps vigil for you;
When your judgment dawns upon the earth,
the world's inhabitants learn justice.
O Lord, you mete out peace to us,
for it is you who have accomplished all we have done.

O Lord, oppressed by your punishment,
we cried out in anguish under your chastising.
As a woman about to give birth
writhes and cries out in her pains,
so were we in your presence, O Lord.
We conceived and writhed in pain,
giving birth to wind;
Salvation we have not achieved for the earth,
the inhabitants of the world cannot bring it forth.
But your dead shall live, their corpses shall rise;
awake and sing, you who lie in the dust.
For your dew is a dew of light,
and the land of shades gives birth. ✛

Psalm 102:13-14ab and 15, 16-18, 19-21

R. (20b) **From heaven the Lord looks down on the earth.**

You, O LORD, abide forever,
   and your name through all generations.
You will arise and have mercy on Zion,
   for it is time to pity her.
For her stones are dear to your servants,
   and her dust moves them to pity. **R.**
The nations shall revere your name, O LORD,
   and all the kings of the earth your glory,
When the LORD has rebuilt Zion
   and appeared in his glory;
When he has regarded the prayer of the destitute,
   and not despised their prayer. **R.**
Let this be written for the generation to come,
   and let his future creatures praise the LORD:
"The LORD looked down from his holy height,
   from heaven he beheld the earth,
To hear the groaning of the prisoners,
   to release those doomed to die." **R.**

Matthew 11:28

R. Alleluia, alleluia.

Come to me, all you who labor and are burdened,
and I will give you rest, says the Lord. **R.**

✝ *Matthew 11:28-30*
I am meek and humble of heart.

Jesus said:
"Come to me, all you who labor and are burdened,
   and I will give you rest.
Take my yoke upon you and learn from me,
   for I am meek and humble of heart;
   and you will find rest for yourselves.
For my yoke is easy, and my burden light." ✝

FRIDAY, JULY 15
ST. BONAVENTURE

✝ *Isaiah 38:1-6, 21-22, 7-8*
I have heard your prayer and seen your tears.

When Hezekiah was mortally ill,
   the prophet Isaiah, son of Amoz, came and said to him:
   "Thus says the LORD: Put your house in order,
   for you are about to die; you shall not recover."

Then Hezekiah turned his face to the wall and prayed to the LORD:

"O LORD, remember how faithfully and wholeheartedly
I conducted myself in your presence,
doing what was pleasing to you!"
And Hezekiah wept bitterly.

Then the word of the LORD came to Isaiah: "Go, tell Hezekiah:
Thus says the LORD, the God of your father David:
I have heard your prayer and seen your tears.
I will heal you: in three days you shall go up to the LORD's temple;
I will add fifteen years to your life.
I will rescue you and this city from the hand of the king of Assyria;
I will be a shield to this city."

Isaiah then ordered a poultice of figs to be taken
and applied to the boil, that he might recover.
Then Hezekiah asked,
"What is the sign that I shall go up to the temple of the LORD?"

Isaiah answered:
"This will be the sign for you from the LORD
that he will do what he has promised:
See, I will make the shadow cast by the sun
on the stairway to the terrace of Ahaz
go back the ten steps it has advanced."
So the sun came back the ten steps it had advanced. ✛

Isaiah 38:10, 11, 12abcd, 16
R. (see 17b) **You saved my life, O Lord; I shall not die.**
Once I said,
"In the noontime of life I must depart!
To the gates of the nether world I shall be consigned
for the rest of my years." **R.**
I said, "I shall see the LORD no more
in the land of the living.
No longer shall I behold my fellow men
among those who dwell in the world." **R.**
My dwelling, like a shepherd's tent,
is struck down and borne away from me;
You have folded up my life, like a weaver
who severs the last thread. **R.**
Those live whom the LORD protects;
yours is the life of my spirit.
You have given me health and life. **R.**

John 10:27
R. Alleluia, alleluia.
My sheep hear my voice, says the Lord;
I know them, and they follow me. **R.**

† *Matthew 12:1-8*
The Son of Man is Lord of the sabbath.

Jesus was going through a field of grain on the sabbath.
His disciples were hungry
   and began to pick the heads of grain and eat them.
When the Pharisees saw this, they said to him,
   "See, your disciples are doing what is unlawful to do on the sabbath."
He said to them, "Have you not read what David did
   when he and his companions were hungry,
   how he went into the house of God and ate the bread of offering,
   which neither he nor his companions
   but only the priests could lawfully eat?
Or have you not read in the law that on the sabbath
   the priests serving in the temple violate the sabbath
   and are innocent?
I say to you, something greater than the temple is here.
If you knew what this meant, *I desire mercy, not sacrifice,*
   you would not have condemned these innocent men.
For the Son of Man is Lord of the sabbath." ✛

SATURDAY, JULY 16
WEEKDAY, OUR LADY OF MOUNT CARMEL, *[BVM]*

† *Micah 2:1-5*
They covet fields, and seize them; houses, and they take them.

Woe to those who plan iniquity,
   and work out evil on their couches;
In the morning light they accomplish it
   when it lies within their power.
They covet fields, and seize them;
   houses, and they take them;
They cheat an owner of his house,
   a man of his inheritance.
      Therefore thus says the LORD:
Behold, I am planning against this race an evil
   from which you shall not withdraw your necks;
Nor shall you walk with head high,
   for it will be a time of evil.

On that day a satire shall be sung over you,
and there shall be a plaintive chant:
"Our ruin is complete,
our fields are portioned out among our captors,
The fields of my people are measured out,
and no one can get them back!"
Thus you shall have no one
to mark out boundaries by lot
in the assembly of the LORD. ✝

Psalm 10:1-2, 3-4, 7-8, 14
R. (12b) **Do not forget the poor, O Lord!**
Why, O LORD, do you stand aloof?
Why hide in times of distress?
Proudly the wicked harass the afflicted,
who are caught in the devices the wicked have contrived. **R.**
For the wicked man glories in his greed,
and the covetous blasphemes, sets the LORD at nought.
The wicked man boasts, "He will not avenge it";
"There is no God," sums up his thoughts. **R.**
His mouth is full of cursing, guile and deceit;
under his tongue are mischief and iniquity.
He lurks in ambush near the villages;
in hiding he murders the innocent;
his eyes spy upon the unfortunate. **R.**
You do see, for you behold misery and sorrow,
taking them in your hands.
On you the unfortunate man depends;
of the fatherless you are the helper. **R.**

2 Corinthians 5:19
R. Alleluia, alleluia.
God was reconciling the world to himself in Christ,
and entrusting to us the message of reconciliation. **R.**

† *Matthew 12:14-21*
He warned them not to make him known to fulfill what had been spoken.

The Pharisees went out and took counsel against Jesus
to put him to death.

When Jesus realized this, he withdrew from that place.
Many people followed him, and he cured them all,
but he warned them not to make him known.

This was to fulfill what had been spoken through Isaiah the prophet:

Behold, my servant whom I have chosen,
my beloved in whom I delight;
I shall place my Spirit upon him,
and he will proclaim justice to the Gentiles.
He will not contend or cry out,
nor will anyone hear his voice in the streets.
A bruised reed he will not break,
a smoldering wick he will not quench,
until he brings justice to victory.
And in his name the Gentiles will hope. ✛

SUNDAY, JULY 17
SIXTEENTH SUNDAY IN ORDINARY TIME

✝ Genesis 18:1-10a
Lord, do not go on past your servant.

The LORD appeared to Abraham by the terebinth of Mamre,
as he sat in the entrance of his tent,
while the day was growing hot.
Looking up, Abraham saw three men standing nearby.
When he saw them, he ran from the entrance of the tent to greet them;
and bowing to the ground, he said:
"Sir, if I may ask you this favor,
please do not go on past your servant.
Let some water be brought, that you may bathe your feet,
and then rest yourselves under the tree.
Now that you have come this close to your servant,
let me bring you a little food, that you may refresh yourselves;
and afterward you may go on your way."
The men replied, "Very well, do as you have said."

Abraham hastened into the tent and told Sarah,
"Quick, three measures of fine flour! Knead it and make rolls."
He ran to the herd, picked out a tender, choice steer,
and gave it to a servant, who quickly prepared it.
Then Abraham got some curds and milk,
as well as the steer that had been prepared,
and set these before the three men;
and he waited on them under the tree while they ate.

They asked Abraham, "Where is your wife Sarah?"
He replied, "There in the tent."
One of them said, "I will surely return to you about this time next year,
and Sarah will then have a son." ✛

Psalm 15:2-3, 3-4, 5
R. (1a) **He who does justice will live in the presence of the Lord.**
One who walks blamelessly and does justice;
  who thinks the truth in his heart
  and slanders not with his tongue. **R.**
Who harms not his fellow man,
  nor takes up a reproach against his neighbor;
by whom the reprobate is despised,
  while he honors those who fear the LORD. **R.**
Who lends not his money at usury
  and accepts no bribe against the innocent.
One who does these things
  shall never be disturbed. **R.**

† *Colossians 1:24-28*
The mystery hidden from ages has now been manifested to his holy ones.

Brothers and sisters:
Now I rejoice in my sufferings for your sake,
  and in my flesh I am filling up
  what is lacking in the afflictions of Christ
  on behalf of his body, which is the church,
  of which I am a minister
  in accordance with God's stewardship given to me
  to bring to completion for you the word of God,
  the mystery hidden from ages and from generations past.
But now it has been manifested to his holy ones,
  to whom God chose to make known the riches of the glory
  of this mystery among the Gentiles;
  it is Christ in you, the hope for glory.
It is he whom we proclaim,
  admonishing everyone and teaching everyone with all wisdom,
  that we may present everyone perfect in Christ. ✛

See Luke 8:15
R. Alleluia, alleluia.
Blessed are they who have kept the word with a generous heart
and yield a harvest through perseverance. **R.**

† *Luke 10:38-42*
Martha welcomed him. Mary has chosen the better part.

Jesus entered a village
  where a woman whose name was Martha welcomed him.
She had a sister named Mary
  who sat beside the Lord at his feet listening to him speak.
Martha, burdened with much serving, came to him and said,
  "Lord, do you not care
  that my sister has left me by myself to do the serving?
Tell her to help me."
The Lord said to her in reply,
  "Martha, Martha, you are anxious and worried about many things.
There is need of only one thing.
Mary has chosen the better part
  and it will not be taken from her." ✛

MONDAY, JULY 18
WEEKDAY, ST. CAMILLUS DE LELLIS

† *Micah 6:1-4, 6-8*
You have been told, O man, what the LORD requires of you.

Hear what the LORD says:
Arise, present your plea before the mountains,
  and let the hills hear your voice!
Hear, O mountains, the plea of the LORD,
  pay attention, O foundations of the earth!
For the LORD has a plea against his people,
  and he enters into trial with Israel.

O my people, what have I done to you,
  or how have I wearied you? Answer me!
For I brought you up from the land of Egypt,
  from the place of slavery I released you;
and I sent before you Moses,
  Aaron, and Miriam.

With what shall I come before the LORD,
  and bow before God most high?
Shall I come before him with burnt offerings,
  with calves a year old?
Will the LORD be pleased with thousands of rams,
  with myriad streams of oil?
Shall I give my first-born for my crime,
  the fruit of my body for the sin of my soul?

You have been told, O man, what is good,
and what the LORD requires of you:
Only to do the right and to love goodness,
and to walk humbly with your God. ✛

Psalm 50:5-6, 8-9, 16bc-17, 21 and 23
R. (23b) **To the upright I will show the saving power of God.**
"Gather my faithful ones before me,
those who have made a covenant with me by sacrifice."
And the heavens proclaim his justice;
for God himself is the judge. **R.**
"Not for your sacrifices do I rebuke you,
for your burnt offerings are before me always.
I take from your house no bullock,
no goats out of your fold." **R.**
"Why do you recite my statutes,
and profess my covenant with your mouth,
Though you hate discipline
and cast my words behind you?" **R.**
"When you do these things, shall I be deaf to it?
Or do you think that I am like yourself?
I will correct you by drawing them up before your eyes.
He that offers praise as a sacrifice glorifies me;
and to him that goes the right way I will show the salvation of
God." **R.**

Psalm 95:8
R. Alleluia, alleluia.
If today you hear his voice,
harden not your hearts. **R.**

† *Matthew 12:38-42*
*At the judgment the queen of the south will arise
with this generation and condemn it.*

Some of the scribes and Pharisees said to Jesus,
"Teacher, we wish to see a sign from you."
He said to them in reply,
"An evil and unfaithful generation seeks a sign,
but no sign will be given it
except the sign of Jonah the prophet.
Just as Jonah was in the belly of the whale three days and three
nights,
so will the Son of Man be in the heart of the earth
three days and three nights.

At the judgment, the men of Nineveh will arise with this generation
and condemn it, because they repented at the preaching of Jonah;
and there is something greater than Jonah here.
At the judgment the queen of the south will arise with this generation
and condemn it, because she came from the ends of the earth
to hear the wisdom of Solomon;
and there is something greater than Solomon here." ✛

TUESDAY, JULY 19
WEEKDAY

† *Micah 7:14-15, 18-20*
He will cast into the depths of the sea all our sins.

Shepherd your people with your staff,
the flock of your inheritance,
That dwells apart in a woodland,
in the midst of Carmel.
Let them feed in Bashan and Gilead,
as in the days of old;
As in the days when you came from the land of Egypt,
show us wonderful signs.

Who is there like you, the God who removes guilt
and pardons sin for the remnant of his inheritance;
Who does not persist in anger forever,
but delights rather in clemency,
And will again have compassion on us,
treading underfoot our guilt?
You will cast into the depths of the sea
all our sins;
You will show faithfulness to Jacob,
and grace to Abraham,
As you have sworn to our fathers
from days of old. ✛

Psalm 85:2-4, 5-6, 7-8
R. (8a) **Lord, show us your mercy and love.**
You have favored, O LORD, your land;
you have brought back the captives of Jacob.
You have forgiven the guilt of your people;
you have covered all their sins.
You have withdrawn all your wrath;
you have revoked your burning anger. **R.**
Restore us, O God our savior,
and abandon your displeasure against us.

Will you be ever angry with us,
    prolonging your anger to all generations? **R.**
Will you not instead give us life;
    and shall not your people rejoice in you?
Show us, O LORD, your kindness,
    and grant us your salvation. **R.**

John 14:23

R. Alleluia, alleluia.
Whoever loves me will keep my word,
and my Father will love him
and we will come to him. **R.**

† *Matthew 12:46-50*
Stretching out his hands toward his disciples, he said,
"Here are my mother and my brothers."

While Jesus was speaking to the crowds,
    his mother and his brothers appeared outside,
    wishing to speak with him.
Someone told him, "Your mother and your brothers are standing
        outside,
    asking to speak with you."
But he said in reply to the one who told him,
    "Who is my mother? Who are my brothers?"
And stretching out his hand toward his disciples, he said,
    "Here are my mother and my brothers.
For whoever does the will of my heavenly Father
    is my brother, and sister, and mother." ✛

WEDNESDAY, JULY 20
WEEKDAY, ST. APOLLINARIS

† *Jeremiah 1:1, 4-10*
A prophet to the nations I appointed you.

The words of Jeremiah, son of Hilkiah,
    of a priestly family in Anathoth, in the land of Benjamin.

The word of the LORD came to me thus:

Before I formed you in the womb I knew you,
    before you were born I dedicated you,
    a prophet to the nations I appointed you.
"Ah, Lord GOD!" I said,
    "I know not how to speak; I am too young."

But the LORD answered me,
Say not, "I am too young."
    To whomever I send you, you shall go;
    whatever I command you, you shall speak.
Have no fear before them,
    because I am with you to deliver you, says the LORD.

Then the LORD extended his hand and touched my mouth, saying,

See, I place my words in your mouth!
    This day I set you
    over nations and over kingdoms,
To root up and to tear down,
    to destroy and to demolish,
    to build and to plant. ✛

Psalm 71:1-2, 3-4a, 5-6ab, 15 and 17
R. (see 15ab) **I will sing of your salvation.**
In you, O LORD, I take refuge;
    let me never be put to shame.
In your justice rescue me, and deliver me;
    incline your ear to me, and save me. **R.**
Be my rock of refuge,
    a stronghold to give me safety,
    for you are my rock and my fortress.
O my God, rescue me from the hand of the wicked. **R.**
For you are my hope, O LORD;
    my trust, O God, from my youth.
On you I depend from birth;
    from my mother's womb you are my strength. **R.**
My mouth shall declare your justice,
    day by day your salvation.
O God, you have taught me from my youth,
    and till the present I proclaim your wondrous deeds. **R.**

R. Alleluia, alleluia.
The seed is the word of God, Christ is the sower;
all who come to him will live for ever. **R.**

† *Matthew 13:1-9*
The seed produced grain a hundredfold.

On that day, Jesus went out of the house and sat down by the sea.
Such large crowds gathered around him
    that he got into a boat and sat down,
    and the whole crowd stood along the shore.

And he spoke to them at length in parables, saying:
  "A sower went out to sow.
And as he sowed, some seed fell on the path,
  and birds came and ate it up.
Some fell on rocky ground, where it had little soil.
It sprang up at once because the soil was not deep,
  and when the sun rose it was scorched,
  and it withered for lack of roots.
Some seed fell among thorns, and the thorns grew up and choked it.
But some seed fell on rich soil, and produced fruit,
  a hundred or sixty or thirtyfold.
Whoever has ears ought to hear." ✛

THURSDAY, JULY 21
WEEKDAY, ST. LAWRENCE OF BRINDISI

† *Jeremiah 2:1-3, 7-8, 12-13*
They have forsaken me, the source of living waters;
they have dug themselves broken cisterns.

This word of the LORD came to me:
  Go, cry out this message for Jerusalem to hear!

I remember the devotion of your youth,
  how you loved me as a bride,
Following me in the desert,
  in a land unsown.
Sacred to the LORD was Israel,
  the first fruits of his harvest;
Should any presume to partake of them,
  evil would befall them, says the LORD.

When I brought you into the garden land
  to eat its goodly fruits,
You entered and defiled my land,
  you made my heritage loathsome.
The priests asked not,
  "Where is the LORD?"
Those who dealt with the law knew me not:
  the shepherds rebelled against me.
The prophets prophesied by Baal,
  and went after useless idols.

Be amazed at this, O heavens,
  and shudder with sheer horror, says the LORD.

Two evils have my people done:
    they have forsaken me, the source of living waters;
They have dug themselves cisterns,
    broken cisterns, that hold no water. ✢

Psalm 36:6-7ab, 8-9, 10-11
R. (10a) **With you is the fountain of life, O Lord.**
O LORD, your mercy reaches to heaven;
    your faithfulness, to the clouds.
Your justice is like the mountains of God;
    your judgments, like the mighty deep. **R.**
How precious is your mercy, O God!
    The children of men take refuge in the shadow of your wings.
They have their fill of the prime gifts of your house;
    from your delightful stream you give them to drink. **R.**
For with you is the fountain of life,
    and in your light we see light.
Keep up your mercy toward your friends,
    your just defense of the upright of heart. **R.**

See Matthew 11:25
R. Alleluia, alleluia.
Blessed are you, Father, Lord of heaven and earth;
you have revealed to little ones the mysteries of the Kingdom. **R.**

✝ *Matthew 13:10-17*
*Because knowledge of the mysteries of the Kingdom of heaven
has been granted to you, but to them it has not been granted.*

The disciples approached Jesus and said,
    "Why do you speak to the crowd in parables?"
He said to them in reply,
    "Because knowledge of the mysteries of the Kingdom of heaven
    has been granted to you, but to them it has not been granted.
To anyone who has, more will be given and he will grow rich;
    from anyone who has not, even what he has will be taken away.
This is why I speak to them in parables, because
    they look but do not see and hear but do not listen or understand.
Isaiah's prophecy is fulfilled in them, which says:

*You shall indeed hear but not understand,
    you shall indeed look but never see.
Gross is the heart of this people,
    they will hardly hear with their ears,
      they have closed their eyes,
      lest they see with their eyes
    and hear with their ears*

and understand with their hearts and be converted
  and I heal them.

"But blessed are your eyes, because they see,
  and your ears, because they hear.
Amen, I say to you, many prophets and righteous people
  longed to see what you see but did not see it,
  and to hear what you hear but did not hear it." ✛

FRIDAY, JULY 22
St. Mary Magdalene

† Song of Songs 3:1-4b (or 2 Corinthians 5:14-17)
I have found him who my heart loves.

The Bride says:
On my bed at night I sought him
  whom my heart loves—
  I sought him but I did not find him.
I will rise then and go about the city;
  in the streets and crossings I will seek
Him who my heart loves.
  I sought him but I did not find him.
The watchmen came upon me,
  as they made their rounds of the city:
  Have you seen him whom my heart loves?
I had hardly left them
  when I found him whom my heart loves. ✛

Psalm 63:2, 3-4, 5-6, 8-9
R. (2) **My soul is thirsting for you, O Lord my God.**
O God, you are my God whom I seek;
  for you my flesh pines and my soul thirsts
  like the earth, parched, lifeless and without water. **R.**
Thus have I gazed toward you in the sanctuary
  to see your power and your glory,
For your kindness is greater good than life;
  my lips shall glorify you. **R.**
Thus will I bless you while I live;
  lifting up my hands, I will call upon your name.
As the riches of a banquet shall my soul be satisfied,
  and with exultant lips my mouth shall praise you. **R.**
You are my help,
  and in the shadow of your wings I shout for joy.
My soul clings to you;
  your right hand upholds me. **R.**

R. Alleluia, alleluia.
Tell us, Mary, what did you see on the way?
I saw the glory of the risen Christ, I saw his empty tomb. **R.**

† *John 20:1-2, 11-18*
Woman, why are you weeping? Whom are you looking for?

On the first day of the week,
  Mary Magdalene came to the tomb early in the morning,
  while it was still dark,
  and saw the stone removed from the tomb.
So she ran and went to Simon Peter
  and to the other disciple whom Jesus loved, and told them,
  "They have taken the Lord from the tomb,
  and we don't know where they put him."

Mary stayed outside the tomb weeping.
And as she wept, she bent over into the tomb
  and saw two angels in white sitting there,
  one at the head and one at the feet
  where the Body of Jesus had been.
And they said to her, "Woman, why are you weeping?"
She said to them, "They have taken my Lord,
  and I don't know where they laid him."
When she had said this, she turned around and saw Jesus there,
  but did not know it was Jesus.
Jesus said to her, "Woman, why are you weeping?
Whom are you looking for?"
She thought it was the gardener and said to him,
  "Sir, if you carried him away,
  tell me where you laid him,
  and I will take him."
Jesus said to her, "Mary!"
She turned and said to him in Hebrew,
  "Rabbouni," which means Teacher.
Jesus said to her,
  "Stop holding on to me, for I have not yet ascended to the Father.
But go to my brothers and tell them,
  'I am going to my Father and your Father,
  to my God and your God.'"
Mary Magdalene went and announced to the disciples,
  "I have seen the Lord,"
  and then reported what he told her. ✛

SATURDAY, JULY 23
WEEKDAY, ST. BRIDGET, *[BVM]*

† *Jeremiah 7:1-11*
*Has this house which bears my name
become in your eyes a den of thieves?*

The following message came to Jeremiah from the LORD:
Stand at the gate of the house of the LORD,
and there proclaim this message:
Hear the word of the LORD, all you of Judah
who enter these gates to worship the LORD!
Thus says the LORD of hosts, the God of Israel:
Reform your ways and your deeds,
so that I may remain with you in this place.
Put not your trust in the deceitful words:
"This is the temple of the LORD!
The temple of the LORD! The temple of the LORD!"
Only if you thoroughly reform your ways and your deeds;
if each of you deals justly with his neighbor;
if you no longer oppress the resident alien,
the orphan, and the widow;
if you no longer shed innocent blood in this place,
or follow strange gods to your own harm,
will I remain with you in this place,
in the land I gave your fathers long ago and forever.

But here you are, putting your trust in deceitful words to your own
loss!
Are you to steal and murder, commit adultery and perjury,
burn incense to Baal,
go after strange gods that you know not,
and yet come to stand before me
in this house which bears my name, and say:
"We are safe; we can commit all these abominations again"?
Has this house which bears my name
become in your eyes a den of thieves?
I too see what is being done, says the LORD. ✚

Psalm 84:3, 4, 5-6a and 8a, 11
R. (2) **How lovely is your dwelling place, Lord, mighty God!**
My soul yearns and pines
for the courts of the LORD.
My heart and my flesh
cry out for the living God. **R.**

Even the sparrow finds a home,
  and the swallow a nest
  in which she puts her young—
Your altars, O LORD of hosts,
  my king and my God! **R.**
Blessed they who dwell in your house!
  continually they praise you.
Blessed the men whose strength you are!
They go from strength to strength. **R.**
I had rather one day in your courts
  than a thousand elsewhere;
I had rather lie at the threshold of the house of my God
  than dwell in the tents of the wicked. **R.**

James 1:21bc
R. Alleluia, alleluia.
Humbly welcome the word that has been planted in you
and is able to save your souls. **R.**

✝ Matthew 13:24-30
Let them grow together until harvest.

Jesus proposed a parable to the crowds.
"The Kingdom of heaven may be likened to a man
  who sowed good seed in his field.
While everyone was asleep his enemy came
  and sowed weeds all through the wheat, and then went off.
When the crop grew and bore fruit, the weeds appeared as well.
The slaves of the householder came to him and said,
  'Master, did you not sow good seed in your field?
Where have the weeds come from?'
He answered, 'An enemy has done this.'
His slaves said to him, 'Do you want us to go and pull them up?'
He replied, 'No, if you pull up the weeds
  you might uproot the wheat along with them.
Let them grow together until harvest;
  then at harvest time I will say to the harvesters,
  "First collect the weeds and tie them in bundles for burning;
  but gather the wheat into my barn.""" ✝

SUNDAY, JULY 24
SEVENTEENTH SUNDAY IN ORDINARY TIME

† *Genesis 18:20-32*
Let not my Lord grow angry if I speak.

In those days, the LORD said:
"The outcry against Sodom and Gomorrah is so great,
  and their sin so grave,
  that I must go down and see whether or not their actions
  fully correspond to the cry against them that comes to me.
I mean to find out."

While Abraham's visitors walked on farther toward Sodom,
  the LORD remained standing before Abraham.
Then Abraham drew nearer and said:
  "Will you sweep away the innocent with the guilty?
Suppose there were fifty innocent people in the city;
  would you wipe out the place, rather than spare it
  for the sake of the fifty innocent people within it?
Far be it from you to do such a thing,
  to make the innocent die with the guilty
  so that the innocent and the guilty would be treated alike!
Should not the judge of all the world act with justice?"
The LORD replied,
  "If I find fifty innocent people in the city of Sodom,
  I will spare the whole place for their sake."
Abraham spoke up again:
  "See how I am presuming to speak to my Lord,
  though I am but dust and ashes!
What if there are five less than fifty innocent people?
Will you destroy the whole city because of those five?"
He answered, "I will not destroy it, if I find forty-five there."
But Abraham persisted, saying, "What if only forty are found there?"
He replied, "I will forbear doing it for the sake of the forty."
Then Abraham said, "Let not my Lord grow impatient if I go on.
What if only thirty are found there?"
He replied, "I will forbear doing it if I can find but thirty there."
Still Abraham went on,
  "Since I have thus dared to speak to my Lord,
  what if there are no more than twenty?"
The LORD answered, "I will not destroy it, for the sake of the twenty."
But he still persisted:
  "Please, let not my Lord grow angry if I speak up this last time.
What if there are at least ten there?"
He replied, "For the sake of those ten, I will not destroy it." ✛

Psalm 138:1-2, 2-3, 6-7, 7-8

R. (3a) **Lord, on the day I called for help, you answered me.**

I will give thanks to you, O LORD, with all my heart,
   for you have heard the words of my mouth;
   in the presence of the angels I will sing your praise;
I will worship at your holy temple
   and give thanks to your name. **R.**
Because of your kindness and your truth;
   for you have made great above all things
   your name and your promise.
When I called you answered me;
   you built up strength within me. **R.**
The LORD is exalted, yet the lowly he sees,
   and the proud he knows from afar.
Though I walk amid distress, you preserve me;
   against the anger of my enemies you raise your hand. **R.**
Your right hand saves me.
   The LORD will complete what he has done for me;
your kindness, O LORD, endures forever;
   forsake not the work of your hands. **R.**

† Colossians 2:12-14

God has brought you to life along with Christ,
having forgiven us all our transgressions.

Brothers and sisters:
You were buried with him in baptism,
   in which you were also raised with him
   through faith in the power of God,
   who raised him from the dead.
And even when you were dead
   in transgressions and the uncircumcision of your flesh,
   he brought you to life along with him,
   having forgiven us all our transgressions;
   obliterating the bond against us, with its legal claims,
   which was opposed to us,
   he also removed it from our midst, nailing it to the cross. ✛

Romans 8:15bc

R. Alleluia, alleluia.

You have received a Spirit of adoption,
through which we cry, Abba, Father. **R.**

†Luke 11:1-13
Ask and you will receive.

Jesus was praying in a certain place, and when he had finished,
 one of his disciples said to him,
 "Lord, teach us to pray just as John taught his disciples."
He said to them, "When you pray, say:
 Father, hallowed be your name,
  your kingdom come.
  Give us each day our daily bread
  and forgive us our sins
  for we ourselves forgive everyone in debt to us,
  and do not subject us to the final test."

And he said to them, "Suppose one of you has a friend
 to whom he goes at midnight and says,
 'Friend, lend me three loaves of bread,
 for a friend of mine has arrived at my house from a journey
 and I have nothing to offer him,'
 and he says in reply from within,
 'Do not bother me; the door has already been locked
 and my children and I are already in bed.
I cannot get up to give you anything.'
I tell you,
 if he does not get up to give the visitor the loaves
 because of their friendship,
 he will get up to give him whatever he needs
 because of his persistence.

"And I tell you, ask and you will receive;
 seek and you will find;
 knock and the door will be opened to you.
For everyone who asks, receives;
 and the one who seeks, finds;
 and to the one who knocks, the door will be opened.
What father among you would hand his son a snake
 when he asks for a fish?
Or hand him a scorpion when he asks for an egg?
If you then, who are wicked,
 know how to give good gifts to your children,
 how much more will the Father in heaven
 give the Holy Spirit to those who ask him?" ✛

MONDAY, JULY 25
St. James

† 2 Corinthians 4:7-15
Always carrying about in the body the dying of Jesus.

Brothers and sisters:
We hold this treasure in earthen vessels,
    that the surpassing power may be of God and not from us.
We are afflicted in every way, but not constrained;
    perplexed, but not driven to despair;
    persecuted, but not abandoned;
    struck down, but not destroyed;
    always carrying about in the body the dying of Jesus,
    so that the life of Jesus may also be manifested in our body.
For we who live are constantly being given up to death
    for the sake of Jesus,
    so that the life of Jesus may be manifested in our mortal flesh.

So death is at work in us, but life in you.
Since, then, we have the same spirit of faith,
    according to what is written, *I believed, therefore I spoke,*
    we too believe and therefore speak,
    knowing that the one who raised the Lord Jesus
    will raise us also with Jesus
    and place us with you in his presence.
Everything indeed is for you,
    so that the grace bestowed in abundance on more and more people
    may cause the thanksgiving to overflow for the glory of God. ✛

Psalm 126:1bc-2ab, 2cd-3, 4-5, 6

R. (5) **Those who sow in tears shall reap rejoicing.**
When the LORD brought back the captives of Zion,
    we were like men dreaming.
Then our mouth was filled with laughter,
    and our tongue with rejoicing. **R.**
Then they said among the nations,
    "The LORD has done great things for them."
The LORD has done great things for us;
    we are glad indeed. **R.**
Restore our fortunes, O LORD,
    like the torrents in the southern desert.
Those that sow in tears
    shall reap rejoicing. **R.**

Although they go forth weeping,
  carrying the seed to be sown,
They shall come back rejoicing,
  carrying their sheaves. **R.**

See John 15:16
R. Alleluia, alleluia.
I chose you from the world,
to go and bear fruit that will last, says the Lord. **R.**

† *Matthew 20:20-28*
You will drink my chalice.

The mother of the sons of Zebedee approached Jesus with her sons
  and did him homage, wishing to ask him for something.
He said to her,
  "What do you wish?"
She answered him,
  "Command that these two sons of mine sit,
  one at your right and the other at your left, in your Kingdom."
Jesus said in reply,
  "You do not know what you are asking.
Can you drink the chalice that I am going to drink?"
They said to him, "We can."
He replied,
  "My chalice you will indeed drink,
  but to sit at my right and at my left, this is not mine to give
  but is for those for whom it has been prepared by my Father."
When the ten heard this,
  they became indignant at the two brothers.
But Jesus summoned them and said,
  "You know that the rulers of the Gentiles lord it over them,
  and the great ones make their authority over them felt.
But it shall not be so among you.
Rather, whoever wishes to be great among you shall be your servant;
  whoever wishes to be first among you shall be your slave.
Just so, the Son of Man did not come to be served
  but to serve and to give his life as a ransom for many." ✛

TUESDAY, JULY 26
ST. JOACHIM, ST. ANNE

† *Jeremiah 14:17-22*
Remember, Lord, your covenant with us and break it not.

Let my eyes stream with tears
  day and night, without rest,
Over the great destruction which overwhelms
  the virgin daughter of my people,
  over her incurable wound.
If I walk out into the field,
  look! those slain by the sword;
If I enter the city,
  look! those consumed by hunger.
Even the prophet and the priest
  forage in a land they know not.

Have you cast Judah off completely?
  Is Zion loathsome to you?
Why have you struck us a blow
  that cannot be healed?
We wait for peace, to no avail;
  for a time of healing, but terror comes instead.
We recognize, O LORD, our wickedness,
  the guilt of our fathers;
  that we have sinned against you.
For your name's sake spurn us not,
  disgrace not the throne of your glory;
  remember your covenant with us, and break it not.
Among the nations' idols is there any that gives rain?
  Or can the mere heavens send showers?
Is it not you alone, O LORD,
  our God, to whom we look?
  You alone have done all these things. ✛

Psalm 79:8, 9, 11 and 13
R. (9) For the glory of your name, O Lord, deliver us.
Remember not against us the iniquities of the past;
  may your compassion quickly come to us,
  for we are brought very low. **R.**
Help us, O God our savior,
  because of the glory of your name;
Deliver us and pardon our sins
  for your name's sake. **R.**

Let the prisoners' sighing come before you;
  with your great power free those doomed to death.
Then we, your people and the sheep of your pasture,
  will give thanks to you forever;
  through all generations we will declare your praise. **R.**

R. Alleluia, alleluia.
The seed is the word of God, Christ is the sower;
all who come to him will live for ever. **R.**

† *Matthew 13:36-43*
*Just as the weeds are collected now and burned up with fire,
so will it be at the end of the age.*

Jesus dismissed the crowds and went into the house.
His disciples approached him and said,
  "Explain to us the parable of the weeds in the field."
He said in reply, "He who sows good seed is the Son of Man,
  the field is the world, the good seed the children of the Kingdom.
The weeds are the children of the Evil One,
  and the enemy who sows them is the Devil.
The harvest is the end of the age, and the harvesters are angels.
Just as weeds are collected and burned up with fire,
  so will it be at the end of the age.
The Son of Man will send his angels,
  and they will collect out of his Kingdom
  all who cause others to sin and all evildoers.
They will throw them into the fiery furnace,
  where there will be wailing and grinding of teeth.
Then the righteous will shine like the sun
  in the Kingdom of their Father.
Whoever has ears ought to hear." ✛

WEDNESDAY, JULY 27
WEEKDAY

† *Jeremiah 15:10, 16-21*
Why is my pain continuous?—If you repent, you shall stand in my presence.

Woe to me, mother, that you gave me birth!
  a man of strife and contention to all the land!
I neither borrow nor lend,
  yet all curse me.
When I found your words, I devoured them;
  they became my joy and the happiness of my heart,
Because I bore your name,
  O LORD, God of hosts.

I did not sit celebrating
   in the circle of merrymakers;
Under the weight of your hand I sat alone
   because you filled me with indignation.
Why is my pain continuous,
   my wound incurable, refusing to be healed?
You have indeed become for me a treacherous brook,
   whose waters do not abide!
     Thus the LORD answered me:
If you repent, so that I restore you,
   in my presence you shall stand;
If you bring forth the precious without the vile,
   you shall be my mouthpiece.
Then it shall be they who turn to you,
   and you shall not turn to them;
And I will make you toward this people
   a solid wall of brass.
Though they fight against you,
   they shall not prevail,
For I am with you,
   to deliver and rescue you, says the LORD.
I will free you from the hand of the wicked,
   and rescue you from the grasp of the violent. ✛

Psalm 59:2-3, 4, 10-11, 17, 18
R. (17d) God is my refuge on the day of distress.
Rescue me from my enemies, O my God;
   from my adversaries defend me.
Rescue me from evildoers;
   from bloodthirsty men save me. **R.**
For behold, they lie in wait for my life;
   mighty men come together against me,
Not for any offense or sin of mine, O LORD. **R.**
O my strength! for you I watch;
   for you, O God, are my stronghold,
As for my God, may his mercy go before me;
   may he show me the fall of my foes. **R.**
But I will sing of your strength
   and revel at dawn in your mercy;
You have been my stronghold,
   my refuge in the day of distress. **R.**
O my strength! your praise will I sing;
   for you, O God, are my stronghold,
   my merciful God! **R.**

John 15:15b
R. Alleluia, alleluia.
I call you my friends, says the Lord,
for I have made known to you all that the Father has told me. **R.**

✝ *Matthew 13:44-46*
He sells all he has and buys that field.

Jesus said to his disciples:
"The Kingdom of heaven is like a treasure buried in a field,
   which a person finds and hides again,
   and out of joy goes and sells all that he has and buys that field.
Again, the Kingdom of heaven is like a merchant
   searching for fine pearls.
When he finds a pearl of great price,
   he goes and sells all that he has and buys it." ✛

THURSDAY, JULY 28
WEEKDAY

✝ *Jeremiah 18:1-6*
Like the clay in the hand of the potter,
so are you in my hand, house of Israel.

This word came to Jeremiah from the LORD:
Rise up, be off to the potter's house;
   there I will give you my message.
I went down to the potter's house and there he was,
   working at the wheel.
Whenever the object of clay which he was making
   turned out badly in his hand,
   he tried again,
   making of the clay another object of whatever sort he pleased.
Then the word of the LORD came to me:
   Can I not do to you, house of Israel,
   as this potter has done? says the LORD.
Indeed, like clay in the hand of the potter,
   so are you in my hand, house of Israel. ✛

Psalm 146:1b-2, 3-4, 5-6ab
R. (5a) Blessed is he whose help is the God of Jacob.
   *(or **Alleluia**.)*
Praise the LORD, O my soul;
   I will praise the LORD all my life;
   I will sing praise to my God while I live. **R.**
Put not your trust in princes,
   in the sons of men, in whom there is no salvation.

When his spirit departs he returns to his earth;
   on that day his plans perish. **R.**
Blessed he whose help is the God of Jacob,
   whose hope is in the LORD, his God.
Who made heaven and earth,
   the sea and all that is in them. **R.**

   See Acts 16:14b
R. Alleluia, alleluia.
Open our hearts, O Lord,
to listen to the words of your Son. **R.**

† *Matthew 13:47-53*
They put what is good into buckets, what is bad they throw away.

Jesus said to the disciples:
"The Kingdom of heaven is like a net thrown into the sea,
   which collects fish of every kind.
When it is full they haul it ashore
   and sit down to put what is good into buckets.
What is bad they throw away.
Thus it will be at the end of the age.
The angels will go out and separate the wicked from the righteous
   and throw them into the fiery furnace,
   where there will be wailing and grinding of teeth."

"Do you understand all these things?"
They answered, "Yes."
And he replied,
   "Then every scribe who has been instructed in the Kingdom of
      heaven
   is like the head of a household who brings from his storeroom
   both the new and the old."
When Jesus finished these parables, he went away from there. ✛

FRIDAY, JULY 29
STS. MARTHA, MARY AND LAZARUS

† *Jeremiah 26:1-9*
All the people gathered about Jeremiah in the house of the LORD.

In the beginning of the reign of Jehoiakim,
   son of Josiah, king of Judah,
   this message came from the LORD:
      Thus says the LORD:
   Stand in the court of the house of the LORD
   and speak to the people of all the cities of Judah

who come to worship in the house of the LORD;
   whatever I command you, tell them, and omit nothing.
Perhaps they will listen and turn back,
   each from his evil way,
   so that I may repent of the evil I have planned to inflict upon them
   for their evil deeds.
Say to them: Thus says the LORD:
   If you disobey me,
   not living according to the law I placed before you
   and not listening to the words of my servants the prophets,
   whom I send you constantly though you do not obey them,
   I will treat this house like Shiloh,
   and make this the city to which all the nations of the earth
   shall refer when cursing another.

Now the priests, the prophets, and all the people
   heard Jeremiah speak these words in the house of the LORD.
When Jeremiah finished speaking
   all that the LORD bade him speak to all the people,
   the priests and prophets laid hold of him, crying,
   "You must be put to death!
Why do you prophesy in the name of the LORD:
   'This house shall be like Shiloh,' and
   'This city shall be desolate and deserted'?"
And all the people gathered about Jeremiah in the house of the
   LORD. ✝

   Psalm 69:5, 8-10, 14
R. (14c) **Lord, in your great love, answer me.**
Those outnumber the hairs of my head
   who hate me without cause.
Too many for my strength
   are they who wrongfully are my enemies.
   Must I restore what I did not steal? **R.**
Since for your sake I bear insult,
   and shame covers my face.
I have become an outcast to my brothers,
   a stranger to my mother's sons,
Because zeal for your house consumes me,
   and the insults of those who blaspheme you fall upon me. **R.**
But I pray to you, O LORD,
   for the time of your favor, O God!
In your great kindness answer me
   with your constant help. **R.**

John 8:12

R. Alleluia, alleluia.

I am the light of the world, says the Lord;
whoever follows me will have the light of life. **R.**

† *John 11:19-27 (or Luke 10:38-42)*
I have come to believe that you are the Christ, the Son of God.

Many of the Jews had come to Martha and Mary
   to comfort them about their brother [Lazarus, who had died].
When Martha heard that Jesus was coming,
   she went to meet him;
   but Mary sat at home.
Martha said to Jesus,
   "Lord, if you had been here,
   my brother would not have died.
But even now I know that whatever you ask of God,
   God will give you."
Jesus said to her,
   "Your brother will rise."
Martha said to him,
   "I know he will rise,
   in the resurrection on the last day."
Jesus told her,
   "I am the resurrection and the life;
   whoever believes in me, even if he dies, will live,
   and anyone who lives and believes in me will never die.
Do you believe this?"
She said to him, "Yes, Lord.
I have come to believe that you are the Christ, the Son of God,
   the one who is coming into the world." **✝**

SATURDAY, JULY 30
WEEKDAY, ST. PETER CHYSOLOGUS, *[BVM]*

† *Jeremiah 26:11-16, 24*
For in truth it was the LORD who sent me to you,
to speak all these things for you to hear.

The priests and prophets said to the princes and to all the people,
   "This man deserves death;
   he has prophesied against this city,
   as you have heard with your own ears."
Jeremiah gave this answer to the princes and all the people:
   "It was the LORD who sent me to prophesy against this house and
      city
   all that you have heard.

Now, therefore, reform your ways and your deeds;
   listen to the voice of the Lord your God,
   so that the Lord will repent of the evil with which he threatens you.
As for me, I am in your hands;
   do with me what you think good and right.
But mark well: if you put me to death,
   it is innocent blood you bring on yourselves,
   on this city and its citizens.
For in truth it was the Lord who sent me to you,
   to speak all these things for you to hear."

Thereupon the princes and all the people
   said to the priests and the prophets,
   "This man does not deserve death;
   it is in the name of the Lord, our God, that he speaks to us."

So Ahikam, son of Shaphan, protected Jeremiah,
   so that he was not handed over to the people to be put to death. ✝

Psalm 69:15-16, 30-31, 33-34
R. (14c) **Lord, in your great love, answer me.**
Rescue me out of the mire; may I not sink!
   may I be rescued from my foes,
   and from the watery depths.
Let not the flood-waters overwhelm me,
   nor the abyss swallow me up,
   nor the pit close its mouth over me. **R.**
But I am afflicted and in pain;
   let your saving help, O God, protect me.
I will praise the name of God in song,
   and I will glorify him with thanksgiving. **R.**
"See, you lowly ones, and be glad;
   you who seek God, may your hearts revive!
For the Lord hears the poor,
   and his own who are in bonds he spurns not." **R.**

Matthew 5:10
R. Alleluia, alleluia.
Blessed are they who are persecuted for the sake of righteousness
for theirs is the Kingdom of heaven. **R.**

† *Matthew 14:1-12*

Herod had John beheaded; John's disciples came and told Jesus.

Herod the tetrarch heard of the reputation of Jesus
  and said to his servants, "This man is John the Baptist.
He has been raised from the dead;
  that is why mighty powers are at work in him."

Now Herod had arrested John, bound him, and put him in prison
  on account of Herodias, the wife of his brother Philip,
  for John had said to him,
  "It is not lawful for you to have her."
Although he wanted to kill him, he feared the people,
  for they regarded him as a prophet.
But at a birthday celebration for Herod,
  the daughter of Herodias performed a dance before the guests
  and delighted Herod so much
  that he swore to give her whatever she might ask for.
Prompted by her mother, she said,
  "Give me here on a platter the head of John the Baptist."
The king was distressed,
  but because of his oaths and the guests who were present,
  he ordered that it be given, and he had John beheaded in the
    prison.
His head was brought in on a platter and given to the girl,
  who took it to her mother.
His disciples came and took away the corpse
  and buried him; and they went and told Jesus. ✝

SUNDAY, JULY 31
EIGHTEENTH SUNDAY IN ORDINARY TIME

† *Ecclesiastes 1:2; 2:21-23*

What profit comes to a man from all his toil?

Vanity of vanities, says Qoheleth,
  vanity of vanities! All things are vanity!

Here is one who has labored with wisdom and knowledge and skill,
  and yet to another who has not labored over it,
  he must leave property.
This also is vanity and a great misfortune.
For what profit comes to man from all the toil and anxiety of heart
  with which he has labored under the sun?
All his days sorrow and grief are his occupation;
  even at night his mind is not at rest.
This also is vanity. ✝

Psalm 90:3-4, 5-6, 12-13, 14 and 17

R. (1) **If today you hear his voice, harden not your hearts.**
You turn man back to dust,
   saying, "Return, O children of men."
For a thousand years in your sight
   are as yesterday, now that it is past,
   or as a watch of the night. **R.**
You make an end of them in their sleep;
   the next morning they are like the changing grass,
which at dawn springs up anew,
   but by evening wilts and fades. **R.**
Teach us to number our days aright,
   that we may gain wisdom of heart.
Return, O LORD! How long?
   Have pity on your servants! **R.**
Fill us at daybreak with your kindness,
   that we may shout for joy and gladness all our days.
And may the gracious care of the LORD our God be ours;
   prosper the work of our hands for us!
   Prosper the work of our hands! **R.**

† *Colossians 3:1-5, 9-11*
Seek what is above, where Christ is.

Brothers and sisters:
If you were raised with Christ, seek what is above,
   where Christ is seated at the right hand of God.
Think of what is above, not of what is on earth.
For you have died,
   and your life is hidden with Christ in God.
When Christ your life appears,
   then you too will appear with him in glory.

Put to death, then, the parts of you that are earthly:
   immorality, impurity, passion, evil desire,
   and the greed that is idolatry.
Stop lying to one another,
   since you have taken off the old self with its practices
   and have put on the new self,
   which is being renewed, for knowledge,
   in the image of its creator.
Here there is not Greek and Jew,
   circumcision and uncircumcision,
   barbarian, Scythian, slave, free;
   but Christ is all and in all. ✛

Matthew 5:3

R. Alleluia, alleluia.

Blessed are the poor in spirit,
for theirs is the kingdom of heaven. **R.**

† *Luke 12:13-21*

The things you have prepared, to whom will they belong?

Someone in the crowd said to Jesus,
  "Teacher, tell my brother to share the inheritance with me."
He replied to him,
  "Friend, who appointed me as your judge and arbitrator?"
Then he said to the crowd,
  "Take care to guard against all greed,
  for though one may be rich,
  one's life does not consist of possessions."

Then he told them a parable.
"There was a rich man whose land produced a bountiful harvest.
He asked himself, 'What shall I do,
  for I do not have space to store my harvest?'
And he said, 'This is what I shall do:
  I shall tear down my barns and build larger ones.
There I shall store all my grain and other goods
  and I shall say to myself, "Now as for you,
  you have so many good things stored up for many years,
  rest, eat, drink, be merry!"'
But God said to him,
  'You fool, this night your life will be demanded of you;
  and the things you have prepared, to whom will they belong?'
Thus will it be for all who store up treasure for themselves
  but are not rich in what matters to God." ✝

MONDAY, AUGUST 1
St. Alphonsus Liguori

† *Jeremiah 28:1-17*
*The Lord has not sent you, and you have
raised false confidence in this people.*

In the beginning of the reign of Zedekiah, king of Judah,
  in the fifth month of the fourth year,
  the prophet Hananiah, son of Azzur, from Gibeon,
  said to me in the house of the Lord
  in the presence of the priests and all the people:
  "Thus says the Lord of hosts, the God of Israel:
  'I will break the yoke of the king of Babylon.
Within two years I will restore to this place
  all the vessels of the temple of the Lord which Nebuchadnezzar,
  king of Babylon, took away from this place to Babylon.
And I will bring back to this place Jeconiah,
  son of Jehoiakim, king of Judah,
  and all the exiles of Judah who went to Babylon,' says the Lord,
  'for I will break the yoke of the king of Babylon.'"

The prophet Jeremiah answered the prophet Hananiah
  in the presence of the priests and all the people assembled
  in the house of the Lord, and said:
  Amen! thus may the Lord do!
May he fulfill the things you have prophesied
  by bringing the vessels of the house of the Lord
  and all the exiles back from Babylon to this place!
But now, listen to what I am about to state in your hearing
  and the hearing of all the people.
From of old, the prophets who were before you and me prophesied
  war, woe, and pestilence against many lands and mighty kingdoms.
But the prophet who prophesies peace
  is recognized as truly sent by the Lord
  only when his prophetic prediction is fulfilled.

Thereupon the prophet Hananiah took the yoke
  from the neck of the prophet Jeremiah and broke it,
  and said in the presence of all the people:
  "Thus says the Lord: 'Even so, within two years
  I will break the yoke of Nebuchadnezzar, king of Babylon,
  from off the neck of all the nations.'"
At that, the prophet Jeremiah went away.

Some time after the prophet Hananiah had broken the yoke
  from off the neck of the prophet Jeremiah,

The word of the LORD came to Jeremiah:
  Go tell Hananiah this:
  Thus says the LORD:
  By breaking a wooden yoke, you forge an iron yoke!
For thus says the LORD of hosts, the God of Israel:
  A yoke of iron I will place on the necks
  of all these nations serving Nebuchadnezzar, king of Babylon,
  and they shall serve him; even the beasts of the field I give him.

To the prophet Hananiah the prophet Jeremiah said:
  Hear this, Hananiah!
The LORD has not sent you,
  and you have raised false confidence in this people.
For this, says the LORD, I will dispatch you from the face of the earth;
  this very year you shall die,
  because you have preached rebellion against the LORD.
That same year, in the seventh month, Hananiah the prophet died. ✛

Psalm 119:29, 43, 79, 80, 95, 102

R. (68b) **Lord, teach me your statutes.**

Remove from me the way of falsehood,
  and favor me with your law. **R.**
Take not the word of truth from my mouth,
  for in your ordinances is my hope. **R.**
Let those turn to me who fear you
  and acknowledge your decrees. **R.**
Let my heart be perfect in your statutes,
  that I be not put to shame. **R.**
Sinners wait to destroy me,
  but I pay heed to your decrees. **R.**
From your ordinances I turn not away,
  for you have instructed me. **R.**

Matthew 14:13-21

R. Alleluia, alleluia.

One does not live on bread alone,
but on every word that comes forth from the mouth of God. **R.**

† *Matthew 14:13-21*

*Looking up to heaven, he said the blessing and gave the loaves to the disciples,
who in turn gave them to the crowds.*

When Jesus heard of the death of John the Baptist,
  he withdrew in a boat to a deserted place by himself.
The crowds heard of this and followed him on foot from their towns.
When he disembarked and saw the vast crowd,
  his heart was moved with pity for them, and he cured their sick.

When it was evening, the disciples approached him and said,
  "This is a deserted place and it is already late;
  dismiss the crowds so that they can go to the villages
  and buy food for themselves."
He said to them, "There is no need for them to go away;
  give them some food yourselves."
But they said to him,
  "Five loaves and two fish are all we have here."
Then he said, "Bring them here to me,"
  and he ordered the crowds to sit down on the grass.
Taking the five loaves and the two fish, and looking up to heaven,
  he said the blessing, broke the loaves,
  and gave them to the disciples,
  who in turn gave them to the crowds.
They all ate and were satisfied,
  and they picked up the fragments left over—
  twelve wicker baskets full.
Those who ate were about five thousand men,
  not counting women and children. ✛

TUESDAY, AUGUST 2
WEEKDAY, ST. EUSEBIUS OF VERCELLI, ST. PETER JULIAN EYMARD

† Jeremiah 30:1-2, 12-15, 18-22
Because of your numerous sins, I have done this to you.
See! I will restore the tents of Jacob.

The following message came to Jeremiah from the LORD:
  For thus says the LORD, the God of Israel:
  Write all the words I have spoken to you in a book.

  For thus says the LORD:
  Incurable is your wound,
    grievous your bruise;
  There is none to plead your cause,
    no remedy for your running sore,
    no healing for you.
  All your lovers have forgotten you,
    they do not seek you.
  I struck you as an enemy would strike,
    punished you cruelly;
  Why cry out over your wound?
    your pain is without relief.
  Because of your great guilt,
    your numerous sins,
    I have done this to you.

Thus says the LORD:
See! I will restore the tents of Jacob,
   his dwellings I will pity;
City shall be rebuilt upon hill,
   and palace restored as it was.
From them will resound songs of praise,
   the laughter of happy men.
I will make them not few, but many;
   they will not be tiny, for I will glorify them.
His sons shall be as of old,
   his assembly before me shall stand firm;
   I will punish all his oppressors.
His leader shall be one of his own,
   and his rulers shall come from his kin.
When I summon him, he shall approach me;
   how else should one take the deadly risk
   of approaching me? says the LORD.
You shall be my people,
   and I will be your God. ✛

Psalm 102:16-18, 19-21, 29 and 22-23

R. (17) The Lord will build up Zion again, and appear in all his glory.

The nations shall revere your name, O LORD,
   and all the kings of the earth your glory,
When the LORD has rebuilt Zion
   and appeared in his glory;
When he has regarded the prayer of the destitute,
   and not despised their prayer. **R.**
Let this be written for the generation to come,
   and let his future creatures praise the LORD:
"The LORD looked down from his holy height,
   from heaven he beheld the earth,
To hear the groaning of the prisoners,
   to release those doomed to die." **R.**
The children of your servants shall abide,
   and their posterity shall continue in your presence,
That the name of the LORD may be declared on Zion;
   and his praise, in Jerusalem,
When the peoples gather together
   and the kingdoms, to serve the LORD. **R.**

John 1:49b
R. Alleluia, alleluia.
Rabbi, you are the Son of God;
you are the King of Israel. **R.**

✝ Matthew 14:22-36 (or Matthew 15:1-2, 10-14)
Command me to come to you on the water.

Jesus made the disciples get into a boat
 and precede him to the other side of the sea,
 while he dismissed the crowds.
After doing so, he went up on the mountain by himself to pray.
When it was evening he was there alone.
Meanwhile the boat, already a few miles offshore,
 was being tossed about by the waves, for the wind was against it.
During the fourth watch of the night,
 he came toward them, walking on the sea.
When the disciples saw him walking on the sea they were terrified.
"It is a ghost," they said, and they cried out in fear.
At once Jesus spoke to them, "Take courage, it is I; do not be afraid."
Peter said to him in reply,
 "Lord, if it is you, command me to come to you on the water."
He said, "Come."
Peter got out of the boat and began to walk on the water toward Jesus.
But when he saw how strong the wind was he became frightened;
 and, beginning to sink, he cried out, "Lord, save me!"
Immediately Jesus stretched out his hand and caught him,
 and said to him, "O you of little faith, why did you doubt?"
After they got into the boat, the wind died down.
Those who were in the boat did him homage, saying,
 "Truly, you are the Son of God."

After making the crossing, they came to land at Gennesaret.
When the men of that place recognized him,
 they sent word to all the surrounding country.
People brought to him all those who were sick
 and begged him that they might touch only the tassel on his cloak,
 and as many as touched it were healed. ✛

WEDNESDAY, AUGUST 3
WEEKDAY

† *Jeremiah 31:1-7*
With age-old love I have loved you.

At that time, says the LORD,
I will be the God of all the tribes of Israel,
and they shall be my people.
Thus says the LORD:
The people that escaped the sword
have found favor in the desert.
As Israel comes forward to be given his rest,
the LORD appears to him from afar:
With age-old love I have loved you;
so I have kept my mercy toward you.
Again I will restore you, and you shall be rebuilt,
O virgin Israel;
Carrying your festive tambourines,
you shall go forth dancing with the merrymakers.
Again you shall plant vineyards
on the mountains of Samaria;
those who plant them shall enjoy the fruits.
Yes, a day will come when the watchmen
will call out on Mount Ephraim:
"Rise up, let us go to Zion,
to the LORD, our God."

For thus says the LORD:
Shout with joy for Jacob,
exult at the head of the nations;
proclaim your praise and say:
The LORD has delivered his people,
the remnant of Israel. ✢

Jeremiah 31:10, 11-12ab, 13

R. (see 10d) **The Lord will guard us as a shepherd guards his flock.**

Hear the word of the LORD, O nations,
proclaim it on distant isles, and say:
He who scattered Israel, now gathers them together,
he guards them as a shepherd his flock. **R.**
The LORD shall ransom Jacob,
he shall redeem him from the hand of his conqueror.
Shouting, they shall mount the heights of Zion,
they shall come streaming to the LORD's blessings. **R.**

Then the virgins shall make merry and dance,
and young men and old as well.
I will turn their mourning into joy.
I will console and gladden them after their sorrows. **R.**

Luke 7:16
R. Alleluia, alleluia.
A great prophet has arisen in our midst
and God has visited his people. **R.**

✝ *Matthew 15:21-28*
O woman, great is your faith!

At that time, Jesus withdrew to the region of Tyre and Sidon.
And behold, a Canaanite woman of that district came and called out,
"Have pity on me, Lord, Son of David!
My daughter is tormented by a demon."
But Jesus did not say a word in answer to her.
Jesus' disciples came and asked him,
"Send her away, for she keeps calling out after us."
He said in reply,
"I was sent only to the lost sheep of the house of Israel."
But the woman came and did Jesus homage, saying, "Lord, help me."
He said in reply,
"It is not right to take the food of the children
and throw it to the dogs."
She said, "Please, Lord, for even the dogs eat the scraps
that fall from the table of their masters."
Then Jesus said to her in reply,
"O woman, great is your faith!
Let it be done for you as you wish."
And the woman's daughter was healed from that hour. ✛

THURSDAY, AUGUST 4
St. John Vianney

✝ *Jeremiah 31:31-34*
*The days are coming when I will make a new covenant with the house of Israel
and I will remember their sin no more.*

The days are coming, says the LORD,
when I will make a new covenant with the house of Israel
and the house of Judah.
It will not be like the covenant I made with their fathers:
the day I took them by the hand
to lead them forth from the land of Egypt;
for they broke my covenant,
and I had to show myself their master, says the LORD.

But this is the covenant that I will make
  with the house of Israel after those days, says the LORD.
I will place my law within them, and write it upon their hearts;
  I will be their God, and they shall be my people.
No longer will they have need to teach their friends and relatives
  how to know the LORD.
All, from least to greatest, shall know me, says the LORD,
  for I will forgive their evildoing and remember their sin no more. ✙

Psalm 51:12-13, 14-15, 18-19
R. (12a) **Create a clean heart in me, O God.**
A clean heart create for me, O God,
  and a steadfast spirit renew within me.
Cast me not out from your presence,
  and your Holy Spirit take not from me. **R.**
Give me back the joy of your salvation,
  and a willing spirit sustain in me.
I will teach transgressors your ways,
  and sinners shall return to you. **R.**
For you are not pleased with sacrifices;
  should I offer a burnt offering, you would not accept it.
My sacrifice, O God, is a contrite spirit;
  a heart contrite and humbled, O God, you will not spurn. **R.**

Matthew 16:18
R. Alleluia, alleluia.
You are Peter, and upon this rock I will build my Church,
and the gates of the netherworld shall not prevail against it. **R.**

✝ *Matthew 16:13-23*
You are Peter, I will give you the keys to the Kingdom of heaven.

Jesus went into the region of Caesarea Philippi
  and he asked his disciples,
  "Who do people say that the Son of Man is?"
They replied, "Some say John the Baptist, others Elijah,
  still others Jeremiah or one of the prophets."
He said to them, "But who do you say that I am?"
Simon Peter said in reply,
  "You are the Christ, the Son of the living God."
Jesus said to him in reply, "Blessed are you, Simon son of Jonah.
For flesh and blood has not revealed this to you, but my heavenly
    Father.
And so I say to you, you are Peter,
  and upon this rock I will build my Church,
  and the gates of the netherworld shall not prevail against it.

I will give you the keys to the Kingdom of heaven.
Whatever you bind on earth shall be bound in heaven;
    and whatever you loose on earth shall be loosed in heaven."
Then he strictly ordered his disciples
    to tell no one that he was the Christ.

From that time on, Jesus began to show his disciples
    that he must go to Jerusalem and suffer greatly
    from the elders, the chief priests, and the scribes,
    and be killed and on the third day be raised.
Then Peter took Jesus aside and began to rebuke him,
    "God forbid, Lord! No such thing shall ever happen to you."
He turned and said to Peter,
    "Get behind me, Satan! You are an obstacle to me.
You are thinking not as God does, but as human beings do." ✛

FRIDAY, AUGUST 5
WEEKDAY, THE DEDICATION OF THE BASILICA OF ST. MARY MAJOR

† Nahum 2:1, 3; 3:1-3, 6-7
Woe to the city of blood!

See, upon the mountains there advances
    the bearer of good news,
        announcing peace!
Celebrate your feasts, O Judah,
    fulfill your vows!
For nevermore shall you be invaded
    by the scoundrel; he is completely destroyed.
The LORD will restore the vine of Jacob,
    the pride of Israel,
Though ravagers have ravaged them
    and ruined the tendrils.

Woe to the bloody city, all lies,
    full of plunder, whose looting never stops!
The crack of the whip, the rumbling sounds of wheels;
    horses a-gallop, chariots bounding,
Cavalry charging, the flame of the sword, the flash of the spear,
    the many slain, the heaping corpses,
    the endless bodies to stumble upon!
I will cast filth upon you,
    disgrace you and put you to shame;
Till everyone who sees you runs from you, saying,
    "Nineveh is destroyed; who can pity her?
    Where can one find any to console her?" ✛

Deuteronomy 32:35cd–36ab, 39abcd, 41

R. (39c) It is I who deal death and give life.

Close at hand is the day of their disaster,
  and their doom is rushing upon them!
Surely, the LORD shall do justice for his people;
  on his servants he shall have pity. **R.**
"Learn then that I, I alone, am God,
  and there is no god besides me.
It is I who bring both death and life,
  I who inflict wounds and heal them." **R.**
I will sharpen my flashing sword,
  and my hand shall lay hold of my quiver,
"With vengeance I will repay my foes
  and requite those who hate me." **R.**

Matthew 5:10

R. Alleluia, alleluia.

Blessed are they who are persecuted for the sake of righteousness;
for theirs is the Kingdom of heaven. **R.**

† *Matthew 16:24-28*
What can one give in exchange for one's life?

Jesus said to his disciples,
  "Whoever wishes to come after me must deny himself,
  take up his cross, and follow me.
For whoever wishes to save his life will lose it,
  but whoever loses his life for my sake will find it.
What profit would there be for one to gain the whole world
  and forfeit his life?
Or what can one give in exchange for his life?
For the Son of Man will come with his angels in his Father's glory,
  and then he will repay each according to his conduct.
Amen, I say to you, there are some standing here
  who will not taste death
  until they see the Son of Man coming in his Kingdom." ✛

SATURDAY, AUGUST 6
THE TRANSFIGURATION OF THE LORD

† *Daniel 7:9-10, 13-14*
His clothing was snow bright.

As I watched:

Thrones were set up
  and the Ancient One took his throne.

His clothing was bright as snow,
  and the hair on his head as white as wool;
 his throne was flames of fire,
  with wheels of burning fire.
A surging stream of fire
  flowed out from where he sat;
Thousands upon thousands were ministering to him,
  and myriads upon myriads attended him.

The court was convened and the books were opened.
As the visions during the night continued, I saw:

One like a Son of man coming,
  on the clouds of heaven;
When he reached the Ancient One
  and was presented before him,
The one like a Son of man received dominion, glory, and kingship;
  all peoples, nations, and languages serve him.
His dominion is an everlasting dominion
  that shall not be taken away,
  his kingship shall not be destroyed. ✝

Psalm 97:1-2, 5-6, 9

R. (1a and 9a) **The Lord is king, the Most High over all the earth.**
The LORD is king; let the earth rejoice;
  let the many islands be glad.
Clouds and darkness are round about him,
  justice and judgment are the foundation of his throne. **R.**
The mountains melt like wax before the LORD,
  before the LORD of all the earth.
The heavens proclaim his justice,
  and all peoples see his glory. **R.**
Because you, O LORD, are the Most High over all the earth,
  exalted far above all gods. **R.**

✝ *2 Peter 1:16-19*
We ourselves heard this voice come from heaven.

Beloved:
We did not follow cleverly devised myths
  when we made known to you
  the power and coming of our Lord Jesus Christ,
  but we had been eyewitnesses of his majesty.
For he received honor and glory from God the Father
  when that unique declaration came to him from the majestic glory,
  "This is my Son, my beloved, with whom I am well pleased."

We ourselves heard this voice come from heaven
　　while we were with him on the holy mountain.
Moreover, we possess the prophetic message that is altogether reliable.
You will do well to be attentive to it,
　　as to a lamp shining in a dark place,
　　until day dawns and the morning star rises in your hearts. ✛

Matthew 17:5c
R. Alleluia, alleluia.
This is my beloved Son, with whom I am well pleased;
listen to him. **R.**

† *Luke 9:28b-36*
While Jesus was praying his face changed in appearance.

Jesus took Peter, John, and James
　　and went up a mountain to pray.
While he was praying his face changed in appearance
　　and his clothing became dazzling white.
And behold, two men were conversing with him, Moses and Elijah,
　　who appeared in glory and spoke of his exodus
　　that he was going to accomplish in Jerusalem.
Peter and his companions had been overcome by sleep,
　　but becoming fully awake,
　　they saw his glory and the two men standing with him.
As they were about to part from him, Peter said to Jesus,
　　"Master, it is good that we are here;
　　let us make three tents,
　　one for you, one for Moses, and one for Elijah."
But he did not know what he was saying.
While he was still speaking,
　　a cloud came and cast a shadow over them,
　　and they became frightened when they entered the cloud.
Then from the cloud came a voice that said,
　　"This is my chosen Son; listen to him."
After the voice had spoken, Jesus was found alone.
They fell silent and did not at that time
　　tell anyone what they had seen. ✛

SUNDAY, AUGUST 7
NINETEENTH SUNDAY IN ORDINARY TIME

† *Wisdom 18:6-9*
Just as you punished our adversaries,
you glorified us whom you had summoned.

The night of the passover was known beforehand to our fathers,
  that, with sure knowledge of the oaths in which they put their faith,
  they might have courage.
Your people awaited the salvation of the just
  and the destruction of their foes.
For when you punished our adversaries,
  in this you glorified us whom you had summoned.
For in secret the holy children of the good were offering sacrifice
  and putting into effect with one accord the divine institution. ✛

Psalm 33:1, 12, 18-19, 20-22
R. (12b) **Blessed the people the Lord has chosen to be his own.**
Exult, you just, in the LORD;
  praise from the upright is fitting.
Blessed the nation whose God is the LORD,
  the people he has chosen for his own inheritance. **R.**
See, the eyes of the LORD are upon those who fear him,
  upon those who hope for his kindness,
To deliver them from death
  and preserve them in spite of famine. **R.**
Our soul waits for the LORD,
  who is our help and our shield.
May your kindness, O LORD, be upon us
  who have put our hope in you. **R.**

† *Hebrews 11:1-2, 8-19* (or Hebrews 11:1-2, 8-12)
Abraham looked forward to the city whose architect and maker is God.

Brothers and sisters:
Faith is the realization of what is hoped for
  and evidence of things not seen.
Because of it the ancients were well attested.

By faith Abraham obeyed when he was called to go out to a place
  that he was to receive as an inheritance;
  he went out, not knowing where he was to go.
By faith he sojourned in the promised land as in a foreign country,
  dwelling in tents with Isaac and Jacob, heirs of the same promise;
  for he was looking forward to the city with foundations,
  whose architect and maker is God.

By faith he received power to generate,
   even though he was past the normal age
   —and Sarah herself was sterile—
   for he thought that the one who had made the promise was trust-
      worthy.
So it was that there came forth from one man,
   himself as good as dead,
   descendants as numerous as the stars in the sky
   and as countless as the sands on the seashore.

All these died in faith.
They did not receive what had been promised
   but saw it and greeted it from afar
   and acknowledged themselves to be strangers and aliens on earth,
   for those who speak thus show that they are seeking a homeland.
If they had been thinking of the land from which they had come,
   they would have had opportunity to return.
But now they desire a better homeland, a heavenly one.
Therefore, God is not ashamed to be called their God,
   for he has prepared a city for them.

By faith Abraham, when put to the test, offered up Isaac,
   and he who had received the promises was ready to offer his only son,
   of whom it was said,
   "Through Isaac descendants shall bear your name."
He reasoned that God was able to raise even from the dead,
   and he received Isaac back as a symbol ✛

Matthew 24:42a, 44
R. Alleluia, alleluia.
Stay awake and be ready!
For you do not know on what day your Lord will come. **R.**

✝ *Luke 12:32-48* (or Luke 12:35-40)
You also must be prepared.

Jesus said to his disciples:
   "Do not be afraid any longer, little flock,
   for your Father is pleased to give you the kingdom.
Sell your belongings and give alms.
Provide money bags for yourselves that do not wear out,
   an inexhaustible treasure in heaven
   that no thief can reach nor moth destroy.
For where your treasure is, there also will your heart be.

"Gird your loins and light your lamps
    and be like servants who await their master's return from a wedding,
    ready to open immediately when he comes and knocks.
Blessed are those servants
    whom the master finds vigilant on his arrival.
Amen, I say to you, he will gird himself,
    have them recline at table, and proceed to wait on them.
And should he come in the second or third watch
    and find them prepared in this way,
    blessed are those servants.
Be sure of this:
    if the master of the house had known the hour
    when the thief was coming,
    he would not have let his house be broken into.
You also must be prepared, for at an hour you do not expect,
    the Son of Man will come."

Then Peter said,
    "Lord, is this parable meant for us or for everyone?"
And the Lord replied,
    "Who, then, is the faithful and prudent steward
    whom the master will put in charge of his servants
    to distribute the food allowance at the proper time?
Blessed is that servant whom his master on arrival finds doing so.
Truly, I say to you, the master will put the servant
    in charge of all his property.
But if that servant says to himself,
    'My master is delayed in coming,'
    and begins to beat the menservants and the maidservants,
    to eat and drink and get drunk,
    then that servant's master will come
    on an unexpected day and at an unknown hour
    and will punish the servant severely
    and assign him a place with the unfaithful.
That servant who knew his master's will
    but did not make preparations nor act in accord with his will
    shall be beaten severely;
    and the servant who was ignorant of his master's will
    but acted in a way deserving of a severe beating
    shall be beaten only lightly.
Much will be required of the person entrusted with much,
    and still more will be demanded of the person entrusted with
        more." ✛

MONDAY, AUGUST 8
ST. DOMINIC

† *Ezekiel 1:2-5, 24-28c*
Such was the vision of the likeness of the glory of the LORD.

On the fifth day of the fourth month of the fifth year,
    that is, of King Jehoiachin's exile,
The word of the LORD came to the priest Ezekiel,
    the son of Buzi,
    in the land of the Chaldeans by the river Chebar.—
There the hand of the LORD came upon me.

As I looked, a stormwind came from the North,
    a huge cloud with flashing fire enveloped in brightness,
    from the midst of which (the midst of the fire)
    something gleamed like electrum.
Within it were figures resembling four living creatures
    that looked like this: their form was human.

Then I heard the sound of their wings,
    like the roaring of mighty waters,
    like the voice of the Almighty.
When they moved, the sound of the tumult was like the din of an army.
And when they stood still, they lowered their wings.

Above the firmament over their heads
    something like a throne could be seen,
    looking like sapphire.
Upon it was seated, up above, one who had the appearance of a man.
Upward from what resembled his waist I saw what gleamed like
        electrum;
    downward from what resembled his waist I saw what looked like
        fire;
    he was surrounded with splendor.
Like the bow which appears in the clouds on a rainy day
    was the splendor that surrounded him.
Such was the vision of the likeness of the glory of the LORD. ✚

Psalm 148:1-2, 11-12, 13, 14
R. Heaven and earth are filled with your glory. *(or* **Alleluia.***)*
Praise the LORD from the heavens;
    praise him in the heights;
Praise him, all you his angels;
    praise him, all you his hosts. **R.**
Let the kings of the earth and all peoples,
    the princes and all the judges of the earth,

Young men too, and maidens,
  old men and boys, **R.**
Praise the name of the LORD,
  for his name alone is exalted;
His majesty is above earth and heaven. **R.**
And he has lifted up the horn of his people.
Be this his praise from all his faithful ones,
  from the children of Israel, the people close to him.
  Alleluia. **R.**

  See 2 Thessalonians 2:14
R. Alleluia, alleluia.
God has called you through the Gospel
to possess the glory of our Lord Jesus Christ. **R.**

† *Matthew 17:22-27*
They will kill him and he will be raised. The subjects are exempt from the tax.

As Jesus and his disciples were gathering in Galilee,
  Jesus said to them,
  "The Son of Man is to be handed over to men,
  and they will kill him, and he will be raised on the third day."
And they were overwhelmed with grief.

When they came to Capernaum,
  the collectors of the temple tax approached Peter and said,
  "Does not your teacher pay the temple tax?"
"Yes," he said.
When he came into the house, before he had time to speak,
  Jesus asked him, "What is your opinion, Simon?
From whom do the kings of the earth take tolls or census tax?
From their subjects or from foreigners?"
When he said, "From foreigners," Jesus said to him,
  "Then the subjects are exempt.
But that we may not offend them, go to the sea, drop in a hook,
  and take the first fish that comes up.
Open its mouth and you will find a coin worth twice the temple tax.
Give that to them for me and for you." ✤

TUESDAY, AUGUST 9
WEEKDAY, ST. TERESA BENEDICTA OF THE CROSS

† *Ezekiel 2:8—3:4*
He fed me with this scroll, and it was as sweet as honey in my mouth.

The Lord GOD said to me:
As for you, son of man, obey me when I speak to you:
be not rebellious like this house of rebellion,
but open your mouth and eat what I shall give you.

It was then I saw a hand stretched out to me,
in which was a written scroll which he unrolled before me.
It was covered with writing front and back,
and written on it was:
Lamentation and wailing and woe!

He said to me: Son of man, eat what is before you;
eat this scroll, then go, speak to the house of Israel.
So I opened my mouth and he gave me the scroll to eat.
Son of man, he then said to me,
feed your belly and fill your stomach
with this scroll I am giving you.
I ate it, and it was as sweet as honey in my mouth.
He said: Son of man, go now to the house of Israel,
and speak my words to them. ✛

Psalm 119:14, 24, 72, 103, 111, 131
R. (103a) **How sweet to my taste is your promise!**
In the way of your decrees I rejoice,
as much as in all riches. **R.**
Yes, your decrees are my delight;
they are my counselors. **R.**
The law of your mouth is to me more precious
than thousands of gold and silver pieces. **R.**
How sweet to my palate are your promises,
sweeter than honey to my mouth! **R.**
Your decrees are my inheritance forever;
the joy of my heart they are. **R.**
I gasp with open mouth,
in my yearning for your commands. **R.**

Matthew 11:29ab
R. Alleluia, alleluia.
Take my yoke upon you and learn from me,
for I am meek and humble of heart. **R.**

† *Matthew 18:1-5, 10, 12-14*
See that you do not despise one of these little ones.

The disciples approached Jesus and said,
    "Who is the greatest in the Kingdom of heaven?"
He called a child over, placed it in their midst, and said,
    "Amen, I say to you, unless you turn and become like children,
    you will not enter the Kingdom of heaven.
Whoever becomes humble like this child
    is the greatest in the Kingdom of heaven.
And whoever receives one child such as this in my name receives me.

"See that you do not despise one of these little ones,
    for I say to you that their angels in heaven
    always look upon the face of my heavenly Father.
What is your opinion?
If a man has a hundred sheep and one of them goes astray,
    will he not leave the ninety-nine in the hills
    and go in search of the stray?
And if he finds it, amen, I say to you, he rejoices more over it
    than over the ninety-nine that did not stray.
In just the same way, it is not the will of your heavenly Father
    that one of these little ones be lost." ✛

WEDNESDAY, AUGUST 10
ST. LAWRENCE

† *2 Corinthians 9:6-10*
God loves a cheerful giver.

Brothers and sisters:
Whoever sows sparingly will also reap sparingly,
    and whoever sows bountifully will also reap bountifully.
Each must do as already determined, without sadness or compulsion,
    for God loves a cheerful giver.
Moreover, God is able to make every grace abundant for you,
    so that in all things, always having all you need,
    you may have an abundance for every good work.
As it is written:

He scatters abroad, he gives to the poor;
    his righteousness endures forever.

The one who supplies seed to the sower and bread for food
    will supply and multiply your seed
    and increase the harvest of your righteousness. ✛

Psalm 112:1-2, 5-6, 7-8, 9

R. (5) **Blessed the man who is gracious and lends to those in need.**

Blessed the man who fears the LORD,
  who greatly delights in his commands.
His posterity shall be mighty upon the earth;
  the upright generation shall be blessed. **R.**
Well for the man who is gracious and lends,
  who conducts his affairs with justice;
He shall never be moved;
  the just one shall be in everlasting remembrance. **R.**
An evil report he shall not fear;
  his heart is firm, trusting in the LORD.
His heart is steadfast; he shall not fear
  till he looks down upon his foes. **R.**
Lavishly he gives to the poor,
  his generosity shall endure forever;
  his horn shall be exalted in glory. **R.**

John 8:12bc

R. Alleluia, alleluia.

Whoever follows me will not walk in darkness
but will have the light of life, says the Lord. **R.**

✝ *John 12:24-26*

The Father will honor whoever serves me.

Jesus said to his disciples:
"Amen, amen, I say to you,
  unless a grain of wheat falls to the ground and dies,
  it remains just a grain of wheat;
  but if it dies, it produces much fruit.
Whoever loves his life loses it,
  and whoever hates his life in this world
  will preserve it for eternal life.
Whoever serves me must follow me,
  and where I am, there also will my servant be.
The Father will honor whoever serves me." ✝

THURSDAY, AUGUST 11
ST. CLARE

✝Ezekiel 12:1-12

*You shall bring out your baggage like an exile in the daytime
while they are looking on.*

The word of the LORD came to me:
Son of man, you live in the midst of a rebellious house;
  they have eyes to see but do not see,
  and ears to hear but do not hear,
  for they are a rebellious house.
Now, son of man, during the day while they are looking on,
  prepare your baggage as though for exile,
  and again while they are looking on,
  migrate from where you live to another place;
  perhaps they will see that they are a rebellious house.
You shall bring out your baggage like an exile in the daytime
  while they are looking on;
  in the evening, again while they are looking on,
  you shall go out like one of those driven into exile;
  while they look on, dig a hole in the wall and pass through it;
  while they look on, shoulder the burden and set out in the darkness;
  cover your face that you may not see the land,
  for I have made you a sign for the house of Israel.

I did as I was told.
During the day I brought out my baggage
  as though it were that of an exile,
  and at evening I dug a hole through the wall with my hand
  and, while they looked on, set out in the darkness,
  shouldering my burden.

Then, in the morning, the word of the LORD came to me:
  Son of man, did not the house of Israel, that rebellious house,
  ask you what you were doing?
Tell them: Thus says the Lord GOD:
  This oracle concerns Jerusalem
  and the whole house of Israel within it.
I am a sign for you:
  as I have done, so shall it be done to them;
  as captives they shall go into exile.
The prince who is among them shall shoulder his burden
  and set out in darkness,
  going through a hole he has dug out in the wall,
  and covering his face lest he be seen by anyone. ✛

Psalm 78:56-57, 58-59, 61-62
R. (see 7b) **Do not forget the works of the Lord!**
They tempted and rebelled against God the Most High,
  and kept not his decrees.
They turned back and were faithless like their fathers;
  they recoiled like a treacherous bow. **R.**
They angered him with their high places
  and with their idols roused his jealousy.
God heard and was enraged
  and utterly rejected Israel. **R.**
And he surrendered his strength into captivity,
  his glory in the hands of the foe.
He abandoned his people to the sword
  and was enraged against his inheritance. **R.**

Psalm 119:135
R. Alleluia, alleluia.
Let your countenance shine upon your servant
and teach me your statutes. **R.**

† *Matthew 18:21—19:1*
I say to you, not seven times but seventy-seven times.

Peter approached Jesus and asked him,
  "Lord, if my brother sins against me,
  how often must I forgive him?
As many as seven times?"
Jesus answered, "I say to you, not seven times but seventy-seven
    times.
That is why the Kingdom of heaven may be likened to a king
  who decided to settle accounts with his servants.
When he began the accounting,
  a debtor was brought before him who owed him a huge amount.
Since he had no way of paying it back,
  his master ordered him to be sold,
  along with his wife, his children, and all his property,
  in payment of the debt.
At that, the servant fell down, did him homage, and said,
  'Be patient with me, and I will pay you back in full.'
Moved with compassion the master of that servant
  let him go and forgave him the loan.
When that servant had left, he found one of his fellow servants
  who owed him a much smaller amount.
He seized him and started to choke him, demanding,
  'Pay back what you owe.'

Falling to his knees, his fellow servant begged him,
  'Be patient with me, and I will pay you back.'
But he refused.
Instead, he had the fellow servant put in prison
  until he paid back the debt.
Now when his fellow servants saw what had happened,
  they were deeply disturbed,
  and went to their master and reported the whole affair.
His master summoned him and said to him, 'You wicked servant!
I forgave you your entire debt because you begged me to.
Should you not have had pity on your fellow servant,
  as I had pity on you?'
Then in anger his master handed him over to the torturers
  until he should pay back the whole debt.
So will my heavenly Father do to you,
  unless each of you forgives his brother from his heart."

When Jesus finished these words, he left Galilee
  and went to the district of Judea across the Jordan. ✝

FRIDAY, AUGUST 12
WEEKDAY, ST. JANE FRANCES DE CHANTAL

† Ezekiel 16:1-15, 60, 63 (or Ezekiel 16:59-63)
You are perfect because of my splendor which I bestowed on you;
you became a harlot.

The word of the LORD came to me:
Son of man, make known to Jerusalem her abominations.
Thus says the Lord GOD to Jerusalem:
  By origin and birth you are of the land of Canaan;
  your father was an Amorite and your mother a Hittite.
As for your birth, the day you were born your navel cord was not cut;
  you were neither washed with water nor anointed,
  nor were you rubbed with salt, nor swathed in swaddling clothes.
No one looked on you with pity or compassion
  to do any of these things for you.
Rather, you were thrown out on the ground as something loathsome,
  the day you were born.

Then I passed by and saw you weltering in your blood.
I said to you: Live in your blood and grow like a plant in the field.
You grew and developed, you came to the age of puberty;
  your breasts were formed, your hair had grown,
  but you were still stark naked.
Again I passed by you and saw that you were now old enough for love.

So I spread the corner of my cloak over you to cover your nakedness;
    I swore an oath to you and entered into a covenant with you;
    you became mine, says the Lord GOD.
Then I bathed you with water, washed away your blood,
    and anointed you with oil.
I clothed you with an embroidered gown,
    put sandals of fine leather on your feet;
    I gave you a fine linen sash and silk robes to wear.
I adorned you with jewelry: I put bracelets on your arms,
    a necklace about your neck, a ring in your nose,
    pendants in your ears, and a glorious diadem upon your head.
Thus you were adorned with gold and silver;
    your garments were of fine linen, silk, and embroidered cloth.
Fine flour, honey, and oil were your food.
You were exceedingly beautiful, with the dignity of a queen.
You were renowned among the nations for your beauty, perfect as it
        was,
    because of my splendor which I had bestowed on you,
    says the Lord GOD.

But you were captivated by your own beauty,
    you used your renown to make yourself a harlot,
    and you lavished your harlotry on every passer-by,
    whose own you became.

Yet I will remember the covenant I made with you when you were a
        girl,
    and I will set up an everlasting covenant with you,
    that you may remember and be covered with confusion,
    and that you may be utterly silenced for shame
    when I pardon you for all you have done, says the Lord GOD. ✚

Isaiah 12:2-3, 4bcd, 5-6
R. (1c) **You have turned from your anger.**
God indeed is my savior;
    I am confident and unafraid.
My strength and my courage is the LORD,
    and he has been my savior.
With joy you will draw water
    at the fountain of salvation. **R.**
Give thanks to the LORD, acclaim his name;
    among the nations make known his deeds,
    proclaim how exalted is his name. **R.**
Sing praise to the LORD for his glorious achievement;
    let this be known throughout all the earth.

Shout with exultation, O city of Zion,
  for great in your midst
  is the Holy One of Israel! **R.**

  See 1 Thessalonians 2:13
R. Alleluia, alleluia.
Receive the word of God, not as the word of men,
but, as it truly is, the word of God. **R.**

† *Matthew 19:3-12*

Because of the hardness of your hearts Moses allowed you to divorce your wives,
but from the beginning it was not so.

Some Pharisees approached Jesus, and tested him, saying,
  "Is it lawful for a man to divorce his wife for any cause whatever?"
He said in reply, "Have you not read that from the beginning
  the Creator *made them male and female* and said,
  For this reason a man shall leave his father and mother
  and be joined to his wife, and the two shall become one flesh?
So they are no longer two, but one flesh.
Therefore, what God has joined together, man must not separate."
They said to him, "Then why did Moses command
  that the man give the woman a bill of divorce and dismiss her?"
He said to them, "Because of the hardness of your hearts
  Moses allowed you to divorce your wives,
  but from the beginning it was not so.
I say to you, whoever divorces his wife
  (unless the marriage is unlawful)
  and marries another commits adultery."
His disciples said to him,
  "If that is the case of a man with his wife,
  it is better not to marry."
He answered, "Not all can accept this word,
  but only those to whom that is granted.
Some are incapable of marriage because they were born so;
  some, because they were made so by others;
  some, because they have renounced marriage
  for the sake of the Kingdom of heaven.
Whoever can accept this ought to accept it." ✛

SATURDAY, AUGUST 13
WEEKDAY, ST. POPE PONTIAN AND ST. HIPPOLYTUS, *[BVM]*

† *Ezekiel 18:1-10, 13b, 30-32*
I will judge you according to your ways.

The word of the LORD came to me:
Son of man, what is the meaning of this proverb
that you recite in the land of Israel:

"Fathers have eaten green grapes,
thus their children's teeth are on edge"?

As I live, says the Lord GOD:
I swear that there shall no longer be anyone among you
who will repeat this proverb in Israel.
For all lives are mine;
the life of the father is like the life of the son, both are mine;
only the one who sins shall die.

If a man is virtuous—if he does what is right and just,
if he does not eat on the mountains,
nor raise his eyes to the idols of the house of Israel;
if he does not defile his neighbor's wife,
nor have relations with a woman in her menstrual period;
if he oppresses no one,
gives back the pledge received for a debt,
commits no robbery;
if he gives food to the hungry and clothes the naked;
if he does not lend at interest nor exact usury;
if he holds off from evildoing,
judges fairly between a man and his opponent;
if he lives by my statutes and is careful to observe my ordinances,
that man is virtuous—he shall surely live, says the Lord GOD.

But if he begets a son who is a thief, a murderer,
or lends at interest and exacts usury—
this son certainly shall not live.
Because he practiced all these abominations, he shall surely die;
his death shall be his own fault.

Therefore I will judge you, house of Israel,
each one according to his ways, says the Lord GOD.
Turn and be converted from all your crimes,
that they may be no cause of guilt for you.
Cast away from you all the crimes you have committed,
and make for yourselves a new heart and a new spirit.

Why should you die, O house of Israel?
For I have no pleasure in the death of anyone who dies,
  says the Lord God. Return and live! ✛

Psalm 51:12-13, 14-15, 18-19
R. (12a) **Create a clean heart in me, O God.**
A clean heart create for me, O God;
  and a steadfast spirit renew within me.
Cast me not out from your presence,
  and your Holy Spirit take not from me. **R.**
Give me back the joy of your salvation,
  and a willing spirit sustain in me.
I will teach transgressors your ways,
  and sinners shall return to you. **R.**
For you are not pleased with sacrifices;
  should I offer a burnt offering, you would not accept it.
My sacrifice, O God, is a contrite spirit;
  a heart contrite and humbled, O God, you will not spurn. **R.**

See Matthew 11:25
R. Alleluia, alleluia.
Blessed are you, Father, Lord of heaven and earth;
you have revealed to little ones the mysteries of the Kingdom. **R.**

† *Matthew 19:13-15*
Let the children come to me, and do not prevent them;
for the Kingdom of heaven belongs to such as these.

Children were brought to Jesus
  that he might lay his hands on them and pray.
The disciples rebuked them, but Jesus said,
  "Let the children come to me, and do not prevent them;
  for the Kingdom of heaven belongs to such as these."
After he placed his hands on them, he went away. ✛

SUNDAY, AUGUST 14
TWENTIETH SUNDAY IN ORDINARY TIME

† *Jeremiah 38:4-6, 8-10*
A man of strife and contention to all the land.

In those days, the princes said to the king:
  "Jeremiah ought to be put to death;
  he is demoralizing the soldiers who are left in this city,
  and all the people, by speaking such things to them;
  he is not interested in the welfare of our people,
  but in their ruin."

King Zedekiah answered: "He is in your power";
   for the king could do nothing with them.
And so they took Jeremiah
   and threw him into the cistern of Prince Malchiah,
   which was in the quarters of the guard,
   letting him down with ropes.
There was no water in the cistern, only mud,
   and Jeremiah sank into the mud.

Ebed-melech, a court official,
   went there from the palace and said to him:
   "My lord king,
   these men have been at fault
   in all they have done to the prophet Jeremiah,
   casting him into the cistern.
He will die of famine on the spot,
   for there is no more food in the city."
Then the king ordered Ebed-melech the Cushite
   to take three men along with him,
   and draw the prophet Jeremiah out of the cistern before he should
      die. ✛

   Psalm 40:2, 3, 4, 18
R. (14b) **Lord, come to my aid!**
I have waited, waited for the LORD,
   and he stooped toward me. **R.**
The LORD heard my cry.
He drew me out of the pit of destruction,
   out of the mud of the swamp;
he set my feet upon a crag;
   he made firm my steps. **R.**
And he put a new song into my mouth,
   a hymn to our God.
Many shall look on in awe
   and trust in the LORD. **R.**
Though I am afflicted and poor,
   yet the LORD thinks of me.
You are my help and my deliverer;
   O my God, hold not back! **R.**

† *Hebrews 12:1-4*
Let us persevere in running the race that lies before us.

Brothers and sisters:
Since we are surrounded by so great a cloud of witnesses,
   let us rid ourselves of every burden and sin that clings to us
   and persevere in running the race that lies before us
   while keeping our eyes fixed on Jesus,
   the leader and perfecter of faith.
For the sake of the joy that lay before him
   he endured the cross, despising its shame,
   and has taken his seat at the right of the throne of God.
Consider how he endured such opposition from sinners,
   in order that you may not grow weary and lose heart.
In your struggle against sin
   you have not yet resisted to the point of shedding blood. ✛

John 10:27
R. Alleluia, alleluia.
My sheep hear my voice, says the Lord;
I know them, and they follow me. **R.**

† *Luke 12:49-53*
I have come not to establish peace, but rather division.

Jesus said to his disciples:
   "I have come to set the earth on fire,
   and how I wish it were already blazing!
There is a baptism with which I must be baptized,
   and how great is my anguish until it is accomplished!
Do you think that I have come to establish peace on the earth?
No, I tell you, but rather division.
From now on a household of five will be divided,
   three against two and two against three;
   a father will be divided against his son
   and a son against his father,
   a mother against her daughter
   and a daughter against her mother,
   a mother-in-law against her daughter-in-law
   and a daughter-in-law against her mother-in-law." ✛

MONDAY, AUGUST 15
THE ASSUMPTION OF THE BLESSED VIRGIN MARY
(Readings for the Vigil Mass are: 1 Chronicles 15:3-4, 15-16; 16:1-2 •
Psalm 132:6-7, 9-10, 13-14 • 1 Corinthians 15:54b-57 • Luke 11:27-28)

† Revelation 11:19a; 12:1-6a, 10ab
A woman clothed with the sun, with the moon beneath her feet.

God's temple in heaven was opened,
   and the ark of his covenant could be seen in the temple.

A great sign appeared in the sky, a woman clothed with the sun,
   with the moon under her feet,
   and on her head a crown of twelve stars.
She was with child and wailed aloud in pain as she labored to give
      birth.
Then another sign appeared in the sky;
   it was a huge red dragon, with seven heads and ten horns,
   and on its heads were seven diadems.
Its tail swept away a third of the stars in the sky
   and hurled them down to the earth.
Then the dragon stood before the woman about to give birth,
   to devour her child when she gave birth.
She gave birth to a son, a male child,
   destined to rule all the nations with an iron rod.
Her child was caught up to God and his throne.
The woman herself fled into the desert
   where she had a place prepared by God.

Then I heard a loud voice in heaven say:
   "Now have salvation and power come,
      and the Kingdom of our God
      and the authority of his Anointed One." ✛

Psalm 45:10, 11, 12, 16
R. (10bc) **The queen stands at your right hand, arrayed in
   gold.**
The queen takes her place at your right hand in gold of Ophir. **R.**
Hear, O daughter, and see; turn your ear,
   forget your people and your father's house. **R.**
So shall the king desire your beauty;
   for he is your lord. **R.**
They are borne in with gladness and joy;
   they enter the palace of the king. **R.**

† 1 Corinthians 15:20-27
Christ, the firstfruits; then those who belong to him.

Brothers and sisters:
Christ has been raised from the dead,
  the firstfruits of those who have fallen asleep.
For since death came through man,
  the resurrection of the dead came also through man.
For just as in Adam all die,
  so too in Christ shall all be brought to life,
  but each one in proper order:
  Christ the firstfruits;
  then, at his coming, those who belong to Christ;
  then comes the end,
  when he hands over the Kingdom to his God and Father,
  when he has destroyed every sovereignty
  and every authority and power.
For he must reign until he has put all his enemies under his feet.
The last enemy to be destroyed is death,
  for "he subjected everything under his feet." ✛

R. Alleluia, alleluia.
Mary is taken up to heaven;
a chorus of angels exults. **R.**

† Luke 1:39-56
The Almighty has done great things for me; he has raised up the lowly.

Mary set out
  and traveled to the hill country in haste
  to a town of Judah,
  where she entered the house of Zechariah
  and greeted Elizabeth.
When Elizabeth heard Mary's greeting,
  the infant leaped in her womb,
  and Elizabeth, filled with the Holy Spirit,
  cried out in a loud voice and said,
  "Blessed are you among women,
  and blessed is the fruit of your womb.
And how does this happen to me,
  that the mother of my Lord should come to me?
For at the moment the sound of your greeting reached my ears,
  the infant in my womb leaped for joy.
Blessed are you who believed
  that what was spoken to you by the Lord
  would be fulfilled."

And Mary said:

> "My soul proclaims the greatness of the Lord;
>   my spirit rejoices in God my Savior,
>   for he has looked with favor on his lowly servant.
> From this day all generations will call me blessed:
>   the Almighty has done great things for me
>   and holy is his Name.
> He has mercy on those who fear him
>   in every generation.
> He has shown the strength of his arm,
>   and has scattered the proud in their conceit.
> He has cast down the mighty from their thrones,
>   and has lifted up the lowly.
> He has filled the hungry with good things,
>   and the rich he has sent away empty.
> He has come to the help of his servant Israel,
>   for he has remembered his promise of mercy,
>   the promise he made to our fathers,
>   to Abraham and his children forever."

Mary remained with her about three months
and then returned to her home. ✛

TUESDAY, AUGUST 16
WEEKDAY, ST. STEPHEN OF HUNGARY

† *Ezekiel 28:1-10*
*You are a mortal and not God,
however you may think yourself like a god.*

The word of the LORD came to me: Son of man,
say to the prince of Tyre:
Thus says the Lord GOD:
> Because you are haughty of heart,
>   you say, "A god am I!
> I occupy a godly throne
>   in the heart of the sea!"—
> And yet you are a man, and not a god,
>   however you may think yourself like a god.
> Oh yes, you are wiser than Daniel,
>   there is no secret that is beyond you.
> By your wisdom and your intelligence
>   you have made riches for yourself;
> You have put gold and silver
>   into your treasuries.

By your great wisdom applied to your trading
    you have heaped up your riches;
    your heart has grown haughty from your riches—
    therefore thus says the Lord GOD:
Because you have thought yourself
    to have the mind of a god,
Therefore I will bring against you
    foreigners, the most barbarous of nations.
They shall draw their swords
    against your beauteous wisdom,
    they shall run them through your splendid apparel.
They shall thrust you down to the pit, there to die
    a bloodied corpse, in the heart of the sea.
Will you then say, "I am a god!"
    when you face your murderers?
No, you are man, not a god,
    handed over to those who will slay you.
You shall die the death of the uncircumcised
    at the hands of foreigners,
    for I have spoken, says the Lord GOD. ✛

Deuteronomy 32:26-27ab, 27cd-28, 30, 35cd-36ab
R. (39c) **It is I who deal death and give life.**
"I would have said, 'I will make an end of them
    and blot out their name from men's memories,'
Had I not feared the insolence of their enemies,
    feared that these foes would mistakenly boast." **R.**
"'Our own hand won the victory;
    the LORD had nothing to do with it.'"
For they are a people devoid of reason,
    having no understanding. **R.**
"How could one man rout a thousand,
    or two men put ten thousand to flight,
Unless it was because their Rock sold them
    and the LORD delivered them up?" **R.**
Close at hand is the day of their disaster,
    and their doom is rushing upon them!
Surely, the LORD shall do justice for his people;
    on his servants he shall have pity. **R.**

2 Corinthians 8:9
R. Alleluia, alleluia.
Jesus Christ became poor although he was rich
so that by his poverty you might become rich. **R.**

† *Matthew 19:23-30*

It is easier for a camel to pass through the eye of a needle
than for one who is rich to enter the Kingdom of God.

Jesus said to his disciples:
"Amen, I say to you, it will be hard for one who is rich
   to enter the Kingdom of heaven.
Again I say to you,
   it is easier for a camel to pass through the eye of a needle
   than for one who is rich to enter the Kingdom of God."
When the disciples heard this, they were greatly astonished and said,
   "Who then can be saved?"
Jesus looked at them and said,
   "For men this is impossible,
   but for God all things are possible."
Then Peter said to him in reply,
   "We have given up everything and followed you.
What will there be for us?"
Jesus said to them, "Amen, I say to you
   that you who have followed me, in the new age,
   when the Son of Man is seated on his throne of glory,
   will yourselves sit on twelve thrones,
   judging the twelve tribes of Israel.
And everyone who has given up houses or brothers or sisters
   or father or mother or children or lands
   for the sake of my name will receive a hundred times more,
   and will inherit eternal life.
But many who are first will be last, and the last will be first." ✛

WEDNESDAY, AUGUST 17
WEEKDAY

† *Ezekiel 34:1-11*

I will save my sheep, that they may no longer be food for their mouths.

The word of the LORD came to me:
   Son of man, prophesy against the shepherds of Israel,
   in these words prophesy to them, to the shepherds:
   Thus says the Lord GOD: Woe to the shepherds of Israel
   who have been pasturing themselves!
Should not shepherds, rather, pasture sheep?
You have fed off their milk, worn their wool,
   and slaughtered the fatlings,
   but the sheep you have not pastured.
You did not strengthen the weak nor heal the sick
   nor bind up the injured.

You did not bring back the strayed nor seek the lost,
    but you lorded it over them harshly and brutally.
So they were scattered for the lack of a shepherd,
    and became food for all the wild beasts.
My sheep were scattered
    and wandered over all the mountains and high hills;
    my sheep were scattered over the whole earth,
    with no one to look after them or to search for them.

Therefore, shepherds, hear the word of the LORD:
    As I live, says the Lord GOD,
    because my sheep have been given over to pillage,
    and because my sheep have become food for every wild beast,
    for lack of a shepherd;
    because my shepherds did not look after my sheep,
    but pastured themselves and did not pasture my sheep;
    because of this, shepherds, hear the word of the LORD:
    Thus says the Lord GOD:
    I swear I am coming against these shepherds.
I will claim my sheep from them
    and put a stop to their shepherding my sheep
    so that they may no longer pasture themselves.
I will save my sheep,
    that they may no longer be food for their mouths.

For thus says the Lord GOD:
    I myself will look after and tend my sheep. ✛

Psalm 23:1-3a, 3b-4, 5, 6
R. (1) The Lord is my shepherd; there is nothing I shall want.
The LORD is my shepherd; I shall not want.
    In verdant pastures he gives me repose;
Beside restful waters he leads me;
    he refreshes my soul. **R.**
He guides me in right paths
    for his name's sake.
Even though I walk in the dark valley
    I fear no evil; for you are at my side
With your rod and your staff
    that give me courage. **R.**
You spread the table before me
    in the sight of my foes;
You anoint my head with oil;
    my cup overflows. **R.**

Only goodness and kindness will follow me
  all the days of my life;
And I shall dwell in the house of the LORD
  for years to come. **R.**

Hebrews 4:12
R. Alleluia, alleluia.
The word of God is living and effective,
able to discern reflections and thoughts of the heart. **R.**

† *Matthew 20:1-16*
Are you envious because I am generous?

Jesus told his disciples this parable:
"The Kingdom of heaven is like a landowner
  who went out at dawn to hire laborers for his vineyard.
After agreeing with them for the usual daily wage,
  he sent them into his vineyard.
Going out about nine o'clock,
  he saw others standing idle in the marketplace,
  and he said to them, 'You too go into my vineyard,
  and I will give you what is just.'
So they went off.
And he went out again around noon,
  and around three o'clock, and did likewise.
Going out about five o'clock,
  he found others standing around, and said to them,
  'Why do you stand here idle all day?'
They answered, 'Because no one has hired us.'
He said to them, 'You too go into my vineyard.'
When it was evening the owner of the vineyard said to his foreman,
  'Summon the laborers and give them their pay,
  beginning with the last and ending with the first.'
When those who had started about five o'clock came,
  each received the usual daily wage.
So when the first came, they thought that they would receive more,
  but each of them also got the usual wage.
And on receiving it they grumbled against the landowner, saying,
  'These last ones worked only one hour,
  and you have made them equal to us,
  who bore the day's burden and the heat.'
He said to one of them in reply,
  'My friend, I am not cheating you.
Did you not agree with me for the usual daily wage?
Take what is yours and go.

What if I wish to give this last one the same as you?
Or am I not free to do as I wish with my own money?
Are you envious because I am generous?"
Thus, the last will be first, and the first will be last." ✛

THURSDAY, AUGUST 18
WEEKDAY

† *Ezekiel 36:23-28*
I will give you a new heart and place a new spirit within you.

Thus says the LORD:
I will prove the holiness of my great name,
  profaned among the nations,
  in whose midst you have profaned it.
Thus the nations shall know that I am the LORD, says the Lord GOD,
  when in their sight I prove my holiness through you.
For I will take you away from among the nations,
  gather you from all the foreign lands,
  and bring you back to your own land.
I will sprinkle clean water upon you
  to cleanse you from all your impurities,
  and from all your idols I will cleanse you.
I will give you a new heart and place a new spirit within you,
  taking from your bodies your stony hearts
  and giving you natural hearts.
I will put my spirit within you and make you live by my statutes,
  careful to observe my decrees.
You shall live in the land I gave your ancestors;
  you shall be my people, and I will be your God. ✛

Psalm 51:12-13, 14-15, 18-19
R. (Ezekiel 36:25) **I will pour clean water on you and wash
  away all your sins.**
A clean heart create for me, O God,
  and a steadfast spirit renew within me.
Cast me not out from your presence,
  and your Holy Spirit take not from me. **R.**
Give me back the joy of your salvation,
  and a willing spirit sustain in me.
I will teach transgressors your ways,
  and sinners shall return to you. **R.**
For you are not pleased with sacrifices;
  should I offer a burnt offering, you would not accept it.
My sacrifice, O God, is a contrite spirit;
  a heart contrite and humbled, O God, you will not spurn. **R.**

Psalm 95:8

R. Alleluia, alleluia.

If today you hear his voice,
harden not your hearts. **R.**

† *Matthew 22:1-14*

Invite to the wedding feast whomever you find.

J esus again in reply spoke to the chief priests and the elders of the
people in parables saying,
"The Kingdom of heaven may be likened to a king
who gave a wedding feast for his son.
He dispatched his servants to summon the invited guests to the feast,
but they refused to come.
A second time he sent other servants, saying,
'Tell those invited: "Behold, I have prepared my banquet,
my calves and fattened cattle are killed,
and everything is ready; come to the feast."'
Some ignored the invitation and went away,
one to his farm, another to his business.
The rest laid hold of his servants,
mistreated them, and killed them.
The king was enraged and sent his troops,
destroyed those murderers, and burned their city.
Then the king said to his servants, 'The feast is ready,
but those who were invited were not worthy to come.
Go out, therefore, into the main roads
and invite to the feast whomever you find.'
The servants went out into the streets
and gathered all they found, bad and good alike,
and the hall was filled with guests.
But when the king came in to meet the guests
he saw a man there not dressed in a wedding garment.
He said to him, 'My friend, how is it
that you came in here without a wedding garment?'
But he was reduced to silence.
Then the king said to his attendants, 'Bind his hands and feet,
and cast him into the darkness outside,
where there will be wailing and grinding of teeth.'
Many are invited, but few are chosen." ✛

FRIDAY, AUGUST 19
WEEKDAY, ST. JOHN EUDES

† *Ezekiel 37:1-14*

Dry bones, hear the word of the LORD. I will bring you back
from your graves, O my people Israel.

The hand of the LORD came upon me,
and led me out in the Spirit of the LORD
and set me in the center of the plain,
which was now filled with bones.
He made me walk among the bones in every direction
so that I saw how many they were on the surface of the plain.
How dry they were!
He asked me:
Son of man, can these bones come to life?
I answered, "Lord GOD, you alone know that."
Then he said to me:
Prophesy over these bones, and say to them:
Dry bones, hear the word of the LORD!
Thus says the Lord GOD to these bones:
See! I will bring spirit into you, that you may come to life.
I will put sinews upon you, make flesh grow over you,
cover you with skin, and put spirit in you
so that you may come to life and know that I am the LORD.
I prophesied as I had been told,
and even as I was prophesying I heard a noise;
it was a rattling as the bones came together, bone joining bone.
I saw the sinews and the flesh come upon them,
and the skin cover them, but there was no spirit in them.
Then the LORD said to me:
Prophesy to the spirit, prophesy, son of man,
and say to the spirit: Thus says the Lord GOD:
From the four winds come, O spirit,
and breathe into these slain that they may come to life.
I prophesied as he told me, and the spirit came into them;
they came alive and stood upright, a vast army.
Then he said to me:
Son of man, these bones are the whole house of Israel.
They have been saying,
"Our bones are dried up,
our hope is lost, and we are cut off."
Therefore, prophesy and say to them: Thus says the Lord GOD:
O my people, I will open your graves
and have you rise from them,
and bring you back to the land of Israel.

Then you shall know that I am the LORD,
    when I open your graves and have you rise from them,
    O my people!
I will put my spirit in you that you may live,
    and I will settle you upon your land;
    thus you shall know that I am the LORD.
I have promised, and I will do it, says the LORD. ✢

Psalm 107:2-3, 4-5, 6-7, 8-9

R. (1) Give thanks to the Lord; his love is everlasting.
Let the redeemed of the LORD say,
    those whom he has redeemed from the hand of the foe
And gathered from the lands,
    from the east and the west, from the north and the south. **R.**
They went astray in the desert wilderness;
    the way to an inhabited city they did not find.
Hungry and thirsty,
    their life was wasting away within them. **R.**
They cried to the LORD in their distress;
    from their straits he rescued them.
And he led them by a direct way
    to reach an inhabited city. **R.**
Let them give thanks to the LORD for his mercy
    and his wondrous deeds to the children of men,
Because he satisfied the longing soul
    and filled the hungry soul with good things. **R.**

Psalm 25:4b, 5a

R. Alleluia, alleluia.
Teach me your paths, my God,
guide me in your truth. **R.**

† *Matthew 22:34-40*

*You shall love the Lord, your God, with all your heart
and your neighbor as yourself.*

When the Pharisees heard that Jesus had silenced the Sadducees,
    they gathered together, and one of them,
    a scholar of the law, tested him by asking,
    "Teacher, which commandment in the law is the greatest?"
He said to him,
    "You shall love the Lord, your God, with all your heart,
    with all your soul, and with all your mind.
This is the greatest and the first commandment.

The second is like it:
    You shall love your neighbor as yourself.
The whole law and the prophets depend on these two
    commandments." ✛

SATURDAY, AUGUST 20
St. Bernard

† *Ezekiel 43:1-7ab*
The glory of God entered the temple.

The angel led me to the gate which faces the east,
    and there I saw the glory of the God of Israel
    coming from the east.
I heard a sound like the roaring of many waters,
    and the earth shone with his glory.
The vision was like that which I had seen
    when he came to destroy the city,
    and like that which I had seen by the river Chebar.
I fell prone as the glory of the Lord entered the temple
    by way of the gate which faces the east,
    but spirit lifted me up and brought me to the inner court.
And I saw that the temple was filled with the glory of the Lord.
Then I heard someone speaking to me from the temple,
    while the man stood beside me.
The voice said to me:
    Son of man, this is where my throne shall be,
    this is where I will set the soles of my feet;
    here I will dwell among the children of Israel forever. ✛

Psalm 85:9ab and 10, 11-12, 13-14
R. (see 10b) **The glory of the Lord will dwell in our land.**
I will hear what God proclaims;
    the Lord—for he proclaims peace.
Near indeed is his salvation to those who fear him,
    glory dwelling in our land. **R.**
Kindness and truth shall meet;
    justice and peace shall kiss.
Truth shall spring out of the earth,
    and justice shall look down from heaven. **R.**
The Lord himself will give his benefits;
    our land shall yield its increase.
Justice shall walk before him,
    and salvation, along the way of his steps. **R.**

Matthew 23:9b, 10b

R. Alleluia, alleluia.

You have but one Father in heaven;
you have but one master, the Christ. **R.**

† *Matthew 23:1-12*

They preach but they do not practice.

Jesus spoke to the crowds and to his disciples, saying,
   "The scribes and the Pharisees
   have taken their seat on the chair of Moses.
Therefore, do and observe all things whatsoever they tell you,
   but do not follow their example.
For they preach but they do not practice.
They tie up heavy burdens hard to carry
   and lay them on people's shoulders,
   but they will not lift a finger to move them.
All their works are performed to be seen.
They widen their phylacteries and lengthen their tassels.
They love places of honor at banquets, seats of honor in synagogues,
   greetings in marketplaces, and the salutation 'Rabbi.'
As for you, do not be called 'Rabbi.'
You have but one teacher, and you are all brothers.
Call no one on earth your father;
   you have but one Father in heaven.
Do not be called 'Master';
   you have but one master, the Christ.
The greatest among you must be your servant.
Whoever exalts himself will be humbled;
   but whoever humbles himself will be exalted." ✝

SUNDAY, AUGUST 21
TWENTY-FIRST SUNDAY IN ORDINARY TIME

† *Isaiah 66:18-21*

They shall bring all your brothers and sisters from all the nations.

Thus says the LORD:
I know their works and their thoughts,
and I come to gather nations of every language;
   they shall come and see my glory.
I will set a sign among them;
   from them I will send fugitives to the nations:
   to Tarshish, Put and Lud, Mosoch, Tubal and Javan,
   to the distant coastlands
   that have never heard of my fame, or seen my glory;
   and they shall proclaim my glory among the nations.

They shall bring all your brothers and sisters from all the nations
   as an offering to the Lᴏʀᴅ,
   on horses and in chariots, in carts, upon mules and dromedaries,
   to Jerusalem, my holy mountain, says the Lᴏʀᴅ,
   just as the Israelites bring their offering
   to the house of the Lᴏʀᴅ in clean vessels.
Some of these I will take as priests and Levites, says the Lᴏʀᴅ. ✛

Psalm 117:1, 2
R. (Mk 16:15) **Go out to all the world and tell the good news.**
   *(or **Alleluia.**)*
Praise the Lᴏʀᴅ, all you nations;
   glorify him, all you peoples! **R.**
For steadfast is his kindness toward us,
   and the fidelity of the Lᴏʀᴅ endures forever. **R.**

† Hebrews 12:5-7, 11-13
Those whom the Lord loves, he disciplines.

Brothers and sisters,
You have forgotten the exhortation addressed to you as children:
   "My son, do not disdain the discipline of the Lord
     or lose heart when reproved by him;
     for whom the Lord loves, he disciplines;
        he scourges every son he acknowledges."
Endure your trials as "discipline";
   God treats you as sons.
For what "son" is there whom his father does not discipline?
At the time,
   all discipline seems a cause not for joy but for pain,
   yet later it brings the peaceful fruit of righteousness
   to those who are trained by it.

So strengthen your drooping hands and your weak knees.
Make straight paths for your feet,
   that what is lame may not be disjointed but healed. ✛

John 14:6
R. Alleluia, alleluia.
I am the way, the truth and the life, says the Lord;
no one comes to the Father, except through me. **R.**

† *Luke 13:22-30*

They will come from east and west and
recline at table in the kingdom of God.

Jesus passed through towns and villages,
   teaching as he went and making his way to Jerusalem.
Someone asked him,
   "Lord, will only a few people be saved?"
He answered them,
   "Strive to enter through the narrow gate,
   for many, I tell you, will attempt to enter
   but will not be strong enough.
After the master of the house has arisen and locked the door,
   then will you stand outside knocking and saying,
   'Lord, open the door for us.'
He will say to you in reply,
   'I do not know where you are from.'
And you will say,
   'We ate and drank in your company and you taught in our streets.'
Then he will say to you,
   'I do not know where you are from.
Depart from me, all you evildoers!'
And there will be wailing and grinding of teeth
   when you see Abraham, Isaac, and Jacob
   and all the prophets in the kingdom of God
   and you yourselves cast out.
And people will come from the east and the west
   and from the north and the south
   and will recline at table in the kingdom of God.
For behold, some are last who will be first,
   and some are first who will be last." ✛

MONDAY, AUGUST 22
THE QUEENSHIP OF THE BLESSED VIRGIN MARY

† *2 Thessalonians 1:1-5, 11-12*
May the name of our Lord Jesus be glorified in you and you in him.

Paul, Silvanus, and Timothy to the Church of the Thessalonians
   in God our Father and the Lord Jesus Christ:
   grace to you and peace from God our Father
   and the Lord Jesus Christ.

We ought to thank God always for you, brothers and sisters,
   as is fitting, because your faith flourishes ever more,
   and the love of every one of you for one another grows ever greater.

Accordingly, we ourselves boast of you in the churches of God
   regarding your endurance and faith in all your persecutions
   and the afflictions you endure.

This is evidence of the just judgment of God,
   so that you may be considered worthy of the Kingdom of God
   for which you are suffering.

We always pray for you,
   that our God may make you worthy of his calling
   and powerfully bring to fulfillment every good purpose
   and every effort of faith,
   that the name of our Lord Jesus may be glorified in you,
   and you in him,
   in accord with the grace of our God and Lord Jesus Christ. ✛

Psalm 96:1-2a, 2b-3, 4-5
R. (3) Proclaim God's marvelous deeds to all the nations.
Sing to the LORD a new song;
   sing to the LORD, all you lands.
Sing to the LORD; bless his name. **R.**
Announce his salvation, day after day.
Tell his glory among the nations;
   among all peoples, his wondrous deeds. **R.**
For great is the LORD and highly to be praised;
   awesome is he, beyond all gods.
For all the gods of the nations are things of nought,
   but the LORD made the heavens. **R.**

John 10:27
R. Alleluia, alleluia.
My sheep hear my voice, says the Lord;
I know them, and they follow me. **R.**

✝ Matthew 23:13-22
Woe to you, blind guides.

Jesus said to the crowds and to his disciples:
"Woe to you, scribes and Pharisees, you hypocrites.
You lock the Kingdom of heaven before men.
You do not enter yourselves,
   nor do you allow entrance to those trying to enter.

"Woe to you, scribes and Pharisees, you hypocrites.
You traverse sea and land to make one convert,
   and when that happens you make him a child of Gehenna
   twice as much as yourselves.

"Woe to you, blind guides, who say,
  'If one swears by the temple, it means nothing,
  but if one swears by the gold of the temple, one is obligated.'
Blind fools, which is greater, the gold,
  or the temple that made the gold sacred?
And you say, 'If one swears by the altar, it means nothing,
  but if one swears by the gift on the altar, one is obligated.'
You blind ones, which is greater, the gift,
  or the altar that makes the gift sacred?
One who swears by the altar swears by it and all that is upon it;
  one who swears by the temple swears by it
  and by him who dwells in it;
  one who swears by heaven swears by the throne of God
  and by him who is seated on it." ✛

TUESDAY, AUGUST 23
WEEKDAY, ST. ROSE OF LIMA

† *2 Thessalonians 2:1-3a, 14-17*
Hold fast to the traditions that you were taught.

We ask you, brothers and sisters,
  with regard to the coming of our Lord Jesus Christ
  and our assembling with him,
  not to be shaken out of your minds suddenly,
  or to be alarmed either by a "spirit," or by an oral statement,
  or by a letter allegedly from us
  to the effect that the day of the Lord is at hand.
Let no one deceive you in any way.

To this end he has also called you through our Gospel
  to possess the glory of our Lord Jesus Christ.
Therefore, brothers and sisters, stand firm
  and hold fast to the traditions that you were taught,
  either by an oral statement or by a letter of ours.

May our Lord Jesus Christ himself and God our Father,
  who has loved us and given us everlasting encouragement
  and good hope through his grace,
  encourage your hearts and strengthen them
  in every good deed and word. ✛

Psalm 96:10, 11-12, 13
R. (13b) **The Lord comes to judge the earth.**
Say among the nations: The LORD is king.
He has made the world firm, not to be moved;
  he governs the peoples with equity. **R.**

Let the heavens be glad and the earth rejoice;
  let the sea and what fills it resound;
  let the plains be joyful and all that is in them!
Then shall all the trees of the forest exult. **R.**
Before the LORD, for he comes;
  for he comes to rule the earth.
He shall rule the world with justice
  and the peoples with his constancy. **R.**

Hebrews 4:12
R. Alleluia, alleluia.
The word of God is living and effective,
able to discern reflections and thoughts of the heart. **R.**

† *Matthew 23:23-26*
But these you should have done, without neglecting the others.

Jesus said:
"Woe to you, scribes and Pharisees, you hypocrites.
You pay tithes of mint and dill and cummin,
  and have neglected the weightier things of the law:
  judgment and mercy and fidelity.
But these you should have done, without neglecting the others.
Blind guides, who strain out the gnat and swallow the camel!

"Woe to you, scribes and Pharisees, you hypocrites.
You cleanse the outside of cup and dish,
  but inside they are full of plunder and self-indulgence.
Blind Pharisee, cleanse first the inside of the cup,
  so that the outside also may be clean." ✛

WEDNESDAY, AUGUST 24
ST. BARTHOLOMEW

† *Revelation 21:9b-14*
On the foundation of the city were inscribed the names
of the twelve Apostles of the Lamb.

The angel spoke to me, saying,
  "Come here.
I will show you the bride, the wife of the Lamb."
He took me in spirit to a great, high mountain
  and showed me the holy city Jerusalem
  coming down out of heaven from God.
It gleamed with the splendor of God.
Its radiance was like that of a precious stone,
  like jasper, clear as crystal.

It had a massive, high wall,
    with twelve gates where twelve angels were stationed
    and on which names were inscribed,
    the names of the twelve tribes of the children of Israel.
There were three gates facing east,
    three north, three south, and three west.
The wall of the city had twelve courses of stones as its foundation,
    on which were inscribed the twelve names
    of the twelve Apostles of the Lamb. ✛

Psalm 145:10-11, 12-13, 17-18

R. (12) Your friends make known, O Lord, the glorious splendor of your Kingdom.
Let all your works give you thanks, O LORD,
    and let your faithful ones bless you.
Let them discourse of the glory of your Kingdom
    and speak of your might. **R.**
Making known to men your might
    and the glorious splendor of your Kingdom.
Your Kingdom is a Kingdom for all ages,
    and your dominion endures through all generations. **R.**
The LORD is just in all his ways
    and holy in all his works.
The LORD is near to all who call upon him,
    to all who call upon him in truth. **R.**

John 1:49b

R. Alleluia, alleluia.
Rabbi, you are the Son of God;
you are the King of Israel. **R.**

† *John 1:45-51*
Here is a true child of Israel. There is no duplicity in him.

Philip found Nathanael and told him,
    "We have found the one about whom Moses wrote in the law,
    and also the prophets, Jesus son of Joseph, from Nazareth."
But Nathanael said to him,
    "Can anything good come from Nazareth?"
Philip said to him, "Come and see."
Jesus saw Nathanael coming toward him and said of him,
    "Here is a true child of Israel.
There is no duplicity in him."
Nathanael said to him, "How do you know me?"
Jesus answered and said to him,
    "Before Philip called you, I saw you under the fig tree."

Nathanael answered him,
"Rabbi, you are the Son of God; you are the King of Israel."
Jesus answered and said to him,
"Do you believe
because I told you that I saw you under the fig tree?
You will see greater things than this."
And he said to him, "Amen, amen, I say to you,
you will see heaven opened and the angels of God
ascending and descending on the Son of Man." ✛

THURSDAY, AUGUST 25
WEEKDAY, ST. LOUIS, ST. JOSEPH CALASANZ

† 1 Corinthians 1:1-9
In him you were enriched in every way.

Paul, called to be an Apostle of Christ Jesus by the will of God, and
Sosthenes our brother,
to the Church of God that is in Corinth,
to you who have been sanctified in Christ Jesus, called to be holy,
with all those everywhere who call upon the name of our Lord
Jesus Christ, their Lord and ours.
Grace to you and peace from God our Father
and the Lord Jesus Christ.

I give thanks to my God always on your account
for the grace of God bestowed on you in Christ Jesus,
that in him you were enriched in every way,
with all discourse and all knowledge,
as the testimony to Christ was confirmed among you,
so that you are not lacking in any spiritual gift
as you wait for the revelation of our Lord Jesus Christ.
He will keep you firm to the end,
irreproachable on the day of our Lord Jesus Christ.
God is faithful,
and by him you were called to fellowship with his Son, Jesus
Christ our Lord. ✛

Psalm 145:2-3, 4-5, 6-7
R. (1) **I will praise your name for ever, Lord.**
Every day will I bless you,
and I will praise your name forever and ever.
Great is the LORD and highly to be praised;
his greatness is unsearchable. **R.**

Generation after generation praises your works
    and proclaims your might.
They speak of the splendor of your glorious majesty
    and tell of your wondrous works. **R.**
They discourse of the power of your terrible deeds
    and declare your greatness.
They publish the fame of your abundant goodness
    and joyfully sing of your justice. **R.**

Matthew 24:42a, 44
R. Alleluia, alleluia.
Stay awake!
For you do not know when the Son of Man will come. **R.**

† *Matthew 24:42-51*
Stay awake!

Jesus said to his disciples:
"Stay awake!
For you do not know on which day your Lord will come.
Be sure of this:
    if the master of the house
    had known the hour of night when the thief was coming,
    he would have stayed awake
    and not let his house be broken into.
So too, you also must be prepared,
    for at an hour you do not expect, the Son of Man will come.

"Who, then, is the faithful and prudent servant,
    whom the master has put in charge of his household
    to distribute to them their food at the proper time?
Blessed is that servant whom his master on his arrival finds doing so.
Amen, I say to you, he will put him in charge of all his property.
But if that wicked servant says to himself, 'My master is long delayed,'
    and begins to beat his fellow servants,
    and eat and drink with drunkards,
    the servant's master will come on an unexpected day
    and at an unknown hour and will punish him severely
    and assign him a place with the hypocrites,
    where there will be wailing and grinding of teeth." ✢

FRIDAY, AUGUST 26
WEEKDAY

† *1 Corinthians 1:17-25*
We proclaim Christ crucified, foolishness to Gentiles,
but to those who are called, the wisdom of God.

Brothers and sisters:
Christ did not send me to baptize but to preach the Gospel,
  and not with the wisdom of human eloquence,
  so that the cross of Christ might not be emptied of its meaning.

The message of the cross is foolishness to those who are perishing,
  but to us who are being saved it is the power of God.
For it is written:

  I will destroy the wisdom of the wise,
    and the learning of the learned I will set aside.

Where is the wise one?
Where is the scribe?
Where is the debater of this age?
Has not God made the wisdom of the world foolish?
For since in the wisdom of God
  the world did not come to know God through wisdom,
  it was the will of God through the foolishness of the proclamation
  to save those who have faith.
For Jews demand signs and Greeks look for wisdom,
  but we proclaim Christ crucified,
  a stumbling block to Jews and foolishness to Gentiles,
  but to those who are called, Jews and Greeks alike,
  Christ the power of God and the wisdom of God.
For the foolishness of God is wiser than human wisdom,
  and the weakness of God is stronger than human strength. ✛

  Psalm 33:1-2, 4-5, 10-11
R. (5) **The earth is full of the goodness of the Lord.**
Exult, you just, in the LORD;
  praise from the upright is fitting.
Give thanks to the LORD on the harp;
  with the ten-stringed lyre chant his praises. **R.**
For upright is the word of the LORD,
  and all his works are trustworthy.
He loves justice and right;
  of the kindness of the LORD the earth is full. **R.**

The LORD brings to nought the plans of nations;
  he foils the designs of peoples.
But the plan of the LORD stands forever;
  the design of his heart, through all generations. **R.**

Luke 21:36
R. Alleluia, alleluia.
Be vigilant at all times and pray,
that you may have the strength to stand before the Son of Man. **R.**

† *Matthew 25:1-13*
Behold, the bridegroom! Come out to meet him!

Jesus told his disciples this parable:
"The Kingdom of heaven will be like ten virgins
  who took their lamps and went out to meet the bridegroom.
Five of them were foolish and five were wise.
The foolish ones, when taking their lamps,
  brought no oil with them,
  but the wise brought flasks of oil with their lamps.
Since the bridegroom was long delayed,
  they all became drowsy and fell asleep.
At midnight, there was a cry,
  'Behold, the bridegroom! Come out to meet him!'
Then all those virgins got up and trimmed their lamps.
The foolish ones said to the wise,
  'Give us some of your oil,
  for our lamps are going out.'
But the wise ones replied,
  'No, for there may not be enough for us and you.
Go instead to the merchants and buy some for yourselves.'
While they went off to buy it,
  the bridegroom came
  and those who were ready went into the wedding feast with him.
Then the door was locked.
Afterwards the other virgins came and said,
  'Lord, Lord, open the door for us!'
But he said in reply,
  'Amen, I say to you, I do not know you.'
Therefore, stay awake,
  for you know neither the day nor the hour." ✝

SATURDAY, AUGUST 27
St. Monica

✝ *1 Corinthians 1:26-31*
God chose the weak of the world.

Consider your own calling, brothers and sisters.
Not many of you were wise by human standards,
    not many were powerful,
    not many were of noble birth.
Rather, God chose the foolish of the world to shame the wise,
    and God chose the weak of the world to shame the strong,
    and God chose the lowly and despised of the world,
    those who count for nothing,
    to reduce to nothing those who are something,
    so that no human being might boast before God.
It is due to him that you are in Christ Jesus,
    who became for us wisdom from God,
    as well as righteousness, sanctification, and redemption,
    so that, as it is written,
Whoever boasts, should boast in the Lord. ✝

Psalm 33:12-13, 18-19, 20-21
R. (12) **Blessed the people the Lord has chosen to be his own.**
Blessed the nation whose God is the LORD,
    the people he has chosen for his own inheritance.
From heaven the LORD looks down;
    he sees all mankind. **R.**
But see, the eyes of the LORD are upon those who fear him,
    upon those who hope for his kindness,
To deliver them from death
    and preserve them in spite of famine. **R.**
Our soul waits for the LORD,
    who is our help and our shield,
For in him our hearts rejoice;
    in his holy name we trust. **R.**

John 13:34
R. Alleluia, alleluia.
I give you a new commandment:
love one another as I have loved you. **R.**

† *Matthew 25:14-30*

Since you have been faithful in small matters,
come, share your master's joy.

Jesus told his disciples this parable:
"A man going on a journey
    called in his servants and entrusted his possessions to them.
To one he gave five talents; to another, two; to a third, one—
    to each according to his ability.
Then he went away.
Immediately the one who received five talents went and traded with
      them,
    and made another five.
Likewise, the one who received two made another two.
But the man who received one went off and dug a hole in the ground
    and buried his master's money.
After a long time
    the master of those servants came back and settled accounts with
      them.
The one who had received five talents
    came forward bringing the additional five.
He said, 'Master, you gave me five talents.
See, I have made five more.'
His master said to him, 'Well done, my good and faithful servant.
Since you were faithful in small matters,
    I will give you great responsibilities.
Come, share your master's joy.'
Then the one who had received two talents also came forward and said,
    'Master, you gave me two talents.
See, I have made two more.'
His master said to him, 'Well done, my good and faithful servant.
Since you were faithful in small matters,
    I will give you great responsibilities.
Come, share your master's joy.'
Then the one who had received the one talent came forward and said,
    'Master, I knew you were a demanding person,
    harvesting where you did not plant
    and gathering where you did not scatter;
    so out of fear I went off and buried your talent in the ground.
Here it is back.'
His master said to him in reply, 'You wicked, lazy servant!
So you knew that I harvest where I did not plant
    and gather where I did not scatter?
Should you not then have put my money in the bank
    so that I could have got it back with interest on my return?

Now then! Take the talent from him and give it to the one with ten.
For to everyone who has,
  more will be given and he will grow rich;
  but from the one who has not,
  even what he has will be taken away.
And throw this useless servant into the darkness outside,
  where there will be wailing and grinding of teeth.'" ✛

SUNDAY, AUGUST 28
Twenty-second Sunday in Ordinary Time
† Sirach 3:17-18, 20, 28-29
Humble yourself and you will find favor with God.

My child, conduct your affairs with humility,
  and you will be loved more than a giver of gifts.
Humble yourself the more, the greater you are,
  and you will find favor with God.
What is too sublime for you, seek not,
  into things beyond your strength search not.
The mind of a sage appreciates proverbs,
  and an attentive ear is the joy of the wise.
Water quenches a flaming fire,
  and alms atone for sins. ✛

Psalm 68:4-5, 6-7, 10-11
R. (see 11b) **God, in your goodness, you have made a home for the poor.**
The just rejoice and exult before God;
  they are glad and rejoice.
Sing to God, chant praise to his name;
  whose name is the LORD. **R.**
The father of orphans and the defender of widows
  is God in his holy dwelling.
God gives a home to the forsaken;
  he leads forth prisoners to prosperity. **R.**
A bountiful rain you showered down, O God, upon your inheritance;
  you restored the land when it languished;
your flock settled in it;
  in your goodness, O God, you provided it for the needy. **R.**

† *Hebrews 12:18-19, 22-24a*
You have approached Mount Zion and the city of the living God.

Brothers and sisters:
You have not approached that which could be touched
  and a blazing fire and gloomy darkness
  and storm and a trumpet blast
  and a voice speaking words such that those who heard
  begged that no message be further addressed to them.
No, you have approached Mount Zion
  and the city of the living God, the heavenly Jerusalem,
  and countless angels in festal gathering,
  and the assembly of the firstborn enrolled in heaven,
  and God the judge of all,
  and the spirits of the just made perfect,
  and Jesus, the mediator of a new covenant,
  and the sprinkled blood that speaks more eloquently than that of
    Abel. ✛

Matthew 11:29ab
R. Alleluia, alleluia.
Take my yoke upon you, says the Lord,
and learn from me, for I am meek and humble of heart. **R.**

† *Luke 14:1, 7-14*
Everyone who exalts himself will be humbled,
everyone who humbles himself will be exalted.

On a sabbath Jesus went to dine
  at the home of one of the leading Pharisees,
  and the people there were observing him carefully.

He told a parable to those who had been invited,
  noticing how they were choosing the places of honor at the table.
"When you are invited by someone to a wedding banquet,
  do not recline at table in the place of honor.
A more distinguished guest than you may have been invited by him,
  and the host who invited both of you may approach you and say,
  'Give your place to this man,'
  and then you would proceed with embarrassment
  to take the lowest place.
Rather, when you are invited,
  go and take the lowest place
  so that when the host comes to you he may say,
  'My friend, move up to a higher position.'
Then you will enjoy the esteem of your companions at the table.

For every one who exalts himself will be humbled,
  but the one who humbles himself will be exalted."
Then he said to the host who invited him,
  "When you hold a lunch or a dinner,
  do not invite your friends or your brothers
  or your relatives or your wealthy neighbors,
  in case they may invite you back and you have repayment.
Rather, when you hold a banquet,
  invite the poor, the crippled, the lame, the blind;
  blessed indeed will you be because of their inability to repay you.
For you will be repaid at the resurrection of the righteous." ✛

MONDAY, AUGUST 29
The Passion of St. John the Baptist

† 1 Corinthians 2:1-5
I came to you proclaiming Jesus Christ, and him crucified.

When I came to you, brothers and sisters,
  proclaiming the mystery of God,
  I did not come with sublimity of words or of wisdom.
For I resolved to know nothing while I was with you
  except Jesus Christ, and him crucified.
I came to you in weakness and fear and much trembling,
  and my message and my proclamation
  were not with persuasive words of wisdom,
  but with a demonstration of spirit and power,
  so that your faith might rest not on human wisdom
  but on the power of God. ✛

Psalm 119:97, 98, 99, 100, 101, 102
R. (97) **Lord, I love your commands.**
How I love your law, O LORD!
  It is my meditation all the day. **R.**
Your command has made me wiser than my enemies,
  for it is ever with me. **R.**
I have more understanding than all my teachers
  when your decrees are my meditation. **R.**
I have more discernment than the elders,
  because I observe your precepts. **R.**
From every evil way I withhold my feet,
  that I may keep your words. **R.**
From your ordinances I turn not away,
  for you have instructed me. **R.**

Matthew 5:10

R. Alleluia, alleluia.

Blessed are those who are persecuted for the sake of righteousness,
for theirs is the Kingdom of heaven. **R.**

† *Mark 6:17-29*

I want you to give me at once on a platter the head of John the Baptist.

Herod was the one who had John the Baptist arrested and bound
    in prison
  on account of Herodias,
   the wife of his brother Philip, whom he had married.
John had said to Herod,
  "It is not lawful for you to have your brother's wife."
Herodias harbored a grudge against him
  and wanted to kill him but was unable to do so.
Herod feared John, knowing him to be a righteous and holy man,
  and kept him in custody.
When he heard him speak he was very much perplexed,
  yet he liked to listen to him.
She had an opportunity one day when Herod, on his birthday,
  gave a banquet for his courtiers,
  his military officers, and the leading men of Galilee.
Herodias' own daughter came in
  and performed a dance that delighted Herod and his guests.
The king said to the girl,
  "Ask of me whatever you wish and I will grant it to you."
He even swore many things to her,
  "I will grant you whatever you ask of me,
  even to half of my kingdom."
She went out and said to her mother,
  "What shall I ask for?"
She replied, "The head of John the Baptist."
The girl hurried back to the king's presence and made her request,
  "I want you to give me at once
  on a platter the head of John the Baptist."
The king was deeply distressed,
  but because of his oaths and the guests
  he did not wish to break his word to her.
So he promptly dispatched an executioner with orders
  to bring back his head.
He went off and beheaded him in the prison.

He brought in the head on a platter and gave it to the girl.
The girl in turn gave it to her mother.
When his disciples heard about it,
  they came and took his body and laid it in a tomb. ✛

TUESDAY, AUGUST 30
WEEKDAY

† *1 Corinthians 2:10b-16*
Natural persons do not accept what pertains to the Spirit of God:
spiritual persons, however, can judge everything.

Brothers and sisters:
The Spirit scrutinizes everything, even the depths of God.
Among men, who knows what pertains to the man
  except his spirit that is within?
Similarly, no one knows what pertains to God except the Spirit of God.
We have not received the spirit of the world
  but the Spirit who is from God,
  so that we may understand the things freely given us by God.
And we speak about them not with words taught by human wisdom,
  but with words taught by the Spirit,
  describing spiritual realities in spiritual terms.

Now the natural man does not accept what pertains to the Spirit of
    God,
  for to him it is foolishness, and he cannot understand it,
  because it is judged spiritually.
The one who is spiritual, however, can judge everything
  but is not subject to judgment by anyone.

For "who has known the mind of the Lord, so as to counsel him?"
But we have the mind of Christ. ✛

  Psalm 145:8-9, 10-11, 12-13ab, 13cd-14
R. (17) **The Lord is just in all his ways.**
The LORD is gracious and merciful,
  slow to anger and of great kindness.
The LORD is good to all
  and compassionate toward all his works. **R.**
Let all your works give you thanks, O LORD,
  and let your faithful ones bless you.
Let them discourse of the glory of your Kingdom
  and speak of your might. **R.**
Making known to men your might
  and the glorious splendor of your Kingdom.

Your Kingdom is a Kingdom for all ages,
  and your dominion endures through all generations. **R.**
The LORD is faithful in all his words
  and holy in all his works.
The LORD lifts up all who are falling
  and raises up all who are bowed down. **R.**

  Luke 7:16
R. Alleluia, alleluia.
A great prophet has arisen in our midst
and God has visited his people. **R.**

† *Luke 4:31-37*
I know who you are—the Holy One of God!

Jesus went down to Capernaum, a town of Galilee.
He taught them on the sabbath,
  and they were astonished at his teaching
  because he spoke with authority.
In the synagogue there was a man with the spirit of an unclean demon,
  and he cried out in a loud voice,
  "What have you to do with us, Jesus of Nazareth?
Have you come to destroy us?
I know who you are—the Holy One of God!"
Jesus rebuked him and said, "Be quiet! Come out of him!"
Then the demon threw the man down in front of them
  and came out of him without doing him any harm.
They were all amazed and said to one another,
  "What is there about his word?
For with authority and power he commands the unclean spirits,
  and they come out."
And news of him spread everywhere in the surrounding region. ✝

WEDNESDAY, AUGUST 31
WEEKDAY

† *1 Corinthians 3:1-9*
We are God's co-workers; you are God's field, God's building.

Brothers and sisters,
  I could not talk to you as spiritual people,
  but as fleshly people, as infants in Christ.
I fed you milk, not solid food,
  because you were unable to take it.
Indeed, you are still not able, even now,
  for you are still of the flesh.

While there is jealousy and rivalry among you,
  are you not of the flesh, and walking
  according to the manner of man?
Whenever someone says, "I belong to Paul," and another,
  "I belong to Apollos," are you not merely men?

What is Apollos, after all, and what is Paul?
Ministers through whom you became believers,
  just as the Lord assigned each one.
I planted, Apollos watered, but God caused the growth.
Therefore, neither the one who plants nor the one who waters is
    anything,
  but only God, who causes the growth.
He who plants and he who waters are one,
  and each will receive wages in proportion to his labor.
For we are God's co-workers;
  you are God's field, God's building. ✝

Psalm 33:12-13, 14-15, 20-21
R. (12) **Blessed the people the Lord has chosen to be his own.**
Blessed the nation whose God is the LORD,
  the people he has chosen for his own inheritance.
From heaven the LORD looks down;
  he sees all mankind. **R.**
From his fixed throne he beholds
  all who dwell on the earth,
He who fashioned the heart of each,
  he who knows all their works. **R.**
Our soul waits for the LORD,
  who is our help and our shield,
For in him our hearts rejoice;
  in his holy name we trust. **R.**

Luke 4:18
R. Alleluia, alleluia.
The Lord sent me to bring glad tidings to the poor
and to proclaim liberty to captives. **R.**

† *Luke 4:38-44*
*To the other towns also I must proclaim the Good News of the Kingdom of God,
because for this purpose I have been sent.*

After Jesus left the synagogue, he entered the house of Simon.
Simon's mother-in-law was afflicted with a severe fever,
  and they interceded with him about her.
He stood over her, rebuked the fever, and it left her.
She got up immediately and waited on them.

At sunset, all who had people sick with various diseases brought
   them to him.
He laid his hands on each of them and cured them.
And demons also came out from many, shouting, "You are the Son of
   God."
But he rebuked them and did not allow them to speak
   because they knew that he was the Christ.

At daybreak, Jesus left and went to a deserted place.
The crowds went looking for him, and when they came to him,
   they tried to prevent him from leaving them.
But he said to them, "To the other towns also
   I must proclaim the good news of the Kingdom of God,
   because for this purpose I have been sent."
And he was preaching in the synagogues of Judea. ✛

Time to Order
***Reading God's Word* 2023.**

Available September 2022.

**An order form is available
on the last page of this book.**

THURSDAY, SEPTEMBER 1
WEEKDAY

† *1 Corinthians 3:18-23*
All belong to you, and you to Christ, and Christ to God.

Brothers and sisters:
Let no one deceive himself.
If anyone among you considers himself wise in this age,
    let him become a fool, so as to become wise.
For the wisdom of this world is foolishness in the eyes of God,
    for it is written:

> *God catches the wise in their own ruses,*

and again:

> *The Lord knows the thoughts of the wise, that they are vain.*

So let no one boast about human beings, for everything belongs to you,
    Paul or Apollos or Cephas,
    or the world or life or death,
    or the present or the future:
    all belong to you, and you to Christ, and Christ to God. ✛

Psalm 24:1bc-2, 3-4ab, 5-6
R. (1) **To the Lord belongs the earth and all that fills it.**
The LORD's are the earth and its fullness;
    the world and those who dwell in it.
For he founded it upon the seas
    and established it upon the rivers. **R.**
Who can ascend the mountain of the LORD?
    or who may stand in his holy place?
He whose hands are sinless, whose heart is clean,
    who desires not what is vain. **R.**
He shall receive a blessing from the LORD,
    a reward from God his savior.
Such is the race that seeks for him,
    that seeks the face of the God of Jacob. **R.**

Matthew 4:19
R. Alleluia, alleluia.
Come after me, says the Lord,
and I will make you fishers of men. **R.**

† *Luke 5:1-11*
They left everything and followed Jesus.

While the crowd was pressing in on Jesus and listening to the
    word of God,
  he was standing by the Lake of Gennesaret.
He saw two boats there alongside the lake;
  the fishermen had disembarked and were washing their nets.
Getting into one of the boats, the one belonging to Simon,
  he asked him to put out a short distance from the shore.
Then he sat down and taught the crowds from the boat.
After he had finished speaking, he said to Simon,
  "Put out into deep water and lower your nets for a catch."
Simon said in reply,
  "Master, we have worked hard all night and have caught nothing,
  but at your command I will lower the nets."
When they had done this, they caught a great number of fish
  and their nets were tearing.
They signaled to their partners in the other boat
  to come to help them.
They came and filled both boats
  so that the boats were in danger of sinking.
When Simon Peter saw this, he fell at the knees of Jesus and said,
  "Depart from me, Lord, for I am a sinful man."
For astonishment at the catch of fish they had made seized him
  and all those with him,
  and likewise James and John, the sons of Zebedee,
  who were partners of Simon.
Jesus said to Simon, "Do not be afraid;
  from now on you will be catching men."
When they brought their boats to the shore,
  they left everything and followed him. ✚

FRIDAY, SEPTEMBER 2
WEEKDAY

† *1 Corinthians 4:1-5*
The Lord will manifest the motives of our hearts.

Brothers and sisters:
Thus should one regard us: as servants of Christ
  and stewards of the mysteries of God.
Now it is of course required of stewards
  that they be found trustworthy.
It does not concern me in the least
  that I be judged by you or any human tribunal;

I do not even pass judgment on myself;
I am not conscious of anything against me,
but I do not thereby stand acquitted;
the one who judges me is the Lord.
Therefore, do not make any judgment before the appointed time,
until the Lord comes,
for he will bring to light what is hidden in darkness
and will manifest the motives of our hearts,
and then everyone will receive praise from God. ✝

Psalm 37:3-4, 5-6, 27-28, 39-40
R. (39a) The salvation of the just comes from the Lord.
Trust in the LORD and do good,
that you may dwell in the land and be fed in security.
Take delight in the LORD,
and he will grant you your heart's requests. **R.**
Commit to the LORD your way;
trust in him, and he will act.
He will make justice dawn for you like the light;
bright as the noonday shall be your vindication. **R.**
Turn from evil and do good,
that you may abide forever;
For the LORD loves what is right,
and forsakes not his faithful ones.
Criminals are destroyed
and the posterity of the wicked is cut off. **R.**
The salvation of the just is from the LORD;
he is their refuge in time of distress.
And the LORD helps them and delivers them;
he delivers them from the wicked and saves them,
because they take refuge in him. **R.**

John 8:12
R. Alleluia, alleluia.
I am the light of the world, says the Lord;
whoever follows me will have the light of life. **R.**

† Luke 5:33-39
When the bridegroom is taken away from them, then they will fast.

The scribes and Pharisees said to Jesus,
"The disciples of John the Baptist fast often and offer prayers,
and the disciples of the Pharisees do the same;
but yours eat and drink."
Jesus answered them, "Can you make the wedding guests fast
while the bridegroom is with them?

But the days will come, and when the bridegroom is taken away
    from them,
  then they will fast in those days."
And he also told them a parable.
"No one tears a piece from a new cloak to patch an old one.
Otherwise, he will tear the new
  and the piece from it will not match the old cloak.
Likewise, no one pours new wine into old wineskins.
Otherwise, the new wine will burst the skins,
  and it will be spilled, and the skins will be ruined.
Rather, new wine must be poured into fresh wineskins.
And no one who has been drinking old wine desires new,
  for he says, 'The old is good.'" ✝

SATURDAY, SEPTEMBER 3
St. Pope Gregory the Great

✝ 1 Corinthians 4:6b-15
We go hungry and thirsty and we are poorly clad.

Brothers and sisters:
Learn from myself and Apollos not to go beyond what is written,
  so that none of you will be inflated with pride
  in favor of one person over against another.
Who confers distinction upon you?
What do you possess that you have not received?
But if you have received it,
  why are you boasting as if you did not receive it?
You are already satisfied; you have already grown rich;
  you have become kings without us!
Indeed, I wish that you had become kings,
  so that we also might become kings with you.

For as I see it, God has exhibited us Apostles as the last of all,
  like people sentenced to death,
    since we have become a spectacle to the world,
    to angels and men alike.
We are fools on Christ's account, but you are wise in Christ;
  we are weak, but you are strong;
  you are held in honor, but we in disrepute.
To this very hour we go hungry and thirsty,
  we are poorly clad and roughly treated,
    we wander about homeless and we toil, working with our own
      hands.
When ridiculed, we bless; when persecuted, we endure;
  when slandered, we respond gently.

We have become like the world's rubbish, the scum of all,
   to this very moment.

I am writing you this not to shame you,
   but to admonish you as my beloved children.
Even if you should have countless guides to Christ,
   yet you do not have many fathers,
   for I became your father in Christ Jesus through the Gospel. ✛

Psalm 145:17-18, 19-20, 21

R. (18) **The Lord is near to all who call upon him.**

The Lord is just in all his ways
   and holy in all his works.
The Lord is near to all who call upon him,
   to all who call upon him in truth. **R.**
He fulfills the desire of those who fear him,
   he hears their cry and saves them.
The Lord keeps all who love him,
   but all the wicked he will destroy. **R.**
May my mouth speak the praise of the Lord,
   and may all flesh bless his holy name forever and ever. **R.**

John 14:6

R. Alleluia, alleluia.

I am the way and the truth and the life, says the Lord;
no one comes to the Father except through me. **R.**

† *Luke 6:1-5*

Why are you doing what is unlawful on the sabbath?

While Jesus was going through a field of grain on a sabbath,
   his disciples were picking the heads of grain,
   rubbing them in their hands, and eating them.
Some Pharisees said,
   "Why are you doing what is unlawful on the sabbath?"
Jesus said to them in reply,
   "Have you not read what David did
   when he and those who were with him were hungry?
How he went into the house of God, took the bread of offering,
   which only the priests could lawfully eat,
   ate of it, and shared it with his companions?"
Then he said to them, "The Son of Man is lord of the sabbath." ✛

SUNDAY, SEPTEMBER 4
TWENTY-THIRD SUNDAY IN ORDINARY TIME

† *Wisdom 9:13-18b*
Who can conceive what the LORD intends?

Who can know God's counsel,
  or who can conceive what the LORD intends?
For the deliberations of mortals are timid,
  and unsure are our plans.
For the corruptible body burdens the soul
  and the earthen shelter weighs down the mind
    that has many concerns.
And scarce do we guess the things on earth,
  and what is within our grasp we find with difficulty;
  but when things are in heaven, who can search them out?
Or who ever knew your counsel, except you had given wisdom
  and sent your holy spirit from on high?
And thus were the paths of those on earth made straight. ✛

Psalm 90:3-4, 5-6, 12-13, 14 and 17
R. (1) **In every age, O Lord, you have been our refuge.**
You turn man back to dust,
  saying, "Return, O children of men."
For a thousand years in your sight
  are as yesterday, now that it is past,
  or as a watch of the night. **R.**
You make an end of them in their sleep;
  the next morning they are like the changing grass,
which at dawn springs up anew,
  but by evening wilts and fades. **R.**
Teach us to number our days aright,
  that we may gain wisdom of heart.
Return, O LORD! How long?
  Have pity on your servants! **R.**
Fill us at daybreak with your kindness,
  that we may shout for joy and gladness all our days.
And may the gracious care of the LORD our God be ours;
  prosper the work of our hands for us!
  Prosper the work of our hands! **R.**

† *Philemon 9-10, 12-17*

Receive him no longer as a slave but as a beloved brother.

I, Paul, an old man,
and now also a prisoner for Christ Jesus,
urge you on behalf of my child Onesimus,
whose father I have become in my imprisonment;
I am sending him, that is, my own heart, back to you.
I should have liked to retain him for myself,
so that he might serve me on your behalf
in my imprisonment for the gospel,
but I did not want to do anything without your consent,
so that the good you do might not be forced but voluntary.
Perhaps this is why he was away from you for a while,
that you might have him back forever,
no longer as a slave
but more than a slave, a brother,
beloved especially to me, but even more so to you,
as a man and in the Lord.
So if you regard me as a partner, welcome him as you would me. ✛

Psalm 119:135
R. Alleluia, alleluia.
Let your face shine upon your servant;
and teach me your laws. **R.**

† *Luke 14:25-33*

Anyone of you who does not renounce all possessions cannot be my disciple.

Great crowds were traveling with Jesus,
and he turned and addressed them,
"If anyone comes to me without hating his father and mother,
wife and children, brothers and sisters,
and even his own life,
he cannot be my disciple.
Whoever does not carry his own cross and come after me
cannot be my disciple.
Which of you wishing to construct a tower
does not first sit down and calculate the cost
to see if there is enough for its completion?
Otherwise, after laying the foundation
and finding himself unable to finish the work
the onlookers should laugh at him and say,
'This one began to build but did not have the resources to finish.'
Or what king marching into battle would not first sit down
and decide whether with ten thousand troops

he can successfully oppose another king
advancing upon him with twenty thousand troops?
But if not, while he is still far away,
he will send a delegation to ask for peace terms.
In the same way,
anyone of you who does not renounce all his possessions
cannot be my disciple." ✝

MONDAY, SEPTEMBER 5
WEEKDAY

✝ *1 Corinthians 5:1-8*
Clean out the old yeast; for our Paschal Lamb, Christ, has been sacrificed.

Brothers and sisters:
It is widely reported that there is immorality among you,
and immorality of a kind not found even among pagans—
a man living with his father's wife.
And you are inflated with pride.
Should you not rather have been sorrowful?
The one who did this deed should be expelled from your midst.
I, for my part, although absent in body but present in spirit,
have already, as if present,
pronounced judgment on the one who has committed this deed,
in the name of our Lord Jesus:
when you have gathered together and I am with you in spirit
with the power of the Lord Jesus,
you are to deliver this man to Satan
for the destruction of his flesh,
so that his spirit may be saved on the day of the Lord.

Your boasting is not appropriate.
Do you not know that a little yeast leavens all the dough?
Clear out the old yeast, so that you may become a fresh batch of dough,
inasmuch as you are unleavened.
For our Paschal Lamb, Christ, has been sacrificed.
Therefore, let us celebrate the feast,
not with the old yeast, the yeast of malice and wickedness,
but with the unleavened bread of sincerity and truth. ✝

Psalm 5:5-6, 7, 12
R. (9) Lead me in your justice, Lord.
For you, O God, delight not in wickedness;
no evil man remains with you;
the arrogant may not stand in your sight.
You hate all evildoers. **R.**
You destroy all who speak falsehood;

The bloodthirsty and the deceitful
   the LORD abhors. **R.**
But let all who take refuge in you
   be glad and exult forever.
Protect them, that you may be the joy
   of those who love your name. **R.**

   John 10:27
R. Alleluia, alleluia.
My sheep hear my voice, says the Lord;
I know them, and they follow me. **R.**

†*Luke 6:6-11*
*The scribes and the Pharisees watched him closely
to see if he would cure on the sabbath.*

On a certain sabbath Jesus went into the synagogue and taught,
   and there was a man there whose right hand was withered.
The scribes and the Pharisees watched him closely
   to see if he would cure on the sabbath
   so that they might discover a reason to accuse him.
But he realized their intentions
   and said to the man with the withered hand,
   "Come up and stand before us."
And he rose and stood there.
Then Jesus said to them,
   "I ask you, is it lawful to do good on the sabbath
   rather than to do evil,
   to save life rather than to destroy it?"
Looking around at them all, he then said to him,
   "Stretch out your hand."
He did so and his hand was restored.
But they became enraged
   and discussed together what they might do to Jesus. ✛

TUESDAY, SEPTEMBER 6
WEEKDAY

† *1 Corinthians 6:1-11*
A believer goes to court against a believer and that before unbelievers.

Brothers and sisters:
How can any one of you with a case against another
   dare to bring it to the unjust for judgment
   instead of to the holy ones?
Do you not know that the holy ones will judge the world?
If the world is to be judged by you,
   are you unqualified for the lowest law courts?

Do you not know that we will judge angels?
Then why not everyday matters?
If, therefore, you have courts for everyday matters,
   do you seat as judges people of no standing in the Church?
I say this to shame you.
Can it be that there is not one among you wise enough
   to be able to settle a case between brothers?
But rather brother goes to court against brother,
   and that before unbelievers?

Now indeed then it is, in any case,
   a failure on your part that you have lawsuits against one another.
Why not rather put up with injustice?
Why not rather let yourselves be cheated?
Instead, you inflict injustice and cheat, and this to brothers.
Do you not know that the unjust will not inherit the Kingdom of God?
Do not be deceived;
   neither fornicators nor idolaters nor adulterers
   nor boy prostitutes nor sodomites nor thieves
   nor the greedy nor drunkards nor slanderers nor robbers
   will inherit the Kingdom of God.
That is what some of you used to be;
   but now you have had yourselves washed, you were sanctified,
   you were justified in the name of the Lord Jesus Christ
   and in the Spirit of our God. ✛

   Psalm 149:1b-2, 3-4, 5-6a and 9b
R. (see 4) **The Lord takes delight in his people.**
Sing to the LORD a new song
   of praise in the assembly of the faithful.
Let Israel be glad in their maker,
   let the children of Zion rejoice in their king. **R.**
Let them praise his name in the festive dance,
   let them sing praise to him with timbrel and harp.
For the LORD loves his people,
   and he adorns the lowly with victory. **R.**
Let the faithful exult in glory;
   let them sing for joy upon their couches;
Let the high praises of God be in their throats.
   This is the glory of all his faithful. Alleluia. **R.**

   See John 15:16
R. Alleluia, alleluia.
I chose you from the world,
that you may go and bear fruit that will last, says the Lord. **R.**

† *Luke 6:12-19*

He spent the night in prayer. He chose Twelve, whom he also named Apostles.

Jesus departed to the mountain to pray,
   and he spent the night in prayer to God.
When day came, he called his disciples to himself,
   and from them he chose Twelve, whom he also named Apostles:
   Simon, whom he named Peter, and his brother Andrew,
   James, John, Philip, Bartholomew,
   Matthew, Thomas, James the son of Alphaeus,
   Simon who was called a Zealot,
   and Judas the son of James,
   and Judas Iscariot, who became a traitor.

And he came down with them and stood on a stretch of level ground.
A great crowd of his disciples and a large number of the people
   from all Judea and Jerusalem
   and the coastal region of Tyre and Sidon
   came to hear him and to be healed of their diseases;
   and even those who were tormented by unclean spirits were cured.
Everyone in the crowd sought to touch him
   because power came forth from him and healed them all. ✛

WEDNESDAY, SEPTEMBER 7
WEEKDAY

† *1 Corinthians 7:25-31*

Are you bound to a wife? Do not seek a separation.
Are you free of a wife? Then, do not look for a wife.

Brothers and sisters:
In regard to virgins, I have no commandment from the Lord,
   but I give my opinion as one who by the Lord's mercy is trustworthy.
So this is what I think best because of the present distress:
   that it is a good thing for a person to remain as he is.
Are you bound to a wife? Do not seek a separation.
Are you free of a wife? Then do not look for a wife.
If you marry, however, you do not sin,
   nor does an unmarried woman sin if she marries;
   but such people will experience affliction in their earthly life,
   and I would like to spare you that.

I tell you, brothers, the time is running out.
From now on, let those having wives act as not having them,
   those weeping as not weeping,

those rejoicing as not rejoicing,
those buying as not owning,
those using the world as not using it fully.
For the world in its present form is passing away. ✣

Psalm 45:11-12, 14-15, 16-17
R. (11) **Listen to me, daughter; see and bend your ear.**
Hear, O daughter, and see; turn your ear,
    forget your people and your father's house.
So shall the king desire your beauty;
    for he is your lord, and you must worship him. **R.**
All glorious is the king's daughter as she enters;
    her raiment is threaded with spun gold.
In embroidered apparel she is borne in to the king;
    behind her the virgins of her train are brought to you. **R.**
They are borne in with gladness and joy;
    they enter the palace of the king.
The place of your fathers your sons shall have;
    you shall make them princes through all the land. **R.**

Luke 6:23ab
R. Alleluia, alleluia.
Rejoice and leap for joy!
Your reward will be great in heaven. **R.**

† Luke 6:20-26
Blessed are you who are poor. Woe to you who are rich.

Raising his eyes toward his disciples Jesus said:

"Blessed are you who are poor,
    for the Kingdom of God is yours.
Blessed are you who are now hungry,
    for you will be satisfied.
Blessed are you who are now weeping,
    for you will laugh.
Blessed are you when people hate you,
    and when they exclude and insult you,
    and denounce your name as evil
    on account of the Son of Man.

"Rejoice and leap for joy on that day!
Behold, your reward
    will be great in heaven. For their
    ancestors treated the prophets
    in the same way.

But woe to you who are rich,
   for you have received your consolation.
But woe to you who are filled now,
   for you will be hungry.
Woe to you who laugh now,
   for you will grieve and weep.
Woe to you when all speak well of you,
   for their ancestors treated the false
   prophets in this way." ✜

THURSDAY, SEPTEMBER 8
The Nativity of the Blessed Virgin Mary

† Micah 5:1-4a (or Romans 8:28-30)
The time when she who is to give birth has borne.

The LORD says:
You, Bethlehem-Ephrathah,
   too small to be among the clans of Judah,
From you shall come forth for me
   one who is to be ruler in Israel;
whose origin is from of old,
   from ancient times.
(Therefore the Lord will give them up, until the time
   when she who is to give birth has borne,
And the rest of his brethren shall return
   to the children of Israel.)
He shall stand firm and shepherd his flock
   by the strength of the LORD,
   in the majestic name of the LORD, his God;
And they shall remain, for now his greatness
   shall reach to the ends of the earth;
   he shall be peace. ✜

Psalm 13:6ab, 6c
R. (Isaiah 61:10) **With delight I rejoice in the Lord.**
Though I trusted in your mercy,
   let my heart rejoice in your salvation. **R.**
Let me sing of the LORD, "He has been good to me." **R.**

R. Alleluia, alleluia.
Blessed are you, holy Virgin Mary, deserving of all praise;
from you rose the sun of justice, Christ our God. **R.**

† *Matthew 1:1-16, 18-23* (or Matthew 1:18-23)
For it is through the Holy Spirit that this child has been conceived in her.

The Book of the genealogy of Jesus Christ,
the son of David, the son of Abraham.

Abraham became the father of Isaac,
  Isaac the father of Jacob,
  Jacob the father of Judah and his brothers.
Judah became the father of Perez and Zerah,
  whose mother was Tamar.
Perez became the father of Hezron,
  Hezron the father of Ram,
  Ram the father of Amminadab.
Amminadab became the father of Nahshon,
  Nahshon the father of Salmon,
  Salmon the father of Boaz,
  whose mother was Rahab.
Boaz became the father of Obed,
  whose mother was Ruth.
Obed became the father of Jesse,
  Jesse the father of David the king.

David became the father of Solomon,
  whose mother had been the wife of Uriah.
Solomon became the father of Rehoboam,
  Rehoboam the father of Abijah,
  Abijah the father of Asaph.
Asaph became the father of Jehoshaphat,
  Jehoshaphat the father of Joram,
  Joram the father of Uzziah.
Uzziah became the father of Jotham,
  Jotham the father of Ahaz,
  Ahaz the father of Hezekiah.
Hezekiah became the father of Manasseh,
  Manasseh the father of Amos,
  Amos the father of Josiah.
Josiah became the father of Jechoniah and his brothers
  at the time of the Babylonian exile.

After the Babylonian exile,
  Jechoniah became the father of Shealtiel,
  Shealtiel the father of Zerubbabel,
  Zerubbabel the father of Abiud.
Abiud became the father of Eliakim,
  Eliakim the father of Azor,

Azor the father of Zadok.
Zadok became the father of Achim,
  Achim the father of Eliud,
  Eliud the father of Eleazar.
Eleazar became the father of Matthan,
  Matthan the father of Jacob,
  Jacob the father of Joseph, the husband of Mary.
Of her was born Jesus who is called the Christ.

Now this is how the birth of Jesus Christ came about.
When his mother Mary was betrothed to Joseph,
  but before they lived together,
  she was found with child through the Holy Spirit.
Joseph her husband, since he was a righteous man,
  yet unwilling to expose her to shame,
  decided to divorce her quietly.
Such was his intention when, behold,
  the angel of the Lord appeared to him in a dream and said,
"Joseph, son of David,
  do not be afraid to take Mary your wife into your home.
For it is through the Holy Spirit
  that this child has been conceived in her.
She will bear a son and you are to name him Jesus,
  because he will save his people from their sins."
All this took place to fulfill
  what the Lord had said through the prophet:

> *Behold, the virgin shall be with child and bear a son,*
> *and they shall name him Emmanuel,*

which means "God is with us." ✛

FRIDAY, SEPTEMBER 9
St. Peter Claver

† *1 Corinthians 9:16-19, 22b-27*
I have become all things to all, to save at least some.

Brothers and sisters:
If I preach the Gospel, this is no reason for me to boast,
  for an obligation has been imposed on me,
  and woe to me if I do not preach it!
If I do so willingly, I have a recompense,
  but if unwillingly, then I have been entrusted with a stewardship.
What then is my recompense?
That, when I preach, I offer the Gospel free of charge
  so as not to make full use of my right in the Gospel.

Although I am free in regard to all,
    I have made myself a slave to all
    so as to win over as many as possible.
I have become all things to all, to save at least some.
All this I do for the sake of the Gospel,
    so that I too may have a share in it.

Do you not know that the runners in the stadium all run in the race,
    but only one wins the prize?
Run so as to win.
Every athlete exercises discipline in every way.
They do it to win a perishable crown,
    but we an imperishable one.
Thus I do not run aimlessly;
    I do not fight as if I were shadowboxing.
No, I drive my body and train it,
    for fear that, after having preached to others,
    I myself should be disqualified. ✛

Psalm 84:3, 4, 5-6, 12
R. (2) How lovely is your dwelling place, Lord, mighty God!
My soul yearns and pines
    for the courts of the LORD.
My heart and my flesh
    cry out for the living God. **R.**
Even the sparrow finds a home,
    and the swallow a nest
    in which she puts her young—
Your altars, O LORD of hosts,
    my king and my God! **R.**
Blessed they who dwell in your house!
    continually they praise you.
Blessed the men whose strength you are!
    their hearts are set upon the pilgrimage. **R.**
For a sun and a shield is the LORD God;
    grace and glory he bestows;
The LORD withholds no good thing
    from those who walk in sincerity. **R.**

See John 17:17b, 17a
R. Alleluia, alleluia.
Your word, O Lord, is truth;
consecrate us in the truth. **R.**

† *Luke 6:39-42*
Can a blind person guide a blind person?

Jesus told his disciples a parable:
"Can a blind person guide a blind person?
Will not both fall into a pit?
No disciple is superior to the teacher;
  but when fully trained,
  every disciple will be like his teacher.
Why do you notice the splinter in your brother's eye,
  but do not perceive the wooden beam in your own?
How can you say to your brother,
  'Brother, let me remove that splinter in your eye,'
  when you do not even notice the wooden beam in your own eye?
You hypocrite! Remove the wooden beam from your eye first;
  then you will see clearly
  to remove the splinter in your brother's eye." ✦

SATURDAY, SEPTEMBER 10
WEEKDAY, *[BVM]*

† *1 Corinthians 10:14-22*
We, though many, are one Body, for we all partake of the one bread.

My beloved ones, avoid idolatry.
I am speaking as to sensible people;
  judge for yourselves what I am saying.
The cup of blessing that we bless,
  is it not a participation in the Blood of Christ?
The bread that we break,
  is it not a participation in the Body of Christ?
Because the loaf of bread is one,
  we, though many, are one Body,
  for we all partake of the one loaf.

Look at Israel according to the flesh;
  are not those who eat the sacrifices participants in the altar?
So what am I saying?
That meat sacrificed to idols is anything?
Or that an idol is anything?
No, I mean that what they sacrifice,
  they sacrifice to demons, not to God,
  and I do not want you to become participants with demons.
You cannot drink the cup of the Lord and also the cup of demons.
You cannot partake of the table of the Lord and of the table of demons.
Or are we provoking the Lord to jealous anger?
Are we stronger than him? ✦

Psalm 116:12-13, 17-18

R. (17) **To you, Lord, I will offer a sacrifice of praise.**

How shall I make a return to the LORD
    for all the good he has done for me?
The cup of salvation I will take up,
    and I will call upon the name of the LORD. **R.**
To you will I offer sacrifice of thanksgiving,
    and I will call upon the name of the LORD.
My vows to the LORD I will pay
    in the presence of all his people. **R.**

John 14:23

R. Alleluia, alleluia.

Whoever loves me will keep my word,
and my Father will love him,
and we will come to him. **R.**

† *Luke 6:43-49*

Why do you call me, "Lord, Lord," but do not do what I command?

Jesus said to his disciples:
"A good tree does not bear rotten fruit,
    nor does a rotten tree bear good fruit.
For every tree is known by its own fruit.
For people do not pick figs from thornbushes,
    nor do they gather grapes from brambles.
A good person out of the store of goodness in his heart produces good,
    but an evil person out of a store of evil produces evil;
    for from the fullness of the heart the mouth speaks.

"Why do you call me, 'Lord, Lord,' but not do what I command?
I will show you what someone is like who comes to me,
    listens to my words, and acts on them.
That one is like a man building a house,
    who dug deeply and laid the foundation on rock;
    when the flood came, the river burst against that house
    but could not shake it because it had been well built.
But the one who listens and does not act
    is like a person who built a house on the ground
    without a foundation.
When the river burst against it,
    it collapsed at once and was completely destroyed." ✚

SUNDAY, SEPTEMBER 11
TWENTY-FOURTH SUNDAY IN ORDINARY TIME

† Exodus 32:7-11, 13-14
The Lord relented in the punishment
he had threatened to inflict on his people.

The LORD said to Moses,
"Go down at once to your people,
whom you brought out of the land of Egypt,
for they have become depraved.
They have soon turned aside from the way I pointed out to them,
making for themselves a molten calf and worshiping it,
sacrificing to it and crying out,
'This is your God, O Israel,
who brought you out of the land of Egypt!'
I see how stiff-necked this people is," continued the LORD to Moses.
"Let me alone, then,
that my wrath may blaze up against them to consume them.
Then I will make of you a great nation."

But Moses implored the LORD, his God, saying,
"Why, O LORD, should your wrath blaze up against your own
people,
whom you brought out of the land of Egypt
with such great power and with so strong a hand?
Remember your servants Abraham, Isaac, and Israel,
and how you swore to them by your own self, saying,
'I will make your descendants as numerous as the stars in the sky;
and all this land that I promised,
I will give your descendants as their perpetual heritage.'"
So the LORD relented in the punishment
he had threatened to inflict on his people. ✛

Psalm 51:3-4, 12-13, 17 and 19
R. (Lk 15:18) **I will rise and go to my father.**
Have mercy on me, O God, in your goodness;
in the greatness of your compassion wipe out my offense.
Thoroughly wash me from my guilt
and of my sin cleanse me. **R.**
A clean heart create for me, O God,
and a steadfast spirit renew within me.
Cast me not out from your presence,
and your Holy Spirit take not from me. **R.**

O Lord, open my lips,
    and my mouth shall proclaim your praise.
My sacrifice, O God, is a contrite spirit;
    a heart contrite and humbled, O God, you will not spurn. **R.**

† *1 Timothy 1:12-17*
Christ came to save sinners.

Beloved:
I am grateful to him who has strengthened me, Christ Jesus our Lord,
    because he considered me trustworthy
    in appointing me to the ministry.
I was once a blasphemer and a persecutor and arrogant,
    but I have been mercifully treated
    because I acted out of ignorance in my unbelief.
Indeed, the grace of our Lord has been abundant,
    along with the faith and love that are in Christ Jesus.
This saying is trustworthy and deserves full acceptance:
    Christ Jesus came into the world to save sinners.
Of these I am the foremost.
But for that reason I was mercifully treated,
    so that in me, as the foremost,
    Christ Jesus might display all his patience as an example
    for those who would come to believe in him for everlasting life.
To the king of ages, incorruptible, invisible, the only God,
    honor and glory forever and ever. Amen. ✝

2 Corinthians 5:19
R. Alleluia, alleluia.
God was reconciling the world to himself in Christ
and entrusting to us the message of reconciliation. **R.**

† *Luke 15:1-32* (or Luke 15:1-10)
There will be great joy in heaven over one sinner who repents.

Tax collectors and sinners were all drawing near to listen to Jesus,
    but the Pharisees and scribes began to complain, saying,
    "This man welcomes sinners and eats with them."
So to them he addressed this parable.
"What man among you having a hundred sheep and losing one of them
    would not leave the ninety-nine in the desert
    and go after the lost one until he finds it?
And when he does find it,
    he sets it on his shoulders with great joy
    and, upon his arrival home,
    he calls together his friends and neighbors and says to them,
    'Rejoice with me because I have found my lost sheep.'

I tell you, in just the same way
    there will be more joy in heaven over one sinner who repents
    than over ninety-nine righteous people
    who have no need of repentance.

"Or what woman having ten coins and losing one
    would not light a lamp and sweep the house,
    searching carefully until she finds it?
And when she does find it,
    she calls together her friends and neighbors
    and says to them,
    'Rejoice with me because I have found the coin that I lost.'
In just the same way, I tell you,
    there will be rejoicing among the angels of God
    over one sinner who repents."

Then he said,
    "A man had two sons, and the younger son said to his father,
    'Father give me the share of your estate that should come to me.'
So the father divided the property between them.
After a few days, the younger son collected all his belongings
    and set off to a distant country
    where he squandered his inheritance on a life of dissipation.
When he had freely spent everything,
    a severe famine struck that country,
    and he found himself in dire need.
So he hired himself out to one of the local citizens
    who sent him to his farm to tend the swine.
And he longed to eat his fill of the pods on which the swine fed,
    but nobody gave him any.
Coming to his senses he thought,
    'How many of my father's hired workers
    have more than enough food to eat,
    but here am I, dying from hunger.
I shall get up and go to my father and I shall say to him,
    "Father, I have sinned against heaven and against you.
I no longer deserve to be called your son;
    treat me as you would treat one of your hired workers."'
So he got up and went back to his father.
While he was still a long way off,
    his father caught sight of him,
    and was filled with compassion.
He ran to his son, embraced him and kissed him.

His son said to him,
  'Father, I have sinned against heaven and against you;
  I no longer deserve to be called your son.'
But his father ordered his servants,
  'Quickly bring the finest robe and put it on him;
  put a ring on his finger and sandals on his feet.
Take the fattened calf and slaughter it.
Then let us celebrate with a feast,
  because this son of mine was dead, and has come to life again;
  he was lost, and has been found.'
Then the celebration began.
Now the older son had been out in the field
  and, on his way back, as he neared the house,
  he heard the sound of music and dancing.
He called one of the servants and asked what this might mean.
The servant said to him,
  'Your brother has returned
  and your father has slaughtered the fattened calf
  because he has him back safe and sound.'
He became angry,
  and when he refused to enter the house,
  his father came out and pleaded with him.
He said to his father in reply,
  'Look, all these years I served you
  and not once did I disobey your orders;
  yet you never gave me even a young goat to feast on with my
      friends.
But when your son returns,
  who swallowed up your property with prostitutes,
  for him you slaughter the fattened calf.'
He said to him,
  'My son, you are here with me always;
  everything I have is yours.
But now we must celebrate and rejoice,
  because your brother was dead and has come to life again;
  he was lost and has been found.'" ✚

MONDAY, SEPTEMBER 12
WEEKDAY, THE MOST HOLY NAME OF MARY

† *1 Corinthians 11:17-26, 33*
If there are divisions among you, then you do not eat the Lord's supper.

Brothers and sisters:
In giving this instruction, I do not praise the fact
  that your meetings are doing more harm than good.
First of all, I hear that when you meet as a Church
  there are divisions among you,
  and to a degree I believe it;
  there have to be factions among you
  in order that also those who are approved among you
  may become known.
When you meet in one place, then,
  it is not to eat the Lord's supper,
  for in eating, each one goes ahead with his own supper,
  and one goes hungry while another gets drunk.
Do you not have houses in which you can eat and drink?
Or do you show contempt for the Church of God
  and make those who have nothing feel ashamed?
What can I say to you? Shall I praise you?
In this matter I do not praise you.

For I received from the Lord what I also handed on to you,
  that the Lord Jesus, on the night he was handed over,
  took bread and, after he had given thanks,
  broke it and said, "This is my Body that is for you.
Do this in remembrance of me."
In the same way also the cup, after supper, saying,
  "This cup is the new covenant in my Blood.
Do this, as often as you drink it, in remembrance of me."
For as often as you eat this bread and drink the cup,
  you proclaim the death of the Lord until he comes.

Therefore, my brothers and sisters,
  when you come together to eat, wait for one another. ✛

    Psalm 40:7-8a, 8b-9, 10, 17
R. (1 Corinthians 11:26b) **Proclaim the death of the Lord until
  he comes again.**
Sacrifice or oblation you wished not,
  but ears open to obedience you gave me.
Burnt offerings or sin-offerings you sought not;
  then said I, "Behold I come." **R.**

"In the written scroll it is prescribed for me,
To do your will, O my God, is my delight,
and your law is within my heart!" **R.**
I announced your justice in the vast assembly;
I did not restrain my lips, as you, O Lᴏʀᴅ, know. **R.**
May all who seek you
exult and be glad in you
And may those who love your salvation
say ever, "The Lᴏʀᴅ be glorified." **R.**

John 3:16
R. Alleluia, alleluia.
God so loved the world that he gave his only-begotten Son,
so that everyone who believes in him might have eternal life. **R.**

✝ *Luke 7:1-10*
Not even in Israel have I found such faith.

When Jesus had finished all his words to the people,
he entered Capernaum.
A centurion there had a slave who was ill and about to die,
and he was valuable to him.
When he heard about Jesus, he sent elders of the Jews to him,
asking him to come and save the life of his slave.
They approached Jesus and strongly urged him to come, saying,
"He deserves to have you do this for him,
for he loves our nation and he built the synagogue for us."
And Jesus went with them,
but when he was only a short distance from the house,
the centurion sent friends to tell him,
"Lord, do not trouble yourself,
for I am not worthy to have you enter under my roof.
Therefore, I did not consider myself worthy to come to you;
but say the word and let my servant be healed.
For I too am a person subject to authority,
with soldiers subject to me.
And I say to one, 'Go,' and he goes;
and to another, 'Come here,' and he comes;
and to my slave, 'Do this,' and he does it."
When Jesus heard this he was amazed at him
and, turning, said to the crowd following him,
"I tell you, not even in Israel have I found such faith."
When the messengers returned to the house,
they found the slave in good health. ✝

TUESDAY, SEPTEMBER 13
St. John Chrysostom

✝ *1 Corinthians 12:12-14, 27-31a*
Now you are Christ's Body, and individually parts of it.

Brothers and sisters:
As a body is one though it has many parts,
  and all the parts of the body, though many, are one body,
  so also Christ.
For in one Spirit we were all baptized into one Body,
  whether Jews or Greeks, slaves or free persons,
  and we were all given to drink of one Spirit.

Now the body is not a single part, but many.

Now you are Christ's Body, and individually parts of it.
Some people God has designated in the Church
  to be, first, Apostles; second, prophets; third, teachers;
  then, mighty deeds;
  then gifts of healing, assistance, administration,
  and varieties of tongues.
Are all Apostles? Are all prophets? Are all teachers?
Do all work mighty deeds? Do all have gifts of healing?
Do all speak in tongues? Do all interpret?
Strive eagerly for the greatest spiritual gifts. ✛

Psalm 100:1b-2, 3, 4, 5
R. (3) **We are his people: the sheep of his flock.**
Sing joyfully to the Lord, all you lands;
  serve the Lord with gladness;
  come before him with joyful song. **R.**
Know that the Lord is God;
  he made us, his we are;
  his people, the flock he tends. **R.**
Enter his gates with thanksgiving,
  his courts with praise;
Give thanks to him; bless his name. **R.**
The Lord is good,
  the Lord, whose kindness endures forever,
  and his faithfulness, to all generations. **R.**

Luke 7:16
R. Alleluia, alleluia.
A great prophet has arisen in our midst
and God has visited his people. **R.**

† *Luke 7:11-17*
Young man, I tell you, arise!

Jesus journeyed to a city called Nain,
and his disciples and a large crowd accompanied him.
As he drew near to the gate of the city,
a man who had died was being carried out,
the only son of his mother, and she was a widow.
A large crowd from the city was with her.
When the Lord saw her,
he was moved with pity for her and said to her,
"Do not weep."
He stepped forward and touched the coffin;
at this the bearers halted,
and he said, "Young man, I tell you, arise!"
The dead man sat up and began to speak,
and Jesus gave him to his mother.
Fear seized them all, and they glorified God, exclaiming,
"A great prophet has arisen in our midst,"
and "God has visited his people."
This report about him spread through the whole of Judea
and in all the surrounding region. ✛

WEDNESDAY, SEPTEMBER 14
THE EXALTATION OF THE HOLY CROSS

† *Numbers 21:4b-9*
Whenever anyone who had been bitten by a serpent
looked at the bronze serpent, he lived.

With their patience worn out by the journey,
the people complained against God and Moses,
"Why have you brought us up from Egypt to die in this desert,
where there is no food or water?
We are disgusted with this wretched food!"

In punishment the LORD sent among the people saraph serpents,
which bit the people so that many of them died.
Then the people came to Moses and said,
"We have sinned in complaining against the LORD and you.
Pray the LORD to take the serpents from us."
So Moses prayed for the people, and the LORD said to Moses,
"Make a saraph and mount it on a pole,
and if any who have been bitten look at it, they will live."
Moses accordingly made a bronze serpent and mounted it on a pole,
and whenever anyone who had been bitten by a serpent
looked at the bronze serpent, he lived. ✛

Psalm 78:1bc-2, 34-35, 36-37, 38
R. (see 7b) **Do not forget the works of the Lord!**
Hearken, my people, to my teaching;
   incline your ears to the words of my mouth.
I will open my mouth in a parable,
   I will utter mysteries from of old. **R.**
While he slew them they sought him
   and inquired after God again,
Remembering that God was their rock
   and the Most High God, their redeemer. **R.**
But they flattered him with their mouths
   and lied to him with their tongues,
Though their hearts were not steadfast toward him,
   nor were they faithful to his covenant. **R.**
But he, being merciful, forgave their sin
   and destroyed them not;
Often he turned back his anger
   and let none of his wrath be roused. **R.**

† *Philippians 2:6-11*
He humbled himself; because of this God greatly exalted him.

Brothers and sisters:
   Christ Jesus, though he was in the form of God,
      did not regard equality with God something to be grasped.
   Rather, he emptied himself,
   taking the form of a slave,
   coming in human likeness;
   and found human in appearance,
   he humbled himself,
   becoming obedient to death,
      even death on a cross.
Because of this, God greatly exalted him
      and bestowed on him the name
      that is above every name,
      that at the name of Jesus
      every knee should bend,
      of those in heaven and on earth and under the earth,
      and every tongue confess that
      Jesus Christ is Lord,
      to the glory of God the Father. ✛

R. Alleluia, alleluia.
We adore you, O Christ, and we bless you,
because by your Cross you have redeemed the world. **R.**

† *John 3:13-17*
So the Son of Man must be lifted up.

Jesus said to Nicodemus:
"No one has gone up to heaven
    except the one who has come down from heaven, the Son of Man.
And just as Moses lifted up the serpent in the desert,
    so must the Son of Man be lifted up,
    so that everyone who believes in him may have eternal life."

For God so loved the world that he gave his only Son,
    so that everyone who believes in him might not perish
    but might have eternal life.
For God did not send his Son into the world to condemn the world,
    but that the world might be saved through him. ✛

THURSDAY, SEPTEMBER 15
OUR LADY OF SORROWS

† *1 Corinthians 15:1-11*
So we preach and so you believed.

I am reminding you, brothers and sisters,
    of the Gospel I preached to you,
    which you indeed received and in which you also stand.
Through it you are also being saved,
    if you hold fast to the word I preached to you,
    unless you believed in vain.
For I handed on to you as of first importance what I also received:
    that Christ died for our sins in accordance with the Scriptures;
    that he was buried;
    that he was raised on the third day in accordance with the
        Scriptures;
    that he appeared to Cephas, then to the Twelve.
After that, he appeared to more than five hundred brothers at once,
    most of whom are still living, though some have fallen asleep.
After that he appeared to James,
    then to all the Apostles.
Last of all, as to one born abnormally,
    he appeared to me.
For I am the least of the Apostles,
    not fit to be called an Apostle,
    because I persecuted the Church of God.
But by the grace of God I am what I am,
    and his grace to me has not been ineffective.

Indeed, I have toiled harder than all of them;
not I, however, but the grace of God that is with me.
Therefore, whether it be I or they,
so we preach and so you believed. ✛

Psalm 118:1b-2, 16ab-17, 28
R. (1) **Give thanks to the Lord, for he is good.**
Give thanks to the LORD, for he is good,
for his mercy endures forever.
Let the house of Israel say,
"His mercy endures forever." **R.**
"The right hand of the LORD is exalted;
the right hand of the LORD has struck with power."
I shall not die, but live,
and declare the works of the LORD. **R.**
You are my God, and I give thanks to you;
O my God, I extol you. **R.**

The sequence Stabat Mater *may be sung optionally before the Alleluia.*

R. Alleluia, alleluia.
Blessed are you, O Virgin Mary;
without dying you won the martyr's crown
beneath the Cross of the Lord. **R.**

† John 19:25-27 (or Luke 2:33-35)
How that loving mother was pierced with grief and anguish
when she saw the sufferings of her Son (Stabat Mater).

Standing by the cross of Jesus were his mother
and his mother's sister, Mary the wife of Clopas,
and Mary Magdalene.
When Jesus saw his mother and the disciple there whom he loved
he said to his mother, "Woman, behold, your son."
Then he said to the disciple,
"Behold, your mother."
And from that hour the disciple took her into his home. ✛

FRIDAY, SEPTEMBER 16
ST. POPE CORNELIUS AND ST. CYPRIAN

† 1 Corinthians 15:12-20
If Christ has not been raised, your faith is vain.

Brothers and sisters:
If Christ is preached as raised from the dead,
how can some among you say there is no resurrection of the dead?
If there is no resurrection of the dead,
then neither has Christ been raised.

And if Christ has not been raised, then empty too is our preaching;
  empty, too, your faith.
Then we are also false witnesses to God,
  because we testified against God that he raised Christ,
  whom he did not raise if in fact the dead are not raised.
For if the dead are not raised, neither has Christ been raised,
  and if Christ has not been raised, your faith is vain;
  you are still in your sins.
Then those who have fallen asleep in Christ have perished.
If for this life only we have hoped in Christ,
  we are the most pitiable people of all.

But now Christ has been raised from the dead,
  the firstfruits of those who have fallen asleep. ✛

Psalm 17:1bcd, 6-7, 8b and 15
R. (15b) **Lord, when your glory appears, my joy will be full.**
Hear, O LORD, a just suit;
  attend to my outcry;
  hearken to my prayer from lips without deceit. **R.**
I call upon you, for you will answer me, O God;
  incline your ear to me; hear my word.
Show your wondrous mercies,
  O savior of those who flee
  from their foes to refuge at your right hand. **R.**
Hide me in the shadow of your wings,
But I in justice shall behold your face;
  on waking, I shall be content in your presence. **R.**

See Matthew 11:25
R. Alleluia, alleluia.
Blessed are you, Father, Lord of heaven and earth;
you have revealed to little ones the mysteries of the Kingdom. **R.**

✝ Luke 8:1-3
Accompanying them were some women,
who provided for them out of their resources.

Jesus journeyed from one town and village to another,
  preaching and proclaiming the good news of the Kingdom of God.
Accompanying him were the Twelve
  and some women who had been cured of evil spirits and infirmities,
  Mary, called Magdalene, from whom seven demons had gone out,
  Joanna, the wife of Herod's steward Chuza,
  Susanna, and many others
  who provided for them out of their resources. ✛

SATURDAY, SEPTEMBER 17
WEEKDAY, ST. ROBERT BELLARMINE, *[BVM]*

✝ *1 Corinthians 15:35-37, 42-49*
It is sown corruptible; it is raised incorruptible.

Brothers and sisters:
Someone may say, "How are the dead raised?
With what kind of body will they come back?"

You fool!
What you sow is not brought to life unless it dies.
And what you sow is not the body that is to be
   but a bare kernel of wheat, perhaps, or of some other kind.

So also is the resurrection of the dead.
It is sown corruptible; it is raised incorruptible.
It is sown dishonorable; it is raised glorious.
It is sown weak; it is raised powerful.
It is sown a natural body; it is raised a spiritual body.
If there is a natural body, there is also a spiritual one.

So, too, it is written,
   "The first man, Adam, became a living being,"
   the last Adam a life-giving spirit.
But the spiritual was not first;
   rather the natural and then the spiritual.
The first man was from the earth, earthly;
   the second man, from heaven.
As was the earthly one, so also are the earthly,
   and as is the heavenly one, so also are the heavenly.
Just as we have borne the image of the earthly one,
   we shall also bear the image of the heavenly one. ✝

Psalm 56:10c-12, 13-14
R. (14) **I will walk in the presence of God, in the light of the
   living.**
Now I know that God is with me.
   In God, in whose promise I glory,
   in God I trust without fear;
   what can flesh do against me? **R.**
I am bound, O God, by vows to you;
   your thank offerings I will fulfill.
For you have rescued me from death,
   my feet, too, from stumbling;
   that I may walk before God in the light of the living. **R.**

See Luke 8:15

R. Alleluia, alleluia.

Blessed are they who have kept the word with a generous heart
and yield a harvest through perseverance. **R.**

† *Luke 8:4-15*

As for the seed that fell on rich soil, they are the ones who
embrace the word and bear much fruit through perseverance.

When a large crowd gathered, with people from one town after
    another
  journeying to Jesus, he spoke in a parable.
"A sower went out to sow his seed.
And as he sowed, some seed fell on the path and was trampled,
  and the birds of the sky ate it up.
Some seed fell on rocky ground, and when it grew,
  it withered for lack of moisture.
Some seed fell among thorns,
  and the thorns grew with it and choked it.
And some seed fell on good soil, and when it grew,
  it produced fruit a hundredfold."
After saying this, he called out,
  "Whoever has ears to hear ought to hear."

Then his disciples asked him
  what the meaning of this parable might be.
He answered,
  "Knowledge of the mysteries of the Kingdom of God
  has been granted to you;
  but to the rest, they are made known through parables
  so that *they may look but not see, and hear but not understand.*

"This is the meaning of the parable.
The seed is the word of God.
Those on the path are the ones who have heard,
  but the Devil comes and takes away the word from their hearts
  that they may not believe and be saved.
Those on rocky ground are the ones who, when they hear,
  receive the word with joy, but they have no root;
  they believe only for a time and fall away in time of temptation.
As for the seed that fell among thorns,
  they are the ones who have heard, but as they go along,
  they are choked by the anxieties and riches and pleasures of life,
  and they fail to produce mature fruit.
But as for the seed that fell on rich soil,
  they are the ones who, when they have heard the word,

embrace it with a generous and good heart,
and bear fruit through perseverance." ✛

SUNDAY, SEPTEMBER 18
TWENTY-FIFTH SUNDAY IN ORDINARY TIME

✝ Amos 8:4-7
Against those who buy the poor for money.

Hear this, you who trample upon the needy
  and destroy the poor of the land!
"When will the new moon be over," you ask,
  "that we may sell our grain,
  and the sabbath, that we may display the wheat?
We will diminish the ephah,
  add to the shekel,
  and fix our scales for cheating!
We will buy the lowly for silver,
  and the poor for a pair of sandals;
  even the refuse of the wheat we will sell!"
The LORD has sworn by the pride of Jacob:
  Never will I forget a thing they have done! ✛

Psalm 113:1-2, 4-6, 7-8
R. (see 1a, 7b) **Praise the Lord, who lifts up the poor.**
  (or **Alleluia.***)*
Praise, you servants of the LORD,
  praise the name of the LORD.
Blessed be the name of the LORD
  both now and forever. **R.**
High above all nations is the LORD;
  above the heavens is his glory.
Who is like the LORD, our God, who is enthroned on high
  and looks upon the heavens and the earth below? **R.**
He raises up the lowly from the dust;
  from the dunghill he lifts up the poor
to seat them with princes,
  with the princes of his own people. **R.**

✝ 1 Timothy 2:1-8
Let prayers be offered for everyone to God who wills everyone to be saved.

Beloved:
First of all, I ask that supplications, prayers,
  petitions, and thanksgivings be offered for everyone,
  for kings and for all in authority,
  that we may lead a quiet and tranquil life
  in all devotion and dignity.

This is good and pleasing to God our savior,
  who wills everyone to be saved
  and to come to knowledge of the truth.
    For there is one God.
    There is also one mediator between God and men, the man
        Christ Jesus,
    who gave himself as ransom for all.
This was the testimony at the proper time.
For this I was appointed preacher and apostle
  —I am speaking the truth, I am not lying—,
  teacher of the Gentiles in faith and truth.

It is my wish, then, that in every place the men should pray,
  lifting up holy hands, without anger or argument. ✝

See 2 Corinthians 8:9
R. Alleluia, alleluia.
Though our Lord Jesus Christ was rich, he became poor,
so that by his poverty you might become rich. **R.**

*✝ **Luke 16:1-13** (or Luke 16:10-13)*
You cannot serve both God and mammon.

Jesus said to his disciples,
  "A rich man had a steward
  who was reported to him for squandering his property.
He summoned him and said,
  'What is this I hear about you?
Prepare a full account of your stewardship,
  because you can no longer be my steward.'
The steward said to himself, 'What shall I do,
  now that my master is taking the position of steward away from me?
I am not strong enough to dig and I am ashamed to beg.
I know what I shall do so that,
  when I am removed from the stewardship,
  they may welcome me into their homes.'
He called in his master's debtors one by one.
To the first he said,
  'How much do you owe my master?'
He replied, 'One hundred measures of olive oil.'
He said to him, 'Here is your promissory note.
Sit down and quickly write one for fifty.'
Then to another the steward said, 'And you, how much do you owe?'
He replied, 'One hundred kors of wheat.'
The steward said to him, 'Here is your promissory note;
  write one for eighty.'

And the master commended that dishonest steward for acting
    prudently.
For the children of this world
    are more prudent in dealing with their own generation
    than are the children of light.
I tell you, make friends for yourselves with dishonest wealth,
    so that when it fails, you will be welcomed into eternal dwellings.
The person who is trustworthy in very small matters
    is also trustworthy in great ones;
    and the person who is dishonest in very small matters
    is also dishonest in great ones.
If, therefore, you are not trustworthy with dishonest wealth,
    who will trust you with true wealth?
If you are not trustworthy with what belongs to another,
    who will give you what is yours?
No servant can serve two masters.
He will either hate one and love the other,
    or be devoted to one and despise the other.
You cannot serve both God and mammon." ✛

MONDAY, SEPTEMBER 19
WEEKDAY, ST. JANUARIUS

† *Proverbs 3:27-34*
The curse of the LORD is on the house of the wicked.

Refuse no one the good on which he has a claim
    when it is in your power to do it for him.
Say not to your neighbor, "Go, and come again,
    tomorrow I will give," when you can give at once.

Plot no evil against your neighbor,
    against one who lives at peace with you.
Quarrel not with a man without cause,
    with one who has done you no harm.

Envy not the lawless man
    and choose none of his ways:
To the LORD the perverse one is an abomination,
    but with the upright is his friendship.

The curse of the LORD is on the house of the wicked,
    but the dwelling of the just he blesses;
When dealing with the arrogant, he is stern,
    but to the humble he shows kindness. ✛

Psalm 15:2-3a, 3bc-4ab, 5

R. (1) **The just one shall live on your holy mountain, O Lord.**
He who walks blamelessly and does justice;
  who thinks the truth in his heart
  and slanders not with his tongue. **R.**
Who harms not his fellow man,
  nor takes up a reproach against his neighbor;
By whom the reprobate is despised,
  while he honors those who fear the LORD. **R.**
Who lends not his money at usury
  and accepts no bribe against the innocent.
He who does these things
  shall never be disturbed. **R.**

Matthew 5:16

R. Alleluia, alleluia.
Let your light shine before others,
that they may see your good deeds and glorify your heavenly Father. **R.**

† *Luke 8:16-18*
A lamp is placed on a lampstand so that those who enter may see the light.

Jesus said to the crowd:
"No one who lights a lamp conceals it with a vessel
  or sets it under a bed;
  rather, he places it on a lampstand
  so that those who enter may see the light.
For there is nothing hidden that will not become visible,
  and nothing secret that will not be known and come to light.
Take care, then, how you hear.
To anyone who has, more will be given,
  and from the one who has not,
  even what he seems to have will be taken away." ✢

TUESDAY, SEPTEMBER 20
ST. ANDREW KIM TAE-GŎN, ST. PAUL CHŎNG HA-SANG AND COMPANIONS

† *Proverbs 21:1-6, 10-13*
Various proverbs.

Like a stream is the king's heart in the hand of the LORD;
  wherever it pleases him, he directs it.

All the ways of a man may be right in his own eyes,
  but it is the LORD who proves hearts.

To do what is right and just
  is more acceptable to the LORD than sacrifice.

Haughty eyes and a proud heart—
   the tillage of the wicked is sin.

The plans of the diligent are sure of profit,
   but all rash haste leads certainly to poverty.

Whoever makes a fortune by a lying tongue
   is chasing a bubble over deadly snares.

The soul of the wicked man desires evil;
   his neighbor finds no pity in his eyes.

When the arrogant man is punished, the simple are the wiser;
   when the wise man is instructed, he gains knowledge.

The just man appraises the house of the wicked:
   there is one who brings down the wicked to ruin.

He who shuts his ear to the cry of the poor
   will himself also call and not be heard. ✛

   Psalm 119:1, 27, 30, 34, 35, 44
R. (35) **Guide me, Lord, in the way of your commands.**
Blessed are they whose way is blameless,
   who walk in the law of the LORD. **R.**
Make me understand the way of your precepts,
   and I will meditate on your wondrous deeds. **R.**
The way of truth I have chosen;
   I have set your ordinances before me. **R.**
Give me discernment, that I may observe your law
   and keep it with all my heart. **R.**
Lead me in the path of your commands,
   for in it I delight. **R.**
And I will keep your law continually,
   forever and ever. **R.**

   Luke 11:28
R. Alleluia, alleluia.
Blessed are those who hear the word of God
and observe it. **R.**

† *Luke 8:19-21*
My mother and my brothers are those who hear the word of God and act on it.

The mother of Jesus and his brothers came to him
  but were unable to join him because of the crowd.
He was told, "Your mother and your brothers are standing outside
  and they wish to see you."
He said to them in reply, "My mother and my brothers
  are those who hear the word of God and act on it." ✦

WEDNESDAY, SEPTEMBER 21
St. Matthew

† *Ephesians 4:1-7, 11-13*
He gave some as Apostles, others as evangelists.

Brothers and sisters:
I, a prisoner for the Lord,
  urge you to live in a manner worthy of the call you have received,
  with all humility and gentleness, with patience,
  bearing with one another through love,
  striving to preserve the unity of the Spirit
  through the bond of peace:
  one Body and one Spirit,
  as you were also called to the one hope of your call;
  one Lord, one faith, one baptism;
  one God and Father of all,
  who is over all and through all and in all.

But grace was given to each of us
  according to the measure of Christ's gift.

And he gave some as Apostles, others as prophets,
  others as evangelists, others as pastors and teachers,
  to equip the holy ones for the work of ministry,
  for building up the Body of Christ,
  until we all attain to the unity of faith
  and knowledge of the Son of God, to mature manhood,
  to the extent of the full stature of Christ. ✦

Psalm 19:2-3, 4-5ab
R. (5) **Their message goes out through all the earth.**
The heavens declare the glory of God;
  and the firmament proclaims his handiwork.
Day pours out the word to day,
  and night to night imparts knowledge. **R.**
Not a word nor a discourse
  whose voice is not heard;

Through all the earth their voice resounds,
  and to the ends of the world, their message. **R.**

See Te Deum
R. Alleluia, alleluia.
We praise you, O God,
we acclaim you as Lord;
the glorious company of Apostles praise you. **R.**

† *Matthew 9:9-13*
Follow me. And he got up and followed him.

As Jesus passed by,
  he saw a man named Matthew sitting at the customs post.
He said to him, "Follow me."
And he got up and followed him.
While he was at table in his house,
  many tax collectors and sinners came
  and sat with Jesus and his disciples.
The Pharisees saw this and said to his disciples,
  "Why does your teacher eat with tax collectors and sinners?"
He heard this and said,
  "Those who are well do not need a physician, but the sick do.
Go and learn the meaning of the words,
  I desire mercy, not sacrifice.
I did not come to call the righteous but sinners." ✛

THURSDAY, SEPTEMBER 22
WEEKDAY

† *Ecclesiastes 1:2-11*
Nothing is new under the sun.

Vanity of vanities, says Qoheleth,
  vanity of vanities! All things are vanity!
What profit has man from all the labor
  which he toils at under the sun?
One generation passes and another comes,
  but the world forever stays.
The sun rises and the sun goes down;
  then it presses on to the place where it rises.
Blowing now toward the south, then toward the north,
  the wind turns again and again, resuming its rounds.
All rivers go to the sea,
  yet never does the sea become full.
To the place where they go,
  the rivers keep on going.

All speech is labored;
   there is nothing one can say.
The eye is not satisfied with seeing
   nor is the ear satisfied with hearing.

What has been, that will be;
   what has been done, that will be done.
Nothing is new under the sun.
Even the thing of which we say, "See, this is new!"
   has already existed in the ages that preceded us.
There is no remembrance of the men of old;
   nor of those to come will there be any remembrance
   among those who come after them. ✛

Psalm 90:3-4, 5-6, 12-13, 14 and 17bc
R. (1) In every age, O Lord, you have been our refuge.
You turn man back to dust,
   saying, "Return, O children of men."
For a thousand years in your sight
   are as yesterday, now that it is past,
   or as a watch of the night. **R.**
You make an end of them in their sleep;
   the next morning they are like the changing grass,
Which at dawn springs up anew,
   but by evening wilts and fades. **R.**
Teach us to number our days aright,
   that we may gain wisdom of heart.
Return, O LORD! How long?
   Have pity on your servants! **R.**
Fill us at daybreak with your kindness,
   that we may shout for joy and gladness all our days.
   Prosper the work of our hands for us!
   Prosper the work of our hands! **R.**

John 14:6
R. Alleluia, alleluia.
I am the way and the truth and the life, says the Lord;
no one comes to the Father except through me. **R.**

† *Luke 9:7-9*
John I beheaded. Who then is this about whom I hear such things?

Herod the tetrarch heard about all that was happening,
   and he was greatly perplexed because some were saying,
"John has been raised from the dead";
   others were saying, "Elijah has appeared";
   still others, "One of the ancient prophets has arisen."

But Herod said, "John I beheaded.
Who then is this about whom I hear such things?"
And he kept trying to see him. ✛

FRIDAY, SEPTEMBER 23
St. Pius of Pietrelcina

† *Ecclesiastes 3:1-11*
There is a time for everything under the heavens.

There is an appointed time for everything,
    and a time for every thing under the heavens.
A time to be born, and a time to die;
    a time to plant, and a time to uproot the plant.
A time to kill, and a time to heal;
    a time to tear down, and a time to build.
A time to weep, and a time to laugh;
    a time to mourn, and a time to dance.
A time to scatter stones, and a time to gather them;
    a time to embrace, and a time to be far from embraces.
A time to seek, and a time to lose;
    a time to keep, and a time to cast away.
A time to rend, and a time to sew;
    a time to be silent, and a time to speak.
A time to love, and a time to hate;
    a time of war, and a time of peace.

What advantage has the worker from his toil?
I have considered the task that God has appointed
    for the sons of men to be busied about.
He has made everything appropriate to its time,
    and has put the timeless into their hearts,
    without man's ever discovering,
    from beginning to end, the work which God has done. ✛

Psalm 144:1b and 2abc, 3-4
R. (1) **Blessed be the Lord, my Rock!**
Blessed be the Lord, my rock,
    my mercy and my fortress,
    my stronghold, my deliverer,
My shield, in whom I trust. **R.**
Lord, what is man, that you notice him;
    the son of man, that you take thought of him?
Man is like a breath;
    his days, like a passing shadow. **R.**

Mark 10:45
R. Alleluia, alleluia.
The Son of Man came to serve
and to give his life as a ransom for many. **R.**

† *Luke 9:18-22*
You are the Christ of God. The Son of Man must suffer greatly.

Once when Jesus was praying in solitude,
  and the disciples were with him,
  he asked them, "Who do the crowds say that I am?"
They said in reply, "John the Baptist; others, Elijah;
  still others, 'One of the ancient prophets has arisen.'"
Then he said to them, "But who do you say that I am?"
Peter said in reply, "The Christ of God."
He rebuked them and directed them not to tell this to anyone.

He said, "The Son of Man must suffer greatly
  and be rejected by the elders, the chief priests, and the scribes,
  and be killed and on the third day be raised." ✛

SATURDAY, SEPTEMBER 24
WEEKDAY, *[BVM]*

† *Ecclesiastes 11:9—12:8*
Remember your Creator in the days of your youth,
before the dust returns to the earth, and the life breath returns to God.

Rejoice, O young man, while you are young
  and let your heart be glad in the days of your youth.
Follow the ways of your heart,
  the vision of your eyes;
Yet understand that as regards all this
  God will bring you to judgment.
Ward off grief from your heart
  and put away trouble from your presence,
  though the dawn of youth is fleeting.

Remember your Creator in the days of your youth,
  before the evil days come
And the years approach of which you will say,
  I have no pleasure in them;
Before the sun is darkened,
  and the light, and the moon, and the stars,
  while the clouds return after the rain;
When the guardians of the house tremble,
  and the strong men are bent,

And the grinders are idle because they are few,
    and they who look through the windows grow blind;
When the doors to the street are shut,
    and the sound of the mill is low;
When one waits for the chirp of a bird,
    but all the daughters of song are suppressed;
And one fears heights,
    and perils in the street;
When the almond tree blooms,
    and the locust grows sluggish
    and the caper berry is without effect,
Because man goes to his lasting home,
    and mourners go about the streets;
Before the silver cord is snapped
    and the golden bowl is broken,
And the pitcher is shattered at the spring,
    and the broken pulley falls into the well,
And the dust returns to the earth as it once was,
    and the life breath returns to God who gave it.

Vanity of vanities, says Qoheleth,
    all things are vanity! ✚

Psalm 90:3-4, 5-6, 12-13, 14 and 17
R. (1) In every age, O Lord, you have been our refuge.
You turn man back to dust,
    saying, "Return, O children of men."
For a thousand years in your sight
    are as yesterday, now that it is past,
    or as a watch of the night. **R.**
You make an end of them in their sleep;
    the next morning they are like the changing grass,
Which at dawn springs up anew,
    but by evening wilts and fades. **R.**
Teach us to number our days aright,
    that we may gain wisdom of heart.
Return, O Lord! How long?
    Have pity on your servants! **R.**
Fill us at daybreak with your kindness,
    that we may shout for joy and gladness all our days.
And may the gracious care of the Lord our God be ours;
    prosper the work of our hands for us!
    Prosper the work of our hands! **R.**

See 2 Timothy 1:10
R. Alleluia, alleluia.
Our Savior Christ Jesus destroyed death
and brought life to light through the Gospel. **R.**

† *Luke 9:43b-45*
The Son of Man is to be handed over to men.
They were afraid to ask him about this saying.

While they were all amazed at his every deed,
  Jesus said to his disciples,
  "Pay attention to what I am telling you.
The Son of Man is to be handed over to men."
But they did not understand this saying;
  its meaning was hidden from them
  so that they should not understand it,
  and they were afraid to ask him about this saying. ✛

SUNDAY, SEPTEMBER 25
TWENTY-SIXTH SUNDAY IN ORDINARY TIME

† *Amos 6:1a, 4-7*
Their wanton revelry shall be done away with.

Thus says the LORD the God of hosts:
Woe to the complacent in Zion!
Lying upon beds of ivory,
  stretched comfortably on their couches,
they eat lambs taken from the flock,
  and calves from the stall!
Improvising to the music of the harp,
  like David, they devise their own accompaniment.
They drink wine from bowls
  and anoint themselves with the best oils;
  yet they are not made ill by the collapse of Joseph!
Therefore, now they shall be the first to go into exile,
  and their wanton revelry shall be done away with. ✛

Psalm 146:7, 8-9, 9-10
R. (1b) **Praise the Lord, my soul!** *(or* **Alleluia.***)*
Blessed is he who keeps faith forever,
  secures justice for the oppressed,
  gives food to the hungry.
The LORD sets captives free. **R.**
The LORD gives sight to the blind;
  the LORD raises up those who were bowed down.

The LORD loves the just.
  The LORD protects strangers. **R.**
The fatherless and the widow he sustains,
  but the way of the wicked he thwarts.
The LORD shall reign forever;
  your God, O Zion, through all generations. Alleluia. **R.**

✝ *1 Timothy 6:11-16*
Keep the commandment until the appearance of the Lord Jesus Christ.

But you, man of God, pursue righteousness,
  devotion, faith, love, patience, and gentleness.
Compete well for the faith.
Lay hold of eternal life, to which you were called
  when you made the noble confession in the presence of many
    witnesses.
I charge you before God, who gives life to all things,
  and before Christ Jesus,
  who gave testimony under Pontius Pilate for the noble confession,
  to keep the commandment without stain or reproach
  until the appearance of our Lord Jesus Christ
  that the blessed and only ruler
  will make manifest at the proper time,
  the King of kings and Lord of lords,
  who alone has immortality, who dwells in unapproachable light,
  and whom no human being has seen or can see.
To him be honor and eternal power. Amen. ✛

See 2 Corinthians 8:9
R. Alleluia, alleluia.
Though our Lord Jesus Christ was rich, he became poor,
so that by his poverty you might become rich. **R.**

✝ *Luke 16:19-31*
You received what was good, Lazarus what was bad;
now he is comforted, whereas you are tormented.

Jesus said to the Pharisees:
  "There was a rich man who dressed in purple garments and fine
    linen
  and dined sumptuously each day.
And lying at his door was a poor man named Lazarus, covered with
    sores,
  who would gladly have eaten his fill of the scraps
  that fell from the rich man's table.
Dogs even used to come and lick his sores.

When the poor man died,
  he was carried away by angels to the bosom of Abraham.
The rich man also died and was buried,
  and from the netherworld, where he was in torment,
  he raised his eyes and saw Abraham far off
  and Lazarus at his side.
And he cried out, 'Father Abraham, have pity on me.
Send Lazarus to dip the tip of his finger in water and cool my tongue,
  for I am suffering torment in these flames.'
Abraham replied,
  'My child, remember that you received
  what was good during your lifetime
  while Lazarus likewise received what was bad;
  but now he is comforted here, whereas you are tormented.
Moreover, between us and you a great chasm is established
  to prevent anyone from crossing who might wish to go
  from our side to yours or from your side to ours.'
He said, 'Then I beg you, father,
  send him to my father's house, for I have five brothers,
  so that he may warn them,
  lest they too come to this place of torment.'
But Abraham replied, 'They have Moses and the prophets.
Let them listen to them.'
He said, 'Oh no, father Abraham,
  but if someone from the dead goes to them, they will repent.'
Then Abraham said, 'If they will not listen to Moses and the prophets,
  neither will they be persuaded if someone should rise from the
  dead.'" ✛

MONDAY, SEPTEMBER 26
WEEKDAY, ST. COSMAS AND ST. DAMIAN

✝ Job 1:6-22
The LORD gave and the LORD has taken away;
blessed be the name of the LORD!

One day, when the angels of God came to present themselves before
  the LORD,
  Satan also came among them.
And the LORD said to Satan, "Whence do you come?"
Then Satan answered the LORD and said,
  "From roaming the earth and patrolling it."
And the LORD said to Satan, "Have you noticed my servant Job,
  and that there is no one on earth like him,
  blameless and upright, fearing God and avoiding evil?"

But Satan answered the LORD and said,
 "Is it for nothing that Job is God-fearing?
Have you not surrounded him and his family
 and all that he has with your protection?
You have blessed the work of his hands,
 and his livestock are spread over the land.
But now put forth your hand and touch anything that he has,
 and surely he will blaspheme you to your face."
And the LORD said to Satan,
 "Behold, all that he has is in your power;
 only do not lay a hand upon his person."
So Satan went forth from the presence of the LORD.

And so one day, while his sons and his daughters
 were eating and drinking wine
 in the house of their eldest brother,
 a messenger came to Job and said,
 "The oxen were ploughing and the asses grazing beside them,
 and the Sabeans carried them off in a raid.
They put the herdsmen to the sword,
 and I alone have escaped to tell you."
While he was yet speaking, another came and said,
 "Lightning has fallen from heaven
 and struck the sheep and their shepherds and consumed them;
 and I alone have escaped to tell you."
While he was yet speaking, another messenger came and said,
 "The Chaldeans formed three columns,
 seized the camels, carried them off,
 and put those tending them to the sword,
 and I alone have escaped to tell you."
While he was yet speaking, another came and said,
 "Your sons and daughters were eating and drinking wine
 in the house of their eldest brother,
 when suddenly a great wind came across the desert
 and smote the four corners of the house.
It fell upon the young people and they are dead;
 and I alone have escaped to tell you."
Then Job began to tear his cloak and cut off his hair.
He cast himself prostrate upon the ground, and said,

 "Naked I came forth from my mother's womb,
 and naked shall I go back again.

The LORD gave and the LORD has taken away;
   blessed be the name of the LORD!"

In all this Job did not sin,
   nor did he say anything disrespectful of God. ✝

   Psalm 17:1bcd, 2-3, 6-7
R. (6) Incline your ear to me and hear my word.
Hear, O LORD, a just suit;
   attend to my outcry;
   hearken to my prayer from lips without deceit. **R.**
From you let my judgment come;
   your eyes behold what is right.
Though you test my heart, searching it in the night,
   though you try me with fire, you shall find no malice in me. **R.**
I call upon you, for you will answer me, O God;
   incline your ear to me; hear my word.
Show your wondrous mercies,
   O savior of those who flee
   from their foes to refuge at your right hand. **R.**

   Mark 10:45
R. Alleluia, alleluia.
The Son of Man came to serve
and to give his life as a ransom for many. **R.**

✝ *Luke 9:46-50*
The one who is least among all of you is the one who is the greatest.

An argument arose among the disciples
   about which of them was the greatest.
Jesus realized the intention of their hearts and took a child
   and placed it by his side and said to them,
"Whoever receives this child in my name receives me,
   and whoever receives me receives the one who sent me.
For the one who is least among all of you
   is the one who is the greatest."

Then John said in reply,
"Master, we saw someone casting out demons in your name
   and we tried to prevent him
   because he does not follow in our company."
Jesus said to him,
   "Do not prevent him, for whoever is not against you is for you." ✝

TUESDAY, SEPTEMBER 27
St. Vincent de Paul

† *Job 3:1-3, 11-17, 20-23*
Why is light given to the toilers?

Job opened his mouth and cursed his day.
Job spoke out and said:

Perish the day on which I was born,
  the night when they said, "The child is a boy!"

Why did I not perish at birth,
  come forth from the womb and expire?
Or why was I not buried away like an untimely birth,
  like babes that have never seen the light?
Wherefore did the knees receive me?
  or why did I suck at the breasts?

For then I should have lain down and been tranquil;
  had I slept, I should then have been at rest
With kings and counselors of the earth
  who built where now there are ruins
Or with princes who had gold
  and filled their houses with silver.

There the wicked cease from troubling,
  there the weary are at rest.

Why is light given to the toilers,
  and life to the bitter in spirit?
They wait for death and it comes not;
  they search for it rather than for hidden treasures,
Rejoice in it exultingly,
  and are glad when they reach the grave:
Those whose path is hidden from them,
  and whom God has hemmed in! ✛

Psalm 88:2-3, 4-5, 6, 7-8

R. (3) **Let my prayer come before you, Lord.**
O Lord, my God, by day I cry out;
  at night I clamor in your presence.
Let my prayer come before you;
  incline your ear to my call for help. **R.**
For my soul is surfeited with troubles
  and my life draws near to the nether world.
I am numbered with those who go down into the pit;
  I am a man without strength. **R.**

My couch is among the dead,
  like the slain who lie in the grave,
Whom you remember no longer
  and who are cut off from your care. **R.**
You have plunged me into the bottom of the pit,
  into the dark abyss.
Upon me your wrath lies heavy,
  and with all your billows you overwhelm me. **R.**

  Mark 10:45
R. Alleluia, alleluia.
The Son of Man came to serve
and to give his life as a ransom for many. **R.**

† *Luke 9:51-56*
He resolutely determined to journey to Jerusalem.

When the days for Jesus to be taken up were fulfilled,
  he resolutely determined to journey to Jerusalem,
  and he sent messengers ahead of him.
On the way they entered a Samaritan village
  to prepare for his reception there,
  but they would not welcome him
  because the destination of his journey was Jerusalem.
When the disciples James and John saw this they asked,
  "Lord, do you want us to call down fire from heaven
  to consume them?"
Jesus turned and rebuked them,
  and they journeyed to another village. ✛

WEDNESDAY, SEPTEMBER 28
WEEKDAY, ST. WENCESLAUS; ST. LAWRENCE RUIZ AND COMPANIONS

† *Job 9:1-12, 14-16*
How can one be justified before God?

Job answered his friends and said:

I know well that it is so;
  but how can a man be justified before God?
Should one wish to contend with him,
  he could not answer him once in a thousand times.
God is wise in heart and mighty in strength;
  who has withstood him and remained unscathed?

He removes the mountains before they know it;
  he overturns them in his anger.

He shakes the earth out of its place,
and the pillars beneath it tremble.
He commands the sun, and it rises not;
he seals up the stars.

He alone stretches out the heavens
and treads upon the crests of the sea.
He made the Bear and Orion,
the Pleiades and the constellations of the south;
He does great things past finding out,
marvelous things beyond reckoning.

Should he come near me, I see him not;
should he pass by, I am not aware of him;
Should he seize me forcibly, who can say him nay?
Who can say to him, "What are you doing?"

How much less shall I give him any answer,
or choose out arguments against him!
Even though I were right, I could not answer him,
but should rather beg for what was due me.
If I appealed to him and he answered my call,
I could not believe that he would hearken to my words. ✛

Psalm 88:10bc-11, 12-13, 14-15
R. (3) **Let my prayer come before you, Lord.**
Daily I call upon you, O LORD;
to you I stretch out my hands.
Will you work wonders for the dead?
Will the shades arise to give you thanks? **R.**
Do they declare your mercy in the grave,
your faithfulness among those who have perished?
Are your wonders made known in the darkness,
or your justice in the land of oblivion? **R.**
But I, O LORD, cry out to you;
with my morning prayer I wait upon you.
Why, O LORD, do you reject me;
why hide from me your face? **R.**

Philippians 3:8-9
R. Alleluia, alleluia.
I consider all things so much rubbish
that I may gain Christ and be found in him. **R.**

† *Luke 9:57-62*
I will follow you wherever you go.

As Jesus and his disciples were proceeding
on their journey, someone said to him,
"I will follow you wherever you go."
Jesus answered him,
"Foxes have dens and birds of the sky have nests,
but the Son of Man has nowhere to rest his head."
And to another he said, "Follow me."
But he replied, "Lord, let me go first and bury my father."
But he answered him, "Let the dead bury their dead.
But you, go and proclaim the Kingdom of God."
And another said, "I will follow you, Lord,
but first let me say farewell to my family at home."
Jesus answered him, "No one who sets a hand to the plow
and looks to what was left behind is fit for the Kingdom of God." ✢

THURSDAY, SEPTEMBER 29
St. Michael, St. Gabriel and St. Raphael

† *Daniel 7:9-10, 13-14* (or Revelation 12:7-12ab)
Thousands upon thousands were ministering to him.

As I watched:

Thrones were set up
and the Ancient One took his throne.
His clothing was bright as snow,
and the hair on his head as white as wool;
His throne was flames of fire,
with wheels of burning fire.
A surging stream of fire
flowed out from where he sat;
Thousands upon thousands were ministering to him,
and myriads upon myriads attended him.

The court was convened, and the books were opened.
As the visions during the night continued, I saw

One like a son of man coming,
on the clouds of heaven;
When he reached the Ancient One
and was presented before him,
He received dominion, glory, and kingship;
nations and peoples of every language serve him.

His dominion is an everlasting dominion
   that shall not be taken away,
   his kingship shall not be destroyed. ✝

   Psalm 138:1-2ab, 2cde-3, 4-5
R. (1) **In the sight of the angels I will sing your praises, Lord.**
I will give thanks to you, O LORD, with all my heart,
   for you have heard the words of my mouth;
   in the presence of the angels I will sing your praise;
I will worship at your holy temple
   and give thanks to your name. **R.**
Because of your kindness and your truth;
   for you have made great above all things
   your name and your promise.
When I called, you answered me;
   you built up strength within me. **R.**
All the kings of the earth shall give thanks to you, O LORD,
   when they hear the words of your mouth;
And they shall sing of the ways of the LORD:
   "Great is the glory of the LORD." **R.**

   Psalm 103:21
R. Alleluia, alleluia.
Bless the LORD, all you angels,
you ministers, who do his will. **R.**

† *John 1:47-51*
*You will see the sky opened and the angels of God
ascending and descending on the Son of Man.*

Jesus saw Nathanael coming toward him and said of him,
   "Here is a true child of Israel.
There is no duplicity in him."
Nathanael said to him, "How do you know me?"
Jesus answered and said to him,
   "Before Philip called you, I saw you under the fig tree."
Nathanael answered him,
   "Rabbi, you are the Son of God; you are the King of Israel."
Jesus answered and said to him,
   "Do you believe
   because I told you that I saw you under the fig tree?
You will see greater things than this."
And he said to him, "Amen, amen, I say to you,
   you will see heaven opened
   and the angels of God ascending and descending on the Son of
   Man." ✝

FRIDAY, SEPTEMBER 30
St. Jerome

† Job 38:1, 12-21; 40:3-5
*Have you ever in your lifetime commanded the morning
and entered into the sources of the sea?*

The Lord addressed Job out of the storm and said:

Have you ever in your lifetime commanded the morning
   and shown the dawn its place
For taking hold of the ends of the earth,
   till the wicked are shaken from its surface?
The earth is changed as is clay by the seal,
   and dyed as though it were a garment;
But from the wicked the light is withheld,
   and the arm of pride is shattered.

Have you entered into the sources of the sea,
   or walked about in the depths of the abyss?
Have the gates of death been shown to you,
   or have you seen the gates of darkness?
Have you comprehended the breadth of the earth?
   Tell me, if you know all:
Which is the way to the dwelling place of light,
   and where is the abode of darkness,
That you may take them to their boundaries
   and set them on their homeward paths?
You know, because you were born before them,
   and the number of your years is great!

Then Job answered the Lord and said:

Behold, I am of little account; what can I answer you?
   I put my hand over my mouth.
Though I have spoken once, I will not do so again;
   though twice, I will do so no more. ✛

Psalm 139:1-3, 7-8, 9-10, 13-14ab
R. (24b) **Guide me, Lord, along the everlasting way.**
O Lord, you have probed me and you know me;
   you know when I sit and when I stand;
   you understand my thoughts from afar.
My journeys and my rest you scrutinize,
   with all my ways you are familiar. **R.**
Where can I go from your spirit?
   From your presence where can I flee?

If I go up to the heavens, you are there;
  if I sink to the nether world, you are present there. **R.**
If I take the wings of the dawn,
  if I settle at the farthest limits of the sea,
Even there your hand shall guide me,
  and your right hand hold me fast. **R.**
Truly you have formed my inmost being;
  you knit me in my mother's womb.
I give you thanks that I am fearfully, wonderfully made;
  wonderful are your works. **R.**

  Psalm 95:8
R. Alleluia, alleluia.
If today you hear his voice,
harden not your hearts. **R.**

† *Luke 10:13-16*
Whoever rejects me rejects the one who sent me.

Jesus said to them,
  "Woe to you, Chorazin! Woe to you, Bethsaida!
For if the mighty deeds done in your midst
  had been done in Tyre and Sidon,
  they would long ago have repented,
  sitting in sackcloth and ashes.
But it will be more tolerable for Tyre and Sidon
  at the judgment than for you.
And as for you, Capernaum, 'Will you be exalted to heaven?
You will go down to the netherworld.'
Whoever listens to you listens to me.
Whoever rejects you rejects me.
And whoever rejects me rejects the one who sent me." ✛

SATURDAY, OCTOBER 1
St. Thérèse of the Child Jesus

† *Job 42:1-3, 5-6, 12-17*
But now my eye has seen you and I disown what I have said.

Job answered the Lord and said:

I know that you can do all things,
  and that no purpose of yours can be hindered.
I have dealt with great things that I do not understand;
  things too wonderful for me, which I cannot know.
I had heard of you by word of mouth,
  but now my eye has seen you.
Therefore I disown what I have said,
  and repent in dust and ashes.

Thus the Lord blessed the latter days of Job
  more than his earlier ones.
For he had fourteen thousand sheep, six thousand camels,
  a thousand yoke of oxen, and a thousand she-asses.
And he had seven sons and three daughters,
  of whom he called the first Jemimah,
  the second Keziah, and the third Kerenhappuch.
In all the land no other women were as beautiful
  as the daughters of Job;
  and their father gave them an inheritance
  along with their brothers.
After this, Job lived a hundred and forty years;
  and he saw his children, his grandchildren,
  and even his great-grandchildren.
Then Job died, old and full of years. ✛

Psalm 119:66, 71, 75, 91, 125, 130
R. (135) **Lord, let your face shine on me.**
Teach me wisdom and knowledge,
  for in your commands I trust. **R.**
It is good for me that I have been afflicted,
  that I may learn your statutes. **R.**
I know, O Lord, that your ordinances are just,
  and in your faithfulness you have afflicted me. **R.**
According to your ordinances they still stand firm:
  all things serve you. **R.**
I am your servant; give me discernment
  that I may know your decrees. **R.**
The revelation of your words sheds light,
  giving understanding to the simple. **R.**

See Matthew 11:25

R. Alleluia, alleluia.

Blessed are you, Father, Lord of heaven and earth;
you have revealed to little ones the mysteries of the Kingdom. **R.**

† *Luke 10:17-24*

Rejoice because your names are written in heaven.

The seventy-two disciples returned rejoicing and said to Jesus,
  "Lord, even the demons are subject to us because of your name."
Jesus said, "I have observed Satan fall like lightning from the sky.
Behold, I have given you the power
  'to tread upon serpents' and scorpions
  and upon the full force of the enemy
  and nothing will harm you.
Nevertheless, do not rejoice because the spirits are subject to you,
  but rejoice because your names are written in heaven."

At that very moment he rejoiced in the Holy Spirit and said,
  "I give you praise, Father, Lord of heaven and earth,
  for although you have hidden these things
  from the wise and the learned
  you have revealed them to the childlike.
Yes, Father, such has been your gracious will.
All things have been handed over to me by my Father.
No one knows who the Son is except the Father,
  and who the Father is except the Son
  and anyone to whom the Son wishes to reveal him."

Turning to the disciples in private he said,
  "Blessed are the eyes that see what you see.
For I say to you,
  many prophets and kings desired to see what you see,
  but did not see it,
  and to hear what you hear, but did not hear it." ✛

SUNDAY, OCTOBER 2
TWENTY-SEVENTH SUNDAY IN ORDINARY TIME

† *Habakkuk 1:2-3; 2:2-4*

The just one, because of his faith, shall live.

How long, O LORD? I cry for help
  but you do not listen!
I cry out to you, "Violence!"
  but you do not intervene.

Why do you let me see ruin;
   why must I look at misery?
Destruction and violence are before me;
   there is strife, and clamorous discord.
Then the LORD answered me and said:
   Write down the vision clearly upon the tablets,
   so that one can read it readily.
For the vision still has its time,
   presses on to fulfillment, and will not disappoint;
if it delays, wait for it,
   it will surely come, it will not be late.
The rash one has no integrity;
   but the just one, because of his faith, shall live. ✛

Psalm 95:1-2, 6-7, 8-9

R. (8) **If today you hear his voice, harden not your hearts.**
Come, let us sing joyfully to the LORD;
   let us acclaim the Rock of our salvation.
Let us come into his presence with thanksgiving;
   let us joyfully sing psalms to him. **R.**
Come, let us bow down in worship;
   let us kneel before the LORD who made us.
For he is our God,
   and we are the people he shepherds, the flock he guides. **R.**
Oh, that today you would hear his voice:
   "Harden not your hearts as at Meribah,
   as in the day of Massah in the desert,
where your fathers tempted me;
   they tested me though they had seen my works." **R.**

✝2 Timothy 1:6-8, 13-14
Do not be ashamed of your testimony to our Lord.

Beloved:
I remind you to stir into flame
   the gift of God that you have through the imposition of my hands.
For God did not give us a spirit of cowardice
   but rather of power and love and self-control.
So do not be ashamed of your testimony to our Lord,
   nor of me, a prisoner for his sake;
   but bear your share of hardship for the gospel
   with the strength that comes from God.

Take as your norm the sound words that you heard from me,
in the faith and love that are in Christ Jesus.
Guard this rich trust with the help of the Holy Spirit
that dwells within us. ✛

1 Peter 1:25
R. Alleluia, alleluia.
The word of the Lord remains forever.
This is the word that has been proclaimed to you. **R.**

† *Luke 17:5-10*
If you have faith!

The apostles said to the Lord, "Increase our faith."
The Lord replied,
"If you have faith the size of a mustard seed,
you would say to this mulberry tree,
'Be uprooted and planted in the sea,' and it would obey you.

"Who among you would say to your servant
who has just come in from plowing or tending sheep in the field,
'Come here immediately and take your place at table'?
Would he not rather say to him,
'Prepare something for me to eat.
Put on your apron and wait on me while I eat and drink.
You may eat and drink when I am finished'?
Is he grateful to that servant because he did what was commanded?
So should it be with you.
When you have done all you have been commanded,
say, 'We are unprofitable servants;
we have done what we were obliged to do.'" ✛

MONDAY, OCTOBER 3
WEEKDAY

† *Galatians 1:6-12*
*The Gospel preached by me is not of human origin
but through a revelation of Jesus Christ.*

Brothers and sisters:
I am amazed that you are so quickly forsaking
the one who called you by the grace of Christ
for a different gospel (not that there is another).
But there are some who are disturbing you
and wish to pervert the Gospel of Christ.
But even if we or an angel from heaven
should preach to you a gospel

other than the one that we preached to you,
   let that one be accursed!
As we have said before, and now I say again,
   if anyone preaches to you a gospel
   other than the one that you received,
   let that one be accursed!

Am I now currying favor with human beings or God?
Or am I seeking to please people?
If I were still trying to please people,
   I would not be a slave of Christ.

Now I want you to know, brothers and sisters,
   that the Gospel preached by me is not of human origin.
For I did not receive it from a human being, nor was I taught it,
   but it came through a revelation of Jesus Christ. ✢

   Psalm 111:1b-2, 7-8, 9 and 10c
R. (5) **The Lord will remember his covenant for ever.**
   (or **Alleluia.***)*
I will give thanks to the LORD with all my heart
   in the company and assembly of the just.
Great are the works of the LORD,
   exquisite in all their delights. **R.**
The works of his hands are faithful and just;
   sure are all his precepts,
Reliable forever and ever,
   wrought in truth and equity. **R.**
He has sent deliverance to his people;
   he has ratified his covenant forever;
   holy and awesome is his name.
   His praise endures forever. **R.**

   John 13:34
R. Alleluia, alleluia.
I give you a new commandment:
love one another as I have loved you. **R.**

† *Luke 10:25-37*
Who is my neighbor?

There was a scholar of the law who stood up to test Jesus and said,
"Teacher, what must I do to inherit eternal life?"
Jesus said to him, "What is written in the law?
How do you read it?"
He said in reply,
"You shall love the Lord, your God,
with all your heart,
with all your being,
with all your strength,
and with all your mind,
and your neighbor as yourself."
He replied to him, "You have answered correctly;
do this and you will live."

But because he wished to justify himself, he said to Jesus,
"And who is my neighbor?"
Jesus replied,
"A man fell victim to robbers
as he went down from Jerusalem to Jericho.
They stripped and beat him and went off leaving him half-dead.
A priest happened to be going down that road,
but when he saw him, he passed by on the opposite side.
Likewise a Levite came to the place,
and when he saw him, he passed by on the opposite side.
But a Samaritan traveler who came upon him
was moved with compassion at the sight.
He approached the victim,
poured oil and wine over his wounds and bandaged them.
Then he lifted him up on his own animal,
took him to an inn, and cared for him.
The next day he took out two silver coins
and gave them to the innkeeper with the instruction,
'Take care of him.
If you spend more than what I have given you,
I shall repay you on my way back.'
Which of these three, in your opinion,
was neighbor to the robbers' victim?"
He answered, "The one who treated him with mercy."
Jesus said to him, "Go and do likewise." ✣

TUESDAY, OCTOBER 4
St. Francis of Assisi

† *Galatians 1:13-24*
God was pleased to reveal his Son to me,
so that I might proclaim him to the Gentiles.

Brothers and sisters:
You heard of my former way of life in Judaism,
  how I persecuted the Church of God beyond measure
  and tried to destroy it,
  and progressed in Judaism
  beyond many of my contemporaries among my race,
  since I was even more a zealot for my ancestral traditions.
But when he, who from my mother's womb had set me apart
  and called me through his grace,
  was pleased to reveal his Son to me,
  so that I might proclaim him to the Gentiles,
  I did not immediately consult flesh and blood,
  nor did I go up to Jerusalem
  to those who were Apostles before me;
  rather, I went into Arabia and then returned to Damascus.

Then after three years I went up to Jerusalem to confer with Cephas
  and remained with him for fifteen days.
But I did not see any other of the Apostles,
  only James the brother of the Lord.
(As to what I am writing to you, behold,
  before God, I am not lying.)
Then I went into the regions of Syria and Cilicia.
And I was unknown personally to the churches of Judea
  that are in Christ;
  they only kept hearing that "the one who once was persecuting us
  is now preaching the faith he once tried to destroy."
So they glorified God because of me. ✛

Psalm 139:1b-3, 13-14ab, 14c-15
R. (24b) **Guide me, Lord, along the everlasting way.**
O Lord, you have probed me and you know me;
  you know when I sit and when I stand;
  you understand my thoughts from afar.
My journeys and my rest you scrutinize,
  with all my ways you are familiar. **R.**
Truly you have formed my inmost being;
  you knit me in my mother's womb.
I give you thanks that I am fearfully, wonderfully made;
  wonderful are your works. **R.**

My soul also you knew full well;
  nor was my frame unknown to you
When I was made in secret,
  when I was fashioned in the depths of the earth. **R.**

Luke 11:28
R. Alleluia, alleluia.
Blessed are those who hear the word of God
and observe it. **R.**

† Luke 10:38-42
Martha welcomed him into her house. Mary has chosen the better part.

Jesus entered a village
  where a woman whose name was Martha welcomed him.
She had a sister named Mary
  who sat beside the Lord at his feet listening to him speak.
Martha, burdened with much serving, came to him and said,
  "Lord, do you not care
  that my sister has left me by myself to do the serving?
Tell her to help me."
The Lord said to her in reply,
  "Martha, Martha, you are anxious and worried about many things.
There is need of only one thing.
Mary has chosen the better part
  and it will not be taken from her." ✛

WEDNESDAY, OCTOBER 5
WEEKDAY, ST. FAUSTINA KOWALSKA, BL. FRANCIS XAVIER SEELOS

† Galatians 2:1-2, 7-14
They recognized the grace bestowed upon me.

Brothers and sisters:
After fourteen years I again went up to Jerusalem with Barnabas,
  taking Titus along also.
I went up in accord with a revelation,
  and I presented to them the Gospel that I preach to the Gentiles—
  but privately to those of repute—
  so that I might not be running, or have run, in vain.
On the contrary,
  when they saw that I had been entrusted with the Gospel to the
    uncircumcised,
  just as Peter to the circumcised,
  for the one who worked in Peter for an apostolate to the circumcised
  worked also in me for the Gentiles,
  and when they recognized the grace bestowed upon me,

James and Cephas and John,
who were reputed to be pillars,
gave me and Barnabas their right hands in partnership,
that we should go to the Gentiles
and they to the circumcised.
Only, we were to be mindful of the poor,
which is the very thing I was eager to do.

And when Cephas came to Antioch,
I opposed him to his face because he clearly was wrong.
For, until some people came from James,
he used to eat with the Gentiles;
but when they came, he began to draw back and separated himself,
because he was afraid of the circumcised.
And the rest of the Jews acted hypocritically along with him,
with the result that even Barnabas
was carried away by their hypocrisy.
But when I saw that they were not on the right road
in line with the truth of the Gospel,
I said to Cephas in front of all,
"If you, though a Jew,
are living like a Gentile and not like a Jew,
how can you compel the Gentiles to live like Jews?" ✛

Psalm 117:1bc, 2
R. Go out to all the world, and tell the Good News.
Praise the LORD, all you nations,
glorify him, all you peoples! **R.**
For steadfast is his kindness toward us,
and the fidelity of the LORD endures forever. **R.**

Romans 8:15bc
R. Alleluia, alleluia.
You have received a spirit of adoption as sons
through which we cry: Abba! Father! **R.**

† *Luke 11:1-4*
Lord, teach us to pray.

Jesus was praying in a certain place, and when he had finished,
one of his disciples said to him,
"Lord, teach us to pray just as John taught his disciples."
He said to them, "When you pray, say:

Father, hallowed be your name,
your Kingdom come.

Give us each day our daily bread
and forgive us our sins
for we ourselves forgive everyone in debt to us,
and do not subject us to the final test." ✝

THURSDAY, OCTOBER 6
WEEKDAY, ST. BRUNO, BL. MARIE ROSE DUROCHER

✝ *Galatians 3:1-5*
*Did you receive the Spirit from works of the law,
or from faith in what you heard?*

O stupid Galatians!
Who has bewitched you,
 before whose eyes Jesus Christ was publicly portrayed as crucified?
I want to learn only this from you:
 did you receive the Spirit from works of the law,
 or from faith in what you heard?
Are you so stupid?
After beginning with the Spirit,
 are you now ending with the flesh?
Did you experience so many things in vain?—
 if indeed it was in vain.
Does, then, the one who supplies the Spirit to you
 and works mighty deeds among you
 do so from works of the law
 or from faith in what you heard? ✝

Luke 1:69-70, 71-72, 73-75
R. (68) **Blessed be the Lord, the God of Israel; he has come to
 his people.**
He has raised up for us a mighty savior,
 born of the house of his servant David. **R.**
Through his holy prophets he promised of old
 that he would save us from our enemies,
 from the hands of all who hate us.
He promised to show mercy to our fathers
 and to remember his holy covenant. **R.**
This was the oath he swore to our father Abraham:
 to set us free from the hands of our enemies,
 free to worship him without fear,
 holy and righteous in his sight
 all the days of our life. **R.**

See Acts 16:14b

R. Alleluia, alleluia.

Open our hearts, O Lord,
to listen to the words of your Son. **R.**

† *Luke 11:5-13*

Ask and you will receive.

Jesus said to his disciples:
"Suppose one of you has a friend
 to whom he goes at midnight and says,
 'Friend, lend me three loaves of bread,
 for a friend of mine has arrived at my house from a journey
 and I have nothing to offer him,'
 and he says in reply from within,
 'Do not bother me; the door has already been locked
 and my children and I are already in bed.
 I cannot get up to give you anything.'
I tell you, if he does not get up to give him the loaves
 because of their friendship,
 he will get up to give him whatever he needs
 because of his persistence.

"And I tell you, ask and you will receive;
 seek and you will find;
 knock and the door will be opened to you.
For everyone who asks, receives;
 and the one who seeks, finds;
 and to the one who knocks, the door will be opened.
What father among you would hand his son a snake
 when he asks for a fish?
Or hand him a scorpion when he asks for an egg?
If you then, who are wicked,
 know how to give good gifts to your children,
 how much more will the Father in heaven give the Holy Spirit
 to those who ask him?" ✠

FRIDAY, OCTOBER 7
OUR LADY OF THE ROSARY

† *Galatians 3:7-14*
Those who have faith are blessed along with Abraham who had faith.

Brothers and sisters:
Realize that it is those who have faith
  who are children of Abraham.
Scripture, which saw in advance that God
  would justify the Gentiles by faith,
  foretold the good news to Abraham, saying,
  Through you shall all the nations be blessed.
Consequently, those who have faith are blessed
  along with Abraham who had faith.
For all who depend on works of the law are under a curse;
  for it is written, *Cursed be everyone*
  who does not persevere in doing all the things
  written in the book of the law.
And that no one is justified before God by the law is clear,
  for *the one who is righteous by faith will live.*
But the law does not depend on faith;
  rather, *the one who does these things will live by them.*
Christ ransomed us from the curse of the law by becoming a curse
    for us,
  for it is written, *Cursed be everyone who hangs on a tree,*
  that the blessing of Abraham might be extended
  to the Gentiles through Christ Jesus,
  so that we might receive the promise of the Spirit through faith. ✛

  Psalm 111:1b-2, 3-4, 5-6
R. (5) The Lord will remember his covenant for ever.
I will give thanks to the LORD with all my heart
  in the company and assembly of the just.
Great are the works of the LORD,
  exquisite in all their delights. **R.**
Majesty and glory are his work,
  and his justice endures forever.
He has won renown for his wondrous deeds;
  gracious and merciful is the LORD. **R.**
He has given food to those who fear him;
  he will forever be mindful of his covenant.
He has made known to his people the power of his works,
  giving them the inheritance of the nations. **R.**

John 12:31b-32
R. Alleluia, alleluia.
The prince of this world will now be cast out,
and when I am lifted up from the earth
I will draw all to myself, says the Lord. **R.**

† *Luke 11:15-26*
If it is by the finger of God that I drive out demons,
then the Kingdom of God has come upon you.

When Jesus had driven out a demon, some of the crowd said:
"By the power of Beelzebul, the prince of demons,
   he drives out demons."
Others, to test him, asked him for a sign from heaven.
But he knew their thoughts and said to them,
   "Every kingdom divided against itself will be laid waste
   and house will fall against house.
And if Satan is divided against himself, how will his kingdom stand?
For you say that it is by Beelzebul that I drive out demons.
If I, then, drive out demons by Beelzebul,
   by whom do your own people drive them out?
Therefore they will be your judges.
But if it is by the finger of God that I drive out demons,
   then the Kingdom of God has come upon you.
When a strong man fully armed guards his palace,
   his possessions are safe.
But when one stronger than he attacks and overcomes him,
   he takes away the armor on which he relied
   and distributes the spoils.
Whoever is not with me is against me,
   and whoever does not gather with me scatters.

"When an unclean spirit goes out of someone,
   it roams through arid regions searching for rest
   but, finding none, it says,
   'I shall return to my home from which I came.'
But upon returning, it finds it swept clean and put in order.
Then it goes and brings back seven other spirits
   more wicked than itself who move in and dwell there,
   and the last condition of that man is worse than the first." ✛

SATURDAY, OCTOBER 8
WEEKDAY, *[BVM]*

† *Galatians 3:22-29*
Through faith you are all children of God.

Brothers and sisters:
Scripture confined all things under the power of sin,
  that through faith in Jesus Christ
  the promise might be given to those who believe.

Before faith came, we were held in custody under law,
  confined for the faith that was to be revealed.
Consequently, the law was our disciplinarian for Christ,
  that we might be justified by faith.
But now that faith has come, we are no longer under a disciplinarian.
For through faith you are all children of God in Christ Jesus.
For all of you who were baptized into Christ
  have clothed yourselves with Christ.
There is neither Jew nor Greek,
  there is neither slave nor free person,
  there is not male and female;
  for you are all one in Christ Jesus.
And if you belong to Christ, then you are Abraham's descendants,
  heirs according to the promise. ✛

Psalm 105:2-3, 4-5, 6-7
R. (8a) **The Lord remembers his covenant for ever.**
  (or **Alleluia.***)*
Sing to him, sing his praise,
  proclaim all his wondrous deeds.
Glory in his holy name;
  rejoice, O hearts that seek the LORD! **R.**
Look to the LORD in his strength;
  seek to serve him constantly.
Recall the wondrous deeds that he has wrought,
  his portents, and the judgments he has uttered. **R.**
You descendants of Abraham, his servants,
  sons of Jacob, his chosen ones!
He, the LORD, is our God;
  throughout the earth his judgments prevail. **R.**

Luke 11:28
R. Alleluia, alleluia.
Blessed are those who hear the word of God
and observe it. **R.**

† *Luke 11:27-28*
Blessed is the womb that carried you.
Rather, blessed are those who hear the word of God and observe it.

While Jesus was speaking,
a woman from the crowd called out and said to him,
"Blessed is the womb that carried you
and the breasts at which you nursed."
He replied, "Rather, blessed are those
who hear the word of God and observe it." ✛

SUNDAY, OCTOBER 9
TWENTY-EIGHTH SUNDAY IN ORDINARY TIME

† *2 Kings 5:14-17*
Naaman returned to the man of God and acknowledged the Lord.

Naaman went down and plunged into the Jordan seven times
at the word of Elisha, the man of God.
His flesh became again like the flesh of a little child,
and he was clean of his leprosy.

Naaman returned with his whole retinue to the man of God.
On his arrival he stood before Elisha and said,
"Now I know that there is no God in all the earth,
except in Israel.
Please accept a gift from your servant."

Elisha replied, "As the LORD lives whom I serve, I will not take it";
and despite Naaman's urging, he still refused.
Naaman said: "If you will not accept,
please let me, your servant, have two mule-loads of earth,
for I will no longer offer holocaust or sacrifice
to any other god except to the LORD." ✛

Psalm 98:1, 2-3, 3-4
R. (see 2b) **The Lord has revealed to the nations his saving
power.**
Sing to the LORD a new song,
for he has done wondrous deeds;
his right hand has won victory for him,
his holy arm. **R.**
The LORD has made his salvation known:
in the sight of the nations he has revealed his justice.
He has remembered his kindness and his faithfulness
toward the house of Israel. **R.**

All the ends of the earth have seen
   the salvation by our God.
Sing joyfully to the LORD, all you lands:
   break into song; sing praise. **R.**

† 2 Timothy 2:8-13
If we persevere we shall also reign with Christ.

Beloved:
Remember Jesus Christ, raised from the dead, a descendant of David:
   such is my gospel, for which I am suffering,
   even to the point of chains, like a criminal.
But the word of God is not chained.
Therefore, I bear with everything for the sake of those who are chosen,
   so that they too may obtain the salvation that is in Christ Jesus,
   together with eternal glory.
This saying is trustworthy:
   If we have died with him
      we shall also live with him;
   if we persevere
      we shall also reign with him.
   But if we deny him
      he will deny us.
   If we are unfaithful
      he remains faithful,
      for he cannot deny himself. ✛

1 Thessalonians 5:18
R. Alleluia, alleluia.
In all circumstances, give thanks,
for this is the will of God for you in Christ Jesus. **R.**

† Luke 17:11-19
None but this foreigner has returned to give thanks to God.

As Jesus continued his journey to Jerusalem,
   he traveled through Samaria and Galilee.
As he was entering a village, ten lepers met him.
They stood at a distance from him and raised their voices, saying,
   "Jesus, Master! Have pity on us!"
And when he saw them, he said,
   "Go show yourselves to the priests."
As they were going they were cleansed.
And one of them, realizing he had been healed,
   returned, glorifying God in a loud voice;
   and he fell at the feet of Jesus and thanked him.
He was a Samaritan.

Jesus said in reply,
"Ten were cleansed, were they not?
Where are the other nine?
Has none but this foreigner returned to give thanks to God?"
Then he said to him, "Stand up and go;
　your faith has saved you." ✛

MONDAY, OCTOBER 10
WEEKDAY

† *Galatians 4:22-24, 26-27, 31—5:1*
We are children not of the slave woman but of the freeborn woman.

Brothers and sisters:
It is written that Abraham had two sons,
　one by the slave woman and the other by the freeborn woman.
The son of the slave woman was born naturally,
　the son of the freeborn through a promise.
Now this is an allegory.
These women represent two covenants.
One was from Mount Sinai, bearing children for slavery;
　this is Hagar.
But the Jerusalem above is freeborn, and she is our mother.
For it is written:
　Rejoice, you barren one who bore no children;
　　break forth and shout, you who were not in labor;
　for more numerous are the children of the deserted one
　　than of her who has a husband.
Therefore, brothers and sisters,
　we are children not of the slave woman
　but of the freeborn woman.

For freedom Christ set us free; so stand firm
　and do not submit again to the yoke of slavery. ✛

　Psalm 113:1b-2, 3-4, 5a and 6-7
R. (see 2) **Blessed be the name of the Lord forever.**
　(or **Alleluia.**)
Praise, you servants of the LORD,
　praise the name of the LORD.
Blessed be the name of the LORD
　both now and forever. **R.**
From the rising to the setting of the sun
　is the name of the LORD to be praised.
High above all nations is the LORD;
　above the heavens is his glory. **R.**

Who is like the Lᴏʀᴅ, our God,
who looks upon the heavens and the earth below?
He raises up the lowly from the dust;
from the dunghill he lifts up the poor. **R.**

Psalm 95:8
R. Alleluia, alleluia.
If today you hear his voice,
harden not your hearts. **R.**

† *Luke 11:29-32*
*This generation seeks a sign, but no sign will be given it,
except the sign of Jonah.*

While still more people gathered in the crowd, Jesus said to them,
"This generation is an evil generation;
it seeks a sign, but no sign will be given it,
except the sign of Jonah.
Just as Jonah became a sign to the Ninevites,
so will the Son of Man be to this generation.
At the judgment
the queen of the south will rise with the men of this generation
and she will condemn them,
because she came from the ends of the earth
to hear the wisdom of Solomon,
and there is something greater than Solomon here.
At the judgment the men of Nineveh will arise with this generation
and condemn it,
because at the preaching of Jonah they repented,
and there is something greater than Jonah here." ✛

TUESDAY, OCTOBER 11
Wᴇᴇᴋᴅᴀʏ, Sᴛ. Pᴏᴘᴇ Jᴏʜɴ XXIII

† *Galatians 5:1-6*
*Neither circumcision nor uncircumcision counts for anything,
but only faith working through love.*

Brothers and sisters:
For freedom Christ set us free;
so stand firm and do not submit again to the yoke of slavery.

It is I, Paul, who am telling you
that if you have yourselves circumcised,
Christ will be of no benefit to you.
Once again I declare to every man who has himself circumcised
that he is bound to observe the entire law.

You are separated from Christ,
you who are trying to be justified by law;
you have fallen from grace.
For through the Spirit, by faith, we await the hope of righteousness.
For in Christ Jesus,
neither circumcision nor uncircumcision counts for anything,
but only faith working through love. ✢

Psalm 119:41, 43, 44, 45, 47, 48

R. (41a) **Let your mercy come to me, O Lord.**
Let your mercy come to me, O LORD,
your salvation according to your promise. **R.**
Take not the word of truth from my mouth,
for in your ordinances is my hope. **R.**
And I will keep your law continually,
forever and ever. **R.**
And I will walk at liberty,
because I seek your precepts. **R.**
And I will delight in your commands,
which I love. **R.**
And I will lift up my hands to your commands
and meditate on your statutes. **R.**

Hebrews 4:12

R. Alleluia, alleluia.
The word of God is living and effective,
able to discern reflections and thoughts of the heart. **R.**

†*Luke 11:37-41*
Give alms and behold, everything will be clean for you.

After Jesus had spoken,
a Pharisee invited him to dine at his home.
He entered and reclined at table to eat.
The Pharisee was amazed to see
that he did not observe the prescribed washing before the meal.
The Lord said to him, "Oh you Pharisees!
Although you cleanse the outside of the cup and the dish,
inside you are filled with plunder and evil.
You fools!
Did not the maker of the outside also make the inside?
But as to what is within, give alms,
and behold, everything will be clean for you." ✢

WEDNESDAY, OCTOBER 12
WEEKDAY

† *Galatians 5:18-25*
Those who belong to Christ Jesus have crucified their flesh
with its passions and desires.

Brothers and sisters:
If you are guided by the Spirit, you are not under the law.
Now the works of the flesh are obvious:
immorality, impurity, licentiousness, idolatry,
sorcery, hatreds, rivalry, jealousy,
outbursts of fury, acts of selfishness,
dissensions, factions, occasions of envy,
drinking bouts, orgies, and the like.
I warn you, as I warned you before,
that those who do such things will not inherit the Kingdom of God.
In contrast, the fruit of the Spirit is love, joy, peace,
patience, kindness, generosity,
faithfulness, gentleness, self-control.
Against such there is no law.
Now those who belong to Christ Jesus have crucified their flesh
with its passions and desires.
If we live in the Spirit, let us also follow the Spirit. ✛

Psalm 1:1-2, 3, 4 and 6
R. (see John 8:12) **Those who follow you, Lord, will have the
light of life.**
Blessed the man who follows not
the counsel of the wicked
Nor walks in the way of sinners,
nor sits in the company of the insolent,
But delights in the law of the LORD
and meditates on his law day and night. **R.**
He is like a tree
planted near running water,
That yields its fruit in due season,
and whose leaves never fade.
Whatever he does, prospers. **R.**
Not so the wicked, not so;
they are like chaff which the wind drives away.
For the LORD watches over the way of the just,
but the way of the wicked vanishes. **R.**

John 10:27
R. Alleluia, alleluia.
My sheep hear my voice, says the Lord;
I know them, and they follow me. **R.**

† *Luke 11:42-46*
Woe to you Pharisees! Woe also to you scholars of the law!

The Lord said:
"Woe to you Pharisees!
You pay tithes of mint and of rue and of every garden herb,
  but you pay no attention to judgment and to love for God.
These you should have done, without overlooking the others.
Woe to you Pharisees!
You love the seat of honor in synagogues
  and greetings in marketplaces.
Woe to you!
You are like unseen graves over which people unknowingly walk."

Then one of the scholars of the law said to him in reply,
  "Teacher, by saying this you are insulting us too."
And he said, "Woe also to you scholars of the law!
You impose on people burdens hard to carry,
  but you yourselves do not lift one finger to touch them." ✝

THURSDAY, OCTOBER 13
WEEKDAY

† *Ephesians 1:1-10*
God chose us in Christ, before the foundation of the world.

Paul, an Apostle of Christ Jesus by the will of God,
  to the holy ones who are in Ephesus
  and faithful in Christ Jesus:
  grace to you and peace from God our Father and the Lord Jesus
    Christ.

Blessed be the God and Father of our Lord Jesus Christ,
  who has blessed us in Christ
  with every spiritual blessing in the heavens,
  as he chose us in him, before the foundation of the world,
  to be holy and without blemish before him.
In love he destined us for adoption to himself through Jesus Christ,
  in accord with the favor of his will,
  for the praise of the glory of his grace
  that he granted us in the beloved.

In Christ we have redemption by his Blood,
the forgiveness of transgressions,
in accord with the riches of his grace that he lavished upon us.
In all wisdom and insight, he has made known to us
the mystery of his will in accord with his favor
that he set forth in him as a plan for the fullness of times,
to sum up all things in Christ, in heaven and on earth. ✛

Psalm 98:1, 2-3ab, 3cd-4, 5-6
R. (2a) The Lord has made known his salvation.
Sing to the Lᴏʀᴅ a new song,
for he has done wondrous deeds;
His right hand has won victory for him,
his holy arm. **R.**
The Lᴏʀᴅ has made his salvation known:
in the sight of the nations he has revealed his justice.
He has remembered his kindness and his faithfulness
toward the house of Israel. **R.**
All the ends of the earth have seen
the salvation by our God.
Sing joyfully to the Lᴏʀᴅ, all you lands;
break into song; sing praise. **R.**
Sing praise to the Lᴏʀᴅ with the harp,
with the harp and melodious song.
With trumpets and the sound of the horn
sing joyfully before the King, the Lᴏʀᴅ. **R.**

John 14:6
R. Alleluia, alleluia.
I am the way and the truth and the life, says the Lord;
no one comes to the Father except through me. **R.**

†*Luke 11:47-54*
*The blood of the prophets is required, from the blood of Abel
to the blood of Zechariah.*

The Lord said:
"Woe to you who build the memorials of the prophets
whom your fathers killed.
Consequently, you bear witness and give consent
to the deeds of your ancestors,
for they killed them and you do the building.
Therefore, the wisdom of God said,
'I will send to them prophets and Apostles;
some of them they will kill and persecute'
in order that this generation might be charged
with the blood of all the prophets

shed since the foundation of the world,
from the blood of Abel to the blood of Zechariah
who died between the altar and the temple building.
Yes, I tell you, this generation will be charged with their blood!
Woe to you, scholars of the law!
You have taken away the key of knowledge.
You yourselves did not enter and you stopped those trying to enter."
When Jesus left, the scribes and Pharisees
began to act with hostility toward him
and to interrogate him about many things,
for they were plotting to catch him at something he might say. ✛

FRIDAY, OCTOBER 14
WEEKDAY, ST. POPE CALLISTUS I

✝ *Ephesians 1:11-14*
We first hoped in Christ, and you were sealed with the Holy Spirit.

Brothers and sisters:
In Christ we were also chosen,
destined in accord with the purpose of the One
who accomplishes all things according to the intention of his will,
so that we might exist for the praise of his glory,
we who first hoped in Christ.
In him you also, who have heard the word of truth,
the Gospel of your salvation, and have believed in him,
were sealed with the promised Holy Spirit,
which is the first installment of our inheritance
toward redemption as God's possession, to the praise of his glory. ✛

Psalm 33:1-2, 4-5, 12-13
R. (12) **Blessed the people the Lord has chosen to be his own.**
Exult, you just, in the LORD;
praise from the upright is fitting.
Give thanks to the LORD on the harp;
with the ten-stringed lyre chant his praises. **R.**
For upright is the word of the LORD,
and all his works are trustworthy.
He loves justice and right;
of the kindness of the LORD the earth is full. **R.**
Blessed the nation whose God is the LORD,
the people he has chosen for his own inheritance.
From heaven the LORD looks down;
he sees all mankind. **R.**

Psalm 33:22

R. Alleluia, alleluia.

May your kindness, O LORD, be upon us;
who have put our hope in you. **R.**

†*Luke 12:1-7*

Even the hairs of your head have all been counted.

At that time:
So many people were crowding together
  that they were trampling one another underfoot.
Jesus began to speak, first to his disciples,
  "Beware of the leaven—that is, the hypocrisy—of the Pharisees.

"There is nothing concealed that will not be revealed,
  nor secret that will not be known.
Therefore whatever you have said in the darkness
  will be heard in the light,
  and what you have whispered behind closed doors
  will be proclaimed on the housetops.
I tell you, my friends,
  do not be afraid of those who kill the body
  but after that can do no more.
I shall show you whom to fear.
Be afraid of the one who after killing
  has the power to cast into Gehenna;
  yes, I tell you, be afraid of that one.
Are not five sparrows sold for two small coins?
Yet not one of them has escaped the notice of God.
Even the hairs of your head have all been counted.
Do not be afraid.
You are worth more than many sparrows." ✛

SATURDAY, OCTOBER 15
ST. TERESA OF JESUS

†*Ephesians 1:15-23*

He gave Christ as head over all things to the Church, which is his Body.

Brothers and sisters:
Hearing of your faith in the Lord Jesus
  and of your love for all the holy ones,
  I do not cease giving thanks for you,
  remembering you in my prayers,
  that the God of our Lord Jesus Christ, the Father of glory,
  may give you a spirit of wisdom and revelation
  resulting in knowledge of him.

May the eyes of your hearts be enlightened,
  that you may know what is the hope that belongs to his call,
  what are the riches of glory
  in his inheritance among the holy ones,
  and what is the surpassing greatness of his power
  for us who believe,
  in accord with the exercise of his great might,
  which he worked in Christ,
  raising him from the dead
  and seating him at his right hand in the heavens,
  far above every principality, authority, power, and dominion,
  and every name that is named
  not only in this age but also in the one to come.
And he put all things beneath his feet
  and gave him as head over all things to the Church,
  which is his Body,
  the fullness of the one who fills all things in every way. ✝

  Psalm 8:2-3ab, 4-5, 6-7

R. (7) **You have given your Son rule over the works of your hands.**

O Lord, our Lord,
  how glorious is your name over all the earth!
  You have exalted your majesty above the heavens.
Out of the mouths of babes and sucklings
  you have fashioned praise because of your foes. **R.**
When I behold your heavens, the work of your fingers,
  the moon and the stars which you set in place—
What is man that you should be mindful of him,
  or the son of man that you should care for him? **R.**
You have made him little less than the angels,
  and crowned him with glory and honor.
You have given him rule over the works of your hands,
  putting all things under his feet. **R.**

  John 15:26b, 27a

R. Alleluia, alleluia.

The Spirit of truth will testify to me, says the Lord,
and you also will testify. **R.**

† Luke 12:8-12

The Holy Spirit will teach you at that moment what you should say.

Jesus said to his disciples:
"I tell you,
everyone who acknowledges me before others
the Son of Man will acknowledge before the angels of God.
But whoever denies me before others
will be denied before the angels of God.

"Everyone who speaks a word against the Son of Man will be forgiven,
but the one who blasphemes against the Holy Spirit
will not be forgiven.
When they take you before synagogues and before rulers and
authorities,
do not worry about how or what your defense will be
or about what you are to say.
For the Holy Spirit will teach you at that moment what you should
say." ✛

SUNDAY, OCTOBER 16
TWENTY-NINTH SUNDAY IN ORDINARY TIME

† Exodus 17:8-13

As long as Moses kept his hands raised up, Israel had the better of the fight.

In those days, Amalek came and waged war against Israel.
Moses, therefore, said to Joshua,
"Pick out certain men,
and tomorrow go out and engage Amalek in battle.
I will be standing on top of the hill
with the staff of God in my hand."

So Joshua did as Moses told him:
he engaged Amalek in battle
after Moses had climbed to the top of the hill with Aaron and Hur.
As long as Moses kept his hands raised up,
Israel had the better of the fight,
but when he let his hands rest,
Amalek had the better of the fight.
Moses' hands, however, grew tired;
so they put a rock in place for him to sit on.
Meanwhile Aaron and Hur supported his hands,
one on one side and one on the other,
so that his hands remained steady till sunset.
And Joshua mowed down Amalek and his people
with the edge of the sword. ✛

Psalm 121:1-2, 3-4, 5-6, 7-8

R. (see 2) Our help is from the Lord, who made heaven and earth.

I lift up my eyes toward the mountains;
   whence shall help come to me?
My help is from the L$_{ORD}$,
   who made heaven and earth. **R.**
May he not suffer your foot to slip;
   may he slumber not who guards you:
Indeed he neither slumbers nor sleeps,
   the guardian of Israel. **R.**
The L$_{ORD}$ is your guardian; the L$_{ORD}$ is your shade;
   he is beside you at your right hand.
The sun shall not harm you by day,
   nor the moon by night. **R.**
The L$_{ORD}$ will guard you from all evil;
   he will guard your life.
The L$_{ORD}$ will guard your coming and your going,
   both now and forever. **R.**

✝ *2 Timothy 3:14—4:2*

One who belongs to God may be competent, equipped for every good work.

Beloved:
Remain faithful to what you have learned and believed,
   because you know from whom you learned it,
   and that from infancy you have known the sacred Scriptures,
   which are capable of giving you wisdom for salvation
   through faith in Christ Jesus.
All Scripture is inspired by God
   and is useful for teaching, for refutation, for correction,
   and for training in righteousness,
   so that one who belongs to God may be competent,
   equipped for every good work.

I charge you in the presence of God and of Christ Jesus,
   who will judge the living and the dead,
   and by his appearing and his kingly power:
   proclaim the word;
   be persistent whether it is convenient or inconvenient;
   convince, reprimand, encourage through all patience and teaching. ✝

Hebrews 4:12

R. Alleluia, alleluia.
The word of God is living and effective,
discerning reflections and thoughts of the heart. **R.**

† *Luke 18:1-8*
God will secure the rights of his chosen ones who call out to him.

Jesus told his disciples a parable
  about the necessity for them to pray always without becoming
    weary.
He said, "There was a judge in a certain town
  who neither feared God nor respected any human being.
And a widow in that town used to come to him and say,
  'Render a just decision for me against my adversary.'
For a long time the judge was unwilling, but eventually he thought,
  'While it is true that I neither fear God nor respect any human
    being,
  because this widow keeps bothering me
  I shall deliver a just decision for her
  lest she finally come and strike me.'"
The Lord said, "Pay attention to what the dishonest judge says.
Will not God then secure the rights of his chosen ones
  who call out to him day and night?
Will he be slow to answer them?
I tell you, he will see to it that justice is done for them speedily.
But when the Son of Man comes, will he find faith on earth?" ✛

MONDAY, OCTOBER 17
St. Ignatius of Antioch

† *Ephesians 2:1-10*
God brought us to life with Christ and seated us with him in the heavens.

Brothers and sisters:
You were dead in your transgressions and sins
  in which you once lived following the age of this world,
  following the ruler of the power of the air,
  the spirit that is now at work in the disobedient.
All of us once lived among them in the desires of our flesh,
  following the wishes of the flesh and the impulses,
  and we were by nature children of wrath, like the rest.
But God, who is rich in mercy,
  because of the great love he had for us,
  even when we were dead in our transgressions,
  brought us to life with Christ (by grace you have been saved),
  raised us up with him,
  and seated us with him in the heavens in Christ Jesus,
  that in the ages to come
  he might show the immeasurable riches of his grace
  in his kindness to us in Christ Jesus.

For by grace you have been saved through faith,
  and this is not from you; it is the gift of God;
  it is not from works, so no one may boast.
For we are his handiwork, created in Christ Jesus for good works
  that God has prepared in advance,
  that we should live in them. ✢

  Psalm 100:1b-2, 3, 4ab, 4c-5
R. (3b) **The Lord made us, we belong to him.**
Sing joyfully to the LORD all you lands;
  serve the LORD with gladness;
  come before him with joyful song. **R.**
Know that the LORD is God;
  he made us, his we are;
  his people, the flock he tends. **R.**
Enter his gates with thanksgiving,
  his courts with praise. **R.**
Give thanks to him; bless his name, for he is good:
  the LORD, whose kindness endures forever,
  and his faithfulness, to all generations. **R.**

  Matthew 5:3
R. Alleluia, alleluia.
Blessed are the poor in spirit;
for theirs is the Kingdom of heaven. **R.**

† *Luke 12:13-21*
And the things you have prepared, to whom will they belong?

Someone in the crowd said to Jesus,
  "Teacher, tell my brother to share the inheritance with me."
He replied to him,
  "Friend, who appointed me as your judge and arbitrator?"
Then he said to the crowd,
  "Take care to guard against all greed,
  for though one may be rich,
  one's life does not consist of possessions."

Then he told them a parable.
"There was a rich man whose land produced a bountiful harvest.
He asked himself, 'What shall I do,
  for I do not have space to store my harvest?'
And he said, 'This is what I shall do:
  I shall tear down my barns and build larger ones.
There I shall store all my grain and other goods
  and I shall say to myself, "Now as for you,

you have so many good things stored up for many years,
rest, eat, drink, be merry!'"
But God said to him,
'You fool, this night your life will be demanded of you;
and the things you have prepared, to whom will they belong?'
Thus will it be for the one who stores up treasure for himself
but is not rich in what matters to God." ✛

TUESDAY, OCTOBER 18
St. Luke

† 2 Timothy 4:10-17b
Luke is the only one with me.

Beloved:
Demas, enamored of the present world,
deserted me and went to Thessalonica,
Crescens to Galatia, and Titus to Dalmatia.
Luke is the only one with me.
Get Mark and bring him with you,
for he is helpful to me in the ministry.
I have sent Tychicus to Ephesus.
When you come, bring the cloak I left with Carpus in Troas,
the papyrus rolls, and especially the parchments.

Alexander the coppersmith did me a great deal of harm;
the Lord will repay him according to his deeds.
You too be on guard against him,
for he has strongly resisted our preaching.

At my first defense no one appeared on my behalf,
but everyone deserted me.
May it not be held against them!
But the Lord stood by me and gave me strength,
so that through me the proclamation might be completed
and all the Gentiles might hear it. ✛

Psalm 145:10-11, 12-13, 17-18
R. (12) **Your friends make known, O Lord, the glorious splendor of your Kingdom.**
Let all your works give you thanks, O Lord,
and let your faithful ones bless you.
Let them discourse of the glory of your Kingdom
and speak of your might. **R.**
Making known to men your might
and the glorious splendor of your Kingdom.

Your Kingdom is a Kingdom for all ages,
 and your dominion endures through all generations. **R.**
The LORD is just in all his ways
 and holy in all his works.
The LORD is near to all who call upon him,
 to all who call upon him in truth. **R.**

 See John 15:16
R. Alleluia, alleluia.
I chose you from the world,
to go and bear fruit that will last, says the Lord. **R.**

† *Luke 10:1-9*
The harvest is abundant but the laborers are few.

The Lord Jesus appointed seventy-two disciples
 whom he sent ahead of him in pairs
 to every town and place he intended to visit.
He said to them,
 "The harvest is abundant but the laborers are few;
 so ask the master of the harvest
 to send out laborers for his harvest.
Go on your way;
 behold, I am sending you like lambs among wolves.
Carry no money bag, no sack, no sandals;
 and greet no one along the way.
Into whatever house you enter,
 first say, 'Peace to this household.'
If a peaceful person lives there,
 your peace will rest on him;
 but if not, it will return to you.
Stay in the same house and eat and drink what is offered to you,
 for the laborer deserves payment.
Do not move about from one house to another.
Whatever town you enter and they welcome you,
 eat what is set before you,
 cure the sick in it and say to them,
 'The Kingdom of God is at hand for you.'" ✝

WEDNESDAY, OCTOBER 19
St. John de Brébeuf, St. Isaac Jogues and Companions

† *Ephesians 3:2-12*
*The mystery of Christ has now been revealed
and the Gentiles are coheirs in the promise.*

Brothers and sisters:
You have heard of the stewardship of God's grace
  that was given to me for your benefit,
    namely, that the mystery was made known to me by revelation,
    as I have written briefly earlier.
When you read this
  you can understand my insight into the mystery of Christ,
    which was not made known to human beings in other generations
    as it has now been revealed
  to his holy Apostles and prophets by the Spirit,
    that the Gentiles are coheirs, members of the same Body,
    and copartners in the promise in Christ Jesus through the Gospel.

Of this I became a minister by the gift of God's grace
  that was granted me in accord with the exercise of his power.
To me, the very least of all the holy ones, this grace was given,
  to preach to the Gentiles the inscrutable riches of Christ,
    and to bring to light for all what is the plan of the mystery
    hidden from ages past in God who created all things,
  so that the manifold wisdom of God
  might now be made known through the Church
  to the principalities and authorities in the heavens.
This was according to the eternal purpose
  that he accomplished in Christ Jesus our Lord,
  in whom we have boldness of speech
  and confidence of access through faith in him. ✛

  Isaiah 12:2-3, 4bcd, 5-6
R. (see 3) **You will draw water joyfully from the springs of
  salvation.**
God indeed is my savior;
  I am confident and unafraid.
My strength and my courage is the Lord,
  and he has been my savior.
With joy you will draw water
  at the fountain of salvation. **R.**
Give thanks to the Lord, acclaim his name;
  among the nations make known his deeds,
  proclaim how exalted is his name. **R.**

Sing praise to the LORD for his glorious achievement;
    let this be known throughout all the earth.
Shout with exultation, O city of Zion,
    for great in your midst
    is the Holy One of Israel! **R.**

Matthew 24:42a, 44
R. Alleluia, alleluia.
Stay awake!
For you do not know when the Son of Man will come. **R.**

† *Luke 12:39-48*
Much will be required of the person entrusted with much.

Jesus said to his disciples:
"Be sure of this:
    if the master of the house had known the hour
    when the thief was coming,
    he would not have let his house be broken into.
You also must be prepared,
    for at an hour you do not expect, the Son of Man will come."

Then Peter said,
    "Lord, is this parable meant for us or for everyone?"
And the Lord replied,
    "Who, then, is the faithful and prudent steward
    whom the master will put in charge of his servants
    to distribute the food allowance at the proper time?
Blessed is that servant whom his master on arrival finds doing so.
Truly, I say to you, he will put him
    in charge of all his property.
But if that servant says to himself,
    'My master is delayed in coming,'
    and begins to beat the menservants and the maidservants,
    to eat and drink and get drunk,
    then that servant's master will come
    on an unexpected day and at an unknown hour
    and will punish the servant severely
    and assign him a place with the unfaithful.
That servant who knew his master's will
    but did not make preparations nor act in accord with his will
    shall be beaten severely;
    and the servant who was ignorant of his master's will
    but acted in a way deserving of a severe beating
    shall be beaten only lightly.

Much will be required of the person entrusted with much,
and still more will be demanded of the person entrusted with
more." ✛

THURSDAY, OCTOBER 20
Weekday, St. Paul of the Cross

†Ephesians 3:14-21
Rooted and grounded in love, you may be filled with the fullness of God.

Brothers and sisters:
I kneel before the Father,
from whom every family in heaven and on earth is named,
that he may grant you in accord with the riches of his glory
to be strengthened with power through his Spirit in the inner self,
and that Christ may dwell in your hearts through faith;
that you, rooted and grounded in love,
may have strength to comprehend with all the holy ones
what is the breadth and length and height and depth,
and to know the love of Christ that surpasses knowledge,
so that you may be filled with all the fullness of God.

Now to him who is able to accomplish far more than all we ask or
imagine,
by the power at work within us,
to him be glory in the Church and in Christ Jesus
to all generations, forever and ever. Amen. ✛

Psalm 33:1-2, 4-5, 11-12, 18-19
R. (5b) **The earth is full of the goodness of the Lord.**
Exult, you just, in the Lord;
praise from the upright is fitting.
Give thanks to the Lord on the harp;
with the ten-stringed lyre chant his praises. **R.**
For upright is the word of the Lord,
and all his works are trustworthy.
He loves justice and right;
of the kindness of the Lord the earth is full. **R.**
But the plan of the Lord stands forever;
the design of his heart, through all generations.
Blessed the nation whose God is the Lord,
the people he has chosen for his own inheritance. **R.**
But see, the eyes of the Lord are upon those who fear him,
upon those who hope for his kindness,
To deliver them from death
and preserve them in spite of famine. **R.**

Philippians 3:8-9

R. Alleluia, alleluia.

I consider all things so much rubbish
that I may gain Christ and be found in him. **R.**

† *Luke 12:49-53*
I have not come to establish peace but division.

Jesus said to his disciples:
"I have come to set the earth on fire,
  and how I wish it were already blazing!
There is a baptism with which I must be baptized,
  and how great is my anguish until it is accomplished!
Do you think that I have come to establish peace on the earth?
No, I tell you, but rather division.
From now on a household of five will be divided,
  three against two and two against three;
  a father will be divided against his son
  and a son against his father,
  a mother against her daughter
  and a daughter against her mother,
  a mother-in-law against her daughter-in-law
  and a daughter-in-law against her mother-in-law." ✛

FRIDAY, OCTOBER 21
WEEKDAY

† *Ephesians 4:1-6*
There is one Body, one Lord, one faith, one baptism.

Brothers and sisters:
I, a prisoner for the Lord,
  urge you to live in a manner worthy of the call you have received,
  with all humility and gentleness, with patience,
  bearing with one another through love,
  striving to preserve the unity of the spirit
  through the bond of peace;
  one Body and one Spirit,
  as you were also called to the one hope of your call;
  one Lord, one faith, one baptism;
  one God and Father of all,
  who is over all and through all and in all. ✛

Psalm 24:1-2, 3-4ab, 5-6

R. (see 6) **Lord, this is the people that longs to see your face.**

The LORD's are the earth and its fullness;
  the world and those who dwell in it.
For he founded it upon the seas
  and established it upon the rivers. **R.**
Who can ascend the mountain of the LORD?
  or who may stand in his holy place?
He whose hands are sinless, whose heart is clean,
  who desires not what is vain. **R.**
He shall receive a blessing from the LORD,
  a reward from God his savior.
Such is the race that seeks for him,
  that seeks the face of the God of Jacob. **R.**

See Matthew 11:25

R. Alleluia, alleluia.

Blessed are you, Father, Lord of heaven and earth;
  you have revealed to little ones the mysteries of the Kingdom. **R.**

† *Luke 12:54-59*

You know how to interpret the appearance of the earth and sky;
why do you not know how to interpret the present time?

Jesus said to the crowds,
  "When you see a cloud rising in the west
  you say immediately that it is going to rain—and so it does;
  and when you notice that the wind is blowing from the south
  you say that it is going to be hot—and so it is.
You hypocrites!
You know how to interpret the appearance of the earth and the sky;
  why do you not know how to interpret the present time?

"Why do you not judge for yourselves what is right?
If you are to go with your opponent before a magistrate,
  make an effort to settle the matter on the way;
  otherwise your opponent will turn you over to the judge,
  and the judge hand you over to the constable,
  and the constable throw you into prison.
I say to you, you will not be released
  until you have paid the last penny." ✦

SATURDAY, OCTOBER 22
WEEKDAY, ST. POPE JOHN PAUL II, *[BVM]*

† *Ephesians 4:7-16*
Christ is the head from whom the whole Body
grows and builds itself up in love.

Brothers and sisters:
Grace was given to each of us
 according to the measure of Christ's gift.
Therefore, it says:

> *He ascended on high and took prisoners captive;*
>   *he gave gifts to men.*

What does "he ascended" mean except that he also descended
 into the lower regions of the earth?
The one who descended is also the one who ascended
 far above all the heavens,
 that he might fill all things.

And he gave some as Apostles, others as prophets,
 others as evangelists, others as pastors and teachers,
 to equip the holy ones for the work of ministry,
 for building up the Body of Christ,
 until we all attain to the unity of faith
 and knowledge of the Son of God, to mature manhood
 to the extent of the full stature of Christ,
 so that we may no longer be infants,
 tossed by waves and swept along by every wind of teaching
 arising from human trickery,
 from their cunning in the interests of deceitful scheming.
Rather, living the truth in love,
 we should grow in every way into him who is the head, Christ,
 from whom the whole Body,
 joined and held together by every supporting ligament,
 with the proper functioning of each part,
 brings about the Body's growth and builds itself up in love. ✛

 Psalm 122:1-2, 3-4ab, 4cd-5
R. (1) **Let us go rejoicing to the house of the Lord.**
I rejoiced because they said to me,
 "We will go up to the house of the LORD."
And now we have set foot
 within your gates, O Jerusalem. **R.**

Jerusalem, built as a city
  with compact unity.
To it the tribes go up,
  the tribes of the LORD. **R.**
According to the decree for Israel,
  to give thanks to the name of the LORD.
In it are set up judgment seats,
  seats for the house of David. **R.**

Ezekiel 33:11
R. Alleluia, alleluia.
I take no pleasure in the death of the wicked man, says the Lord,
but rather in his conversion that he may live. **R.**

† *Luke 13:1-9*
If you do not repent, you will all perish as they did!

Some people told Jesus about the Galileans
  whose blood Pilate had mingled with the blood of their sacrifices.
He said to them in reply,
  "Do you think that because these Galileans suffered in this way
  they were greater sinners than all other Galileans?
By no means!
But I tell you, if you do not repent,
  you will all perish as they did!
Or those eighteen people who were killed
  when the tower at Siloam fell on them—
  do you think they were more guilty
  than everyone else who lived in Jerusalem?
By no means!
But I tell you, if you do not repent,
  you will all perish as they did!"

And he told them this parable:
  "There once was a person who had a fig tree planted in his orchard,
  and when he came in search of fruit on it but found none,
  he said to the gardener,
  'For three years now I have come in search of fruit on this fig tree
  but have found none.
So cut it down.
Why should it exhaust the soil?'
He said to him in reply,
  'Sir, leave it for this year also,
  and I shall cultivate the ground around it and fertilize it;
  it may bear fruit in the future.
If not you can cut it down.'" ✛

SUNDAY, OCTOBER 23
THIRTIETH SUNDAY IN ORDINARY TIME

† *Sirach 35:12-14, 16-18*
The prayer of the lowly pierces the clouds.

The LORD is a God of justice,
  who knows no favorites.
Though not unduly partial toward the weak,
  yet he hears the cry of the oppressed.
The Lord is not deaf to the wail of the orphan,
  nor to the widow when she pours out her complaint.
The one who serves God willingly is heard;
  his petition reaches the heavens.
The prayer of the lowly pierces the clouds;
  it does not rest till it reaches its goal,
nor will it withdraw till the Most High responds,
  judges justly and affirms the right,
and the Lord will not delay. ✛

Psalm 34:2-3, 17-18, 19, 23
R. (7a) **The Lord hears the cry of the poor.**
I will bless the LORD at all times;
  his praise shall be ever in my mouth.
Let my soul glory in the LORD;
  the lowly will hear me and be glad. **R.**
The LORD confronts the evildoers,
  to destroy remembrance of them from the earth.
When the just cry out, the LORD hears them,
  and from all their distress he rescues them. **R.**
The LORD is close to the brokenhearted;
  and those who are crushed in spirit he saves.
The LORD redeems the lives of his servants;
  no one incurs guilt who takes refuge in him. **R.**

† *2 Timothy 4:6-8, 16-18*
From now on, the crown of righteousness awaits me.

Beloved:
I am already being poured out like a libation,
  and the time of my departure is at hand.
I have competed well; I have finished the race;
  I have kept the faith.
From now on the crown of righteousness awaits me,
  which the Lord, the just judge,
  will award to me on that day, and not only to me,
  but to all who have longed for his appearance.

At my first defense no one appeared on my behalf,
  but everyone deserted me.
May it not be held against them!
But the Lord stood by me and gave me strength,
  so that through me the proclamation might be completed
  and all the Gentiles might hear it.
And I was rescued from the lion's mouth.
The Lord will rescue me from every evil threat
  and will bring me safe to his heavenly kingdom.
To him be glory forever and ever. Amen. ✝

2 Corinthians 5:19
R. Alleluia, alleluia.
God was reconciling the world to himself in Christ,
and entrusting to us the message of salvation. **R.**

†*Luke 18:9-14*
The tax collector, not the Pharisee, went home justified.

Jesus addressed this parable
  to those who were convinced of their own righteousness
  and despised everyone else.
"Two people went up to the temple area to pray;
  one was a Pharisee and the other was a tax collector.
The Pharisee took up his position and spoke this prayer to himself,
  'O God, I thank you that I am not like the rest of humanity—
  greedy, dishonest, adulterous—or even like this tax collector.
I fast twice a week, and I pay tithes on my whole income.'
But the tax collector stood off at a distance
  and would not even raise his eyes to heaven
  but beat his breast and prayed,
  'O God, be merciful to me a sinner.'
I tell you, the latter went home justified, not the former;
  for whoever exalts himself will be humbled,
  and the one who humbles himself will be exalted." ✝

MONDAY, OCTOBER 24
WEEKDAY, ST. ANTHONY MARY CLARET

†*Ephesians 4:32—5:8*
Walk in love, just as Christ.

Brothers and sisters:
Be kind to one another, compassionate,
  forgiving one another as God has forgiven you in Christ.

Be imitators of God, as beloved children, and live in love,
   as Christ loved us and handed himself over for us
   as a sacrificial offering to God for a fragrant aroma.
Immorality or any impurity or greed must not even be mentioned
      among you,
   as is fitting among holy ones,
   no obscenity or silly or suggestive talk, which is out of place,
   but instead, thanksgiving.
Be sure of this, that no immoral or impure or greedy person,
   that is, an idolater,
   has any inheritance in the Kingdom of Christ and of God.

Let no one deceive you with empty arguments,
   for because of these things
   the wrath of God is coming upon the disobedient.
So do not be associated with them.
For you were once darkness,
   but now you are light in the Lord.
Live as children of light. ✠

Psalm 1:1-2, 3, 4 and 6
R. (see Ephesians 5:1) **Behave like God as his very dear children.**
Blessed the man who follows not
   the counsel of the wicked
Nor walks in the way of sinners,
   nor sits in the company of the insolent,
But delights in the law of the LORD
   and meditates on his law day and night. **R.**
He is like a tree
   planted near running water,
That yields its fruit in due season,
   and whose leaves never fade.
   Whatever he does, prospers. **R.**
Not so the wicked, not so;
   they are like chaff which the wind drives away.
For the LORD watches over the way of the just,
   but the way of the wicked vanishes. **R.**

John 17:17b, 17a
R. Alleluia, alleluia.
Your word, O Lord, is truth;
consecrate us in the truth. **R.**

† *Luke 13:10-17*

This daughter of Abraham, ought she not to have been set free on the sabbath day?

Jesus was teaching in a synagogue on the sabbath.
And a woman was there who for eighteen years
 had been crippled by a spirit;
 she was bent over, completely incapable of standing erect.
When Jesus saw her, he called to her and said,
 "Woman, you are set free of your infirmity."
He laid his hands on her,
 and she at once stood up straight and glorified God.
But the leader of the synagogue,
 indignant that Jesus had cured on the sabbath,
 said to the crowd in reply,
 "There are six days when work should be done.
Come on those days to be cured, not on the sabbath day."
The Lord said to him in reply, "Hypocrites!
Does not each one of you on the sabbath
 untie his ox or his ass from the manger
 and lead it out for watering?
This daughter of Abraham,
 whom Satan has bound for eighteen years now,
 ought she not to have been set free on the sabbath day
 from this bondage?"
When he said this, all his adversaries were humiliated;
 and the whole crowd rejoiced at all the splendid deeds done by
  him. ✛

TUESDAY, OCTOBER 25
WEEKDAY

† *Ephesians 5:21-33*

This is a great mystery, but I speak in reference to Christ and the Church.

Brothers and sisters:
Be subordinate to one another out of reverence for Christ.
Wives should be subordinate to their husbands as to the Lord.
For the husband is head of his wife
 just as Christ is head of the Church,
 he himself the savior of the Body.
As the Church is subordinate to Christ,
 so wives should be subordinate to their husbands in everything.
Husbands, love your wives,
 even as Christ loved the Church
 and handed himself over for her to sanctify her,
 cleansing her by the bath of water with the word,

that he might present to himself the Church in splendor,
without spot or wrinkle or any such thing,
that she might be holy and without blemish.
So also husbands should love their wives as their own bodies.
He who loves his wife loves himself.
For no one hates his own flesh
but rather nourishes and cherishes it,
even as Christ does the Church,
because we are members of his Body.

*For this reason a man shall leave his father and his mother
and be joined to his wife,
and the two shall become one flesh.*

This is a great mystery,
but I speak in reference to Christ and the Church.
In any case, each one of you should love his wife as himself,
and the wife should respect her husband. ✛

Psalm 128:1-2, 3, 4-5
R. (1a) Blessed are those who fear the Lord.
Blessed are you who fear the LORD,
who walk in his ways!
For you shall eat the fruit of your handiwork;
blessed shall you be, and favored. **R.**
Your wife shall be like a fruitful vine
in the recesses of your home;
Your children like olive plants
around your table. **R.**
Behold, thus is the man blessed
who fears the LORD.
The LORD bless you from Zion:
may you see the prosperity of Jerusalem
all the days of your life. **R.**

See Matthew 11:25
R. Alleluia, alleluia.
Blessed are you, Father, Lord of heaven and earth;
you have revealed to little ones the mysteries of the Kingdom. **R.**

† Luke 13:18-21
When it was fully grown, it became a large bush.

Jesus said, "What is the Kingdom of God like?
To what can I compare it?
It is like a mustard seed that a man took and planted in the garden.

When it was fully grown, it became a large bush
and *the birds of the sky dwelt in its branches."*

Again he said, "To what shall I compare the Kingdom of God?
It is like yeast that a woman took
and mixed in with three measures of wheat flour
until the whole batch of dough was leavened." ✢

WEDNESDAY, OCTOBER 26
WEEKDAY

† *Ephesians 6:1-9*
Willingly serving the Lord and not human beings.

Children, obey your parents in the Lord, for this is right.
Honor your father and mother.
This is the first commandment with a promise,
that it may go well with you
and that you may have a long life on earth.
Fathers, do not provoke your children to anger,
but bring them up with the training and instruction of the Lord.

Slaves, be obedient to your human masters with fear and trembling,
in sincerity of heart, as to Christ,
not only when being watched, as currying favor,
but as slaves of Christ, doing the will of God from the heart,
willingly serving the Lord and not men,
knowing that each will be requited from the Lord
for whatever good he does, whether he is slave or free.
Masters, act in the same way towards them, and stop bullying,
knowing that both they and you have a Master in heaven
and that with him there is no partiality. ✢

Psalm 145:10-11, 12-13ab, 13cd-14
R. (13c) **The Lord is faithful in all his words.**
Let all your works give you thanks, O LORD,
and let your faithful ones bless you.
Let them discourse of the glory of your Kingdom
and speak of your might. **R.**
Making known to men your might
and the glorious splendor of your Kingdom.
Your Kingdom is a Kingdom for all ages,
and your dominion endures through all generations. **R.**
The LORD is faithful in all his words
and holy in all his works.
The LORD lifts up all who are falling
and raises up all who are bowed down. **R.**

See 2 Thessalonians 2:14

R. Alleluia, alleluia.

God has called us through the Gospel
to possess the glory of our Lord Jesus Christ. **R.**

† *Luke 13:22-30*

*And people will come from the east and the west and
will recline at the table in the Kingdom of God.*

Jesus passed through towns and villages,
   teaching as he went and making his way to Jerusalem.
Someone asked him,
   "Lord, will only a few people be saved?"
He answered them,
   "Strive to enter through the narrow gate,
   for many, I tell you, will attempt to enter
   but will not be strong enough.
After the master of the house has arisen and locked the door,
   then will you stand outside knocking and saying,
   'Lord, open the door for us.'
He will say to you in reply,
   'I do not know where you are from.'
And you will say,
   'We ate and drank in your company and you taught in our streets.'
Then he will say to you,
   'I do not know where you are from.
Depart from me, all you evildoers!'
And there will be wailing and grinding of teeth
   when you see Abraham, Isaac, and Jacob
   and all the prophets in the Kingdom of God
   and you yourselves cast out.
And people will come from the east and the west
   and from the north and the south
   and will recline at table in the Kingdom of God.
For behold, some are last who will be first,
   and some are first who will be last." ✝

THURSDAY, OCTOBER 27
WEEKDAY

† *Ephesians 6:10-20*
Put on the armor of God, that you may be able,
having done everything, to hold your ground.

Brothers and sisters:
Draw your strength from the Lord and from his mighty power.
Put on the armor of God so that you may be able to stand firm
   against the tactics of the Devil.
For our struggle is not with flesh and blood
   but with the principalities, with the powers,
   with the world rulers of this present darkness,
   with the evil spirits in the heavens.
Therefore, put on the armor of God,
   that you may be able to resist on the evil day
   and, having done everything, to hold your ground.
So stand fast with your loins girded in truth,
   clothed with righteousness as a breastplate,
   and your feet shod in readiness for the Gospel of peace.
In all circumstances, hold faith as a shield,
   to quench all the flaming arrows of the Evil One.
And take the helmet of salvation and the sword of the Spirit,
   which is the word of God.

With all prayer and supplication,
   pray at every opportunity in the Spirit.
To that end, be watchful with all perseverance and supplication
   for all the holy ones and also for me,
   that speech may be given me to open my mouth,
   to make known with boldness the mystery of the Gospel
   for which I am an ambassador in chains,
   so that I may have the courage to speak as I must. ✛

   Psalm 144:1b, 2, 9-10
R. (1b) Blessed be the Lord, my Rock!
Blessed be the LORD, my rock,
   who trains my hands for battle, my fingers for war. **R.**
My mercy and my fortress,
   my stronghold, my deliverer,
My shield, in whom I trust,
   who subdues my people under me. **R.**
O God, I will sing a new song to you;
   with a ten-stringed lyre I will chant your praise,
You who give victory to kings,
   and deliver David, your servant from the evil sword. **R.**

See Luke 19:38; 2:14

R. Alleluia, alleluia.

Blessed is the king who comes in the name of the Lord.

Glory to God in the highest and on earth peace to those on whom his
favor rests. **R.**

† *Luke 13:31-35*

It is impossible that a prophet should die outside of Jerusalem.

Some Pharisees came to Jesus and said,
"Go away, leave this area because Herod wants to kill you."
He replied, "Go and tell that fox,
'Behold, I cast out demons and I perform healings today and tomorrow,
and on the third day I accomplish my purpose.
Yet I must continue on my way today, tomorrow, and the following
day,
for it is impossible that a prophet should die
outside of Jerusalem.'

"Jerusalem, Jerusalem,
you who kill the prophets and stone those sent to you,
how many times I yearned to gather your children together
as a hen gathers her brood under her wings,
but you were unwilling!
Behold, your house will be abandoned.
But I tell you, you will not see me until the time comes when you say,
Blessed is he who comes in the name of the Lord." ✛

FRIDAY, OCTOBER 28
St. Simon and St. Jude

† *Ephesians 2:19-22*

Built upon the foundation of the Apostles.

Brothers and sisters:
You are no longer strangers and sojourners,
but you are fellow citizens with the holy ones
and members of the household of God,
built upon the foundation of the Apostles and prophets,
with Christ Jesus himself as the capstone.
Through him the whole structure is held together
and grows into a temple sacred in the Lord;
in him you also are being built together
into a dwelling place of God in the Spirit. ✛

Psalm 19:2-3, 4-5

R. (5a) **Their message goes out through all the earth.**
The heavens declare the glory of God,
  and the firmament proclaims his handiwork.
Day pours out the word to day,
  and night to night imparts knowledge. **R.**
Not a word nor a discourse
  whose voice is not heard;
Through all the earth their voice resounds,
  and to the ends of the world, their message. **R.**

  See Te Deum
R. Alleluia, alleluia.
We praise you, O God,
we acclaim you as Lord;
the glorious company of Apostles praise you. **R.**

† *Luke 6:12-16*
From them Jesus chose Twelve, whom he also named Apostles.

Jesus went up to the mountain to pray,
  and he spent the night in prayer to God.
When day came, he called his disciples to himself,
  and from them he chose Twelve, whom he also named Apostles:
  Simon, whom he named Peter, and his brother Andrew,
  James, John, Philip, Bartholomew, Matthew,
  Thomas, James the son of Alphaeus,
  Simon who was called a Zealot,
  and Judas the son of James,
  and Judas Iscariot, who became a traitor. ✛

SATURDAY, OCTOBER 29
Weekday, *[BVM]*

† *Philippians 1:18b-26*
For to me life is Christ, and death is gain.

Brothers and sisters:
As long as in every way, whether in pretense or in truth,
  Christ is being proclaimed, and in that I rejoice.

Indeed I shall continue to rejoice,
  for I know that this will result in deliverance for me
  through your prayers and support from the Spirit of Jesus Christ.
My eager expectation and hope
  is that I shall not be put to shame in any way,
  but that with all boldness, now as always,

Christ will be magnified in my body,
   whether by life or by death.
For to me life is Christ, and death is gain.
If I go on living in the flesh, that means fruitful labor for me.
And I do not know which I shall choose.
I am caught between the two.
I long to depart this life and be with Christ,
   for that is far better.
Yet that I remain in the flesh is more necessary for your benefit.
And this I know with confidence,
   that I shall remain and continue in the service of all of you
   for your progress and joy in the faith,
   so that your boasting in Christ Jesus may abound on account of me
   when I come to you again. ✝

Psalm 42:2, 3, 5cdef
R. My soul is thirsting for the living God.
As the hind longs for the running waters,
   so my soul longs for you, O God. **R.**
Athirst is my soul for God, the living God.
   When shall I go and behold the face of God? **R.**
I went with the throng
   and led them in procession to the house of God.
Amid loud cries of joy and thanksgiving,
   with the multitude keeping festival. **R.**

Matthew 11:29ab
R. Alleluia, alleluia.
Take my yoke upon you and learn from me,
for I am meek and humble of heart. **R.**

†*Luke 14:1, 7-11*
Everyone who exalts himself will be humbled,
but the one who humbles himself will be exalted.

On a sabbath Jesus went to dine
   at the home of one of the leading Pharisees,
   and the people there were observing him carefully.

He told a parable to those who had been invited,
   noticing how they were choosing the places of honor at the table.
"When you are invited by someone to a wedding banquet,
   do not recline at table in the place of honor.
A more distinguished guest than you may have been invited by him,
   and the host who invited both of you may approach you and say,
   'Give your place to this man,'

and then you would proceed with embarrassment
  to take the lowest place.
Rather, when you are invited,
  go and take the lowest place
  so that when the host comes to you he may say,
  'My friend, move up to a higher position.'
Then you will enjoy the esteem of your companions at the table.
For everyone who exalts himself will be humbled,
  but the one who humbles himself will be exalted." ✛

SUNDAY, OCTOBER 30
THIRTY-FIRST SUNDAY IN ORDINARY TIME

† *Wisdom 11:22—12:2*
You have mercy on all because you love all things that are.

Before the LORD the whole universe is as a grain from a balance
  or a drop of morning dew come down upon the earth.
But you have mercy on all, because you can do all things;
  and you overlook people's sins that they may repent.
For you love all things that are
  and loathe nothing that you have made;
  for what you hated, you would not have fashioned.
And how could a thing remain, unless you willed it;
  or be preserved, had it not been called forth by you?
But you spare all things, because they are yours,
  O LORD and lover of souls,
  for your imperishable spirit is in all things!
Therefore you rebuke offenders little by little,
  warn them and remind them of the sins they are committing,
  that they may abandon their wickedness and believe in you, O
    LORD! ✛

Psalm 145:1-2, 8-9, 10-11, 13, 14
R. (see 1) **I will praise your name forever, my king and my
  God.**
I will extol you, O my God and King,
  and I will bless your name forever and ever.
Every day will I bless you,
  and I will praise your name forever and ever. **R.**
The LORD is gracious and merciful,
  slow to anger and of great kindness.
The LORD is good to all
  and compassionate toward all his works. **R.**
Let all your works give you thanks, O LORD,
  and let your faithful ones bless you.

Let them discourse of the glory of your kingdom
    and speak of your might. **R.**
The LORD is faithful in all his words
    and holy in all his works.
The LORD lifts up all who are falling
    and raises up all who are bowed down. **R.**

† *2 Thessalonians 1:11—2:2*
May the name of Christ be glorified in you and you in him.

Brothers and sisters:
We always pray for you,
    that our God may make you worthy of his calling
    and powerfully bring to fulfillment every good purpose
    and every effort of faith,
    that the name of our Lord Jesus may be glorified in you,
    and you in him,
    in accord with the grace of our God and Lord Jesus Christ.

We ask you, brothers and sisters,
    with regard to the coming of our Lord Jesus Christ
    and our assembling with him,
    not to be shaken out of your minds suddenly, or to be alarmed
    either by a "spirit," or by an oral statement,
    or by a letter allegedly from us
    to the effect that the day of the Lord is at hand. ✝

  John 3:16
R. Alleluia, alleluia.
God so loved the world that he gave his only Son,
so that everyone who believes in him might have eternal life. **R.**

† *Luke 19:1-10*
The Son of Man has come to seek and to save what was lost.

At that time, Jesus came to Jericho and intended to pass through
    the town.
Now a man there named Zacchaeus,
    who was a chief tax collector and also a wealthy man,
    was seeking to see who Jesus was;
    but he could not see him because of the crowd,
    for he was short in stature.
So he ran ahead and climbed a sycamore tree in order to see Jesus,
    who was about to pass that way.
When he reached the place, Jesus looked up and said,
    "Zacchaeus, come down quickly,
    for today I must stay at your house."

And he came down quickly and received him with joy.
When they all saw this, they began to grumble, saying,
"He has gone to stay at the house of a sinner."
But Zacchaeus stood there and said to the Lord,
"Behold, half of my possessions, Lord, I shall give to the poor,
and if I have extorted anything from anyone
I shall repay it four times over."
And Jesus said to him,
"Today salvation has come to this house
because this man too is a descendant of Abraham.
For the Son of Man has come to seek
and to save what was lost." ✝

MONDAY, OCTOBER 31
WEEKDAY

†*Philippians 2:1-4*
Complete my joy by being of the same mind.

Brothers and sisters:
If there is any encouragement in Christ,
any solace in love,
any participation in the Spirit,
any compassion and mercy,
complete my joy by being of the same mind, with the same love,
united in heart, thinking one thing.
Do nothing out of selfishness or out of vainglory;
rather, humbly regard others as more important than yourselves,
each looking out not for his own interests,
but also everyone for those of others. ✝

Psalm 131:1bcde, 2, 3
R. In you, O Lord, I have found my peace.
O LORD, my heart is not proud,
nor are my eyes haughty;
I busy not myself with great things,
nor with things too sublime for me. **R.**
Nay rather, I have stilled and quieted
my soul like a weaned child.
Like a weaned child on its mother's lap,
so is my soul within me. **R.**
O Israel, hope in the LORD,
both now and forever. **R.**

John 8:31b-32

R. Alleluia, alleluia.

If you remain in my word, you will truly be my disciples,
and you will know the truth, says the Lord. **R.**

† *Luke 14:12-14*

Do not invite your friends, but those who are poor and crippled.

On a sabbath Jesus went to dine
  at the home of one of the leading Pharisees.
He said to the host who invited him,
  "When you hold a lunch or a dinner,
  do not invite your friends or your brothers or sisters
  or your relatives or your wealthy neighbors,
  in case they may invite you back and you have repayment.
Rather, when you hold a banquet,
  invite the poor, the crippled, the lame, the blind;
  blessed indeed will you be because of their inability to repay you.
For you will be repaid at the resurrection of the righteous." ✝

TUESDAY, NOVEMBER 1
ALL SAINTS

† *Revelation 7:2-4, 9-14*
I had a vision of a great multitude, which no one could count,
from every nation, race, people and tongue.

I, John, saw another angel come up from the East,
  holding the seal of the living God.
He cried out in a loud voice to the four angels
  who were given power to damage the land and the sea,
  "Do not damage the land or the sea or the trees
  until we put the seal on the foreheads of the servants of our God."
I heard the number of those who had been marked with the seal,
  one hundred and forty-four thousand marked
  from every tribe of the children of Israel.

After this I had a vision of a great multitude,
  which no one could count,
  from every nation, race, people, and tongue.
They stood before the throne and before the Lamb,
  wearing white robes and holding palm branches in their hands.
They cried out in a loud voice:

"Salvation comes from our God, who is seated on the throne,
  and from the Lamb."

All the angels stood around the throne
  and around the elders and the four living creatures.
They prostrated themselves before the throne,
  worshiped God, and exclaimed:

"Amen. Blessing and glory, wisdom and thanksgiving,
    honor, power, and might
    be to our God forever and ever. Amen."

Then one of the elders spoke up and said to me,
  "Who are these wearing white robes, and where did they come from?"
I said to him, "My lord, you are the one who knows."
He said to me,
  "These are the ones who have survived the time of great distress;
  they have washed their robes
  and made them white in the Blood of the Lamb." ✛

Psalm 24:1bc-2, 3-4ab, 5-6

R. (see 6) **Lord, this is the people that longs to see your face.**

The LORD's are the earth and its fullness;
   the world and those who dwell in it.
For he founded it upon the seas
   and established it upon the rivers. **R.**
Who can ascend the mountain of the LORD?
   or who may stand in his holy place?
One whose hands are sinless, whose heart is clean,
   who desires not what is vain. **R.**
He shall receive a blessing from the LORD,
   a reward from God his savior.
Such is the race that seeks him,
   that seeks the face of the God of Jacob. **R.**

✝ *1 John 3:1-3*
We shall see God as he is.

Beloved:

See what love the Father has bestowed on us
   that we may be called the children of God.
Yet so we are.
The reason the world does not know us
   is that it did not know him.
Beloved, we are God's children now;
   what we shall be has not yet been revealed.
We do know that when it is revealed we shall be like him,
   for we shall see him as he is.
Everyone who has this hope based on him makes himself pure,
   as he is pure. ✝

Matthew 11:28

R. Alleluia, alleluia.

Come to me, all you who labor and are burdened,
and I will give you rest, says the Lord. **R.**

✝ *Matthew 5:1-12a*
Rejoice and be glad, for your reward will be great in heaven.

When Jesus saw the crowds, he went up the mountain,
   and after he had sat down, his disciples came to him.
He began to teach them, saying:

   "Blessed are the poor in spirit,
      for theirs is the Kingdom of heaven.
   Blessed are they who mourn,
      for they will be comforted.

Blessed are the meek,
   for they will inherit the land.
Blessed are they who hunger and thirst for righteousness,
   for they will be satisfied.
Blessed are the merciful,
   for they will be shown mercy.
Blessed are the clean of heart,
   for they will see God.
Blessed are the peacemakers,
   for they will be called children of God.
Blessed are they who are persecuted for the sake of righteousness,
   for theirs is the Kingdom of heaven.
Blessed are you when they insult you and persecute you
   and utter every kind of evil against you falsely because of me.
Rejoice and be glad,
   for your reward will be great in heaven." ✝

WEDNESDAY, NOVEMBER 2
THE COMMEMORATION OF ALL THE FAITHFUL DEPARTED (ALL SOULS' DAY)
(Other readings for All Souls include: Wisdom 4:7-14 • Isaiah 25:6ab, 7-9 •
Psalm 25:6 and 7b, 17-18, 20-21 • Psalm 27:1, 4, 7 and 8b and 9a, 13-14 • Romans 5:17-21 •
Romans 6:3-9 • Romans 8:14-23 • Romans 8:31b-35, 37-39 • Romans 14:7-9, 10c-12 •
1 Corinthians 15:20-28 • 1 Corinthians 15:51-57 • 2 Corinthians 4:14—5:1 •
2 Corinthians 5:1, 6-10 • Philippians 3:20-21 • 1 Thessalonians 4:13-18 •
2 Timothy 2:8-13 • Matthew 5:1-12a • Matthew 11:25-30 • Matthew 25:31-46 •
Luke 7:11-17 • Luke 23:44-46, 50, 52-53; 24:1-6a • Luke 24:13-16, 28-35 • John 5:24-29 •
John 6:51-58 • John 11:17-27 • John 11:32-45 • John 14:1-6, or any readings from the
Lectionary for Mass (volume IV), the Masses for the Dead, numbers 1011-1016.)

† Wisdom 3:1-9
As sacrificial offerings he took them to himself.

The souls of the just are in the hand of God,
   and no torment shall touch them.
They seemed, in the view of the foolish, to be dead;
   and their passing away was thought an affliction
   and their going forth from us, utter destruction.
But they are in peace.
For if before men, indeed, they be punished,
   yet is their hope full of immortality;
Chastised a little, they shall be greatly blessed,
   because God tried them
   and found them worthy of himself.
As gold in the furnace, he proved them,
   and as sacrificial offerings he took them to himself.
In the time of their visitation they shall shine,
   and shall dart about as sparks through stubble;

They shall judge nations and rule over peoples,
   and the Lord shall be their King forever.
Those who trust in him shall understand truth,
   and the faithful shall abide with him in love:
Because grace and mercy are with his holy ones,
   and his care is with his elect. ✛

   Psalm 23:1b-3a, 3b-4, 5, 6
R. (1) **The Lord is my shepherd; there is nothing I shall want.**
or
(4ab) **Though I walk in the valley of darkness, I fear no evil,
   for you are with me.**
The Lord is my shepherd; I shall not want.
   In verdant pastures he gives me repose;
Beside restful waters he leads me;
   he refreshes my soul. **R.**
He guides me in right paths
   for his name's sake.
Even though I walk in the dark valley
   I fear no evil; for you are at my side
With your rod and your staff
   that give me courage. **R.**
You spread the table before me
   in the sight of my foes;
You anoint my head with oil;
   my cup overflows. **R.**
Only goodness and kindness follow me
   all the days of my life;
And I shall dwell in the house of the Lord
   for years to come. **R.**

† *Romans 5:5-11* (or Romans 6:3-9)
Justified by his Blood, we will be saved through Christ from the wrath.

Brothers and sisters:
Hope does not disappoint,
   because the love of God has been poured out into our hearts
   through the Holy Spirit that has been given to us.
For Christ, while we were still helpless,
   died at the appointed time for the ungodly.
Indeed, only with difficulty does one die for a just person,
   though perhaps for a good person
   one might even find courage to die.
But God proves his love for us
   in that while we were still sinners Christ died for us.

How much more then, since we are now justified by his Blood,
    will we be saved through him from the wrath.
Indeed, if, while we were enemies,
    we were reconciled to God through the death of his Son,
    how much more, once reconciled,
    will we be saved by his life.
Not only that,
    but we also boast of God through our Lord Jesus Christ,
    through whom we have now received reconciliation. ✛

See John 6:40 (or see Lectionary for Mass (volume IV) no. 668 for more choices)
R. Alleluia, alleluia.
This is the will of my Father, says the Lord,
that everyone who sees the Son and believes in him
may have eternal life. **R.**

✝ John 6:37-40
*Everyone who believes in the Son will have eternal life
and I shall raise him up on the last day.*

Jesus said to the crowds:
    "Everything that the Father gives me will come to me,
    and I will not reject anyone who comes to me,
    because I came down from heaven not to do my own will
    but the will of the one who sent me.
And this is the will of the one who sent me,
    that I should not lose anything of what he gave me,
    but that I should raise it on the last day.
For this is the will of my Father,
    that everyone who sees the Son and believes in him
    may have eternal life,
    and I shall raise him on the last day." ✛

THURSDAY, NOVEMBER 3
WEEKDAY, ST. MARTIN DE PORRES

✝ Philippians 3:3-8a
But whatever gains I had, I even consider as a loss, because of Christ.

Brothers and sisters:
We are the circumcision,
    we who worship through the Spirit of God,
    who boast in Christ Jesus and do not put our confidence in flesh,
    although I myself have grounds for confidence even in the flesh.

If anyone else thinks he can be confident in flesh, all the more can I.
Circumcised on the eighth day,
  of the race of Israel, of the tribe of Benjamin,
  a Hebrew of Hebrew parentage,
  in observance of the law a Pharisee,
  in zeal I persecuted the Church,
  in righteousness based on the law I was blameless.

But whatever gains I had,
  these I have come to consider a loss because of Christ.
More than that, I even consider everything as a loss
  because of the supreme good of knowing Christ Jesus my Lord. ✟

Psalm 105:2-3, 4-5, 6-7
R. (3b) **Let hearts rejoice who search for the Lord.**
  (or **Alleluia.***)*
Sing to him, sing his praise,
  proclaim all his wondrous deeds.
Glory in his holy name;
  rejoice, O hearts that seek the LORD! **R.**
Look to the LORD in his strength;
  seek to serve him constantly.
Recall the wondrous deeds that he has wrought,
  his portents, and the judgments he has uttered. **R.**
You descendants of Abraham, his servants,
  sons of Jacob, his chosen ones!
He, the LORD, is our God;
  throughout the earth his judgments prevail. **R.**

Matthew 11:28
R. Alleluia, alleluia.
Come to me, all you who labor and are burdened,
and I will give you rest, says the Lord. **R.**

✝ *Luke 15:1-10*
There will be more joy in heaven over one sinner who repents.

The tax collectors and sinners were all drawing near to listen to
    Jesus,
  but the Pharisees and scribes began to complain, saying,
  "This man welcomes sinners and eats with them."
So Jesus addressed this parable to them.
"What man among you having a hundred sheep and losing one of them
  would not leave the ninety-nine in the desert
  and go after the lost one until he finds it?
And when he does find it,
  he sets it on his shoulders with great joy

and, upon his arrival home,
he calls together his friends and neighbors and says to them,
'Rejoice with me because I have found my lost sheep.'
I tell you, in just the same way
there will be more joy in heaven over one sinner who repents
than over ninety-nine righteous people
who have no need of repentance.

"Or what woman having ten coins and losing one
would not light a lamp and sweep the house,
searching carefully until she finds it?
And when she does find it,
she calls together her friends and neighbors
and says to them,
'Rejoice with me because I have found the coin that I lost.'
In just the same way, I tell you,
there will be rejoicing among the angels of God
over one sinner who repents." ✛

FRIDAY, NOVEMBER 4
St. Charles Borromeo

† *Philippians 3:17—4:1*
*We await a savior who will change our lowly body
to conform with his glorified Body.*

Join with others in being imitators of me, brothers and sisters,
and observe those who thus conduct themselves
according to the model you have in us.
For many, as I have often told you
and now tell you even in tears,
conduct themselves as enemies of the cross of Christ.
Their end is destruction.
Their God is their stomach;
their glory is in their "shame."
Their minds are occupied with earthly things.
But our citizenship is in heaven,
and from it we also await a savior, the Lord Jesus Christ.
He will change our lowly body
to conform with his glorified Body
by the power that enables him also
to bring all things into subjection to himself.

Therefore, my brothers and sisters,
whom I love and long for, my joy and crown,
in this way stand firm in the Lord, beloved. ✛

Psalm 122:1-2, 3-4ab, 4cd-5

R. (1) **Let us go rejoicing to the house of the Lord.**

I rejoiced because they said to me,
   "We will go up to the house of the LORD."
And now we have set foot
   within your gates, O Jerusalem. **R.**
Jerusalem, built as a city
   with compact unity.
To it the tribes go up,
   the tribes of the LORD. **R.**
According to the decree for Israel,
   to give thanks to the name of the LORD.
In it are set up judgment seats,
   seats for the house of David. **R.**

1 John 2:5

R. Alleluia, alleluia.

Whoever keeps the word of Christ,
the love of God is truly perfected in him. **R.**

† *Luke 16:1-8*

For the children of this world are more prudent in dealing
with their own generation than are the children of light.

Jesus said to his disciples, "A rich man had a steward
   who was reported to him for squandering his property.
He summoned him and said,
   'What is this I hear about you?
Prepare a full account of your stewardship,
   because you can no longer be my steward.'
The steward said to himself, 'What shall I do,
   now that my master is taking the position of steward away from me?
I am not strong enough to dig and I am ashamed to beg.
I know what I shall do so that,
   when I am removed from the stewardship,
   they may welcome me into their homes.'
He called in his master's debtors one by one.
To the first he said, 'How much do you owe my master?'
He replied, 'One hundred measures of olive oil.'
He said to him, 'Here is your promissory note.
Sit down and quickly write one for fifty.'
Then to another he said, 'And you, how much do you owe?'
He replied, 'One hundred measures of wheat.'
He said to him, 'Here is your promissory note;
   write one for eighty.'

And the master commended that dishonest steward for acting
   prudently.
For the children of this world
   are more prudent in dealing with their own generation
   than the children of light." ✛

SATURDAY, NOVEMBER 5
WEEKDAY, *[BVM]*

† Philippians 4:10-19
I have the strength for everything through him who empowers me.

Brothers and sisters:
I rejoice greatly in the Lord
   that now at last you revived your concern for me.
You were, of course, concerned about me but lacked an opportunity.
Not that I say this because of need,
   for I have learned, in whatever situation I find myself,
   to be self-sufficient.
I know indeed how to live in humble circumstances;
   I know also how to live with abundance.
In every circumstance and in all things
   I have learned the secret of being well fed and of going hungry,
   of living in abundance and of being in need.
I have the strength for everything through him who empowers me.
Still, it was kind of you to share in my distress.

You Philippians indeed know that at the beginning of the Gospel,
   when I left Macedonia,
   not a single church shared with me
   in an account of giving and receiving, except you alone.
For even when I was at Thessalonica
   you sent me something for my needs,
   not only once but more than once.
It is not that I am eager for the gift;
   rather, I am eager for the profit that accrues to your account.
I have received full payment and I abound.
I am very well supplied because of what I received from you
   through Epaphroditus,
   "a fragrant aroma," an acceptable sacrifice, pleasing to God.
My God will fully supply whatever you need,
   in accord with his glorious riches in Christ Jesus. ✛

Psalm 112:1b-2, 5-6, 8a and 9

R. Blessed the man who fears the Lord. *(or* **Alleluia.***)*

Blessed the man who fears the LORD,
  who greatly delights in his commands.
His posterity shall be mighty upon the earth;
  the upright generation shall be blessed. **R.**
Well for the man who is gracious and lends,
  who conducts his affairs with justice;
He shall never be moved;
  the just one shall be in everlasting remembrance. **R.**
His heart is steadfast; he shall not fear.
Lavishly he gives to the poor;
  his generosity shall endure forever;
  his horn shall be exalted in glory. **R.**

2 Corinthians 8:9

R. Alleluia, alleluia.

Jesus Christ became poor although he was rich,
so that by his poverty you might become rich. **R.**

† *Luke 16:9-15*

If, therefore, you are not trustworthy with dishonest wealth,
who will trust you with true wealth?

Jesus said to his disciples:
"I tell you, make friends for yourselves with dishonest wealth,
  so that when it fails, you will be welcomed into eternal dwellings.
The person who is trustworthy in very small matters
  is also trustworthy in great ones;
  and the person who is dishonest in very small matters
  is also dishonest in great ones.
If, therefore, you are not trustworthy with dishonest wealth,
  who will trust you with true wealth?
If you are not trustworthy with what belongs to another,
  who will give you what is yours?
No servant can serve two masters.
He will either hate one and love the other,
  or be devoted to one and despise the other.
You cannot serve God and mammon."

The Pharisees, who loved money,
  heard all these things and sneered at him.

And he said to them,
> "You justify yourselves in the sight of others,
> but God knows your hearts;
> for what is of human esteem is an abomination in the sight of
> God." ✛

SUNDAY, NOVEMBER 6
THIRTY-SECOND SUNDAY IN ORDINARY TIME

† *2 Maccabees 7:1-2, 9-14*
The King of the world will raise us up to live again forever.

It happened that seven brothers with their mother were arrested
> and tortured with whips and scourges by the king,
> to force them to eat pork in violation of God's law.
One of the brothers, speaking for the others, said:
> "What do you expect to achieve by questioning us?
We are ready to die rather than transgress the laws of our ancestors."

At the point of death he said:
> "You accursed fiend, you are depriving us of this present life,
> but the King of the world will raise us up to live again forever.
It is for his laws that we are dying."

After him the third suffered their cruel sport.
He put out his tongue at once when told to do so,
> and bravely held out his hands, as he spoke these noble words:
> "It was from Heaven that I received these;
> for the sake of his laws I disdain them;
> from him I hope to receive them again."
Even the king and his attendants marveled at the young man's
> courage,
> because he regarded his sufferings as nothing.

After he had died,
> they tortured and maltreated the fourth brother in the same way.
When he was near death, he said,
> "It is my choice to die at the hands of men
> with the hope God gives of being raised up by him;
> but for you, there will be no resurrection to life." ✛

Psalm 17:1, 5-6, 8, 15
R. (15b) **Lord, when your glory appears, my joy will be full.**
Hear, O LORD, a just suit;
> attend to my outcry;
> hearken to my prayer from lips without deceit. **R.**

My steps have been steadfast in your paths,
  my feet have not faltered.
I call upon you, for you will answer me, O God;
  incline your ear to me; hear my word. **R.**
Keep me as the apple of your eye,
  hide me in the shadow of your wings.
But I in justice shall behold your face;
  on waking I shall be content in your presence. **R.**

† *2 Thessalonians 2:16—3:5*
*May the Lord encourage your hearts and strengthen them
in every good deed and word.*

Brothers and sisters:
May our Lord Jesus Christ himself and God our Father,
  who has loved us and given us everlasting encouragement
  and good hope through his grace,
  encourage your hearts and strengthen them in every good deed
    and word.

Finally, brothers and sisters, pray for us,
  so that the word of the Lord may speed forward and be glorified,
  as it did among you,
  and that we may be delivered from perverse and wicked people,
  for not all have faith.
But the Lord is faithful;
  he will strengthen you and guard you from the evil one.
We are confident of you in the Lord that what we instruct you,
  you are doing and will continue to do.
May the Lord direct your hearts to the love of God
  and to the endurance of Christ. ✛

Revelation 1:5a, 6b
R. Alleluia, alleluia.
Jesus Christ is the firstborn of the dead;
to him be glory and power, forever and ever. **R.**

†*Luke 20:27-38* (or *Luke 20:27, 34-38)*
He is not God of the dead, but of the living.

Some Sadducees, those who deny that there is a resurrection,
  came forward and put this question to Jesus, saying,
  "Teacher, Moses wrote for us,
  If someone's brother dies leaving a wife but no child,
  his brother must take the wife
  and raise up descendants for his brother.
Now there were seven brothers;
  the first married a woman but died childless.

Then the second and the third married her,
    and likewise all the seven died childless.
Finally the woman also died.
Now at the resurrection whose wife will that woman be?
For all seven had been married to her."
Jesus said to them,
    "The children of this age marry and remarry;
    but those who are deemed worthy to attain to the coming age
    and to the resurrection of the dead
    neither marry nor are given in marriage.
They can no longer die,
    for they are like angels;
    and they are the children of God
    because they are the ones who will rise.
That the dead will rise
    even Moses made known in the passage about the bush,
    when he called out 'Lord,'
    the God of Abraham, the God of Isaac, and the God of Jacob;
    and he is not God of the dead, but of the living,
    for to him all are alive." ✛

MONDAY, NOVEMBER 7
WEEKDAY

✝ *Titus 1:1-9*
Appoint presbyters in every town, as I directed you.

Paul, a slave of God and Apostle of Jesus Christ
    for the sake of the faith of God's chosen ones
    and the recognition of religious truth,
    in the hope of eternal life
    that God, who does not lie, promised before time began,
    who indeed at the proper time revealed his word
    in the proclamation with which I was entrusted
    by the command of God our savior,
    to Titus, my true child in our common faith:
    grace and peace from God the Father and Christ Jesus our savior.

For this reason I left you in Crete
    so that you might set right what remains to be done
    and appoint presbyters in every town, as I directed you,
    on condition that a man be blameless,
    married only once, with believing children
    who are not accused of licentiousness or rebellious.
For a bishop as God's steward must be blameless, not arrogant,
    not irritable, not a drunkard, not aggressive,

not greedy for sordid gain, but hospitable, a lover of goodness,
temperate, just, holy, and self-controlled,
holding fast to the true message as taught
so that he will be able both to exhort with sound doctrine
and to refute opponents. ✛

Psalm 24:1b-2, 3-4ab, 5-6
R. (see 6) **Lord, this is the people that longs to see your face.**
The LORD's are the earth and its fullness;
   the world and those who dwell in it.
For he founded it upon the seas
   and established it upon the rivers. **R.**
Who can ascend the mountain of the LORD?
   or who may stand in his holy place?
He whose hands are sinless, whose heart is clean,
   who desires not what is vain. **R.**
He shall receive a blessing from the LORD,
   a reward from God his savior.
Such is the race that seeks for him,
   that seeks the face of the God of Jacob. **R.**

Philippians 2:15d, 16a
R. Alleluia, alleluia.
Shine like lights in the world,
as you hold on to the word of life. **R.**

† *Luke 17:1-6*

If your brother wrongs you seven times in one day, and returns to you
seven times saying, "I am sorry," you should forgive him.

Jesus said to his disciples,
  "Things that cause sin will inevitably occur,
   but woe to the one through whom they occur.
It would be better for him if a millstone were put around his neck
   and he be thrown into the sea
   than for him to cause one of these little ones to sin.
Be on your guard!
If your brother sins, rebuke him;
   and if he repents, forgive him.
And if he wrongs you seven times in one day
   and returns to you seven times saying, 'I am sorry,'
   you should forgive him."

And the Apostles said to the Lord, "Increase our faith."
The Lord replied, "If you have faith the size of a mustard seed,
   you would say to this mulberry tree,
   'Be uprooted and planted in the sea,' and it would obey you." ✛

TUESDAY, NOVEMBER 8
WEEKDAY

† *Titus 2:1-8, 11-14*
We live devoutly in this age, as we await the blessed hope,
the appearance of our savior Jesus Christ.

Beloved:
You must say what is consistent with sound doctrine,
  namely, that older men should be temperate, dignified,
  self-controlled, sound in faith, love, and endurance.
Similarly, older women should be reverent in their behavior,
  not slanderers, not addicted to drink,
  teaching what is good, so that they may train younger women
  to love their husbands and children,
  to be self-controlled, chaste, good homemakers,
  under the control of their husbands,
  so that the word of God may not be discredited.

Urge the younger men, similarly, to control themselves,
  showing yourself as a model of good deeds in every respect,
  with integrity in your teaching, dignity, and sound speech
  that cannot be criticized,
  so that the opponent will be put to shame
  without anything bad to say about us.

For the grace of God has appeared, saving all
  and training us to reject godless ways and worldly desires
  and to live temperately, justly, and devoutly in this age,
  as we await the blessed hope,
  the appearance of the glory of the great God
  and of our savior Jesus Christ,
  who gave himself for us to deliver us from all lawlessness
  and to cleanse for himself a people as his own,
  eager to do what is good. ✦

Psalm 37:3-4, 18, 23, 27 and 29
R. (39a) **The salvation of the just comes from the Lord.**
Trust in the LORD and do good,
  that you may dwell in the land and be fed in security.
Take delight in the LORD,
  and he will grant you your heart's requests. **R.**
The LORD watches over the lives of the wholehearted;
  their inheritance lasts forever.
By the LORD are the steps of a man made firm,
  and he approves his way. **R.**

Turn from evil and do good,
  that you may abide forever;
The just shall possess the land
  and dwell in it forever. **R.**

  John 14:23
R. Alleluia, alleluia.
Whoever loves me will keep my word,
and my Father will love him,
and we will come to him. **R.**

† *Luke 17:7-10*
We are unprofitable servants; we have done what we were obliged to do.

Jesus said to the Apostles:
"Who among you would say to your servant
  who has just come in from plowing or tending sheep in the field,
  'Come here immediately and take your place at table'?
Would he not rather say to him,
  'Prepare something for me to eat.
Put on your apron and wait on me while I eat and drink.
You may eat and drink when I am finished'?
Is he grateful to that servant because he did what was commanded?
So should it be with you.
When you have done all you have been commanded, say,
  'We are unprofitable servants;
  we have done what we were obliged to do.'" ✛

WEDNESDAY, NOVEMBER 9
THE DEDICATION OF THE LATERAN BASILICA
† *Ezekiel 47:1-2, 8-9, 12*
*I saw water flowing from the temple, and all who were touched by it were saved
(see Roman Missal, antiphon for the blessing and sprinkling of water
during the season of Easter).*

The angel brought me
  back to the entrance of the temple,
  and I saw water flowing out
  from beneath the threshold of the temple toward the east,
  for the façade of the temple was toward the east;
  the water flowed down from the southern side of the temple,
  south of the altar.
He led me outside by the north gate,
  and around to the outer gate facing the east,
  where I saw water trickling from the southern side.

He said to me,
"This water flows into the eastern district down upon the Arabah,
and empties into the sea, the salt waters, which it makes fresh.
Wherever the river flows,
every sort of living creature that can multiply shall live,
and there shall be abundant fish,
for wherever this water comes the sea shall be made fresh.
Along both banks of the river, fruit trees of every kind shall grow;
their leaves shall not fade, nor their fruit fail.
Every month they shall bear fresh fruit,
for they shall be watered by the flow from the sanctuary.
Their fruit shall serve for food, and their leaves for medicine." ✛

Psalm 46:2-3, 5-6, 8-9

R. (5) **The waters of the river gladden the city of God, the
holy dwelling of the Most High!**

God is our refuge and our strength,
an ever-present help in distress.
Therefore, we fear not, though the earth be shaken
and mountains plunge into the depths of the sea. **R.**
There is a stream whose runlets gladden the city of God,
the holy dwelling of the Most High.
God is in its midst; it shall not be disturbed;
God will help it at the break of dawn. **R.**
The LORD of hosts is with us;
our stronghold is the God of Jacob.
Come! behold the deeds of the LORD,
the astounding things he has wrought on earth. **R.**

† 1 Corinthians 3:9c-11, 16-17
You are God's temple.

Brothers and sisters:
You are God's building.
According to the grace of God given to me,
like a wise master builder I laid a foundation,
and another is building upon it.
But each one must be careful how he builds upon it,
for no one can lay a foundation other than the one that is there,
namely, Jesus Christ.

Do you not know that you are the temple of God,
and that the Spirit of God dwells in you?
If anyone destroys God's temple,
God will destroy that person;
for the temple of God, which you are, is holy. ✛

2 Chronicles 7:16

R. Alleluia, alleluia.

I have chosen and consecrated this house, says the Lord,
that my name may be there forever. **R.**

† *John 2:13-22*
Jesus was speaking about the temple of his Body.

Since the Passover of the Jews was near,
  Jesus went up to Jerusalem.
He found in the temple area those who sold oxen, sheep, and doves,
  as well as the money-changers seated there.
He made a whip out of cords
  and drove them all out of the temple area, with the sheep and oxen,
  and spilled the coins of the money-changers
  and overturned their tables,
  and to those who sold doves he said,
  "Take these out of here,
  and stop making my Father's house a marketplace."
His disciples recalled the words of Scripture,
  Zeal for your house will consume me.
At this the Jews answered and said to him,
  "What sign can you show us for doing this?"
Jesus answered and said to them,
  "Destroy this temple and in three days I will raise it up."
The Jews said,
  "This temple has been under construction for forty-six years,
  and you will raise it up in three days?"
But he was speaking about the temple of his Body.
Therefore, when he was raised from the dead,
  his disciples remembered that he had said this,
  and they came to believe the Scripture
  and the word Jesus had spoken. **✢**

THURSDAY, NOVEMBER 10
St. Pope Leo the Great

† *Philemon 7-20*
Have him back, no longer as a slave but more than a slave,
a brother, beloved especially to me.

Beloved:
I have experienced much joy and encouragement from your love,
  because the hearts of the holy ones
  have been refreshed by you, brother.
Therefore, although I have the full right in Christ
  to order you to do what is proper,

I rather urge you out of love,
being as I am, Paul, an old man,
and now also a prisoner for Christ Jesus.
I urge you on behalf of my child Onesimus,
whose father I have become in my imprisonment,
who was once useless to you but is now useful to both you and me.
I am sending him, that is, my own heart, back to you.
I should have liked to retain him for myself,
so that he might serve me on your behalf
in my imprisonment for the Gospel,
but I did not want to do anything without your consent,
so that the good you do might not be forced but voluntary.
Perhaps this is why he was away from you for a while,
that you might have him back forever,
no longer as a slave but more than a slave, a brother,
beloved especially to me, but even more so to you,
as a man and in the Lord.
So if you regard me as a partner, welcome him as you would me.
And if he has done you any injustice
or owes you anything, charge it to me.
I, Paul, write this in my own hand: I will pay.
May I not tell you that you owe me your very self.
Yes, brother, may I profit from you in the Lord.
Refresh my heart in Christ. ✛

Psalm 146:7, 8-9a, 9bc-10
R. (5a) **Blessed is he whose help is the God of Jacob.**
(or **Alleluia.**)
The LORD secures justice for the oppressed,
gives food to the hungry.
The LORD sets captives free. **R.**
The LORD gives sight to the blind.
The LORD raises up those who were bowed down;
the LORD loves the just.
The LORD protects strangers. **R.**
The fatherless and the widow he sustains,
but the way of the wicked he thwarts.
The LORD shall reign forever;
your God, O Zion, through all generations. Alleluia. **R.**

John 15:5
R. Alleluia, alleluia.
I am the vine, you are the branches, says the Lord:
whoever remains in me and I in him will bear much fruit. **R.**

† *Luke 17:20-25*
The Kingdom of God is among you.

Asked by the Pharisees when the Kingdom of God would come,
Jesus said in reply,
"The coming of the Kingdom of God cannot be observed,
and no one will announce, 'Look, here it is,' or, 'There it is.'
For behold, the Kingdom of God is among you."

Then he said to his disciples,
"The days will come when you will long to see
one of the days of the Son of Man, but you will not see it.
There will be those who will say to you,
'Look, there he is,' or 'Look, here he is.'
Do not go off, do not run in pursuit.
For just as lightning flashes
and lights up the sky from one side to the other,
so will the Son of Man be in his day.
But first he must suffer greatly and be rejected by this generation." ✛

FRIDAY, NOVEMBER 11
St. Martin of Tours

† *2 John 4-9*
Whoever remains in the teaching has the Father and the Son.

[Chosen Lady:]
I rejoiced greatly to find some of your children walking in the truth
just as we were commanded by the Father.
But now, Lady, I ask you,
not as though I were writing a new commandment
but the one we have had from the beginning:
let us love one another.
For this is love, that we walk according to his commandments;
this is the commandment, as you heard from the beginning,
in which you should walk.

Many deceivers have gone out into the world,
those who do not acknowledge Jesus Christ as coming in the flesh;
such is the deceitful one and the antichrist.
Look to yourselves that you do not lose what we worked for
but may receive a full recompense.
Anyone who is so "progressive"
as not to remain in the teaching of the Christ does not have God;
whoever remains in the teaching has the Father and the Son. ✛

Psalm 119:1, 2, 10, 11, 17, 18

R. (1b) **Blessed are they who follow the law of the Lord!**

Blessed are they whose way is blameless,
 who walk in the law of the LORD. **R.**
Blessed are they who observe his decrees,
 who seek him with all their heart. **R.**
With all my heart I seek you;
 let me not stray from your commands. **R.**
Within my heart I treasure your promise,
 that I may not sin against you. **R.**
Be good to your servant, that I may live
 and keep your words. **R.**
Open my eyes, that I may consider
 the wonders of your law. **R.**

Luke 21:28

R. Alleluia, alleluia.

Stand erect and raise your heads
because your redemption is at hand. **R.**

† *Luke 17:26-37*

So it will be on the day the Son of Man is revealed.

Jesus said to his disciples:
"As it was in the days of Noah,
 so it will be in the days of the Son of Man;
 they were eating and drinking,
 marrying and giving in marriage up to the day
 that Noah entered the ark,
 and the flood came and destroyed them all.
Similarly, as it was in the days of Lot:
 they were eating, drinking, buying,
 selling, planting, building;
 on the day when Lot left Sodom,
 fire and brimstone rained from the sky to destroy them all.
So it will be on the day the Son of Man is revealed.
On that day, someone who is on the housetop
 and whose belongings are in the house
 must not go down to get them,
 and likewise one in the field
 must not return to what was left behind.
Remember the wife of Lot.
Whoever seeks to preserve his life will lose it,
 but whoever loses it will save it.
I tell you, on that night there will be two people in one bed;
 one will be taken, the other left."

And there will be two women grinding meal together;
   one will be taken, the other left."
They said to him in reply, "Where, Lord?"
He said to them, "Where the body is,
   there also the vultures will gather." ✣

SATURDAY, NOVEMBER 12
St. Josaphat

✝ *3 John 5-8*
We ought to support such persons,
so that we may be co-workers in the truth.

Beloved, you are faithful in all you do for the brothers and sisters,
   especially for strangers;
   they have testified to your love before the Church.
Please help them in a way worthy of God to continue their journey.
For they have set out for the sake of the Name
   and are accepting nothing from the pagans.
Therefore, we ought to support such persons,
   so that we may be co-workers in the truth. ✣

Psalm 112:1-2, 3-4, 5-6
R. Blessed the man who fears the Lord. *(or* **Alleluia.***)*
Blessed the man who fears the LORD,
   who greatly delights in his commands.
His posterity shall be mighty upon the earth;
   the upright generation shall be blessed. **R.**
Wealth and riches shall be in his house;
   his generosity shall endure forever.
Light shines through the darkness for the upright;
   he is gracious and merciful and just. **R.**
Well for the man who is gracious and lends,
   who conducts his affairs with justice;
He shall never be moved;
   the just one shall be in everlasting remembrance. **R.**

See 2 Thessalonians 2:14
R. Alleluia, alleluia.
God has called us through the Gospel,
to possess the glory of our Lord Jesus Christ. **R.**

† *Luke 18:1-8*

Will not God then secure the rights of his chosen ones
who call out to him day and night?

Jesus told his disciples a parable
  about the necessity for them to pray always without becoming
    weary.
He said, "There was a judge in a certain town
  who neither feared God nor respected any human being.
And a widow in that town used to come to him and say,
  'Render a just decision for me against my adversary.'
For a long time the judge was unwilling, but eventually he thought,
  'While it is true that I neither fear God nor respect any human being,
  because this widow keeps bothering me
  I shall deliver a just decision for her
  lest she finally come and strike me.'"
The Lord said, "Pay attention to what the dishonest judge says.
Will not God then secure the rights of his chosen ones
  who call out to him day and night?
Will he be slow to answer them?
I tell you, he will see to it that justice is done for them speedily.
But when the Son of Man comes, will he find faith on earth?" ✛

SUNDAY, NOVEMBER 13
THIRTY-THIRD SUNDAY IN ORDINARY TIME

† *Malachi 3:19-20a*
The sun of justice will shine on you.

Lo, the day is coming, blazing like an oven,
  when all the proud and all evildoers will be stubble,
and the day that is coming will set them on fire,
  leaving them neither root nor branch,
  says the LORD of hosts.
But for you who fear my name, there will arise
  the sun of justice with its healing rays. ✛

Psalm 98:5-6, 7-8, 9

R. (see 9) **The Lord comes to rule the earth with justice.**
Sing praise to the LORD with the harp,
  with the harp and melodious song.
With trumpets and the sound of the horn
  sing joyfully before the King, the LORD. **R.**
Let the sea and what fills it resound,
  the world and those who dwell in it;
let the rivers clap their hands,
  the mountains shout with them for joy. **R.**

Before the LORD, for he comes,
  for he comes to rule the earth;
he will rule the world with justice
  and the peoples with equity. **R.**

†2 Thessalonians 3:7-12
If anyone is unwilling to work, neither should that one eat.

Brothers and sisters:
You know how one must imitate us.
For we did not act in a disorderly way among you,
  nor did we eat food received free from anyone.
On the contrary, in toil and drudgery, night and day
  we worked, so as not to burden any of you.
Not that we do not have the right.
Rather, we wanted to present ourselves as a model for you,
  so that you might imitate us.
In fact, when we were with you,
  we instructed you that if anyone was unwilling to work,
  neither should that one eat.
We hear that some are conducting themselves among you in a
    disorderly way,
  by not keeping busy but minding the business of others.
Such people we instruct and urge in the Lord Jesus Christ to work
    quietly
  and to eat their own food. ✝

Luke 21:28
R. Alleluia, alleluia.
Stand erect and raise your heads
because your redemption is at hand. **R.**

†Luke 21:5-19
By your perseverance you will secure your lives.

While some people were speaking about
  how the temple was adorned with costly stones and votive offerings,
Jesus said, "All that you see here—
  the days will come when there will not be left
  a stone upon another stone that will not be thrown down."

Then they asked him,
  "Teacher, when will this happen?
And what sign will there be when all these things are about to
    happen?"

He answered,
"See that you not be deceived,
for many will come in my name, saying,
'I am he,' and 'The time has come.'
Do not follow them!
When you hear of wars and insurrections,
do not be terrified; for such things must happen first,
but it will not immediately be the end."
Then he said to them,
"Nation will rise against nation, and kingdom against kingdom.
There will be powerful earthquakes, famines, and plagues
from place to place;
and awesome sights and mighty signs will come from the sky.

"Before all this happens, however,
they will seize and persecute you,
they will hand you over to the synagogues and to prisons,
and they will have you led before kings and governors
because of my name.
It will lead to your giving testimony.
Remember, you are not to prepare your defense beforehand,
for I myself shall give you a wisdom in speaking
that all your adversaries will be powerless to resist or refute.
You will even be handed over by parents, brothers, relatives, and
friends,
and they will put some of you to death.
You will be hated by all because of my name,
but not a hair on your head will be destroyed.
By your perseverance you will secure your lives." ✛

MONDAY, NOVEMBER 14
WEEKDAY

† *Revelation 1:1-4; 2:1-5*
Realize how far you have fallen and repent.

The revelation of Jesus Christ, which God gave to him,
to show his servants what must happen soon.
He made it known by sending his angel to his servant John,
who gives witness to the word of God
and to the testimony of Jesus Christ by reporting what he saw.
Blessed is the one who reads aloud
and blessed are those who listen to this prophetic message
and heed what is written in it, for the appointed time is near.

John, to the seven churches in Asia: grace to you and peace
  from him who is and who was and who is to come,
  and from the seven spirits before his throne.

I heard the Lord saying to me:
"To the angel of the Church in Ephesus, write this:

"'The one who holds the seven stars in his right hand
  and walks in the midst of the seven gold lampstands says this:
  "I know your works, your labor, and your endurance,
  and that you cannot tolerate the wicked;
you have tested those who call themselves Apostles but are not,
  and discovered that they are impostors.
Moreover, you have endurance and have suffered for my name,
  and you have not grown weary.
Yet I hold this against you:
  you have lost the love you had at first.
Realize how far you have fallen.
Repent, and do the works you did at first.
Otherwise, I will come to you
  and remove your lampstand from its place, unless you repent.""'" ✛

Psalm 1:1-2, 3, 4 and 6

R. (Revelation 2:17) **Those who are victorious I will feed from
  the tree of life.**
Blessed the man who follows not
  the counsel of the wicked
Nor walks in the way of sinners,
  nor sits in the company of the insolent,
But delights in the law of the LORD
  and meditates on his law day and night. **R.**
He is like a tree
  planted near running water,
That yields its fruit in due season,
  and whose leaves never fade.
  Whatever he does, prospers. **R.**
Not so the wicked, not so;
  they are like chaff which the wind drives away.
For the LORD watches over the way of the just,
  but the way of the wicked vanishes. **R.**

John 8:12

R. Alleluia, alleluia.
I am the light of the world, says the Lord;
whoever follows me will have the light of life. **R.**

† *Luke 18:35-43*
What do you want me to do for you? Lord, please let me see.

As Jesus approached Jericho
a blind man was sitting by the roadside begging,
and hearing a crowd going by, he inquired what was happening.
They told him,
"Jesus of Nazareth is passing by."
He shouted, "Jesus, Son of David, have pity on me!"
The people walking in front rebuked him,
telling him to be silent,
but he kept calling out all the more,
"Son of David, have pity on me!"
Then Jesus stopped and ordered that he be brought to him;
and when he came near, Jesus asked him,
"What do you want me to do for you?"
He replied, "Lord, please let me see."
Jesus told him, "Have sight; your faith has saved you."
He immediately received his sight
and followed him, giving glory to God.
When they saw this, all the people gave praise to God. ✛

TUESDAY, NOVEMBER 15
WEEKDAY, ST. ALBERT THE GREAT

† *Revelation 3:1-6, 14-22*
If anyone hears my voice and opens the door,
I will enter his house and dine with him.

I, John, heard the Lord saying to me:
"To the angel of the Church in Sardis, write this:

"'The one who has the seven spirits of God
and the seven stars says this: "I know your works,
that you have the reputation of being alive, but you are dead.
Be watchful and strengthen what is left, which is going to die,
for I have not found your works complete in the sight of my God.
Remember then how you accepted and heard; keep it, and repent.
If you are not watchful, I will come like a thief,
and you will never know at what hour I will come upon you.
However, you have a few people in Sardis
who have not soiled their garments;
they will walk with me dressed in white,
because they are worthy.

"'The victor will thus be dressed in white,
   and I will never erase his name from the book of life
   but will acknowledge his name in the presence of my Father
   and of his angels.

"'Whoever has ears ought to hear what the Spirit says to the churches.'"

"To the angel of the Church in Laodicea, write this:

"'The Amen, the faithful and true witness,
   the source of God's creation, says this:
   "I know your works;
   I know that you are neither cold nor hot.
I wish you were either cold or hot.
So, because you are lukewarm, neither hot nor cold,
   I will spit you out of my mouth.
For you say, 'I am rich and affluent and have no need of anything,'
   and yet do not realize that you are wretched,
   pitiable, poor, blind, and naked.
I advise you to buy from me gold refined by fire so that you may be
      rich,
   and white garments to put on
   so that your shameful nakedness may not be exposed,
   and buy ointment to smear on your eyes so that you may see.
Those whom I love, I reprove and chastise.
Be earnest, therefore, and repent.

"'Behold, I stand at the door and knock.
If anyone hears my voice and opens the door,
   then I will enter his house and dine with him,
   and he with me.
I will give the victor the right to sit with me on my throne,
   as I myself first won the victory
   and sit with my Father on his throne.

"'Whoever has ears ought to hear
   what the Spirit says to the churches.'" ✛

   Psalm 15:2-3a, 3bc-4ab, 5
R. (Revelation 3: 21) **I will seat the victor beside me on my
   throne.**
He who walks blamelessly and does justice;
   who thinks the truth in his heart
   and slanders not with his tongue. **R.**

Who harms not his fellow man,
   nor takes up a reproach against his neighbor;
By whom the reprobate is despised,
   while he honors those who fear the LORD. **R.**
Who lends not his money at usury
   and accepts no bribe against the innocent.
He who does these things
   shall never be disturbed. **R.**

   1 John 4:10b
R. Alleluia, alleluia.
God loved us, and sent his Son
as expiation for our sins. **R.**

† *Luke 19:1-10*
The Son of Man has come to seek and to save what was lost.

At that time Jesus came to Jericho and intended to pass through
   the town.
Now a man there named Zacchaeus,
   who was a chief tax collector and also a wealthy man,
   was seeking to see who Jesus was;
   but he could not see him because of the crowd,
   for he was short in stature.
So he ran ahead and climbed a sycamore tree in order to see Jesus,
   who was about to pass that way.
When he reached the place, Jesus looked up and said,
   "Zacchaeus, come down quickly,
   for today I must stay at your house."
And he came down quickly and received him with joy.
When they saw this, they began to grumble, saying,
   "He has gone to stay at the house of a sinner."
But Zacchaeus stood there and said to the Lord,
   "Behold, half of my possessions, Lord, I shall give to the poor,
   and if I have extorted anything from anyone
   I shall repay it four times over."
And Jesus said to him,
   "Today salvation has come to this house
   because this man too is a descendant of Abraham.
For the Son of Man has come to seek
   and to save what was lost." ✠

WEDNESDAY, NOVEMBER 16
WEEKDAY, ST. MARGARET OF SCOTLAND, ST. GERTRUDE

† *Revelation 4:1-11*

Holy is the Lord God almighty, who was, and who is, and who is to come.

I, John, had a vision of an open door to heaven,
and I heard the trumpetlike voice
that had spoken to me before, saying,
"Come up here and I will show you what must happen afterwards."
At once I was caught up in spirit.
A throne was there in heaven, and on the throne sat one
whose appearance sparkled like jasper and carnelian.
Around the throne was a halo as brilliant as an emerald.
Surrounding the throne I saw twenty-four other thrones
on which twenty-four elders sat,
dressed in white garments and with gold crowns on their heads.
From the throne came flashes of lightning,
rumblings, and peals of thunder.
Seven flaming torches burned in front of the throne,
which are the seven spirits of God.
In front of the throne was something that resembled
a sea of glass like crystal.

In the center and around the throne,
there were four living creatures
covered with eyes in front and in back.
The first creature resembled a lion, the second was like a calf,
the third had a face like that of a man,
and the fourth looked like an eagle in flight.
The four living creatures, each of them with six wings,
were covered with eyes inside and out.
Day and night they do not stop exclaiming:
"Holy, holy, holy is the Lord God almighty,
who was, and who is, and who is to come."
Whenever the living creatures give glory and honor and thanks
to the one who sits on the throne, who lives forever and ever,
the twenty-four elders fall down
before the one who sits on the throne
and worship him, who lives forever and ever.
They throw down their crowns before the throne, exclaiming:

"Worthy are you, Lord our God,
to receive glory and honor and power,
for you created all things;
because of your will they came to be and were created." ✝

Psalm 150:1b-2, 3-4, 5-6
R. (1b) **Holy, holy, holy Lord, mighty God!**
Praise the LORD in his sanctuary,
  praise him in the firmament of his strength.
Praise him for his mighty deeds,
  praise him for his sovereign majesty. **R.**
Praise him with the blast of the trumpet,
  praise him with lyre and harp,
Praise him with timbrel and dance,
  praise him with strings and pipe. **R.**
Praise him with sounding cymbals,
  praise him with clanging cymbals.
Let everything that has breath
  praise the LORD! Alleluia. **R.**

See John 15:16
R. Alleluia, alleluia.
I chose you from the world,
to go and bear fruit that will last, says the Lord. **R.**

✝ *Luke 19:11-28*
Why did you not put my money in a bank?

While people were listening to Jesus speak,
  he proceeded to tell a parable because he was near Jerusalem
  and they thought that the Kingdom of God
  would appear there immediately.
So he said,
  "A nobleman went off to a distant country
  to obtain the kingship for himself and then to return.
He called ten of his servants and gave them ten gold coins
  and told them, 'Engage in trade with these until I return.'
His fellow citizens, however, despised him
  and sent a delegation after him to announce,
  'We do not want this man to be our king.'
But when he returned after obtaining the kingship,
  he had the servants called, to whom he had given the money,
  to learn what they had gained by trading.
The first came forward and said,
  'Sir, your gold coin has earned ten additional ones.'
He replied, 'Well done, good servant!
You have been faithful in this very small matter;
  take charge of ten cities.'
Then the second came and reported,
  'Your gold coin, sir, has earned five more.'

And to this servant too he said,
  'You, take charge of five cities.'
Then the other servant came and said,
  'Sir, here is your gold coin;
  I kept it stored away in a handkerchief,
  for I was afraid of you, because you are a demanding man;
  you take up what you did not lay down
  and you harvest what you did not plant.'
He said to him,
  'With your own words I shall condemn you,
  you wicked servant.
You knew I was a demanding man,
  taking up what I did not lay down
  and harvesting what I did not plant;
  why did you not put my money in a bank?
Then on my return I would have collected it with interest.'
And to those standing by he said,
  'Take the gold coin from him
  and give it to the servant who has ten.'
But they said to him,
  'Sir, he has ten gold coins.'
He replied, 'I tell you,
  to everyone who has, more will be given,
  but from the one who has not,
  even what he has will be taken away.
Now as for those enemies of mine who did not want me as their king,
  bring them here and slay them before me.'"

After he had said this,
  he proceeded on his journey up to Jerusalem. ✝

THURSDAY, NOVEMBER 17
ST. ELIZABETH OF HUNGARY

✝ *Revelation 5:1-10*
The Lamb that was slain purchased us with his Blood from every nation.

I, John, saw a scroll in the right hand of the one who sat on the
  throne.
It had writing on both sides and was sealed with seven seals.
Then I saw a mighty angel who proclaimed in a loud voice,
  "Who is worthy to open the scroll and break its seals?"
But no one in heaven or on earth or under the earth
  was able to open the scroll or to examine it.
I shed many tears because no one was found worthy
  to open the scroll or to examine it.

One of the elders said to me, "Do not weep.
The lion of the tribe of Judah, the root of David, has triumphed,
    enabling him to open the scroll with its seven seals."

Then I saw standing in the midst of the throne
    and the four living creatures and the elders
    a Lamb that seemed to have been slain.
He had seven horns and seven eyes;
    these are the seven spirits of God sent out into the whole world.
He came and received the scroll from the right hand
    of the one who sat on the throne.
When he took it,
    the four living creatures and the twenty-four elders
    fell down before the Lamb.
Each of the elders held a harp and gold bowls filled with incense,
    which are the prayers of the holy ones.
They sang a new hymn:

"Worthy are you to receive the scroll
    and break open its seals,
    for you were slain and with your Blood you purchased for God
    those from every tribe and tongue, people and nation.
You made them a kingdom and priests for our God,
    and they will reign on earth." ✛

Psalm 149:1b-2, 3-4, 5-6a and 9b
R. (Revelation 5:10) **The Lamb has made us a kingdom of priests to serve our God.** *(or Alleluia.)*
Sing to the LORD a new song
    of praise in the assembly of the faithful.
Let Israel be glad in their maker,
    let the children of Zion rejoice in their king. **R.**
Let them praise his name in the festive dance,
    let them sing praise to him with timbrel and harp.
For the LORD loves his people,
    and he adorns the lowly with victory. **R.**
Let the faithful exult in glory;
    let them sing for joy upon their couches;
Let the high praises of God be in their throats.
    This is the glory of all his faithful. Alleluia. **R.**

Psalm 95:8
R. Alleluia, alleluia.
If today you hear his voice,
harden not your hearts. **R.**

† *Luke 19:41-44*
If you only knew what makes for peace.

As Jesus drew near Jerusalem,
he saw the city and wept over it, saying,
"If this day you only knew what makes for peace—
but now it is hidden from your eyes.
For the days are coming upon you
when your enemies will raise a palisade against you;
they will encircle you and hem you in on all sides.
They will smash you to the ground and your children within you,
and they will not leave one stone upon another within you
because you did not recognize the time of your visitation." ✛

FRIDAY, NOVEMBER 18
WEEKDAY, THE DEDICATION OF THE BASILICAS OF ST. PETER AND ST. PAUL, ST. ROSE PHILIPPINE DUCHESNE
(For the memorial of the Dedication: Acts 28:11-16, 30-31 •
Psalm 98:1, 2-3ab, 3cd-4, 5-6 • Matthew 14:22-33 [679].)

† *Revelation 10:8-11*
I took the small scroll and swallowed it.

I, John, heard a voice from heaven speak to me.
Then the voice spoke to me and said:
"Go, take the scroll that lies open in the hand of the angel
who is standing on the sea and on the land."
So I went up to the angel and told him to give me the small scroll.
He said to me, "Take and swallow it.
It will turn your stomach sour,
but in your mouth it will taste as sweet as honey."
I took the small scroll from the angel's hand and swallowed it.
In my mouth it was like sweet honey,
but when I had eaten it, my stomach turned sour.
Then someone said to me, "You must prophesy again
about many peoples, nations, tongues, and kings." ✛

Psalm 119:14, 24, 72, 103, 111, 131
R. (103a) **How sweet to my taste is your promise!**
In the way of your decrees I rejoice,
as much as in all riches. **R.**
Yes, your decrees are my delight;
they are my counselors. **R.**
The law of your mouth is to me more precious
than thousands of gold and silver pieces. **R.**
How sweet to my palate are your promises,
sweeter than honey to my mouth! **R.**

Your decrees are my inheritance forever;
 the joy of my heart they are. **R.**
I gasp with open mouth
 in my yearning for your commands. **R.**

John 10:27
R. Alleluia, alleluia.
My sheep hear my voice, says the Lord;
I know them, and they follow me. **R.**

† *Luke 19:45-48*
You have made it a den of thieves.

Jesus entered the temple area and proceeded to drive out
 those who were selling things, saying to them,
 "It is written, *My house shall be a house of prayer,*
 but you have made it a den of thieves."
And every day he was teaching in the temple area.
The chief priests, the scribes, and the leaders of the people, meanwhile,
 were seeking to put him to death,
 but they could find no way to accomplish their purpose
because all the people were hanging on his words. ✟

SATURDAY, NOVEMBER 19
WEEKDAY, *[BVM]*

† *Revelation 11:4-12*
These two prophets tormented the inhabitants of the earth.

I, John, heard a voice from heaven speak to me:
Here are my two witnesses:
 These are the two olive trees and the two lampstands
 that stand before the Lord of the earth.
If anyone wants to harm them, fire comes out of their mouths
 and devours their enemies.
In this way, anyone wanting to harm them is sure to be slain.
They have the power to close up the sky
 so that no rain can fall during the time of their prophesying.
They also have power to turn water into blood
 and to afflict the earth with any plague as often as they wish.

When they have finished their testimony,
 the beast that comes up from the abyss
 will wage war against them and conquer them and kill them.
Their corpses will lie in the main street of the great city,
 which has the symbolic names "Sodom" and "Egypt,"
 where indeed their Lord was crucified.

Those from every people, tribe, tongue, and nation
   will gaze on their corpses for three and a half days,
   and they will not allow their corpses to be buried.
The inhabitants of the earth will gloat over them
   and be glad and exchange gifts
   because these two prophets tormented the inhabitants of the earth.
But after the three and a half days,
   a breath of life from God entered them.
When they stood on their feet, great fear fell on those who saw them.
Then they heard a loud voice from heaven say to them, "Come up
    here."
So they went up to heaven in a cloud as their enemies looked on. ✝

Psalm 144:1, 2, 9-10
R. (1b) **Blessed be the Lord, my Rock!**
Blessed be the LORD, my rock,
   who trains my hands for battle, my fingers for war. **R.**
My mercy and my fortress,
   my stronghold, my deliverer,
My shield, in whom I trust,
   who subdues my people under me. **R.**
O God, I will sing a new song to you;
   with a ten-stringed lyre I will chant your praise,
You who give victory to kings,
   and deliver David, your servant from the evil sword. **R.**

See 2 Timothy 1:10
R. Alleluia, alleluia.
Our Savior Jesus Christ has destroyed death
and brought life to light through the Gospel. **R.**

† *Luke 20:27-40*
He is not God of the dead, but of the living.

Some Sadducees, those who deny that there is a resurrection,
   came forward and put this question to Jesus, saying,
   "Teacher, Moses wrote for us,
If someone's brother dies leaving a wife but no child,
his brother must take the wife
and raise up descendants for his brother.
Now there were seven brothers;
   the first married a woman but died childless.
Then the second and the third married her,
   and likewise all the seven died childless.
Finally the woman also died.
Now at the resurrection whose wife will that woman be?

For all seven had been married to her."
Jesus said to them,
"The children of this age marry and remarry;
but those who are deemed worthy to attain to the coming age
and to the resurrection of the dead
neither marry nor are given in marriage.
They can no longer die,
for they are like angels;
and they are the children of God
because they are the ones who will rise.
That the dead will rise
even Moses made known in the passage about the bush,
when he called 'Lord'
the God of Abraham, the God of Isaac, and the God of Jacob;
and he is not God of the dead, but of the living,
for to him all are alive."
Some of the scribes said in reply,
"Teacher, you have answered well."
And they no longer dared to ask him anything. ✛

SUNDAY, NOVEMBER 20
OUR LORD JESUS CHRIST, KING OF THE UNIVERSE
† 2 Samuel 5:1-3
They anointed David king of Israel.

In those days, all the tribes of Israel came to David in Hebron and
said:
"Here we are, your bone and your flesh.
In days past, when Saul was our king,
it was you who led the Israelites out and brought them back.
And the LORD said to you,
'You shall shepherd my people Israel
and shall be commander of Israel.'"
When all the elders of Israel came to David in Hebron,
King David made an agreement with them there before the LORD,
and they anointed him king of Israel. ✛

Psalm 122:1-2, 3-4, 4-5
R. (see 1) **Let us go rejoicing to the house of the Lord.**
I rejoiced because they said to me,
"We will go up to the house of the LORD."
And now we have set foot
within your gates, O Jerusalem. **R.**
Jerusalem, built as a city
with compact unity.

To it the tribes go up,
  the tribes of the Lord. **R.**
According to the decree for Israel,
  to give thanks to the name of the Lord.
In it are set up judgment seats,
  seats for the house of David. **R.**

† *Colossians 1:12-20*
He transferred us to the kingdom of his beloved Son.

Brothers and sisters:
Let us give thanks to the Father,
  who has made you fit to share
  in the inheritance of the holy ones in light.
He delivered us from the power of darkness
  and transferred us to the kingdom of his beloved Son,
  in whom we have redemption, the forgiveness of sins.

    He is the image of the invisible God,
      the firstborn of all creation.
    For in him were created all things in heaven and on earth,
      the visible and the invisible,
      whether thrones or dominions or principalities or powers;
      all things were created through him and for him.
    He is before all things,
      and in him all things hold together.
    He is the head of the body, the church.
    He is the beginning, the firstborn from the dead,
      that in all things he himself might be preeminent.
    For in him all the fullness was pleased to dwell,
      and through him to reconcile all things for him,
      making peace by the blood of his cross
      through him, whether those on earth or those in heaven. ✙

Mark 11:9, 10
R. Alleluia, alleluia.
Blessed is he who comes in the name of the Lord!
Blessed is the kingdom of our father David that is to come! **R.**

† *Luke 23:35-43*
Lord, remember me when you come into your kingdom.

The rulers sneered at Jesus and said,
  "He saved others, let him save himself
  if he is the chosen one, the Christ of God."
Even the soldiers jeered at him.

As they approached to offer him wine they called out,
   "If you are King of the Jews, save yourself."
Above him there was an inscription that read,
   "This is the King of the Jews."

Now one of the criminals hanging there reviled Jesus, saying,
   "Are you not the Christ?
Save yourself and us."
The other, however, rebuking him, said in reply,
   "Have you no fear of God,
   for you are subject to the same condemnation?
And indeed, we have been condemned justly,
   for the sentence we received corresponds to our crimes,
   but this man has done nothing criminal."
Then he said,
   "Jesus, remember me when you come into your kingdom."
He replied to him,
   "Amen, I say to you,
   today you will be with me in Paradise." ✛

MONDAY, NOVEMBER 21
THE PRESENTATION OF THE BLESSED VIRGIN MARY
(THIRTY-FOURTH OR LAST WEEK IN ORDINARY TIME)

† *Revelation 14:1-3, 4b-5*
His name and his Father's name are written on their foreheads.

I, John, looked and there was the Lamb standing on Mount Zion,
   and with him a hundred and forty-four thousand
   who had his name and his Father's name written on their foreheads.
I heard a sound from heaven
   like the sound of rushing water or a loud peal of thunder.
The sound I heard was like that of harpists playing their harps.
They were singing what seemed to be a new hymn before the throne,
   before the four living creatures and the elders.
No one could learn this hymn except the hundred and forty-four
      thousand
   who had been ransomed from the earth.
These are the ones who follow the Lamb wherever he goes.
They have been ransomed as the first fruits
   of the human race for God and the Lamb.
On their lips no deceit has been found; they are unblemished. ✛

Psalm 24:1bc-2, 3-4ab, 5-6

R. (see 6) **Lord, this is the people that longs to see your face.**

The LORD's are the earth and its fullness;
   the world and those who dwell in it.
For he founded it upon the seas
   and established it upon the rivers. **R.**
Who can ascend the mountain of the LORD?
   or who may stand in his holy place?
He whose hands are sinless, whose heart is clean,
   who desires not what is vain. **R.**
He shall receive a blessing from the LORD,
   a reward from God his savior.
Such is the race that seeks for him,
   that seeks the face of the God of Jacob. **R.**

Matthew 24:42a, 44

R. Alleluia, alleluia.

Stay awake!
For you do not know when the Son of Man will come. **R.**

† *Luke 21:1-4*
He noticed a poor widow putting in two small coins.

When Jesus looked up he saw some wealthy people
   putting their offerings into the treasury
   and he noticed a poor widow putting in two small coins.
He said, "I tell you truly,
   this poor widow put in more than all the rest;
   for those others have all made offerings from their surplus wealth,
   but she, from her poverty, has offered her whole livelihood." ✣

TUESDAY, NOVEMBER 22
ST. CECILIA

† *Revelation 14:14-19*
The time to reap has come, because the earth's harvest is fully ripe.

I, John, looked and there was a white cloud,
   and sitting on the cloud one who looked like a son of man,
   with a gold crown on his head and a sharp sickle in his hand.
Another angel came out of the temple,
   crying out in a loud voice to the one sitting on the cloud,
   "Use your sickle and reap the harvest,
   for the time to reap has come,
   because the earth's harvest is fully ripe."
So the one who was sitting on the cloud swung his sickle over the
      earth,
   and the earth was harvested.

Then another angel came out of the temple in heaven
    who also had a sharp sickle.
Then another angel came from the altar, who was in charge of the fire,
    and cried out in a loud voice
    to the one who had the sharp sickle,
    "Use your sharp sickle and cut the clusters from the earth's vines,
    for its grapes are ripe."
So the angel swung his sickle over the earth and cut the earth's
    vintage.
He threw it into the great wine press of God's fury. ✝

Psalm 96:10, 11-12, 13
R. (13b) **The Lord comes to judge the earth.**
Say among the nations: The LORD is king.
He has made the world firm, not to be moved;
    he governs the peoples with equity. **R.**
Let the heavens be glad and the earth rejoice;
    let the sea and what fills it resound;
    let the plains be joyful and all that is in them!
Then shall all the trees of the forest exult. **R.**
Before the LORD, for he comes;
    for he comes to rule the earth.
He shall rule the world with justice
    and the peoples with his constancy. **R.**

Revelation 2:10c
R. Alleluia, alleluia.
Remain faithful until death,
and I will give you the crown of life. **R.**

† *Luke 21:5-11*
There will not be left a stone upon another stone.

While some people were speaking about
    how the temple was adorned with costly stones and votive offerings,
Jesus said, "All that you see here—
    the days will come when there will not be left
    a stone upon another stone that will not be thrown down."

Then they asked him,
    "Teacher, when will this happen?
And what sign will there be when all these things are about to
    happen?"
He answered,
"See that you not be deceived,
    for many will come in my name, saying,
    'I am he,' and 'The time has come.'

Do not follow them!
When you hear of wars and insurrections,
   do not be terrified; for such things must happen first,
   but it will not immediately be the end."
Then he said to them,
   "Nation will rise against nation, and kingdom against kingdom.
There will be powerful earthquakes, famines, and plagues
   from place to place;
   and awesome sights and mighty signs will come from the sky." ✢

WEDNESDAY, NOVEMBER 23
WEEKDAY, ST. POPE CLEMENT I, ST. COLUMBAN, BL. MIGUEL AGUSTÍN PRO

† *Revelation 15:1-4*
They sang the song of Moses and the song of the Lamb.

I, John, saw in heaven another sign, great and awe-inspiring:
   seven angels with the seven last plagues,
   for through them God's fury is accomplished.

Then I saw something like a sea of glass mingled with fire.
On the sea of glass were standing those
   who had won the victory over the beast
   and its image and the number that signified its name.
They were holding God's harps,
   and they sang the song of Moses, the servant of God,
   and the song of the Lamb:

   "Great and wonderful are your works,
     Lord God almighty.
   Just and true are your ways,
     O king of the nations.
   Who will not fear you, Lord,
     or glorify your name?
   For you alone are holy.
     All the nations will come
     and worship before you,
     for your righteous acts have been revealed." ✢

Psalm 98:1, 2-3ab, 7-8, 9
R. (Revelation 15:3b) **Great and wonderful are all your works,
   Lord, mighty God!**
Sing to the LORD a new song,
   for he has done wondrous deeds;
His right hand has won victory for him,
   his holy arm. **R.**

The LORD has made his salvation known:
  in the sight of the nations he has revealed his justice.
He has remembered his kindness and his faithfulness
  toward the house of Israel. **R.**
Let the sea and what fills it resound,
  the world and those who dwell in it;
Let the rivers clap their hands,
  the mountains shout with them for joy. **R.**
Before the LORD, for he comes,
  for he comes to rule the earth;
He will rule the world with justice
  and the peoples with equity. **R.**

Revelation 2:10c
R. Alleluia, alleluia.
Remain faithful until death,
and I will give you the crown of life. **R.**

† *Luke 21:12-19*

You will be hated by all because of my name,
but not a hair on your head will be destroyed.

Jesus said to the crowd:
"They will seize and persecute you,
  they will hand you over to the synagogues and to prisons,
  and they will have you led before kings and governors
  because of my name.
It will lead to your giving testimony.
Remember, you are not to prepare your defense beforehand,
  for I myself shall give you a wisdom in speaking
  that all your adversaries will be powerless to resist or refute.
You will even be handed over by parents,
  brothers, relatives, and friends,
  and they will put some of you to death.
You will be hated by all because of my name,
  but not a hair on your head will be destroyed.
By your perseverance you will secure your lives." ✣

THURSDAY, NOVEMBER 24

St. Andrew Dũng-Lac and Companions, Thanksgiving Day, U.S.A.

For Thanksgiving Day, use any readings from the Mass "In Thanksgiving to God," *Lectionary for Mass* (volume IV), numbers 943-947.

† *Revelation 18:1-2, 21-23; 19:1-3, 9a*
Fallen is Babylon the great.

I, John, saw another angel coming down from heaven,
  having great authority,
  and the earth became illumined by his splendor.
He cried out in a mighty voice:

"Fallen, fallen is Babylon the great.
  She has become a haunt for demons.
She is a cage for every unclean spirit,
  a cage for every unclean bird,
  a cage for every unclean and disgusting beast."

A mighty angel picked up a stone like a huge millstone
  and threw it into the sea and said:

"With such force will Babylon the great city be thrown down,
  and will never be found again.
No melodies of harpists and musicians,
  flutists and trumpeters,
  will ever be heard in you again.
No craftsmen in any trade
  will ever be found in you again.
No sound of the millstone
  will ever be heard in you again.
No light from a lamp
  will ever be seen in you again.
No voices of bride and groom
  will ever be heard in you again.
Because your merchants were the great ones of the world,
  all nations were led astray by your magic potion."

After this I heard what sounded like
  the loud voice of a great multitude in heaven, saying:

"Alleluia!
Salvation, glory, and might belong to our God,
  for true and just are his judgments.
He has condemned the great harlot
  who corrupted the earth with her harlotry.
He has avenged on her the blood of his servants."

They said a second time:

"Alleluia! Smoke will rise from her forever and ever."

Then the angel said to me, "Write this:
   Blessed are those who have been called
   to the wedding feast of the Lamb." ✝

Psalm 100:1b-2, 3, 4, 5
R. (Revelation 19:9a) **Blessed are they who are called to the wedding feast of the Lamb.**
Sing joyfully to the LORD, all you lands;
   serve the LORD with gladness;
   come before him with joyful song. **R.**
Know that the LORD is God;
   he made us, his we are;
   his people, the flock he tends. **R.**
Enter his gates with thanksgiving,
   his courts with praise;
Give thanks to him; bless his name. **R.**
For he is good:
   the LORD, whose kindness endures forever,
   and his faithfulness, to all generations. **R.**

Luke 21:28
R. Alleluia, alleluia.
Stand erect and raise your heads
because your redemption is at hand. **R.**

† *Luke 21:20-28*
*Jerusalem will be trampled underfoot by the Gentiles
until the times of the Gentiles are fulfilled.*

Jesus said to his disciples:
"When you see Jerusalem surrounded by armies,
   know that its desolation is at hand.
Then those in Judea must flee to the mountains.
Let those within the city escape from it,
   and let those in the countryside not enter the city,
   for these days are the time of punishment
   when all the Scriptures are fulfilled.
Woe to pregnant women and nursing mothers in those days,
   for a terrible calamity will come upon the earth
   and a wrathful judgment upon this people.

They will fall by the edge of the sword
and be taken as captives to all the Gentiles;
and Jerusalem will be trampled underfoot by the Gentiles
until the times of the Gentiles are fulfilled.

"There will be signs in the sun, the moon, and the stars,
and on earth nations will be in dismay,
perplexed by the roaring of the sea and the waves.
People will die of fright
in anticipation of what is coming upon the world,
for the powers of the heavens will be shaken.
And then they will see the Son of Man
coming in a cloud with power and great glory.
But when these signs begin to happen,
stand erect and raise your heads
because your redemption is at hand." ✝

FRIDAY, NOVEMBER 25
WEEKDAY, ST. CATHERINE OF ALEXANDRIA

✝ Revelation 20:1-4, 11—21:2
*The dead were judged according to their deeds. I saw a new Jerusalem,
coming down out of heaven from God.*

I, John, saw an angel come down from heaven,
holding in his hand the key to the abyss and a heavy chain.
He seized the dragon, the ancient serpent,
which is the Devil or Satan,
and tied it up for a thousand years and threw it into the abyss,
which he locked over it and sealed,
so that it could no longer lead the nations astray
until the thousand years are completed.
After this, it is to be released for a short time.

Then I saw thrones; those who sat on them were entrusted with
judgment.
I also saw the souls of those who had been beheaded
for their witness to Jesus and for the word of God,
and who had not worshiped the beast or its image
nor had accepted its mark on their foreheads or hands.
They came to life and they reigned with Christ for a thousand years.

Next I saw a large white throne and the one who was sitting on it.
The earth and the sky fled from his presence
and there was no place for them.
I saw the dead, the great and the lowly, standing before the throne,
and scrolls were opened.

Then another scroll was opened, the book of life.
The dead were judged according to their deeds,
  by what was written in the scrolls.
The sea gave up its dead;
  then Death and Hades gave up their dead.
All the dead were judged according to their deeds.
Then Death and Hades were thrown into the pool of fire.
(This pool of fire is the second death.)
Anyone whose name was not found written in the book of life
  was thrown into the pool of fire.

Then I saw a new heaven and a new earth.
The former heaven and the former earth had passed away,
  and the sea was no more.
I also saw the holy city, a new Jerusalem,
  coming down out of heaven from God,
  prepared as a bride adorned for her husband. ✛

Psalm 84:3, 4, 5-6a and 8a
R. (Revelation 21:3b) **Here God lives among his people.**
My soul yearns and pines
  for the courts of the LORD.
My heart and my flesh
  cry out for the living God. **R.**
Even the sparrow finds a home,
  and the swallow a nest
  in which she puts her young—
Your altars, O LORD of hosts,
  my king and my God! **R.**
Blessed they who dwell in your house!
  continually they praise you.
Blessed the men whose strength you are!
  They go from strength to strength. **R.**

Luke 21:28
R. Alleluia, alleluia.
Stand erect and raise your heads
because your redemption is at hand. **R.**

† *Luke 21:29-33*

When you see these things happening, know that the Kingdom of God is near.

Jesus told his disciples a parable.
"Consider the fig tree and all the other trees.
When their buds burst open,
 you see for yourselves and know that summer is now near;
 in the same way, when you see these things happening,
 know that the Kingdom of God is near.
Amen, I say to you, this generation will not pass away
 until all these things have taken place.
Heaven and earth will pass away,
 but my words will not pass away." ✛

SATURDAY, NOVEMBER 26
WEEKDAY, *[BVM]*

† *Revelation 22:1-7*

Night will be no more, for the Lord God shall give them light.

John said:
An angel showed me the river of life-giving water,
 sparkling like crystal, flowing from the throne of God
 and of the Lamb down the middle of the street.
On either side of the river grew the tree of life
 that produces fruit twelve times a year, once each month;
 the leaves of the trees serve as medicine for the nations.
Nothing accursed will be found anymore.
The throne of God and of the Lamb will be in it,
 and his servants will worship him.
They will look upon his face, and his name will be on their foreheads.
Night will be no more, nor will they need light from lamp or sun,
 for the Lord God shall give them light,
 and they shall reign forever and ever.

And he said to me, "These words are trustworthy and true,
 and the Lord, the God of prophetic spirits,
 sent his angel to show his servants what must happen soon."
"Behold, I am coming soon."
Blessed is the one who keeps the prophetic message of this book. ✛

Psalm 95:1-2, 3-5, 6-7ab

R. (1 Corinthians 16:22b, see Revelation 22:20c) **Marana tha!**
 Come, Lord Jesus!

Come, let us sing joyfully to the LORD;
 let us acclaim the Rock of our salvation.
Let us come into his presence with thanksgiving;
 let us joyfully sing psalms to him. **R.**
For the LORD is a great God,
 and a great king above all gods;
In his hands are the depths of the earth,
 and the tops of the mountains are his.
His is the sea, for he has made it,
 and the dry land, which his hands have formed. **R.**
Come, let us bow down in worship;
 let us kneel before the LORD who made us.
For he is our God,
 and we are the people he shepherds, the flock he guides. **R.**

Luke 21:36

R. Alleluia, alleluia.
Be vigilant at all times and pray
that you may have the strength to stand before the Son of Man. **R.**

✝ *Luke 21:34-36*

*Be vigilant that you may have the strength to escape
the tribulations that are imminent.*

Jesus said to his disciples:
"Beware that your hearts do not become drowsy
 from carousing and drunkenness
 and the anxieties of daily life,
 and that day catch you by surprise like a trap.
For that day will assault everyone
 who lives on the face of the earth.
Be vigilant at all times
 and pray that you have the strength
 to escape the tribulations that are imminent
 and to stand before the Son of Man." ✛

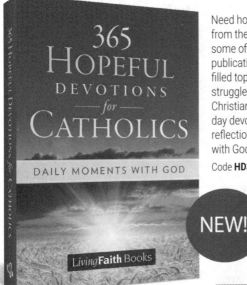
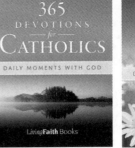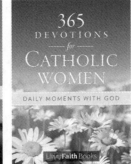

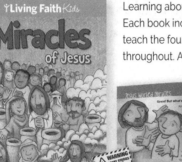

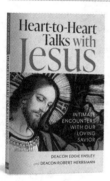

Apply your faith to the everyday experiences of life!

Use these beautiful, full-color illustrated booklets for your personal growth, for reflection and prayer, and for sharing your faith with others in your family, household, or community.

All title full-color, 32 pages 6⅜" x 6"

Receive an **ADDITIONAL 10%** off our already low prices
when you order two or more different titles!

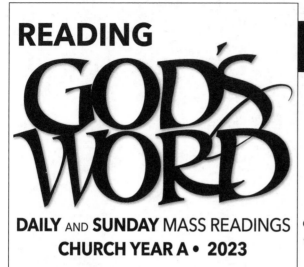

READING GOD'S WORD

DAILY AND **SUNDAY** MASS READINGS
CHURCH YEAR A • 2023

Paper • $18.95 + shipping • Order Code RGW23
Payment in full must be included in your mail order.

Great gift for family, friends, catechists, parish staff & YOU!

Please send _____ **copies of RGW23 to:**

_____
SEND TO

_____
PHONE (DAYTIME)

_____
P.O. BOX   (must include street address below)

_____
STREET ADDRESS

_____
CITY, STATE, ZIP   (Please Note: U.S. Customers Only)

PLEASE NOTE shipping and handling fees to a single address.	If your subtotal is:	
	$20.00 or less,	add $5.00
	$20.01-$40.00,	add $6.00
	$40.01-$70.00,	add $7.00
	$70.01 or more,	add 10%

SUBTOTAL _____

SHIPPING _____

Sales tax _____

States with applicable sales tax:
CA, CO, CT, IL, IN, MA, MN, MO,
NC, NY, NJ, OH, PA and TX

TOTAL _____
Prices subject to change.

LF Book Orders
1564 Fencorp Drive, Fenton, MO 63026-2942
800-325-9414 • 8 AM-5 PM (Central Time) Monday-Friday

RGW22